WORKING CAPITAL MANAGEMENT AND CONTROL

Principles and Applications

WORKING CAPITAL MANAGEMENT AND CONTROL

Principles and Applications

(REVISED SECOND EDITION)

Satish B Mathur
PhD (Business Management), CAIIB
Mentor, Mathur Management Consultants (MMC), Lucknow
Former Professor of Finance and Accounting
Indian Institute of Management, Lucknow, (IIML)
Senior Member of Faculty
Administrative Staff College of India, (ASCI), Hyderabad
and
State Bank Staff College, (SBSC), Hyderabad, India

With a Foreword
by

Dr. C Rangarajan
Chairman, Economic Advisory Council to the Prime Minister
Government of India, New Delhi, (India)
Former Governor, Reserve Bank of India, Mumbai, and
Governor, Andhra Pradesh, Hyderabad

NEW AGE MANAGEMENT

An Imprint of

NEW AGE INTERNATIONAL (P) LIMITED, PUBLISHERS
LONDON • NEW DELHI • NAIROBI
Bangalore • Chennai • Cochin • Guwahati • Hyderabad • Kolkata • Lucknow • Mumbai
Visit us at **www.newagepublishers.com**

Published by New Age International (P) Ltd., Publishers
First Edition: 2002
Revised Second Edition: 2013
Reprint: 2018

GLOBAL OFFICES

- **New Delhi** **NEW AGE INTERNATIONAL (P) LIMITED, PUBLISHERS**
  7/30 A, Daryaganj, New Delhi-110002, (INDIA)
  Tel.: (011) 23253771, 23253472, **Telefax:** 23267437, 43551305
  E-mail: contactus@newagepublishers.com • Visit us at www.newagepublishers.com
- **London** **NEW AGE INTERNATIONAL (UK) LTD.**
  27 Old Gloucester Street, London, WC1N 3AX, UK
  E-mail: info@newacademicscience.co.uk • Visit us at www.newacademicscience.co.uk
- **Nairobi** **NEW AGE GOLDEN (EAST AFRICA) LTD.**
  Ground Floor, Westlands Arcade, Chiromo Road (Next to Naivas Supermarket)
  Westlands, Nairobi, KENYA, **Tel.:** 00-254-713848772, 00-254-725700286
  E-mail: kenya@newagepublishers.com

BRANCHES

- **Bangalore** 37/10, 8th Cross (Near Hanuman Temple), Azad Nagar, Chamarajpet, Bangalore- 560 018
  Tel.: (080) 26756823, **Telefax:** 26756820, **E-mail: bangalore@newagepublishers.com**
- **Chennai** 26, Damodaran Street, T. Nagar, Chennai-600 017, **Tel.:** (044) 24353401, **Telefax:** 24351463
  E-mail: chennai@newagepublishers.com
- **Cochin** CC-39/1016, Carrier Station Road, Ernakulam South, Cochin-682 016, **Tel.:** (0484) 2377303, **Telefax:** 4051304
  E-mail: cochin@newagepublishers.com
- **Guwahati** Hemsen Complex, Mohd. Shah Road, Paltan Bazar, Near Starline Hotel, Guwahati-781 008,
  Tel.: (0361) 2513881, **Telefax:** 2543669, **E-mail: guwahati@newagepublishers.com**
- **Hyderabad** 105, 1st Floor, Madhiray Kaveri Tower, 3-2-19, Azam Jahi Road, Near Kumar Theater, Nimboliadda Kachiguda, Hyderabad-500 027, **Tel.:** (040) 24652456, **Telefax:** 24652457
  E-mail: hyderabad@newagepublishers.com
- **Kolkata** RDB Chambers (Formerly Lotus Cinema) 106A, 1st Floor, S N Banerjee Road, Kolkata-700 014
  Tel.: (033) 22273773, **Telefax:** 22275247, **E-mail: kolkata@newagepublishers.com**
- **Lucknow** 16-A, Jopling Road, Lucknow-226 001, **Tel.:** (0522) 2209578, 4045297, **Telefax:** 2204098
  E-mail: lucknow@newagepublishers.com
- **Mumbai** 142C, Victor House, Ground Floor, N.M. Joshi Marg, Lower Parel, Mumbai-400 013
  Tel.: (022) 24927869, **Telefax:** 24915415, **E-mail: mumbai@newagepublishers.com**
- **New Delhi** 22, Golden House, Daryaganj, New Delhi-110 002, **Tel.:** (011) 23262368, 23262370, **Telefax:** 43551305
  E-mail: sales@newagepublishers.com

ISBN: 978-81-224-2835-3
C-18-02-11087

Printed in India at Saras Graphics Rai, Haryana.
Typeset at In-house, Delhi

NEW AGE INTERNATIONAL (P) LIMITED, PUBLISHERS
7/30 A, Daryaganj, New Delhi-110002
Visit us at **www.newagepublishers.com**
(CIN: U74899DL1966PTC004618)

Dedicated

to

my Students, and

to the loving memory of

my revered parents

Late Shrimati Heera Devi Mathur

and

Late Shri Bhagwati Lal Mathur

FOREWORD

Raj Bhawan
Hyderabad-500 041

Dr. C. Rangarajan

August 20, 2001

सत्यमेव जयते

GOVERNOR
ANDHRA PRADESH

I am happy to write this foreword for S.B. Mathur's book "Working Capital Management and Control: Principles and Applications." There are several books on working capital management, but most of them have been written in the context of the Western conditions. Dr. Satish B. Mathur, by virtue of having been a practising banker, with the State Bank of India, for over 27 years, has made the full use of his long and varied experience and expertise in the field, in writing this useful book.

The book has been written in an easy-to-understand style. The large number of apt and appropriate illustrations and live examples, mostly drawn from author's own personal experience, as a professional banker, go to clarify and elucidate the concepts. These make the book a useful guide to management of working capital. Needless to say, assessment of the level of working capital, methods of financing and control over the use of funds are of extremc importance both to borrowers and lenders.

The book is a detailed study on the management and control of working capital, which I am sure, will be widely read, with immense benefit by bankers, business managers and students.

(C. Rangarajan)

PREFACE TO THE SECOND REVISED EDITION

The response to the First Edition of the book, from the students and the academia, as also from the practising executives of banks and business, has been very heartening and inspiring. I sincerely thank them all.

As the First Edition of the book was published way back in the year 2002, I have gone through the entire book over again very minutely and meticulously, and have endeavoured to update the various facts and figures, wherever it was considered necessary.

A new portion on 'Models of Cash Management' has been added to the Chapter Four on 'Management of Cash', as sub-section 4.12 of the book. Relevant thematic quotations and 'The Learning Points' have also been incorporated at the beginning of each chapter, which will further facilitate in the understanding of the contents of each chapter.

The Second Edition of the book, I fondly hope, will prove to be still more useful to the readers. But then, as there is no room on earth bigger than the room for improvement, I most earnestly solicit valuable suggestions from my worthy readers, with a view to bringing about further improvement in the next edition of the book. The readers may feel free to contact the author at 09839227181, or email < satishb_mathur@yahoo.co.in > and < satishb_mathur@rediffmail.com >. My postal address is 2/55, Vivek Khand, Gomti Nagar, Lucknow-226 010.

Satish B. Mathur

PREFACE TO THE FIRST EDITION

Many of my students colleagues and well-wishers, in the banks and the academia, particularly Dr. Prasanna Chandra, former Professor of Finance at IIM, Bangalore, have been pressing me for quite some time, to venture into writing of a comprehensive book on "Working Capital Management and Control", in the Indian context and conditions, citing suitable illustrative live cases, drawn from the Indian experience. They were, perhaps, thinking that, with the vast and varied experiences undergone by me as a professional banker in the premier banking institution of the country, the State Bank of India, for over 27 years, in several senior positions and postings, I may be able to do full justice to the subject.

And, their such a high opinion of, and expectation from me, perhaps, been more a deterrent than a facilitating factor in my daring such a demanding endeavour on my part. Besides, my varied experience and the wide-spread knowledge in the area had, in fact, made the task appear to me to be too stupendous, difficult and demanding, to even make a humble beginning in this direction. But then, it took me long precious five years to realise that howsoever long and difficult a journey may be, it can be completed only after the first step is taken; that is, a small beginning is made. And thus, the hard and strenuous, concerted and concentrated efforts, made in the right direction, and in right earnest, have made it possible for me to place the book, my humble work, right before you.

One's own baby, the book in the instant case, is the most beloved and beautiful the world over. But then, the real judges are, definitely and decidedly, the readers themselves. And, if they would think that the book has presented the difficult and dull subject like the management and control of working capital, in a quite easy-to-understand, interesting and absorbing manner, I would think that my job has really been well done. And, if the readers, like the students (of B.Com. and M.Com., MBA and PGP, degrees and diplomas), and the Chartered Accounts, the professional and practising bankers and industrialists, all in one voice, experience that, while reading the book, they tend to feel as if, the author had personally been talking to them, instead, on a one to one basis, I would sincerely thank them all, and think that my sincere and strenuous efforts have been amply rewarded.

Further, as the term lending institutions, like ICICI Bank, IDBI Bank, and IFCI have also, of late, decided to finance even the working capital requirements of borrowers, under one roof, an attempt has been made to make the book a helpful and handy guide, for their executives, too, to get inducted and introduced to the tricks of the trade, in the discharge of their day-to-day business activities, in this rather new area, too. And, I sincerely feel that even the practising professionals of the commercial banks may find the book quite relevant for reference and refreshing purposes.

A summary, containing just the gist and the essence of each Chapter, from Chapters Two to Twelve [each titled as "A Synoptic Note: Chapter at a Glance"], may be found to be very useful and valuable for the students and the practising professionals in the banks and business alike. And, even the Professors, teaching the topics, may find the synopsis immensely useful for preparing the required transparencies or slides on the Power-Point Software, on the same or similar lines, for use in their lecture sessions.

Satish B. Mathur

ACKNOWLEDGEMENTS

I am extremely grateful to my students, friends and well-wishers for their having given me the idea and encouragement for writing the book. And, I lack words, indeed, to express my deep sense of sincere gratefulness and indebtedness to my dearest and closest friend, Dr. Prasanna Chandra, former Professor of Finance at IIM, Bangalore, for his profuse and perpetual praise and pep, which gave me the much needed strength and stimulus, for making uninterrupted and untiring, sustained and sincere efforts, in completing the tough task, as also for keeping the self-imposed tight time schedule.

I am immensely grateful to Meera Mathur, my wife, for her self-less sacrifice and unstinted support, significant suggestions and valuable views, from time to time. My hearty gratitude is due to my lovely dear daughters—Archana Mathur and Kartika Mathur, for their free and frank opinion, and constructive suggestions, which have gone a long way in making the book so very reader-friendly, lucid and easy-to-understand, even by non-experts and non-finance executives, in the business and industry.

I profusely thank Mr. Saumya Gupta, Managing Director, New Age International (P) Limited in taking an active and sincere interest in the publication of the book.

Satish B. Mathur

CONTENTS

PART FOUR
SOME OTHER SHORT-TERM FINANCING

PART ONE

FUND-BASED WORKING CAPITAL FINANCING

1

WORKING CAPITAL MANAGEMENT AND CONTROL: AN OVERVIEW

Good management is better than good income. — **Portuguese Proverb**

Our income is like our shoes; if too small, they gall and pinch us; but if too large, they cause us to stumble and trip. — **Charles Caleb Colton**

If you can actually count your money, then you're not a rich man. — **J. Paul Getty**

The Learning Points

The chapter aims at giving an overview of effective management and control of the various components of working capital, along with the scheme of the book, as to where to find what, viz.:

- Components of Working Capital and their Management
- Operating Cycle Approach
- Rationale behind effective management and control of working capital
- Assessment of Working Capital Requirements and Formulation of Working Capital Policies
- Sources of Working Capital Financing (Short-term and Long-term Sources of Funds)
- Financing of Working Capital by Banks
- Mechanism of Managing Credit Risks by Banks
- Effective Supervision and Follow-up of Advances by Banks
- Non-fund based Working Capital Finance by Banks, viz. Letters of Credit and Bank Guarantees

1.1 WHAT IS 'WORKING CAPITAL MANAGEMENT'?

Working capital management involves the management and control of the gross current assets [as against the net working capital (NWC)]. And, the current assets mainly comprise cash, sundry debtors [also known as Accounts Receivable (ARs) and Bills Receivable (BRs)], and inventories. Thus, the working capital management comprises the management of all these components, individually and collectively. The detailed discussions pertaining to the management and control of Cash (in hand, in bank, as also in transit), Sundry Debtors, and Inventories (comprising raw materials, consumable stores and spares, work-in-process, and finished goods), are contained in Chapters 4, 5 and 6, respectively.

1.2 OPERATING CYCLE APPROACH

With the help of the operating cycle method, we are able to estimate and almost ascertain the duration of one operating cycle; that is, the time taken by a particular manufacturing company in completing one full cycle, starting right from cash, to the purchase of raw materials and their processing (known as the work-in-process stage), and the final conversion into finished goods which, after the sales, in cash and/or on the realization of the sale proceeds even of the credit sales, over again gets converted into cash, and when again, the next round of the operating cycle may start, afresh. Thus, the time taken in the completion of one cycle of operation, as aforesaid, is known as the duration of the operating cycle.

We have, therefore, also examined, in Chapter 3, how, with the completion of each operating cycle, the profitability of the company goes up. Thus, we may be able to fully comprehend as to how, by making each and every component of the operating cycle cover more mileage during the period, say, one year, the total number of operating cycle may be maximized, and the company's profitability and prospects therewith. Therefore, the imperative need and the vital importance of an effective management and control of the working capital, in particular, can hardly be over-emphasized.

It would, therefore, augur well if we examine, in greater detail, the rationale behind attaching such a high importance to the management and control of the working capital, in general, and those of its each and every component, in particular.

1.3 WHY WORKING CAPITAL MANAGEMENT?

Effective management and control of the various components of working capital has been rated as one of the most important and vital functions of financial management in any of the industrial and business units, based on varied parameters, discussed hereunder:

A. Flexibility

Working capital management is highly flexible in nature, so much so that it can very easily be adapted to suit even extreme conditions, like rising and falling demands in peak and off seasons, buoyant and sluggish economic and market conditions, etc. Further, if some inappropriate policy or procedure is detected at a later stage, remedial and right steps can be adopted henceforth. This, however, is not the position in the case of project management.

B. Level of investments in various components of current assets

Investment in current assets constitute a very substantial percentage (usually more than 50%), of the total investment in most of the Indian companies and firms.

The quantum, and percentage (in terms of total assets) of current assets in some of the Indian industries, in the large scale sector, during the year 1996-97, presented in **Table 1.1**, may bring home the point clearly.

Table 1.1: Level of Current Assets in some of the Indian Companies during the Year 1996-97

(Rupees in crores)

Name of the Company	*Inventories*	*Sundry Debtors*	*Cash*	*Total Current Assets*	*Percentage of Total Assets*
BHEL	1,877 (23.7%)	3239 (40.8%)	350 (4.4%)	5466	68.9%
L & T	4034 (41.7%)	873 (9.0%)	278 (2.9%)	5185	53.6%
VOLTAS	287 (29.1%)	186 (18.9%)	29 (2.9%)	502	50.9%
GNFC	191 (12.7%)	159 (10.5%)	10 (0.7%)	360	23.9%

BHEL Bharat Heavy Electricals Limited
L & T Larsen and Toubro Limited
VOLTAS Voltas Limited
GNFC Gujarat Narmada Fertilizers Company Limited

C. Criticality

The undermentioned fact itself can bring home the extent of cruciality and criticality of Working Capital Management.

In early nineties, an empirical study had revealed that most of the Indian companies had reported some losses, as per the un-audited Balance Sheet and Profit and Loss Account for the respective half-year period. And, it further reported that if the companies reduced the level of their inventories just by 1%, most of the loss-making companies would have shown at least some marginal profits. Thus, if only one of the components of the Working Capital can make such a dramatic difference, the importance of meticulous management of all the components of the Working Capital (viz. Current Assets, Current Liabilities and even a portion of the deferred liabilities) can very well be imagined and appreciated.

D. Quantum of efforts and time

Empirical study and observations have revealed that a major portion of the time of the finance managers, in most of the companies, is devoted (and rightly so) to the management of the various components of the working capital, with a view to maximise their profitability, and their prospects and prosperity.

1.4 ASSESSMENT OF WORKING CAPITAL REQUIREMENTS AND FORMULATION OF WORKING CAPITAL POLICIES

Further, depending upon the levels of sundry debtors and inventories, a matching level of funds are also required to finance them, which, again, in turn, means an outflow of funds by way of interest paid, and/or involves some opportunity cost. Therefore, the management of working capital would also involve the management of funds (both short-term and long-term sources of funds), required for financing the working capital. Thus, the management of working capital, in its totality, means management of current assets and the entire current liabilities, as also a portion of long-term or deferred liabilities, which caters to the financial requirements of working capital.

A further question that may arise is as to what should be the optimal level of finance and the optimal level of the mix of the short-term and long-term sources of funds, to finance the company's working capital requirements, as also as how to keep the various items of current assets at the optimal and minimal levels. Such issues have been addressed to in Chapter 2.

1.5 SOURCES OF WORKING CAPITAL FINANCING: SHORT-TERM AND LONG-TERM SOURCES OF FUNDS

The various short-term sources of financing the working capital requirements [like accruals, trade credits, loans from banks and financial institutions, public deposits, inter-corporate deposits (ICDs), Commercial Papers (CPs), rights debentures, factoring, etc.], have been discussed, in detail, in Chapter 7-Part 'A'. And, Chapter 7-Part 'B' has been devoted entirely to the discussions on the long-term sources of financing the working capital like retained earnings, shares, etc.

1.6 WORKING CAPITAL FINANCING BY BANKS

It is a well known fact that working capital financing by the commercial banks (as also, of late, by other financial institutions like ICICI Bank, IDBI Bank, IFCI, etc.), still contributes a major portion of such financing. Accordingly, the assessment and disbursement of working capital loans by banks (and the other financial institutions), have exclusively been discussed, separately in detail, in Chapter 8, wherein all the three methods of assessing the working capital requirements [viz. (*i*) Projected Balance Sheets (PBS) method, (*ii*) Cash Budget (CB) method, and (*iii*) Projected Yearly Turnover (PYT) method] have separately been dealt with. A separate section has also been devoted towards the end of Chapter 8, which deals exclusively with the "Assessment of the Working Capital requirements of SSI Sector" (as per Nayak Committee), *w.e.f.* June 1993.

1.7 MANAGEMENT OF CREDIT RISKS

Management of Credit Risks is a matter of great concern and prime importance for the banks, granting working capital loans to industries and merchants alike. A detailed discussion on the principles and practices, strategies and policies, followed by banks, have been discussed in Chapter 9. A special care has, however, been taken to see to it that the confidential nature of details of the scoring pattern, etc., of specific banks and financial institutions, do not get disclosed, even tacitly. The various pertinent parameters, considered by banks and financial institutions, have, however, been discussed, in detail, which may prove to be of great help to the executives of the banks and industries alike. The overall management of Credit Risks, *inter alia*, include the management of

(*i*) Financial Risks, both in quantitative and qualitative terms,

(*ii*) Industrial Risks, and

(*iii*) Managerial Risks, including the quality and competence, credibility and integrity, of the management.

The mechanism of pricing of the bank credits, *i.e.* the rate of interest to be applicable on the respective loan accounts, depending upon the credit rating given by the banks to the respective companies, has also been explained at the end of Chapter 9.

1.8 EFFECTIVE SUPERVISION AND FOLLOW-UP OF ADVANCES

Besides the realistic credit appraisal, assessment of the working capital needs, and the phased disbursement of the working capital loan, the effectiveness of the post-disbursement supervision and follow-up of the advances, are of prime importance and significance for banks and other financial institutions. And, it is in this respect that the timely detection of early symptoms of sickness, and prompt execution of the necessary remedial measures assume great importance. A sincere effort has, therefore, been made to discuss such sensitive and vital topics, in detail, in Chapter 10, which may be found to be of great practical application and use in the day-to-day working of the executives of banks and industries alike. An attempt has also been made to enlist the various steps and measures to be taken in this regard. The long and varied experiences of the author as a senior executive with the State Bank of India, for over 27 years (1961-1988) and as a senior professor in the finance area, dealing with senior practising executives of banks and industries, as also the administrators like IAS and IPS officers, get clearly reflected in Chapter 10, which is expected to serve as a useful and handy handbook for the practising executives and administrators, as also the prospective MBA/PGP graduates alike. If this happens to come true, all the efforts of the author could be deemed to have been amply rewarded.

1.9 NON-FUND BASED WORKING CAPITAL FINANCING

(*i*) Letters of Credit (L/C), and

(*ii*) Bank Guarantees (B/Gs).

Part II of the book, comprising Chapters 11 and 12, deal with 'Non-fund based Working Capital Financing,' like Letters of Credit and Bank Guarantees. Both these topics have been dealt with in the book, mainly from practical and pragmatic points of view, which may prove to be of great help and guidance to the executives, both in banks and industries.

The relevant legal aspects, their implications and ramifications, have also been dealt with in sufficient detail, quoting and illustrating with relevant case laws. These may, sometimes, be found to be of some guidance and assistance even to some legal experts, engaged by the banks and industries, to plead their cases more effectively. These case laws are based on sound legal precedents.

1.10 CASE STUDIES WITH SUGGESTED APPROACHES

Some integrated case studies on working capital management and control, as well as some suggested approaches thereto, have been given in Chapters 13 and 14, which comprise Part III of the book.

1.11 EXPORT FINANCING

Export financing, both pre-shipment and post-shipment financing, has been dealt with, in detail, in Chapter 15.

1.12 WORKING CAPITAL FINANCE FOR INFORMATION TECHNOLOGY AND SOFTWARE INDUSTRIES

The concluding Chapter 16, introduces the topic of "Financing Working Capital Requirements of Information Technology (IT) and Software Industries", which has, of late, assumed a much greater importance in the current scenario of our national economy, going global.

1.13 CONCLUDING REMARKS

In summary, it may well be said that the progress and prosperity, financial health and stability, of an industrial or business organization largely depend on the effective management and control of the various facets of the working capital. Thus, a careful study of the following chapters and an appropriate application of the principles and practices discussed therein, may go a long way in achieving the desired results, by the executives of banks and industries alike.

Further, at the end of each chapter, a synoptic note has been provided with the idea that after having read and studied the respective chapter, with the minute details contained therein, the synoptic note may well serve the purpose of giving a summary of the chapter (the chapter at a glance), which may facilitate the formulation and execution of the necessary action points in the day-to-day working.

A set of questions has also been given at the end of each chapter, so as to help the practising executives, as also the promising students, to have a fair amount of self-assessment about the clear understanding and assimilation of the text.

The practical problems, given at the end of the relevant chapters, may help the readers to achieve the required perfection and expertise in the various areas of management and control of working capital.

2

WORKING CAPITAL POLICY

In all things there is a law of cycles. **Publius Cornelius Tacitus**

Successful people make money. It's not that people who make money become successful, but that successful people attract money. They bring success to what they do. **Wayne Dyer**

The Learning Points

The chapter aims at developing the knowledge and facilitating the understanding of:

- Elements of Gross and Net Working Capital
- Distinguishing features of Working Capital and Project Management
- Special features of Current Assets
- Importance and advantages of Synergy inherent in Team Spirit
- Mechanism of Assessment of Working Capital Requirements
- How to ascertain the Optimal Level of Current Assets
- Different Policies of Financing Working Capital
- Distinction between Operating Cycle and Cash Cycle
- Time-Series Analysis and Cross-section Analysis

Working capital management, or short-term financial management, largely deals with the management and control of current assets and current liabilities. As against long-term financial management where cash flows are extended from 5 to 15 years, or even more, short-term financial management involves cash flows within the operating cycle of the company, usually not exceeding the period of one year, in the usual course of business.

2.1 GROSS WORKING CAPITAL VS. NET WORKING CAPITAL

Theoretically speaking, there are two concepts of working capital, viz.;

(*i*) Gross working capital comprising of total current assets; and

(*ii*) Net working capital, *i.e.* current assets less current liabilities.

The main items that comprise **current assets** are

(*i*) Cash:

(*a*) in hand;

(*b*) in bank; and

(*c*) in transit.

(*ii*) Investments:

Only short-term investments, like quoted shares of other companies intended for sale, are treated as Current Assets, and long-term investments, like all unquoted shares, and quoted shares of subsidiary companies are treated as Miscellaneous Assets.

(*iii*) Inventories, comprising:

(*a*) raw materials, and consumable stores and spares;

(*b*) work-in-process; and

(*c*) finished goods.

(*iv*) Sundry debtors, also known as Bills Receivable or Accounts Receivable.

(*v*) Loans and advances, given by the company to others.

All items (excluding No. *v*) are included in the operating cycle.

Items comprising **current liabilities** are:

(*i*) Sundry Creditors, also known as Bills Payable or Accounts Payable.

(*ii*) Trade Advances received by the company for supply of goods and/or for rendering services.

(*iii*) Short-term borrowings from commercial banks or other financial institutions.

(*iv*) Short-term loans from other sources.

(*v*) Provisions made for;

(*a*) payment of taxes;

(*b*) bad debts to be written off; and

(*c*) fluctuations in exchange rates; etc.

But, in practice, the working capital management is concerned with the management of total current assets and total current liabilities, which, in fact, varies, depending upon the level of current assets required. Thus, the term, 'net working capital', is only an accounting concept, not having much of economic or financial significance.

In fact, working capital management mainly pertains to the management of current assets. But it also involves management of current liabilities, because they arise due to the volume and value of the current assets required. It is, therefore, a good business sense to keep the level of current assets to the minimal level, whereby the level of current liabilities would automatically be low enough, and the interest outgo and the opportunity cost, too, therewith.

2.2 WORKING CAPITAL MANAGEMENT VS. PROJECT MANAGEMENT

In project management, a lot of deliberations and discussions, planning and pondering, must take place at the pre-implementation stage, including the conception of the project stage. After the project commences and is half way through, not much of changes or modifications are possible, except giving up the whole project, half-way, if that comes to mitigating the imminent losses.

Examples:

Take, for instance, the case of Scooters (India) Limited. Its "Vijaya" brand scooter had not been well received in the market, and ultimately its production had to be given up. However, its "Vikram" brand three wheelers have since been doing well in the market, so much so that once a sick industrial unit, in the public sector, has since been revived under the effective and efficient leadership of the former CMD, Dr Arun Sahay, and has now started showing a net profit after wiping off the entire accumulated losses. A commendable feat, indeed, which, naturally reminds us of the success story of Crysler Motors Company (USA) which, too, was revived, under the unmatched leadership of the management wizard, Lee Iacocca.

I also know of a company, which had established its factory in a rural area, around 100 kms. away from Hyderabad, with a view to availing of the various concessions and subsidies available for encouraging industrial development of rural and/or backward areas. But, later, it was found that as all the required raw materials had to be transported from Hyderabad and all the finished goods had to be brought back to Hyderabad for sale, the entire amount of subsidy fell short of meeting the involved transport expenses alone. But, now nothing could be done.

There are umpteen number of cases which could be cited, but I feel, the point has already been brought home well.

But, this is not the case in the working capital management. If you have taken a decision regarding inventory management policy or credit management policy, and you later find that some changes or amendments are needed, you may introduce the proposed changes instantaneously. This is the beauty and ample advantage of working capital management. That is why, as you must have yourself seen, a lot of valuable time of the finance executives are gainfully and meaningfully invested in the management and monitoring of various components and facets of working capital, like arranging short-term sources of funds, negotiating gainful terms of credit, management of cash (inflows and outflows), control and follow-up of sundry debtors, management and control of inventories (raw materials, work-in-process, finished goods), etc.

The other reason why the finance executives devote considerable time in effective control and supervision of the working capital components is that the inventories and sundry debtors account for a very large and substantial portion of the total assets and investments of the company, mostly next to the capital employed in the company's fixed assets.

Moreover, with the expected changes in the market conditions, and the resultant level of sales, the level of holdings of the current assets have also to be geared up and adjusted accordingly. And, this has the cascading effect mainly on the various items of current liabilities, though some long-term sources of funds also get affected, depending upon the working capital policy of the company, mainly in regard to the proportion of the mix between the short-term and long-term sources of funds, to finance the working capital. This point shall be discussed in greater details in the following pages of the chapter.

2.3 SPECIAL FEATURES OF CURRENT ASSETS

Before we discuss the working capital policy, management and control, we should better identify the folllowing two main characteristics of current assets, viz.

(*i*) Current assets have a much shorter life span, and

(*ii*) They get transformed into other forms of assets (and ultimately in cash) much more quickly.

They get converted into cash in the ordinary course of business, and within the operating cycle, which may vary from product to product, but largely not exceeding 12 months.

The concept of operating cycle can be comprehensively understood with the help of the diagram (Fig. 2.1).

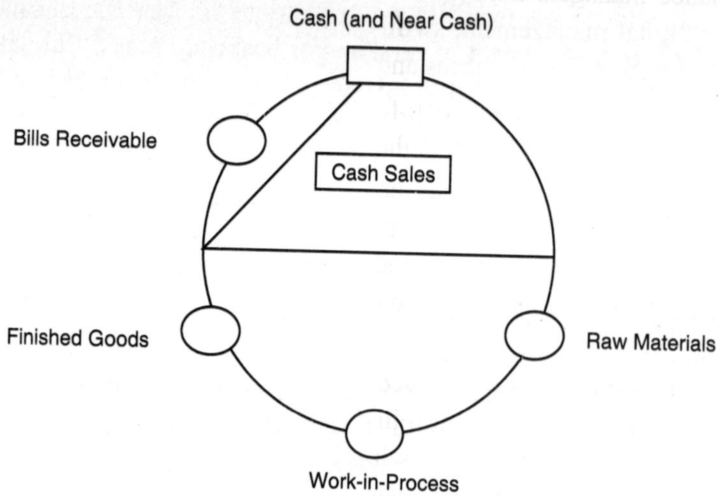

Fig. 2.1

(*i*) The lower half of the circle (comprising raw materials, work-in-process and finished goods), constitutes "inventories".

(*ii*) And, the upper half, mostly comprises "Quick Assets" (*i.e.* Total Current Assets less Inventories).

A manufacturing unit starts from cash, used for the purchase of raw materials (stocked to cover one to three months of requirement for production), which, in turn, are processed (comprising work-in-process, generally ranging from 10–30 days or so), and finally they reach the finished goods stage, ready for sale in the market.

Some sales, effected on cash basis (though mostly a smaller portion of the total sales), get converted into cash immediately. But, a major portion of the sales is usually effected on some varying credit terms (except in the case of industries which are fortunate enough to be in the sellers' market, like Domestic Gas Services, Petrol Pumps, etc.). These, however, get converted into cash after realisation, say, within a month or two or even more, depending upon the credit terms. The cycle begins from the starting point, *i.e.* cash. The total time taken from the cash stage, *i.e.* from the purchase of raw materials, till the realisation of the sale proceeds of the credit sales, is known as the operating cycle period or time. And, lower the operating cycle period, greater is the turnover (times) and higher is the value added, and the volume of the resultant profit. The main effectiveness of working capital management is that the resources (cash, etc.) should cover more mileage in a shorter time; that is, they should work smarter, not necessarily harder. We shall discuss this aspect of working capital management in a much greater detail a little later in this chapter.

The aforesaid two special characteristics of current assets have some distinct ramifications, too. **For example:**

(*i*) The finance managers have to be ever alert to take financial decisions, pertaining to working capital management, swiftly and frequently, and repeatedly, too, keeping pace with the changing circumstances and scenario of the market and the economy.

(*ii*) The subtle distinction between profitability and the net present value (NPV) of money is considered rather insignificant, in the case of management of working capital.

(*iii*) As the aggregate current assets have various components (viz. cash and marketable securities, raw materials, work-in-process, finished goods, and bills receivable), and all these are closely interconnected and interdependent, each and every item of the current assets has to be managed and controlled with equal rigour and in a systematic and synchronised manner.

For example, if some items of finished goods get accumulated, or become slow moving or even non-moving items, some strategies, like liberalization of the credit policy and/or allowing some relaxation in credit collection, or giving some off-season or clearance sales discount, etc., could be adopted for an overall financial gain to the company and the release of blocked funds in finished goods. Similarly, if the company is facing some cash crunch, adoption of some policy of cash discount, to induce prompt payment, could be considered.

2.4 SYNERGY OF TEAM SPIRIT

This also necessitates the full coordination and cooperation of respective functionaries as a well-knit team to realise the economy and advantages of synergy created thereby.

For example, the purchase and production departments, as well as production and marketing departments, etc., should work in unison. Because, if the purchase department procures materials not required for production and fails to procure some materials required for production, well in time, production of the company may get adversely affected as also the financial gains that go therewith. Similarly, if the production department feels happy about having achieved its budgeted level of production, but produces only such items which are not in demand in the market (or vice versa), it is not that the marketing division alone will suffer the adverse consequences; the loss will be of the company as a whole. This is the reason productivity and profitability of a company is not just the sum total of different sections or departments as such, the activities and productivity of all the departments should also match with each other. This underlines the need for creation, development and sustenance of team spirits. For a detailed discussion on these points, readers may like to refer to the author's book titled '*Mentoring Mantras for Indian Managers*', Matrix Publishers, New Delhi, 2010. The following table should make it clear appropriately.

Accordingly, it is suggested, just by way of an illustrative example, that any of the undernoted specific tasks, must be performed and decisions taken in perfect cooperation and coordination of the respective departments, noted thereagainst.

Table 2.1

Tasks	*Functionaries to be Involved in Performance and Decision Making*
Purchase	By purchase, materials and production departments.
Materials	By materials, purchase and production departments.
Production	By production, purchase, materials and marketing departments.
Finished Goods	By production and marketing (and sales) departments.
Bills Receivables	By marketing (and sales) and finance departments.

Finally, the finance department should continue to perform the overall coordination and control functions, as hitherto.

2.5 ASSESSMENT OF WORKING CAPITAL REQUIREMENTS

There are several determinant factors which can influence the assessment of the quantum of working capital requirements of a company. These may largely depend upon one or more of the undernoted factors:

- Nature of Business;
- Seasonal Industries;
- Production Policy;
- Market Conditions; and
- Supply Conditions (of Materials).

Nature of Business

The quantum of working capital requirement is closely related to the nature of business of the company which, in turn, is related to the operating cycle. For example, in a bakery unit, the requirement may be very low, as the operating cycle may be hardly for one or two days.

Similarly, in case of an electric supply company, or a transport company, or for a company which is still in the sellers' market, the working capital requirement may be much less as the operating cycle is much shorter, mainly due to the fact that most of their sales are on cash basis. And, so the whole time lag between credit sales and collection of bills are saved. As against this, a company, manufacturing heavy machine tools or turbines, has a much longer operating cycle, as it sells mostly on credit, and, consequently requires a much higher level of working capital.

The following table shows the proportionate levels of investments in current assets and fixed assets for different groups of industries, and clarifies the above assumption.

Table 2.2: Percentages of Current Assets and Fixed Assets

Current Assets (%)	*Fixed Assets (%)*	*Industrial Groups*
10–20	80–90	Hotels and Restaurants
20–30	70–80	Electricity Generation and Distribution
30–40	60–70	Aluminium, Shipping
40–50	50–60	Iron and Steel, Basic Industrial Chemicals
50–60	40–50	Tea Plantation
60–70	30–40	Cotton Textiles, Sugar
70–80	20–30	Edible Oils, Tobacco
80–90	10–20	Trading, Construction

Seasonal Industries

Seasonal industries, manufacturing fans and fridges, room heaters and geysers, room coolers and air-conditioners, woollen clothes and blankets, may require a much higher level of working capital requirements in peak seasons, and much lower requirements during the slack (off) seasons. That is why, the commercial banks stipulate fluctuating working capital limits for such companies for peak and slack seasons.

Production Policy

Most of the companies may find it a better financial decision to keep on manufacturing goods even in the off season so as to keep on working above the break-even point (BEP), to meet, at least, the fixed costs, on a continuous basis. As an additional strategy, they may also prefer to offer some attractive off-season discount, well below the fixed cost, so as to yield some amount by way of contributions. This may have the incidence of adding to the profitability of the company. This way, the working capital requirements, even of seasonal industries, may remain almost stable and uniform throughout the year.

As against the seasonal industries, the units manufacturing items like furniture or tube lights and fittings, would have stable and uniform sales round the year and correspondingly, the level of production activities too. Therefore, for such industries, the working capital requirements may be almost uniform throughout.

Market Conditions

In a fiercely competitive market condition, the companies may have to keep sufficient quantities of finished goods in their ready stock so as to be able to supply them to the prospective buyers off the shelf and thereby try to get an edge over their competitors. Besides, with a view to push up the sales and to withstand stiff competition, a company may have to offer relatively further liberalised credit terms, whereby a larger amount of money may get blocked in the sundry debtors, for quite a long time. Thus, the additional inventory of finished goods, and the larger amount of sundry debtors, may proportionately increase the quantum of working capital requirements.

As against this, if the products of a company have a marked edge in the market, as compared to their competitors, it may not be required to have huge stocks of finished goods, as the customers may prefer to wait for sometime for a better quality of goods. Besides, taking advantage of this envious position in the market, they may even insist on some advance payment or cash sales, at least in part. These special features will well reduce the level of working capital requirements of such companies.

Supply Conditions of Materials

If the required raw materials, consumable stores and spares are in short and scarce supply, or if the lead time (due to the long distance of the point of supply or the high demand of these materials), is long enough, the working capital need may go higher. Such higher level of inventory of raw materials and consumable stores and spares may have to be stocked to ensure uninterrupted production throughout the year. Similar will be the position if the supply of the material is seasonal (*e.g.* agricultural products like wheat, cotton, rice, etc.), but the production process is uniform throughout the year. That is, the company may have to store sufficiently large stocks of materials during the harvesting season, when these are available in plenty and at much cheaper rates. Reverse, however, will be the case if these materials are in ample supply and that too at a nearby place, resulting in zero or minimal lead time.

2.6 OPTIMAL LEVEL OF CURRENT ASSETS

The quantum of working capital requirement is directly dependent on the policy of the company regarding the level of current assets, as to how much stocks of inventories of raw materials and finished goods may be considered to be sufficiently and reasonably safe, so as to fairly avoid the possible risk of stock outs (in the case of raw materials), and loss of business (in the case of finished goods), and the resultant losses.

Based upon these criteria, the working capital policy may broadly be divided into three categories, viz.

(*a*) Conservative or liberal or flexible policy.

(*b*) Aggressive or strict or restrictive policy.

(*c*) Moderate or middle-of-the-road policy.

Under the conservative policy, the company may prefer to have somewhat heavy cash balance and bank balance in current account, or investments in readily marketable securities, as also higher stocks of raw materials and finished goods, with a view to considerably reduce the risks of stock outs and loss of sales. Such companies may also prefer to have a rather liberal credit policy, resulting in a substantial amount of funds locked up in sundry debtors. All these investments in the various components of current assets will naturally require correspondingly higher levels of current liabilities, and the working capital requirements.

As against this, the level of current assets, and accordingly the working capital requirement, will, of course, be of a much lower order in case the company adopts an aggressive or restrictive working capital policy. But again, too much of a restrictive working capital policy may result in a disproportionately heavier losses by way of stock-out risks, and the consequential loss of production and lowering of the profitability of the company.

And, in the case of adoption of a moderate policy, the requirement of working capital is moderate—that is, neither too high nor too low, but just right.

Thus, we see that both the conservative and aggressive policies have their own comparative advantages and disadvantages in terms of carrying costs and stock out (or shortage) costs.

Thus, the essence of working capital policy or mainly the current assets policy is to determine the optimal level of current assets, which is the point of trade off between the inventory carrying costs and the stock out costs (in terms of loss of production and loss of sales and the resultant loss of customers' goodwill). A graphic presentation of how these two different costs behave, in relation to the level of current assets, is given below:

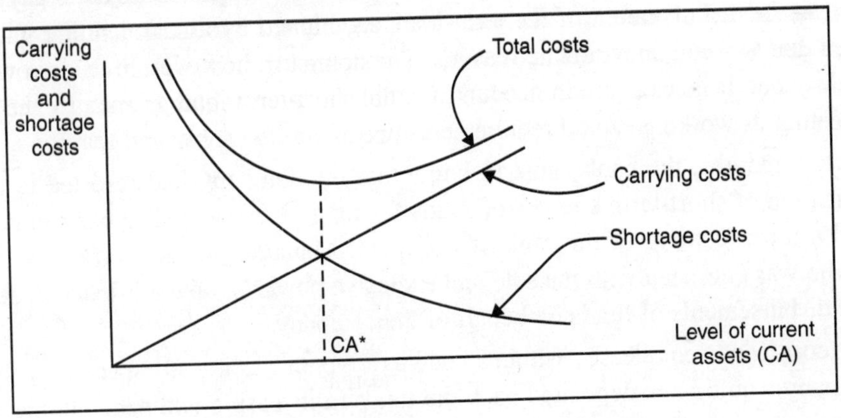

Fig. 2.2: Carrying costs and shortage costs

The optimal level of current assets is represented by CA* (in the above Figure 2.2), inasmuch as the total of both the costs (inventory carrying costs and stock out costs), are minimum at this level.

It has, however, been observed that in most of the cases the curve of total costs is fairly flat, around the optimal level, whereby it becomes very difficult to identify the optimal level in a precise manner. It should, however, be considered to be a sufficiently helpful guideline if we are able to get a range of optimal level rather than a precise optimal point.

2.7 WORKING CAPITAL FINANCING POLICY

After having established the optimal level of current assets, as per the current assets policy, the company must determine and decide about the sources of financing the current assets. This would, in essence, mean to arrive at a crucial decision as to what should be the optimal mix of long-term and short-term sources of funds, to finance the company's working capital requirements.

As a matter of principle, all the fixed assets of a company must be financed invariably and exclusively from the long-term sources, *i.e.* out of term loans (deferred liabilities) and equity. Because, financing of some items of fixed assets out of short-term loan (or working capital loan), is considered to be diversion of funds, and it is viewed by the commercial banks with great disfavour and distrust.

Example:

The case of J.K. Synthetics Limited, as published in the newspapers, is an apt illustrative example of diversion of funds and its far reaching ramifications.

J.K. Synthetics Limited imported certain items of machinery, which were lying at the port, incurring heavy demurrages. The company was not able to arrange for funds to pay the required import duty, as the disbursement of the term-loan, sanctioned by a term lending institution, had been delayed due to some unavoidable reasons. The company, however, in its own wisdom, paid the import duty out of its cash credit account, *i.e.* the short-term loan granted by the commercial bank, for meeting its working capital requirements only.

After a few months, the bank came to know that the company had resorted to diversion of funds (application of short-term sources of funds for long-term uses). The bank thus, got alerted and deputed a top executive of the rank of a General Manager, in the Corporate Office of the Company, who was entrusted with the sole and exclusive power to take all financial decisions and authorise all disbursements of funds on behalf of the company.

Had the term-loan been released within a couple of months, as it was expected by the company, and the company would have deposited back the funds in its cash credit account, the bank would not have ever sensed the irregularity on this count, and the company would have continued to enjoy the full trust and credibility with the bank.

But, once the diversion of funds came to the knowledge of the bank, all the goodwill and credit-worthiness of the company, established by the company during the course of long and steady dealings with the bank, got shattered and demolished with a single stroke of distrust. This factor led to the cause of decay and downfall of the company, so much so that one of the blue chip companies of the J.K. Group got a beating in the stock exchanges, too, in that the price of its shares of the face value of Rs. 10 each dropped down from around Rs. 100 to even below par. Therefore, it would always augur well for the companies not to indulge in the risky action of diversion of funds.

Now, a question arises as to whether the company should finance its working capital requirements out of:

(*i*) short-term sources of funds only; or

(*ii*) long-term sources of funds only; or

(*iii*) out of an optimal mix of both (*i*) and (*ii*).

If the entire working capital requirement is decided to be met by short-term sources only, it may not be free from risks emanating from the Reserve Bank of India directives to impose ceilings on the level of bank credit, in respect of each borrower. Such directives had been of different features in the past.

For example, in 1973-74 the Reserve Bank of India had decided that the level of credit limit of each borrower will be frozen at the level of drawings as on the specified Friday, immediately preceding the issue of the Reserve Bank of India directive.

But this, in effect, meant that the borrowers, who managed their working capital more effectively and smartly, by keeping it at a minimal level (to reduce the quantum of interest outgo and the corresponding rise in their profit), instead of having been rewarded, were punished by way of pruning their credit limits and eligibility.

After having suffered due to such directives of the Reserve Bank of India, the borrowers tended to avail of their working capital limit to a rather fuller extent and lent the surplus funds at a higher rate of interest, thereby increasing the quantum of other income. The Reserve Bank of India ultimately realised its mistake and subsequently decided to freeze the limit at the level of the highest outstandings on the account, during the period of the last three years or so.

This was, obviously, more equitable and reasonable. But, thereafter, the borrowers adopted a counter strategy. They would withdraw the full amount of the sanctioned working capital limit, at least for a day, and pay heavy interest thereon (but only for a single day), so that, in the event of issuance of a Reserve Bank of India directive, their eligibility will continue to be up to the level of their sanctioned credit limit.

It, however, is yet to be seen as to what further novel strategy would the Reserve Bank of India adopt to counter the aforesaid strategy adopted by most of the companies.

Another risk attached with too much dependence, exclusively on short-term sources, like working capital loan from the bank, may be said to be depending on the whims and fancies of different bank managers with divergent mind sets. Besides, the periodical submission of detailed information and reports, as per the requirements of the bank, from time to time, is yet another hindering factor.

As against this, when you finance your working capital requirements substantially from long-term sources, the banks hold you in a very high credit ratings, and may request you to avail of some credit facilities from them, too, as we also tend to invite people for dinner, who are well fed at their own homes.

Therefore, the prudence and pragmatism of financing working capital requirements with an optimal mix of short-term and long-term sources of funds, can hardly be over-emphasized. The question that ultimately arises now is as to how to determine the optimal level of, and the proportion of such financing, from short-term and long-term sources of funds.

With a view to arrive at a definite decision in this regard, let us first try to understand the concepts of:

(*i*) Permanent (or core) Current Assets; and

(*ii*) Temporary (or fluctuating) Current Assets.

As we all know, the permanent (or core) current assets (out of the total current assets) is said to be the lowest level of the company's current assets charged to the bank (or the corresponding level of the working capital loan), below which it has never gone for the last few years. This also represents the working capital requirement of the company even at the lowest level of its sales cycle. Thus, the entire core assets, which will be of the nature of permanent current assets of the company, must invariably and exclusively be financed by long-term sources, like equity, debentures (rights issue), etc.

Now, the question arises as to what level should be considered to be optimal in the case of financing of the temporary (or fluctuating levels of) current assets of the company, which keep on changing in accordance with the seasonal demands, or even some other market factors, affecting the demand.

At this stage, the following two strategic decisions emerge in certain terms:

(*i*) All the fixed assets of the company must invariably and exclusively be financed from long-term sources only.

(*ii*) The entire permanent (or core) current assets of the company must also be financed by long-term sources only.

These strategies are based on the Matching Principle, discussed hereunder:

Matching Principle

According to the matching principle, the due dates of repayment of all the advances—both short-term and long-term obtained for acquiring the respective assets—both current assets and fixed assets, should match with the time of generation of or conversion into cash, out of such assets. That is, while the fixed assets and the permanent (core) current assets must be financed by long-term sources of finance, the temporary (fluctuating) current assets alone may be financed by the short-term sources of funds, or by a suitable mix of both the short-term and long-term sources of finance.

Thus, the only decision that now remains to be taken is as to what should be the proportion of short-term and long-term sources of funds to finance the temporary or flexible components of the current assets, which keep varying, depending upon the level of sales and the matching level of production.

Three possible situations emerge for financing the flexible components of current assets:

(*i*) The entire temporary (flexible) components of the current assets should also be financed entirely from long-term sources of funds. But then, in such a case, the company will be left with surplus funds in all the situations when the current assets would remain at the lower levels than the peak level. And, such surplus funds, if parked for a short period, may give a return of a much lower proportion than the rate of interest payable on the funds borrowed.

This would result in a net loss to the company at almost regular intervals, whenever the demand of the product would get sluggish (and thereby the quantum of production and the corresponding demand of the raw materials). Therefore, this strategy does not seem to be sound and prudent enough.

(*ii*) The second situation may be just the opposite of the first one. That is, the entire fluctuating levels of current assets must be financed exclusively by short-term sources only. But then, this is fraught with great risk of imposition of credit squeeze policy by the Reserve Bank of India (RBI), based on some different criteria. Under such situation also, the company would be facing some avoidable financial difficulties, which may, in a way, be called a self-created and self-imposed one, as it would be based upon the apparently imprudent policy of financing the entire fluctuating current assets by short-term sources only.

(*iii*) Now, ultimately, we are left with the third option of the middle-of-the-road strategy. That is, the fluctuating components of the current assets must be financed with a suitable mix of both long-term and short-term sources of funds. Thus, when the level of demand, and the matching level of production (depending upon the expected sales), would be at somewhat lower or even at the lowest level, the surplus, arising out of the long-term sources of funds, may be invested for a suitable short-term. And, in the case of peak levels of demand, the short-term sources of funds would be fully availed of.

All considered, the third strategy seems to be the most suitable one to be adopted.

All the three aforesaid situations can very well be illustrated with the help of a graphic presentation, given hereafter.

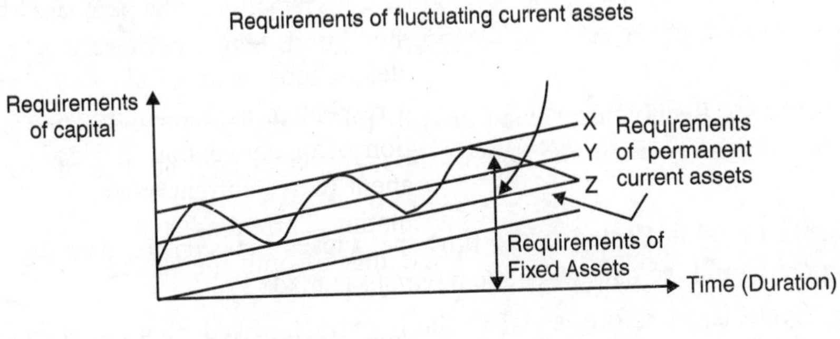

Fig. 2.3: Three Strategies Indicated by Lines Marked X, Y and Z

Operating Cycle

We have seen, in the previous pages, that the operating cycle in a manufacturing company comprises cash (and near cash), inventories (raw materials, consumable stores and spares, work-in-process and finished goods) and sundry debtors. A trading company, however, where the manufacturing activity is not involved, has a much shorter span of operating cycle as it is exclusive of the raw materials and work-in-process stages.

These items are financed partly from the owners' equity and partly by the bank and other creditors. Besides, the company also gets raw materials from the suppliers on credit, for which the payment is to be made after the expiry of the stipulated credit period, say, one month, two months or three months. Thus, the funds are required only to finance all the items contained in the operating cycle (including raw materials purchased on cash payment basis) but excluding the quantum of raw materials obtained on credit, as these are payable at a later date.

2.8 OPERATING CYCLE AND CASH CYCLE

We may, therefore, conclude that all the aforesaid items, including the items of raw materials, consumable stores and spares, etc., constitute the operating cycle. As against this, however, the cash cycle comprises the items included in the operating cycle, less the items of raw materials, and consumable stores and spares, obtained on credit, payable and, therefore, involving cash out flows, only at a later date.

Therefore, we may summarise that:

Operating Cycle = Raw Materials (and consumable stores and spares)
+ Work-in-process
+ Finished Goods
+ Bills Receivable
+ Minimal amount of Cash Balance required for meeting the day-to-day requirements.

Thus, the **Operating Cycle** = RM + W – I – P + FG + BR + Cash Balance.

And, **Cash Cycle** = [RM + W – I – P + FG + BR + Cash Balance] (less) BP (Bills Payable or Accounts Payable or Sundry Creditors).

Further, the **Inventory Period** is the period that elapses between the purchase of raw materials and the sale of finished goods, and not the finished goods stage, because this itself comprises finished goods inventory.

And, the **Accounts Receivable Period** or Bills Receivable period or Sundry Debtors period, is the period that elapses between the date of the credit sales and the date of realization of the sale proceeds.

The **Accounts Payable Period** is the time that lapses between the date the raw materials are received on credit and the date when the payment is made.

Operating Cycle is, therefore, equal to the inventory period plus the accounts receivable period.

Cash Cycle is, however, equal to the operating cycle less the accounts payable period.

Thus, the

$$\text{Inventory Period} = \frac{\text{Average Inventory}}{\text{Annual Cost of Good Solid/365 (or 360, if 360 days are taken to a year)}} \text{(Days)}$$

$$\text{Accounts Receivable Period} = \frac{\text{Average Accounts Receivable}}{\text{Annual (Credit) Sales/365}} \text{(Days)}$$

$$\text{Accounts Payable Period} = \frac{\text{Average Accounts Payable}}{\text{Annual (Credit) Purchases/365}} \text{(Days)}$$

If we take these figures from the balance sheet of the company, we may have to take the average by adding the closing balances of the two successive years divided by two [or the opening and closing balances of the same (current) year] divided by two. But, with a view to get a more accurate and realistic picture, we may take the total of month-end figures for the last twelve months divided by 12, or better still, if we take the weekly figures for the last 52 weeks and divide the total by 52.

For this, we may have to call for the respective break-ups from the company. It would, however, be readily available for the executives of the company.

Now, let us understand the concept with the help of an **illustrative example** of XYZ Company.

Data from the Balance Sheet of the Company (Rs.)

Descriptions	*Opening Balance*	*Closing Balance*
Inventory	100	110
Accounts Receivable	90	96
Accounts Payable	80	86

Data from the Profit and Loss Account of the Company

Total Annual Sales	Rs. 1400
Annual (Credit) Sales	Rs. 1000
Cost of Goods Sold	Rs. 860
Annual (Credit) Purchases	Rs. 730

I. Inventory Period $= \frac{(100+110) \div 2}{860 \div 365} = \frac{105}{2.36}$

$= 44.50$ (days)

II. Accounts Receivable Period $= \frac{(90+96) \div 2}{1000 \div 365} = \frac{93}{2.74}$

$= 33.94$ (days)

III. Accounts Payable Period $= \frac{(80+86) \div 2}{730 \div 365} = \frac{83}{2.00}$

$= 41.50$ (days)

IV. Operating Cycle $= (I) + (II)$

$= 44.50 + 33.94 = 78.44$ (days)

V. Cash Cycle $= (I) + (II)$ less (III)

$= 78.44 (-) 41.50$

$= 36.94$ (days).

2.9 TIME-SERIES ANALYSIS VS. CROSS-SECTION ANALYSIS

Analysis and monitoring of the behaviour of each component of the operating cycle individually and separately, as also of the operating cycle as a whole, is of great help in the management and control of working capital and operating cycle time. In this regard, the

(*i*) time-series analysis (like the intra-firm comparison); and the

(*ii*) cross-section analysis (like the inter-firm comparison); may also be of great help.

In the time series analysis the aggregate period of the operating cycle and the periods of the individual components thereof are compared over a period of time in respect of the same company. This is like the intra-firm comparison.

In the cross-section analysis, however, like the inter-firm comparison, the duration of the operating cycle as also that of its individual components of this company is compared with those of some other companies of comparable nature in regard to the line of business and the scale of operations. And, based upon the respective analysis and findings, suitable corrective steps are enunciated and initiated, and that too, promptly.

To quote Lee Iacocca, the management wizard, taking and acting on the business decision is like "shooting a flying duck"; you shoot it here and now, or else it flies away, and thus the business opportunity. He further elaborates that if a problem be given to the MBA students of say, Harvard Business School, they may provide you with a thorough analysis and the most appropriate decision in the matter, but then, they may take far too long to do so, and by then the business scenario itself would have undergone a sea change. Therefore, time is money, and specially so, in money matters (*financial management*).

A SYNOPTIC NOTE
(CHAPTER 2 AT A GLANCE)

WORKING CAPITAL POLICY

1. WORKING CAPITAL MANAGEMENT

Working Capital Management means management of Current Assets and Current Liabilities as also long-term sources of funds, *i.e.* Deferred Liabilities and Owners' Equity, used to finance Current Assets.

Gross Working Capital = Total Current Assets

Net Working Capital = Current Assets (Less) Current Liabilities.

2. COMPONENTS OF CURRENT ASSETS

(*i*) Cash (in hand, in bank and in transit)

(*ii*) Investments (short-term only, and not long-term)

(*iii*) Inventories (raw materials and consumable stores and spares, work-in-process, and finished goods)

(*iv*) Sundry Debtors (also known as Bills Receivable and Accounts Receivable)

(*v*) Loans and Advances, granted by the Company.

3. COMPONENTS OF CURRENT LIABILITIES

(*i*) Sundry Creditors, also known as Bills Payable and Accounts Payable

(*ii*) Trade·Advances, given to the company for the supply of goods

(*iii*) Short-term Borrowings from banks and others

(*iv*) Provisions for taxes, bad debts, exchange rate fluctuations, etc.

Better business sense, however, calls for keeping the current assets at the minimal level, whereby minimum sources of funds, both current and non-current liabilities, may be required to finance them, and thereby, the "inventory carrying costs", and the "interest outgo" may as well be kept at the minimal level.

4. WORKING CAPITAL MANAGEMENT VS. PROJECT MANAGEMENT

(*i*) While working capital management is flexible enough, the project management is inflexible, with respective ramifications, applicable in both the cases.

(*ii*) Current assets get converted into cash in the usual course of business during the operating cycle, usually within one year, whereas the returns on projects keep coming in small doses, spread over a period of time, say, 5 – 10 years.

5. THE OPERATING CYCLE COMPRISES

(*a*) (*i*) Cash and near cash, viz. Government Securities, Quoted Shares of Non-Subsidiary Companies, etc.;

(*ii*) Raw Materials;

(*iii*) Work-in-process;

(*iv*) Finished Goods; and

(*v*) Bills Receivable.

(*b*) The operating cycle of a trading company, however, is much shorter, inasmuch as it does not involve any raw material or work-in-process.

(*c*) Cash Cycle = Operating Cycle (less) Bills Payable.

(*d*) Quick Assets = Current Assets (less) Inventories.

6. TEAM SPIRIT

The synergy of team spirit, among various functionaries like, purchase, materials, production and marketing departments, is the essence of effective working capital management and control, and the resultant optimal profit.

The finance department, of course, performs the overall coordination role.

7. QUANTUM OF WORKING CAPITAL REQUIREMENTS

It largely depends on:

(*i*) Nature of business (e.g. Bakery, Automobiles, Heavy Engineering Goods);

(*ii*) Seasonal character of industry (e.g. fans and fridges; rugs and woollens);

(*iii*) Production Policy (e.g. varying with peak and slack season);

(*iv*) Market conditions (like competition, etc.); and

(*v*) Supply condition of materials.

8. OPTIMAL LEVEL OF CURRENT ASSETS

The best working capital policy may be said to be the golden mean of the "conservative policy" and the "aggressive policy". That is, where the inventory carrying costs and the stock-out costs are at the minimal levels. Simply speaking, it should be "neither too much, nor too little".

9. WORKING CAPITAL FINANCING POLICY

The best policy may be an optimal mix of short-term sources of funds and long-term sources of funds. That is, the core (or permanent) Current Assets (CAs) [besides the entire fixed assets] must necessarily be financed from the long-term sources, based on the "Matching Principle". Besides, a reasonable portion of the temporary (or fluctuating) current assets may as well be financed from long-term sources of funds, such that during the time of lower demand of the product, and the corresponding lower level of production, the resultant surplus funds could be temporarily parked in some suitable short-term investments. The remaining portion of the fluctuating current assets must, of course, be financed out of the short-term sources of funds.

However, care should always be taken not to use the short-term sources of funds for acquiring fixed assets, inasmuch as this does amount to diversion of funds, which is viewed by the commercial banks with great disfavour, e.g. the case of J.K. Synthetics Limited.

10. TIME-SERIES ANALYSIS VS. CROSS-SECTION ANALYSIS

The time-series analysis (the intra-firm comparison) gives us the idea as to how the company has been able to perform this year, as compared to the previous year(s).

As against this, the cross-section analysis or the inter-firm comparison indicates as to how has the company performed this year in comparison to the performance of other companies, in the similar line of business, and of the similar scale of operation.

But, just doing such an analysis is not good enough. We should, instead, ensure that a suitable action is taken, based on the reasoned analysis, and that too promptly and in time. Because, time is money, and specially so, in the matters of money, *i.e.* financial management.

QUESTIONS

(For Self-Assessment)

1. What are the main features of current assets?

   What are their chief ramifications in the management of working capital?
2. What are the various factors that are considered for assessment of the working capital requirements?
3. (*a*) What do you mean by the conservative and aggressive (flexible and restrictive) policies?

   (*b*) How do these affect (or determine) the levels of the various components of current assets?

4. "For a growing firm, the level of total assets keep on changing over a period of time". Do you agree? Explain, by citing suitable illustrative examples.
5. What do you mean by the term "Operating Cycle"? Explain, with the help of suitable illustrative examples.
6. (*a*) Distinguish between "Operating Cycle" and "Cash Cycle" by citing suitable illustrative examples.
   (*b*) What is the rationale behind drawing such a distinction?
7. Distinguish between "Permanent Current Assets" (also known as Core Current Assets) and "Temporary Current Assets".
8. "Current Assets" must be financed with an optimal mix of short-term sources of funds and long-term sources of funds, in the most appropriate proportions." Do you agree? Give reasons for your answer.
9. (*a*) Some persons may argue that the Working Capital Requirements, being of short-term nature, should be exclusively financed from short-term sources of funds. Do you agree? Give reasons for your answer.
   (*b*) What would be your reasoned recommendations regarding the mode of financing Working Capital requirements?
10. What do you mean by "Matching Principle"? Explain the concept by citing suitable illustrative examples.
11. (*a*) Distinguish between the following two concepts of Working Capital:
    (*i*) Gross Working Capital; and
    (*ii*) Net Working Capital.
    (*b*) Which one of the two concepts have the greater relevance for the management of Working Capital? Give reasons for your answer.
12. Distinguish between short-term investments and long-term investments, by giving suitable examples to illustrate your points.
13. What are the main components of inventories? Explain, with the help of some suitable illustrative examples in each case.
14. What are the main components of
    (*a*) Working Capital Management, and
    (*b*) (*i*) Current Assets, and
    (*ii*) Current Liabilities?
    Give suitable examples in each case.
15. Bring out the main distinguishing features between
    (*a*) Working Capital Management, and
    (*b*) Project Management.
16. "For the operation of an effective working capital management at the optimal level, all the respective departments/functionaries, like the purchase, materials, production, marketing, besides the finance, must work in close coordination and as a well-knit team." Discuss.
17. "The quantum of Working Capital requirement depends upon various factors like:
    (*a*) Nature of business,
    (*b*) Seasonal nature of industries,

(*c*) Production Policy,

(*d*) Market Conditions, and

(*e*) Supply Conditions (of materials)".

Do you agree with the above statement? Give reasons for your answer, citing suitable illustrative examples in each case.

18. (*i*) What do you understand by the undernoted 'types' of working capital policy?

(*a*) Conservative (or Liberal or Flexible) Policy;

(*b*) Aggressive (or Strict or Restrictive) Policy; and

(c) Moderate (or middle-of-the-road) Policy.

Explain, by giving suitable illustrative examples, in each case.

(*ii*) Which one of the aforesaid three policies, in your considered opinion, would be the most suitable one, in most of the cases? Give reasons for your answer.

19. (*a*) Which one of the following strategies, in your considered opinion, should be adopted for financing the working capital requirements of most of the companies:

(*i*) From short-term sources of funds only;

(*ii*) From long-term sources of funds only; and

(*iii*) Out of an optimal mix of (*i*) and (*ii*), above? Give reasons for your answer.

(*b*) Please examine the positive and negative aspects of each of the above financing strategies, and then come to some specific logical conclusions, with convincing reasons, in favour of your concrete and specific contentions and stands.

20. What do you understand by the following terms?

(*i*) Time-Series Analysis, and

(*ii*) Cross-section Analysis, in regard to the

(*a*) Operating Cycle, as also

(*b*) Its various components, individually?

Explain your points, by giving suitable illustrative examples, in each case.

PROBLEMS FOR PRACTICE

1. **Some financial information for Akash Automobiles Limited is given hereunder:**

Extracts from the Balance Sheet of the Company as on:		**(*Rs. in lakh*)**
	31.3.2008	*31.3.2009*
Raw Materials	80	85
Work-in-progress	40	45
Finished Goods	60	65
Bills Receivable	200	230
Bills Payable	100	110

Extracts from the Profit and Loss Account of the Company for the year ended 31.3.2009

	(*Rs. in lakh*)
Sales	1600
Cost of goods sold	1200

Required

Compute the duration of
(*i*) Operating Cycle, and
(*ii*) Cash Cycle, of the Company.

2. **Some relevant financial information for Kartika Kosmetics Limited is as follows:**

Extracts from the Balance Sheet of the Company as on:

		(*Rs. in lakh*)
	(*30.06.2008*)	(*30.6.2009*)
Raw Materials	35	38
Work-in-progress	12	14
Finished Goods	25	28
Bills Receivable	96	105
Bills Payable	48	55

Extracts from the Profit and Loss Account of the Company for the year ended 30.6.2009

	(*Rs. in lakh*)
Sales	600
Cost of goods sold	430

Required

Compute the duration of
(*i*) Operating Cycle, and
(*ii*) Cash Cycle, of the Company.

3

ANALYSIS OF THE COMPONENTS OF CURRENT ASSETS

Life is like riding a bicycle. You don't fall off unless you stop peddling.

Claude D. Pepper

The highest use of capital is not to make more money, but to make money do more for the betterment of life.

Henry Ford

If you cannot make money on one dollar, if you do not coax one dollar to work hard for you, you won't know how to make money out of one hundred thousand dollars.

E.S. Kinnear

The Learning Points

The chapter aims at developing the knowledge and facilitating the understanding of:

- Various Components of Current Assets and their Analysis
- Operating Cycle Analysis
- Weighted Operating Cycle Analysis
- Working Capital Leverage Analysis

3.1 OPERATING CYCLE ANALYSIS

Operating Cycle Analysis (OCA) has been of immense benefit in determining the duration of the period that a single operating cycle takes to complete. This gives us the idea about the length of time each component of the working capital involved in the operating cycle, will require investment (or blockage) of funds therein. This means that, if the operating cycle is of a longer duration, more funds are required to finance the components, which, in turn, will involve higher costs in the form of inventory carrying costs and interest outgo or opportunity costs. The reverse will be the position if the operating cycle period is shorter. Therefore, "shorter the better" should be the motto in the management of the operating cycle, and that of working capital which goes with it.

Let us try to understand the principles and procedures involved, a little more clearly, with the help of the following diagram (Figure 3.1):

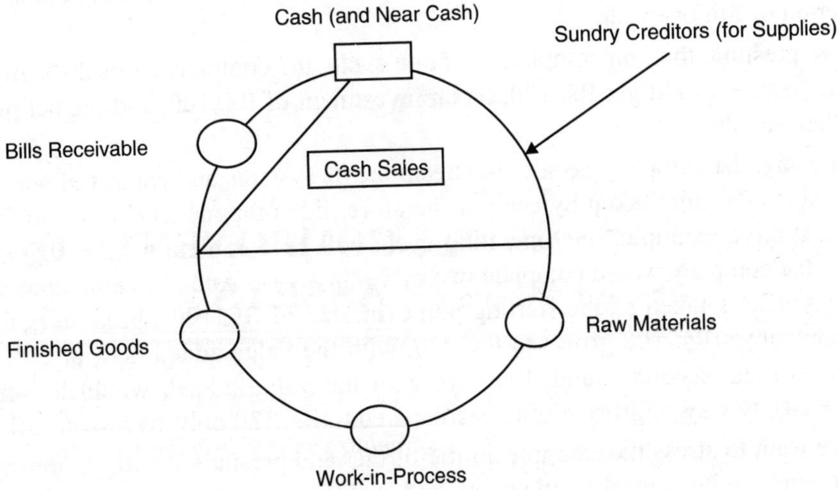

Fig. 3.1: Operating Cycle

As is evident from the above figure, the process starts with the investment (or outflow) of cash for the purchase of raw materials and ends-up in the collection of the bills receivable (or inflow) of cash. Thus, from the stage of cash outflow to cash inflow, involving four stages in all, one cycle is complete, and this is known as one operating cycle.

Now, let us presume that in the process of production, (*i*) stocks of raw materials remain for four months; (*ii*) work-in-process takes one month; (*iii*) finished goods are stored for four months; and (*iv*) the collection period, on an average, ranges up to three months.

Thus, the time taken in completing one round; comprising four stages, from the cash outflow to cash inflow takes 4 + 1 + 4 + 3 = 12 months, in all.

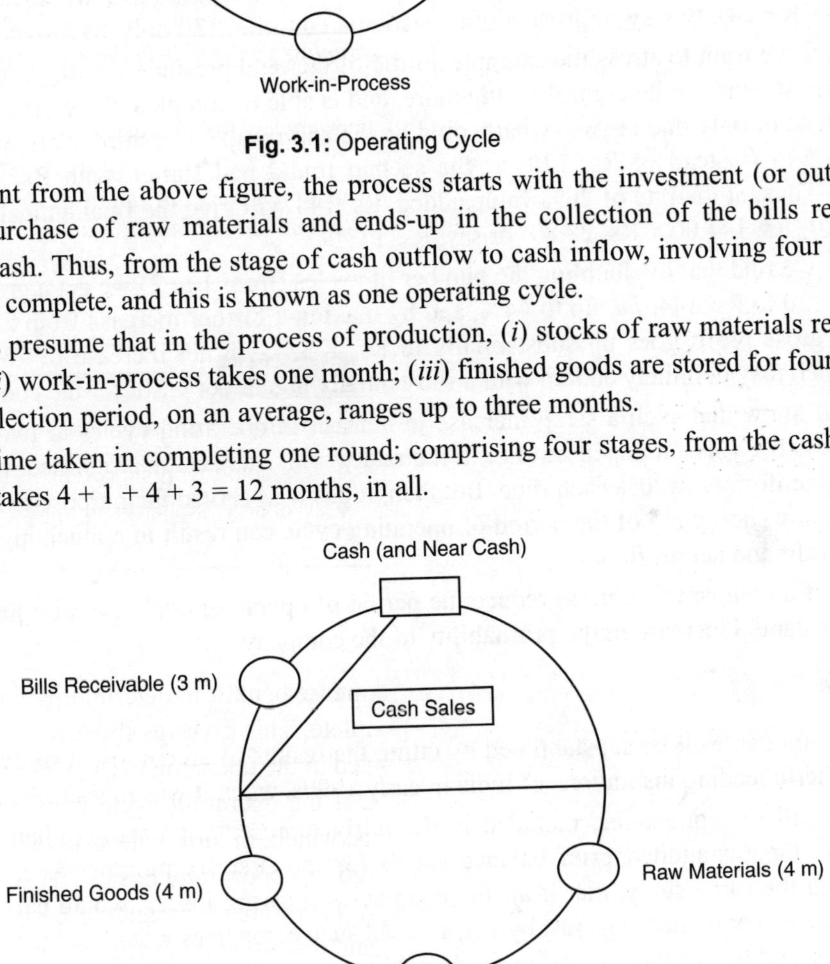

Fig. 3.2: Duration of operating cycle

In this way, the company is able to complete one full circle, *i.e.* one single operating cycle, during the period of full one year.

And, if we presume that, on completion of one cycle, the company earns 20% gross profit, at the end of the year, it would get Rs. 120, on an investment of Rs. 100, and the net profit will be even lesser than Rs. 20.

But, supposing, the company decides to streamline its systems and control of working capital, it is able to reduce the time taken by each of the aforesaid components (i to iv) to 50%, just by way of an illustrative example, one operating cycle will be complete in (2 + 0.5 + 2 + 1.5) 6 months. Thus, the company would complete two cycles in a year. And, for computing the quantum of turnover, Rs. 120 is taken as the starting point (instead of Rs. 100), because at the end of 6 months the company's Rs. 100 grows to Rs. 120, with the value added (say, at 20%). Thus, on the completion of the second round, Rs. 120, with the value added, would become Rs. 144 (Rs. 120 + Rs. 24) by way of gross profit, as compared to Rs. 120 only, as shown earlier.

And, if we want to stress the example a little further and presume that the company is able to tighten and streamline the control a little more, and is able to complete three operating cycles in a year, instead of only one or two, what would be the end result? The third cycle would again start from Rs. 144 (instead of Rs. 120, as the second round had started with Rs. 120, instead of Rs. 100). Thus, at the rate of 20% value added, Rs. 144 will give the final annual gross return of Rs. 172.80 (Rs. 144.00 + Rs. 28.80) or say, Rs. 173.

Thus, we find that by doubling the number of cycles (from 1 to 2) we get a gross profit raised from Rs. 120 to Rs. 144, *i.e.* up to 44%, and by making a further increase from 2 to 3 cycles per year, the gross profit goes up substantially to Rs. 173, *i.e.* a net increase of 73% in the gross profit, which may definitely end up with a substantially higher net profit for the company.

We all know that such a steep increase in number in operating cycles to two or three folds may be possible only on paper, but not in the real world. Increase may not necessarily be in the linear way uniformly @20% each time. But then, it has well served the purpose to bring home the point how any shortening of the period of operating cycle can result in a much higher percentage of gross profit and net profit.

Thus, if a company is able to reduce the period of operating cycle even by just 10%, it may mean a substantial increase in the profitability of the company.

Example

This point can well be substantiated by citing the results of an empirical study conducted by one of the term lending institutions of India in early 1990s, when it was revealed as under:

Almost all the companies, included in the fairly representative sample, had shown losses, based upon their unaudited brief balance sheets for the first six months. And, it was further observed, in the same study, that if all the companies showing losses, would care to reduce the level of their inventory holdings just by say, 1 %, all such companies would be ble to wipe off their entire losses, and would show some profit, though it may only be marginal.

Thus, if tightening of control of only one of the components of the operating cycle, and that too, just by 1 %, can show such an encouraging end-result, the importance of an all out effort to minimize the operating cycle time (by reducing it gradually by 10% to 15% or so) can hardly be over-emphasized. And, I believe that the statement that "there is no room on earth bigger than the room for improvement", may motivate and bestir even the complacent profit making companies to tighten their belts, and endeavour to achieve higher and higher standards of efficiency and effectiveness, profitability and prosperity, on an on-going basis, mainly by managing their working capital, so as to enable it to cover more mileage.

We may, therefore, define the duration of the operating cycle (D_{oc}) as the sum total of the time involved in all the four stages, viz.,

(*i*) the duration of the raw materials stage (including consumable stores and spares) – (D_{rm});

(*ii*) the duration of the work-in-process stage (D_{wip});

(*iii*) the duration of the finished goods stage (D_{fg}); and

(*iv*) the duration of the accounts receivable (or bills receivable or sundry debtors) stage (D_{ar}).

And, to compute the duration of the cash cycle (D_{cc}), we would just substract the period of accounts payable (or bills payable or sundry creditors) from the above aggregate figure.

To sum up, we may rewrite the two formulas as under:

(*i*) $D_{oc} = D_{rm} + D_{wip} + D_{fg} + D_{ar}$; and

(*ii*) $D_{cc} = [D_{rm} + D_{wip} + D_{fg} + D_{ar}]$ (less) $[D_{ap}]$.

Now, let us try to understand what does the duration of each of these four stages, of the four components, of the operating cycle, represent. We would also like to see as to how do we arrive at the duration of the cash cycle.

(*i*) **Duration of the Raw Material (and Consumable Stores and Spares) Stage:** This reflects the number of days for which raw materials, consumable stores and spares, etc. remain in the inventory before these are issued for production purposes. This may be calculated as under:

$$D_{rm} = \frac{\text{Average stocks or raw materials (and stores, etc.)}}{\text{Average raw materials (and stores, etc.) consumed per day}}.$$

(*ii*) **Duration of the Work-in-Process Stage:** This indicates the number of days that elapses in the work-in-process stage. It may be computed as under:

$$D_{wip} = \frac{\text{Average work-in-process inventory}}{\text{Average work-in-process value of raw materials committed per day}}.$$

(*iii*) **Duration of the Finished Goods Stage:** This represents the number of days for which the finished goods remain in the inventory, before they are sold out. This may be calculated as under:

$$D_{fg} = \frac{\text{Average stocks of finished goods}}{\text{Average cost of goods sold per day}}.$$

(*iv*) **Duration of the Sundry Debtors (or Bills Receivable or Accounts Receivable) Stage:** This indicates the number of days required to collect the sundry debtors. This may be computed as under:

$$D_{ar} = \frac{\text{Average sundry debtors (or accounts receivable or bills payable)}}{\text{Average credit sales per day}}.$$

(*v*) **Duration of the Sundry Creditors (or Accounts Payable or Bills Payable) Stage:** This denotes the number of days for which the suppliers' credit is available to the company. This may be arrived at as under:

$$D_{ap} = \frac{\text{Average sundry creditors (or accounts payable or bills payable)}}{\text{Average credit purchases per day}}.$$

Now, let us try to understand the calculation of the operating cycle as well as that of the cash cycle with the help of an **illustrative example.**

Example

The relevant pieces of the information in respect of Jyotsna Javeri (P) Limited are given hereunder:

- Average stocks of raw materials and consumable stores as well as spares : 240
- Average work-in-process inventory : 330
- Average stocks of finished goods : 200
- Average sundry debtors or bills receivable, or accounts receivable : 360
- Average sundry creditors or bills payable, or accounts payable : 220
- Average raw materials and stores, etc., consumed per day : 10
- Average work-in-process value of raw materials committed per day : 15
- Average cost of goods sold per day : 20
- Average credit sales per day : 18
- Average credit purchases per day : 11

On the basis of the aforesaid pieces of information, please calculate the duration of the various components of the (*i*) operating cycle and (*ii*) cash cycle.

Solution

(*i*) Duration of raw materials and consumable stores and spares (D_{rm}) = 240 ÷ 10 = 24 days

(*ii*) Duration of work-in-process stage (D_{wip}) = 330 ÷ 15 = 22 days

(*iii*) Duration of finished goods stage (D_{fg}) = 200 ÷ 20 = 10 days

(*iv*) Duration of sundry debtors or bills receivable or accounts receivable stage (D_{ar}) = 360 ÷ 18 = 20 days

(*v*) Duration of sundry creditors or bills payable or accounts payable (D_{ap}) = 220 ÷ 11 = 20 days.

The duration of the operating cycle D_{oc} $= D_{rm} + D_{wip} + D_{fg} + D_{ar}$

$= 24 + 22 + 10 + 20$

$= 76$ days.

And, the duration of the cash cycle (D_{cc}) is:

$$= D_{rm} + D_{wip} + D_{fg} + D_{ar} - D_{ap}$$
$$= 24 + 22 + 10 + 20 - 20$$
$$= 56 \text{ days}$$

(or $D_{cc} = D_{oc} - D_{ap} = 76 - 20 = 56$ days)

But, as we have found, the operating cycle analysis, or even cash cycle analysis, concentrates only on the duration or the time dimension of investment of funds in the respective components thereof. But, in fact, there may be a vast difference, in terms of value or quantum of investment among the various items of each of these components, *i.e.* at each of the stages of the operating cycle, as also of the cash cycle.

Thus, the calculation on the basis of the value of each component of the operating cycle may prove to be of much greater value and importance in the working capital management and control. Such extended analysis is referred to as the **weighted** operating cycle analysis and **weighted** cash cycle analysis.

3.2 WEIGHTED OPERATING CYCLE ANALYSIS

Calculation of the Weighted Operating Cycle

Step 1: Calculate the durations of the various stages of the operating cycle

The durations of the following stages may be easily computed with the help of the formula described in the previous pages.

D_{rm} (duration of the raw materials and stores etc. stage)

D_{wip} (duration of the work-in-process stage)

D_{fg} (duration of the finished goods stage)

D_{ar} (duration of the sundry debtors stage)

D_{ap} (duration of the sundry creditors stage)

Step 2: Determine the weights for the various stages of the operating cycle

The weights applicable to the various stages of the operating cycle should represent the proportions of the costs incurred up to that stage in relation to the selling price of the product. Hence, the weights, too, may have to be calculated as under:

Stage	**Weight**
Raw materials and stores stage	$W_{rm} = \dfrac{\text{Costs of raw materials (and stores, etc.) per unit}}{\text{Selling price per unit}}$
Work-in-process stage	$W_{wip} = \dfrac{\text{Costs of raw materials (and stores, etc.) per unit}}{\text{Selling price per unit}}$

Finished goods stage $W_{fg} = \dfrac{\text{Costs of goods sold per unit}}{\text{Selling price per unit}}$

Sundry debtors (or accounts receivable or bills receivable) stage

$$W_{ar} = \frac{\text{Selling price per unit}}{\text{Selling price per unit}}$$

Sundry debtors (or accounts receivable or bills receivable) stage

$$W_{ap} = \frac{\text{Costs of raw materials (and stores, etc., per unit)}}{\text{Selling price per unit}}$$

Step 3: Calculate the weighted operating cycle

The duration of the weighted operating cycle may be arrived at as under:

$D_{woc} = W_{rm} (D_{rm}) + W_{wip} (D_{wip}) + W_{fg} (D_{fg}) + W_{ar} (D_{ar})$

Step 4: Calculate the weighted cash cycle

[Similarly, the weighted cash cycle may be calculated as under:

$D_{wcc} = [D_{woc}] (-) [W_{ap} (D_{ap})]$

Let us now look into the detailed procedure of calculation of the weighted operating cycle and weighted cash cycle with the help of an illustrative example.

Example

The relevant pieces of information of Prashant Coolers (P) Limited, that is, the duration (or period) of each of the components of the operating cycle, as well as those of the cash cycle, are given hereunder:

D_{rm} = 36 days

D_{wip} = 24 days

D_{fg} = 12 days

D_{ar} = 36 days

D_{ap} = 24 days

The cost and price structures of the company are:

- Cost of raw materials and stores, etc. per unit : Rs. 60
- Processing cost per unit : Rs. 36
- Selling, administration, and financial costs per unit : Rs. 12
- Selling price per unit : Rs. 120

Based on the cost and price structures of the company, the weights applicable to the different stages of the operating cycle may be calculated as under:

$$W_{rm} = \frac{\text{Costs of raw materials and stores etc. per unit}}{\text{Selling price per unit}} = \frac{60}{120} = 0.50$$

$$W_{wip} = \frac{\text{Costs of raw materials and stores per unit} + 0.5 \text{ processing cost per unit}}{\text{Selling price per unit}} = \frac{60 + 18}{120} = 0.65$$

$$W_{fg} = \frac{\text{Costs of goods sold per unit}}{\text{Selling price per unit}} = \frac{108}{120} = 0.90$$

$$W_{ar} = \frac{\text{Selling price per unit}}{\text{Selling price per unit}} = \frac{120}{120} = 1.00$$

$$W_{ap} = \frac{\text{Costs of raw materials and stores etc. per unit}}{\text{Selling price per unit}} = \frac{60}{120} = 0.50$$

Now that both the durations of the various components of the operating cycle and the weights associated therewith are given, the duration of the weighted operating cycle can well be calculated as under:

$$\begin{aligned} D_{woc} &= W_{rm}(D_{rm}) + W_{wip}(D_{wip}) + W_{fg}(D_{fg}) + W_{ar}(D_{ar}) \\ &= 0.50\,(36) + 0.65\,(24) + 0.90\,(12) + 1.00\,(36) \\ &= 18 + 15.6 + 10.8 + 36 \\ &= 80.4 \text{ days (or say, 81 days).} \end{aligned}$$

And, accordingly, the duration of the weighted cash cycle will be

$$\begin{aligned} D_{wcc} &= D_{woc} - (W_{ap} \times D_{ap}) \\ &= 80.4 - (0.50 \times 24) \\ &= 80.4 - 12 \\ &= 68.4 \text{ days (or say, 69 days).} \end{aligned}$$

Application of Weighted Operating Cycle (in Assessing the Working Capital Requirement)

The concept of the weighted operating cycle has been very effectively and usefully applied for estimating the working capital requirement of a company. As we all know:

Working capital requirement = Sales per day × Weighted operating cycle + Cash balance requirement

Example

Let us understand the process of estimating the working capital requirement of a company with the help of an illustrative example. The following pieces of information (financial figures) of Talwar Motors Limited are available:

Sales per day	= Rs. 40 million [1 million = 10 lakh]
Cash balance requirement	= Rs. 140 million
Weighted operating cycle	= 64 days

Please estimate the working capital requirement of the company.

Solution

Rs. 40 million × 64 + Rs. 140 million = Rs. 2560 million + Rs. 140 million = Rs. 2700 million.

We shall now attempt to solve an integrated **illustrative example.**

AN INTEGRATED EXERCISE

The following information is available for VXL Limited:

• Average stock of raw materials and stores	240
• Average work-in-process inventory	330
• Average finished goods inventory	200
• Average accounts receivable	360
• Average accounts payable	220
• Average raw materials and stores consumed per day	10
• Average work-in-process value of raw materials committed per day	15
• Average cost of goods sold per day	20
• Average credit sales per day	18
• Average credit purchases per day	11

The cost and price structure of VXL Limited is as follows:

• Raw materials and stores cost per unit	: Rs. 60.00
• Processing cost per unit	: Rs. 36.00
• Selling, administration and financial costs per unit	: Rs. 12.00
• Sales price per unit	: Rs. 120.00

- Sales per annum — 730 million units (assume 365 days to a year)
- Cash balance requirement — Rs. 70 million

Required

On the basis of the above information, please calculate:

(*a*) the duration of the weighted operating cycle;

(*b*) the duration of the weighted cash cycle; and

(*c*) the working capital requirement of the company.

Solution

(*a*) D_{rm} = 240 ÷ 10 = 24 days

(*b*) D_{wip} = 330 ÷ 15 = 22 days

(*c*) D_{fg} = 200 ÷ 20 = 10 days

(*d*) D_{ar} = 360 ÷ 18 = 20 days

D_{oc} = (*a* + *b* + *c* + *d*) = 76 days

(*e*) D_{ap} = 220 ÷ 11 = 20 days

D_{cc} = (D_{oc} – D_{ap}) = 56 days

(*i*) [W_{rm} 60 ÷ 120 = 0.50] × 24 = 12 days

(*ii*) [W_{wip} (60 + 36/2) ÷ 120 = 0.65] × 22 = 14.3 days (or 14 days)

(*iii*) [W_{fg} (108 ÷ 120) = 0.90] × 10 = 9 days

(*iv*) [W_{ar} (120 ÷ 120) = 1.00] × 20 = 20 days

[W_{oc} = (*i* + *ii* + *iii* + *iv*) = 55.3 days (or 55 days) **[Ans. (a)]**

(*v*) [W_{ap} = [(60 ÷ 120) = 0.50] × 20 = 10 days

[W_{cc} = (W_{oc} – W_{ap}) = (55.3 – 10) = 45.3 days (or 45 days) **[Ans. (b)]**

Working Capital Requirement of the Company = (Sales per day × W_{oc})
+ Cash Balance Requirement
= (Rs. 120 × 730 million × 55.3) ÷ 365 + Rs. 70 million
= (Rs. 240 million × 55.3) + Rs. 70 million
= Rs. 13,272 million + Rs. 70 million
= Rs. 13,342 million. **[Ans. (c)]**

3.3 WORKING CAPITAL LEVERAGE

Working Capital Leverage measures the sensitivity of return on investment (ROI) *i.e.* the earning power, to the changes in the level of current assets (CA_s).

This can easily be determined with the help of the following formula:

$$\text{Working Capital Leverage (WCL)} = \frac{\text{Percentage change in ROI}}{\text{Percentage change in CA}}$$

With a view to express the formula for using figures of the undernoted relevant items, we shall use the symbols noted thereagainst.

CA = Total value of current assets
[Gross working capital and not net working capital].

ΔCA = Change in the level of current assets

FA = Value of net fixed assets (not gross fixed assets)

TA = Value of total assets, *i.e.* CA + FA

EBIT = Earnings (Profits) before interest and taxes

ROI = Return on Investment, *i.e.* EBIT ÷ TA.

Let us now consider a case where the current assets are reduced by ΔCA, without, in any way, adversely affecting the earning capacity of the company. The percentage increase in ROI in this case will be equal to:

$$\left[\left(\frac{\text{EBIT}}{\text{TA}-\Delta\text{CA}}-\frac{\text{EBIT}}{\text{TA}}\right)\div\frac{\text{EBIT}}{\text{TA}}\right]$$

This expression, on simplification, will become:

$$\frac{\Delta\,\text{CA}}{\text{TA}-\Delta\,\text{CA}}$$

The percentage decrease in the current assets is simply:

Δ CA/CA

Hence,

$$\text{WCL}=\frac{\Delta\,\text{CA}}{\text{TA}-\Delta\,\text{CA}}\div\frac{\Delta\,\text{CA}}{\text{CA}}$$

$$=\frac{\text{CA}}{\text{TA}-\Delta\,\text{CA}}$$

And, in case there is an increase in the current assets, instead:

$$\text{WCL}=\frac{\text{CA}}{\text{TA}+\Delta\,\text{CA}}$$

Let us now try to have a better understanding with the help of an illustrative example:

Example

Some available pieces of information for ABC Limited and XYZ Limited are given hereunder:

Rs. in million

Descriptions	*ABC Limited*	*XYZ Limited*
Current Assets (CA)	Rs. 200	Rs. 80
Net Fixed Assets (FA)	Rs. 80	Rs. 200
Total Assets (TA)	Rs. 280	Rs. 280
Earnings Before Interest and Taxes (EBIT)	Rs. 70	Rs. 70
ROI	25%	25%

Required

Compute the working capital leverage with a reduction of 20% in current assets.

Solution

It will be equal to:

$$\text{WCL} = \frac{\text{CA}}{\text{TA} - 0.2\,\text{CA}}$$

For the two companies, ABC Limited and XYZ Limited, the WCL values are as follows:

$$\text{WCL (ABC Limited)} = \frac{200}{280-40} = \frac{200}{240} = 0.8333 \text{ or } 83.33\%$$

$$\text{WCL (XYZ Limited)} = \frac{80}{280-16} = \frac{80}{264} = 0.3030 \text{ or } 30.30\%$$

Thus, we find that the sensitivity of ROI to changes in the level of CA is far greater for ABC Limited than for XYZ Limited.

Similarly, the WCL for a 20% increase in current assets will be equal to:

$$\text{WCL} = \frac{\text{CA}}{\text{TA} + 0.2\,\text{CA}}$$

$$\text{WCL (ABC Limited)} = \frac{200}{280+40} = \frac{200}{320} = 0.625 \text{ or } 62.5\%$$

$$\text{WCL (XYZ Limited)} = \frac{80}{280+16} = \frac{80}{296} = 0.2703 \text{ or } 27.03\%$$

In the case of increase in CA also we find that the sensitivity of ROI to increase in the level of CA is far greater for ABC Limited than for XYZ Limited.

It may, therefore, well be inferred that in a company, if the value of total current assets (CAs) is proportionately substantially higher than its total investments in Non-Current Assets (NCAs), the sensitivity of ROI or WCL (Working Capital Leverage) will be much higher than if the position is just the reverse, as we have seen in the cases of ABC Limited and XYZ Limited.

A SYNOPTIC NOTE
(CHAPTER 3 AT A GLANCE)

ANALYSIS OF THE COMPONENTS OF CURRENT ASSETS

1. OPERATING CYCLE ANALYSIS

By finding out the aggregate duration of the operating cycle [comprising the total of the duration of each component of the operating cycle, *i.e.* raw materials, work-in-process, finished goods and bills receivable], we can determine the total time taken in the completion of one full circle.

Higher the operating cycle time, greater is the requirement of the working capital. It means higher inventory carrying cost and higher outgo of interest, as well as loss by way of opportunity cost, by investing as much higher sources of funds, both current liabilities and non-current liabilities.

Therefore, "lower (or shorter) the operating cycle, the better it is." But then, the level of inventory should not be too low, to create an on-going fire-fighting and crisis management exercise, throughout the year for procuring raw materials, etc. Therefore, here again, not the "minimal" but the "optimal" operating cycle should be the motto. This should be indeed the guiding principle.

However, lower the duration of the operating cycle, the greater will be the number of cycles completed, during the year. With each completed cycle, the value addition will increase progressively. The gross and net profits of the company will also go up.

All considered, our sincere attempt should be to effectively manage and control each and every item of the operating cycle, individually as also collectively, inasmuch as even 1 % reduction in the duration of just a single component of the operating cycle (like the inventories) may make a substantial difference in the bottom-line, especially of large scale companies, as has been revealed by a study made by one of the term lending institutions in India.

Thus, we may conclude that "eternal vigilance is the price of profitability", paving way for prosperity of the company.

2. WEIGHTED OPERATING CYCLE ANALYSIS

The weighted operating cycle analysis is a further improvement and refinement over the operating cycle approach. This is so, because, in the operating cycle analysis we take into consideration the period/duration of each stage of the various components of the operating cycle, viz. the duration at the inventories stage, work-in-process stage, finished goods stage, and bills receivable stage in absolute terms, *i.e.* in terms of number of days.

But, we do not give any weightage to any of the respective duration stages, which they rightly deserve, depending upon their individual percentage value, *i.e.* of blockage of funds at each stage, in terms of the percentage of sale value or the selling price of the finished goods.

To arrive at the weighted operating cycle (WOC) we may follow the undernoted steps:

(*i*) First, calculate the duration (in number of days) of the various stages of the Operating Cycle (OC).

(*ii*) Then, determine the weights for each stage of the operating cycle in terms of the selling price of the finished goods.

(*iii*) Now, you may easily calculate the weighted operating cycle.

And, with the help of the weighted operating cycle (WOC), you may assess the working capital requirement of the firms in a more realistic manner.

3. WORKING CAPITAL LEVERAGE

It measures the sensitivity of return on investment (ROI), *i.e.* the earning power of the company to the proportionate changes in the level of current assets.

The formula for calculating the working capital leverage (WCL) is:

Percentage change in ROI ÷ Percentage change in current assets

$$= \left[\left(\frac{EBIT}{TA - \Delta CA} - \frac{EBIT}{TA}\right) + \frac{EBIT}{TA}\right]$$

(And, on simplification, we get)

$$\frac{\Delta CA}{TA - \Delta CA}$$

And, the percentage decrease in CA = ΔCA + CA

Hence, WCL = [ΔCA/(TA – ΔCA)] + [ΔCA/CA]

= CA/(TA – ΔCA)

[This is so in the case of decrease in the level of CA].

And, in case there is an increase in the level of CA, the formula will change correspondingly to WCL = [CA/(TA + ΔCA)].

We may further observe that

If, in a company, the value of total current assets is proportionately higher than its total investment in net fixed assets and other non-current assets (NCAs), taken together, the WCL (or the sensitivity of ROI) will be comparatively much higher than in case the position is just the reverse.

QUESTIONS

(For Self-Assessment)

1. (*a*) What do you mean by "weighted operating cycle" approach?
   (*b*) Do you think that this is a significant improvement on the usual "Operating Cycle" approach?
2. What do you mean by the term "working capital leverage"? Explain the concept as also discuss the relative formula, by citing suitable illustrative example.

PROBLEMS FOR PRACTICE

1. The following information is available for Rakesh Olympics Limited:

• Average stock of raw materials and stores	400
• Average work-in-process inventory	500
• Average finished goods inventory	300
• Average accounts receivable	450
• Average accounts payable	250
• Average raw materials and stores consumed per day	18
• Average work-in-process value of raw materials committed per day	21
• Average cost of goods sold per day	25
• Average credit sales per day	30
• Average credit purchases per day	15

Required

Calculate the duration of the (*i*) operating cycle; and (*ii*) cash cycle of the company.

2. The cost/price structure for Rakesh Olympics Limited is as follows:

• Raw materials and stores cost per unit	Rs. 70
• Processing cost per unit	Rs. 30
• Selling, administration, and financial costs per unit	Rs. 15
• Sales price per unit	Rs. 140

Other information is the same as in Problem 1.

Required

Calculate the (*i*) weighted operating cycle; and
(*ii*) weighted cash cycle of the company.

3. The following information is available for two companies, ABC Limited and XYZ Limited

	ABC LTD.	XYZ LTD.
• Current Assets	Rs. 240 lakh	Rs. 100 lakh
• Net Fixed Assets	Rs. 160 lakh	Rs. 200 lakh
• Total Assets	Rs. 400 lakh	Rs. 300 lakh
• Profit Before Interest and Tax (PBIT)	Rs. 80 lakh	Rs. 75 lakh
• Return on Investment (ROI)	20%	25%

Required

Find out the working capital leverage in respect of both the companies, for:

(*i*) 25 per cent reduction in current assets, and

(*ii*) 20 per cent increase in current assets.

4. The following information is available for VXL Limited:

• Average stock of raw materials and stores	240
• Average work-in-process inventory	330
• Average finished goods inventory	200
• Average accounts receivable	360
• Average accounts payable	220
• Average raw materials and stores consumed per day	10
• Average work-in-process value of raw materials committed per day	15
• Average cost of goods sold per day	20
• Average credit sales per day	18
• Average credit purchases per day	11

The cost/price structure for VXL Limited is as follows:

• Raw materials and stores cost per unit:	Rs. 60.00
• Processing cost per unit:	Rs. 36.00
• Selling, administration and financial costs per unit:	Rs. 12.00
• Sales price per unit:	Rs. 120.00
• Sales per annum:	730 lakh units (assume 365 days to a year)
• Cash balance requirement:	Rs. 7 crore.

Required

On the basis of the above information calculate:

(*a*) the duration of the weighted operating cycle;

(*b*) the duration of the weighted cash cycle; and

(*c*) the working capital requirement, of the company.

4

MANAGEMENT OF CASH

Ready money is Aladdin's lamp. **Lord Byren**

Yesterday is a cancelled check: Forget it. Tomorrow is a promissory note: Don't count on it. Today is ready cash: Use it! **Edwin C. Bliss**

Money in the bank is like toothpaste in the tube. Easy to take out, hard to put back. **Earl Wilson**

Money is usually attracted, not pursued. **Jim Rohn**

The Learning Points

The chapter aims at developing the knowledge and facilitating the understanding of:

- Mechanism of Cash Budgeting
- Methods of Long-term Cash Forecasting
- Types of Reports and Statements for Control
- Imperative Need of Effective Management and Control of Sundry Debtors
- Distinction between Current Account and Cash Credit Account
- Advantages of Depositing Margin Money in Cash Credit Account
- Effective Management and Control of Payments
- Mechanism and Principles of Playing the Float
- Safe Avenues of Investment of Surplus Funds

Cash, being the most liquid asset, is always required for the day-to-day business operations. But the funds, in the form of cash, do not earn any interest. These, instead, cost loss of interest by way of opportunity cost, that is, by the amount of loss sustained by foregoing the alternative investment opportunity. Therefore, a prudent management invariably prefers to keep the hard cash at the minimum possible level, so as to maintain the required liquidity, and thereby the solvency of the firm, at the lowest possible cost. That is why, most of the companies generally hold cash to the extent of 1–3% only of their total assets at any point in time.

Broadly speaking, cash management comprises of three main functions:

1. To evolve and establish a reliable forecasting and reporting system,
2. To improve and streamline the system and mechanism of cash collection as well as cash payments, and
3. To achieve optimum savings and gainful investment of surplus cash for an appropriate period, till such cash would not be required for some purchases and payments.

4.1 CASH BUDGETING

To achieve the first objective, we should evolve and establish a dependable system of cash budgeting, based on some scientific and logical basis, and by using some relevant available data pertaining to possible cash receipts and cash payments. Cash budgeting, also known as short-term cash forecasting, has proved to be of great help and benefit in the following areas:

(*i*) In estimating, in a reasonably accurate way, cash requirements based on the items and amount of expected cash payments;

(*ii*) In estimating the extent of short-fall, if any, and to arrange for its financing from some reliable and cheaper sources of finance well in time;

(*iii*) In preparing a detailed purchase and payment schedule for acquiring some capital goods (fixed assets);

(*iv*) In planning and phasing the purchase of raw materials, etc.;

(*v*) In evolving and implementing credit policies, based upon the market trend and the company's liquidity position; and

(*vi*) In checking and verifying the accuracy, or otherwise, of the company's long-term cash forecasting, and making the necessary amendments, both in the cash forecast figures as well as in the system evolved for the purpose.

For preparing the Cash Budget or short-term forecasting, different companies may opt for different ranges of periods, further sub-divided into shorter periods, to suit the specific requirements.

But, as has usually been observed, most of the companies prepare cash budget for a period of one year, further subdivided into quarters, which, in turn, are again sub-divided into months. Some companies also prepare cash budgets on quarterly basis, further subdivided into months, and even weeks, depending upon their own specific requirements of greater details and shorter periods.

Thus, some companies, in very special cases (facing a high degree of liquidity crunch), may prefer to prepare even weekly cash budgets, further subdivided into daily basis. Thus, we may say that the details and the period may vary from company to company, to suit their specific requirements and financial position.

Table 4.1: Items of Cash Receipts and Payments and the Basis of Their Estimation

Items	*Basis of Estimation*
Cash Sales	Estimated sales and its bifurcation into cash and credit sales
Collection of Sundry Debtors (Bills Receivable, Accounts Receivable)	Estimated sales, its bifurcation into cash and credit sales and pattern of collection
Receipts of interest and dividend	Company's portfolio of shares and securities and income expected therefrom
Increase in loans/deposits, and issue of securities	Financial Plan
Sales of assets	Proposed disposal of assets
Cash Purchases	Estimated purchases, its bifurcation into cash and credit purchases, as also the terms of credit purchases
Payment for Purchases	Estimated purchases, its bifurcation into cash and credit purchases, as also the terms of credit purchases
Wages and Salaries	Manpower employed and wages and salaries payable
Manufacturing Expenses	Production Plan
General Administration and Selling Expenses	Administration and sales personnel and proposed sales promotion and distribution expenditure
Capital Equipment Purchases	Capital expenditure budget and payment pattern associated with the purchases of capital equipments
Repayment of loans and sale of Securities and Shares	Financing Plan

Receipts and Payments Method

The most important and primary method of short-term cash forecasting is the receipts and payments method. Under this method, the timings and quantum of the expected cash receipts and cash payments, during the budget period, are computed. It includes all types of receipts and payments, irrespective of their classifications (into expenses and expenditures, etc.) on the strict principles of accounting. The various items of cash receipts and payments, and the bases on which these may be estimated, are given in Table 4.1.

It may, thus, be observed that while preparing the cash budget on the basis of the receipts and payments method, mainly the following information may be required:

(*i*) Estimated sales (cash and credit sales)

(*ii*) Production plans,

(*iii*) Purchase plan,

(*iv*) Financing plan, and

(*v*) Capital expenditure budget.

Out of all these items, the most important and pivotal item seems to be the estimate of sales (both cash sales and credit sales) because, the various other plans and estimates are directly based upon the sales figures. Therefore, the companies should take some special care while estimating the level of sales, to make it nearly accurate. Thus, within a period of 2/3 years, after periodical review of the gaps between the estimated and actual figures, and by taking the required corrective steps from time-to-time the system of sales estimates may get stabilised.

With the help of some illustrative examples, let us now try to understand and appreciate the mechanism of preparation of Cash Budget, on the basis of receipts and payments method.

Examples

A. VXL Company Limited manufactures nuts and bolts. Its estimated sales for the period January through June next year are: Rs. 1,20,000 per month from January through March, and Rs. 1,44,000 per month from April through June. The sales for the months of November and December of the current year are expected at Rs. 1,20,000 each. Cash and credit sales are expected to be 25 per cent and 75 per cent, respectively.

The receivables from credit sales are expected to be collected as follows:

60 per cent of the receivables, on an average, one month after the date of sale and the balance 40 per cent, two months after the date of sale. No bad debt losses are expected to occur.

Other anticipated receipts are:

(*i*) Rs. 6,000 from the sale of a machine in February; and

(*ii*) Rs. 3,000 interest on securities in May.

Required

Given this information, prepare the budgeted cash receipts.

B. VXL Company Limited plans to purchase materials worth Rs. 48,000 in January and February, and materials worth Rs. 58,000 each month from March through June next year. The payments for these purchases are made approximately a month after the purchase. The purchases for the month of December of the current year have been estimated at Rs. 40,000, for which payment will be made in January next year. Miscellaneous cash purchases of Rs. 3,000 per month are planned from January through June. Wage payments are expected to be Rs. 18,000 per month from January through June. Manufacturing expenses are expected to be Rs. 23,000 per month from January through June. General administrative and selling expenses are expected to be Rs. 12,000 per month. Dividend payment of Rs. 24,000 and tax payment of Rs. 25,000 are scheduled in the month of June next year. A machine worth Rs. 90,000 is proposed to be purchased on cash payment basis in the month of March, next year.

Required

From the above information, compute the budgeted cash payments.

C. Now, assuming that the cash balance on January 1, next year, is Rs. 25,000 and the minimum cash balance required by the company is Rs. 24,000.

Required

(*i*) Prepare a summary statement, calculating the surplus/deficit in relation to the required minimum cash balance.

(*ii*) Further, find out whether any cash shortage is expected to occur during some month(s). And, if so, in which of the month(s) and, what are the specific reason(s) for such cash shortage(s), if any?

(*iii*) Do you think that the management can adopt some suitable measures to avoid or overcome such cash shortage(s), if any? Be specific in your suggestions.

Solutions

A.

Table 4.2: Budgeted Cash Receipts

(*Rs. in lakh*)

Sl. No.	*Items of Cash Receipts*	*Jan.*	*Feb.*	*March*	*April*	*May*	*June*
1	Sales	1.20	1.20	1.20	1.44	1.44	1.44
2	Credit Sales	0.90	0.90	0.90	1.08	1.08	1.08
3	Collection of Accounts						
	(*i*)	0.36 Nov	0.36 Dec	0.36 Jan	0.36 Feb	0.36 Mar	0.432 Apr
	(*ii*)	0.54 Dec	0.54 Jan	0.54 Feb	0.54 Mar	0.648 Apr	0.648 May
	(*i*) + (*ii*)	0.90	0.90	0.90	0.90	1.008	1.08
4	Cash Sales	0.30	0.30	0.30	0.36	0.360	0.36
5	Receipt from Sale of machines		0.06				
6	Interest on Securities					0.030	
	Total Cash Receipts (3 + 4 + 5 + 6)	**1.20**	**1.26**	**1.20**	**1.26**	**1.398**	**1.44**

B.

Table 4.3: Budgeted Cash Payments

(*Rs. in lakh*)

Sl. No.	*Items of Cash Payments*	*Jan.*	*Feb.*	*March*	*April*	*May*	*June*
1.	Material Purchases	0.48	0.48	0.58	0.58	0.58	0.58
2.	Credit Material Purchases	0.48	0.48	0.58	0.58	0.58	0.58
3.	Payment of Accounts Payable	0.40	0.48	0.48	0.58	0.58	0.58

(*Contd.*)

Sl. No.	Items of Cash Payments	Jan.	Feb.	March	April	May	June
4.	Miscellaneous Cash Purchases	0.03	0.03	0.03	0.03	0.03	0.03
5.	Wages	0.18	0.18	0.18	0.18	0.18	0.18
6.	Manufacturing Expenses	0.23	0.23	0.23	0.23	0.23	0.23
7.	General Administrative and Selling Expenses	0.12	0.12	0.12	0.12	0.12	0.12
8.	Dividend						0.24
9.	Tax						0.25
10.	Machine			0.90			
	Total (Items 3 to 10)	**0.96**	**1.04**	**1.94**	**1.14**	**1.14**	**1.63**

C.

Table 4.4: Summary Cash Forecast

(Rs. in lakh)

Sl.No.	Items	Jan.	Feb.	March	April	May	June
1.	Opening Cash Balance (Each Month)	0.25	0.49	0.71	(0.03)	0.09	0.348
2.	Receipts (Each Month)	1.20	1.26	1.20	1.26	1.398	1.44
3.	Payments (Each Month)	0.96	1.04	1.94	1.14	1.14	1.63
4.	Net Cash Flow (2-3) (Each Month)	0.24	0.22	(0.74)	0.12	0.258	(0.19)
5.	Closing Cash Balance (Each Month End) (1+4)	0.49	0.71	(0.03)	0.09	0.348	0.158
6.	Minimum Cash Balance required	0.24	0.24	0.24	0.24	0.24	0.24
7.	Surplus or deficit in relation to the minimum cash balance required (Each Month) (5-6)	0.25	0.47	(0.27)	(0.15)	0.108	(0.082)

From the summary of Cash Budget (Table 4.4), we see that a shortage of cash to the extent of Rs. 27,000, is expected during the month of March, which as a result of business operations, gets wiped off by May, due to some cash inflows.

We further see that the aforesaid cash shortage of Rs. 27,000 only is expected to occur mainly due to the proposed capital expenditure to the tune of Rs. 90,000 in the month of March. Such cash shortage can very well be avoided by the company by adopting one or more suggestions as under:

(*i*) By postponing the entire proposed capital expenditure, just by two months, that is to May, instead of March, or

(*ii*) By postponing only a portion of the payment (say, to the tune of Rs. 30,000) and by paying only a sum of Rs. 60,000 in the month of March itself, and the balance Rs. 30,000 in the month of May.

(*iii*) By resorting to some short-term loan for a period of two months only.

(*iv*) By delaying the payment of some sundry creditors (suppliers of materials) but only to the extent the credibility of the company may not get adversely affected.

(*v*) By speeding up the collection machinery so as to realise some sundry debtors expeditiously.

Cash shortage to the tune of just Rs. 820 is also expected to occur in the month of June, mainly due to the payment of dividend (Rs. 24,000) or payment of tax (Rs. 25,000).

(*i*) As for the payment of tax for the quarter ending 30th June, it cannot be postponed any further as it may entail some penalty for default. As against this, payment of dividend (Rs. 24,000) may be easily deferred by a month, as no such expenditure (like payment of dividend and/or tax) is expected next month.

(*ii*) Or else, an ad-hoc short-term loan or temporary irregularity (over drawings) on the account of the company could be permitted by the bank, to be adjusted in about a month's time. Here, we must also bear in mind that all the dividend warrants, sent to the shareholders, may not be presented by all of them during the month of June itself.

Variance in Cash Budget

As we look at the above statements of Cash Receipts and Cash Payments, as also the Summary Statement, we may, at times, get an impression as if these present a picture of precision. But, in fact, these are only expectations and projections, which may not necessarily get reflected exactly as such in the actual practice too. Instead, there are bound to be some variations, either way, depending upon the difference in the expected levels of cash inflows and outflows of the company. To take care of such an eventuality, it would augur well if the companies, instead of preparing just one Cash Budget, prefer to prepare at least three sets of Cash Budget, based upon different sets of assumptions, depending upon three different scenarios, viz.

(*i*) Normal conditions,

(*ii*) Pessimistic conditions, and

(*iii*) Optimistic conditions.

And, accordingly, different sets of contingency plans must also be prepared, so as to meet the specific eventualities taking place in actual business transactions (cash inflows and cash outflows).

Advantages and Disadvantages of the System

With a view to evaluate the related advantages and disadvantages, we may enlist some of these, though only illustratively, so as to decide upon the degree of dependability on these.

Advantages

(*i*) It provides a comprehensive picture of cash inflows and cash outflows, as well as resultant surplus or deficit. It enables the companies to plan, well in advance, for parking the surplus funds more gainfully as also to obtain the required finance promptly and at the lowest possible cost.

(*ii*) It may also alert the management of any possible deficit so as to control the cost and cash outflows, well in time, on a day-to-day basis.

Disadvantages

(*i*) The system may not prove to be reliable in the eventuality of undue delays in receipt of dues (cash inflows) or sudden demand for payment (cash outflows) due to some unexpected, but urgent purchases of materials, machines, etc.

(*ii*) The system does not reveal and reflect the changes in the movements of the working capital components, mainly in regard to the inventories and sundry debtors (bills receivable or accounts receivable).

Accordingly, a long-term cash forecasting may provide some help in overcoming such disadvantages.

4.2 LONG-TERM CASH FORECASTING

While the short-term cash forecasting usually covers a one-year period, the long-term forecasting may be done for a period of 2-3 years, or even five years. This way, it provides a larger perspective and picture of the company's cash position (surplus or deficit), and accordingly we can prepare the required investment and financing plans.

Such forecasts are of special significance in the case of planning for

(*i*) capital investments, and

(*ii*) long-term financing.

Here, one may argue that the long-term cash forecasting can well be prepared on the basis of the receipts and payments method itself. But, even for some obvious and valued reasons, long-term cash forecasting is done, based on "adjusted net income method".

This method largely resembles the funds flow statement, in that it estimates the company's (heavy) expenditure, expected in the future as also whether such expenditure can be met from internal generation of cash surplus.

Pro forma and Preparation of Adjusted Net Income Forecast

A pro forma for the preparation of the adjusted net income forecast is given hereunder. It should, however, be borne in mind that the relevant information for the purpose would be available only from the (short-term) cash budgets, as discussed earlier.

Table 4.5: Pro forma for the Adjusted Net Income Method

	2009	2010	2011	2012	2013
Sources					
Net Income after taxes (PAT)					
Non-cash charges					
(Depreciation, amortisation, etc.)					
Increase in borrowings					
Sales of equity shares					
Miscellaneous					
Uses					
Capital expenditures					
Increase in current assets					
Repayment of borrowings					
Dividend Payment					
Miscellaneous					
Surplus/Deficit					
Opening Cash Balance					
Closing Cash Balance					

4.3 REPORTS AND STATEMENTS FOR CONTROL

A. Monthly Performance Report on Cash Budget

As in the case of performance budgeting, periodical performance report must be submitted to the management, in the case of Cash Budgeting, giving therein the budgeted figures, the actual figures and the variances, if any, against each item, for control purposes. Specific reasons and convincing comments should also be incorporated in respect of each variance, both favourable and unfavourable, so that the consolidating and corrective steps, may be taken to make the cash budgeting exercise more scientific, and the estimates more accurate and dependable. This may prove to be of great help to formulate the company's financial policy and decision-making. Such reports may normally be sent on a monthly basis. In case, it is considered necessary, due to some financial crunch, the frequency of the report could well be made weekly, or even daily, depending upon the break-ups given in the Cash Budget documents.

B. Daily Cash Report

This report contains, on a daily basis, the opening cash balance, receipts, payments and the closing cash balance, showing the amount of cash surplus or deficit, as the case may be, so as to take suitable steps to ensure smooth running of the business.

C. Daily Treasury Report

This report is prepared on a more comprehensive manner than the Daily Cash Report. It provides a detailed picture of changes in cash, marketable securities, sundry debtors and sundry creditors.

4.4 EFFECTIVE MANAGEMENT AND CONTROL OF SUNDRY DEBTORS (ACCOUNTS RECEIVABLE OR BILLS RECEIVABLE)

Effective monitoring of sundry debtors (accounts receivable or bills receivable), with a view to expediting collections, is of vital importance in any cash management exercise. This may involve various steps, like prompt and accurate billing and expeditious dispatch of goods of right quality and in right quantity, so as to avoid any possible delay in the payment, due to the resultant dispute. A detailed discussion in this regard is available in Chapter 5, 'Management of Credit' [or 'Accounts Receivable', or 'Bills Receivable'].

Prompt Collection of Cheques

Immediately on receipt of the cheques, and/or bank drafts, they must be promptly deposited in the bank for credit of the proceeds to the company's account, because the avoidable delay, even of a single day, may postpone the credit of the proceeds in the company's account, costing the avoidable loss of interest to the company. In fact, as a former bank executive, I would suggest that some cheques of large amounts, of course, in small numbers, may be sent to the bank the same day, even beyond the stipulated time, fixed by the bank for the purpose of acceptance of the cheques. The bank official may accept such cheques, if you have maintained good relation with them.

In metropolitan cities, like Mumbai, Kolkata, Delhi, Chennai, three clearings take place, instead of the usual two. There is an additional clearing, known as the 'High Value Clearing', wherein only large amounts of cheques/drafts say, of Rs. 0.50 million and above, are accepted.

Now, however, the facility of 'High Value Clearing' has been extended to various cities, and the minimum value of the 'High Value Cheques' has also been reduced to Rs. 10 lakh only. In such cases, the proceeds of the high value cheques, deposited in time, are credited to the respective payee's account the same day.

This facility must meticulously be availed of and special care must be taken to ensure that no cheques, below the minimum acceptable amount, gets included in the list, whereby the whole lot of all the cheques, including even the eligible (high value) ones, may be refused by the bank.

Companies may also prefer to negotiate with the bankers for grant of a Demand Draft Purchased (DDP) limit of a specified amount, depending upon their genuine business requirements, under which the proceeds of the outstation cheques and bank drafts may be credited to the company's account the same day.

Now that most of the branches of all the major banks have since been switched over to on-line-system, the payment of the cheque(s), drawn on any of the branches, of the same bank, who have switched over to on-line-system, can be paid immediately at any of its branches all over India, just by pressing a button on the computer.

Alternatively, the banks may grant an overdraft limit against the outstation cheques and bank drafts (as is done in the case of supply/trade bills) under which the cheques may be sent on a collection basis, but an overdraft to the extent of say, 75 per cent of the total amount of cheques/drafts deposited, could be allowed on the account immediately on the deposit of the cheques/drafts with the bank. Such overdraft would, of course, get adjusted when the proceeds of such outstation cheques/drafts are credited to the accounts, and the Drawing Power (D.P.) on the account adjusted accordingly.

One more practical tip. The duplicate key(s) of the safe/drawer of the official concerned, who keeps the custody of the cheques/drafts overnight, must be available with the Chief Manager or such other responsible officer, so that if, for some unavoidable reason, the official concerned fails to attend the office the next day, the process of depositing the cheques/drafts is not interrupted.

Further, all the cheques received during the day, after the banking hours, must be kept ready, in every respect, the same evening, so that they may be deposited in the bank in the early banking hours, the very next day. This should facilitate the smooth working of the bank. The bank official may also are normally cooperative and accept a small number of cheques of relatively large amounts, even if received a little later in the day, *i.e.* a little after the stipulated time for acceptance of such cheques by the bank.

It has been observed that some companies do incorporate some unnecessary details (like the name and code number of the customer, the order number and date, etc.) in the bank's pay-in-slips for deposit of the cheques/drafts, involving wastage of the precious little time, causing some avoidable delay in the deposit of the cheques/drafts with the bank. Such practices, if prevailing, must be stopped forthwith, and only the bare minimum particulars, required by the bank, need be incorporated in the bank's pay-in-slip. Other particulars/details, required by the company for its own record and reconciliation, must be recorded and maintained in its own books and/or computers.

Decentralisation of Collections

A company, with its business, spread over a vast area, and its branches or offices located at different places, would do well to decentralise its collections, whereby it may drastically reduce the avoidable delays involved in the credit of the proceeds of the cheques in its account, centrally maintained with the corporate office. Under such an arrangement, the various branches and offices of the company receive the cheques directly from the customers for depositing them with their banks the same day. And, on realization of the proceeds of the cheques, they may be remitted for credit to the Head Office Account, by way of telegraphic transfer (as was the practice in the past) daily, weekly or fortnightly, as per the quantum of collections and the local requirements of funds for expenses. Such a practice, however, is no longer in vogue. Instead, due to the technological advancements the credit balances in the collection accounts, maintained at all the large centres, are transferred instantaneously, at the close of business the same day. The amounts in the collection accounts at rather smaller centres, however, are transferred by fax the same day. Telegraphic transfers have, thus, now virtually become a thing of the past, except in the case of some remote villages only.

Some big borrowers are known to have had the arrangement with the bank, as detailed hereunder:

A company enjoyed cash credit limit of several millions of rupees in their account with a bank maintained with its branch, located at the company's corporate office. All the drawings were made on this account. And the company maintained collection accounts at a large number of locations, spread all over the country. No remittance from these collection accounts were, however, made on a periodical basis. But, the company was not a looser on this count. Because, the interest was mutually agreed to be payable by the company on the amount of the net debit balance (*i.e.* the debit balance in the company's Head Office account, less the aggregate credit balances in all its collection accounts, maintained at the different branches of the same bank at different locations), on a day-to-day basis.

But, such special facilities may not be made available by the banks to the clientele. Therefore, all the companies and firms should arrange for the remittance of the funds from their respective collection accounts to their main corporate account. Such an arrangement is very beneficial, expeditious and even cost-effective, by virtue of the technological advancements now prevalent and popular in the banking system, too.

The company should, however, insist on periodical audit of its various collection accounts, maintained by its different branches/officers at different locations, to verify whether all the instructions, regarding periodical remittance of the specified (excess) amounts of collections have been meticulously carried out by the bank at all times. It should further be periodically ascertained through reconciliation of bank accounts, that each and every item of such remittances have been correctly and promptly credited to the company's main account at the Head Office.

Any discrepancy, if at all observed, must be pointed out to the bank in writing to make officers and staff alert and prompt in doing the needful.

4.5 CURRENT ACCOUNT *vs.* CASH CREDIT ACCOUNT

It has been observed that some of the Public Sector Undertakings (PSUs) prefer to keep two separate accounts at the same branch, viz.

(*i*) Current Account, meant for all deposits and some specified expenses only. This account, on an average, has a substantially high credit balance.

(*ii*) Cash Credit Account, which is a loan account, usually having very high debit balances, are also maintained simultaneously, mostly at the same branch.

Thus, the company does not earn any income by way of interest on the credit balance in its current account. As against this, the company keeps on paying huge amount by way of interest on the debit balance outstanding in its Cash Credit Account.

Let us fully understand and appreciate the financial implications of such an arrangement with the help of an **illustrative example.**

Example

A Public Sector Undertaking (PSU) maintained a Current Account and a Cash Credit Account at the same branch of the bank. As per the Balance Sheet, as on the 31st March, the position of its two accounts were as under:

Current Account	Rs. 4000 million (Credit)
(Interest earned on deposit - NIL)	
Cash Credit Account	Rs. 400 million (Debit)
(Interest paid on Advance @ 20% per annum)	

The simplest thing that the company could have easily done was to get Rs. 400 million transferred to the Cash Credit Account (first over telephone, and soon followed by a confirmation letter). This way, the PSU would have saved (and, in effect, earned) an interest outgo on Rs. 400 million @ 20% per annum, which comes to a substantial amount of Rs. 80 million per annum (just by way of a telephone call, followed by a confirmation letter).

Better still, if the remaining credit balance of Rs. 3600 million would have been gainfully invested in some suitable short-term schemes, including the term-deposits with the bank, breaking the entire amount for different maturity periods keeping in view the requirement of the company. Bank Term Deposit Receipts (TDRs) are considered to be preferable, as they are most secured and liquid investments, with the twin facility of getting advance payment or the provision of pre-mature payment, and, at the same time, earning some amount by way of interest too.

When these facts and features were brought to the notice of the Director (Finance) of the PSU, he was sharp enough to appreciate the point, and initiated the necessary action, whereby the cash and bank balance, as shown in the Balance Sheet of the company, drastically came down from Rs. 4,000 million to just Rs. 7.5 million and Rs. 5 million during the next two years.

Some senior finance executives have confided with me that the rationale behind maintaining two separate accounts (Current Account and Cash Credit Account) is that some specific transactions, under certain heads only, are effected through one of these accounts specified for the identified purposes. This way, it facilitated their exercise pertaining to the reconciliation of the bank accounts.

If this be the case, the company may instruct the bank to transfer the entire credit balance in its current account to its cash credit account, at the end of each day, thereby reducing the amount of debit balance in the cash credit account, and thus effecting a substantial saving on the amount of interest outgo.

4.6 DEPOSITING MARGIN MONEY IN CASH CREDIT ACCOUNT

There are some other ways also of effecting some savings on account of amount of interest payable. For example, on margin money to be deposited with the bank for the issuance of Letters of Credit (L/Cs) and Bank Guarantees (BIGs), etc. Depending upon the credit rating, companies are required to deposit margin money with the bank to the extent of 10%, 20%, 50% (or even more) of the amount for which the Letter of Credit (L/C) or Bank Guarantee (BIG) is required to be issued. In the long past, such margin money was being retained by the banks in current account, maintained exclusively for the purpose, styled as "Margin Money Account for Letters of Credit and Bank Guarantees", with no interest payable thereon. But, these days such margin money is being retained by the banks usually by way of term deposits, earning interest as per the prevailing rate. This arrangement has now become somewhat better for companies. But then, there is yet another way whereby the company may save interest at an even higher rate. That is, by requesting the bank to retain the margin money by way of noting a lien on the loan account (cash credit account of the company), it may very well make a clear saving of interest outgo at the prevailing rate of interest, applicable on the cash credit account. The procedure to be followed by the bank, under such an arrangement, can well be understood with the help of a practical case given hereunder:

Margin Money Makes Money — A Mini Case Study

Diamond Pearl Export House Ltd. enjoyed a Cash Credit Limit of Rs. 100 million with the Bank of Lucknow, and was being charged interest thereon @ 15% per annum, with quarterly rests (*i.e.* compounded quarterly).

Mr Onkar Kaveri, Director (Finance) of the Company, made the undernoted announcement in the Board meeting of the company on the 12th November, 2009:

> The Company, hitherto, had been depositing the margin money against Letters of Credit in the Current Account with the bank, whereby it was not earning any interest thereon. This time, I had a detailed discussion with the Branch Manager of the Bank, who ultimately agreed to open a Letter of Credit for Rs. 10 million for one year on retention of 20% margin thereon by way of Term Deposit for one year, earning an interest @ 10% p.a., with quarterly rests (*i.e.* compounded quarterly). And, this has resulted in a substantial financial gain to the company.

All the members of the Board were extremely happy to know this.

Issues to be discussed

(*a*) If you were one of the members of the Board, present in the meeting, what better suggestions would you have given, for further negotiation with the bank, in this regard, such that the quantum of the Company's financial gain would have been still higher.

By citing a suitable illustrative example, explain the full procedure for the bank to follow in this regard and the effect that it will have on the Company's Cash Credit Account, *i.e.* working capital finance account. You may presume that the Drawing Power (D.P.) on the Cash Credit Account is Rs. 90 million and the debit balance on the account is Rs. 75 million.

(*b*) Compute the financial gain that would accrue to the company as a result of the deal negotiated by Mr Kaveri.

(*c*) Compute the financial gain that would accrue to the company as a result of your suggestion.

For the sake of simplicity and with a view to understand the principles and procedures involved in the case, you may calculate the amount of interest at the simple rate of interest instead of the compound rate easily and more clearly.

A Suggested Solution

The company is now a net gainer of Rs. 0.20 million, by way of simple interest @ 10% p.a. on Rs. 2 million. And, by way of interest, compounded quarterly, for a period of one year, the gain will naturally be even higher. As against this, when the margin money was being kept in the current account, the income by way of interest was 'nil'. But then, where did the amount of Rs. 2 million come from? Obviously from the cash credit account, which attracted interest @ 15% p.a. Even if the amount were to come from internal savings or from somewhere else, the opportunity cost will be, at least, the rate of interest applicable on the cash credit account.

Thus, the company, even now, is a net loser of interest to the extent of 5% (15% – 10%). But, by availing of the facility of noting the amount of the margin money, by way of a lien on the cash credit account, instead, the company would save interest at the full rate applicable on the cash credit account, *i.e.* @ 15% p.a.

How? Let us try to understand by way of an illustrative example, by actually showing as to how the position will appear in the books of the bank.

As already stated earlier, the limit is Rs. 100 million and the Drawing Power is Rs. 90 million.

A. The position of the cash credit account (in situation "A" (*i.e.* when the margin money is deposited by way of Term Deposit Receipt (TDR), would be as under:

Particulars	*Debit*	*Credit*	*Balance (Amount in Million)*
To Bfd. Amount			Rs. 75 (Debit)
To Margin Money	Rs. 2		Rs. 77 (Debit)

Thus, the company will have to pay interest on Rs. 77 million (*i.e.* on Rs. 2 million more than Rs. 75 million), @ 15% p.a., which amounts to Rs. 0.30 million. The company will, however, earn interest on Term Deposit Receipt (TDR) @ 10% on 2 million, amounting to Rs. 0.20 million. Thus, the company will be a net loser of Rs. 0.10 million.

B. But, in case a lien of Rs. 2 million is noted in the Cash Credit Account, a different picture would emerge as under: Let us call it situation "B".

Limit	:	Rs. 100 million
Drawing Power	:	Rs. 90 million
Lien	:	Rs. 2 million

Therefore, the Effective Drawing Power (EDP) would be Rs. 88 million

[Rs. 90 million (–) Rs. 2 million = Rs. 88 million]

Thus, the position of Cash Credit Account in situation "B" would be as under:

Particulars	*Debit*	*Credit*	*Balance (Amount in Million)*
To Bfd. Amount			As. 75 (Debit)

Thus, the company pays interest on the debit balance of Rs. 75 million only in situation "B", as against Rs. 77 million in situation "A", resulting in a net saving of interest on Rs. 2 million @ 15 %, *i.e.* Rs. 0.30 million, as against the income of Rs. 0.20 million only, by way of interest @ 10% p.a. on the Term Deposit. Thus, there is a net gain of Rs. 0.10 million more.

For the sake of simplicity and only to bring home the relative point, the amount of interest has been calculated only at simple rate of interest, and not at compound rate. We may, however, calculate the amount of interest on compounding basis also, when the savings to the company on account of interest will be even higher.

Further, as for the balance of withdrawable amount, available on the account, it will be the same in both the cases, *i.e.* Rs. 13 million.

How? Because, the available balance = D.P. (less) Debit Balance.

In situation "A", it would be Rs. 90 million – Rs. 77 million = Rs. 13 million.

In situation "B" also, it (EDP) would be Rs. 88 million – Rs. 75 million = Rs. 13 million.

Thus, the company is a net gainer in case "B", and the bank alone is the loser.

That is why, as of now, some banks are reluctant to allow the facility of noting of the lien, for the amount of margin money, on the cash credit account, except, to valued customers. They, however, readily agree to keep the margin money by way of Term Deposits.

4.7 MANAGEMENT AND CONTROL OF PAYMENTS

A prudent business man would always prefer to make the payment only on the last day, when it is due, and never earlier. But, we should always remember that sometimes, our over-enthusiasm to cut it too fine, may usually prove to be too costly.

Payment of Taxes

Take for example, the payment of advance income tax per quarter. Instead of paying say, on the 1st July, it would be most beneficial for the company to pay the tax for the respective quarter on September 30. But then, with a view to, avoid the last day rush, and to circumvent the eventuality of some unexpected bank holiday or lightning strike, etc., it may prove to be a pragmatic and prudent act to pay the taxes only a couple of days earlier, so as to avoid default and delay and the consequent penalty.

Payments to Sundry Creditors

Similarly, for the supply of materials, so as to match with our expected cash position at the material time, and avoid any shortfall in cash position, necessitating some borrowings at a higher rate of interest, or to run the risk of losing credit-worthiness and reputation in the market, we should plan the payments to our sundry creditors.

Some may tend to argue that it would mean a better business sense to pay to the creditors as late as possible. Because, as we stand to lose some amount of interest when our own funds get unduly blocked in sundry debtors, we may be a gainer, instead, in case we delay the payments to our creditors. But then, this one can prove counter-productive and you may get the required materials or services at a relatively higher cost or of an inferior quality, or even both.

Mini Case-one

It reminds me of a real life experience of a colleague of mine. I was directing an in-company Management Development Programme (MDP) on "finance for Non-Finance Executives" (FNFE), for a Public Sector Undertaking (PSU). The travel involved some eight hour journey by road. While I preferred to engage a taxi from the taxi stand myself, a colleague of mine instead, asked the PSU to arrange for him a taxi. While my journey (though I was all alone), was trouble-free, my colleague had a tough time, as the taxi, arranged by the PSU, was an old one, requiring some repairs and renovations.

However, at the end of the journey, it was revealed, by the taxi driver himself, that as the PSU usually delayed the payments by say, six months or even more, we made it a point to provide only such taxis to them, which would not be so efficient and trouble-free. This shows that over-delayed payments to the sundry creditors has the incidence on price raise or performance or even both.

Mini Case-two

I would like to share with you yet another practical experience to point out as to how the practice of prompt payment to the sundry creditors may prove to be beneficial in the long run.

A company, established in Chennai (formerly known as Madras) was regularly buying some vital items from a vendor, who was decidedly the best choice, and so the company could never afford to offend him by over-delaying the payments.

The Director (Finance) of the company, therefore, issued strict instructions to all the members of the staff concerned, in the finance and purchase departments, that all payments of the specific vendor should be made promptly, even a day before the due date, invariably, without fail. And, if there was any cash problem in the company at the time of payment, even short-term borrowings, even at a much higher rate of interest, could be resorted to. And, this was good enough as, in a private sector company, you may not expect to go scot-free if you were to borrow at an unduly higher cost, instead of managing your cash better, by way of proper planning of your receipts and payments. This practice continued uninterruptedly for about six months. In the seventh month, the Director (Finance) instructed the General Manager (Finance) to personally visit the office of the vendor company concerned to negotiate with it to grant them the facility of extended credit period of say 45 days, instead of the usual 30 days, as the company had been particularly prompt in payments for the last six months in a row and accordingly, it would be ensured again that the payments are made mostly on the 44th day and never even on the 46th day. And, the deal was struck to the mutual advantage of both the parties.

Here, I may further add that by adopting the strategy of prompt payment to the sundry creditors, we also, at the same time, ensure an innovative source of finance, easily available to us in times of difficulty. Because, if you had been a prompt payment party all through, all the sundry creditors would voluntarily supply you the required material for a much longer credit period, at no extra cost, till your financial position improves and restored to the normal efficiency level.

Centralised Payments

It proves to be highly beneficial if the payments and disbursements are centralised at the corporate office of the company. The multifaceted advantages include, *inter alia*:

(*a*) Concentration of the company's funds at a single point, *i.e.* at the corporate office;

(*b*) Phasing and scheduling of all payments—effectively and systematically;

(*c*) This may, as well, reduce the unproductive lying of funds, spread over several offices of the company;

(*d*) And, above all, the short-term investment of surplus funds can also be better planned and managed at the one central point at the corporate office.

It may be beneficial if purchases, or at least their payments, are scheduled, in advance, in such a way that the due dates of payments almost perfectly match with the position of inflows of cash, so that most of the payments may fall due when the company's cash position is most favourable. And, correspondingly, no payment may fall due, when the company is likely to pass through the phase of some cash crunch. It may sound difficult but it is not impossible.

4.8 PLAYING THE FLOAT

While issuing a cheque, the company reduces the balance in its books the same day. But, in fact, the cheque may be presented in the bank a day or more later. Thus, for the intervening period, the books of the company may show a lower balance than that in the books of the bank. Similarly, when the company receives a cheque, it increases the balance in its books the same day, though the bank may credit the company's account in its books a day or more later, only on the realisation of the amount of the relative cheque. Thus, the balance in the books of the bank may be accordingly lower by the matching amount.

Payment float

Till the amount of cheque(s) issued by the company is not paid by the bank, it is referred to as the "payment float".

Collection float

As against this, till the proceeds of the amount of the cheques, received by the company and deposited with the bank, are not collected (realised) by the bank, and credited to the company's account, it is known as the "collection float".

Net float

And, the net difference between the "Payment Float" and the "Collection Float" is known as the "Net Float".

So, when the balance shown in the books of the bank is higher than that in the books of the company, the "Net Float" will be positive. And, when the position is just the reverse, that is, when the balance, appearing in the books of the bank, is lower than that appearing in the books of the company, the "Net Float" will be negative.

Thus, so long as the position is of positive (net) float, even though the books of the company may show a lower balance, there should be no cause for alarm. Because, by the time, the cheques issued by the company are presented to the bank for payment, there would be significant balance in the company's account with the bank to meet the amount. And, thus the cheques will be honoured and would not bounce back.

Playing the float

Therefore, it may be a prudent step for the company to issue some cheques even beyond the balance appearing in its own books, so long as the company's account with the bank shows a sufficiently higher balance. This practice of issuing cheques beyond the balance available in the company's books, is known as "playing the float".

However, playing the float to the full extent may often be risky, because, sometimes the cheques issued by the company may be presented by some payees promptly or, at least, a little earlier than expected. And, similarly, some of the cheques received by the company and deposited with the bank may be collected by the bank with some amount of unexpected, and even some undue delay. Therefore, to avoid such an embarrassing situation, it is better to play the float but, of course, within some safe limits; that is, up to 50 to 60% of the net positive float, and not more. This way, the company may get some more mileage with lesser funds being actually available with it and that too at no extra cost, at no unmanageable risk, either.

Let us try to have a fuller and clearer understanding of the accounting procedure and mechanism involved in the activity of "Playing the Float", with the help of an example.

Example

Locks and Keys Company Limited issues cheques aggregating Rs. 30,500 daily and it takes five days for its cheques to be cleared and debited to its account with the bank. The company receives cheques aggregating Rs. 35,500 daily and it takes four days for these cheques to be realised and credited to its account.

Assuming a balance of Rs. 15,500 in the books of the company and those of the bank to begin with, show the balances in their respective accounts. What will be the balance in the steady state situation?

Suggested Solution

Table 4.6: Balance in the Books of the Company and in the Books of the Bank

Day	Books of the Company (Rs.)			Day	Books of the Bank (Rs.)		
	Debit	*Credit*	*Balance*		*Debit*	*Credit*	*Balance*
0		BFD	15500	0		BFD	15500
1	30500	35500	20500*	1			15500@
2	30500	35500	25500*	2			15500@
3	30500	35500	30500*	3			15500@
4	30500	35500	35500*	4			15500@
5	30500	35500	40500*	5		35500	51000$
6	30500	35500	45500*	6	30500	35500	56000#
7	30500	35500	50500*	7	30500	35500	61000#

* Balance decreased by the amount of cheques issued (Rs. 30,500) and increased by the amount of cheques received (Rs. 35,500). Therefore, the net effect is the increase of Rs. 5,000 whereby the closing balance has gone up by Rs. 5,000 per day).

@As neither cheques issued are debited nor cheques deposited are credited for the first-four days, the closing balance remains unchanged at Rs. 15,500.

$The cheques deposited with the bank on day one is credited to the company's account whereby the balance goes up by Rs. 35,500 making the closing balance stand at Rs. 51,000.

#The cheques deposited with the bank on day two (Rs. 35,500) is credited to the account and the cheques issued on day one (Rs. 30,500) is debited to the account, resulting in a net increase of Rs. 5,000 to the closing balance, hereafter per day.

Steady State Situation

Thus, we find that from (and including) day five onwards, the credit balance available in the books of the bank are uniformly higher by a sum of Rs. 10,500 on each day. Such a situation is known as the "Steady State" situation, which commences and continues from day five onwards.

This so happens because from this (fifth) day the balances, both in the books of the company and in the books of the bank, go on registering an equal increase @ Rs. 5,000 per day every day henceforth. So, the difference between these two accounts stand static at Rs. 10,500, as aforesaid.

4.9 INVESTMENT OF SURPLUS FUNDS

There may be several occasions when the companies may be having some surplus funds, which they may, of course, require, but after some time. Therefore, it would be a prudent financial decision to invest such surplus funds in some safe avenues of investment, which may be secure and relatively liquid, and which may earn some reasonable interest, too, during the intervening period. There are, in fact, several options available to the companies, depending upon the varying degree of risks and liquidity and the matching income generation.

To illustrate the point, we may take two extreme examples. While the bank term deposits for periods ranging from 15 days to three years, or even more, are almost risk-free, the yield is sure but small, as the rate of interest is relatively lower. On the other extreme is the investment in quoted shares, specially blue chip shares (falling in the category A) which are most liquid as they are heavily transacted on a daily basis, and the possibility of making huge profit on their sale at a much higher price, a little later, too, is too high. But, at the same time, the element of risk of losing heavily, due to a crash in the prices of the shares, so purchased by the company, is also too high.

Let us take a recent example. Till a couple of years back, the sensex at the Bombay Stock Exchange (BSE) hovered above 20,000 points. But since late 2008, it started coming down steadily, so much so that it had fallen to 8,160.40 points, its lowest in the past three and a half years, on Monday, the 9th March, 2009. (Source: *The Hindustan Times*, Lucknow edition, 10th March, 2009). However, since April 2009 (after Manmohan Singh became the Prime Minister) the Sensex (bench mark index) at the Bombay Stock Exchange (BSE), had again started showing a steady rising trend, so much so that, as on Wednesday, the 30th September, 2009, it had breached the psychological level of 17,000 points, and had hit a 16-month high, to close at 17,127 points. This is more than double the position that was obtaining just six months earlier, *i.e.* on Monday, the 9th March, 2009 (*i.e.*, 8,160 points). Earlier, on Tuesday, the 22nd September, 2009, Nifty, the favourite 50-share index, had crossed the crucial psychological 5,000 mark and had closed at 5,020 points. [Source: *The Economic Times,* dated the 23rd September and 1st October, 2009, respectively]. However, the share-markets have again turned extremely volatile since May-June 2010.

The aforementioned facts and figures clearly show the volatile (unpredictable) nature of sensex, and correspondingly, of frequent fluctuations in the market price (rise and fall) of shares in the stock exchanges, and the resultant risks involved in the investment of short-term surplus funds by the companies in quoted shares (even in blue chip shares).

Thus, it may be pragmatic and prudent to select some such avenues of investment where both the elements of risk, and the related gain, are neither too high nor too low, but moderate.

There are, in fact, various schemes and avenues for parking the surplus funds for a short period, with fairly reasonable business risk and gain.

Let us now discuss several such schemes, one after the other, weighing, at the same time, the relative advantages and disadvantages (negative and positive features) connected with each scheme, so as to facilitate the decision-making process of companies.

4.10 SOME OTHER SAFE AND GAINFUL AVENUES

Units of the Unit 1964 Scheme

This scheme of the Unit Trust of India (UTI), commonly known as the Unit Scheme 1964 (US64, for short), had been the most popular mutual fund scheme in India. It comprised the following features:

(*i*) Most importantly, it was an open ended scheme. That is, it could be purchased and sold back to the UTI itself at the pre-announced sale and purchase prices. Such announcements were made by the UTI periodically (usually on a monthly basis).

(*ii*) The face value of each unit was Rs. 10. But, as we all know, the sale and purchase prices were not determined on the basis of the Net Asset Value (NAV) of the units, which should have actually been the case, as it was, and also is, usually so in the cases of all the other such truly open-ended funds schemes. It was, instead, determined administratively by the UTI, taking into account the element of accrued interest (nay, dividend) from time to time, usually at monthly intervals. Thus, as the dividend on the US64 was declared as on June 30, each year, the selling price of the unit was the lowest in the month of July. And, as the time passed by, the amount of dividend, accruing to the unit periodically, got added to its sale value and, accordingly, the price went up gradually with the passage of time. Thus, its selling price towards the end of the year, *i.e.* in the month of June, each year, was the highest. And, taking into account the spread of profit, the purchase price of the unit was also determined by the UTI simultaneously.

Thus, the US64 scheme proved to be the most convenient and attractive, and therefore, most popular avenue for parking of funds gainfully for a short period of time. It is because of the aforesaid reasons, as also for the various other reasons. For example, there was also an active secondary market for selling and buying units in stock exchanges, of course, through some brokers. And, this strategy seemed to be more gainful.

For example, if the sale and purchase price fixed by the UTI was, say, Rs. 15.90 and Rs. 15.10, respectively (of the US64 of the face value of Rs. 10.00), the unit could be traded in the stock exchanges at around Rs. 15.50 with the variance of a few paise only between the buying and selling rates.

Besides, the units also appreciated in value at a pre-determined rate, as between July and June each year, the UTI made an upward revision in its selling and repurchase prices.

Performance of US64

As we are already aware, US64 ran into some rough weather in 1998, and again in 2001, when its Net Asset Value (NAV) dropped well below par, *i.e.* around Rs. 9.50.

Deepak Parekh Committee, in its report, submitted much earlier, had already suggested that the UTI should also make its NAV public, periodically, as all the other Mutual Funds (MFs) are required to do. But, the UTI did not agree, on the plea that by virtue of being established under a specific law, it enjoyed a special privileged position. But when some other reliable sources made the NAV of US64 public, the US64 price in the stock exchanges got a beating, and many investors preferred to encash the US64 units and to invest the funds in some other reliable and gainful avenues.

Ultimately, the Government of India had to come to UTI's rescue and the commercial banks, including State Bank of India, were asked, through Reserve Bank of India, to provide the required funds to the UTI. But the State Bank of India and the other commercial banks did not oblige.

Thus, ultimately, to meet the high demand for payment of US64 units, the UTI had perforce to sell most of the shares, held in its portfolio, at a much lower price, as the Sensex was, at a very low level. This obviously meant further losses to the UTI.

As against other Mutual Funds (MFs), the UTI maintained the rate of dividend payment at the predetermined rate of 20%, for quite some time, despite the fact that its NAV dropped even below par. To arrest the depleting confidence of the public in US64 in particular, and in the UTI in general, the dividend was paid at the same rate of 20% that year, too, of course, subject to income tax.

This, however, at the post-tax rate, comes to around 13.5%. Accordingly, the very next year, the UTI declared a dividend of 13.5%, free of income tax, which again meant the pre-tax value of around 20% at the then prevailing rate of income tax at 33%.

The NAV of US64 again dropped to around Rs. 14.00 in April 2000, from Rs. 17.50 just a month ago, which, of course, was not far below the repurchase price of Rs. 14.45 for April, 2000.

In this way, the UTI has done well to wipe out the negative reserves of Rs. 1098 crore of 1998. And, in the financial year 1999, the scheme earned Rs. 2200 crore, which was sufficient to payout the dividend at 16.2%, though the UTI actually declared a dividend of 13.5% only, in line with one of the recommendations of the Deepak Parekh Committee. The UTI suffered a far more severe setback in June 2001, when it declared the freez of the repurchase of the US64 units.

(For a detailed discussion on this issue, please refer to the Appendices 4.1 and 4.2 at the end of the chapter).

All considered, the US64 may no longer be said to be a very safe and attractive scheme.

Ready Forward

Under the ready forward deal, a commercial bank (or some other organization) may enter into an arrangement with a company, intending to park its surplus funds for a short period, under which the bank may sell some securities to the company, on the understanding that the bank will repurchase the same securities from the company at a later date at a pre-determined mutually agreed prices *i.e.* both selling and repurchase prices. That is why it is termed as "Ready Forward". Ready forwards, however, are permitted only in a limited number of specified securities. Under this arrangement, the company does not earn by way of interest. The income, however, takes place in the form of the price difference (spread) between the buying and selling rates. Such income is also taxable as usual.

The rate of return on a ready forward deal is directly related to the conditions prevailing in the money market, which is generally tight during the busy season, as also at the time of the annual closing.

Treasury Bills

Treasury bills are the obligations of the government for a short-term period of less than one year ranging from 91 days to its multiples like 182 days and 364 days. Instead of attracting a specific interest rate (also known as coupon rate), it is issued at a discount and redeemed at the face value, and the difference between these two rates constitute the income or surplus. Thus, the rate of interest, in effect, is the function of the rate of discount and the period of maturity. The yield of treasury bills are somewhat low, as compared to other more gainful avenues of short-term investments. But then, it has several other attractive features, as detailed hereafter.

(*i*) As the treasury bills are issued in a bearer form, they can be transacted easily, as the title can be transferred merely by delivery of the documents, without any endorsement, whatsoever.

(*ii*) The treasury bills can be readily sold off in the secondary market any time, and with great ease, as these are very actively transacted in the stock exchanges. The Discount and Finance House of India is a major market maker of treasury bills.

(*iii*) As the treasury bills are issued by the government, these are virtually free of any risk, whatsoever.

Certificates of Deposits (CDs)

Certificates of Deposits (CDs) represent the receipts of funds deposited with a bank for a specified period, like the Bank Term Deposit Receipts (TDRs), but with a difference; as against the bank TDRs, the CDs are negotiable.

It may be issued in two forms:

(*i*) In registered form, in which case the transfer of title can take place by endorsement and delivery of the document; and

(*ii*) In bearer form, the title can be transferred merely by delivery of the documents; no endorsement is required in such cases. The bearer form of CDs is, therefore, more popular, as it can be transacted in the secondary market more readily and with much greater ease, for the aforesaid reasons.

As against the Treasury Bills, the CDs are issued with a specifically stated rate of interest (instead of at a discount). Thus, on maturity of the CDs, the investor gets the principal amount, together with the interest accrued during the period of deposit at the explicit rate of interest.

The popularity of this form of short-term investment of surplus funds can be attributed to the following main reasons:

(*i*) These can be issued by the banks in the required denominations and for a specific period of maturity, as per the specific requirements of each company.

(*ii*) CDs are very liquid, as these are activity transacted, with great ease, in the secondary market.

(*iii*) These are virtually risk-free, too.

(*iv*) The CDs earn a higher rate of interest, as compared to Treasury Bills and even Bank Term Deposits.

Commercial Papers (CPs)

Commercial Paper (CP) is an unsecured money-market instrument. It is issued in the form of a Promissory Note. CP, as a privately placed instrument, was introduced in India in 1990 to enable the highly rated corporate borrowers to diversify the sources of their short-term borrowings, as also to provide an additional instrument to the investors, to park their surplus funds for a short period.

The Reserve Bank of India (RBI), in the mid-term review of the monetary and credit policy for the year 2000-2001 (announced in October, 2000), had initiated several measures to keep pace with the developments in the financial market. In fact, the guidelines, pertaining to the issuance of the Commercial Papers (CPs) are modified/amended by the Reserve Bank of India (RBI), from time to time. The Master Circular of the RBI dated the Ist July, 2009, issued by its Financial Markets Department, incorporates all the existing guidelines/instructions/directives, updated upto the 30th June, 2009. This Master Circular of the RBI has been placed on the RBI website at <www.mastercircular.rbi.org.in>.

Some of the salient features of such modifications (as amended upto the 30th June, 2009, vide RBI Financial Markets Department Master Circular letter dated the 1st July, 2009) are as follows:

(*i*) The Commercial Paper (CP) is since being treated as a "Stand Alone" facility.

(*ii*) A provision has been made for providing a "Stand By" facility, too.

(*iii*) The CPs can now be issued in de-materialized (demat) form, too.

(*iv*) The responsibilities of the Issuing and Paying Agents (IPAs), have been enlarged.

The detailed guidelines for the issuance of the CPs have been discussed hereunder:

(i) Eligibility

(*a*) The Tangible Net Worth (TNW) of the company, as per its latest audited balance-sheet, should not be less than Rs. 4 crore;

(*b*) The company should have been sanctioned a working capital limit by the bank(s) and/or the all India financial institutions (FIs) and

(*c*) The borrowal account of the company should have been classified as a 'Standard Asset' by the financing bank(s)/financial institutions.

It may, thus, be observed that the minimum fund-based working capital limit of Rs. 4 crore enjoyed by the company, has since been dispensed with.

(ii) Credit Rating Requirements

The minimum credit rating of the company should be P-2 of Credit Rating Information Services of India Limited (CRISIL) or such equivalent rating by any of the other Credit Rating Agencies (CRAs), specified by the Reserve Bank of India (RBI), e.g. Investment Information and Credit Rating Agency of India Limited (ICRA), Credit Analysis and Research Limited (CARE), FITCH Ratings India Private Limited, or such other Credit Rating Agencies (CRAs). Such credit ratings of each company should, however, be duly reviewed periodically by the CRA concerned on the specified due dates. This indicates that the CRAs, at the time of the rating, should clearly indicate the date when the rating falls due for the review, and revision, whenever necessary. Besides, the issuers of the CPs should also ensure that at the time of issurance of the CPs, the ratings so obtained are current and have not fallen due for review/renewed.

It may, thus, be observed that there has been no other change in this regard.

(iii) Maturity

The Commercial Papers (CPs) can be issued for maturities, ranging from a minimum period of 7 days (reduced from 15 days) to a maximum period of up to one year from the date of the issue. The maturity date of the CP, however, should not go beyond the date up to which the credit rating of the issuing company is valid.

There has, however, been no other change in this regard. We may, thus, observe that the minimum maturity period of CPs has since been reduced from 15 days to only 7 days. There has, however, been no change in regard to the maximum maturity period of CPs.

(iv) Denomination

Commercial Paper (CP) can be issued in the denomination of Rs. 5 lakh or in multiples thereof. The amount to be invested by a single investor, however, should not be less than Rs. 5 lakh (face value).

While there has been no other change in regard to the denomination, the minimum investment by a single investor has since been reduced from Rs. 25 lakh to Rs. 5 lakh only.

(v) Limits and the Amount of Issue

(*a*) CPs can now be issued as a 'stand alone' facility.

(*b*) The aggregate amount of the CP issued by the issuer, should be within the limit, as approved by the Board of Directors of the company, issuing the CP, or the quantum indicated by the Credit Rating Agency for the specified rating, whichever is lower.

(*c*) Banks and FIs will, however, have the flexibility to fix suitable working capital limits, by duly taking into account the resource pattern of the companies financing, including the CPs.

It may, thus, be observed that the linkage of the issuance of the CPs with the fund-based working capital limit has since been removed. That is why, it has since been termed as a 'Stand Alone' product. Thus, the working capital limit will now have to be fixed by the banks/FIs by taking into account the resource pattern of the company, including the CPs.

(vi) Issuance of CPs by FIs

An FI can issue the CP within the overall umbrella limit fixed by the RBI, *i.e.*, the issue of CPs together with the other instruments, viz. Term Money Borrowings, Term Deposits, Certificate of Deposits, and Inter-corporate Deposits, should not exceed 100 per cent of its net owned funds, as per its latest audited balance sheet.

(vii) Time Limit for Raising Total Amount of CPs

The total amount of CP, proposed to be issued, should be raised within a period of two weeks from the date on which the issuer opens the issue for subscription. CP may be issued on a single date, or even in parts on different dates, provided that, in the latter case, each CP should have the same maturity date. Further, every issue of CP, including renewal, should be treated as a fresh issue.

(viii) Who can Act as the Issuing and Paying Agent (IPA)?

Only a Scheduled Bank can act as an IPA for the issuance of the CPs.

(ix) Investment in CPs

CP may be issued to, and held by, individuals, banking companies, other corporate bodies, registered or incorporated in India, and unincorporated bodies, Non-Resident Indians (NRIs), and Foreign Institutional Investors (FIIs). However, the investments by FIIs should be within the limits set for their investments by Securities and Exchange Board of India (SEBI).

(x) Mode of Issuance

(*i*) CPs can be issued either in the form of a promissory note [as per the format prescribed by the RBI for the purpose (specimen of the pro forma has been given as Appendix 4.3, at the end of the Chapter), or in a Dematerialised (demat) form, through any of the depositories approved by, and registered with, the Securities and Exchange Board of India (SEBI). The existing stocks of the CPs can, however, continue to be held in the physical or demat form, as agreed to by the issuer and the investor].

(*ii*) CPs will be issued at discount on the face value, as determined by the issuer. Thus, the implicit interest rate is the function of the quantum of the discount and the period of maturity.

(*iii*) No issuer of the SP should have the issue of CP underwritten or co-accepted.

It is, thus, worth noting that the issuance of the CPs in the demat form is an additional provision.

(xi) Preference for Dematerialised Form

While the option is available to both the issuers and the subscribers, to issue/hold CPs in dematerialised or physical form, the issuers and the subscribers are encouraged to prefer exclusive reliance on dematerialised form of the issue/holding. However, with effect from the 30th June, 2001, Banks, Financial Institutions and PDs are required by the Reserve Bank of India (RBI) to make fresh investments and hold the CPs only in dematerialized form.

(xii) Payment of CPs

The initial investor in CP shall pay the discounted value of the CP by means of a crossed account payee cheque for credit to the account of the issuer company, through the IPA.

On the date of maturity, when the CP is held in the physical form, the holder of the CP shall present the instrument (CP) to the issuer through the IPA for the payment. However, when the CP is held in demat form, the holder of the CP will have to get it redeemed (paid) through the depository and receive the payment from the IPA.

(xiii) Stand-by Facility

In view of the CP being a 'stand alone' product now, it would no longer be obligatory in any manner on the part of the banks and the FIs to provide the stand-by facility to the issuer of the

CP. Banks and FIs, however, have the flexibility, to provide for an issue of CP, the credit enhancement to the company issuing the CP, by way of a stand-by assistance/credit, back-stop facility, etc., based on their own commercial judgement, subject to the prudential norms, as applicable, and with the specific approval of the Board (*i.e.,* of the Boards of the banks and FIs).

(xiv) Roles and Responsibilities of (a) the Issuers, (b) the IPAs, and (c) the Credit Rating Agencies (CRAs)

The roles and responsibilities of (*a*) the Issuers, (*b*) the IPAs and (*c*) the Credit Rating Agencies (CRAs) have been discussed hereafter, one after the other.

(a) Of the Issuers (Companies)

With the simplification in the procedures for the issuance of the CPs, the issuers would now have more flexibility. The issuers would, however, have to ensure that the guidelines and procedures laid down for the issuance of the CPs have been strictly adhered to.

(b) Of the Issuing and Paying Agents (IPAs)

(*i*) IPA would ensure that the issuer has the minimum credit rating, as stipulated by the RBI and that the amount mobilized through the issuance of the CP is within the quantum indicated by the CRA, for the specified rating, or as approved by its Board of Directors, whichever is lower.

(*ii*) IPA has to verify all the documents, submitted by the issuer, viz. copy of the board resolution, signatures of the authorized executants (when the CP is being issued in the physical form), and to issue a certificate to the effect that the documents are in order. It should also certify that it has a valid agreement with the issuer.

(*iii*) The certified copies of the original documents, duly verified by the IPA, should be held by the IPA in his personal custody.

(*iv*) Every CP issue should be reported to the Chief General Manager, Financial Markets Department, Reserve Bank of India, Central Office, Fort, Mumbai 400 001.

(*v*) The IPAs, who are the members of the NDS, are required to report the details of every issuance of the CP to the NDS, within two days of the date of completion of the issue of each CP.

(*vi*) Further, all the scheduled banks, acting as IPAs, will continue to report the details of issuance of each CP to the RBI, as hitherto, within three days from the date of completion of the issue, incorporating all the required details, on the pro forma prescribed by the RBI for the purpose, till such time as NDS reporting stabilizes, to the satisfaction of the RBI.

(c) Of the Credit Rating Agencies (CRAs)

(*i*) The 'Code of Conduct', prescribed by the SEBI for the CRAs, for the purpose of undertaking the rating of the capital market instruments, shall be applicable to them (CRAs) also for the rating of CPs.

(*ii*) Further, the Credit Rating Agency (CRA) would henceforth have the discretion to determine the validity period of the rating, depending upon its own perception about the (financial) strength of the issuer company. Accordingly, the CRA shall, at the time of rating, clearly indicate the date when the rating is due for review.

(*iii*) While the CRA can decide the validity period of the credit rating, they would have to closely monitor the rating, assigned to the issuer companies *vis-à-vis* their track record at regular intervals, and would be required to make their revision in their ratings, and make these public too, through their publications and website.

(xv) Procedure for Documentation

(*i*) The 'Fixed Income Money Market and Derivatives Association of India' (FIMMDA) may prescribe, in consultation with the RBI, for operational flexibility and smooth functioning of CP market, any standard procedure and documentation that are to be followed by the participants (in CP), in consonance of with the international best practices. The Issuers/ IPAs may refer to the detailed guidelines issued by the FIMMDA in this regard on the 5th July, 2001.

(*ii*) Further, any violation of these guideline will attract penalties, and may also include debarring of the entity (Issuer/IPA concerned) from the CP market.

(xvi) Defaults in CP Market

In order to monitor defaults in the redemption (repayment) of CP, the scheduled banks, acting as IPA for such CP, are advised to immediately report the matter, on its occurrence, with full particulars of such default in the repayment of the CP to the Financial Markets Department, Reserve Bank of India, Central Office, Mumbai, in the format prescribed by the RBI for the purpose.

(xvii) Non-Applicability of Certain Other Directions

Nothing contained in the Non-Banking Financial Companies Acceptance of Public Deposits (Reserve Bank) Directions, 1998, shall apply to any Non-Banking Financial Company (NBFC) insofar as it relates to acceptance of deposits by issuance of CP in accordance with these guidelines.

Public Deposits

Public deposits or term deposits are in the nature of unsecured deposits, solicited by the companies (both large and small) from the general public, primarily for the purpose of financing their working capital requirements. As of now, there is no ceiling stipulated on the interest rate payable on such public deposits, inasmuch as such ceiling has since been withdrawn since mid-1996. Accordingly, the rates of interest offered on the public deposits by the companies usually fall in line with the pattern of the rates of interest, prevailing at the material time and determined by the market forces.

Regulations

Such fixed (public) deposits, accepted by the companies, are governed by the Companies (Acceptance of Deposits) Amendment Rules, 1978.

The salient features of such regulations are:

(*i*) No company can issue public deposits for more than 25 per cent of its share capital and free reserves.

(*ii*) The public deposit can be issued for a period ranging from minimum six months to maximum three years. Public deposits for a period of three months, however, can as well be issued, but only for an amount up to 10 per cent of the company's share capital and free reserves.

(*iii*) The companies issuing public deposits are required to set aside, by way of deposit and/or investment, by April, 30 each year, an amount equal to 10 per cent of the deposits which are due for payment by March, 31 of the next year. This amount is to be earmarked for the exclusive purpose of repaying the amount of deposits as and when these may fall due for payment.

(*iv*) Lastly, the companies, soliciting and accepting the public deposits from the general public, are required to make true, fair, and honest disclosures about certain vital and relevant facts in regard to their financial position and performance.

Advantages and disadvantages of public deposits:

(A) From the points of view of the company

Advantages

(*i*) The procedure for soliciting and accepting public deposits is a rather simple one, involving no restrictive conditions and/or covenants, whatsoever.

(*ii*) As the public deposits are unsecured, assets of the company remain available with them, for being offered as a security (by way of hypothecation and/or mortgage) for the purpose of obtaining in future some further financial assistance from some other sources, as and when required.

(*iii*) Inasmuch as the amount of interest, payable on public deposits, is tax-deductible, the post-tax cost to the company becomes fairly reasonable.

Disadvantages

(*i*) Only a limited amount of funds can be raised by way of public deposits.

(*ii*) Such funds are available only for a shorter period, ranging from six months to three years.

(B) From the points of view of the investors:

Advantages

(*i*) The rate of interest offered by the companies on their public deposits is relatively higher, as compared to the various other avenues of investments.

(*ii*) The period of maturity, too, is relatively short-ranging from six months to three years.

Disadvantages

(*i*) The public deposits, offered by the company being unsecured, are not backed up by any tangible security. Accordingly, these are fraught with grave financial risks of default in payments on the due dates or even later. The example of the Century Consultants Limited (CCL), Lucknow, is a case in point.

It would, therefore, augur well if the investors are cautious enough to invest their hard earned savings only in some reputed companies of high and undisputedly sound and stable financial standing. By way of some illustrative examples, the names of some such companies may be said to be RIL, L&T, Infosys, Wipro, Colgate, P&G, Ranbaxy.

(*ii*) The income by way of interest, in the hands of the investors, is taxable. And, therefore, the post-tax yield on such investment should be taken into account, while taking the investment decisions.

Inter-Corporate Deposits (ICDs)

As the name itself suggests, an inter-corporate deposit is the deposit made by one corporate body (company) with another company. Such deposits are usually made for a maximum period of six months.

Such deposits may generally be of three types:

(*i*) ***Call Deposits:*** Such deposits are called so because, these are expected to be payable on call, that is whenever its repayment (or refund) is demanded, of course, on just one day's notice. But, in actual practice, the lender has to wait for at least 2/3 days (instead of just a single day), to get the amount paid back.

(*ii*) ***Three-months Deposits:*** These inter-corporate deposits are made for a period of three months. Such deposits have been found to be most popular among the corporate bodies for parking the surplus funds available with some companies, and correspondingly, for tiding over the short-term financial crunch faced by some others.

(*iii*) ***Six-months Deposits:*** Generally, the inter-corporate deposits are made for a maximum period of six months and that, too, with the 'A' category companies only.

As the inter-corporate deposits are in the nature of unsecured deposits, due care has to be taken to assess and ascertain the creditworthiness and willingness of the company concerned, with whom deposits are intended to be made. Further, the undernoted provisions, contained under Section 372 A [inserted by the Companies (Amendment) Act, 1999 (replacing the provisions earlier contained in Sections 370 and 372 of the Companies Act, 1956)], should invariably be adhered to:

A company cannot make deposits (investments), loans and guarantees, all the three taken together, of more than 60% of its net worth [comprising paid-up share capital (*i.e.* paid up portion only of equity and preference shares) plus free reserves (*i.e.* the reserves which have not been earmarked for specific purposes, like capital redemption reserves, investment allowance reserves, foreign exchange fluctuation reserves, capital reserves, etc.)], or cent per cent of its free reserves, whichever is more.

This limit can, however, be crossed but under some special circumstances, and only with the specific prior permission of the Government of India, and a special resolution passed by the company, granting permission to exceed such stipulated ceiling on inter-corporate deposits.

Badla Financing

Let us, first of all, understand what is meant by '*badla*'. In stock exchanges, one particular day of a week is identified as the weekly settlement day, which varies in one stock exchange to the other. **For example,** while in the Bombay Stock Exchange (BSE) the weekly settlement day is Friday, in the National Stock Exchange (NSE) it is Wednesday. On these specific weekly days, all transactions of sale and purchase of shares and securities are settled and squared up. But there may be such occasions where the person, who has bought some shares, through a stock broker, does not want to take delivery of his shares, during the preceding week (maybe, because the price of such shares, might have fallen down). He, therefore, wants to carry over the transaction to the next settlement period, *i.e.* to the next week, in the hope that the prices of such shares may again go up in the future. This is known as forward transaction or *badla* transaction.

Such carry forwards are permitted only in BSE (and not in NSE) and that, too, in the case of some specified shares and securities only, classified in category "A", depending upon their quantum of transactions, both in quantity and volume. Thus, the list has to be periodically revised, depending upon the changes in the quantum and volume of some shares, whereby the shares of some companies may be excluded from the list and those of some other companies may be added thereto.

But, when a carry forward is permitted, the seller of the shares would stand to lose (the opportunity to book the profit). So, with a view to compensate him, some *badla* changes are paid to him for the deal of carry forward. The rate of *badla* charges, however, depends upon the demand and supply position of funds, which, in turn, is determined on the next preceding business day of the settlement.

Financing such payments is known as *badla* financing, that is, lending money to a stock market operator, to enable him to carry forward his transaction from one settlement period to the other.

"*Badla*" financing, however, necessarily takes place;

(*i*) through a broker, and that, too,

(*ii*) against the security of the shares already purchased by the stock market operator.

Thus, a company, having surplus funds, may provide say, a sum of, Rs. 100 million for *badla* financing through a broker. The lending company may also specify the shares, in which case alone the *badla* financing is to be provided, *e.g.* the shares of L&T or Reliance Industries Limited.

The one single greatest advantage of *Badla* financing is that it offers a very attractive rate of interest. But, coupled with this gain, there are several risks, too; for example,

(*i*) The stock market operator may decline to honour his commitment; or

(*ii*) The broker himself may become a defaulter.

Therefore, with a view to guard against such risks involved, the following precautionary and safety measures must be taken by the company to safeguard its own interest:

(*i*) *Badla* financing must be done only through reputed and financially strong brokers.

(*ii*) Only such shares, which are considered to be intrinsically sound, should be specified for the purpose.

(*iii*) Adequate margin must also be retained in case the *badla* financing is being offered in the case of some highly volatile and risky shares.

(*iv*) It must invariably be insisted upon that the *badla* financing would be provided only after taking the actual possession of the relative share certificates (physically or in the demated form).

(*v*) And, above all, the main purpose of such dealing should be the reasonable gain (by way of reasonable return on the employment of the surplus funds), and not the greed to make a fast buck.

Purchase and Discount of Bills

Banks provide finance to the companies and firms by way of purchase and/or discount of bills of exchange drawn by their borrowers (sellers) on the respective buyers, representing genuine trade transactions. The sellers are known as the drawers of the bills and the buyers are known as the drawees of the bills.

Such Bills of Exchange are broadly of two types:

(*i*) Demand Bills; and

(*ii*) Time (Usance) Bills.

Demand bills are drawn specifically made payable to the payee, named therein, on demand. Time bills, however, are drawn and made payable after a specified number of days or months from the date of the bill or from the date of its acceptance by the drawees for its payment. When the amount of the demand bills is paid in advance in full, by the banks, it is technically known as the purchase or negotiation of the bill.

And, accordingly, the banks in such cases, become the "holders in due course," as against mere 'holders' of the bills, whereby they assume the owner's rights on the goods involved. That is why, such advances are known as Secured Advances. And, if only a percentage of the amount, mentioned in the bill, is advanced against, the banks remain only "holders" of the bills (only as collecting agents and not owners of goods) and, therefore, such advances are treated as unsecured advances.

As against Demand Bills, when the advance is granted by the bank against Time Bills, such a transaction is technically known as discounting of the bills. This is so, as, such bills are advanced against at a discount (and not for the full amount mentioned in the bill, as is the position in case of Demand Bills). And, the quantum of discount depends on the rate of interest and the period of the respective time bills. For example, if a Time Bill is drawn payable after three months from the date of the bill, and if the rate of interest charged on the cash credit account of the borrower is 16% per annum, the rate of discount will be 4% (3 months × 16/12). This means that a Time Bill of Rs. 100 is discounted at 4%, *i.e.* only a sum of Rs. 96 is payable to the borrower as against the time bills of Rs. 100 being discounted.

Detailed discussion on the following issues has been provided in Chapter 11, Letters of Credit:

(*i*) Definition of Bills of Exchange;

(*ii*) Clean and Documentary Bills;

(*iii*) Mode of calculation of due date of Time Bills, etc., as per the Negotiable Instruments Act; and

(*iv*) Stamp duties exigible on time bills, as stipulated in the Indian Stamp Act.

As the banks provide finance against demand and time bills, as aforesaid, the firms and companies, having some surplus funds for investment for a short duration, may, likewise, deploy their surplus funds for the purchase/discount of demand/time bills. Such purchase/discount of bill may be safely considered as a better option to the lending money in the inter-corporate deposit market, inasmuch as such bills are self-liquidating instruments, provided of course, these represent genuine trade transactions, *i.e.* covering actual sale and purchase of goods in the normal course of business.

The companies/firms would, therefore, do well to ensure that the bills being discounted/ purchased, are genuine trade bills, representing genuine trade transactions.

The following examples, may provide some insight into developing the skills to detect whether the bills are genuine trade bills or just accommodation bills.

4.11 MINI CASE STUDIES

Mini Case Study No. 1

"HAVE YOU CHANGED YOUR LINE OF BUSINESS"

Mr. Ashok, the Managing Director of YRV Rubber Industries (P) Ltd., manufacturing rubber goods, approached me to grant an overdraft of Rs. 5 million on the company's account. When I sought details of the account, I found that it was already irregular by Rs. 4 million. I, therefore, expressed my inability to grant any further overdraft on the account. Thereupon, he asked me that if he were to bring the trade bills aggregating the required amount, would he be able to draw the amount? I immediately responded that as he already has a bill limit, sanctioned in his favour, he could do so as a matter of right. But, when he left, I wondered why should he ask me such an obvious question?

Soon he came with two trade bills, aggregating Rs. 6 million, against which a further drawing power of Rs. 4.5 million (after deducting 25% margin) was allotted to the company. But, after adjustment of the existing irregularity of Rs. 4 million on the account, he could hardly draw another Rs. 0.5 million only. This obviously did not serve his purpose. So, he went back again and brought yet another trade bill worth Rs. 6 million. When the third bill came to my notice for allowing further drawing power on the account, it struck me that if the company had three bills aggregating Rs. 12 million, why did he not submit all these bills in one go? It, thus, occurred to me that all these three bills may not be representing genuine trade transactions. So, I asked Mr. Ashok if he changed his line of business?" He was taken aback and responded, with an expression of wonder in his eyes, "No Sir, I am still continuing the same business of manufacturing rubber goods". Thereupon, I told him that I was, instead, fully convinced that he had since changed his line of business, *i.e.* from manufacturing rubber goods to manufacturing of (trade) bills.

I, accordingly, issued instructions for the cancellation of the drawing power even of Rs. 4.5 million granted to the company earlier, and sent all the three bills on collection basis. However, as expected, these bills were returned unpaid, incontrovertibly proving that my suspicion that all these were fake bills was justified. Such an activity is known as Kite Flying.

On further scrutiny of the trade bills account of the company, I found that most of its bills, pertaining to a party in Chandigarh, were generally returned unpaid. I, therefore, got further suspicious that the Chandigarh party may be fictitious, too. Therefore, I immediately contacted the Chief Manager of Chandigarh branch over telephone, and my suspicion also came out to be true. I, therefore, immediately took necessary precautionary measures in regard to the conduct of all the accounts of the company and instructed all the members of the staff to be extra careful while dealing with this company.

I took this opportunity of scrutinizing the trade bills accounts of all the borrowers and detected one more case, where the trade bills, drawn by one of our borrowers, on a buyer company at Allahabad, were mostly received unpaid. I, therefore, issued suitable instructions that the trade bills drawn on the particular party at Allahabad should not be advanced against. Instead, these must invariably be sent on collection basis.

It was, on this day, that I could personally understand fully well the importance of scrutinizing the ledgers and registers at the branch by the Chief Manager himself at periodical intervals and on a continuing basis.

However, the art and skill to be used for supervision is covered in my other book, 'Principles of Managerial Excellence—*The Indian Experience*', Himalaya Publishing House, Mumbai, 2010.

Mini Case Study No. 2

"TDR IS BETTER OR BLUE CHIP SHARE"

(A Case Study on Investment of Surplus Funds)

"Arijit Enterprises (P) Ltd.", has the facility of a cash credit limit of Rs. 500 lakh with a bank. As on September 30, 2009 (the annual closing day) the company's Cash Credit account showed a debit balance of Rs. 100 lakh, including interest charged thereon @15% per annum. The company has an ambitious expansion plan. It has already placed orders for the supply of plant and machinery worth Rs. 400 lakh. As per the agreement, the supply is expected to arrive any time during the period June-July 2010. The company has also been sanctioned a term loan of Rs. 300 lakh by the same branch of the bank and the balance amount of Rs. 100 lakh is payable by the company as a margin thereon. A new factory building is also under the initial stages of construction at an estimated cost of Rs. 100 lakh, being fully financed by the company from its internal cash generation.

As the construction work is already in progress and the plant and machinery are also expected to arrive any time, the company has been prudent enough to keep the required sum of Rs. 200 lakhs in the current account of the same branch of the bank.

One of the approaches to the Case Study, as suggested by the author.
Please note that there is no single approach/solution to a case study.

In the Board meeting of the company, held on October 30, 2009, Mr. Avinash Prakash, one of the directors of the company, suggested that the surplus funds must be gainfully invested in quoted shares of blue-chip companies. Another Director, Ms. Kalpana Satlaj, however, strongly opposed the suggestion, and suggested that the surplus funds should, instead, be invested with the bank in its Term Deposit Schemes.

She even quoted the rates of interest payable by the bank on the term deposits of respective maturity periods (given hereunder) and also explained, in detail, the various other available facilities of loan, on some easy terms. She further suggested that the company should obtain two Term Deposit Receipts (TDRs), both maturing after 180 days, but each for Rs. 100 lakh only, as these amounts were earmarked for two separate specific purposes.

Period	*Rate of Interest*
30 days to 45 days	3.50% p.a.
46 days to 179 days	4.75% p.a.
180 days to 1 year	5.75% p.a.
Over 1 year up to 3 years	6.50% p.a.
Over 3 years	7.25% p.a.

Required

(*i*) What would have been the arguments of Ms. Kalpana Satlaj

(*a*) Against the suggestions of Mr. Avinash Prakash, and

(*b*) In favour of her own suggestions?

(*ii*) If you were on the Board of the Company, what further improvements you would have suggested over those of Ms. Kalpana Satlaj and Mr. Avinash Prakash?

"TDR is Better or Blue Chip Share": A Suggested Approach*

(*i*) (*a*) Ms. Kalpana Satlaj would have argued that the share market is very volatile and thus, may involve great risks too. The shares of some blue chip companies may give us very high profits. True. But then, the possibility of heavy losses, sometimes, may not be ruled out, either. Take, for example, the case of a relatively lesser volatile shares of Larsen and Toubro (L & T). Reliance Industries Limited (RIL) is reported to have cornered (though indirectly), a large number of shares of L & T, with a view to gain full control over the management of the affairs of L & T, allegedly for accruing some substantial financial gains to its other group companies. But then, as per the court rulings, such L & T shares could not be transferred and registered in the name of RIL. Consequently, the RIL had to get such shares sold out in the stock market. And, incidentally, as the market price of the L & T shares ruled at a much higher level than these shares had been bought for, the RIL, in the process, had a substantial profit. But then, if unfortunately (for RIL, that is), L & T shares would

*One of the approaches to the case study, as suggested by the author.

Please note that there is no single approach/solution to a case study.

have been transacted at a much lower price than the purchase price, at the material time of the sale; RIL would have sustained huge financial loss, instead. In early 1998, while the L & T shares were quoted at around Rs. 300, a couple of years earlier these had shot up well above Rs. 600, sometime, in the year 1998-99. And again, as on Friday, the 5th October 2001, these were quoted at around Rs. 160 to Rs. 165, at both the BSE and NSE.

Similarly, the market prices of software company shares, like those of Infosys and Wipro, suddenly dropped dramatically, immediately after the terrorist attack in New York on the Twin Towers of the World Trade Centre (WTC), and some other places in the USA.

There are umpteen such examples in the annals of the Stock Exchanges in India, but just these illustrative examples are sufficient enough to bring home the point that the investments of short-term funds in the shares, even those of the blue-chip companies, may not be considered prudent by any standard, due to the inherent risks involved therein.

(*b*) As against this, the arguments in favour of investment of such short-term surplus funds in the banks' Term Deposit Receipts (TDRs) may be far too many, some of which have been stated hereunder:

Most importantly, such an investment is extremely safe, and enjoys the utmost liquidity; one may take some loans against this, and may even prefer to take the repayment thereof prematurely, *i.e.* well before the due dates. Of course, it involves loss of some amount of interest. And the banks would comply with either of these instructions of yours immediately and instantaneously.

As against this, the sale-proceeds of the shares may usually take at least three to four days, in most of the cases, even if the shares were sold in the dematted form. And, even if you act safely and sell the shares say, a fortnight, in advance, you may have to keep the sale proceeds lying idle for quite some time if, for some unknown and unavoidable reasons, the occasion for making the required payment gets slightly deferred.

Further, you may have to sell the shares, per force, at the required time, even if their price be lower than the purchase price, resulting in a substantial financial loss, and the resultant deficit, to meet the expected expenditure, for which it had specifically been provided for.

(*ii*) If I were on the Board of Directors of the company, I would prefer to go a step further, and suggest that the entire debit balance of Rs. 100 lakh, outstanding in the company's cash credit account, must be got wiped off by depositing the entire amount of Rs. 100 lakh, by transfer from the company's current account, and thereby to save the interest outgo @ 15% p.a. on the full amount.

But, it would augur well if the company takes care to explain the position to the Bank Manager, and obtain his/her confirmation, preferably in writing, that the amount was kept for the sole purpose of meeting the margin money on the term loan, and it would be withdrawn for the purpose, on the arrival of goods, and for affecting the required payment thereof. This I suggest as this bank managers may create some problem at a later date on the plea that the bank's cash credit account cannot be used for payments, for acquiring fixed assets, inasmuch as it is a short-term finance, meant for meeting only the short-term applications, *i.e.* for the purchase of current assets only.

How best to invest the balance amount of Rs. 100 lakhs meant for meeting the expenses for the construction purposes?

As the construction work progresses, in phases, the expenses are also required to be incurred in the correspondingly phased manner. Therefore, it is better if the amount is suitably divided and invested in the Bank's TDRs, with the maturity period, corresponding with the phased progress and the corresponding financial requirements, in the construction work, so that the eventuality of taking loans against the TDRs, or even taking some pre-mature payments thereof, could be avoided, as far as possible.

Some banks have the facility of flexible deposits, *e.g.* the Khazana Scheme of Central Bank of India, which has a hybrid facility of saving bank account and the term deposit account, blended and twined together.

Lastly, as the "eternal vigilance is the price of profitability", it would mean a much better business sense to be alert enough to keep up-to-date about the investment opportunities and the relative advantages of the various deposit schemes, new and old, innovative and conservative, so as to take an appropriate investment decision at the material time.

4.12 MODELS OF CASH MANAGEMENT

Cash Budget is a managerial tool, whereby the companies come to know the period for which they are to have surplus funds, which must be gainfully invested in some safe and beneficial short-term investment schemes. Hard cash, as such, does not earn any interest. Further, through the their Cash Budgets, the companies come to know as to which period they are about to face the problem of some shortage of funds, which may have to be arranged to make payments of the instalments on term loans and to pay to the short-term lenders, like the banks and sundry creditors, when these may fall due. But then, hard cash is a necessary evil, in that all the companies have to necessarily have some hard cash too, to meet their day-to-day expenses. Therefore, a prudent business sense requires some minimal hard cash, and the surplus must be gainfully invested in some safe and beneficial short-term investment schemes. Now, the problem that may, naturally, arise is as to what should be the optional mix of cash holdings and short-term investment components in marketable securities.

There are many models, developed by various finance experts, which address this vital problem of the optional mix, and they have suggested their own models to solve this issue. However, in this section, we propose to discuss only the following two cash models:

(*a*) The Baumol Model; and

(*b*) The Miller and Orr Model.

4.12.1 Baumol Model

William J. Baumol, has applied the concept and principles of Economic Order Quantity (EOQ), which is commonly used in the management of inventories to determine the cash conversion size (which, in turn, affects the average cash holding of the company). The main purpose of such an analysis is to balance the income foregone in the case when the company holds cash balances, instead of investing the surplus cash in some marketable securities. It also takes into account the transaction costs incurred when the marketable securities are again converted into cash.

An **example** of the situation prevailing in Anurag Furniture Limited (AFL), should illustrate the nature of this analysis.

1. AFL needs Rs. 15 lakh in cash, to meet its requirements for various transactions which has been represented by the symbol 'T'. This amount is required by the company to meet its transactions for three months, which corresponds with its planning period, for taking liquidity decisions. Further, this amount, as of now, is held by the company in the form of marketable securities.

2. For the purpose of meeting its projected requirements of cash, the company can sell its marketable securities, in one of the five sizes of lots, viz. Rs. 1,00,000. Rs. 2,00,000, Rs. 3,00,000, Rs. 4,00,000 and Rs. 5,00,000. The quantum of such cash conversions of the marketable securities has been represented by the symbol 'C', and is shown in line 1 of Table 4.7.

3. Further, the number of times the marketable securities are converted into cash is simply T ÷ C. The value of T ÷ C, when T = Rs. 15 lakh, and C, varying in the range of Rs. 1,00,000, Rs. 2,00,000, Rs. 3,00,000, Rs. 4,00,000, and Rs. 5,00,000 is shown in line 2 of Table 4.7.

4. It has been presumed that the cash payments are made by the company evenly, over the full planning period of three months. If such be the case, the cash balance of the company will behave in the saw-tooth manner, as has been represented in **Figure 4.1**. Therefore, the average cash balance will simply be C ÷ 2. The average cash balances, corresponding with the various sizes of cash conversions, is shown in line 3 of Table 4.7.

5. On its marketable securities the company can earn an annual yield of 16 per cent. Accordingly, the rate of interest for the period of three months planning comes to 4 per cent (16 ÷ 4 = 4). This quarterly yield has been represented by the symbol 'I'. Further, as the average cash balance is C ÷ 2, the interest income foregone will be C ÷ 2 × 0.04. This has been shown in line 4 of Table 4.7.

6. The conversion of marketable securities into cash involves a fixed cost of Rs. 500 per transaction, represented by the symbol 'b'. However, 'b' is independent of the size of the marketable securities required to be converted into cash. Thus, the total conversion cost during the period of planning will be equal to number of cash order × cost per transaction. This has been shown in line 5 of Table 4.7. Generally speaking, the total conversion cost is '(T ÷ C) b'.

7. The total cost of ordering and holding ('TC') has been shown in line 6 of Table 4.7.

Table 4.7: Establishing the Optimal Cash Conversion Size

1. Cash conversion size (the amount of marketable securities that will be converted into cash).	Rs. 1,00,000	Rs. 2,00,000	Rs. 3,00,000	Rs. 4,00,000	Rs. 5,00,000
2. Number of conversions during the planning period of three months. (15,00,000 ÷ line 1)	15.00	7.50	5.00	3.75	3.00
3. Average cash balance (line 1 ÷ 2)	Rs. 50,000	1,00.000	1,50.000	2,00,000	2,50.000
4. Interest income foregone (line 3 × 0.04)	Rs. 2,000	4,000	6,000	8,000	10,000
5. Cost of cash conversion (Rs. 500 × line 2)	Rs. 7,500	3,750	2,500	1,875	1,500
6. Total cost of ordering cash and holding cash (line 4 + line 5)	Rs. 9,500	**7,750**	8,500	9,875	11,500

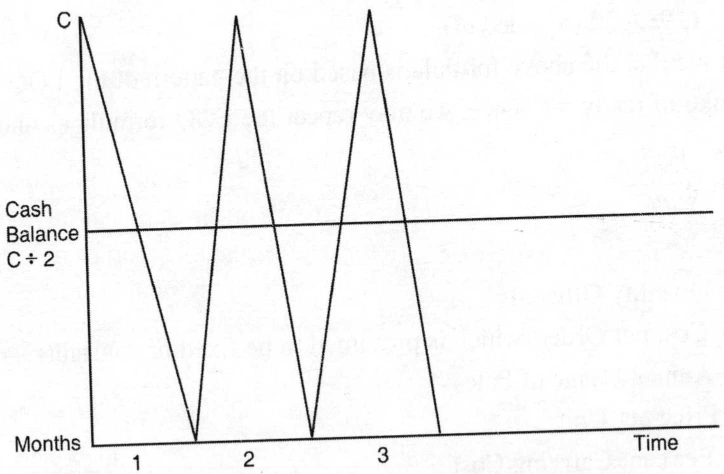

Fig. 4.1 Cash balance according to baumol model

When we look at the total cost, given in line 6 of Table 4.7, we see that the total cost is minimum, when C (conversion order) is Rs. 2,00,000. Thus, we find that, at the beginning of the planning period, the company should convert only Rs. 2,00,000 of marketable securities into cash. Moreover, the remaining amount should also be converted into cash in the lots of Rs. 2,00,000, as and when indicated by the need of disbursement of the company.

The aforementioned analysis may be represented in the form of a **general model** by applying the following symbols presented in our aforementioned illustration:

C = Amount of marketable securities converted into cash per order

I = Interest rate earned per planning period on investment in marketable securities

T = Projected cash requirements during the planning period

TC = Total of conversion and holding cost

The total cost (TC) may be expressed as follows:

$$TC = \underset{\text{(Interest income foregone)}}{I(C \div 2)} + \underset{\text{(Conversion costs)}}{b(T \div C)}$$

The value of 'C', which minimises 'TC' may be derived from the following equation:

$$C = \sqrt{\frac{2bT}{I}}$$

By applying the above equation to the situation of Anurag Furniture Limited (AFL), we get

$$C = \sqrt{\frac{2 \times 500 \times 15,00,000}{0.04}} \qquad (0.04 = 4\%)$$

$$= 1,93,649.1673$$

or 1, 93, 650 (rounded of)

Thus, we see that the above formula is based on the pattern of the EOQ formula.

For the sake of ready reference, we may repeat the EOQ formula as under:

$$Q = \sqrt{\frac{2FU}{PC}}$$

where

Q = Quantity Ordered

F = Cost per Order (which is presumed to be fixed or constant)

U = Annual Usage of Sales

P = Price per Unit

C = Per cent Carrying Cost

(*i.e.* PC = Inventory Carrying Cost itself.)

Thus, we arrive at the Economic Order Quantity (EOQ), where the Total Cost (Ordering Cost + Inventory Carrying Cost) is the minimum.

Similarly, by applying the relevant data in the aforementioned formula

$$\left(C = \sqrt{\frac{2bT}{I}}\right),$$

we are able to find where the Total Cost 'C' (*i.e.* the income foregone in the case when the company holds cash balance, instead of investing the surplus cash in some marketable securities), and the transaction costs incurred (when the marketable securities are again converted into cash), both taken together, is at the minimum possible level. That is to say that, in what circumstances the 'Interest Income Foregone' + 'Conversion Costs' are minimized.

Here, we find that the solution obtained by applying the formula above *i.e.*, $C = \sqrt{\frac{2bT}{I}}$

$\left[C = \sqrt{2 \times 500 \times 15{,}00{,}000 \div (0.04)}\right]$ comes to Rs. 1,93,650, which slightly differs from the solution obtained by us earlier, *i.e.* Rs. 2,00,000, as per line 1 of Table 4.7. This is so because, the **general equation** assumes that the conversion can take place in any amount, while the numerical analysis of Anurag Furniture Limited (AFL), assumes that the marketable securities can be sold only in one in one of the five distinct lots *i.e.* in the lots of Rs. 1,00,000, Rs. 2,00,000, Rs. 3,00,000, Rs. 4,00,000, and Rs. 5,00,000.

4.12.2 Miller and Orr Model

Miller and Orr Model, on the other hand, has expanded further on the Baumol Model of William J. Baumol, in that Miller and Orr consider a **stochastic generating process** for the periodical changes in the cash balance. As against the entirely deterministic assumptions of the Baumol Model, Miller and Orr assume that the changes in the cash balances in over a given period are random, both in size and direction, *i.e.,* in both upward and downward directions. Thus, as the period increases, the cash balance changes from a normal distribution.

Given the changing behaviour of cash balance, Miller and Orr Model endeavours to answer the following questions:

(*a*) When should transfers be effected between marketable securities and cash?

(*b*) What should be the size (magnitude) of these transfers?

According to Miller and Orr Model, any upward changes in the level of cash balance are permitted till the cash balance reaches an "**Upper Control Limit**" (UL). As and when this level reaches, the cash balance is required to be reduced to a "**Return Point**" (RP), by investing UL – RP in the marketable securities. As against this, any downward changes in the level of cash balance are permitted only till the cash balance touches a "**Lower Control Limit**" (LL). And, as and when such level is reached, sufficient quantum of marketable securities should be sold out or disposed of so as to restore the level of cash balance to its "**Return Point**" (RP).

The results of the analysis, based on the Miller and Orr Model, are as follows:

$$\text{RP} = \sqrt[3]{\frac{3b\delta^2}{4I}} + \text{LL}$$

$UL = 3RP - 2LL$

where

RP = Return Point

b = Fixed cost per order for converting marketable securities into cash

I = Daily interest rate earned on marketable securities

δ^2 = Variance of daily changes in the expected cash balance

LL = Lower control limit

UL = Upper control limit

Let us take an illustrative example to explain the point clearly.

Example

The following information is available in regard to Aishwarya Appliances Company Limited about its liquidity position:

1. An annual yield of 12 per cent is available on its marketable securities. On a daily basis, the yield, 'I' (taking 360 days in a year), works out to:
   $0.12 \div 360 = 0.000333$ or 0.0333 per cent.
2. The fixed cost of effecting a marketable securities transaction 'b', is Rs. 1,600.
3. The standard deviation, 'δ', of the change in daily cash balance is Rs. 5,000.
4. The management of Aishwarya Appliances Company Limited has decided to maintain a minimum cash balance of Rs. 50,000.

Solution

Based on the aforementioned information, the 'Return Point' and the 'Upper Control Limit', for Aishwarya Appliances Company Limited, by applying the Miller and Orr Model, are as follows:

$$RP = \sqrt[3]{\frac{3(1,600)(5,000)^2}{4 \times 0.000333}} + 50,000$$

$$= 94,962.50$$

$$UL = 3RP - 2LL$$

$$= (3 \times 94,962.50) - (2 \times 50,000) = 1,84,887.50.$$

This means that when the cash balance reaches the 'Upper Control Limit' of Rs. 1,84,887.50, the management *i.e.* the Finance Manager, in this case, should buy marketable securities of the value of Rs. 89,925 (Rs. 1,84,887.50 – Rs. 94,962.50 = Rs. 89,925). As against this, when the cash balance touches the 'Lower Control Limit' of Rs. 50,000, the management, (*i.e.* the Finance Manager, in this case) should sell the marketable securities with a view to restore the cash balance to the 'Return Point' level of Rs. 94,962.50. Further, so long as the cash balance lies between the 'Upper Control Limit', *i.e.* Rs.1,84,887.50 and the 'Lower Control Limit', *i.e.* Rs. 50,000, no transaction, pertaining to the marketable securities, should be taken up. This course of action, on the part of the company, will minimise the total of the transaction costs and the interest income foregone taken together.

A SYNOPTIC NOTE

(CHAPTER 4 AT A GLANCE)

MANAGEMENT OF CASH

1. CASH: A NECESSARY EVIL

Cash is a necessary evil. While all business establishments do have to keep some hard cash (in hand and/or in the bank), it does not yield any return by way of interest, whatsoever. It should, therefore, be kept at the minimal level.

2. CASH BUDGETING

Cash budget is a handy tool and technique to forecast the inflows and outflows of cash over a period of time, and thereby to determine the minimal level of cash to be maintained by the company. Most of the companies do the short-term cash budgeting on an yearly basis, subdivided into quarterly and/or monthly basis. Some of the companies, facing some cash crunch, however, may find it useful to prepare the cash budget on weekly or even daily basis.

3. RECEIPT AND PAYMENT METHOD

This is the most important and primary method of short-term cash forecasting. Under this method, the various receipts and payments (comprising both the expenditure and expenses), *i.e.* inflows and outflows of funds, are accounted for, as per the expected timings (months) of their actual occurrences.

To make such estimates more realistic, some reasonable basis must be formulated for each item of receipts and payments. For example

(*i*) Collection of sundry debtors must be based on the extent of cash and credit sales and the pattern of realisation of dues.

(*ii*) Salaries and wages must be based on manpower employed, and the salary and wages payable to them, etc.

With a view to achieve the above objectives, some basic information may be required. For example

(*i*) Estimated Sales (Cash and Credit Sales),

(*ii*) Purchase Plan,

(*iii*) Financing Plan, and

(*iv*) Capital Expenditure Budget.

And, out of these, the estimated sales is the most crucial factor, inasmuch as it is on the quantum of expected sales that the quantum of production actually depends. It is on production, in turn, that the quantum of purchases and stocking of raw materials etc., depends.

Further, on the basis of all this required information/estimated data, the companies prepare the following statements:

(*i*) Cash Receipt Budget;

(*ii*) Cash Payment Budget; and

(*iii*) Summary Statement.

And, the summary statement finally gives us the quantum and period of occurrences of cash surplus or cash deficit.

Further, based on such an information, we may take suitable financial decisions whether to postpone some heavy capital expenditure by a month or two, or to expedite the collection mechanism, or to borrow some short-term loans, or to arrange for some temporary overdrafts from the bank, or to somewhat delay the payments, at least, of some of the sundry creditors, without, of course, adversely affecting the company's own credit worthiness.

In the initial couple of years, the cash budgets may show some wide variances between budgeted and actual figures. But, with the passage of time, and by learning from the experiences, the officers of the company may be able to streamline the cash budgeting system, whereby the fluctuations may be contained and kept well within control.

4. VARIANCE IN CASH BUDGET

It may augur well if, instead of preparing a single cash budget, the companies may prefer to prepare a set of the undernoted three sets of the budget, based on different sets of assumptions and estimates, while taking into account the:

(*i*) Normal conditions,

(*ii*) Pessimistic conditions, and

(*iii*) Optimistic conditions.

5. LONG-TERM CASH FORECASTING

Such a cash budget is prepared for a period of two to three years, or say, for five years or so. Such a cash budget, however, is usually required mainly for taking capital investment decisions.

Long-term cash budget should better be prepared on "Adjusted Net Income Method", which largely resembles the funds flow statement.

6. REPORTS AND STATEMENTS FOR CONTROL

The following periodical reports and statements must be submitted to the controlling authorities, and on time, as and when they fall due:

(*i*) Monthly Performance Report on Cash Budget,

(*ii*) Daily Cash Report, and

(*iii*) Daily Treasury Report.

7. EXPEDITIOUS REALISATION OF RECEIPTS

With a view to have a comfortable cash balance position, all companies must pay special attention to the following sources of receipts:

(*i*) Management and control of sundry debtors,

(*ii*) Expeditious realisation of cheques/bank drafts, and

(*iii*) Decentralisation of collections.

8. CURRENT ACCOUNT VS. CASH CREDIT ACCOUNT

It is a drain on the company's profit to keep any credit balance in its current accounts overnight, inasmuch as it does not yield any interest, whatsoever. It would, therefore, be a better business sense to get the entire credit balance in the current account transferred to the company's cash credit account, so as to save the amount of interest payable thereon.

And, in case there is some surplus cash available to the company for a shorter span of time, it must be gainfully parked temporarily in some safe and sure evenues of short-term investments.

9. DEPOSITING MARGIN MONEY IN CASH CREDIT ACCOUNT

It will be highly beneficial for the company to deposit the margin money, on letters of credit or bank guarantees, by way of getting a lien noted in its cash credit account for the required amount, instead of depositing the money in the bank's term deposit account.

10. MANAGEMENT AND CONTROL OF PAYMENTS

This aspect of financial management is also equally crucial for the management of cash of the company. Therefore, instead of making payment of taxes on the day date, it may well be paid just a couple of days in advance, so as to avoid the last day rush and the risk of default, and the penalty that may go therewith. Similarly, the payment to the sundry creditors may, as well, be delayed but by a few days only, and in such cases only when the company may be facing some cash crunch. But, the over-delayed payment may ultimately prove to be very costly. Similarly, the prompt payment to the sundry creditors may have its own prize and reward too.

11. CENTRALISED PAYMENTS VS. DECENTRALISED PAYMENTS

Both the centralised and decentralised systems of payments have their own respective advantages and disadvantages.

Therefore, an optimal mix of both these systems, depending upon the special circumstances and conditions of each company, may be the best financial policy.

12. PLAYING THE FLOAT

WHAT IS MEANT BY FLOAT?

(*i*) When a company issues cheques, it debits the aggregate amount in its books the same day, though these cheques may generally be presented and debited in the company's account with the bank on some later date.

(*ii*) Similarly, when the company receives cheques/bank drafts in payment of its dues, it credits the amount of these instruments in its books the same day, while the respective amounts are generally credited to its account with the bank on some later dates. Thus, the time gap is known as the "Payment Float", in the first instance and the time gap pertaining to the second above condition is referred to as the "Collection Float".

And, if the difference between the two, *i.e.* the payment float, and the collection float, is positive, it is known as "Positive Net Float", and if the resultant balance is negative, it is known as the "Negative Net Float".

Thus, in the case of the "Positive Net Float", the credit balance in the company's bank account will be higher than what it should be in its own books. Thus, the company can very well issue some cheques against the (excess) amount of credit balance in the bank's books. The act of doing so is known as "Playing the Float".

Further, as this extra amount becomes available to the company for its use, free of interest, it would be a good business sense to make full use of it. But then, one should not overplay it. It will augur well if the company issues cheques with some restraints, *i.e.* say, up to 50 to 60% of the "Positive Net Float", available, and not up to the fullest extent, inasmuch as sometime the net difference may get narrowed down too.

13. INVESTMENT OF SURPLUS FUNDS FOR SHORT-TERM

SOME SAFE AND SURE AVENUES OF INVESTMENT FOR PARKING SURPLUS FUNDS FOR A SHORT-TERM

(a) UTI'S US 1964

(*i*) It was an open-ended mutual fund scheme with the face value of Rs. 10 each.

(*ii*) It was sold and purchased by the UTI at pre-announced sale and purchase prices, fixed administratively, usually monthly, and were based not on its Net Asset Value (NAV).

(*iii*) Its sales and purchases in the secondary market, however, were more gainful.

The UTI's US64 ran into some deep trouble in 1998, when its NAV had actually fallen below par, at around Rs. 9.50. And, it again faced even deeper trouble in June 2001. Thus, it is not a safe and gainful investment.

(b) READY FORWARD

This represents the deal of sale of some specified securities to be purchased back by the seller itself at a later date (*i.e.* forward), at ready.(*i.e.* predetermined) price. That is how, the term is referred to as, "Ready Forward".

Under this arrangement, the banks and some other organizations may sell some of the specified securities only to a company, at a certain price, but on the condition that the same securities will be bought back by the seller, on a stipulated date, and at a somewhat higher price, mutually agreed upon at the time of the sale itself.

In this way the bank may unload some of the specified securities, purchased by it to meet its requirements of Statutory Liquidity Ratio (SLR) to invest/advance the funds, so generated, elsewhere, at a higher yield. And, the company concerned is also able to park its surplus funds for a short period, safely and with sure liquidity.

The price difference between the purchase and resale price is the yield to the company, instead of the interest on the invested amount.

(c) TREASURY BILLS

Investments of treasury bills are safe, as these are issued by the Reserve Bank of India on behalf of the Government of India.

These are issued for a period of 91 days, 182 days and 364 days, and at a discount. Thus, the rate of interest is the function of the rate of discount and the period of maturity.

These are issued in bearer form to make transfer and transactions easy.

Besides, these are actively traded in the secondary market, too.

(d) CERTIFICATES OF DEPOSITS (CDs)

The certificates of deposits, like TDRs, are issued by the banks for a specified amount and for a specified period. But unlike the TDRs, they are negotiable, too.

It may be issued in "bearer" form, too, besides in the registered form.

The bearer form of CDs are more popular as its title may be transferred by delivery only—as no endorsement is required on bearer instruments.

Further, these are traded even in the secondary market. These are issued at a specified rate of interest, where the yield is somewhat higher than that in the case of TDRs and Treasury Bills.

(e) COMMERCIAL PAPERS (CPs)

These are the unsecured money market instruments, issued in the form of promissory notes, in physical or dematerialised form, and at a discount on the face value.

Eligibility

(*i*) Tangible Net Worth (TNW) of the company should be minimum Rs. 4 crore.

(*ii*) It should be enjoying a working capital facility; its account being classified as the "standard asset".

(*iii*) Its minimum credit rating should be P-2 of CRISIL, or equivalent thereof.

(*iv*) It can be issued for a period ranging from 7 days to one year, in the denominations of Rs. 5 lakh or multiples thereof.

(*v*) A single investor can now invest minimum Rs 5 lakh in the CP (reduced from Rs. 25 lakh).

(*vi*) It is now a "stand-alone" facility. Banks and FIs may, however, decide, at their sole discretion, to provide a "standby" financial assistance to the issuing company.

(*vii*) The under-noted eligibility criteria/conditions have since been lifted:

(*a*) Listing of the company's shares in some stock exchange;

(*b*) Minimum Current Ratio (CR) to be 1.33; and

(*c*) The company that enjoy Health Code NO.1.

(f) Public Deposits

Public deposits are unsecured deposits, solicited and accepted by large and small companies, mainly for meeting their working capital requirements. These are usually issued for a period ranging from minimum six months to maximum three years.

Public deposits can be issued for a maximum amount equal to 25 per cent of the company's share capital and free reserves. Such deposits for a minimum period of three months can be issued by the companies, but only up to 10 per cent of its share capital and free reserves.

The rate of interest payable on public deposits are determined by the prevailing market conditions and the pattern followed by other companies, though the ceiling stipulated on the rate of interest payable on such deposits has been withdrawn since mid-1996.

An amount equal to 10 per cent of the amount of the deposits, maturing and falling due for payment after the 31st March next year, has to be deposited and/or invested on April, 30 each year, and kept specifically earmarked for the purpose of meeting the repayments of the public deposits, as and when these may fall due.

Most importantly, the companies are required to make some true and fair disclosures about certain vital and relevant facts, pertaining to its financial position, performance and prospects.

(g) INTER-CORPORATE DEPOSITS (ICDs)

These are the unsecured deposits made by one corporate body with another. The maturity period, however, varies from minimum "one-day notice" to maximum six months.

There are three types of ICDs:

(*i*) Call Deposits—payable on demand, on one-day notice.

But, usually, it takes around two to three days to effect the actual payment.

(*ii*) Three-month Deposits.

(*iii*) Six-month Deposits, which is the maximum permitted maturity period.

As these are unsecured deposits, care should be taken to select the financially safe and sound corporate bodies to invest with.

Besides, the company's total investments in ICDs plus the loans and guarantees, should not exceed 60% of its net worth, *i.e.* paid-up share capital + free reserves, or up to cent per cent of its free reserves, whichever is more, as per Section 372Aof the Companies Act, 1956.

(h) BADLA FINANCING

Financing the *Badla* transactions or forward-trading, is a process under which the brokers are permitted to carry forward the payments pertaining to the share transactions, but, in the case of category "A" shares only, to the next week-end settlement date.

But, as the stock market is too volatile, such investments, though high yielding, may be quite risky, too.

Thus, the following safeguard measures must be taken by the companies:

(*i*) The financing should be done through reputed and honest brokers, with stable financial position.

(*ii*) The company may even stipulate that the shares of some specific companies only should be financed, and that too to the investors of known integrity.

(*iii*) Badla financing should be provided only after taking the possession of the respective shares in physical or demated forms.

(*iv*) Above all, the aim should be to make some reasonable 'gain' and not to crave for an undue "greed".

(i) PURCHASE/DISCOUNT OF DEMAND/TIME BILLS

As the demand bills and time (usance) bills are purchased and discounted, by the bank, such a facility may be granted even by the companies, which are flush with surplus funds, though temporarily.

Care should, however, be taken that such "finance" is made available against genuine trade transactions and not against fictitious bills. Further, such facilities should be granted only to such companies whose financial stability and integrity are well-established, so as to avoid any possible risks involved in such business transactions.

14. MODELS OF CASH MANAGEMENT

(*a*) William J. Baumol has developed a model, which is based on the concept of the **Economic Order Quantity (EOQ)**, usually used in the management of inventories, to determine the cash conversion size which, in turn, influences the average holding of cash of a company.

(*b*) Miller and Orr, however, have further developed on the Baumol model and have taken into account a **stochastic generating process**, instead, for the periodical changes in the cash balance.

QUESTIONS
(For Self-assessment)

1. Despite knowing it fully well that the cash in hand and/or with the banks (in the current account) does not earn any interest, all the companies and firms, worldover, have invariably been found to be holding cash. What could be the compelling reason and rationale behind this?

2. "Cash budgeting or short-term cash forecasting (budgeting) is the principal tool of cash management." Discuss.

3. Discuss the 'receipts and payments' method of cash budgeting.

4. (*a*) What are the major sources of

(*i*) Cash Receipts; and

(*ii*) Cash payments?

(*b*) How can these be estimated with almost near accuracy?

5. Various types of cash reports are prepared and submitted periodically to the management for controlling and reviewing cash forecast on a continuous basis. Discuss the three main reports submitted in this regard.
6. What necessary steps would you suggest to be taken by the companies to improve the efficiency and effectiveness of their cash management?
7. (*i*) What do you mean by:
   (*a*) Payment float,
   (*b*) Collection float,
   (*c*) Net float,
   (*d*) Positive 'net-float',
   (*e*) Negative 'net-float', and
   (*f*) Steady state situation?

   (*ii*) Explain each of the terms by citing some suitable illustrative examples.
8. (*a*) What do you mean by the term 'playing the float'?
   Explain by using some appropriate illustrative examples.

   (*b*) In your own considered opinion, what would be your specific suggestions to the companies, in regard to, 'playing the float'? Give reasons for your answer.
9. What is meant by the term 'Optimal Cash Balance'?
10. What are the various options or opportunities available to the companies to park their surplus funds for a short-term, so as to gain a reasonable income by way of interest, and, at the same time, maintain sufficient safety and liquidity of the invested funds?
11. If you were the Director (Finance) of a company, what specific strategies would you formulate and adopt in regard to the investment of surplus funds available with the company, but only for a short period of say, six months from now? Give specific reasons for adopting a specific step and strategy in each case.
12. Write short notes on:
    (*a*) US64 Scheme,
    (*b*) Ready Forward,
    (*c*) Treasury Bills,
    (*d*) Certificates of Deposits (CDs),
    (*e*) Commercial Papers (CPs),
    (*f*) Inter-Corporate Deposits (ICDs),
    (*g*) Badla Financing,
    (*h*) Discounting of (time) Bills, and
    (*i*) Purchase of Demand Drafts.
13. What will be the value of 'C' (*i.e.* the amount of marketable securities converted into cash per order), according to the Baumol model?
14. What are the important features of Miller and Orr Model? Discuss.

PROBLEMS FOR PRACTICE

1. KLM Company (P) Limited is preparing its cash budget for the period July through December, this year. The following information is available:
   (a) The estimated sales for the period, July through December, are as follows: Rs. 1,80,000 per month for July and August, and Rs. 2,10,000 per month from September through December.
   (b) The sales for the months of May and June have been Rs. 1,50,000 each.
   (c) The division of sales between cash and credit sales is: 25 per cent cash and 75 per cent credit.
   (d) Credit collection pattern is: 30 per cent after one month and 70 per cent after two months.
   (e) Bad debt losses are nil.
   (f) Other anticipated receipts are: (i) Rs. 75,000 from the sale of a machine in August, and (ii) Rs. 8,000 interest on securities in December.
   (g) The estimated purchases of materials on credit are: Rs. 70,000 per month from June to August and Rs. 95,000 per month from September to December.
   (h) The payments for the purchases are made in about a month's time after the purchase.
   (i) The purchases for the month of June have been Rs. 65,000 for which payments will be made in July.
   (j) Miscellaneous cash purchases of Rs. 7,000 per month are planned for July through December.
   (k) Wage payments are expected to be Rs. 40,000 per month, July through December.
   (l) Manufacturing expenses are expected to be Rs. 40,000 per month, July through December.
   (m) General administrative and selling expenses are expected to be Rs. 20,000 per month.
   (n) Dividend payment of Rs. 50,000 and tax payment of Rs. 45,000 are scheduled in December.
   (o) A machine worth Rs. 95,000 is planned to be purchased in cash in October.

   The cash balance, as on the 1st of July is Rs. 45,000. The minimum cash balance required by the company is Rs. 35,000.

Required

1. Prepare a statement showing the surplus/deficit in relation to the minimum cash balance required by the company.

2. Mr John has a tea-stall on the high way. He has asked you to prepare a cash budget for him for the quarter, October through December, this year, with the following information
   (a) Sales are expected to be: Rs. 70,000 in October, Rs. 80,000 in November, and Rs. 60,000 in December. All sale transactions will be in cash and credit in the ratio of 20 : 80.
   (b) His estimated credit purchases are: Rs. 30,000 in October, Rs. 35,000 in November and Rs. 40,000 in December. Payments for purchases are usually made after one month. The outstandings on account of the credit purchases in September are Rs. 35,000.
   (c) The rent per month is Rs. 7,000 and his personal withdrawal per month is Rs. 6,000.
   (d) Salaries and other expenses, payable in cash, are expected to be: Rs. 20,000 in October, Rs. 23,000 in November, and Rs. 25,000 in December.
   (e) He plans to buy in October furniture worth 40,000 on cash payment basis.
   (f) The cash balance, at present, is Rs. 6,000. He, however, prefers to have cash balance at Rs. 10,000.

Required

What will be the surplus/deficit of cash in relation to his planned cash balance?

3. JKL Industries Ltd. issues cheques of Rs. 70,000 daily and it takes 7 days for its cheques to be cleared. The company receives cheques amounting to Rs. 80,000 daily and it takes 6 days for these cheques to be realised.

Required

Assuming that there is a balance of Rs. 40,000 in the books of the firm and the bank, to begin with;

(*i*) Show the balances in the books of the firm as well as the bank.

(*ii*) What will be the balance in the steady state situation?

4. Moon and Star Sports Ltd. issues cheques aggregating Rs. 50,000 daily and it takes 6 days for its cheques to be cleared and debited to its account with the bank. The company receives cheques aggregating Rs. 60,000 daily and it takes 4 days for these cheques to be realised and credited to its account.

Required

(*i*) Assuming a balance of Rs. 70,000 in the books of the company and the bank, to begin with, show the balance in the books of the company and the books of the bank.

(*ii*) What will be the balance in the 'steady state situation'?

5. Seven Sisters Associates issues cheques aggregating Rs. 47,000 daily and it takes 7 days for its cheques to be cleared and debited to its account with the bank. The firm receives cheques aggregating Rs. 59,000 daily and it takes 5 days for these cheques to be realised and credited to its account.

Required

(*a*) Assuming a balance of Rs. 35,000 in the books of the firm and the bank, to begin with, show the balances in the books of the firm and the books of the bank.

(*b*) What will be the balance in the 'steady state situation'?

6. (*i*) Ashoka Automobiles Limited will need Rs. 30 lakhs in cash. This amount will be required by the company to meet its transactions for three months, which correspond with its planning period, for taking liquidity decisions. Further, this amount, as of now, is held by the company in the form of marketable securities.

(*ii*) For the purpose of meeting its projected requirements of cash, the company can sell its marketable securities, in one of the five sizes of lots, viz. Rs. 2,00,000, Rs. 4,00,000, Rs. 6,00,000, Rs. 8,00,000 and Rs. 10,00,000.

Required

(*a*) Compute the number of times the marketable securities will be converted into cash during the planning period of three months.

(*b*) It has been presumed that the cash payments are made by the company evenly, over the full planning period of three months. Compute the average cash balances, corresponding with the various sizes of each conversion.

(*c*) On its marketable securities, the company can earn an annual yield of 16 per cent. Compute the rate of interest for the three months period of planning, as also the amount of interest income foregone by the company.

(*d*) The conversion of marketable securities into cash involves a fixed cost of Rs. 1,000 per transaction, which is independent of the size of the marketable securities required to be converted into cash. Compute the cost of conversion of the marketable securities into cash.

(*e*) Compute the total ordering cost and cost of holding cash.

(*f*) At what stage the total ordering cost and cost of holding cash will be minimized?

7. The following information is available in regard to Shalini Saris Company Limited:

(*i*) An annual yield of 18 per cent is available on its marketable securities.

(*ii*) The fixed cost of effecting one marketable securities transaction is Rs. 240.

(*iii*) The standard deviation of the change in daily cash balance is Rs. 7,500.

(*iv*) The management of the company has decided to maintain a minimum cash balance of Rs. 75,000.

Required

(*a*) Taking 360 days in a year, compute the yield of the company on a daily basis.

(*b*) (*i*) Based on the aforementioned information, compute the 'Return Point' and the 'Upper Control Limit', for the Company, by applying the Miller and Orr Model.

(*ii*) Also find out, when the cash balance reaches the 'Upper Control Limit', agrregating what amount the management should buy marketable securities? Give reasons for your answer.

(*iii*) Further, compute the amount when the cash balance touches the 'Lower Control Limit', the management should sell the marketable securities aggregating what amount, with a view to restoring the cash balance to the 'Return Point' level.

(*iv*) It is said that 'so long as the cash balance lies between the 'Upper Control Limit' and the 'Lower Control Limit', no transaction, pertaining to the marketable securities, should take place.' Do you agree with this view? Give reasons for your answer.

Appendix 4.1

PROBLEMS OF UTI : ROOTS AND REMEDIES

(a) General Problems

(*i*) Most of the scholars and academics, experts and experienced people, have opined that the UTI would not have come down to such a pitiable position, had its US64 units been priced on the basis of its Net Asset Value (NAV), instead of the administrative pricing mechanism.

(*ii*) Further, the declaration of systematic and continuous dividend of 20%, irrespective of its NAV and the income generated, was a further faulty mechanism against all the principles of finance, specially when its NAV had reportedly gone down below par during the crisis that UTI had faced earlier.

(*iii*) It has also been argued that had the UTI been subjected to the regulation and scrutiny of the Securities Exchange Board of India (SEBI), as was proposed in 1993, and again by the Deepak Parekh Committee in 1999, the situation would not have come to such a pitiable position.

Just take one token example of the public issue of Usha Rectifier (now renamed as Usha India). The company had been able to manipulate the price of its shares up to Rs. 200 and Rs. 250, just prior to their coming up with the mega public issue of Rs. 10 (face value) shares at a hefty premium of Rs. 40, *i.e.* at a price of Rs. 50. The issue was highly under-subscribed, far below the stipulated 90% mark.

But, the application money was not refunded by the company to the investors, on the plea that no such conditions were stipulated in their application/public issue proposal, submitted to the SEBI. Then, who is responsible for such a gross lapse on the part of the SEBI? What exemplary action SEBI authorities have so far taken against their own negligent and delinquent employees and senior officers?

(b) Corruption—The Most Fundamental Problem

Besides the aforesaid valid, oft-repeated and well known causes of the problems being faced by the UTI, specially in regard to its US64 units, in my considered opinion, the element of 'Corruption', prevalent at various levels, high and low, in the UTI, seems to be the most fundamental cause of the pitiable position of the premier Mutual Fund Company of India.

While I was engaged in the empirical study of the causes of industrial sickness and turnaround strategies, I observed that corruption of the bank officials had also been one of the main and major causes of industrial sickness. And now, it occurs to me, on the basis of the press reports, that the officials of the UTI are no exception.

The press reports reveal that a maximum number of transfers of the officers of the UTI has recently taken place, and the UTI, in turn, tries to convince the people that this is the routine periodical exercise. Whatever be the true state of affairs, there cannot be two opinions that such transfers can, at best, transfer the problems, but can never transform the system.

Let us look into some illustrative (not exhaustive) but revealing facts, which came in the papers, about the UTI, which were, *prima facie* and obviously bad decisions. Such decisions cannot be said to be accidental but deliberate and wilful. And, if the UTI people have taken such decisions, it can, at best, be taken for two distinct reasons:

(*a*) The people, who took the decisions, were lacking the general knowledge and common sense, and the required expertise, or (*b*) Alternatively, it was done deliberately, and, therefore, obviously, for some sort of personal (financial) gains.

And, the first option does not seem to be plausible, inasmuch as the personnel of the UTI are considered to be experts in the line of such deals. Thus, the second option, that is some connivance and underhand deals, seems to be apparent and obvious.

For example, the unhealthy link between the UTI and CCL (Century Consultants Limited), Lucknow, is not far to seek. The reports, published in the newspapers on July 13, 2001 say that the UTI officials had invested the UTI's money, mostly of the small investors, to the tune of Rs. 50 crore in the Cyberspace shares—a company owned by the Joharis of CCL. The UTI officials are reported to have bought 29 lakh shares of Cyberspace between August 1999 to 2000 of which while 17 lakh shares were bought from the secondary markets, investments in another 12 lakh preferential shares were made by the UTI officials at a time when the Cyberspace scrips were nose-diving in July 2000. Don't these bare facts smack of something fishy.

Most of the papers have reported that a large scale redemption to the tune of Rs. 4,151 crore to be exact had taken place, during the period of two months April-May 2001, and that some big corporations had accounted for around 90% of such redemption [The *Economic Times*, 14 July, 2001]. Incidentally, during the whole fiscal year 2001, the redemption had aggregated to only Rs. 5,962 crores.

These facts alone go to indicate that there had been some connivance between the UTI and Corporate Houses, and the information of the impending freezing of the redemption after June 2001 must have been conveyed to them surreptitiously, of course, by some highly-placed officers in the UTI; that is, by the persons, who were in the full knowledge of such impending decisions. This may, thus, well be termed as the "inside trading", as some papers have reported. Otherwise, why else the corporates would have encashed their US64 units, in bulk, to reinvest the proceeds in some other avenues of short-term parking of surplus funds, where the return was far less than usually expected from the US64.

SOME SUGGESTED SOLUTIONS TO THESE PROBLEMS

(a) Clear the Cob-Web of Corruption first, through determined deterrent punishment, even on circumstantial evidences

It is very disheartening and disturbing to note that the financial institutions wait and look for some documentary evidence before initiating any disciplinary proceedings against their corrupt employees and officers. In my personal considered opinion, this may somewhat amount to expecting the thief to leave behind the detailed inventory of the articles stolen as also his address and the mobile number so as to facilitate his prosecution. During my over 27 years of service in the State Bank of India, when one corrupt Branch Manager had demanded the balance amount of the bribe money by writing a letter to the person concerned under his handwriting and his full signature, he was immediately dismissed from the Bank's service. But, this may be the rarest of the rare and, perhaps, the solitary exception. I earnestly feel that if circumstantial evidence can prove even the cases of murder, and the culprits are hanged or sentenced for life, the corrupt practices of dishonest persons can as well be proved on the basis of the circumstantial evidence, in the departmental proceedings, and suitable disciplinary action can well be taken against them. Otherwise, the unhealthy and dangerous trend of even the honest people getting converted into the dishonest lot can hardly be arrested.

All considered, I am of the firm opinion that if some circumstantial evidence can, *prima facie*, be established in respect of the malpractices of any official, he or she should be put under suspension, immediately. As we all know, suspension is not considered to be a punishment, but only as a preventive measure. And, if the charges of corruption are proved, the minimum punishment to be meted out to such people should be nothing short of dismissal and forfeiture of all retirement benefits, whatsoever.

(b) Restraint in Government Directions

The use or misuse of UTI funds, time and again, by the Government of India, as a tool to control abnormal trades in the stock markets [the most recent case being that of payment default crisis in Calcutta Stock Exchange (CSE)] also constitutes an avoidable burden on it. Because, in this bailout exercise, the UTI, on verbal instructions from the Ministry of Finance, Government of India, had reportedly purchased mainly four scrips, for over Rs. 55 crore, viz. the scrips of HFCL, Global Tele System, DSQ Software and Zee Telefilms.

UTI reportedly purchased about 1.46 lakh shares of HFCL at an average price of Rs. 439.20 per share for an aggregate amount of Rs. 6.41 crores. And, the current market price of the share is as low as around Rs. 75. Similarly, the share of DSQ software, purchased by UTI at an average price of Rs. 250.14 for an aggregate amount of Rs. 33.27 crores was quoted at Rs. 61.85 [press reports dated July 14, 2001].

ALTERNATIVES TO AVERT SOME OF THE PROBLEMS

Better late than never

(*a*) It is a belated but right decision to change over to the NAV-based pricing mechanism of US64 (w.e.f. 1st January, 2002), instead of the irrational and unreasonable administered pricing system.

(*b*) Further, it will augur well for the investors if the US64 is also brought under the purview of the control and regulation of SEBI, but then, provided the regulatory authority (SEBI) itself takes care not to fail in disciplining its own regulators to discharge their duties honestly and sincerely, and the callous actions and decisions on their part should earn the deserved deterrent disciplinary actions.

(*c*) The Government of India, Ministry of Finance, would do well not to unnecessarily intervene and interfere in the affairs of the UTI, and should not force or direct the UTI authorities to come to the rescue of the Stock Exchanges, and/or arrest some drastic fluctuations or irregularities, whereby the UTI authorities (in order to save their own position), mostly succumb to such pressures, even though they may have to knowingly and deliberately take some obviously wrong, non-business-like and unprofessional decisions of buying and selling some of the shares, just to keep their, 'bosses' happy and in good humour.

(*d*) The UTI, and all the Mutual Fund Companies, should exercise more than ordinary care in recruiting and appointing competent and professional executives and officers, they should be properly groomed and trained, before they are entrusted any onerous responsibility and authority to take high-value decisions in regard to the funds generated out of the small savings of small investors.

(*e*) And, above all, with a view to avoid any further erosion of trust in the UTI and, more importantly, to restore the confidence and reliance in the professionalism and transparency of the top executives and senior officers of the UTI, the most crucial step and action to be taken in the present juncture, in my personal considered opinion, is that some streamlined system should be in place to determine whether the officers concerned had taken the decision in a professional and proficient manner, and no mala fide intentions were involved, even if the decision, genuinely taken, turned out to be a wrong and losing proposition. But then, the officers concerned should learn from their own mistakes, as well as those of the others, and should see to it that these are never repeated. But then, if any *prima facie* circumstantial evidence is found, smacking of the lack of bonafide and honesty in any of the decisions or actions of any of the officials, of any category and grade, they must be immediately suspended, and disciplinary proceedings should be urgently initiated and promptly concluded, and some deterrent actions should be taken against them, so that other officers may refrain from indulging in any mal-practices, whatsoever.

Most of the national newspapers had flashed the front page news on July 21, 2001, that the former UTI Chairman Mr P.S. Subramanyam, the Executive Directors, Mr M.M. Kapoor, and Mr S.K. Basu, and some other officers had since fallen in the CBI net "for allegedly squandering public funds worth Rs. 32. 8 crore" (The *Hindustan Times*, Lucknow, July 21) and inquiries and investigations, search and research, are in progress. And, there can hardly be any difference of opinion that the offences and negligence, if proved, should be dealt with, and drastic and deterrent action, have to be taken ruthlessly.

UTI should become self-sustaining, rather than usually looking for the Government's Support, from time to time

The UTI is gradually becoming a drag on the tax-payer's money, surely and undoubtedly. But, if the Government directs the UTI to wilfully take some ill-conceived and apparently non-business-like decisions, as aforesaid, it is under moral obligation to bail it out of the resultant losses inflicted on it. That is what the Government seems to be doing, too. In the earlier crisis, the RBI reportedly asked SBI and other public sector banks to bail UTI out of the crisis, though SBI had reportedly not obliged last time. But then, this time, many Public Sector Banks, including State Bank of India, have agreed to lend money to UTI at below PLR (Prime Lending Rate), its (UTI's) financial position being far from satisfactory. This will have an adverse effect on the income of the banks, earning much less interest, which, in turn, will be again a drag on the public fund.

Further, the favour shown by the Government of India, during the previous crisis of UTI, by making the income (not dividend) on US64 tax-free had, in effect, meant that the income of 13.50 per cent was equivalent to around 20% taxable income. And, the exemption from the income tax, naturally, had the direct effect on the reduction in the income tax collection to that extent which, in turn, had to be compensated by taxing the general public more harshly, both intensively and extensively.

It may not be an exaggeration to say that in India, most of the financial and economic decisions are taken on political considerations, and in the case of UTI, too, the story is not different. Unless this unhealthy trend is set in order, the UTI's state of affairs cannot be streamlined and stabilised, enabling it to turn around and stand on its own feet, without any external support, including that of the Government.

UTI's Relief Package: How Plausible, How Painful?

The UTI's most eagerly awaited and recently announced relief package, specially to soothe the small investors, seems to be yet another attempt to swindle them over again. The UTI offered to repurchase its US64 units up to 3000 units per investor, with effect from the 1st August, 2001 and up to 31st May, 2003, at a repurchase price of Rs. 10.00 per unit. And, with a view to add some sugar to the bitter pill (of relief), it is proposed to increase the repurchase price of the unit by 10 paise every month till the closure of the package in May 2003. This arrangement seemingly amounts to a return of 12% per annum, *i.e.* an increase of Rs. 1.20 in the future purchase price, from Rs. 10 to Rs. 11.20, during the period of 12 months. This prima facie seems quite reasonable at the present interest rate structure on deposits. But, the UTI's wishful thinking is that the poor small investors, who have invested their small but hard earned savings, by purchasing the US64 units at a price of say, Rs. 14.25 per unit in May 2001 (as the big corporate houses had reportedly sold their US64 Units to UTI in April-May, 2001 at an average price of Rs. 14.25 per unit), may not be intelligent and wise enough, even after having lost so heavily, to see through the fact that the effective rate of interest at 10 paise per month per unit (*i.e.* on Rs. 14.25) comes to just around 7% per annum.

The plight of the small investors does not seem to end even here. Because, if a unit holder gets his 1000 units, at Rs. 14.25 per unit, redeemed @ Rs. 10 instead, he would lose [(Rs. 14.25 – Rs. 10.00) × (1000)] Rs. 4,250 straight.

The "game" does not seem to be still over. The dicey thing is that the UTI gave a further allurement to the small investors that from January 2002, the UTI would switch over to Net Asset Value (NAV) – based pricing, and the investors would be able to sell these units to UTI at the NAV-based price, or Rs. 10.00, whichever was higher.

And, look at the optimistic note struck in the nicely worded statement of the newly appointed Chairman of the UTI, Mr M. Damodaran (after the unceremonious exit of Mr P.S. Subramanyam), as has been reported in newspapers dated July 16, 2001, and I quote:

"Our expectation is that after looking at the graded system, the small investors will remain with the scheme for a long-term", as if there seemed to be still some fond hope that the NAV of US64 units, was to appreciate in the near future. The stark reality, reportedly, was that the NAV of US64 units, by the end of December 2001, was expected to be as low as around Rs. 7.40 only.

That is why, perhaps, some of the investors' creative brain choose to expand the UTI to mean **"Un-Trusted Institution"** and some even changed the name of the UTI as **"DTI"**, meaning **"Don't Trust It"**. These may, however, sound some extreme expressions, uttered in the fits of anger and anguish, but the pain and pangs, inherent in such statements, could be felt and heard, loud and clear.

All considered, I am inclined to be in full agreement with the concluding sentence of the editorial in the *Hindustan Times*, Lucknow, dated the July 17, 2001, reading as under:

"The package has to be more attractive to benefit small investors who lost out when the corporates and banks sucked the UTI dry."

Do the Investors, especially the small ones, still have some trust left in the UTI? What does the UTI hold for them in the near future?

The Unit Trust of India has, in fact, acted in the most unexpected and irresponsible manner and, the trust and confidence of the general public, stand shattered, due to its own misdeeds and doings, so much so that the small investors feel cheated and betrayed.

Thus, with a view to avoid any further damage, the aforesaid suggestions and steps need serious consideration and implementation by all the authorities concerned, I reiterate that all the cases of corruption have to be dealt with in the most deterrent manner so as to arrest and, at least, mitigate, if not, eliminate, the cases of corruption. Further, the relief package needs to be reconsidered and made somewhat realistic and based on the principles of justice, so that the small investors may not feel cheated and swindled.

Unless such minimal, though major, steps are taken, immediately and urgently, the already shattered confidence in the UTI in particular, and the Mutual Fund Companies in general, instead of being restored, may get further shattered and eroded, up to a point of no return, which may, in turn, prove to be most dangerous and detrimental to the growth and development of our national economy.

I fondly hope that the authorities in the UTI and all the other places would act swiftly and surely. Amen!

[This discussion is based on the author's interview published in the journal "ICFAI READER", September 2001, pp. 18–22].

Appendix 4.2

DID UTI SUCCUMB TO PRESSURE?

"No one can make you feel inferior without your consent", so said Eleanor Roosevelt, in *Catholic Digest*, August 1960, p. 102. In a similar vein, I wish to say, "No one can force you to do wrong things, without your consent". Thus, it will be quite naive to take any serious note of the allegation of S.P. Subramanyam, the Ex-chairman, UTI, to the effect that he had taken some obviously wrong and grossly unwise decisions in regard to some investments like in the shares of Cyberspace, etc., at an unreasonably high price and, that too, at a very wrong time (as reported in the press), under pressure from the Ministry of Finance and/ or the Minister of Finance himself. Such a poor plea seems to be blantantly bogus, and maliciously misplaced, to put it mildly. The advocate of Subramanyam seems to be working on the management "*mantra*" that: "Aggression is the best defence". But, in the instant case, it has proved to be a dull and dead defence, instead.

And, as if it was not enough, some Members of the Parliament (MPs) preferred to raise the issue of involvement of the Prime Minister's Office (PMO), too. And, perhaps, pointing out an accusing finger against our Prime Minister, too, though obliquely and tacitly only. These people, the law-makers and the law interpreters (MPs and lawyers) seem to lack the common sense, and the natural instinct and intuitive power, to tell the difference in "right" and "wrong", between "honest" and "dishonest".

I am not holding any brief on behalf of the Prime Minister's Office (PMO) or the Prime Minister (PM), nor even of the Union Finance Ministry (UFM) nor the Finance Minister. But, the act of levelling serious allegations, based on as flimsy a ground as just some phone calls, by itself, exposes the bankruptcy of the logical thinking and rational reasoning. If the Union Finance Ministry and the Minister(s) have to oversee the working of UTI, and other financial institutions, should ascertain from the Chairman, UTI the present position and advise him to act rightly.

Such allegations got a severe and strong jolt when it transpired that no one tried to ascertain none of the from the Prime Minister's Office (PMO), but the fact was the other way round. The principles of justice and jurisprudence and, at least, the common and civic sense, demand that we must first try to find out why did the "wrong" person at all called the "right" person, as also as to what for, and, above all, as to what was the response of the "right" person, and what did actually transpire between them. My humble submission to such people will be: "Don't dare charging "good" persons, for "bad" reasons, "right" persons for "wrong" reasons. Instead, first learn the art and skill of telling honest persons from dishonest ones. And, then act and allege, if at all warranted.

And, how about the (so called) Chief Executive Officers (CEOs), who succumb to the slightest pressure from the top, and yield fast enough, to please the "boss", as if they do not have a spine or a super supple spine? Do they, at all, deserve the "Chair", if they want to stick to it, without sticking to the principles of honesty and uprightness?

In this context, I instantaneously get reminded of R. K. Talwar, the former Chairman, State Bank of India. It is a well-known "secret" that Talwar was under great pressure from Sanjay Gandhi, when he was somehow yielding some great powers, though in an extra-constitutional capacity. But then, Mr. Talwar is known to have once said that "Talwar is made of steel. He can break but can't bend". He did not bend and budge even an inch. And, he had to pay a very high price for that. Yes, you have guessed it right. He was forcibly eased out, at the instance of Sanjay Gandhi. But, he preferred to stick to the principles of honesty, and uprightness, rather than sacrificing and crucifying them, so as to continue as the Chairman, State Bank of India, and keep on suffering such imminent humiliations. And, as I gather from very reliable sources, Talwar is still remembered with great respect and reverence by all the employees and officers of the State Bank of India, and all of them speak, with one voice, that he had been, by far the best Chairman of the State Bank of India, so long and so far. And I, too, hold it to be true, till today.

It will, thus, augur well if the Chief Executive Officers (CEOs) remember the golden words of Dolores Ibarruri, put so succinctly: "It is better to die on one's feet rather than to live on one's knees". Amen!

[This discussion is based on the author's article published in the *Times of India*, Lucknow, August 21, 2001, p. 2].

Appendix 4.3

(Stamp to be affixed as in force in the State in which the CP is to be issued)

Name of the Issuing Company/Institution
____

Serial No.______________

Issued at ____________ Date of Issue________________

(Name of Place)

Date of Maturity____________________, without days of grace

(If such date happens to fall on a holiday, payment shall be made on the immediate preceding working day).

For value received__________________________we hereby

(Name of the Issuing Company/Institution)

Promise to pay_______________________________or Order on the maturity,

(Name of the Investor)

as specified above, the sum of Rs.________________________________

(in words)

upon presentation and surrender of the Commercial Paper to

(Name of the Issuing and Paying Agent)

For and on behalf of____

(Name of the Issuing Company/Institution)

Authorized Signatory

All endorsements upon the Commercial Paper must be clean and distinct.

Each endorsement should be written within the space alloted.

Pay to_________________________or Order

(Name of the Transfree)

the amount within named (mentioned).

For and on behalf of

1.______________________

(Name of the Transferor)

2.______________________

3.______________________

4.______________________

5.______________________

6.______________________

7.______________________

8.______________________

9.______________________

5

MANAGEMENT OF CREDIT

[Or of Sundry Debtors or Bills Receivable or Accounts Receivable]

It is only the poor who pays cash, and that not from virtue, but because they are refused credit.
Anatole France

Creditors have better memories than debtors. **Benjamin Franklin**

If you don't have some bad loans you are not in business. **Paul Volcker**

The Learning Points

The aim of this chapter is to develop the knowledge and facilitate an understanding of:

- Mechanism of Formulating Appropriate Credit Policy—Steps and Strategies
- A General Pattern of Follow-up Measures
- Need for Streamlining Enquiry Systems
- Some Main Causes of High Sundry Debtors, viz. Internal Causes, External Causes, Dispute as the Cause, and Miscellaneous Causes
- Appreciating the Ramifications of, and need for avoiding High Sundry Debtors
- Formulation of Credit Policy by Top Management: Strict, Liberal and Moderate (or middle-of-the-road)
- Mechanism and Cost of Cash Discount
- Effective Management Control System (MCS) for Sundry Debtors
- Management practice of Sundry Debtors (Bills Receivable) in India, and Some Suggestions for Improvement

When the finished goods are sold on credit, the entire sales, both on cash and credit bases, are recorded as sales in the profit and loss account. But, while the cash sales get represented in terms of cash in hand or in bank or in some assets purchased on cash basis, etc., the credit sales are reflected in the value of Sundry Debtors (SDs), as referred to in India, also known as Trade Debtors (TDs), Accounts Receivable (ARs), Bills Receivable (BRs) on the assets side of the balance sheet. This is what happens in the books of the seller. But, in the books of the buyer, the purchases made on credit basis are accounted for as Sundry Creditors (SCs) [also known as Trade Creditors (TCs), Accounts Payable (APs) and Bills Payable (BPs)].

With a view to fully understand and appreciate the high need for effective monitoring and follow-up of sundry debtors, it may be pertinent to mention here that generally speaking, after the company's investment in plant and machinery, and stocks of inventory (mostly in that order), the sundry debtors constitute the third largest and most important item of assets of the company.

Therefore, the imperative need of effective monitoring and control of all the items of Sundry Debtors assumes a highly important and strategic position in the area of corporate financial management.

All industrialists and business persons, if left to themselves, prefer to sell their entire goods on cash down basis. This way, the risk of bad debts gets completely eliminated and so will be the loss of interest on the blocked funds. Besides, the liquidity of the company becomes also high, and so is the productivity, profitability and prosperity therewith. But then, such conditions could be insisted upon, only by the companies whose products be in the sellers' market. But, as most of the companies usually remain in the buyers' market, they have to compulsorily give some trade credits, as per the prevailing market conditions and trade practices and policies adopted by their competitors, to stay and survive in the market. Usually, trade credits are given to different parties for different periods, which generally ranges from 15 to 60 days. But, in the case of Public Sector Undertakings (PSUs), and government departments, the period may vary from 3 to 6 months, or even more.

5.1 CREDIT POLICY

While formulating credit policies, we should vary the quantum and period of credit, party-wise. For this purpose, we may broadly classify our parties (customers, clientale) under four different categories, on the basis of their integrity and ability, to pay in full and in due time. Accordingly, these may be classified as under:

Category	*Degree of Risks*
A	No risk
B	Little risk
C	Some risk
D	High risk

But, such an exercise should not be taken as just a one time exercise. Such classifications must, instead, be reviewed periodically, and revised upward or downward, as the case may be. That is, if the performance of a particular party in category A seems to be declining, in terms of promptness in payment, it could well be brought down from Category A to say, Category B. And, similarly, based upon the past performance, as per the company's records, if some perceptible improvement is observed in some category B, or even category C parties, these could be promoted to Category A and B respectively, as the case may be.

All the sundry debtors of the company may remain under continuous observation and scrutiny, and some urgent remedial measures of applying some restrictions or liberalisation could be effected at the earliest.

A **live example** may bring home the point more clearly. While I was directing a Management Development Programme (MDP) on Finance for Non-Finance Executives (FNFE) at the Administrative Staff College of India (ASCI), Hyderabad, one of the participants, Managing Director of a company, confided with me that a substantial sum of Rs. 20 million of his company had been blocked and became long overdue in the account of a single sundry debtor. He sought my sound and sincere advice in the matter. I remember to have suggested to him that so long as one of your hands is lying under a heavy stone, you must keep the stone held up with your other hand and you should not release the hold unless you have been able to take out your hand completely out of the danger of being crushed under it. Under the present circumstances, you cannot afford to take the stand of stopping any further credit supplies to the party, and press him for cash down payment henceforth. Because, in that event, he may stop all the dealings with you and may not pay back a single rupee out of the long standing overdues to the extent of Rs. 20 million. If you have some thousand rupees blocked with just one of your sundry debtors, you may control him, but then, if you have a few million rupees outstanding with one single company, it controls you, instead. Such a stand could and should have, in fact, been taken much earlier, when just a couple of defaults (in payment) were committed by the party. But, as of now, you stand to lose everything by taking such a position, now that it had already become too late. You may have to, instead, settle down by continuing to allow the credit facility and, at the same time, requesting the party concerned to pay at least 5 to 10% of the long outstanding dues, too, along with the payments of the current credit sales, in due time.

But, by learning a couple of lessons from such practical cases, we must always monitor our sundry debtors on an effective and continuous basis. It is only in this way that we may be able to keep the bad debts at the minimal level.

We would now discuss, in detail, about the various ways and means, steps and strategies, that can be adopted to achieve the desired goal of keeping the sundry debtors at the minimal level.

5.2 STEPS AND STRATEGIES

Step 1

Prompt despatch of goods and invoice: The very first step towards effective supervision and follow-up of sundry debtors is that the goods along with invoice should be despatched promptly. Because, the 15th day or 60th day, whatever, can be counted only after the goods and invoice have been despatched. Thus, a small delay even of a day or two can further delay the payment of the sundry debtors by many more days.

Step 2

Correct and unambiguous invoicing: It is of crucial importance that the order number, particulars (quality and quantity) of goods, and such other details are incorporated in the invoice correctly, so as to facilitate the buyer company to connect the matter appropriately. Any error in these particulars, howsoever small, may result in a significant financial loss, sometime, due to avoidable correspondence and resultant delay in payment.

Step 3

Avoid disputes: We should take extra care and due precaution at all times, and despatch the goods of the agreed quality only (not even a shade less or more), so as to avoid all the possible disputes.

Example

I am saying, based upon my experience in SONY STEELS COMPANY LTD. (name changed), which took place some two decades ago. The company accumulated a hefty amount (over a period of time), by way of long overdue sundry debtors, mostly due to one single reason, *i.e.* dispute about the despatch of a lower quality of goods than agreed upon, while charging for the higher quality. And, the position had become so serious that once the company had to sell all its scraps even to meet the financial requirements of paying the monthly salary and wages to its staff and officers. The company had, by then, realised its mistake when it was too late, and deputed some young university students during their summer vacation to contact such parties, who had some dispute or the other as the cause for non-payment of the dues, so as to settle the disputes on the spot. To facilitate and hasten the process, the company had also instructed those young boys and girls (of course, in confidence) to settle the dispute on the spot, if the amount was somewhere within up to 20% of the invoice value. And, if it was settled for any lesser discount, it was a bonus. They were, however, required to make a reference to the corporate office of the company, only in such cases where the sundry debtor was found insisting for more than 20% discount, so as to get a prior approval in the matter. This way, the company could realise a very large portion of its long outstanding sundry debtors, which went a long way in tiding over its financial difficulties. Such sane and sound step, also had yet another vital beneficial result, in that the high risk of huge losses by way of bad debts could as well be avoided. We should remember 'longer the period of overdue sundry debtors, higher is the risk of bad debts, too'.

Step 4

Standard (printed) invoice proforma with a tear-off portion: With a view to ensure that all the relevant particulars have been incorporated in the invoice (of course, meticulously and correctly), it would augur well if the company takes care to evolve an all-comprehensive proforma of its invoices, so that no relevant particulars may be lost sight of. Besides, with a view to ensure that the invoice, along with the relative bill of exchange and such other documents have been duly received by the party, an acknowledgement slip could also be provided as a tear off portion of the relative forwarding letter itself, wherein all the relevant particulars, details of the various documents, etc., as also the full and correct postal address of the seller company are computer-printed at the appropriate place. This way, the buyer company, at the receiving end, would have to just put its rubber stamp (not even signature) on the acknowledgement slip, and to slip the (acknowledgement) slip in the window envelope and post it. A specimen proforma of the suggested forwarding letter along with the tear off portion containing the acknowledgement slip is placed at Appendix 5.1 at the end of this chapter.

I am suggesting such steps, based on my personal experience, where the efforts of typing an acknowledgement letter are involved, mostly the buyer companies are found to be adopting the easiest course of action. That is, they just do not send any acknowledgement, whatsoever.

Step 5

Entries in the (i) Master Register (all comprehensive), and (ii) Ledger Accounts (party-wise): With a view to exercising effective control on all the sales, on a day-to-day basis, companies may maintain a Master Register, wherein all the particulars of the sales effected on a particular day should be entered, in serial order.

To facilitate calculation of the due dates of payment, separate sections in the register, or separate files in the computer, should be maintained for parties enjoying the credit for different periods, viz. 15 days, 30 days, 45 days, 60 days, 75 days, 90 days, 180 days, and so on. A specimen proforma each of the suggested 'Master Register' and the 'Ledger Accounts' (party-wise) is placed at Appendix 5.2 and Appendix 5.3 at the end of the chapter.

It will be still better, if separate sub-sections are also maintained for parties falling under different categories like A, B and C, presuming that the parties falling under category 'D' they being high risk parties will not be given any credit, whatsoever. This may facilitate the company's effective follow-up programme in a scientific and systematic manner, on the basis of the ABC analysis, whereby the quantum of pressure and frequency and rigour of monitoring could be gradually increased in the case of B (as compared to A) and C (as compared to B) categories of sundry debtors.

In case of category A, too much of close follow-up may not be required until their payment pattern calls for their degradation from category A to category B, and so on. Similarly, the parties under category B may require somewhat closer follow-up, while those under category C may require a still closer and more frequent follow-up measures as also a constant watch and vigil over the payment pattern, so as to decide whether some restrictions are required to be imposed on their credit terms, so that the situation may not get worsened and go out of control, beyond any remedy.

5.3 A GENERAL PATTERN OF FOLLOW-UP MEASURES

A general pattern of follow-up of sundry debtors are discussed hereafter, followed by some special strategies to be evolved for some special and specific cases, desiring special attention and specific treatment.

The idea behind having different sections or registers or different folios in computer is that the actual due date can easily be calculated from the date of sale, as the same section/file will have the same due date for the same date of sale. That is, in a section/file of 30 days credit period, the due date is 30 days after the date of sale and so on.

Step 1

By way of a general follow-up, usually a week before the due date of payment, a routine type of computer printed reminder could be sent, somewhat on the following lines:

M/S.

____

____

____

Dear Sirs,

Your Order No. ________________ dated ________________ for Rs. __________
Our Bill/Invoice No. ________________ dated ________________ for Rs. __________

This is just to bring to your kind notice that the Bill/Invoice, as per the details given above, is due for payment a week after the date of the letter, and we hope that by the time the letter reaches you, you might have already paid the bill. If so please ignore this letter. But, in case, due to some other pressing preoccupations, it has escaped your notice, may we request you to please do so now.

Thanking you,

Yours faithfully,
*
(Authorised Officer)

---

* Computer Print-out; requiring no signature.

Step 2

Further, if the bill does not appear to have been paid even after a week or a fortnight of the stipulated due date, a second reminder may be sent with a slightly firm language used, and a copy thereof may be endorsed to the Sales Officer/Sales Representative for necessary follow-up action.

Step 3

If, this reminder does not evoke the desired results, a third strict reminder may have to be sent, with a copy thereof endorsed to the Sales Officer/Sales Manager concerned, to personally follow-up the matter with the party(ies) concerned, during their immediately next visit to the area, so as to obtain the payment, at the earliest. And, in the mean time, the goods despatch section may be instructed to suspend the supply of goods to such party(ies), till further instructions, so as to avoid the situation of accumulation of some huge over-due amounts (as had happened in the case of a company, as aforesaid).

A proforma each, of such letters, is given at Appendix 5.4 and Appendix 5.5, at the end of the chapter. These are, however, intended to be only illustrative, and may have to be suitably modified in the case of each company to meet its specific requirements.

Step 4

And, even if such strict and firm dealings do not activate the parties, legal notice may have to be served on some of them, just as test case, so that they (and even other buyers) may not get an impression that they may go scot free so easily.

Step 5

Similarly, in some cases, just by way of setting an example, and creating some sense of fear, even civil suits may be filed, though not with the intention of bringing it to its logical conclusion, but only as a demonstration of your strong will that you mean business.

Here, I may like to share a practical case which has some great learning value.

Example

In one of the Management Development Programmes (MDPs) on "Working Capital Management and Control" at ASCI, Hyderabad, while I was discussing the aforesaid strategies and steps for an effective follow-up of sundry debtors, one of the participants raised his point of dissent and argued that such strategies could not work in his specific case. Explaining further, he stated that he was from a very large company (name withheld for obvious reasons) looking after the marketing of some turn-key projects in the middle east worth Rs. 1000 million to Rs. 5000 million or even more.

And, he rightly pointed out that such routine reminders may offend his valued clientele. And, I readily agreed with him, and, instead, suggested to him one of the pragmatic strategies, that had occurred to me instantaneously, which goes as follows:

"When a Sheikh from the Middle East, the key person buying the turn-key project from your company, happens to visit India, on some official tour, arrange to publish a full page advertisement in national dailies of repute like the *Economic Times*, *Financial Express*, *Times of India*, *Hindustan Times*, *The Hindu*, *Statesman*, etc., extending a very warm welcome to him. And, on his arrival, throw a very grand get-together and dinner party, exclusively in his honour. And, in a lighter vein, I added that when he may be feeling a little 'high', just whisper into his ears to release at least Rs. 1000 million, as a part payment of the bill, to tide over your financial difficulties. And, in all probability, he may call his aide and give the necessary instructions to him to issue a cheque for the required amount. And, your job gets done, so easily and well".

And, the whole class had a hearty laugh, and, in the whole process some valuable learning had taken place for all the participants and for me too. That is, "Don't treat all persons on the same level, but only equals equally". Here also we must apply the underlying idea behind the ABC analysis, so as to treat the different 'classes' of clients differently, even in the case of follow-up reminders for realisation of the sundry debtors.

As has already been stated, along with the Master Register, the companies must also maintain a separate ledger account for each party giving the date of sale, particulars of sale, date of payment or return of the bills, etc. This way, you will be able to form an opinion regarding each party which may, in turn, facilitate the review and revision of the categorisation of each party periodically, to adopt specific strategies for the continuation of the terms of the credit sales or otherwise, depending upon the review data, as is evident by the ledger account of the party concerned.

A pro forma each of the 'Master Register' and the 'Ledger Accounts' is given at the end of the chapter as Appendices 5.2 and 5.3. These, however, are only illustrative and subject to changes and modifications, to meet the specific requirements of different companies.

5.4 STREAMLINED ENQUIRY SYSTEMS

Due care must be taken by the companies to identify one specific official to attend to all the enquiries pertaining to sundry debtors, and all the other officials of the company must know it. This can include the telephone operator even. Thus, any call coming for such enquiries may invariably be put through to the right person, and even if, by chance, it gets connected to some wrong number, the person concerned would be able to transfer the call to the right person. Now, in almost all the companies, the relevant particulars will be made available to the person just with the press of a button on the computer, for clarification of any doubt or for replying to any query pertaining to bills, etc., with great ease.

Further, the official concerned would do well if he could note down all the queries made by various sundry debtors so that when all these are listed category-wise, the study and analysis may throw-up some light on how to streamline the pro forma invoice or such other systems, so that much of the queries could be eliminated.

Incidentally, it may be mentioned here that such enlisting of various complaints received on different counts, may also be used to enable us to take some suitable remedial measures pertaining to after-sales service, quality control, delayed despatch, etc. We should, therefore, treat all the complaints as a free and franks feedback, an opportunity to introspect and improve upon.

Besides, this will also enable the official of the company to raise some of his own queries or else to seek some clarification or even to remind about some long overdue payments, etc. But, care must be taken that you raise your query only after all the queries of the caller have been answered to his entire satisfaction.

5.5 FINDING FACTS ON TELEPHONE

And, one more piece of friendly advice; 'Phone yourself to find yourself'.

As the top executive of the company with a view to verify yourself, as you may contact the enquiry officer on telephone without divulging your identity to the officer concerned by changing your voice a little or by muffling it by putting some cloth or your hanky on the mouthpiece, and raise some queries, feigning yourself to be one of the company's sundry debtors. This way, you may get a first-hand information whether the system is fine enough or something is required to be done to set it right. And, please do take care, that no one should come to know of your 'strategy', otherwise it may not work with full force and efficiency, next time. Therefore, even if you have to make some suggestions for improvement, you must try to find out the deficiency, if any, by raising some questions yourself that your aforesaid strategy may remain a closely guarded secret for ever.

I say so because, in some of the companies in India, I have seen that the CEO or one of the top executives visits the site of a branch of the company, feigning himself to be a common customer and immediately on finding some people doing something wrong, he will catch him and fix him, after disclosing his identity. True, the job is done, but once only, because, other offices/branches of the company may get alerted on hearing of such incidents.

5.6 SOME MAIN CAUSES OF HIGH SUNDRY DEBTORS

During the course of my empirical study of some sick industrial units, I found that a large number of sundry debtors, with huge amounts of overdues, was one of the main causes of their sickness, I could, thereby, identify some main causes of high sundry debtors, which are given below:

(A) Internal Causes (IC)

IC-1 Ambiguous/Incorrect invoicing regarding quantity, price, etc.

IC-2 Delay in the despatch of documents/goods.

IC-3 Lack of effective monitoring of Sundry Debtors like, age-wise/party-wise analysis and vigorous follow-up, etc.

IC-4 Lacunae in the monitoring mechanism/credit policy, regarding credit period/cash discount, etc.

IC-5 Goods despatched with insufficient documents, *e.g.* valid purchase order, etc.

IC-6 Defective supplies, *e.g.* sub-standard quality/quantity, insufficient after-sales services, etc.

IC-7 Relevant documents and/or information not readily available for vigorous follow-up.

IC-8 Ambiguity/deficiency in the terms and conditions, fixation/re-fixation of prices, and such unresolved issues, causing further delays.

IC-9 Overbilling regarding excise duty/sales tax etc., due to changes in laws, non-compliance of the terms and conditions of the purchase order, especially regarding excise duty/sales tax, etc.

IC-10 Holding back of 5 to 10 per cent of the amount of the bill, pending installation and commissioning, completion of the project, expiry of the warranty period and such other mutually agreed terms and conditions.

IC-11 Any other internal cause(s); (please specify).

(B) External Causes (EC)

EC-1 Damage/loss during transit

EC-2 Lack of co-ordination in the buyers' organisations

EC-3 Lack of liquidity with the buyers

EC-4 Buyer's insolvency/liquidation

EC-5 Buyers' reluctance to take delivery of the documents from the bank

EC-6 Instalments due but not collected by the collecting agent

EC-7 Instalments collected but not remitted by the collecting agent for credit of the company's account

EC-8 Any other external cause(s) (please specify).

(C) Dispute Being the Cause (DC)

DC-1 Buyers' unreasonable rejections on untenable grounds of deficiency in the quality/quantity of goods supplied

DC-2 Buyers unduly delaying the inspection of finished goods, before despatch

DC-3 Charges like freight, insurance, postage, demmurages, bank charges, etc., disallowed/ deducted by the buyers, and are being contested by us.

DC-4 Litigation

DC-5 Any other cause(s) for dispute (please specify).

(D) Miscellaneous Causes (MC): (please specify)

MC-1

MC-2

MC-3

(E) General Comments, If any

As you may observe from the above list, I have tried to divide the main causes of high sundry debtors into four categories, viz.,

(*i*) Internal causes (IC 1 to 11) where the reasons could be the negligence or slackness on the part of some in-house staff.

(*ii*) External causes (EC 1 to 8) where the reasons lie somewhere outside the control of the company and its staff.

(*iii*) Dispute being the cause (DC 1 to 5) where the dispute regarding quality and/or quantity or such other factors may be the main causes.

(*iv*) Miscellaneous causes (MC 1 to 3) where the causes are such which do not fall under any of the aforesaid three categories.

The added advantage of the listing of the causes, with code numbers given in the parentheses, would be to facilitate all the different departments to submit the periodical performance reports in regard to the sundry debtors, with the specific reasons, quoted at the appropriate places, by way of the code numbers only, like IC-3, EC-5, DC-2 etc. or MC-1 (to be specified).

Besides, such a list may force the concerned departmental heads to identify the specific reasons to be quoted in their periodical reports, instead of the usual practice of giving some causes or the other, mostly in general terms, which does not convey much sense. But, this practice may facilitate the analysis of the various causes of high sundry debtors, which, in turn, may go a long way in evolving some appropriate remedial measures, promptly and well in time.

5.7 RAMIFICATIONS OF HIGH SUNDRY DEBTORS

With a view to understand and fully realise the implications and ramifications of an effective monitoring and follow-up of sundry debtors, which, in turn, is expected to result in early realisation of the sundry debtors, let us take an illustrative example.

Example

The annual credit sales of Gama Garments (P) Ltd. is Rs. 360 million and the average outstanding of sundry debtors, as of now, is to the extent of 60 days' credit sales (taking only 360 days to a year). Thus, in terms of amount, the average sundry debtors outstanding comes to 360 × 60/360 = Rs. 60 million.

But, supposing the company streamlines and strengthens its credit realisation efforts and the average sundry debtors outstandings come down, say by 10 days, *i.e.* to 50 days, and in terms of money, they are 360 × 50/360 *i.e.* 150 million. Thus, on an average, the outstanding of Rs. 10 million more (Rs. 60 million – Rs. 50 million) gets released earlier, which, in turn, means a net saving of Rs. 1.5 million, just by way of interest @ say, 15% (Rs. 10 million × 0.15). [Note: Rs. 1 million = Rs. 10 lakh].

It means a net saving of Rs. 1,25,000 per month and a net saving of Rs. 4,167 (approximately) per day, taking 30 days to a month, which, of course, is quite a substantial amount. And, if the company's scale of operations is still higher, and its annual sales are around ten times higher or even 100 times higher, the daily savings in terms of money, would have been as much greater, *i.e.* Rs. 41,667 (approx.) and Rs. 4,16,667 (approx.), respectively, per day. Further, by virtue of effective and speeded up collection mechanism, the quantum of bad debts would also be expected to come down substantially, resulting in further boosting up of the company's profitability, and the prospects that go therewith. Besides, it also means that the liquidity position of the company would become as much stronger. And, the resultant financial gains may go still further if we take into account the element of opportunity cost and benefit connected therewith.

To sum up, we find that the imperative need and utmost desirability of effective monitoring and follow-up of sundry debtors can hardly be over-emphasised, inasmuch as it results in a number of advantages and financial gains that go therewith. **For example:**

(*i*) As timely and early payment is assured, the estimates of cash budgeting may be as much easier and more realistic and accurate.

(*ii*) The liquidity position of the company would be as much higher and its credibility and credit-worthiness therewith.

(*iii*) The substantial amount of interest saved (and its opportunity cost avoided) will go a long way to enhance the gross income as also the net profitability of the company, and thereby the company's and the shareholder's wealth.

(*iv*) And finally, the risk of bad debts and its erosion of the profitability, due to the writing off of a high quantum of bad debts, may also go down in a similar, though not necessarily in equal, proportions.

(*v*) Thus, by way of the total cascading effect of all these strategic actions, the financial gains and the market image of the company, the market price of its shares in the stock exchanges and its overall ratings and reputation, prospects and prosperity will get enhanced inasmuch as all these go together.

5.8 FORMULATION OF CREDIT POLICY

Credit policies need to be necessarily formulated by the top management, of course, in consultation with the lower levels of management, as they are expected to have the real feel and first hand experience and information about the market trends as also about the traders and the competitors.

The credit policy can broadly be classified under three categories:

(*i*) Strict,

(*ii*) Liberal, and

(*iii*) Moderate (or middle-of-the-road).

And, each of these can further be bifurcated

(*i*) In terms of number of days of credit given, *i.e.* credit period, viz. 15 days, 30 days, 45 days, 60 days, etc., and

(*ii*) In terms of quality and category of the sundry debtors that are offered credit, that is, to the category A & B only, or to A, B and C also, or even A, B, C and a portion of D, too.

If the credit period is extended from 30 days to 45 days or 60 days, it would mean the liberalisation of the credit policy. As against this, the strict credit policy would mean just the opposite, *i.e.* reduction in the number of days.

Similarly, the inclusion of a portion of category 'C' parties in the earlier list of sundry debtors, comprising only A and B categories of sundry debtors, and so on, would mean liberalisation of the credit policy. And, the review and revision of the credit policy in the reverse order (that is, exclusion of the entire category C parties from the current list of A, B and C categories), would mean a strict credit policy.

However, there may not be any dispute on the point that, with a view to take some 'Fair Business Risks', following the 'middle-of-the-road' policy, or the 'moderate credit policy', will augur well, inasmuch as this will be neither too liberal, resulting in higher sales but higher quantum of bad debts, too nor too strict to lower down the sales and the profitability therewith. Thus, the 'middle-of-the-road policy' or the 'golden mean' may be the optimal level where the additional sales and profitability may be higher than the percentage of extra risks of bad debt losses, connected with the liberalisation of the credit policy. To arrive at such a decision, on some systematic and scientific basis, some mathematical calculations and study may be of great help. This, however, we propose to discuss a little later in this chapter.

5.9 CASH DISCOUNT

Cash discount is a very common mechanism of effecting and encouraging speedy payments but, of course, at a price. Therefore, before taking a decision about the period and quantum of giving cash discount, we must first try to understand and appreciate the financial implications of such a stand taken, mainly in terms of the quantum of interest gained or lost.

This can be best understood by taking some **illustrative examples.**

(a) 1/10, net 30

This expression means that 1% cash discount is given if payment is made within 10 days (say, of the date of the bill), otherwise the full amount of the invoice/bill is payable, if the payment is made within 30 days. Now, let us compute the gain or loss in terms of the quantum of interest involved in the instant case.

As a cash discount of 1% is available if the bill is paid within 10 days, a prudent buyer prefers to pay on the last possible day, *i.e.* on the 10th day only, to avail of the maximum benefit of the offer. Now that he pays on the 10th day, instead of on the 30th day means that the seller loses 1% by way of interest on the full amount in only 20 days. Thus, the annual loss to the seller would come to $(0.01 \times 360) \div 20 = 0.18$ or 18% p.a. taking 360 days in a year. And, accordingly, the gain to the buyer, by virtue of making an early payment, comes slightly more, as he has to pay only Rs. 99, as against the invoice value of Rs. 100. That is, the seller stands to gain net Re. 1 on payment of only Rs. 99. Thus, his percentage gain on Rs. 99, on an annual basis, would come to a still higher level, *i.e.* $(0.01 \times 360 \times 100) \div (20 \times 99) = [360 \div (20 \times 99)] = 18.18\%$ p.a.

Such a higher gain is available only to the buyer, as he gains 1% on payment or investment of Rs. 99 only. But, so far as the seller is concerned, he has to forego Re. 1 out of the total amount in question, *i.e.* Rs. 100, the full value of the invoice, and not on Rs. 99, as is the position in the case of the buyer.

Such subtle distinction must always be borne in mind, inasmuch as in some of the textbooks the authors have preferred to compute the same percentage of gain or loss *i.e.* @ 18% p.a. for both the buyer and the seller. But then, I have a different view, as I go by the aforesaid logic.

Now, let us solve some such problems by way of reinforcement of the concept, from the points of view of both [A] the seller and [B] the buyer, separately:

(b) Exercise

(Please take 360 days to a year)

(*a*) 2/15, net 45 (*b*) 3/20, net 60 (*c*) 1/9, net 45 (*d*) 2/30, net 75

Suggested Solutions

(A) From the point of view of the Seller:

(*a*) (0.02 × 360)/(45 – 15) = 0.24 or 24% p.a.

(*b*) (0.03 × 360)/(60 – 20) = 0.27 or 27% p.a.

(*c*) (0.01 × 360)/(45 – 9) = 0.10 or 10% p.a.

(*d*) (0.02 × 360)/(75 – 30) = 0.16 or 16% p.a.

(B) From the point of view of the Buyer:

(*a*) (0.02 × 360 × 100) ÷ [(45 – 15) (100 – 2)] = 0.2449 or 24.49% p.a.

(*b*) (0.03 × 360 × 100) ÷ [(60 – 20) (100 – 3)] = 0.2784 or 27.84 % p.a.

(*c*) (0.01 × 360 × 100) ÷ [(45 – 9) (100 – 1)] = 0.1010 or 10.10% p.a.

(*d*) (0.02 × 360 × 100) ÷ [(75 – 30) (100 – 2)] = 0.1633 or 16.33% p.a.

5.10 MANAGEMENT CONTROL SYSTEM (MCS) AND SUNDRY DEBTORS

As per the Companies Act, 1956, all companies are required to show Sundry Debtors into two categories, viz.

(*i*) Bills outstanding up to 6 months, and

(*ii*) Bills outstanding for over 6 months (which at times, can be even for one year, two years, or even more).

These are all the legal and statutory requirements. But, an enlightened management must be concerned about the financial health of its company on a continuous basis. To this end, the age analysis of the sundry debtors must be done on a regular basis so as to study the number and the aggregate value of the bills, outstanding for various ranges of period, viz. (*i*) 15-30 days, (*ii*) 30–45 days, (*iii*) 45–60 days, (*iv*) 60–75 days, (*v*) 75–90 days, (*vi*) 90–180 days, (*vii*) over 180 day, (*viii*) over 1 year, (*ix*) over 2 years and (*x*) over 3 years, etc. Such an analysis should be done, not only in terms of number of bills and the value thereof (in terms of rupees), but percentage-wise also, indicating the percentage of the total number of bills and that of the total amount involved in the bills, outstanding for different periods of time.

An illustrative example, given in the following page (at Table 5.1) may clearly indicate that, while the perusal of only column (*f*), showing the total amount, does not seem to signify much, instantaneously, just a glance at column (*g*), showing the percentages, gives a complete and easily comprehensible position of the outstanding sundry debtors (period-wise) [as also party-wise, as has been shown in Table 5.1].

The illustrative example, thus, very pointedly indicates that the analysis, in percentage terms, makes a better sense to understand the extent of the problem as also to indicate suitable remedial measures, inasmuch as the amount mentioned in much larger figures may seem rather difficult to comprehend and appreciate instantaneously.

Such an analysis should be done, not only percentage-wise but also party-wise. That is, for different segments of buyers (sundry debtors) separately. Because, as we have generally observed, the undernoted groups of buyers have, by and large, a very different payment-period pattern, in relation to each other. But, on the whole, the payment patterns of almost all the buyers, in each of these four separate segments, are almost uniform.

Such indicative figures are given hereunder:

Four Segments of the Buyers	***The usual Payment Pattern (No. of Days)***
(*i*) Government Departments	120–180 days
(*ii*) Public Sector Undertakings	60–90 days
(*iii*) Private Sector Companies	30–45 days
(*iv*) Others	up to 30 days

The various points, discussed above, can better be understood and appreciated through Table 5.1 given hereunder:

Table 5.1: Classification of the Sundry Debtors, Period-wise, Percentage-wise and Party-wise

(Rs. in Million)

Period (*a*)	*Govt. Dept.* (*b*)	*Public Sector* (*c*)	*Private Sector* (*d*)	*Others* (*e*)	*Total (Rs.)* (*f*)	*Percentage (%)* (*g*)
Up to 30 days	5	7	56	123	191	16
30 – 45 days	10	12	103	57	182	15
45 – 60 days	15	69	61	14	159	13
60 – 75 days	20	10	23	5	58	5
75 – 120 days	124	15	4	–	143	12
120 – 150 days	55	17	–	–	72	6
150 – 180 days	206	4	–	–	210	18
Over 180 days	175	6	3	1	185	15
Total	**610** **51%**	**140** **12%**	**250** **21%**	**200** **16%**	**1200** **100%**	**100**

It may augur well if an incisive analysis and study is done by further subdividing the parties (sundry debtors) under each category into yet another set of groups on the basis of:

A. The extent of the credit risks [(A, B, C and D) or (nil, little, some or high risks), respectively], involved in the case of each party in each segment, separately, and

B. Under groups 1, 2 and 3, based on the different ranges of period of credit allowed to them.

A still further break-up of the bills, outstanding for different periods, like 181 days to 1 year, 1–2 years, 2–3years, etc., may also give some valuable insight into the present status, enabling us to formulate and implement some suitable strategies to realise such overdues swiftly and surely.

Now, when we look at the total value of the bills outstanding under the four different categories, viz. Rs. 610, Rs. 140, Rs. 250 and Rs. 200 (million), out of the total bills outstanding for Rs. 1200 (million), we are not able to derive much of a sense from these figures, just at a glance. But, the moment we look at the percentage figures, we are able to clearly see, and that, too, so easily and soon enough, that a little more than half of the total amount of the bills outstanding pertain to the government departments followed by the private sector, and not public sector, as was usually expected, *i.e.* at 21% or around 1/5th of the total outstandings in the sundry debtors. Then comes the number of others and the public sector, in that order, at around almost the same level at 16% and 12% respectively. Similarly, we may further classify all the outstanding bills into A, B and C categories, facilitated by the application of the ABC analysis, for deciding upon the strategies and pressure to be applied by close follow-up, too, and in that order.

Similar is the case when we look at the absolute total amount, pertaining to various blocks of period, viz. 15 to 30 days to over 180 days, etc., in the instant case. A very clear picture does not emerge. But, the moment we convert these figures into percentage terms, we just jump at the clear conclusion in that here again the overall trend can be easily divided into three main segments (percentage-wise) viz. the blocks of period with outstandings ranging from (*a*) 15% to 18%; and (*b*) 12% to 13% and the balance (*c*) 5% to 6%. And thus, these percentages get easily categorised into A, B and C classes, making the application of the principle of ABC analysis so easy and facile.

The percentage figures also reveal an alarming position, in that the outstandings under the longest period block constitute the highest percentage of total outstandings at 18% and 15%. Further, these figures also suggest that, as the outstandings of over 180 days are as high as 15% of the total outstandings, these figures require to be further classified into 180 days to 1 year, 1–2 years, 2–3 years, and over 3 years, etc., with a view to assess the status, and adopt suitable strategies, and swift action accordingly.

But now, when we analyse and study these percentages, not in totality, but under the different segments (party-wise) we find that the maximum portion, *i.e.* more than half of the total outstandings pertain to government department, which fact, of course, is usual and expected, and thus not at all alarming. Besides, as most of the outstandings of the longest period also pertain to the government department segment, the position does not seem to be as alarming and panicky as we had concluded only a little while ago, in the earlier paragraph itself. This is so because, the usual pattern of payments, made by the government department segment is around 180 days and even more. And, therefore, except for the outstandings of over 180 days, accounting for 15% of the total outstandings, no other outstanding need much of a special attention. But then, it cannot be left unattended, either. This figure requires further classifications under the periods of 181 days to 1 year, 1–2 years, and 2–3 years, and over 3 years, as aforesaid, and suitable strategies have be evolved, followed by specific and swift action.

Thus, we are able to fully comprehend and appreciate the worth and value of the simple, but significant statement that the classification of the sundry debtors should not be done only period-wise, and in absolute terms alone, but party-wise and percentage-wise too, which proves to be a very prudent and pragmatic step to assess the position accurately, and to act swiftly, with a view to achieve the desired results of fast realisation of the outstanding bills, and keep the bad debts at the minimal level.

Day's Sales Outstanding (DSO)

There is yet another method of monitoring and follow-up of sundry debtors, commonly known as 'Day's Sales Outstanding' (DSO).

The 'day's sales outstanding' at a given time 't' may be said to be the ratio of sundry debtors outstanding at the material time to the average daily (credit) sales [not total sales] during the preceding month or two months' period or quarter, or say 30 days, 60 days and 90 days, or such other suitable period. It may be represented as under:

DSOt = Sundry Debtors at time 't'/Average daily (Credit) Sales.

Let us try to understand this method/tool better with the help of an illustrative example.

Example

Suppose the monthly credit sales of Pankaj Home Appliances, and the month-end sundry debtors outstanding for the period 1st January to 31st December, 2009, are as given in Table 5.2.

Table 5.2: Sales and Sundry Debtors (Bills Receivable) Data

Month (in the year 2009)	*Credit Sales*	*Sundry Debtors (Receivables)*	*Month (in the year 2009)*	*Credit Sales*	*Sundry Debtors (Receivables)*
January	200	450	July	250	407
February	210	420	August	255	415
March	215	380	September	270	425
April	206	365	October	285	444
May	225	355	November	290	460
June	240	375	December	310	475

And, if we decide to calculate the 'Day's Sales Outstanding' (DSO) on a quarterly basis, *i.e.* at the end of each quarter, the following picture emerges:

Quarter

One $380 \div [(200 + 210 + 215) \div 91]$

$380 \div (625 \div 91) = 55.33$ days or say, 55 days

Two $375 \div [(206 + 225 + 240) \div 91]$

$375 \div (671 \div 91) = 50.88$ days or say, 51 days

Three $425 \div [(250 + 255 + 270) \div 92]$

$425 \div (775 \div 92) = 50.48$ days or say, 50 days

Four $475 \div [(285 + 290 + 310) \div 92]$

$475 \div (885 \div 92) = 49.38$ days or say, 49 days

The nominators represent the sundry debtors outstanding at the end of each quarter and the denominators represent the sum total of the credit sales of the respective three months.

Here, we should remember that the resultant ratios do not mean anything in isolation. To see whether the level of sundry debtors is under control or not, we should first decide upon a standard or the norm whereby we may infer the position to be under control, if the resultant figure is less than or at least equal to the norm. And, if it happens to be above the set norm, the position may be inferred to have worsened. Therefore, the efforts of collection may have to be tightened and geared up to control the situation from going from bad to worse.

Thus, in the above case, if we set the norm (of course, based upon the market trend, pertaining to the specific industry at the material time), at say, 55 days, the aforesaid figures would indicate that the position is well within control, inasmuch as while the average collection period is well within the norm *i.e.* 55 days, it, gradually comes down from 55 days in the first quarter to 49 days in the last quarter. But then, a prudent management should not feel complacent at this. A better business sense should always urge you to improve the position further because "there is no room on earth bigger than the room for improvement".

5.11 DECISION-MAKING

Sundry debtors management requires a lot of decision-making exercises, in several areas, by the personnel at different levels: top level, middle level and junior level.

5.11.1 Credit Policy

Formulation of credit policy comes within the purview of the top management. It comprises various aspects of credit policy, which are discussed hereafter, one by one.

Assessment of Credit-Worthiness of the Sundry Debtors

This decision is the most crucial one to make, as it is the starting point of the whole chain of events, right from the point of sales on credit to the point of final realisation of the proceeds of the credit sales.

Here also the main problem area is to take a decision while selecting a new party for dealings for the first time. This may involve various facets of enquiries and studies, with a view to assessing and evaluating the credit-worthiness and financial stability and strength of each company under consideration. While assessing the extent and quantum of credit risks involved, which differ from case to case, one must guard against some usual types of errors of judgement that may take place sometimes.

They are:

(*i*) Either 'A' category of customers may be classified as category B or even C.

(*ii*) Or vice versa, *i.e.* a category B (or even category C) customer may be erroneously classified in A category.

And, both these errors may prove a little costly in that either a good business may be lost (and the financial gains therewith), or the company may accumulate some more bad debts, eroding its profitability.

Such errors may take place but only in some cases, and not in general, provided due care is taken at the time of the evaluation of the credit-worthiness of the parties. In such cases, the periodical review of the payment pattern of the respective parties may be helpful in reclassification of some parties, thereby rectifying the error, if any, hopefully well in time.

Compilation of Opinion Report on Financial Status of the Company

A. Annual Reports

As a first step, we may like to have a look at the Annual Reports of the company for the last 2–3 years, and analyse and interpret the relevant ratios, based on the Balance Sheet and the Profit & Loss Account of the company. Care should, however, be taken to read the foot-notes, auditors' report, directors' report, etc., as also to call for some required break-ups to be able to ascertain the financial health and stability of the company on a near accurate basis.

Some of the ratios that may be found to be of some special value in this regard may be the current ratio, quick ratio (or acid-test ratio), return on net worth, debt equity ratio, EBIT to total assets ratio, sundry debtors and sundry creditors' position (in number of days, of annual sales and credit purchases respectively), etc.

B. Trade and Local Enquiries

Trade enquiries and sharing of the experiences with the existing parties, who have been selling their goods to the party under enquiry, on credit basis, may be helpful in forming some realistic impressions about the possibility of the party being somewhat reasonably safe or otherwise. Such enquiries may, however, be available to you, only after you have been able to take the relative existing parties in full confidence, before they may venture to share their free and frank opinion about the credit-worthiness, etc., of the party under enquiry.

C. Bank Enquiries

Confidential enquiries from the party's bankers may also yield some valuable database and vital information to form a realistic valid impression and opinion about the company. But, if you just write a letter to the bank requesting for a credit report on the party concerned, the bank may, at its sole discretion, decide to send a report and oblige you. But then, the banker's written report may not provide much of the desired clue, or even a small clue, because it may use certain set terminologies, which may have different bases and connotations, varying from bank to bank.

Besides, they also use extremely safe and cautious language, saying somewhat like: "the information is of a very secret and confidential nature, and is, therefore, being given in strict confidence, and at the same time, without any obligation on the part of its validity, etc." And, in the end it will state that in their considered opinion, the company seems to be enjoying 'satisfactory', 'fair', or 'good' credit rating in the market, which may actually mean Rs. 1 million, Rs. 5 million and Rs. 50 million, respectively, in one bank and Rs. 5 million, Rs. 10 million, and Rs. 100 million, etc., respectively, in the other.

Therefore, the best way, in my considered view, based on my personal experience, with the State Bank of India, would be to personally meet the Manager of the branch of the bank concerned, build up some rapport with him or her, and gradually take the person in confidence. And, only then, and that too, with mutual trust and in good faith, ask for the free and frank opinion and advice of the banker, of course, without any commitment, whatsoever, as also with a sincere undertaking not to be quoted or shared elsewhere. This may prove to be a very fruitful and beneficial exercise. And remember, if any information is shared by the banker, after having built such a trust and faith, we must take care to prove ourselves being worthy of the trust and faith reposed by the banker in us. This is of great essence and value in the business world.

Yet, another useful strategy could be to ascertain the financial strength and stability of the prospective customer from his or her banker, not directly, but through your own banker, who has met your credit needs, as he or she would also be equally interested in your safety to keep his own credit, granted to you, safeguarded.

D. Six C's

You may also do as the bankers do. That is, to test the credit-worthiness of the prospective buyers on the basis of the Six C's, dealt with hereunder:

(*i*) **Character:** This is of prime importance, inasmuch as it refers to the moral integrity, noble intentions and willingness on the part of the buyers to honour the obligation of making the full payment on the due date. Because, there may be cases where the buyer may be able to pay but may not have the good intentions to do so.

(*ii*) **Capability:** Only second in importance is the capacity or the financial capability of the customer to make payment on the due date. This may be ascertained from the profitability and prospects of the company, based mainly on the net cash position, after assessing the total inflows and outflows of cash.

(*iii*) **Capital:** This, of course, refers to the capital base and capital structure of the company, as also the strength and position of its reserves and surplus. This is to say that, even if, sometimes, due to some external unfavourable factors, beyond the control of the buyer company, it is not in a sufficiently strong financial position to make the payment, out of the current generation of surplus cash, it may afford to make the payment out of its reserves and surplus, till its present financial position improves.

(*iv*) **Collateral:** Some of the companies, depending upon their strength and stability in the market, may insist on some collateral (additional) security, by way of some security deposits or bank guarantees to guard against any default in the payment at any stage. The practice, adopted by NIRMA UDYOG LIMITED, a reputed company, manufacturing detergent powders and soaps, with the brand name 'NIRMA', is a good illustrative example. They keep on insisting that the buyer company must make a security deposit equivalent to the amount of its two months' supply to meet its requirement of the company's products, before single supply could be effected. And, the next order for the supply may be compiled with only if the previous supply has, already been paid in full. Besides, any default or even undue delay in making the payment of any bill may render the particular customer liable for cancellation of the agency arrangement for ever. Such strict stipulations can, however, be made only by the company who controls a major share of the market, whose products are very popular and in high demand, so much so that it may virtually be said to be almost in the sellers' market. But, some such precautionary measures, like putting a halt to any further supplies on credit, if the earlier supplies have already fallen overdue for payment, can well be said to be a prudent preventive measure. The case of a company having accumulated long outstanding bills to the tune of Rs. 20 million, discussed in the previous pages, is a good illustrative example.

(*v*) **Condition:** The term 'condition' here refers only to the economic conditions and climate prevailing at the material time, which may have favourable or unfavourable impact on the financial position and prospects of a particular customer, at least in the near future. That is, supposing the companies like DCL Polyester and INDO RAMA SYNTHETICS are your regular customers, you may have to think twice before deciding to continue to keep the credit supplies going on as usual, if such companies are passing through a phase of slump and sluggishness in the market. The supplies may, however, be resumed in full force only after the economic conditions for such industries change for the better.

(*vi*) **Case history [Past experience]:** If a credit decision is to be taken in the case of a customer, who has had some dealings with your company in the past, too, your own first hand experience and information may be the most handy, reliable and valuable data to determine and decide this way or that way. The detailed pattern of performance of each customer recorded in the separate ledger accounts of each customer may provide a wealth of reliable information, like timeliness or delay or default in the payments, raising of flimsy and untenable objections, showing a tendency of resorting to some legal remedies, etc., may be sufficient data to take a decision, which may not be far wrong in most of the cases.

In case of a customer, with whom we are to deal for the first time, more than ordinary care and caution needs to be taken. In such cases, it may augur well if, at the very first stage, we adopt the policy of going slow and steady for quite a reasonable time, so that we may get a fair feel of the firm to decide on the quantum of credit risk involved therewith. Besides, the practical advantage of regular periodical review and revision of the categorisation of the customers under categories A, B, C and D, can hardly be over emphasised. In such cases, the first impression of our own sales personnel, based upon their personal interviews and interactions with the prospective new customer, and the market reports, obtained through personal trade enquires made from some of our reliable and regular customers, may also prove to be of immense use and great value.

E. Share Market Report

For listed companies, *i.e.* the companies whose shares are listed in some stock-exchange(s) (and are actively traded) the market data, like market price and prospects, price-earning ratios, dividend policy and pattern, may as well be a good indicator of the credit risks, if any.

5.11.2 Types of Credit Policy

Different dimensions of the credit policy may vary in different degrees and shades. It may be categorised under three broad types:

(*i*) **Liberal Credit Policy:** A credit policy may be termed as liberal wherein some other concessions and facilities are granted to the buyers, with the expectation that this way the sales may pick up, and thereby the cost of extra concessions granted can well be taken care of, by the additional yield, resulting from the extra sales generated. But then, such liberalisation may as well lead to some additional quantum of bad debts, related with the extra sales effected, as also the resultant higher blockage of funds in sundry debtors, and a higher cost of collection, too. Therefore, all such inter-related facts and factors must be duly considered while taking a decision regarding adoption and execution of a specific credit policy, most suited under the given circumstances.

(*ii*) **Strict Credit Policy:** Under such credit policy, as against the liberal one, the minimum possible concessions and relaxations are granted to the customers. And, as a result thereof, the sales may get somewhat adversely affected. But, at the same time, the risk of bad debts may as well be minimised, and so will be the extent of blockage of funds in sundry debtors and the collection efforts and expenses too. Thus, the decision should be based on the trade-off position of the positive and negative factors.

(*iii*) **Medium (Moderate) Credit Policy:** Such a credit policy adopts the middle-of-the-road approach whereby a balance is tried to be struck in such a way that both the quantum of additional sales and the resultant risk of bad debts may be kept at the optimal levels, *i.e.* neither too high nor too low; but in about just the right measure.

5.12 PARAMETERS OF CREDIT POLICY

The various dimensions on the basis of which a company may adopt a rather liberal, strict or medium (moderate) credit policy may be broadly classified under four different parameters. They are:

(*i*) Standard of credit,

(*ii*) Period of credit,

(*iii*) Cash discount, and

(*iv*) Effective monitoring and follow-up (*i.e.* collection efforts).

Let us discuss all these four different parameters of credit policy one after the other.

A. Standard of Credit

The main and most important question that may arise, while arriving at the credit policy decision, is as to what standard could be considered as the most appropriate and optimal one, with a view to accept or reject a customer for credit sales. Here, the company has a variety of choices, of offering credit sales, ranging from 'none' to 'all' and to 'some only'. The first two options, obviously, do not seem to be right, as these may either adversely affect the volume and value of the sales, or else, may run the high risk of the quantum of bad debts. Thus, both these steps are generally not advisable unless either the company enjoys the envious privilege of being in the sellers' market, or else, it is in such a desperate situation that its sales may drastically drop down unless a very liberal credit policy is adopted.

But, by and large, the 'golden mean' may be considered to be the most suitable and acceptable strategy. It, however, is generally easier said than done. But, at the same time, some action has to be taken, if one has chosen to be in the business.

The extent of the resultant gain or loss, in the event of relaxing a prevalent credit policy, could well be estimated in monetary terms on the basis of certain formula, and calculations given hereunder:

$$\Delta NP = [\Delta S (1 - V) - \Delta Sbn] - K\Delta I$$

where;

ΔNP = Change in net profit

ΔS = Increase in sales

V = Ratio of variable costs to sales

bn = Ratio of bad debt losses on new sales

K = Cost of capital

ΔI = Increase in investment (or blockage of funds) in sundry debtors.

Here, it may be mentioned that ΔI is equal to $\Delta S/360 \times ACP \times V$, where $\Delta S/360$ = Average change (increase) in sales per day (presuming 360 days to a year, to facilitate calculations, otherwise here the denominator can as well be taken as 365 instead of 360), and ACP = Average collection period.

Thus, we see that, on the right hand side of the equation, $\Delta S (1 - V)$ represents the increase in gross profit (or contribution), *i.e.* sales, less variable costs, resulting from the increase in the sales. And, ΔSbn denotes the extent of losses due to bad debts, resulting from the increased sales. Therefore $\Delta S (1 - V) \Delta Sbn]$ indicates the operating profit, resulting from the increased sales, after allowing for the quantum of the resultant bad debt losses.

The term, $K\Delta I$, however, represents the pre-tax (not post-tax) opportunity cost of capital, *i.e.* the additional funds locked up in the sundry debtors. All considered, the end result of the final calculations would represent the resultant net profit (or loss), depending upon whether the end-result is a positive or a negative figure, respectively. Thus, it would become far easier for us to take a decision whether it is gainful or otherwise to take the decision to relax the credit standard or not.

Let us try to explain and elucidate the point still further with the help of two **illustrative examples**.

Example I

The present level of the annual sales of Moon & Sun Company is Rs. 200 million. The company, as usual, has categorised its customers into four categories of credit, viz. A, B, C and D; that is, the credit rating diminishes in that order. Thus the customers in category 'A' would be enjoying the highest credit rating and those in the category 'D' would enjoy the lowest one. Further, the company, as of now, gives credit to its customers in category A and B to an unlimited extent, whereas to those in category C are given credit only to a limited extent. And, so far as the customers in category D are concerned, they, being high risks, are not extended any credit whatsoever. But, as a result of such a strict credit policy, the company is estimated to be losing its sales to the extent of Rs. 25 million to the customers in category C and Rs. 20 million to the customers in category D. The company was, therefore, considering to relax its credit standard in such a way that all the customers in category C would be extended unlimited credit and even the customers in category D would now be extended limited credit, instead of none at all, as of now. And, as a result of such a relaxation and liberalisation of the credit standard, the sales are expected to go up by Rs. 35 million and, at the same time, the resultant losses on the increased bad debts are estimated to be to the extent of 15 per cent. The contribution margin ratio (1 – V) is estimated to be 30 per cent and the average collection period (ACP) at 54 days, and the (pre-tax) cost of funds (K), is 20 per cent. The rate of income tax is 40 per cent.

Required

Should the company go ahead with the proposed relaxation? Give reasons for your specific answer.

Solution

As per the information given above, we can very well assess the effect of relaxing the credit policy, on the net profit of the company, by application of the aforesaid formula and computing the various values appropriately, and thereafter, calculating the end-result as has been worked out hereafter:

The formula reads as under:

$$\begin{aligned} \Delta NP &= [\Delta S\,(1 - V) - \Delta Sbn] - K\Delta I \\ &= [35\text{ m}\,(1 - 0.70) - 35\text{ m} \times 0.15]\ (-)\ [(0.20 \times 35/360) \times (54 \times 0.70)] \\ &= [10.5\text{ m} - 5.25\text{ m}] - [0.735\text{ m}] \\ &= 5.25\text{ m} - 0.735\text{ m} \\ &= \text{Rs. } 4.515\text{ million} \end{aligned}$$

Further, as the net result is a positive figure, it means that the end-result is profit. Therefore, the obvious decision will be to go for the proposed change.

But, one more consideration may be found to be of great relevance here.

And that is that, what would actually be the PAT (Profit After Tax) and whether the PAT is attractive and substantial enough. Thus, we find that the PAT

$$= 4.515\text{ M} \times (1 - 0.40) = \text{Rs. } 27.090\text{ million}$$

And, as the PAT is also a substantial amount, the final decision remains the same, that is the change is desirable.

Example II

Now, supposing that in Example I, the resultant losses on the increased bad debts are estimated to be 18 per cent, the contribution margin rate is estimated to be 20 per cent the pre-tax cost of fund is 24 per cent, and the other data remains unchanged, the end-result will be as under:

Solution

$$\Delta NP = [35 \text{ m } (1 - 0.80) - 35 \text{ m} \times 0.18] (-) [0.24 \times 35 \text{ m}/360 \times 54 \times 0.70]$$
$$= [7.00 - 6.30] - 0.8820$$
$$= 0.7000 - 0.8820$$
$$= (-)\ 0.1820$$

As the end result is a negative figure, it means that the proposed change leads to a net loss and hence it is not desirable to implement the proposed change.

Here, it may be reiterated that, as the end-result in itself is a net loss, the question of ascertaining the post-tax position does not arise, as no tax is payable on losses.

Some textbooks, however, calculate the position on post-tax basis, *ab initio*, in that while they deduct the income tax in the first part of the equation, *i.e.*

$$[\{\Delta S\ (1 - V) - \Delta Sbn\}\ (1 - t)],$$

they take K as the post-tax cost of the capital. But, I somehow do not agree to such a contention, inasmuch as the question of calculating the post-tax position would arise only when, at the pre-tax stage, there is some profit. And, in the case of there being some profit, we should deduct the income tax payable from the operating profit so as to decide whether the post-tax profit is good enough to take the extra risk. Further, when the lenders (banks or others) quote the rate of interest chargeable, they do not quote a post-tax rate but only the pre-tax rate. Therefore, taking the post-tax rate, as the cost of capital (K), does not seem to be proper or even plausible.

B. Period of Credit

The duration of time (say, 30 days, 45 days, 60 days, etc.) allowed to the customers, to make the payment of our bills, representing the cost of the goods, supplied on credit, is referred to as the credit period. It has generally been seen' that the credit period ranges from 15 days to 60 days or even more. And, in the case of government departments, it may be even 90 days, 180 days, or even more. The credit period, however, is based mainly on two considerations:

(*i*) the trade practices in the particular line of business, and

(*ii*) the degree of trust and credit-worthiness on the part of the customers concerned.

If a company does not extend any credit and insists only on cash payment, the credit period obviously is nil or zero. But, in case a credit period of 30 days is stipulated, it may conventionally be represented as 'net/30', if no cash discount is granted by way of an incentive to make an early payment. However, if the payment condition is stipulated as '2/10, net 30', it goes to indicate that a discount of 2 per cent is allowed on the invoice value, if the payment is made within 10 days, otherwise the full payment has to be made within 30 days, suggesting thereby that any further delay may attract payment of some extra amount by way of overdue interest, at the stipulated rate. In actual practice, however, a minor delay of 4/5 days or so is generally condoned.

It, however, is quite obvious that if the credit period is extended a little further, the chances of some incremental sales taking place is almost certain. But then, this may also entail cost of capital for that much extended period. Besides, longer the credit period, higher may be the risk of bad debts, too. This factor, however, is not being taken into account in our instant discussions hereafter.

Extension of the credit period boosts up the sales in two ways:

(*i*) the existing customers tend to purchase a little more quantity, and value, and

(*ii*) some new customers also get attracted and come within the fold of the company's clientele.

But, the flip side of such a liberalisation in the credit policy is that the company's valuable financial resources get blocked in sundry debtors by as much longer time, resulting in the corresponding loss of interest and involving some opportunity cost. As against this, resorting to a stricter credit policy naturally means shortening of the credit period, *i.e.* reducing it to 30 days from 45 days, or to 45 days from 60 days, etc., resulting in a corresponding drop in sales, in that some of the existing customers may be lost and new customers may hardly get attracted. But, at the same time, it may reduce the element of loss of interest, or opportunity cost, and the incidence of losses, on account of bad debts. Therefore, striking a golden mean may seem to be of essence in the art and skill of decision making in this area. That is, care should be taken to find out whether the incremental income is sufficient enough to take care of the loss of interest and the opportunity cost that go with such a decision, as also the element of the relative increase in the quantum and value of bad debts, though it has not formed a part of the undernoted formula, to facilitate the process of decision making in this area.

Thus, we observe that the resultant effect of such a change, *i.e.* lengthening of or shortening of the credit period, in our credit policy may seem to be somewhat similar to that of effecting some relaxation in our credit standard. We may, therefore, use the same formula here also, so as to assess the change in profit, resulting from the change in credit period, and, accordingly, take a definite and desirable decision. The formula is:

$$\Delta NP = [\Delta S (1 - V) - \Delta Sbn] - K \Delta I$$

But then, there is a catch here; a subtle difference in calculating the 'I' in the instant case, in that here 'I' will have to be calculated, instead, as under:

ΔI = $(ACP_n - ACP_o)(So)/360 + V(ACP_n)(\Delta S/360)$
(taking 360 days to a year), where:

ΔI = Increase in investment

ACP_n = New average collection period (after the credit period has been extended)

AC_{po} = Old average collection period

So = Old (Current) Sales

V = Ratio of variable costs to sales

ΔS = Increase in sales

Thus, we see that, while the first part of the above equation on the right hand side reflects the extent of the resultant increase in the blockage of funds in the sundry debtors, for a longer period, on the basis of the current sales, the second part represents the blockage of funds in sundry debtors as a result of the increased sales.

Here, it may be observed that in the first part of the equation, the sales have been computed at the selling price because of the blockage of funds including the portion of profit, for some days. But, so far as the second part is concerned, only the cost of sales, *i.e.* only the variable cost, has been taken into account. And rightly so, because, if the incremental sale, due to the change in the credit policy, turns out to be a losing proposition, the company will lose only the cost of sales, and, therefore, the element of profit should not be taken into account, for taking a decision in this regard.

Let us now try to understand the concept and application of the formula with the help of an **illustrative example**.

Example

Tirupati Equipment Ltd., as per the extant credit policy, extended 40 days of credit to its customers. Its level of sales, as of now, is Rs. 60 million, the cost of capital of the company is 15 per cent p.a., and the ratio of variable cost to sales is 80 per cent. The company is contemplating to extend the credit period from 40 days to 75 days, whereby the sales are expected to go up by Rs. 6 million. The resultant bad debt portion is also expected to be 10 per cent. The company has to pay income tax @ 35% (please take 360 days in a year).

Required

As per the information given above;

(*i*) What would be the effect of extending the credit period on the Profit Before Tax (PBT) as also on the Profit After Tax (PAT)?

(*ii*) Further, what should be your expert advice to the company in regard to the proposed change in the credit period, giving specific reasons for your considered opinion?

A Suggested Solution

By computing the relative information/data in the formula, we get the value as under:

$$(6 \times 0.20 - 6 \times 0.10) - 0.15\ [\{(75 - 40) \times 60\} + (0.80 \times 75 \times 6)/360]$$
$$= (1.20 - 0.60) - 0.15\ [(35 \times 60)/360 + (0.80 \times 75 \times 6)/360]$$
$$= 0.60 - 0.15\ [(35/6) + (360/360)]$$
$$= 0.60 - 0.15\ [5.833 + 1]$$
$$= 0.60 - 0.15\ [6.833]$$
$$= [0.60]\ (-)\ [1.02495]$$

= (–) 0.42495 m (Loss) **or 0.425 m (Loss)**

Thus, as the end-result is a loss, the change is not desirable. And, therefore, the computation of PAT position is deemed unnecessary.

C. Cash Discount

Some companies offer cash discount to their customers to give some financial incentive to their customers to pay the bills well before the usual credit period granted. Under such an arrangement, the terms of payment are such that the buyer gets a cash discount at a certain percentage (say, 2%), if he makes the payment well before the usual credit period granted (*e.g.* if he pays within 10 days, while the usual credit period granted is say, 30 days). If this is the stipulation, it is usually represented, as per the prevailing practice, as '2/10, net 30'.

It means that the buyer gets a discount of 2 per cent, if he makes the payment within 10 days from the date of the bill, or else, he will have to pay the full amount of the bill, if the payment is made after 10 days but within 30 days.

We must, therefore, appreciate that to obtain an early payment of the bill, some discount is given, which means that there is a price to be paid to obtain an early payment.

Now, let us compute the price (or the rate of interest, as in effect, it is the interest only), that is being paid by the seller to the buyer for making an early payment.

We here presume that all the buyers are prudent enough to pay the bill only on the 10th day (and not earlier) so as to reap the maximum benefit out of the cash discount offered. And, if they were to decide, not to avail of the cash discount, they would, invariably, pay bills on the very last day, *i.e.* on the 30th day only.

Example

(A) From the point of view of the seller:

(*i*) 2/10, Net 30

In effect, it means that a discount of 2 per cent is to be given if the bill is paid earlier, just by 20 days only, *i.e.* 30 less 10 = 20 days). That is, the loss, by way of interest, to the seller (on Rs. 100) for 20 days is 2 per cent. Thus, the rate of interest per annum (presuming 360 days to a year) would come to:

$(2 \times 360)/[100\ (30 - 10)] = 720/2000 = 0.36$ or 36% .

(*ii*) Similarly, in the case of '1/15, net 45', the cost (to the seller) by way of interest, will be:

$(1 \times 360)/[100 \times (45 - 15)] = 360/3000 = 0.12$ or 12%.

(*iii*) And, in the case of '2/9, net 45', the cost (to the seller) by way of interest, would be:

$(2 \times 360)/[100\ (45 - 9)] = 720/3600 = 0.20$ or 20%.

(*iv*) And, '1.5/15, net 60' would mean:

$(1.5 \times 360)/[100\ (60 - 15)] = 540/4500 = 0.12$ or 12%.

(B) From the point of view of the buyer:

But, does it mean that the percentage of savings made by the buyer is also the same, as the percentage of the cost incurred by the seller, or else, it is a little more or less? Let us, find it out, based upon the very first illustrative example, given above. That is, '2/10, net 30'.

Here, from the point of view of the buyer, he stands to gain Rs. 2 when he has to actually pay (Rs. 100 – 2) = Rs. 98 only, instead of Rs. 100. That is, on an investment or payment of Rs. 98 only, he stands to gain Rs. 2 in 20 days. So, on an annualised basis, he stands to gain

$(2 \times 360)/98 \times 20 = 36.666$ per cent or say, 36:73 per cent.

Thus, we see that the buyer is a gainer by a slightly higher percentage, as compared to the seller, because the buyer gains the same amount by investing or paying a little lesser amount than Rs. 100 *i.e.* Rs. 98 only. But, the loss of the seller is on the full amount of Rs. 100, *i.e.* instead of getting Rs. 100, he gets a little less, *i.e.* Rs. 98 in the example under consideration.

In the same way, we may calculate the percentage of savings accruing to the buyers in the remaining three examples too.

When to offer, or avail of, Cash Discount

Now, when it would be prudent enough for the seller to offer such cash discount? The answer is simple enough. The cash discount should be given only when the seller's company faces some financial crunch, and it would not be a losing proposition if the extent of cash discount given is around the same as the rate of interest applicable on the advances procured by the company. But, if it is more, then only such companies, who face some cash crises, should offer it, to receive prompt payment and thereby tide over its financial difficulties, and continue its level of operation.

Accordingly, if the buyer companies have sufficient cash surplus, it would make a wise business sense to avail of the cash discount provided, of course, the average yield here is higher than in other avenues of investments.

If a company decides to liberalise its cash discount policy, it will mean that

(*i*) the discount percentage would be increased, or

(*ii*) the discount period may be enhanced.

Such steps may increase the sales, because the cash discount has the effect of reduction in the price of goods. Further, the average collection period may also come down, as the buyer is encouraged to pay promptly and early to avail of the cash discount. It may also reduce the incidence of bad debts. All these advantages are, however, available but at a price, that is, the increased cost of discount to the seller.

D. Effective Monitoring and Follow-up (i.e. Collection Efforts)

We have already examined the vital importance and imperative need of effective monitoring and follow-up of the sundry debtors with a view to ensure early realisation of the bills, and thereby shorten the collection period, while keeping the risk of bad debts at the minimal level. But, on the flip side, this may result in some reduction in sales and increase in collection expenses. And, correspondingly, some slackness in monitoring and follow-up system may increase the sales and save some collection expenses, too, but at a price. That is, this may result in some increase in the average collection period, resulting in some loss of interest and bad debt risks. But, as all of us may agree, we should be neither too strict nor too lax and liberal in this area. We should, instead, attempt to strike a golden mean, which may, on the whole, prove to be most profitable. With this end in view, we may take the help of the following formula:

$$\Delta \text{NP} = [\Delta \text{S} (1 - \text{V}) - \Delta \text{BD}] (-) \text{K} \Delta \text{I},$$

where:

Δ NP = Change in profit

Δ S = Increase in sales

V = Variable cost to sales ratio

K = Cost of capital

Δ I = Increase in blockage of funds (investment) in sundry debtors

Δ BD = Increase in loss by way of bad debts, to be written off.

Let us explain it further with the help of an illustrative example.

Example

Tirumala & Brothers, a company manufacturing room air-coolers, is contemplating to liberalize its monitoring efforts and strategies. Its present sales ranges to Rs. 50 million, its average collection period (ACP) is 30 days, its variable costs to sales ratio (V) is 75 per cent, its cost of capital is 15 per cent, and its bad debt ratio is 8 per cent. The proposed relaxation, however, is estimated to push up the sales by Rs. 10 million, increase in the average collection period (ACP) is 45 days and the bad debt ratio to 10 per cent. The rate of tax may be taken at 40 per cent, and 360 days to a year.

With the information, given above, and computing the relative values in the formula, we get the value as under:

$$\Delta \text{NP} = [10 \text{ m } (0.25) - \{60 \text{ m } (0.10) - 50 \text{ m } (0.08)\} - [0.15 \{50 \text{ m } (45 - 0)\}360] + [10 \text{ m } (45 \times 0.75)/360]$$

$$= [2.5 \text{ m} - \{(6 \text{ m} - 4 \text{ m})\} - [0.15 \{50 \text{ m } (15)\}\backslash 360] + [10 \text{ m } (45 \times 0.75)/360]$$

$$= [(2.5 \text{ m} - 2 \text{ m})] - [0.15 \{50 \text{ m } (15)\}/360] + [10 \text{ m } (45 \times 0.75)/360]$$

$$= 0.5 \text{ m} - 0.15 [2.0833 + 0.9375]$$

$$= 0.5 \text{ m} - 0.15 (3.0208)$$

$$= 0.5 \text{ m} - 0.453120 \text{ m}$$

$$= (+) 0.046880 \text{ m}$$ **or Rs. 46,880**

As the end-result is a positive figure, *i.e.* profit, we must take the post-tax profit (PAT), which would come to:

Rs. 46,880 (1–0.40) = **Rs. 28,128.**

As the end-result (naturally, at the post-tax level, too) is a positive figure, we may go ahead with the proposal.

But, if the end-result at the pre-tax level itself would have been negative, suggesting a loss, the income tax was not required to be deducted, and the decision had been not to go ahead with the relaxation proposal.

But, supposing if the PAT position would have been a meagre amount, like Rs. 100 or so, the question could be whether it would be prudent to go ahead with the relaxation or not. We should not go ahead with the relaxation, as our estimates of increase in sales or bad debt risks, etc. cannot be said to be exact. Therefore, unless the possibility of the net profit is a substantial amount, which may not come down so much as to result in a loss, even if our estimates prove to be slightly off the mark, we should not go ahead with the proposed relaxation. And, in fact, this alone is the rationale, to find out the post-tax profit. Because, if the incidence of tax is very high, even a higher magnitude of profit may not seem to be attractive enough at the post-tax (PAT) level.

5.13 DECISION-MAKING FOR GRANTING CREDIT

The main purpose of assessing the credit-worthiness of a prospective customer is to assess whether he is worthy for granting the credit or not. Such a decision can easily be taken with the help of a decision tree each to suit the two different circumstances, viz.:

(*i*) where the possibility of repeat order is nil, and

(*ii*) when the repeat order is possible.

(i) Where the possibility of repeat order is nil, the decision tree would look as under:

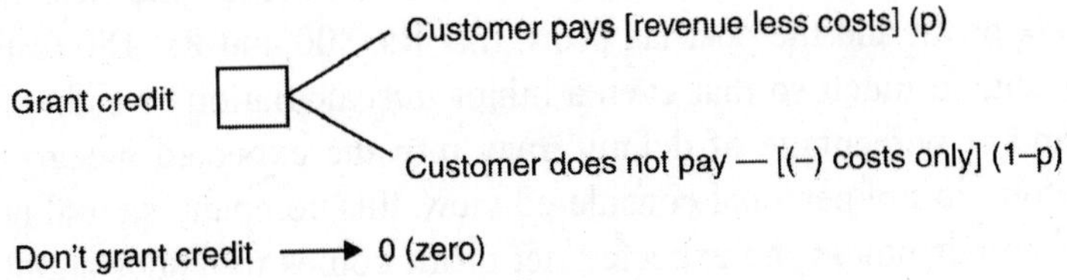

Fig. 5.1

[where, 'p' is the probability that the customer pays his dues].

Thus, '1 – p' is the probability that the customer does not pay his dues.

Revenue represents the total sales revenue arising out of the sales, and the cost is only the variable cost of goods sold, because it is presumed here that the fixed cost is already recovered in full at the earlier level of sales itself.

Now, if we take a decision not to offer any credit, there would be no effect, whatsoever—neither favourable nor unfavourable—on the profitability of the company, as no action, whatsoever, is going to be taken. But, if we were to decide to offer the credit, it would be prudent enough to calculate the end-result with the help of the decision tree given in Fig. 5.1.

The expected profit or loss would be [p (REV – COST) – (1 – p) (cost)].

Here, it may be observed that we are taking the total sales revenue, less cost of sales, in the first half of the statement, inasmuch as in case the dues are duly paid, the company would stand to earn the whole profit, too, built up in the sales (invoice) price. But, in case the customer defaults, the company would stand to lose only the cost of sales (the variable cost alone). That is why, to calculate the amount of loss, in the event of the customer defaulting, we have taken only the cost of sales, the variable cost alone.

Now, let us explain the point a little further with the help of an illustrative example.

Example

Sunbeam Limited is considering whether to offer credit to a customer or not. The probability of payment by the customer is expected to be 75 per cent and, accordingly, the probability that he would not pay is 25 per cent. The revenue from the incremental sale to this customer is expected to be Rs. 2000 and the cost of sales would be Rs. 1200. The rate of income tax may be taken at 0.40.

Solution

By computing the relative values in the above formula (decision tree) we get:

0.75 (2000 – 1200) – 0.25 (1200)

= 0.75 (800) less 0.25 (1200)

= 600.00 – 300.00 = Rs. 300

Profit After Tax (PAT) would be Rs. 300 (1 – 0.40)

= Rs. 180

As the net result is a positive figure (that is indicating profit), the company may decide to offer the credit to the customer. But then, this seems to be a boarder line case, anyway. Because, the amount of pre-tax profit and the post-tax profit (*i.e.* Rs. 300 and Rs. 180 respectively) are too small and insignificant, so much so that even a minor miscalculation or estimates, of amount of incremental sales and/or percentage of default, may turn the expected meagre profit into some loss, instead. Therefore, in my personal considered view, this company should not decide to offer the credit to this customer unless the expected net profit comes to a substantial amount, to take care of the minor variations in our estimates of sales and/or default.

(ii) In Case of Repeat Order: Now, let us see what happens in the case of the possibility of a repeat order.

Here, it must be remembered that repeat order will be accepted only when the first credit sales are paid in full in due time. Further, it may as well be taken that as the customer is said to have not defaulted in the case of the first order, the possibility that he may default, in the case of the second order, will relatively be much less than was expected in the case of the first order.

The expected profit, in such cases may be computed on the basis of the undernoted formula and decision tree:

Expected profit on the first order + (probability of payment of the repeat order) × (expected profit on the repeat order).

Example

Let us take an example. Here we would presume all the figures to be the same (as in the above example) except that the 'incidence of default in the case of the repeat order is expected to be reduced from 25 per cent to 15 per cent. Now, by computing the values of these figures in the formula (decision tree), we get:

$$\{0.75\ (2000 - 1200) - 0.25\ (1200)\} + \{0.85\ (2000 - 1200) - 0.15\ (1200)$$
$$= (600 - 300) + (680 - 180)$$
$$= 300 + 500 = \text{Rs. } 800$$

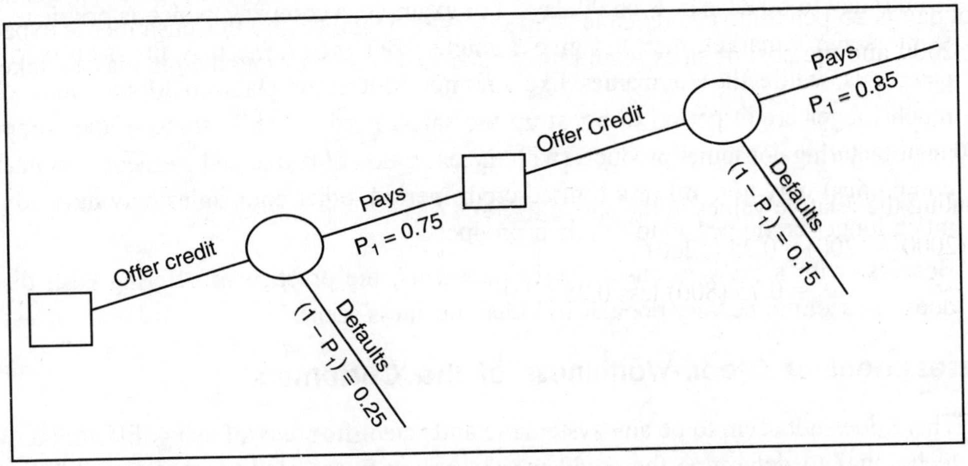

Fig. 5.2: A decision tree for granting credit (in the case of repeat order)

Therefore, if the first order was supplied on credit, the repeat order may as well be complied with, on credit, as the resultant pre-tax profit is Rs. 800 and the post-tax profit (PAT) would be Rs. 480 (Rs. 800 × 0.60).

5.14 MANAGEMENT OF SUNDRY DEBTORS (BILLS RECEIVABLE OR ACCOUNTS RECEIVABLE) IN INDIA

We have so far discussed about the various principles of management and control of sundry debtors. Now, we would like to critically examine as to what are the actual practices and policies that are generally being followed by the various companies in India. For the purpose of the study we shall take up the issues under three broad categories:

(A) Credit Policy,

(B) Assessment of Credit-worthiness of the customers (present and prospective), and

(C) Monitoring and control of sundry debtors.

(A) Credit Policy

(*i*) Very few companies have been found to have systematically formulated and documented their credit policies. In most of the cases these are made on an ad-hoc basis and mostly remain as unwritten conventions and practices.

(*ii*) In some of the companies, the credit policy and philosophy have been stated, in general terms, which do not signify any specific stand or standard to be followed by the operating staff. For example, if a company states its credit policy, "Our credit policy aims at maximising the growth of sales with the minimal bad debt risks", it does not convey much as a guideline or guiding principle of any practical use and utility.

(*iii*) The credit periods offered by various companies differ to a very great extent, ranging from 0 day to 60 days or even 90 days. For example, a company, which is privileged to be in the seller's market, may not give a single day's credit, *i.e.* may insist on cash down payments, while the companies like Premier Motors or Daewoo Motors may offer a much longer credit period to boost up the sales. Further, while some of the companies, manufacturing consumer products (with the exception of textile and garment manufacturing companies) may give nil or a limited credit period, other companies may have to give a much longer credit period to sell their products.

(*iv*) Besides, with a view to ensure early payments, the practice of offering cash discount does not seem to be very popular in Indian business scenario.

(B) Assessment of Credit-Worthiness of the Customers

(*i*) There does not seem to be any systematic and scientific study of using different tools and techniques to determine the credit-worthiness or financial strength and stability of the customers, both present and prospective. In fact, the financial position of the present customers should also be reviewed and revised on a regular basis, based upon our own experiences, of their past performance and dealings with us. But this seldom seems to have been resorted to in most of the companies.

(*ii*) No serious and sincere effort seems to have been made to meticulously analyse the balance sheet and profit and loss account of the companies with a view to make a realistic assessment and appraisal of their financial position. It has hardly been observed that some companies have asked for some break-ups of certain items, say, of inventories or bad debts, to see through the elements of window dressing, if any.

(*iii*) Prospective customers are required to give, at least, two or three references, but no serious attempt seems to have been made by most of the companies to verify the position from such references.

(*iv*) Independent credit rating agencies, like CRISIL and ICRA, have, of late, appeared on the scene but the credibility and dependability of their credit ratings may be a little doubtful. The credit rating agencies had given satisfactory credit rating to 'MS Shoes' and 'CRB Finance Company', but their assessment had proved to be totally wrong and contrary to facts. Besides, the practice of seeking professional help from such credit rating companies to ascertain and assess the financial position of the prospective customers does not seem to be very common, as opposed to the conditions prevailing in the USA, and other developed countries.

(*v*) Some companies attempt to get the opinion of the bankers on the prospective customers from the latters' bank, but, as has already been observed earlier, their opinions, though given in strict confidence and without any obligation, are written in such general and vague terms that these do not seem to be of much help and practical utility.

(C) Monitoring and Control of Sundry Debtors

Though the various tools and techniques, systems and strategies, of effective monitoring of sundry debtors are very well known to the executives of most of the companies, very few companies have been found to have evolved some systematic mechanism of effective monitoring and follow-up of sundry debtors on some sound, systematic and scientific lines. A lot seems to have been left to be desired. Some companies have been found to be working out the average collection period, but not party-wise. They do the ageing analysis but only in absolute terms and not in terms of percentage, etc.

5.15 SOME SUGGESTIONS FOR IMPROVEMENT

1. At the very outset, I would like to reiterate that the companies in India must realise and fully appreciate the imperative need of management and control of sundry debtors, which is so crucial for the financial liquidity and stability of any business entity, be it a manufacturing unit or even a trading company.

   As we have already seen earlier, an Indian company blocked a huge sum in the sundry debtors, mostly due to disputes arising out of the supply of sub-standard goods, instead of the agreed quality, and it had to pay the salary and wages for a particular month out of the sale proceeds of the accumulated scraps.

   I also know of a Small Scale Industrial Unit, 'Windy Fans' (not the real name), which had fallen sick, mainly on account of lack of effective monitoring and follow-up of its sundry debtors. [For further details, please refer to the Case Study, incorporated in the author's book titled "*Sickness in Small Scale Sector: Causes and Cures*" [Concept Publishing Company, New Delhi - 110 059 (1999), pp. 129-133].

   After the first stage has been achieved, that is, the importance and urgency of effective monitoring and control of sundry debtors have been fully realised by all the officials concerned, at different levels, half of the battle is won.
2. At the next stage, the company must formulate its credit policy in clear and unambiguous terms, which must be articulated in writing. It should further be ensured that it is understood and appreciated by all the officials concerned, for their meticulous and effective implementation and compliance. Besides, the credit policy should also be periodically revised, depending upon the changing circumstances/conditions, both internal and external.
3. Then we come to the third stage, when the various tools and techniques for the purpose, as discussed, in detail, in earlier pages, must be effectively implemented.

For example

(*i*) Periodical review of the sundry debtors, based on the past performance and records of different companies, and revising the credit ratings/gradings, accordingly.

(*ii*) Ageing - analysis of sundry debtors should invariably be done, not only period-wise but also party-wise, taking suitable steps for realisation of the overdues at the earliest.

4. Development of a team spirit and the culture of coordination and cooperation amongst different departments, like materials and purchases, production and sales, and above all, the finance department is the most felt need of the hour. If, we Indians, being excellent solo performers, are also excellent team workers, we can definitely do wonders. Introduction of the scheme of reward and punishment to the whole integrated team of different departments (instead of excellent individual official/worker) may go a long way in realisation of such a dynamic and deserving dream.

   [For further detailed discussions on the strategies of building an effective team, please refer to the author's book titled '*Mentoring Mantras for Indian Managers*', Matrix Publishers, New Delhi, 2010, chapter titled "Three Plus Three Makes Nine"].
5. While considering the credit and grading categories of the prospective customers, care should be taken to analyse and interpret their balance sheets, and profit and loss accounts, more thoroughly and meticulously, by obtaining further break-ups and such other relevant information, wherever required. This, however, is not being done in most of the companies, as of now.
6. Pertinent enquiries must be made from the referees mentioned by the prospective customers, coupled with periodical trade enquires from other customers, in the area. And, most importantly, the required follow-up actions should also follow such enquiries.
7. And, above all, a well designed and defined collection plan and programme must be evolved and improved upon, from time to time, as we go on gaining, rewarding and revealing experiences with the passage of time.

Appendix 5.1

To [Name and complete postal address of the Buyer Company/Firm]

Dear Sirs,

Your Order No. ____________ dated ____________ for Rs. ____________

Our Invoice/Bill No. ____________ dated ____________ for Rs. ____________

In terms of your above-noted valued order, we are pleased to advise you having despatched today the relative goods to your address by goods/passenger train/truck (lorry).

The above-noted invoice and other documents, detailed hereunder, are being sent herewith:

1. Bill of Exchange No. ____________ dated ____________ for Rs. ____________
2. Railway Receipt /Truck Receipt No. ____________ dated ____________
3. Inspection Note No. ____________ dated ____________
4. Transit Insurance Policy No. /Cover Note No. ____________ dated ____________
5. ____________
6. ____________

Please arrange to pay the amount of the bill within 30 days [enter here the specific credit period allowed to the respective buyers, viz. 30, 45, 60, 90 days, etc.] from the date of the invoice by Bank Draft made payable at ____________.

Overdue interest will be charged @ 15 per cent per annum from the due date specified above.

Meanwhile, please acknowledge receipt of the documents on the tear-off portion of the letter, which may be posted to us just by slipping the tear-off slip in a window envelop, duly stamped.

Thanking you in anticipation,

Yours faithfully,

*

Authorised Signatory

* Computer Print Out; Requiring No Signature.

Tear-off slip [to be duly completed by the Seller Company]

Received from M/s (Name of the Seller Company ____________, ____________), the Bill/Invoice No. ____________ dated ____________ for Rs. ____________ in compliance of our Order No. ____________ dated ____________ along with the undernoted documents.

1. Bill of Exchange No. ____________ dated ____________ for Rs. ____________
2. Railway Receipt/Truck Receipt No. ____________ dated ____________
3. Inspection Note No. ____________ dated ____________
4. Transit Insurance Policy No./Cover Note No. ____________ dated ____________
5. ____________
6. ____________

To be mailed to:

Name and complete address of the seller (Drawer company/firm) ____________

Rubber Stamp of the buyer (drawee) Company/firm with the date of receipt [Signature is optional]

Appendix 5.2

SUNDRY DEBTORS' MASTER REGISTER

[Separate Section/Register/Computer File may be maintained for different credit periods allowed, viz. 30, 45, 60, 90 days, etc.]

Credit Period ———— Days

Date	*Sl. No.*	*Name of the Buyer*	*Buyer's Code No.*	*Buyer's Order No. and Date*	*Our Bill/ Invoice No. and Date*	*Amount (Rs.)*
1	2	3	4	5	6	7

1st Reminder sent on	*Date of Payment*	*2nd Reminder sent on*	*3rd Reminder sent on*	*Legal Notice served on*	*Further Actions to be initiated (to be specified)*	*General Remarks*
8	9	10	11	12	13	14

Appendix 5.3

LEDGER ACCOUNTS–(PARTY-WISE)

Name of the Buyer: ____________________

Buyer's Code No. : ____________________

Sl. No.	*Sl. No. [As per Master Register]*	*Date and No. of Order*	*Date of Bill/ Invoice*	*Amount (Rs.)*	*Date of Payment of the Bill*	*Payment delayed by – days*
1	2	3	4	5	6	7

Reason(s) for the delay, if any	*Reminder I sent on*	*Reminder II sent on*	*Reminder III sent on*	*Legal Notice Served on*	*Legal action initiated, if any*	*General Remarks*
8	9	10	11	12	13	14

Appendix 5.4

REMINDER II*

To
[Name and Address of the
Buyer Company/Firm]

Dear Sirs,

Your Order No. ______________________ dated ________________ for Rs. ______________
Our Invoice/Bill No. ___________________ dated ________________ for Rs. ______________

We may bring to your kind notice that our above-noted bill, which has already fallen due for payment a fortnight back, from the date of this letter, still remains outstanding, in our books, despite our reminder sent to you three weeks earlier.

In case you have since paid the bill, please let us know the particulars thereof. If, however, the bill still remains unpaid, please do pay it now, along with the amount of overdue interest, without any further delay.

We hope, we will not have to remind you again in this regard.

Thanking you in anticipation,

Yours faithfully,

@

Authorised Signatory

@Computer Print Out; Requiring No Signature.

Copy forwarded, for information and further necessary follow-up action, ensuring early payment of the bill, to:

(*a*) The Area Sales Manager, and

(*b*) The Area Sales Officer/Sales Representative concerned.

Signature
Authorised Signatory

---

*The specimen pro forma of the (routine) Reminder I has already been given in the foregoing page.

Appendix 5.5

REMINDER III

To,
[Name and Address of the
Buyer Company/Firm]

Dear Sirs,

Your Order No. ____________________ dated ______________ for Rs. __________
Our Invoice/Bill No. ________________ dated ______________ for Rs. __________

We are constrained to observe that our above-noted invoice/bill, which has already fallen overdue for payment, has not been paid by you so far, despite our repeated reminders and personal approaches made by our representative(s) on several occasions, from time to time.

In case, however, you have, in the mean time, paid the bill, along with the amount of the overdue interest, please advise us the details thereof. But, if you have failed to do so even till date, please arrange to pay the same forthwith, under an urgent advice to us, failing which we may be reluctantly compelled to initiate further necessary actions, including legal action, for the realisation of our bill.

We earnestly hope that you would not prefer to compel us to resort to some extreme steps.

Yours faithfully,

Signature
Authorised Signatory

Copy forwarded, for information, and further intensified follow-up actions, including making personal contacts/visits to the party, for an early realisation of the overdue bill to:

1. The Area Sales Manager, concerned, and
2. The Area Sales Officer/Sales Representative concerned.

Signature
Authorised Signatory

Copy forwarded to
The General Manager, Credit Sales Department, with instructions to suspend all credit supplies to the addressee company/firm till further specific written instructions, in this regard.

Signature
Authorised Signatory

A SYNOPTIC NOTE
(CHAPTER 5 AT A GLANCE)

MANAGEMENT OF CREDIT

1. Why Management and Control of Credit?

Sundry debtors generally constitute the third largest item of the aggregate assets of a company, *i.e.* after Plant and Machinery, and Inventories. Hence, its management and control is essential.

2. Credit Policy

The sundry debtors of a company are usually classified under four categories, based on the degree of risks involved, viz.

(*i*) Category A, Representing "No Risk".
(*ii*) Category B, Representing "Little Risk".
(*iii*) Category C, Representing "Some Risk".
(*iv*) Category D, Representing "High Risk".

The sundry debtors, pertaining to each category/classification should, however, be periodically reviewed and revised.

3. Steps and strategies for effective management and control of sundry debtors

(*i*) Prompt despatch of goods and invoice.
(*ii*) Correct and unambiguous invoicing.
(*iii*) Despatch of right quality of goods in right quantity and at right price, to avoid any possible dispute.
(*iv*) Standard (Printed) invoice proforma containing full particulars, with tear-off portion, for acknowledgement purpose.
(*v*) Maintenance of:
 (*a*) Master Register (separate file/section, as per credit periods allowed)
 (*b*) Ledger Accounts (party-wise)
(*vi*) Periodical analysis of historical data about paying pattern of the respective parties, for reclassification/re-categorization as A, B, C and D.

4. Effective follow-up for speedy collection of bills

(*i*) A routine reminder (a week before the due date).
(*ii*) A second reminder (a fortnight after the due date).
(*iii*) A third strict reminder (after a month), with a copy endorsed to the sales manager/sales representative, for stoppage of further supplies, on credit, forthwith.
(*iv*) A forewarning regarding imminent issue of legal notice.
(*v*) Issuance of legal notice and ultimately filing of civil suits, against some parties, to serve as test cases, as also as deterrents.

But we are to remember not to treat all sundry debtors equally, or in the same way. They are to be treated differently. Treat only equals equally.

(*vi*) Streamline the enquiry system.

Take a phone call to find out the facts.

5. Some main causes of high sundry debtors, classified under four heads

(*i*) Internal causes (IC).

(*ii*) External causes (EC).

(*iii*) Dispute as a cause (DC).

(*iv*) Miscellaneous causes (MC).

Periodical analysis of the causes of overdue bills, and review of each party's performance and re-categorization, wherever necessary.

6. Ramifications of high sundry debtors

(*i*) Loss of interest, and/or opportunity cost.

(*ii*) Liquidity constraint and cash crunch.

(*iii*) Hampers accurate cash budgeting, and increases incidence of bad debts.

(*iv*) Adversely affects the company's profitability and its prospects, that go therewith.

7. Formulation of credit policy

(*i*) Three types of credit policies:

(*a*) Liberal;

(*b*) Strict; and

(*c*) Moderate (*i.e.* middle-of-the-road), *i.e.* neither too liberal nor too strict.

(*ii*) In terms of:

(*a*) Standard of credit, *i.e.* criteria and standard for categorization of clients into A, B, C and D.

(*b*) Period of credit allowed.

(*c*) Effective credit monitoring and follow-up (*i.e.* collection efforts).

(*d*) Cash discount offered.

8. Management of control systems (MCS) of sundry debtors

Age-Analysis

(*a*) Period-wise,

(*b*) Party-wise (viz. Government Departments, Public Sector Undertakings, Private Sector and others) and also in,

(*c*) Percentage terms (instead of in absolute terms only).

9. Assessment of credit-worthiness of customers (sundry debtors) through

(*i*) Annual reports (analysis and interpretation of ratios); viz. current ratio, quick ratio, return on net worth, debt equity ratio, EBIT to total assets, sundry debtors vs. sundry creditors, etc.,

(*ii*) Trade and local enquiries,

(*iii*) Bank enquiries [both in writing and, more importantly, verbally and on personal and confidential terms],

(*iv*) Six C's, viz.,

(*a*) Character – integrity

(*b*) Capability – financial strength and stability

(*c*) Capital Base – financial standing

(*d*) Collaterals (securities)

(*e*) Conditions (economic and market conditions)

(*f*) Case History (past performance of parties)

(*v*) Share market report.

10. Management and control of sundry debtors in india

(*i*) Credit policy

(*a*) Very few Indian companies systematically formulate and document their credit policies in clear terms.

(*b*) And, usually, these are stated in vague and general terms.

(*c*) The practice of offering cash discount is rather rare.

(*ii*) Assessment of credit-worthiness of customers:

(*a*) Usually no scientific or systematic studies are made professionally, by using the required tools and techniques.

(*b*) Balance sheet and, profit and loss account of companies are not analyzed and studied meticulously, by asking for further break-ups, etc., wherever required.

(*c*) Prospective customers are usually required to give two/three references. But, their standings are seldom seriously verified from the respective references.

(*d*) The credibility and dependability of credit rating agencies like ICRA, CRISIL, etc. are not very high in India.

(*iii*) Effective monitoring and control of sundry debtors:

These are known well to the executives of companies. But, unfortunately, these are seldom done well in a professional and scientific manner.

11. Some suggestions for improvement

(*i*) The executives of Indian companies must fully understand the importance and implications of effective management and control of sundry debtors, and therefore, start taking it up with the desired seriousness and sincerity.

(*ii*) They must take every care to avoid dispute regarding quantity and quality of goods, and their prices.

(*iii*) Many companies, specially in small scale sector, had fallen sick mainly for neglecting this vital segment of financial management.

And, once this much has been achieved, the companies must proceed further.

(*iv*) (*a*) Companies must formulate credit policy in clear and concrete terms. Credit policy should be periodically reviewed and revised, too, depending upon trade/market conditions.

(*b*) The credit ratings/categorization must be periodically reviewed and revised.

(*c*) Age-analysis should be done, not only period-wise but also party-wise; not only in absolute terms but in percentage terms, too. Suitable corrective steps must be taken in due time.

(*d*) Above all, a culture of cooperation and team spirit must be developed among production and marketing, etc.

(*e*) The study of annual reports of the prospective customers, as also of the existing clients, must be done meticulously and regularly.

(*f*) Thorough enquiries must be made from traders and referees, bankers and other creditors.

(*g*) A well-designed and defined collection plan and programme must be evolved, and the follow-up action must be taken expeditiously.

QUESTIONS
(For Self-assessment)

1. There are several terms of payment prevalent in the business world. Name the major terms of payment in practice and briefly describe each one, separately.

2. What are the ramifications of enhancing and reducing the credit period? Explain, by citing some illustrative examples.

3. Distinguish between (*i*) liberal and (*ii*) strict credit standards and policies, by citing suitable examples in each case. Explain the effects of liberal and strict credit terms in each case, separately.

4. What do you mean by (*i*) liberalising and (*ii*) restricting the credit policies, in terms of the following:

(*a*) Period of credit,

(*b*) Cash discount,

(*c*) Credit standards, and

(*d*) Collection efforts.

5. Proper assessment of credit risks is considered to be one of the most crucial factors in the area of management of credit. Do you agree? Give reasons for your answer.

6. What are the two main types of errors that may creep in, while assessing the credit risks? Explain each of them by citing suitable illustrative examples.

7. (*a*) What are the six 'C's of Credit'? Discuss each of them, separately, by citing suitable illustrative examples in each case.

(*b*) Do you think of dimensions other than 'Six C's', while assessing a prospective customer? Give reasons for your answer.

8. (*a*) Bank reference is considered to be one of the major factors for assessing the credit-worthiness of a prospective customer. Do you agree? Give reasons for your answer.

(*b*) What are the main shortcomings and limitations connected with obtaining bank references and what are the pragmatic approaches for overcoming them?

9. (*a*) Credit management practices, in Indian companies, suffer from several deficiencies. What are these and what are the adverse effects of each of them in actual practice?

(*b*) What are the specific suggestions that you would like to make with a view to streamlining and strengthening the present practices of management of credit (Sundry Debtors) by the industries in India?

10. 'Ageing Analysis' is an effective tool for monitoring and follow-up of sundry debtors. However, for better results, it is desirable to do the ageing analysis:
    (*i*) Not only 'period-wise', but also 'party-wise', and
    (*ii*) Not only in 'absolute terms' (of Rs.) but also in 'percentage terms'.
    Explain and illustrate, by using suitable examples.
    You may assume the various factors, viz. period, parties, percentage, amount, etc., for the purpose.

PROBLEMS FOR PRACTICE

1. Aditya and Company currently provides 30 days of credit to its customers. Its present level of sales is Rs. 70 lakh. The firm's cost of capital is 12 per cent and the ratio of variable costs to sales is 0.75. The company is considering extending its credit period to 45 days. Such an extension is likely to push the sales up by Rs. 5 lakh. The bad debt proportion on additional sales would be 9 per cent. The income tax rate is 35%.

Required

(*a*) What would be the effect of extending the credit period on profit before tax (PBT) and profit after tax (PAT) of the company, assuming 360 days to a year?

(*b*) Is the proposed change under consideration desirable? Give reasons for your specific recommendations.

2. What is the annual percentage interest cost (at simple rate of interest; not compounded) associated with the following credit terms:
   (*i*) to the buyer company, and
   (*ii*) to the seller company, separately (assume 360 days in a year).
   (*a*) 1/10, net 40
   (*b*) 2/15, net 60
   (*c*) 3/20, net 60
   (*d*) 1/5, net 20
3. (*a*) Firms experiencing cash crunch usually resort to giving some cash discount, as it ensures prompt payment, though at a price, in terms of loss of interest.
   Calculate the cost of credit in terms of loss of interest per annum to the selling firms in the following cases (assuming 360 days in a year):
   (*i*) 1/10, net 50 days
   (*ii*) 2/15, net 75 days
   (*iii*) 2/15, net 45 days
   (*iv*) 1.5/15, net 50 days.
   (*b*) What would be the percentage gain to the buyer firms per annum in the above cases?
4. Arjun Sports Limited is considering to extend credit facility to two companies, viz.
   (*i*) Sanjay Co. (P) Ltd., and
   (*ii*) Krishna Co. (P) Ltd.

The probability that the two companies would pay is 70% and 40% respectively; and accordingly, the probability that they would not pay is 30% and 60% respectively. The revenue from the sales is expected to be Rs. 36,000 and the cost of sales is estimated to be Rs. 18,000.

The Chairman of Arjun Sports Ltd. has approached you to give him an expert financial advice as to whom should he offer or refuse credit, based on the exact amount of expected profit or loss, resulting therefrom, in each case, as per the foregoing information.

Required

What would be your specific reasoned recommendations in each case?

5. "Alka Automobiles Limited" (AAL) is considering to extend credit facility to two companies, viz.
   (*i*) VXL Co. (P) Ltd., and
   (*ii*) UXL Co. (P) Ltd.

The probability that the two companies would pay is 80% and 75%, respectively; and accordingly, the probability that they would not pay is 20% and 25% respectively. The revenue from the sales is expected to be Rs. 55 lakh and the cost of sales is estimated to be Rs. 43 lakh.

The Managing Director of AAL has approached you to give him an expert financial advice as to whom should he offer or refuse credit, based on the exact amount of expected profit or loss, resulting therefrom, in each case, as per the foregoing information.

Required

What would be your specific recommendations in each case? Give reasons for your recommendations.

6. 'His and Her Garments Ltd.' (HHGL) is considering to extend credit facility to two companies, viz.
   (*i*) ABC Co. (P) Ltd., and
   (*ii*) PQR Co. (P) Ltd.

The probability that the two companies would pay is 75% and 55%, respectively; and accordingly, the probability that they would not pay is 25% and 45%, respectively. The revenue from the sales is expected to be Rs. 21,000 and the cost of sales is estimated to be Rs. 12,000.

The Chairman and Managing Director (CMD) of HHGL has approached you to give him an expert financial advice as to whom should the credit facility be offered or refused, based on the exact amount of expected profit or loss, resulting therefrom, in each case, as per the foregoing information.

Required

What would be your specific reasoned recommendations in each case?

7. The present sales of Nirmal Industries (P) Limited are Rs. 200 lakh. The firm has classified its customers into three credit categories: A, B and C. The firm extends unlimited credit to the customers in category A, limited credit to the customers in category B, and no credit to the customers in category C. As a result of this credit policy, the firm is foregoing sales to the extent of Rs. 20 lakh to the customers in category B and Rs. 40 lakh to the customers in category C. The firm is considering the adoption of a more liberal credit policy under which the customers in category B would be extended unlimited credit and the customers in category C would be provided limited credit. Such a relaxation would increase the sales by Rs. 40 lakh, on which bad debt losses would be 10 per cent. The collection period is 45 days, and the cost of funds is 20 per cent per annum. The contribution margin ratio for the firm is 20%.

Required

(*a*) What will be the effect of relaxing the credit policy on the pre-tax profit and the net profit of the firm, assuming 360 days in a year, and the rate of income tax @ 40%?

(*b*) Whether the proposed change under consideration is desirable? Give reasons for your specific recommendations.

8. The present sales of Parijat Pharmaceuticals and Sisters are Rs. 100 lakh. The firm has classified its customers into four credit categories: A, B, C and D. The firm extends unlimited credit to the customers in category A, limited credit to the customers in category B, and no credit to the customers in categories C and D. As a result of this credit policy, the firm is foregoing sales to the extent of Rs. 10 lakh to the customers in category B and Rs. 20 lakh to the customers in category C. The firm is considering the adoption of a more liberal credit policy under which the customers in category B would be extended unlimited credit and the customers in category C would be provided limited credit. Such a relaxation would increase the sales by Rs. 20 lakh, on which the bad debt losses would be 12 per cent. The contribution margin ratio for the firm is 15 per cent, the average collection period is 50 days, and the cost of funds is 16 per cent per annum.

Required

(*a*) What will be the effect of relaxing the credit policy on the pre-tax profit and net profit of the firm, assuming 360 days in a year, and income tax @ 33%?

(*b*) Is the proposed change under consideration desirable? Give reasons for your specific recommendations.

9. The present sales of Kavery Krafts Ltd., are Rs. 200 lakh. The firm classifies its customers into credit categories: A, B, C and D. The firm extends unlimited credit to the customers in category A, limited credit to the customers in category B, and no credit to the customers in categories C and D. As a result of this credit policy, the firm foregoes sales to the extent of Rs. 20 lakh to the customers in category B and Rs. 40 lakh to the customers in category C. The firm is considering the adoption of a more liberal credit policy, under which the customers in category B would be extended unlimited credit and customers in category C would be provided limited credit. Such a relaxation would increase the sales by Rs. 40 lakh on which bad debt losses would be 20 per cent. The contribution margin ratio for the firm is 30 per cent, the average collection period is 55 days, and the cost of funds is 1.5 per cent per month.

Required

(*i*) What will be the effect of relaxing the credit policy on the pre-tax profit and the net profit of the firm, assuming 360 days in a year and the rate of income tax @ 30%?

(*ii*) Is the proposed change under consideration desirable? Give reasons for your specific recommendations.

10. The current level of sales of Sunshine Batteries Limited is Rs. 60 million. The company has classified its customers into credit categories: A, B and C. The company extends unlimited credit to their customers in category A, limited credit to customers in category B, and no credit to customers in category C. As a result of this credit policy, the company seems to be losing sales to the extent of Rs. 6 million to the customers in category B and Rs. 15 million to the customers in category C. The firm is considering the adoption of a more liberal credit policy under which the customers in category B would be extended unlimited credit and the customers in category C would be provided limited credit. Such a relaxation is expected to increase the sales by Rs. 20 million on which bad debt losses would be 10 per cent. The contribution margin ratio for the company is 20 per cent, the average collection period is 50 days, and the cost of capital is 14 per cent p.a. The tax rate for the company is 33 per cent.

Required

(*a*) What will be the effect of relaxing the credit policy on the profitability of the company at the

(*i*) pre-tax (PBT) level, and

(*ii*) post-tax (PAT) level?

(*b*) Should the company go ahead with the proposed relaxation? Give reasons for your answer.

11. Gomti Garments currently provide 30 days of credit to its customers. Its present level of sales is Rs. 20 million. The firm's cost of capital is 14 per cent and the ratio of variable costs to sales is 0.75. The firm is considering to extend its credit period to 45 days. Such a relaxation is expected to boost its sales by Rs. 2.0 million. The bad debt proportion on additional sales would be 6 per cent. The tax rate is 30 per cent.

Required

(*a*) What will be the effect of relaxing the credit policy on the profitability of the company at the (*i*) Pre-tax (PBT) level; and (*ii*) Post-tax (PAT) level?

(*b*) Should the company go ahead with the proposed relaxation? Give reasons for your answer.

12. The present credit terms of Aditya Awaran Agencies Limited are 1/15, net 45. Its sales are Rs. 15 million, its average collection period is 30 days, its variable cost to sales ratio is 0.70 and its cost of funds is 16 per cent. The proportion of sales on which customers currently take discount is 0.5. The company is considering to relax its discount terms to 2/25, net 45. Such a relaxation is expected to increase the sales by Rs. 1.5 million, reduce the average collection period to 27 days, and increase the proportion of discount sales to 0.9.

What will be the effect of relaxing the discount policy on its net profit? The tax rate is 40 per cent (assuming 360 days in a year).

13. Manisha Amol Enterprises is considering to relax its collection efforts. Presently its sales are Rs. 60 million, its average collection period is 30 days, its variable costs to sales ratio is 0.80, its cost of capital is 16 per cent, and its bad debt ratio is 0.05. The relaxation in collection efforts is expected to push the sales up by Rs. 6 million, increase the average collection period to 45 days, and raise the bad debts ratio to 0.07. The tax rate of the firm is 40 per cent.

Required

What will be the effect of relaxing the collection effort on

(*i*) the gross profit (PBT) and

(*ii*) the net profit (PAT) of the firm?

14. The current credit terms of Windy Fans are 1/10, net 40. The total sales for the year are Rs. 50 million. Forty per cent of the customers pay on the tenth day and avail of the discount; the remaining sixty per cent pay on an average 60 days after their purchases.

Calculate the average collection period and the average blockage of funds.

15. Ashirvad Associates sells on terms 1/10, net 20. The total sales for the year are Rs. 20 million. The cost of goods sold is Rs. 10.0 million. Customers accounting for 25 per cent of the sales take discount and pay on the tenth day, while others take an average of 30 days to pay.

Calculate

(*a*) the average collection period, and

(*b*) the average blockage of funds in receivables.

16. Suruchi Enterprises is considering a change in its credit terms from the present 1/15, net 45, to 2/15, net 60. This change is expected to

(*a*) increase the total sales from Rs. 60 million to Rs. 80 million;

(*b*) decrease the proportion of customers taking discount from 0.80 to 0.70, and

(*c*) increase the average collection period from 30 days to 40 days. The gross profit margin for the firm is 16 per cent and the cost of capital is 15 per cent. The tax rate is 30 per cent.

Compute

(*a*) the expected change in profit, and

(*b*) the expected cost of increasing the cash discount.

17. The Finance Manager of a company is wondering whether credit should be granted to a new customer who is expected to make a repeat order. On the basis of the credit evaluation, the Finance Manager feels that the probability that the customer will pay is 0.90 and, accordingly, the probability that the customer will default is 0.10. Once the customer pays for the first purchase, the probability that he will pay for the repeat purchase increases to 0.95. The revenues from sales will be Rs. 15,000 and the cost of sale would be Rs. 9,500 — these figures apply to both the initial and the repeat purchases.

Should the credit be granted? Give reasons for your answer.

18. A firm is considering whether to sell goods to a customer on credit. The revenues from the sale will be Rs. 20,000 and the cost of sale will be Rs. 15,000.

What should be the minimum probability that the customer will pay in order to sell profitably?

19. What is the interest cost on an annual percentage basis, associated with the following credit terms for the seller, assuming 360 days in a year?

(*a*) 1/10, net 50

(*b*) 2/15, net 45

(*c*) 3/20, net 60

(*d*) 2/7, net 25.

20. What will be the percentage interest gain on annual basis associated with the following credit terms to the buyers, assuming 360 days in a year?

(*a*) 3/15, net 60

(*b*) 2/9, net 36

(*c*) 11/20, net 50

(*d*) 1/30, net 90.

6

MANAGEMENT OF INVENTORIES

> *God gave man the challenge of raw materials — not the ease of finished things. He left the pictures unpainted and the music unsung and the problems unsolved, that man might know the joys and glories of creation.*
> **Source Unknown**
>
> *Money is like manure. If you spread it around it does a lot of good. But if you pile it up in one place it stinks like hell.*
> **Clint Murchison Jr.**

The Learning Points

The chapter aims at developing knowledge and facilitating understanding of:

- Various components of inventories
- Compulsive need for Stocking of Investories
- Mechanism of Computing Economic Order Quantity (EOQ)
- Principles of Basic Economic Order Quantity (EOQ) Model
- Comparison between Trial and Error method, and Economic Order Quantity Formula
- Mechanism of Devising Economic Order Quantity Formula
- Distinction between Economic Order Quantity and Optimum Order Quantity
- Finding A New Clue to EOQ
- Appreciating different Components of Inventory Carrying Costs
- Elements of Lead Time, Order Point, Safety Stock and other Variable Factors affecting EOQ
- Mechanism of doing ABC Analysis or VED Analysis, and the principles behind Categorization of Items for ABC Analysis
- Management and Control of Inventory through Ratio Analysis
- Distinction between Just-in-Time (JIT) system and Just-in-Case (JIC) system
- Evolving effective system for Inventory Management, Monitoring and Control, and Strategies for achieving success
- Prevalent practices of Inventory Management and Control in India, and some suggestions for improvement

6.1 COMPONENTS OF INVENTORIES

The term 'inventory' comprises three components. They are:

1. Raw materials (also consumable stores and spares),

2. Work-in-process (also known as stock-in-process or goods-in-process), and
3. Finished goods.

Let us now discuss all these three items, one by one.

1. Raw materials are those basic inputs which are used to manufacture the finished products.
2. Work-in-process, however, is the intermediary stage that comes after the stage of raw materials, but just before the stage of finished goods.
3. The finished goods, in turn, comprise the end-products, that is, the goods at their final stage of production, ready for sale in the market.

Let us bring home the point with the help of an **example**.

Supposing a company is in the business of production of breads. In this case, the wheat flour, baking powder, etc., would comprise the raw materials. And, when the flour is put in the relative moulds which, in turn, are placed in oven, this stage is known as the work-in-process stage. And, when the bread is fully baked and is ready for sale, of course, after being wrapped in the packing paper, it comprises the finished goods of the company.

In the case of manufacturing companies, inventory comprises raw materials, work-in-process and finished goods, while in the case of trading concerns or trade merchants or retail traders, the inventory comprises only the finished goods. In this way, all the three components, as aforesaid, comprise the items of inventory for the manufacturing concerns, and the finished goods, like the breads alone, comprise the inventory for a retail trader for selling breads.

The importance and imperative need for effectively managing and controlling all the items of inventory in a company can be judged from the fact that generally these comprise the largest component of the total assets of a company, second only to the items of plant and machinery. In terms of percentage of the total assets of a manufacturing company, all the three components of inventory, taken together, generally account for around 25 to 30 per cent of the total assets of the company. Thus, the importance of effectively managing and controlling the inventory of a company can hardly be over-emphasised.

It may be pertinent to mention that the task of inventory management and control is the joint responsibility of the purchase department, materials department, production department and marketing department. While the policy pertaining to the raw materials is to be formulated by the purchase department, in coordination with the materials and production departments, the policy in regard to the inventory of finished goods is to be formulated by the production department in coordination with the marketing department. The policy in regard to the work-in-process, however, is finalised by the production department alone.

As already explained, keeping in view the vital importance of inventory management and control, in financial terms, the role of finance manager can be said to be the central coordinating role, among all the aforesaid four different departments, with a view to ensure that the inventory management and control are being exercised effectively at the various stages and in all the departments on the desired lines. Here, the main responsibility of finance manager is to apprise the non-finance executives so as at least to understand the basis of mechanism and its overall implication in regard to the control of various items of inventory, as these have direct effect on the financial gains of the company. That is why, it is said that the management of inventory, and management of working capital as a whole is not the responsibility of the finance manager alone, but also of the purchase department, materials department, production department, and marketing departments. That is why, the imperative need of the day is that we should become excellent in terms of team work and for individual performance.

The readers, interested in knowing more about building an effective team, may like to read the chapter titled "Three Plus Three Makes Nine", in the book by the author titled "*Mentoring Mantras for Indian Managers*", Matrix Publishers, New Delhi, 2010.

6.2 WHY DO WE NEED INVENTORY?

Before we attempt to answer this question, let us first understand that, generally speaking, the entire stocks of inventory can be divided into two main categories. They are:

(*a*) (*i*) 'Process' Inventories, and (*ii*) 'Movement' Inventories

(*b*) 'Organisation' Inventories

(a) (i) Process Inventories

These inventories comprise the various items of raw materials, lying at the various stages of production, till these reach the final stage, to become the finished goods. Supposing, a company is manufacturing iron nails, and its basic raw material is iron rods. In the drawing machine, these rods may be drawn (stretched) and, thus, these may become thinner and thinner in three to four processes, when these may come to the required diameter. Then, these thinner iron rods are to be cut into pieces of the required length of the nails. And then, while one end may be made pointed, the other end may be flattened to become the head of the nail. After completing all these processes the stocks of finished goods are ready for transportation to godowns or to company's sales outlets.

Thus, as the production process involves several stages, the aggregate quantum and value of raw materials, lying at different stages of production, taken together, comprise the stocks of process inventory.

And, thus, if the entire process (from the raw material stage till the stage immediately preceding the finished goods stage) takes say, ten days, and the average production of the item is 1000 units per day, the average quantity of such process inventories would be equal to:

Average stocks-in-process, multiplied by the time (days) required to complete all the processes, *i.e.* 1000×10 days = 10,000 units.

The relative formula that, emerges is:

$$\begin{bmatrix}\text{Average production process} \\ \text{(in terms of units or in terms of} \\ \text{total cost of such units)}\end{bmatrix} \times \begin{bmatrix}\text{Total time required for} \\ \text{completing all the} \\ \text{involved processes}\end{bmatrix}$$

That is, as per the above example, it would come to 1000 × 10 = 10,000 units.

And, presuming that the cost per unit is Rs. 5, the total value of the process inventory comes to:

(1000 units × Rs. 5 × 10 days) = Rs. 50,000

(a) (ii) Movement Inventories

Movement inventories are usually referred to as the inventories of finished goods, to be transferred from a factory to the company's godowns, warehouses or sales depots. Thus, if the average daily sales at the company's sales depot are 250 units and the transit time (for transporting the finished goods from the factory to the sales depots) is 10 days, the average movement inventories, as per the aforesaid formula, would be:

250 units × 10 days = 2500 units, or

250 units × Rs. 5 × 10 days = Rs. 12,500.

(b) Organisation of Inventories

Organisation of inventories, comprise the items of raw materials and finished goods stored and stocked in the company's godowns, to be supplied to the factory or to the sales depots, as and when required in specific quantity, weight, volume, etc. of the specific items of raw materials and finished goods.

The moment the stocks of raw materials and finished goods are issued from the company's godown(s), these items are excluded from the organisation inventories and these, in turn, are included in the process inventories, though these raw materials may actually be put into the production process a little later, or in the movement inventories, even if the stocks of the finished goods may be lying in the company's show-rooms, unsold.

Now, a question that may arise could be that if the inventory carrying cost is so huge and material to affect the profitability of the company, favourably or unfavourably, why should the companies, at all, have organisation inventories, too, in addition to the process inventories and movement inventories. And, the answer, too, is very simple and logical. That is, to make the decision-making process of planning (of purchases of raw materials and level of stocking of various items of finished goods) and scheduling of successive operations of production, even more free and flexible. This also facilitates bifurcation of the functions of purchase of raw materials and production plan into two separate departments, to be managed by the respective experts in each department.

Thus, while the production department may just give its production schedule to the purchase department, it would be the sole responsibility of the purchase department to decide about the quantum of such purchases and the stockists to purchase from. This means, if the stocks sometimes are available at a cheaper price during the harvesting seasons of the respective agricultural products, etc., the purchase department may even purchase the materials in a much larger quantity than required by the production department just for a fortnight or a month. The purchase department can decide whether to go in for such purchases to avail of the bulk discount or the cash discount, etc., whenever offered. Similarly, the purchase department may make purchases locally for a week only, to meet the immediate demands of production, if, by that time, bulk purchases may be made available at a much cheaper rate. Similarly, in an inflationary condition, the purchase people may exercise their prudence and expertise to buy larger quantity than required, if goods are available sufficiently at lower prices, taking into account the quantum of inflation, etc. That is, it would augur well if the purchase people could also know the fundamentals of cost-benefit analysis to be made in this regard, as also as to what factors should be taken into consideration, like time-value of money, rate of inflation and the total inventory carrying costs, etc.

This much about the rationale behind keeping the organisation inventory of stocks of raw materials, and delinking the purchase functions and the production functions.

Now, let us discuss about the rationale behind keeping organisation inventories of finished goods. It is a well-known fact that, in order to have some edge over the competitors, companies have to keep some items in ready stock so as to be able to supply these to the customers from the shelf, at least to meet their immediate requirements, and the balance to be supplied later. This is important because, keeping huge numbers of items in ready stock is fraught with grave risks of obsolescence, expiry of shelf-life, etc. Further, by virtue of having some organisation inventory of finished foods, the companies are able to delink the production schedule from marketing activities.

Thus, by delinking the purchase activities from those of production and production activities from those of marketing, the companies may be able to optimise their profitability by enabling the experts in different departments to plan things in such a way that the profitability of the company could be optimised and each departmental experts can concentrate on their respective work, of course, keeping the overall interests and requirements of other departments in view inasmuch as all the departments are inter-dependent with each other.

At this stage, it may be quite pertinent to examine the rationale behind keeping the in-process inventory, too, though these do not constitute a part of the organisation inventory as such.

Let us, at the very outset, clarify that though the in-process inventory refers to work-in-process inventory only, it is different from the process or movement inventory, discussed earlier, even though a part of the work-in-process inventory may represent process or movement inventory, too.

Now, as regards the rationale behind keeping the in-process inventory, it may be mentioned here that it provides some flexibility and latitude in the scheduling of production, so as to ensure efficient production schedule and higher capacity utilisation of plant and machinery. Further, in case there is no stock of in-process inventory, some bottlenecks may be caused sometime somewhere in the production process, which may ultimately result in delay in production and non-utilisation of the installed capacity at the optimum possible level. These factors will naturally adversely affect the financial gains of the company.

6.3 ECONOMIC ORDER QUANTITY (EOQ)

In regard to the management of inventories, specially the inventories of raw materials, two primary questions arise. They are:

(*a*) Order size, *i.e.* what should be the ideal size of the order? and

(*b*) Order level, *i.e.* at what level of the stocks should the next order be placed?

But, before deliberating to find out answers to the above questions, let us first try to understand the distinguishing features of the three types of costs involved in the management of inventories:

(*i*) Ordering costs,

(*ii*) (Inventory) carrying costs, and

(*iii*) Shortage costs.

Let us now discuss these costs, in detail, one by one.

1. Ordering Costs

Ordering costs pertain to the placement of an order for the purchase of certain items of raw materials. These include the expenses in respect of the following items:

(*i*) Cost of requisitioning the items(s).

(*ii*) Cost of preparation of purchase order, *i.e.* drafting, typing, despatch, postage, etc.

(*iii*) Cost of sending reminders to get the dispatch of items(s) expedited.

(*iv*) Cost of transportation of goods.

(*v*) Cost of receiving and verifying the goods.

(*vi*) Cost of unloading the item(s) of goods.

(*vii*) Storage and stacking charges, etc.

However, in case of items manufactured in-house, *i.e.* by the same company, the ordering costs would comprise the following costs:

(*i*) Requisitioning cost.

(*ii*) Set-up cost.

(*iii*) Cost of receiving and verifying the items.

(*iv*) Cost of placing and arranging/stacking items in our store, etc.

2. Carrying Costs of inventories

Inventory carrying costs include expenses incurred on the following items:

(*i*) Capital cost (*i.e.* interest on capital locked up in inventories).

(*ii*) Storage cost.

(*iii*) Cost of insurance, fire and theft insurance of stocks.

(*iv*) Obsolescence cost.

(*v*) Taxes, etc.

It may, however, be mentioned here that the carrying costs usually constitute around 25 per cent of the value of inventories held.

3. Shortage Costs (or costs of stockout)

Shortage costs or costs of stockout are such costs which a company incurs in case of shortage of certain items of raw materials required for production, or the shortage of certain items of finished goods to meet the immediate demands of the customers.

Shortage of inventories of raw materials may affect the company in one or more of the following ways:

(*i*) It may have to pay somewhat higher price, connected with immediate procurements.

(*ii*) It may have to compulsorily resort to some different production schedules, which may not be as efficient and economical.

Stock out of finished goods, however, may result in the dissatisfaction of customers and the resultant loss of sales.

However, it is relatively very difficult to measure the shortage cost when it results due to the failure to meet the demands of customers instantaneously out of the existing stocks. This is so because, such costs may have the ramifications, both in the short-term as also in the long-term. Besides, these costs are somewhat intangible in nature, and consequently difficult to assess quantitatively.

It has also been observed that some of the companies, with a view to reduce the total ordering costs, prefer to order larger quantities. But, in this way the level of inventory becomes higher, thus increasing the inventory carrying costs. Further, if the company decides to carry a safety stock of inventory so as to mitigate or reduce the stock out costs, or shortage costs, its carrying costs, in turn, goes up further.

Thus, with a view to keep the total costs, pertaining to management of inventory, at the minimum level, we may have to arrive at the optimal level where the total costs, *i.e.* total ordering costs plus total inventory carrying costs, are minimal.

To achieve this end-result, we may have to work out the Economic Order Quantity (EOQ).

6.4 BASIC ECONOMIC ORDER QUANTITY (EOQ) MODEL

At the very outset, I would like to clarify here that we are going to discuss only the basic EOQ model, one of the simplest inventory models. There are, in fact, a large number of other inventory models, depending upon various variables and assumptions. We, however, propose to discuss only the basic EOQ model in this book.

Assumptions of the Basic EOQ Model

It may be further clarified here that the basic EOQ model is based on various assumptions, which are given hereunder:

(*i*) The estimate of usage (demand or consumption) of the items of inventory for a given period (usually one year) is known accurately.

(*ii*) The usage (demand or consumption of the various items of inventory) is equal (even) throughout the period.

(*iii*) There is no lead time involved. That is, the item of inventory can be supplied immediately on receipt of the order itself; there being virtually no time lag between placing of an order and the receipt of the goods. Consequently, there is no likelihood of stock out, at any stage. Therefore, the shortage cost, or stock out cost, is not being taken into account, as if it is 'nil'.

(*iv*) Thus, there remains only two distinct costs involved in computing the total costs, pertaining to inventory, viz.:

(*a*) Ordering cost, and

(*b*) Inventory carrying cost.

(*v*) Further, the cost of every order remains uniformly the same, irrespective of the size of the order.

(*vi*) And, finally, the inventory carrying cost is a fixed percentage of the average value of inventory.

6.5 EOQ FORMULA vs. TRIAL AND ERROR METHOD

It may be observed that the EOQ can be ascertained in two distinct ways:

(*i*) By trial and error methods, discussed immediately hereafter, and

(*ii*) By use of a definite formula, discussed thereafter.

Trial and Error Methods

Let us understand the 'trial and error' methods with the help of an **illustrative example.**

Example 1

The annual sales of Friends Electricals (Private) Limited, is estimated at 1800 units, the cost price per unit is Rs. 80.00. The ordering cost per order is Rs. 60.00 and the inventory carrying cost per unit is Rs. 2.00.

Solution

The company has a number of options. For example, it may decide to procure its entire annual requirement of 1800 units in one go, in which case the ordering cost will be minimal but the inventory carrying cost will be the highest. Similarly, if it were to order for its monthly requirements, the ordering cost will be twelve times higher, but the inventory carrying cost will be much less. Thus, the total costs, *i.e.* ordering costs and carrying costs will vary in the aforesaid manner in all the cases, when the numbers of orders vary from 1 to 12. But, the main purpose behind the exercise is to find out that specific number of order and the quantity ordered each time on which the carrying cost depends, such that the total of both these costs is at the minimal level.

Now, let us work out the total costs at different numbers of order and the level of stocks of inventory, with the 'trial and error' approach, instead of taking the help of the EOQ formula.

The information given in the example is:

Annual Sales or Usage (U)	— 1800 units
Inventory Carrying Cost per unit (C)	— Rs. 2.00
Ordering Cost per order (F)	— Rs. 60.00

Table 6.1: Total Costs at Different Number(s) of Order

Quantity Ordered (Q)	1800	900	600	450	360	300	225	200	180	150
Average Inventory (Q/2)	900	450	300	225	180	150	112.5	100	90	75
No. of Orders (U/Q)	1	2	3	4	5	6	8	9	10	12
(*i*) Annual Carrying Cost (Rs.) [C × (Q/2)]	1800	900	600	450	360	300	225	200	180	150
(*ii*) Annual Ordering Cost (Rs.) [F × (U/Q)]	60	120	180	240	300	360	480	540	600	720
TOTAL (Annual) Cost (Rs.) (*i* + *ii*)	**1860**	**1020**	**780**	**690**	**660**	**660**	**705**	**740**	**780**	**870**

Thus, we find that the total cost at Rs. 660.00 is the lowest in two different cases, viz. when 5 or 6 orders are placed. The EOQ comes to 360 units *i.e.*(1800 ÷ 5) or 300 units *i.e.* (1800 ÷ 6), respectively, when 5 or 6 orders are placed. That is, in the case of placing 5 orders per annum, while the ordering cost is less as compared to 6 orders, the inventory carrying cost is naturally relatively higher, because the quantity per order will be higher when lesser number of orders are placed.

But, as we have just seen, the trial and error method is a little too cumbersome, tedious and time consuming, and specially so when, in the actual practice, the various factors, given in the above example, are not so simple and in round figures.

Therefore, it will be worth while to take the help of the EOQ formula to compute the EOQ, even with a more complicated data, as we face in the real life.

EOQ Formula

The EOQ formula is:

$$Q = \sqrt{(2FU) \div (PC)}$$

where: Q = Quantity Ordered

F = Cost per Order (which is presumed to be fixed or constant)

U = Annual Usage or Sales

P = Price per Unit

C = Per cent Carrying Cost (*i.e.* PC = Inventory Carrying Cost, itself).

By computing the given values in the formula, we get

$$Q = \sqrt{(2 \times 60 \times 1800) \div (2)}$$

$$Q = 328.63$$

or say, 329.

Therefore, the number of orders required to be placed during the year will be 1800 ÷ 329, which comes to 5.47 orders. But, the number of orders will have to be an integer, that is, it would be either 5 or 6.

And, by computing the total cost in the event of placing 5 and 6 orders separately, we get the total cost at the same 660 in both the cases. Therefore, EOQ will be 1800 ÷ 6 = 300 units, as also 1800 ÷ 5 = 360 units.

Example 2

Let us now work out yet another example, where all the figures are the same as in Example 1, except that the inventory carrying cost is Rs. 3.00 per unit.

Thus, the only change that will occur will be in the column 'Annual Carrying Cost', which would go up by 150% in this case.

Solution

The detailed figures are given in Table 6.2 hereunder:

Table 6.2

Quantity Ordered (Q)	1800	900	600	450	360	300	256	225	200	180	150
Average Inventory (Q/2)	900	450	300	225	180	150	128	112.5	100	90	75
No. of Orders (U/Q)	1	2	3	4	5	6	7	8	9	10	12
(*i*) Annual Carrying Cost (Rs.) [C × (Q/2)]	2700	1350	900	675	540	450	384	337.5	300	270	225
(*ii*) Annual Ordering Cost (Rs.) [F × (U/Q)]	60	120	180	240	300	360	420	480	540	600	720
TOTAL (Annual) Cost (Rs.) (*i* + *ii*)	**2760**	**1470**	**1080**	**915**	**840**	**810**	**804**	**817.5**	**840**	**870**	**945**

Thus, we find that the total cost is the lowest at Rs. 804.00 when seven orders are placed per annum.

Incidentally, we further observe that even in the case of placing 6 and 8 orders the total cost is only slightly higher at Rs. 810.00 and Rs. 817.50 respectively. And, in the case of placement of even 5 or 9 orders, the total cost go up but only marginally at Rs. 840.00 in each case. Thus, we can conclude that it would not make much of a difference whether we place 5, 6, 7, 8 or 9 orders, per annum, when the order size will be 360, 300, 256, 225 and 200, respectively. The total costs, however, are different in each case, but they will fall in the range of Rs. 804.00 to Rs. 840.00 only, which is not a very significant difference. So, we can safely say that there is not an 'Economic Order Point (EOP)', but an 'Economic Order Range (EOR)'. A much detailed discussion on this point appears a little later in this Chapter.

Let us now solve Example 2 with the help of the formula. By computing the respective values in the formula, we get:

$$Q = \sqrt{(2FU) \div (PC)}$$

$$Q = \sqrt{2 \times 60 \times 1800 \div (3)}$$

$$Q = 268.33$$

Or say 269 units (Unit being an integer)

Thus, we get the number of orders to be placed per annum at 1800 ÷ 269 = 6.69, or say, 7 orders (an integer).

Therefore, the EOQ will be equal to 1800 ÷ 7 = 257.14 or say 257 (an integer).

6.6 EOQ FORMULA—HOW DERIVED?

Now, let us see how the EOQ formula has evolved.

We have already seen that the total costs involved comprise only two costs, *i.e.*

Total costs = Ordering cost + Carrying cost.

Now, let us see as to what actually is the ordering cost?

As we have already presumed, as stated above, the ordering cost is constant irrespective of the order size, the total ordering cost will be simply the number of orders × cost per order.

Now, how to estimate the number of orders. This, too, is simple enough. It can well be found out by dividing the quantum of annual usage (U), with the quantity ordered (Q), per order.

And, how to compute the second cost, *i.e.* the inventory carrying cost? We have already presumed it to be a fixed percentage of the average value of inventory. So, we should try to find out the average value of inventory. It would be nothing but just half of the quantity ordered. This would be so, because we shall place the next order only when the level of stock holding shall be 'nil'.

Supposing the ordered quantity (Q) is 50 kg. and it lasts just for 5 days. Thus, on the start of the day one, it would be 50 kgs, on the start of the second day it would be 40 kgs, and so on, so that on the start of the fifth day it would be 10 and at end of the fifth day it would come to zero, when the next order is placed and the stocks are replenished (50 kgs. again) instantaneously, at the start of the sixth day, as we have already presumed earlier (though it does not happen so in the real life situations). Thus, the average value of inventory held over a period of 5 days, as presumed, will be as under:

Table 6.3

At the end of the day	*The balance stocks would be (in kg.)*
1	40
2	30
3	20
4	10
5	NIL
TOTAL	**100 ÷ 4 = 25** **50 ÷ 2 = 25**

So the average inventory holding, spread over a period of five days, comes to [(40 + 30 + 20 + 10) ÷ (4)] = 25, which, in turn, is equal to Q/2, *i.e.* 50 ÷ 2 = 25.

Thus, the EOQ formula evolved is as under:

$$TC = \left(\frac{U}{Q} \times F\right) + \left(\frac{Q}{2} \times P \times C\right)$$

(*i.e.* Total Cost = (Ordering Cost) + (Inventory Carrying Cost), where

U = Annual consumption (usage)

Q = Quantity ordered

F = Cost per order (which is fixed, *i.e.* constant)

C = Per cent carrying cost

P = Price per unit.

The first term on the right hand side gives us the Ordering Cost which is equal to number of orders (U/Q) multiplied by (fixed) cost per order (F). And the second term, on the right hand side, represents the (inventory) Carrying Cost which is equal to average value of inventory holding (Q/2) multiplied by price per unit (P) which comes to QP/2 and again multiplied by percentage carrying cost (C). And, ordering cost + carrying cost gives us the total cost. Simple!

Now, the question that remains to be addressed, is to find out the exact order quantity which will be most economical (EOQ), *i.e.* where the total costs (ordering costs + carrying costs) will be minimal.

To find this out the following formula will be of great help.

$$Q = \sqrt{\frac{2FU}{PC}}$$

Now, let us try to understand as to how the EOQ formula has evolved.

To find it out, let us examine the various steps involved in evolving the above formula:

As we already know, we find out the Total Cost (TC) as under:

$$TC = \frac{U}{Q} \times F + \frac{Q}{2} \times P \times C$$

Differentiating the equation with respect to Q, we get.

$$\frac{dTC}{dQ} = (-)\frac{UF}{Q^2} + \frac{PC}{2} = 0$$

or $$(-)2UF + Q^2PC = 0$$

or $$Q^2PC = 2UF$$

or $$Q^2 = \frac{2UF}{PC}$$

or $$Q = \sqrt{\frac{2UF}{PC}}$$

Now, let us understand the application of the EOQ formula by taking an **illustrative example** of Virtual Company (P) Limited.

Example 3

Annual sales of the Virtual Company (P) Limited is 50,000 units. The ordering cost per order is Rs. 5,000. Purchase price per unit is Rs. 20. Inventory carrying cost is 25 per cent of the inventory value.

Solution

That is; U = 50,000 units
F = Rs. 5,000
P = Rs. 20
C = 25 per cent

Now, by computing these values in the EOQ formula, we get

$$Q = \sqrt{\frac{2\,FU}{PC}}$$

$$= \sqrt{\frac{2 \times 5{,}000 \times 50{,}000}{20 \times 0.25}}$$

$$\therefore \text{ EOQ} = 10{,}000 \text{ units.}$$

6.7 ECONOMIC ORDER QUANTITY (EOQ) AND OPTIMUM ORDER QUANTITY (OOQ)

The standard EOQ analysis is based on the assumption that no discount is given, howsoever large the order size be. But, in most of the cases, some discount is given by way of an incentive to the buyers to order for a larger quantity, so as to avail of some bulk discount. Thus, we should try to modify the standard EOQ formula so as to find out the EOQ as also to assess whether it would be economical to avail of the bulk discount or not.

To arrive at the required data we should follow the following steps:

Step 1

First, find out the EOQ by applying the standard EOQ formula.

Let us call it Q@.

Step 2

If Q@, *i.e.* the usual EOQ itself is equal to or larger than the minimum quantity upon which the discount is available, the EOQ will be the OOQ, *i.e.* the required quantity to be ordered and to avail of the bulk discount too.

Step 3

And, if the EOQ, *i.e.* Q@ is less than the minimum order size, on which the discount is available, we may have to calculate whether the quantum of bulk discount is sufficient enough to trade off the higher inventory carrying cost plus slightly lower ordering cost (because, bigger the order size, smaller will be the number of orders required to be placed).

Let us call the minimum quantity on which the discount is available as Q@ @. Therefore, we should see whether any change in the savings (due to the increase in the order size and higher inventory carrying cost, and the corresponding decrease in the number of orders and the resultant savings in the ordering cost, and the total discount available on such purchases, would prove to be profitable or otherwise.

To compute this, we may apply the under-noted formula:

$$\Delta\pi = UD + \left[\frac{U}{Q@} - \frac{U}{Q@@}\right]F - \left[\frac{Q@@(P-D)C}{2} - \frac{Q@PC}{2}\right]$$

where

$\Delta\pi$ = Change in profit

U = Annual usage/requirement

D = Discount per unit when quantity discount is available

Q@ = Economic Order Quantity (EOQ) when no quantity discount is available

Q@@ = Minimum order size required for quantity discount

F = Fixed cost per order

P = Unit purchase price without discount

C = Inventory carrying cost expressed as percentage

Thus, we see that on the right hand side of the above equation:

(*i*) the first term denotes savings in price,

(*ii*) the second term represents savings in ordering cost, and

(*iii*) the third term represents an increase in the inventory carrying cost.

Step 4

Thus, if the change in profit comes to a positive figure, Q@@ will be the optimal order quantity (OOQ), which means that the quantum of total discount on the larger size of order is more than the resultant higher inventory carrying cost and slightly lower ordering cost taken together. And, accordingly, if the change in profit, thus arrived at, is negative, *i.e.* loss, the Q@, *i.e.* the standard EOQ itself, will be the Optimal Order Quantity (OOQ).

Let us bring home the point by means of an **illustrative example** given hereunder:

Example 1

The respective data pertaining to IXL Company Ltd. are as follows:

U	annual usage	= 25,000 units
F	fixed cost per order	= Rs. 300
P	purchase price per unit	= Rs. 60
C	inventory carrying cost	= 25% of the value of inventory
Q@@	minimum order size required to be eligible for the quantity discount)	= 1,000 units
D	discount per unit	= Rs. 4

Solution

Let us now compute the EOQ, without quantity discount:

$$Q@ = \sqrt{\frac{2\,FU}{PC}}$$

$$= \sqrt{(2 \times 300 \times 25000) \div (60 \times 0.25)}$$

$$= \sqrt{10{,}00{,}000}$$

$$= 1{,}000$$

As the Economic Order Quantity (EOQ), without quantity discount, is 1,000 units, which is equal to the minimum quantity eligible for the quantity discount, *i.e.* 1,000 the EOQ itself will be the Optimum Order Quantity (OOQ).

Example 2

We take another example where every figure is the same as in Example 1, except that the minimum order size required to be eligible for quantity discount is 10,000 units, instead of 1,000 units, what would be the OOQ in this case?

Solution

Step 1

EOQ = 1,000 units (as already calculated in Solution 1).

Step 2

But EOQ (1,000 units) is less than the minimum quantity eligible for the discount.

Step 3

We will, therefore, take the help of the following formula and compute the relative values therein, to arrive at a decision:

$$\begin{aligned}
\Delta\pi &= UD + [(U \div Q\text{@}) - (U \div Q\text{@@})]\,F - [\{Q\text{@@}\,(P - D)C\} \div 2] \\
&\quad \{Q\text{@}\,PC \div 2\} \\
&= (25000 \times 4) + [(25000 \div 1000) - (25000 \div 10000)]\ 300\ (-) \\
&\quad [\{1000\,(60 - 4) \times 0.25\} \div 2\ (-)\ \{(1000 \times 60 \times 0.25) \div 2\}] \\
&= 100000 + [25 - 2.5]\ 300\ (-)\ [(10000 \times 56 \times 0.25) \div 2\ (-)\ (1000 \times 15) \div 2] \\
&= [100000 + 6750]\ (-)\ [70000 - 7500] \\
&= 106750 - 62500 \\
&= \text{Rs. } 44250.
\end{aligned}$$

Step 4

Now that, the resultant figure is a positive one, it suggests that by ordering 10,000 units, the company stands to gain Rs. 44,250.

Therefore, the company should go in for 10,000 units. Thus, the OOQ in this case is 10,000 units.

Economic Order Quantity (EOQ) and Inflation

The EOQ analysis presumes that the cost price per unit is constant. This implies that the incidence of inflation has not been taken into account. In order to account for inflation, what we have to do is to first substract the rate of inflation from C the annual inventory carrying cost expressed as a percentage and apply the standard EOQ formula with this simple modification only.

Why do we substract the rate of inflation from C? The reason is simple enough. In an inflationary condition, the purchase price of inventory goes up and to some extent, it offsets the inventory carrying cost.

6.8 A NEW CLUE TO EOQ

One day, I thought of examining whether the formula for finding out the Economic Order Quantity (EOQ) viz. $\sqrt{\dfrac{2FU}{PC}}$ [where F is the fixed cost per order, U is the annual usage, P is the purchase price per unit, and C is the inventory carrying cost], was actually giving us the one and only one quantity, where the total costs (ordering cost and inventory carrying cost), were the minimal, of course, presuming that certain other variables remained unchanged.

So, I took an illustrative example, given hereunder, and started working it out, not only with the help of the formula, but also by trial and error method, side by side, and the result was, as worked out, in detail, immediately thereafter.

Example

Find out the 'Economic Order Quantity' in respect of a company whose:

Annual usage (U) is	15,000 units
Inventory carrying cost (PC) per unit is	Rs. 2, and
Ordering cost (F) per order is	Rs. 40.

Suggested Solution (step-by-step)

Step 1

Find out the EOQ, first with the help of the formula:

$$\text{EOQ} = \sqrt{\frac{2\text{FU}}{\text{PC}}} = \sqrt{\frac{2 \times 40 \times 15{,}000}{2}}$$

$$= 774.59 = \text{or say } 775\text{, an integer.}$$

Step 2

Then, find out the number of orders per annum based on the EOQ, *i.e.* $\frac{15{,}000}{775} = 19.35$ or say, 20 orders (an integer).

Step 3

Now, calculate the EOQ by finding out the Total Costs at 17, 18, 19, 20 and 21, 22, 23 orders, *i.e.* at 3 lower and 3 higher nos. of orders than 20 orders.

Table 6.4

No. of Orders	17	18	19	20	21	22	23
(*i*) Ordering cost	680	720	760	800	840	880	920
(*ii*) Carrying cost of quantity per order,	(1764.70)	(1666.66)	(1578.95)	(1500)	(1428.57)	(1363.64)	(1304.35)
(*iii*) or say, integers (rounded off)	1765	1667	1579	1500	1429	1364	1304
Total (*i* + *iii*)	**2445**	**2387**	**2339**	**2300**	**2269**	**2244**	**2224**

Thus, we see that there is a difference of just Rs. 39, or even less (which is quite insignificant) in the case of number of orders being in the range of 19 to 21 and the corresponding quantity being in the range of 2269 to 2339.

Thus, we may fairly conclude that the total costs of inventory are fairly insensitive to moderate changes in the order size. It may, therefore, be appropriate to say that there is an 'Economic Order Range (EOR)' and not an 'Economic Order Point (EOP)'. In the instant case, the EOR comes to 19 to 21 orders 2269 to 2331.

This illustrative example throws yet another conclusion that the EOQ, found out by the universally accepted formula, as aforesaid, *i.e.* 775 units is, in fact, not the real EOQ, *i.e.* where the total costs are minimal. The real EOQ is 750 units, instead. That is, while at 750 units per order the number of orders comes to 20, in case of 775 units per order, the number of order comes to 19.35, *i.e.* say, 20 again (as the number of orders can't be a non-integer, and so has to be rounded off to the nearest integer). Thus, while in both the cases the ordering cost remains the same, the inventory carrying cost at 775 units per order is decidedly higher than 750 units.

Under the circumstances, it will augur well if we do not straightaway conclude that the EOQ is the exact quantity where the total costs are minimal. Instead, we should follow the following steps:

Step 1

After arriving at the EOQ (775 in the instant case) find out the number of orders required at such a point.

Step 2

If the resultant number of orders happens to be a non-integer, *i.e.* 19.35, then round it off to the nearest integer, *i.e.* 20.

Step 3

And, then again calculate the resultant quantity required per order, *i.e.* 750 as against 775 in the instant case. It is only then that we can arrive at the actual EOQ.

We thus get at a new clue to EOQ. Or, at least, in this way we have been able to put across an old well known fact, in a new, different and succinct manner.

6.9 COMPONENTS OF INVENTORY CARRYING COSTS

Inventory carrying costs comprise various items, some of which are given hereunder:

(*i*) **Storage Costs:** That is, the rental payable will be proportionately higher as more space would be required to store higher level of inventory.

(*ii*) **Handling Charges:** When higher stocks are stored, handling charges, like unloading and stacking charges, at the time of receipt of the goods, etc., involving manpower may also go up.

(*iii*) **Insurance Premium:** Similarly, the amount of insurance premium payable for fire insurance, theft insurance, flood and such other natural calamity insurance, etc., will also be higher.

(*iv*) **Wastages:** It has generally been observed that if more than sufficient stocks of inventory are stored, there is a usual tendency to consume more than what is actually required, resulting in extra avoidable wastages.

To bring home the point, let us take a common place example. Supposing there is a huge stock of medical bills pro forma, these may, at times, be used even as paper plates, etc. But, if these proforma were in short supply, people may take care not to waste a single form.

(*v*) **Damage and Deterioration:** In the event of storing more than required level of stocks of raw materials and finished goods, there is a chance that the goods may deteriorate in quality, like the whiteness of papers gets diminished (it turns yellowish) with the passage of time. Some chemicals or medicines also have limited shelf-life, whereafter these may turn useless. Stocks of cement, in rainy season, are fraught with grave risk of turning into stones, and, thus becoming useless.

(*vi*) **Technical Obsolescence:** In the modern age of technological advancements, the pace of goods and commodities becoming obsolete has become fast enough. Thus, more than necessary stocks run the risk of becoming obsolete and consequently of much lesser value and use.

(*vii*) **Blockage of Funds:** And, above all, more than necessary funds, blocked in inventory, may pose liquidity problems to the companies. It may involve some loss by way of payment of interest as well as opportunity costs.

Advantages of High Inventories

But, at the same time, it may be argued that there are several reasons which may justify stocking of higher level of inventories of raw materials and finished goods.

Bulk Purchase

For example, you may get bulk discount, making the average costs of the stocks much cheaper. But then, one should not lose sight of the fact that, in such a case, there are several inventory carrying costs involved (like wastages, damages and deterioration, loss of interest and opportunity cost, etc.), which may offset the advantages of bulk purchases.

An arrangement may be arrived at to make some bulk purchases on an annual basis, but on the condition that the supply will be spread over on a monthly basis. This may serve the twin purpose of enabling the buyer to avail of the bulk discount, without involving any avoidable extra inventory carrying costs and, at the same time, facilitating the seller to regulate its production and supplies accordingly, without making bulk supply, in one go.

Several other arguments could as well be advanced in favour of carrying higher level of inventory. **For example**:

(*i*) Purchases during the harvesting season of crops may be much cheaper.

But, we should not lose sight of the risk of damages and deterioration of stocks and the loss by way of interest and opportunity cost.

(*ii*) The possibility cf stock will be minimal and consequently the stock out cost. But again, care must be taken to see that such savings do not fall short of the extra higher inventory carrying costs involved.

(*iii*) In an inflationary economy, it may be prudent to stock more than required level of inventories of raw materials. But, the extra interest payable and/or loss by way of opportunity cost may nullify such advantages.

(*iv*) There may be less number of orders required to be placed, saving a lot on ordering cost, and consequently on follow-up problems of delivery and handling charges, etc. But, much can be argued against such arguments too.

Similarly, one may argue that it may make much sense to stock higher level of inventories of finished goods also, whereby one may meet the supply of customers out of the shelf, and thereby may have an edge over the competitors.

Example

We must, however, bear in mind the case of a company, which had reaped some advantages in the initial stages. But then, all these gains were wiped off once the stocks of such extra finished goods became obsolete and costlier, due to technological advancement, making the substitute products cheaper and even better.

In conclusion, the 'golden mean' can be the main *'mantra'* in deciding upon the optimal levels of stocks of raw materials and finished goods.

6.10 LEAD TIME

Lead time is the time lag that takes place between the placement of an order and the actual supply/delivery made in the company's godown. Supposing, an order is processed at our end and is placed to the supplier today. The supplier's office will also take its own time in processing the order plus loading, transporting and unloading, etc. Supposing it takes, around 15 days in completing all these processes and the goods are delivered and stored in our godown(s) on the 16th day in the instant case, the lead time would be said to be 16 days.

But, as we have seen earlier, the standard EOQ model presumes as if there is no lead time involved. And thus, the order can well be placed when the inventory level comes to zero. But, the factual position is otherwise. Therefore, we should decidedly take into account the lead time, too, while computing EOQ. This can well be done by introducing a slight modification in the standard EOQ analysis to arrive at a realistic ordering point, so as to take care of the lead time involved and thereby to mitigate the risk of shortage of stocks, involving stockout costs.

6.11 ORDER POINT

This can well be done by ensuring that the order is placed when sufficient balance of stock is still left to take care of the lead time. But, for doing so accurately, we may have to know the rate of usage of materials as also the lead time, exactly and in definite terms. In that case, the ordering level would simply be as under:

Lead time (in number of days for procurement) multiplied by average usage per day.

i.e. Order Point = Lead time (in days) × Daily usage.

6.12 SAFETY STOCK

But then, in actual practice, one can neither estimate the lead time nor the daily usage so accurately and exactly. We can, at best, make some reasonable estimates. But, in that case, the possibility of some error, howsoever small, can hardly be eliminated completely.

And, therefore, we should, to be on the safer side, take into account the element of such uncertainty, too. Accordingly, we should always keep some safety stock with us to meet such eventualities.

And, as such, the order point should be computed by adding the quantum of sufficient safety stocks, too.

Thus, the order point can well be computed as:

EOQ + [Lead Time (in days) × Daily Usage] + Safety Stock.

How to compute the safety stock? In fact, it is a managerial decision and, therefore, it largely depends upon the inventory policy as also the organisational culture of the company. It may accordingly be high or low, or even medium.

Example

It has, however, been usually observed that in most of the Indian companies, and specially so in the Public Sector Undertakings (PSUs), there is a general tendency, on the part of the management, to keep sufficiently high level of safety stocks. The main reason for such a situation is said to be the fact that, while no questions are asked if more than necessary stocks of inventories are held in a company, several accusing fingers are raised, in case there happens to be a stock out, even for a day, resulting in some loss in production, which, in turn, adversely affects the profitability of the company. Let us, now examine the wisdom, or otherwise, of such tendencies in our companies.

Let us presume that the Chairman and Managing Director (CMD) of a company asks his Materials Manager that in case a safety stock of only 15 days is kept, what is the likelihood of stock out risk, in terms of days of production loss. And, the response is, say, 7 days on an average, and 10 days in extreme cases. However, the risk goes on reducing when the safety stock is kept for 1 month, 1.5 months, 2 months and 2.5 months, and the corresponding stock out risk, comes down to say 6 days, 4 days, 2 days and almost 'nil', respectively, and that, too, in extreme cases.

Thus, to be on the safer side, the CEO may decide to keep a safety stock of, say, full 3 months, whereby the possibility of stock out is considered to be zero. Some other CEOs may prefer to have a safety stock of even 3.5 months or even 4 months, in such a case.

Some of us may tend to feel that, such CEO's, perhaps, have little idea about the high inventory carrying cost involved in such a decision, and its cascading effect on the profitability of the company. But, in my considered view, this is not the case. In fact, the anxiety (or over-anxiety), on the part of the CEO, that he may lose his job, in the event of even a single day's stock out, he wants to play it safe, nay, over safe rather. And, rightly so, inasmuch as, in most of the cases (of even a single day's stock out) some questions may be asked, even in the Parliament, raising accusing fingers at the CEO, in the name of national loss, damaging the national economy, etc.

To conclude, let us examine the situation from another angle. Supposing, there is the production loss to the extent of Rs. 10 million per day. But, at the same time, let us take the inventory carrying cost to be to the tune of say, Rs. 5 million per day. Thus, if there is a stock out of even 6 days in extreme cases, if the safety stock is kept for one month only, such loss may amount to Rs. 60 million [(Rs. 10 million (per day) × 6 (days)]. But, if we consider the savings made in the area of inventory carrying cost by having a safety stock of only one month, instead of say, full three months, it may amount to Rs. 5 million multiplied by 60 (taking 30 days to a month), *i.e.* Rs. 300 million, resulting in a net saving of Rs. 240 million (Rs. 300 million less Rs. 60 million).

In a private sector company, the enlightened management may appreciate the business sense involved in such an argument. However, it is very difficult to say whether the government and other related parties like M.Ps, ministers and administrators would also take their stands on similar lines. Perhaps not. But then, they must, if they want to sustain themselves and survive in the business world. Otherwise, as Mr Roosy Mody, the former M.D. of TISCO, has so succinctly put it, "The government has no business to be in the business of business". Let the PSUs and the government wake up and realise their mistake and make amends, sooner the better.

This, however, does not mean that we should try to cut it too fine. Otherwise, a lot of valuable time of the Materials Manager and the Purchase Department would get wasted in the fire-fighting operations in procuring the materials, in the nick of time, and incur the avoidable expenses relating to such crash purchases.

The best policy, to keep the safety stock, would ideally be neither 'too much', nor 'too little', but 'just right'. But, it is easy said than done. However, I am of the considered opinion that, by some trial and error method, we may be able to arrive at a nearly optimal level of safety stocks, in due course of time.

6.13 OTHER VARIABLE FACTORS AFFECTING EOQ

In finding out the EOQ or order level or safety stock, etc., we have, in the preceding pages, made certain assumptions that some other factors do not vary, though in practice they do. Therefore, it would always be prudent enough to consider the following variable factors, too, while taking a particular decision. They are:

1. **Restrictions Imposed by the Reserve Bank of India (RBI) and the Government:** The Reserve Bank of India (RBI), and the Government of India, with a view to arrest inflation or steep rise in the prices of certain essential commodities, like food grains (rice, wheat, maize, etc.), onion, etc., may resort to some changes in their Selective Credit Control Policies, instructing the banks to retain higher percentage as margin on such stocks advanced against, as also by fixing some ceiling on the maximum amount that could be advanced against the security of some commodities specified, to a single borrower, as also to fix a lower ceiling on holding of such stocks by a single party, so as to restrict hoarding, and consequently the steep rise in the price. Such a statutory restriction exercise limitation on companies in formulating their inventory policy.
2. **Expected Scarcity:** In case certain material is expected to be in short supply in the near future, it would be a prudent policy to stock a larger quantity of such material so as to avoid the stock out risk, as far as possible.

For example, Tata Engineering and Locomotive Company (TELCO), now Tata Motors, had procured stocks of Fuel Injection (FI) pumps for its trucks, produced by MICO industries, in a much larger quantity, the moment it sensed that some staff problem was brewing in their factory and that, most likely, this may ultimately culminate in strike by the workers, and/or lock out by the management, adversely affecting its own production of trucks for want of the Fuel Injection (FI) pumps of MICO.

3. **Fluctuating Prices:** Sometimes the price of certain commodity is expected to rise or fall, in the near future. Accordingly, the stocks of inventory of such items should be kept flexible, and adjusted accordingly, *i.e.* retaining higher or lower levels of such inventory.
4. **Risk of Obsolescence:** Certain items of raw materials may become obsolete with the passage of time. For example, jute packing has since been replaced by polythene matting in the carpet industries. The risk of obsolescence may be even higher and costlier in the case of finished goods in the modern age of technological advancements and stiff global competition. Such stocks should naturally be kept at the minimal possible level.

Example

I know of a company which had in their ready stock certain items of pump-sets, so as to make the supply of the goods to the customers, out of the shelf, and thereby to have an edge over the competitors. But then, the item had soon become obsolete, and the company had to suffer heavy losses, on this count alone.

Here, it may be emphasised that even if the policy of meeting the customers' demand is immediately taken to be the company's marketing strategy, instead of having a huge ready stocks of such finished goods, it would augur well if only a percentage of the market requirements could be kept in the ready stock to be supplied to the customers immediately, and the balance quantity could be produced on an emergency basis and supplied in a week's time or so. This way, the company may meet the competitive challenges, and avoid the risk of obsolescence.

6.14 ABC ANALYSIS (OR VED ANALYSIS)

ABC analysis is a very effective and useful tool for monitoring and control of inventories. As you must have observed, generally speaking, a very small percentage of the total number of items of inventory (say 10%) may account for a much larger percentage (say 65%) in terms of value. As against this, in case of certain other items of inventory, a very large percentage of the total number of items of inventory (say 70%) may account for a much smaller percentage (say 10%) in terms of their total value. And, likewise, a medium percentage of some items (say 20%) may account for a medium percentage (say 25%) in terms of their total value. These are classified under A, C and B categories. ABC analysis is also referred to as VED (Vital, Essential and Desirable) analysis.

We may put the aforesaid statements in a tabular form as under:

Table 6.5

Percentage, in Terms of Number of Items of Inventories (%)	*Percentage in Terms of Value of Inventories (%)*
A (V) 10	65
B (E) 20	25
C (D) 70	10
Total 100	**100**

The main (or even sole) purpose of classifying the inventories into A, B and C categories is to vary the pressure and intensity of control, in terms of the value of the items of inventory.

To put it differently, while the entire stocks (say 100%) of the items in Category 'A' must be very closely monitored and controlled, the monitoring and control of 10% of the items of Category 'C', could be considered enough to serve the purpose. And, in the case of 'B' category of items, the monitoring and control of, say, 25% of the item alone may be taken as sufficient.

The resultant effect of such a strategy is reflected, in Table 6.6:

Table 6.6

Category	*No. of Items (%)*	*In Terms of % of Total Value*	*% of Number of Items Monitored i.e. of Column (1)*	*% of Value that Get Monitored and Controlled in this Way, i.e. % of Column (2)*
0	1	2	3	4
A (V)	10%	65%	100% *i.e.* 10%	100% *i.e.* 65%
B (E)	20%	25%	25% *i.e.* 5%	25% *i.e.* 6.25% (or say, 6%)
C (D)	70%	10%	10% *i.e.* 7%	10% *i.e.* 0.7% or say, 1%
TOTAL	**100%**	**100%**	**22%**	**72%**

Thus, we see that, by effectively monitoring and controlling around 20% of the number of items of stocks, we have, as a result, exercised control on more than 70% of the total value of inventories. This is also based on the principle of increasing the pressure and intensity of control in accordance with the increasing value of items concerned. And, this is so, because usually, in our over-anxiety and over-enthusiasm of controlling everything, we may end up by controlling nothing.

After making an empirical study of items of inventory of a large number of companies, it has been observed that items in Category A generally account for 15% to 20% of the total number of items of inventory, but, in terms of the total annual usage value, these account for 60% to 75%. Similarly, items in Category B account for 20% to 30% (and 20% to 30%), and Category C items for 40% to 60% (and 10% to 15%) in terms of their total number (and their total annual usage), respectively.

In a tabular form, it may be presented as under:

Table 6.7

Category	*Percentage in Terms of Number (%)*	*Percentage in Terms of Total Annual Usage Value (%)*
A (V)	15–20	60–75
B (E)	20–30	20–30
C (D)	40–60	10–15

But, in inventory management, prudence is of essence. **For example**, as we know, during the rainy season, there is disruption of rail and road transport say, from Assam side. It would, therefore, augur well to stock sufficiently larger quantum of safety stocks, to take care of such eventualities.

Further, sensing that some staff trouble was brewing in MICO, the prudent management of TELCO, now Tata Motors, Jamshedpur, stored sufficiently large quantum of safety stocks of the injection fuel pumps, failing which their own production of trucks would have adversely suffered, in the event of strike or lockout, etc., in MICO, as mentioned earlier.

Several companies have saved a lot of money by implementing innovative and creative suggestions for keeping inventory at the lowest possible level. A **live example** of inventory management in TELCO (now Tata Motors), Jamshedpur, may illustrate the point well.

Example

In the year 1988, TELCO (now Tata Steel), held only six days' stock of category 'A' items (Super A, B, and C categories of items are excluded from the example). And, in the sessions on "Group Creative Problem Solving Exercise", conducted at ASCI, Hyderabad, the General Manager of TELCO proposed a problem as to how to reduce the holding of stocks of 'A' items of inventories from 6 to 5 days or 4 days, and this was, ultimately, selected by the group for the creative problem solving exercise. The participants came forward with several suggestions, by implementation of some of which the company could succeed in further lowering the level of stocks of 'A' items of inventories to 5 days and later even to 4 days. Sharing of one of such suggestions may prove to be of great learning value.

TELCO received different components of their trucks from several vendors, most of whom were located in or around Mumbai. In order to explain the arrangements prevalent at the material time, let me take an illustrative example. Supposing there had been 100 vendors (say, V_1 to V_{100}), and there were 10 truck owners (say, T_1 to T_{10}). And, 10 venders each were attached to the respective truck owners. For example; V_1 to V_{10} were tied up with T_1,' V_{11} to V_{20} were tied up with T_2, and so on. Now, if the supplies, meant for TELCO, were received from V_1, V_{25}, V_{49} and V_{63}, these will have to be necessarily loaded in the truck of T_1, T_3, T_5 and T_7 respectively, as per the extant arrangement. Thus, none of these four trucks will be have a full truck load. So, they will wait for a day or two, or would reluctantly load the goods meant for some other destinations, even requiring some detour, too. This would, naturally, cause some delay of a couple of days or more, than the journey time usually taken to reach Jamshedpur, where the TELCO factory was located.

The single suggestion made by the group was just to discontinue the tie-up arrangements of the vendors with each truck owners. Thus, all the goods, meant for TELCO, received at the point of loading, were to be first loaded to the full, in the truck standing there first in the queue, and only thereafter, the further supplies were to be loaded in the second one, and so on. Thus, it was found that usually three to four trucks were loaded and, thus, the wastage of time, due to avoidable detouring involved, was saved. This suggestion, when implemented, reduced the stocking time of 'A' category inventories from six days to five days immediately, and later, when some other suggestions were also implemented, it came down to even four days.

I would now like to share one more secret, lying behind the success of this story. That is, while the discussion was going on, and the participants were making suggestions, the General Manager from TELCO, whose proposed problem was selected for the creative problem solving exercise (as aforesaid) had always been found saying that 'this would not work', or 'we have already tried it', etc. He, however, had to be counselled not to make such judgemental remarks, as it could hamper the free flow of creative ideas to solve the problem, as is the basic ground rule, to be meticulously followed while conducting the brainstorming sessions.

This is so, because, when we work in an organisation for quite sometime, we tend to put on some blinkers, such that we tend not to see beyond the existing rules and practices, and consequently develop a sense of resistance to change. But, when the gentleman stopped such discouraging stance on his part, the group could come out with quite a few winner ideas, as aforesaid. This I have stated just to emphasise that one of the primary conditions, for the success of any creative problem solving exercise, is to refrain from passing judgemental remarks, and thereby interrupte the free flow (free-wheeling) of ideas.

(Readers, interested in knowing something more, in greater detail, about the techniques of creative problem solving, may please refer to the chapter on "Brainstorming for Organisation Development" in the author's book titled "*Mentoring Mantras for Indian Managers*", Matrix Publishers, New Delhi, 2010.

6.15 CATEGORISATION OF ITEMS FOR ABC ANALYSIS

Now, let us see how do we usually proceed to classify the various items of inventories into three categories, viz. A, B and C. The procedure involves the following steps:

Step 1

Rank all the items of inventory, in a descending order, based upon their annual usage value, and serially number them, from 1 onward.

Step 2

Record the totals of annual consumption values of all the items separately and express them as a percentage of the total value of consumption.

Step 3

(*a*) Observe the percentage column and find out the cut-off point where the difference between the two successive percentages is rather significant and marked.

(*b*) At the same time, please bear in mind that the cut-off point so arrived at comprises a reasonable number of items of inventory.

Step 4

We may finalise the classification of items of inventory into A, B and C categories, giving the number of units of inventory and their values in percentage terms, under all the three categories, with the laid down principles and objectives of the ABC analysis (or VED analysis), in the desired manner.

It may, however, be mentioned here that there is no fixed rule or rigid principle for classifying various items into A, B and C categories. In fact, it is a managerial decision, and, therefore, may vary from person to person. But, this should not, at the same time, suggest that any classification can be justified on the basis of the managerial decision and discretion. It may vary, but only marginally, as the principle and rationale of selective approach to inventory, monitoring and control, must always be borne in mind, and taken full care of, to justify the acceptance of classification and reasonably.

Let us now understand the procedure more clearly with the help of an **illustrative example**:

Example

The information, about the annual usages and price for 12 items used by a firm is given hereunder:

Item	*Annual Usage (Number of Units)*	*Price per Unit (Rs.)*
(a)	*(b)*	*(c)*
1.	6155	0.40
2.	61200	0.75
3.	16800	5.00
4.	3000	0.35
5.	55800	1.20
6.	22680	0.60
7.	26640	5.00
8.	14760	1.20
9.	20520	0.90
10.	90000	0.30
11.	29940	0.40
12.	24660	0.70

Required

(*a*) Rank the items of inventory on the basis of their annual usage value;

(*b*) Record the percentages of usage of the items;

(*c*) Show the cumulative percentages of usage of items;

(*d*) Classify items into three categories, viz. A, B and C; and

(*e*) Justify the rationale behind the cut-off levels, between these categories (A, B and C) selected by you.

Solution

Approach I

Step A

Table 6.8

Item	Annual Usage (Number of Units)	Price per Unit (Rs.)	Annual Usage Value (Rs.)	Rank
(a)	(b)	(c)	(d)	(e)
1.	6160	0.40	2464	11
2.	61200	0.75	45900	4
3.	16880	5.00	84400	2
4.	3000	0.35	1050	12
5.	55800	1.20	66960	3
6.	22680	0.60	13608	9
7.	26640	5.00	133200	1
8.	14760	1.20	17712	7
9.	20520	0.90	18468	6
10.	90000	0.30	27000	5
11.	29940	0.40	11976	10
12.	24660	0.70	17262	8
	TOTAL		440000	

Step B

Table 6.9

7Rank	Item (Sl. No.)	Annual Usage Value (Rs.)	Annual Usage, in Percentage	Cumulative Percentage (%)
(a)	(b)	(c)	(d)	(e)
1.	7	133200	30.27	30.27
2.	3	84400	19.18	49.45
3.	5	66960	15.22	64.67
4.	2	45900	10.43	75.10
5.	10	27000	6.14	81.24
6.	9	18468	4.20	85.44
7.	8	17712	4.03	89.47
8.	12	17262	3.92	93.39
9.	6	13608	3.09	96.48
10.	11	11976	2.72	99.20
11.	1	2464	0.56	99.76
12.	4	1050	0.24	100.00
	TOTAL	440000	100.00	

Step C

Table 6.10

Category	*Item Nos.*	*No. of Items*	*% of Total Items*	*Cumulative Percentage of Annual Usage*	*Net %*
(a)	*(b)*	*(c)*	*(d)*	*(e)*	*(f)*
A	7, 3, 5, 2	4	33.3	75.10	75.10 (Say, 75%)
B	10, 9, 8, 12	4	33.3	93.39	18.29 (Say, 18%)
C	6, 11, 1, 4	4	33.3	100.00	6.61 (Say, 7%)

Step D

Thus, we find that under each of the A, B and C, categories equal number of items, *i.e.* 4 item or 1/3rd portion or 33.33% of total 12 items have fallen and in terms of percentages, too, they are 75%, 18% and 7%, which are reasonable and justifiable for categorisation, based upon the main principle and purpose of the ABC analysis.

But, it must be borne in mind that such identically equal number of items may not necessarily come under each of the categories A, B and C, as has, incidentally, happened in the case of the given illustrative example.

Rationale behind some other alternative categorisations

Approach II

(A). So far as the classification of items under Category 'A' is concerned, there may not be much of a difference of opinion inasmuch as the relative difference in the last rank of item included in category 'A', *i.e.* item number 4 and the immediately next item (number 5 in rank) being classified under Category 'B', is a significant over 4%. Besides, it is well below 10%, cut-off point.

One may still argue for the inclusion of item number 5 too under Category 'A'. But, in that event, though in terms of percentage of value, there is an increase of around 6% (81%, raised from 75%), the increase in terms of percentage of number of total items is around 9% (42%, raised from 33%). And, therefore, it may be a prudent business sense to arrest the temptation of very closely monitoring and controlling a large number of items, inasmuch as "in our over-anxiety to control everything, we may end up controlling nothing".

Therefore, the Approach (II) does not seem be much justifiable.

Let us look at a couple of other alternative approaches, too, detailed hereunder:

Approach III

Table 6.11

Cut-off Point for Category	*No. of Items*	*% of total No. of Items*	*% of Total Value*
A	(1 to 3) 3	25	64.67
B	(4 to 8) 5	42	28.72
C	(9 to 12) 4	33	6.61
TOTAL	**12**	**100**	**100.00**

Approach IV

Table 6.12

Cut-off Point for Category	*No. of Items*	*% of total No. of Items*	*% of Total Value*
A	(1 to 4) 4	33	75.10
B	(5 to 9) 5	42	21.38
C	(10 to 12) 3	25	3.52
TOTAL	**12**	**100**	**100.00**

When we compare the two approaches (III and IV), we find that while the percentage of the number of items (5 or 42%) in category 'B' remains the same in both the cases, the value of 'B' category items is around 25% higher in the Approach 'III', which is a plus point for this Approach 'III', as against the Approach 'IV'. Further, while the percentage of the number of items in Category 'A' in Approach 'III' is around 32% less, as compared to Approach 'IV', the percentage of value is only around 16% less.

Thus, on both these counts, we find that the Approach 'III' is more rational, reflecting a much better business sense. As regards the number of items in Category 'C', it comes down by 8 per cent (from 33% to 25%) in Approaches 'III' and 'IV' respectively, which is quite against the general principles lying behind the ABC analysis. Therefore, Approach 'III' seems to be a better choice than Approach 'IV', on this count.

Further, when we look at the Category 'A' items in these two approaches, we find that while the number of items in Approach 'III' goes up from 3 to 4 in Approach 'IV' (an increase of 33.3%), the percentage increase in terms of value goes up only from 64.67% to 75.10%, *i.e.* just by 10.43 per cent, which is comparatively too low to justify inclusion of one more number of item in Category 'A'.

Thus, in the case of items of Category 'A' also, the approach 'III' seems to be making a better business sense.

All considered, on final analysis, the Approach 'III' seems to be a better managerial decision. Besides, we may further observe that the relative difference, in percentage terms, between the adjacent items, right from rank number 5 to number 10, is of around 2% to less than even 1%. Thus, if we include the item at rank number 5 in Category 'A', we may have to include all the other items up to rank number 10 in Category 'A', whereby the whole purpose behind the ABC analysis gets defeated.

Therefore, in my modest personal opinion, there does not seem to be much of a justification to include rank number 5 in Category 'A'.

But, so far as the classification under Category 'B' is concerned, one may argue that, if item number 5 has been classified under Category 'B', the other items up to rank number 10, *i.e.,* rank number 5 to number 10 should be classified under Category 'B'. And, there seems to be much force and weight in such an argument. This way, while Category 'B' includes as many as 6 items, Category 'C' is left with just two items.

All considered, this seems to be a very apt illustrative example to demonstrate how the process of classification of items under Categories 'A', 'B' and 'C', is not based on any rigid or fixed laid down principle but, instead, it is more a managerial and discretionary decision to take, keeping the various other relevant facts and factors, too, in one's view.

Thus, one more alternative categorization could be, as under, if a particular team of managers may so desire and decide:

Approach V

Table 6.13

Category	*Rank No. of Items*	*No. of Items in Each Category*	*% of Total Items*	*% of Value of Items Under Each Category*
A	1 to 4	4	33	75
B	5 to 10	6	50	24
C	11 & 12	2	17	1

The moot question that may arise now in the instant case is that as to how successfully one could justify keeping only 1% of the total annual usage value in Category 'C' thereby over-burdening the Category 'B' with 50% of the total number of items, accounting for only 24% of the annual usage value.

I, however, would prefer to leave the matter on to the judgment and discretion of the readers to take their own managerial decision in the case, depending upon their own personal business sense. However, in my own considered view, the Approach 'III' seems to be the most acceptable, rational and reasonable one.

6.16 INVENTORY CONTROL THROUGH RATIO ANALYSIS

Analysis of the following ratios, in addition to the Current and Quick Ratios may be found to be helpful in effective monitoring and control of inventory:

(a) Turnover Ratio (Times)

(*i*) of Total Inventory $= \dfrac{\text{Cost of goods sold}}{\text{Average total inventories (at cost)}}$

(*ii*) of Raw Materials Inventory $= \dfrac{\text{Annual consumption of raw materials}}{\text{Average raw materials inventory (at cost)}}$

(*iii*) of Work-in-process Inventory $= \dfrac{\text{Cost of manufacturing}}{\text{Average work-in-process inventory (at cost)}}$

(*iv*) of Finished Goods Inventory $= \dfrac{\text{Cost of manufacturing}}{\text{Average finished goods inventory (at cost)}}$

(b) Age Analysis

(*i*) Average age of Raw Materials Inventory $= \dfrac{\text{Average raw materials inentory (at cost)}}{\text{Average daily consumption of raw materials}}$

(*ii*) of Finished Goods Inventory $= \dfrac{\text{Average finished goods inventory (at cost)}}{\text{Average cost of products manufactured per day}}$

(c) Index

(*i*) of Out-of-stock $= \dfrac{\text{Number of times out of stock}}{\text{Number of times requisitioned}}$

(*ii*) of Spare Parts $= \dfrac{\text{Value of spare parts inventory}}{\text{Value of capital equipments}}$.

6.17 JUST-IN-TIME (JIT) SYSTEM vs. JUST-IN-CASE (JIC) SYSTEM

JIT system of inventory was first developed in Japan by Taichi Okno. It implies that a company must evolve a system, to maintain a minimal level of inventories in stock, whereby the inventory carrying cost could be minimized, and, at the same time, the risk of loss due to stock out position could as well be avoided. This, however, could be possible only if the suppliers were able to meticulously keep up the stipulated delivery time schedule and thereby the stocks (of parts and components) could reach the factory premises 'just-in-time', when these are required for assembly or production purposes.

The difference between the traditional system of inventory management and control and JIT system is that, while in the former system we have to keep a reasonable amount of safety stock to meet the exigencies of extended lead time, or strike in the supplier's industries, etc., in JIT system almost 'nil' safety stocks are required as the supply chain has been worked out meticulously and the time schedule is adhered to by all the suppliers religiously.

As against the JIT system, the most relaxed and lax system of inventory management and control could well be termed as the JIC (Just-in-Case) system.

I know of a company (name not being disclosed for obvious reasons) where the inventory of some spare parts, even of high value, were lying in stocks for the last, around 10 to 20 years, as these had never been required to be replaced. Still, these were not being sold off, simply on the ground that, in the 21st or 25th year or even later, these parts may be required. And, as per our Indian mind-set, we call for explanation regarding stock out but no questions are asked for carrying even fabulously higher quantity and value of inventories. This unhealthy practice has to be given up, sooner the better.

JIT system sounds appealing but, in fact, it is very hard to implement, inasmuch as it requires a complete overhauling of the entire system of production and management, and, above all, the mind-set, both of the management and the workers, as also of the suppliers.

Some illustrative (not exhaustive) examples of the required prerequisites for the success of a JIT system are:

(*i*) The high dependability and efficiency on the part of all the suppliers, because, even a slight delay on the part of a single supplier may disturb the whole supply chain and production schedule.

(*ii*) All the suppliers should preferably be located in the vicinity of the factory premises.

(*iii*) A reliable transport system is a must.

(*iv*) There has to be sufficient number of doors and approaches and conveniently positioned storage facilities, docks, and godowns, so as to perfectly match the production and assembly requirements, at various stages, and the schedule of supplies of parts, spares, etc.

To bring home the advantages of JIT system, let us use the undernoted formula:

$$\text{Average Inventory} = \frac{\sqrt{(2FU) \div PC}}{2} + \text{Safety Stock.}$$

And, as against the traditional system of inventory management and control, under the JIT system the ordering cost is brought to the minimal level (as the one time order system of pre-settled arrangement of supplies is sufficient enough to ensure timely supplies), and the minimal (or nil) level of safety stock required, as a very high level of dependability and efficiency and sense of responsibility (based on a long-term relationship) on the part of each and every vendor (supplier) are the prerequisites for the success of the JIT system.

Under the circumstances, as all the components of the equation on the right hand side come down to a minimal level and, as the minimum level of inventory is required to be carried, to avoid the risk of stock outs, the total inventory carrying cost comes down drastically. And, as a result, the profitability of the company goes up correspondingly.

It may, however, be recalled that JIT system in Japan, too, was mostly confined to the automobile industries, and that, too, in regard only to the parts and components, mainly to feed the assembly line. And, of late, as it was found that in the JIT system, on several occasions the trucks had to leave for their destinations half-full or even quarter full, to meet the dead line of time schedule of supplies, it ended up in a much higher transportation cost, eroding the overall advantages of the JIT system. And, above all, this meant avoidable increase in the level of pollution by automobiles, as it had to undertake much more number of trips, for the aforesaid reason. And, therefore, the Japanese companies, by virtue of their high sense of responsibility and commitment to the nation, relaxed the JIT system a bit and now they are said to be maintaining, 4/5 hours of their requirements of inventory, as a safety stock, too.

6.18 EVOLVING AN EFFECTIVE SYSTEM OF INVENTORY MANAGEMENT, MONITORING AND CONTROL

A company, with a view to implement an effective and efficient system of inventory management, monitoring and control, may do well to initiate the under-noted steps:

(*i*) It should endeavour hard, on a continuous basis, to avoid (or at least, mitigate), the usual imbalances of raw materials and work-in-process, as these, in turn, reduce the utility of stocks.

(*ii*) Extra efforts are required to reduce the work-in-process time, so as to convert the items of work-in-process into finished goods (ready for sale), at a much faster pace.

(*iii*) The management should always be alert and vigilant enough to dispose of any surplus stock of inventories and spare-parts, preferably before these become obsolete or of a very low value. And, even obsolete items may be disposed of at the best available price, at the material time, sooner the better. We should act fast and should not work in a sluggish manner, as we have seen earlier, in the case of a PSU.

(*iv*) Continuous exercise must go on, with a view to reduce the production cycle time, by effective management of each of its components, viz. cash and near cash, bills receivable, together with each item of inventory, viz. raw materials, work-in-process and finished goods.

(*v*) Suitable changes in the production design are desirable so as to facilitate the use of standard parts and components to a maximum possible extent, as these may well be available off-the-shelf any time.

(*vi*) Most importantly, the production schedules must be followed, strictly and religiously, by all concerned (workers and officers). All of them must realise its implications and ramifications to the full, and, therefore, develop the required mind-set to ensure its implementation.

(*vii*) The exercise of classifying the stocks of inventory into fast moving, slow moving and non-moving groups of items, must go on, on a continuous basis, and urgent and fast measures must be taken to look into the roots of the causes thereof, and to remedy them fast. Alternatively, sincere efforts must be made to dispose them of, sooner the better, by offering an attractively lower price.

(*viii*) Seasonal industries, manufacturing air-conditioners and fans, heaters and geysers, woollens and blankets, etc., must take suitable steps, like giving off-season discounts, etc., so as to even out the fluctuations in the level of sales in the peak-season and off-season to the maximum possible extent.

(*ix*) It may augur well for companies to resist the temptation of availing of the credit facilities from banks on the security of such items of finished goods, which have already been rejected by the specific buyer firm for whom it had been specially made, inasmuch as these have to be ultimately sold as scraps at a much lesser value.

I know of a company which had been manufacturing aluminium components and parts for supply to one of the State Electricity Boards. A huge stock of such items of finished goods, already rejected by the Board earlier, were pledged to the bank at their full cost of production, as if these were genuine products, ready for supply to the Board. But, soon the reality of such non-moving stocks got revealed and the borrower company got exposed, and lost its credit-worthiness and trust-worthiness, in the eyes of the bank. As we all know it very well, it takes several long years to build the trust and confidence, but it hardly takes any time to break and demolish it once for an.

6.19 STRATEGIES FOR ACHIEVING SUCCESS IN INVENTORY MANAGEMENT AND CONTROL

The main objectives of inventory management and control system are:

(*i*) to keep the total inventory carrying costs to the minimal level and, at the same time,

(*ii*) to keep the stock out risk, too, at the lowest.

With a view to achieving these objectives, the following strategies may be of immense help:

1. Rationality

Complete Understanding and Commitment of One and All: The most important prerequisite for the success of any monitoring and control system of inventory is that all the members of the staff, at various levels, must be fully aware of the various steps that are to be taken for the purpose. They should also be able to appreciate full well the rationale behind meticulous application of various monitoring strategies.

Let us share an interesting episode, which may bring home the desirability of knowing some task and the rationale behind it, too, so as to motivate the people to implement them meticulously, and with unfailing enthusiasm.

Example

An Army Officer instructed his group of men to dig a ditch, at a particular place, 10 feet deep and again at a distance of every 10 feet, therefrom, and then call him. The army men complied with the instructions. But, whenever, the officer was called, he peeped into the ditch and went away, without telling anything except asking his men to go on digging, as already instructed. Within half an hour or so, these army men got bored and worn out, and ultimately they all gave up the task.

As against this, another Army Officer, assigned with the same job, had, instead, asked his men to dig ten feet deep and thereafter, at a distance of ten feet each, and call him as soon as they are able to locate a junction box, which was located at a depth of ten feet and at a distance of ten feet each, from the specified starting point. And, after a couple of hours, the men of the other (first) group, sitting idle for so long, came running towards this (second) group of men, who were dancing with joy and shouting aloud, "we have got it; we have done it". The officer concerned also came running, after hearing the shouts of joy and victory, of his men. And, let me confide with you, they had dug up a large number of ditches untiringly and with great enthusiasm, all through. And, that was just because they were not only given an instruction to follow just blindly, but with the full knowledge and understanding of the rationale behind the instructions.

Therefore, in an organisation, too, it will augur well if the rationale behind the laid down systems and procedures are also explained to, and appreciated by, all the members of the staff and officers at all levels, so as to ensure their full commitment and meticulous compliance of the laid down instructions.

2. Flexibility

The inventory control system should be flexible enough so as to be able to adapt to the changing circumstances and conditions with ease, with minor adjustments and modifications in the system, as and when required. Here, it must be realised that it may not be too practical to expect that such a system could be evolved which may take care of all the contingencies and complexities. It would be sufficient if almost 90% of the system can be adapted in the changed situations and conditions and the remaining 10% could very well be handled on case to case basis, or by introducing some slight modification/relaxation in the system, as and when required.

3. Punctuality

Timely and effective action is essential in management of inventory. As we have seen, the value of inventory declines mostly due to the following reasons:

(*i*) Obsolescence, specially in the modern technological advancements and fast changes in technology.

(*ii*) Change in the fashion or the taste of the people.

(*iii*) Deterioration in quality due to the passage of time, like those of paper, medicines, and a variety of other stocks, which have a limited shelf-life.

(*iv*) Sharp fluctuations in price due to some inherent volatility of some goods or else due to the changes in the government policies of import and export, excise and custom duties, selective credit control by the Reserve Bank of India (RBI), etc.

It would augur well if some in-built mechanism/system is in place so as to give a warning signal in respect of ensuing deterioration in the quality or obsolescence or price fluctuations, etc., so that all the people concerned may be alerted well in time to take the required remedial actions, promptly and effectively.

6.20 INVENTORY MANAGEMENT IN INDIA

Now, let us briefly examine the generally prevailing practices in India, so far as management and control of inventory are concerned. Later, we would also attempt to make some practical and useful suggestions, as to what can be done by us to streamline and strengthen our inventory management systems and control mechanism.

Present Practices

1. The most vital area, requiring urgent attention, is the fact that, by and large, most of the companies have a tendency to hold a much higher level of inventory than could be considered desirable and optimal. Some common arguments, advanced in favour of keeping such a high level of inventory, are given hereunder:
   (*a*) As we have already stated in the previous pages, it is a common practice in India, specially in the public sector undertakings, that hardly anyone raises any question about the inherent losses in carrying higher levels of inventory. But, every case of loss, howsoever small, arising out of stock out, even for a day or so, resulting in production losses, is usually made a big issue. Such non-business-like Indian mind-set needs to be changed fast, sooner the better.
   (*b*) Till recently, the procedure for the issue of import licenses was so tedious and time consuming that the companies preferred to stock imported goods, in a much higher quantity than reasonably required. But, now that the system has rather been streamlined and simplified, some improvements have, of late, been observed in this area.
   (*c*) Again, till the recent past, the rate of inflation in India was very high, mostly in two degits. Accordingly, some of the companies had a tendency to stock more goods than reasonably necessary, inasmuch as the high rate of inflation could, in turn, take care of the higher inventory carrying cost. But now that the rate of inflation has gone down steeply, such a tendency is on the decline.
   (*d*) Besides, a large number of vendors (suppliers) in India have been found to be not so very reliable and responsible, to strictly adhere to the delivery schedule and quality of their products. Such a tendency has compelled the companies to keep a much higher level of safety stock to meet any exigencies.
   (*e*) More importantly, lack of standardization of most of the products, has also forced companies to carry a large variety of stores which, in turn, enhances the quantum of inventory, and carrying costs therewith.
2. Yet, another segment of shortcomings, observed in the inventory management in the Indian companies, has been that we Indians have generally been found great in planning and analysing but rather poor and sluggish in implementation and execution of any action plan or procedure.
   (*a*) For example, we do undertake the ABC analysis exercise, but hardly take care to follow it up, and update, review and revise the categorization at regular periodical intervals.
   (*b*) Likewise, we also undertake the FSN analysis, *i.e.* analysis of goods under three different categories, viz. fast moving (F), slow moving (S) and non-moving (N) items of raw materials and finished goods, but, most of the companies have been found to be too slow in deciding about the disposal of non-moving items or to evolve some suitable strategies to clear the slow moving stocks, fast enough, so that the financial

resources, avoidably blocked in these items, could be got released and invested or employed in some other economic and profitable areas.

(*c*) Indian companies have usually been found to be undertaking Inventory Turnover Analysis, but generally, on an aggregate basis. It would augur well if such an analysis is done even of individual items of raw materials and finished goods, specially of high value items, so that the advantages, on the pattern of ABC analysis, could be reaped in such areas too.

6.21 ROOMS FOR IMPROVEMENT—SOME SUGGESTIONS

Under the foregoing circumstances, we observe that there is a vast scope for bringing about lot many changes and improvements in the area of inventory management and control. Some of the strategies and steps could be suggested as follows:

(*a*) More importantly, we should not only end up in analyzing things; we should be action-oriented too. That is, we should not stop only at doing the ABC (VED) analysis or FSN analysis. We should, instead, periodically review it too, and should take prompt remedial measures to bring about the desirable results, wherever necessary.

(*b*) As we have already observed, we, Indians, are excellent solo performers but not so good team workers. We have to change our individualistic approach, attitude and mind-set, and must learn to work in coordination and cooperation with the related and inter-dependent departments, like purchase and production, production and marketing, etc., and work under a system of overall coordination and control by the finance department.

(*c*) The companies must treat the vendor as a part of themselves. They should develop a long-term relationship and bondage with the vendors, specially the key-vendors, so as to ensure strict adherence to the delivery schedule and quality control.

(*d*) As Lee Iacocca has aptly opined, the timely decision making and quick action is of essence in any business organization. We should, therefore, act fast to dispose of the obsolete items and the surplus stocks of raw materials and finished goods by adopting suitable strategies and action plan in these areas. This will go a long way in substantially reducing the quantum of our inventory, and thereby the total inventory carrying costs, etc. which may, in turn, result in higher profitability and brighter prospects of the organizations. Incidentally, the whole procedure of disposal of surplus and obsolete items of inventories need to be simplified, facilitating quick and easy action plan.

(*e*) Another key to an ongoing process of improvement is that we should set challenging but achievable levels of performance in all the segments of business management, including in the area of inventory management and control. We should also aim at JIT inventory, or quite near it, so as to be globally competitive in the modern age of globalization and 'a great global village' concept.

(*f*) In the modern age of rapid growth and technological advancements, we should also endeavour to march ahead in the area of computerization of the entire system of management of inventory to bring about a marked improvement in the efficiency and effectiveness of an overall management and control of inventories.

But it is not enough just to computerize the management of inventories. We should, at the same time, have a complete and comprehensive, accurate and dependable data base. I have personally observed in a few companies, who had their godowns and store-houses, spread over a vast area in a particular state, or even all over the country, but they have not been supplied the relative data base from most of their departments and store-houses, for a couple of years or even more now. We should, therefore, fully appreciate and understand the implications of computerization and should act in coordination and in the right direction in the right earnest, so as to reap the immense benefit of computerization and such other automation and mechanization and technological advancements, in the area of inventory management and control.

A SYNOPTIC NOTE (CHAPTER 6 AT A GLANCE)

MANAGEMENT OF INVENTORIES

1. Inventories comprise
   (*i*) Raw materials and consumable stores and spares, *i.e.* the basic inputs used to manufacture the finished goods.
   (*ii*) Work-in-process [also known as stock-in-process or goods-in-process], *i.e.* the intermediary stage between raw materials and finished goods.
   (*iii*) Finished goods, *i.e.* the end-products, ready for sale.
   For merchants, the inventories comprise only finished goods.
2. Inventory management is most important as it involves around 25% to 30% of the total investments, *i.e.* only next to the fixed assets.
3. Inventory management is the role and responsibility of purchases and production, as also of the manufacturing and marketing functions. Finance department, however, performs the coordinating role. Therefore, they all should work as a well-knit team.
4. Two main types of inventories:
   (*i*) (*a*) "Process" inventories, *i.e.* the raw materials lying at the various "stages of production", prior to getting converted into finished goods.
   (*b*) "Movement" inventories, *i.e.* the items of finished goods, transported from factory to the company's warehouse/selling points.
   (*ii*) 'Organization' Inventories, *i.e.* the raw materials and finished goods stocked in the company's godowns, to be supplied to the factory and sale depots respectively from time to time.
5. Rationale for storing sufficient stocks of organization inventories:
   To delink (*a*) purchase and production, and (*b*) production and marketing, to ensure professional and expert decision making and optimizing profitability.
   In-process Inventory: It is a part of, but also apart from, the process inventories.
6. Economic Order Quantity (EOQ):
   To know the optimal
   (*i*) Order Size, and
   (*ii*) Order Level.

7. First, let us understand the three different types of costs:
   (*i*) Ordering Cost, *i.e.* requisitioning, placing order, sending reminders, transporting, loading, unloading, stacking, etc.
   (*ii*) Inventory Carrying Cost, *i.e.* cost of capital, storage, insurance, taxation as also obsolescence cost. It usually constitutes 25% of the total value of inventories.
   (*iii*) Stock out, or Shortage Cost, *i.e.* shortage of raw materials, resulting in the loss of production, crash purchases in cash, at higher cost, adopting sub-optimal production schedule, etc.

   Shortage of finished goods may lead to customer dissatisfaction and loss of business; with the long-term ramifications, which are somewhat intangible.

   A moderate (middle-of-the-road) policy of storing, only some quantity of finished goods, to meet some immediate need, followed by fresh production, on priority basis.

   This would avoid:
   (*a*) Extra (finished goods) inventory carrying cost; and
   (*b*) The risk of obsolescence.
8. Basic EOO model

   It is based on the following assumptions:
   (*i*) The quantum of the usual annual usage of the items of inventories is known, in accurate term.
   (*ii*) The usage is usually uniform throughout the year.
   (*iii*) The lead-time, *i.e.* time gap between ordering and receiving, is NIL.
   (*iv*) Therefore, there is no risk of stockout, either. That is, the stockout cost is NIL.
   (*v*) Thus, only two costs are involved:
      (*a*) Ordering cost, and
      (*b*) Inventory carrying cost.
   (*vi*) Further,
      (*a*) Ordering cost is uniform, irrespective of the order size, and
      (*b*) The Inventory carrying cost is a fixed percentage of the average value of inventories.
9. EOQ formula vs. trial and error method

   Trial and error method is a very cumbersome and time-consuming process. The formula, however, makes the procedure rather simple enough.

   $$EOQ = \sqrt{2(FU) \div PC}$$
10. In practice, there is no single Economic Order Point (EOP). There is, instead, an Economic Order Range (EOR).
11. EOQ vs. OOQ (Optimal Order Quantity):

    [That is, when bulk (quantity) discount is available].
    (*a*) When the quantity discount is available at a lower level than the EOQ, then EOQ itself will be the OOQ, too.
    (*b*) But, if it is higher than OOQ, OOQ will be the EOQ or the quantity eligible for bulk discount, depending upon which one of these two will be beneficial, *i.e.* when the resultant difference will be a positive (+ve) figure.

12. A new clue to EOQ:

    That is, after finding out the EOQ in terms of the nearest integer figure, we should find out the number of orders. And, this again, should be converted into the nearest integer number. Based on this figure as the number of orders, we should calculate the EOQ, which will be the EOQ in real terms. Besides, we should bear in mind the concepts of EOP and EOR, too, at this stage.

13. Components of inventory carrying costs:

    (*i*) Storage cost

    (*ii*) Handling charges

    (*iii*) Insurance charges

    (*iv*) Wastages

    (*v*) Damage/deterioration

    (*vi*) Technical obsolescence, blockage of funds and cost of capital, and opportunity cost connected therewith.

14. Advantages of high inventory:

    (*a*) High stocks of raw materials

    (*i*) Bulk purchase at cheaper rate with quantity discount. Better, if bulk annual purchase is ordered, but the delivery and payments are to be made in phases, to the mutual advantages of both the parties. It is an optimal strategy.

    (*ii*) Seasonal purchases, being cheaper and sure.

    (*iii*) No stock out cost and risk.

    (*iv*) In inflationary economy, it may be gainful.

    (*v*) Savings of ordering cost and the connected hazels of loading and unloading, etc.

    (*b*) High stocks of finished goods:

    (*i*) It may facilitate instant delivery, out of the shelf, and, thus, have an edge over the competitors. But it is better to have only a small ready stock and the rest to be produced on receipt of the order, on a priority basis].

    (*ii*) Thus, the 'Golden Mean' is the most basic management mantra, pertaining to the management of inventory.

15. Lead time

    It represents the time lag between placement of order and the actual receipt of goods.

    This could as well be taken into account by modifying the EOQ formula, just slightly.

16. Order point

    Thus, as a prudent manager, we should place the next order well in advance, when there is some stock left, being sufficient enough to take care of the lead time.

17. Safety stock

    And, it would be a better business sense to have some safety stock too, so as to take care of some possible fluctuations in both: (*i*) the lead-time, and accordingly; (*ii*) the order point.

    Thus, Order Point will be = EOQ + [Lead-time (in days) × Daily usage] + Safety stock.

    Estimating and ascertaining the safety stock is a managerial judgement–decision/discretion. But, the safety stock should not be too high, nor too low. It should be sufficient enough, just about right.

    That is, somewhere between JIT and JIC (Just-in-Time and Just-in-Case) extreme situations.

18. Some other variable factors affecting EOQ:
    (*i*) Selective credit control: Restrictions imposed by the Reserve Bank of India and the Government of India, prescribing a ceiling for stocking (and advancing against) certain commodities, holding the price line and avoiding artificially created shortage/scarcity, and the resultant acceleratingly rising prices.
    (*ii*) Expected scarcity/delay in supply.
    (*iii*) Fluctuating prices, *i.e.* rising and falling prices, suggesting higher or lower levels of inventory.
    (*iv*) Risk of obsolescence.
19. ABC analysis or VED, *i.e.* vital, essential and desirable, analysis:
    These concepts can well be used in various areas, besides the management and control of inventories. For example:
    (*i*) for management of credits and follow-up with different categories of creditors, etc.
    (*ii*) for periodical inspection and verification of stocks.
    (*iii*) for general supervision and follow-up, etc.
20. Creative problem solving techniques in management.
21. Principles and procedure of categorization of items of inventory under categories A, B and C; or V, E and D.
22. Inventory management and control through ratio analysis:
    A. Some relevant ratios are:
        (*i*) Current ratio
        (*ii*) Quick ratio
        (*iii*) Turn-over ratios, viz. of
            (*a*) Total inventory
            (*b*) Raw materials
            (*c*) Work-in-process
            (*d*) Finished goods.
        (*iv*) Age analysis, *i.e.* average age of
            (*a*) Raw material inventory, and
            (*b*) Finished goods inventory, *i.e.* fast moving, slow moving, and non-moving items of raw materials and finished goods. This is known as 'FSN' analysis.
    B. Detailed analysis of some high value items of raw materials and finished goods is desirable.
    C. Indices
        (*i*) Index of out of stock, *i.e.* number of items out-of-stock/number of times requisitioned.
        (*ii*) Index of spare parts, *i.e.* value of spare parts inventory/value of capital equipment.
23. Evolving an effective system of inventory management and control
    (*i*) Avoid (or mitigate) imbalances of raw materials and work-in-process.
    (*ii*) Reduce work-in-process time.
    (*iii*) Dispose of slow and non-moving items of raw materials and spare parts, fast enough.
    (*iv*) Reduce operating (or production) cycle time by controlling each of its components (items).
    (*v*) Change the production design so as to use standard parts and spares.

(*vi*) Developing mind-set of staff to strictly follow stipulated production schedule.

(*vii*) Periodical review of Fast, Slow, and Non-moving (FSN) items of raw materials and finished goods, and take timely policy decisions, and ensure its effective and prompt implementation.

(*viii*) Giving incentives like off-season discount, specially by seasonal industries, to evenly spread the production level and thereby operating at well above break-even-point (BEP) levels, throughout the year.

(*ix*) Resisting the general temptation to stock the rejected items of finished goods, and to take loan against it.

24. Strategies for ensuring success in inventory management:

(*i*) Rationality: Complete understanding of the rationale behind the systems to monitor and control the inventories.

(*ii*) Flexibility: Inventory control system should be flexible enough to adapt to the changing circumstances and conditions, with ease and speed.

(*iii*) Punctuality: Timely and effective action is the essence of management and control. The management should, therefore, immediately respond to:

(*a*) Possible obsolescence of any item, due to change in:

(*i*) Technology, and

(*ii*) Fashion and design, taste, etc.

(*b*) Any deterioration in the quality of raw materials, like paper and cement, as also of the finished goods.

(*c*) Sharp fluctuation in the prices of raw materials, etc., due to import policies, etc.

25. Inventory management in India

(*i*) General tendency to hold much higher level of inventory, always to be on the EXTRA safe side.

Because, while no questions are asked for such lapses, serious objections are raised for stock outs, without taking into account the relative optimal resultant profitability and savings of inventory carrying cost vs. stock out cost.

(*ii*) Now that the rate of inflation is very much in control, and the import policy has also been liberalized and streamlined, such excuses for holding high level of inventory is no longer valid.

(*iii*) The non-dependability of vendors, in terms of both quality and timely delivery, however, still exists to prompt huge stockings of inventory by way of safety stocks.

(*iv*) Lack of standardization of a large number of components of products force companies to stock a variety of items, aggregating huge amounts and involving high inventory carrying cost.

(*v*) Indians are generally found to be fond of planning but are found to be slow in implementation and action. That is, though they do the ABC and FSN analysis meticulously and/or classify the customers into A, B, C and D categories, quite professionally, they hardly review and reclassify them periodically. Thus, the whole time consuming exercise ultimately proves to be a thorough waste of time.

(*vi*) Most of the Indian companies do not do any further detailed ABC and/or FSN analysis of specific high value items of raw materials and finished goods individually, in addition to the overall analysis, in aggregate.

26. Scope for improvement—Some suggestions

(*i*) We should become action-oriented too, instead of being analysis prone.

(*ii*) Besides being an excellent solo-performers, we should become excellent team-workers.

(*iii*) We should treat our vital vendors as a part of the company, and not alien to our company.

(*iv*) We should take timely decision and should also act fast.

(*v*) We should always be on the look out of rooms for improvement and must bring in excellence. We should have challenging but achievable goals, and must aim at achieving JIT systems of inventory. This is now a MUST in the present age of global competition, when the whole world is 'a great global village'.

(*vi*) We must keep pace with the fast changing technologies, lest we are left behind.

(*vii*) We should computerize our inventory management and control systems.

And, to begin with, we should fast build up a sound and complete database.

QUESTIONS
(For self-assessment)

1. (*a*) Name the three main components of inventory.

(*b*) Are the bond papers, ceiling fans, woollen suit lengths and Maruti 800 cars are raw materials or finished goods? Give specific reasons for your answer, citing illustrative examples to bring home your points of view.

2. Why, at all, are we required to keep stocks of inventories of;

(*a*) raw materials, and

(*b*) finished goods?

3. (*a*) Distinguish between 'process or movement' inventories, and 'organization' inventories.

(*b*) What is the rationale behind keeping stocks of 'organization' inventories of both raw materials and finished goods?

4. The basic EOQ model is based on several assumptions. What are they?

5. Write down the formula for EOQ. Explain, how the formula has been derived?

6. The basic EOQ model does not take into account the elements of inflation. What adjustments/ modifications, in your considered view, need to be made in the basic EOQ model to take care of the elements of inflation?

7. What do you understand by the terms:

(*a*) ordering cost,

(*b*) inventory carrying costs, and

(*c*) shortage costs or stockout costs?

Clarify your points, by citing suitable illustrative examples, in each case.

8. What are the various factors/elements involved in the inventory carrying costs? Explain with the help of some illustrative examples.

9. (*a*) Explain the following terms with the help of some illustrative examples:

(*i*) lead time,

(ii) order point, and

(iii) safety stock.

(b) How is the reorder level ascertained? Explain with the help of an illustrative example.

10. (a) What do you understand by the term 'ABC Analysis'? Explain with the help of an illustrative example the procedure adopted for doing the ABC analysis.

(b) What purpose does ABC analysis serve in the context of inventory policy, monitoring, management and control? Explain, with the help of some suitable illustrative examples.

(c) In what other two areas (other than the area of inventory management) can the ABC analysis be used with immense advantage? Name them and explain each of them with the help of some illustrative examples.

11. It is often said that the undernoted three elements are the essence of inventory management; viz.;

(i) appreciation of the rationale behind the various steps and strategies of inventory management by all concerned,

(ii) elements of inherent flexibility in inventory management systems, and

(iii) promptness and action orientation in taking remedial measures.

Do you agree? Give reasons for your answer, with the help of some illustrative examples.

12. The state of affairs in the area of management of inventory in most of the Indian companies leaves a lot to be desired.

(a) What are the various factors responsible for such dismal state of affairs?

(b) What corrective steps would you suggest to streamline and improve the system of inventory management and control in India?

13. Distinguish between EOQ and OOQ (Optimum Order Quantity) when quantity discount is available. Elucidate your point by citing suitable illustrative examples.

14. Distinguish between JIT (Just-in-Time) and JIC (Just-in-Case) approaches towards inventory management and control.

(i) Cite suitable illustrative examples to clarify your point.

(ii) Which one of the above noted two approaches, in your considered opinion, should be adopted by any company? Give reasons for your answer.

15. (a) What are the comparative advantages and disadvantages of carrying too high or too low stocks of inventories of:

(i) raw materials, and

(ii) finished goods?

Explain, with the help of some illustrative examples.

(b) What, in your considered view, would be the right approach in this area? Give convincing reasons for your answer.

16. (a) Distinguish between JIT (Just-in-Time) and JIC (Just-in-Case) systems of inventory management and control.

(b) Do you think that there are some distinct differences in the public sector and private sector undertakings, in regard to their respective approaches, in general, pertaining to the management of inventories?

17. (*a*) "The present practices of Inventory Management and Control in most of the Indian companies leave much to be desired". Do you agree? Give reasons for your answer.

(*b*) What are the different specific suggestions that you would like to offer for bringing in some significant improvements in this area?

18. "Determining the optimal level of current assets involves a trade off between carrying cost and shortage cost". Explain with the help of a suitable example.

PROBLEMS FOR PRACTICE

1. VXL Associates, a trading firm, wants to arrive at the Economic Order Quantity (EOQ) for a certain type of water-lifting pumps. The firm sells 7500 numbers of this pump annually at a price of Rs. 6000 per piece. The purchase price per pump to the firm is, however, Rs. 4500. The cost of carrying a pump is Rs. 900 per year and the cost of placing an order is Rs. 60.

(*a*) What is the total cost associated with placing four, six, seven, eight and nine orders per year?

(*b*) What is the quantum of the Economic Order Quantity?

2. Tarun Traders is trying to determine the Economic Order Quantity (EOQ) for a certain type of transformers. The firm sells 500 numbers of this transformer annually at a price of Rs. 400 per piece. The purchase price per transformer to the firm is, however, Rs. 300. The cost of carrying a transformer is Rs. 60 per year and the cost of placing an order is Rs. 40.

(*a*) What is the total cost associated with placing five, eight, ten and twelve orders per year?

(*b*) What is the quantum of the Economic Order Quantity?

3. UXL Industries is trying to determine the Economic Order Quantity (EOQ) for certain type of washing machines. The firm sells 2000 washing machines annually at a price of Rs. 1600 per piece. The purchase price per washing machine to the firm is, however, 1200. The cost of carrying a washing machine is Rs. 240 per year and the cost of placing an order is Rs. 60.

(*a*) What is the total cost associated with placing four, six, eight and ten orders per year?

(*b*) What is the quantum of the Economic Order Quantity?

4. It is said that the total costs of inventory are fairly insensitive to moderate changes in the order size. It may, therefore, be appropriate to say that there is an 'Economic Order Range', and not an Economic Order Point.

Required

Find out the 'Economic Order Range' in respect of Popular Electricals Limited, whose:

Annual usage is	15000 units;
Inventory carrying cost per unit is	Rs. 2.00; and
Ordering cost per order is	Rs. 40.00.

5. The relative pieces of information pertaining to Gomti Electricals Limited are given hereunder:

Annual usage	50000 units
Ordering cost per order	Rs. 50.00
Purchase price per unit	Rs. 100.00
Inventory carrying Cost	20% of the value of inventory
Rate of discount per unit	Rs. 10.00

Compute the Optimum Order Quantity (OOQ) when the minimum order size required to be eligible for the quantity discount is:

(a) 2000 units;
(b) 4000 units;
(c) 6000 units;
(d) 12000 units; and
(e) 15000 units.

6. The information about annual usages and price for 16 items used by a firm is given hereunder:

Item	Annual Usage (Number of Units)	Price per Unit (Rs.)
1.	1400	220.00
2.	915	150.00
3.	6000	202.00
4.	9750	418.00
5.	1200	525.00
6.	125	160.00
7.	300	442.00
8.	450	101.00
9.	1500	94.00
10.	1300	20.00
11.	8900	72.00
12.	11600	715.00
13.	90600	5.00
14.	530	640.00
15.	945	420.00
16.	4000	10.00

Required

A. Rank the items of inventory on the basis of annual usage value;
B. Record the percentages of usage of items;
C. Show the cumulative percentages of usage of items;
D. Classify the items into three categories: A, B and C; and
E. Justify the rationale behind the cut-off levels, between these three categories (A, B and C) selected by you.

7. Krishna Safe Works is trying hard to work out the economic order quantity for certain types of wardrobes. The firm sells 300 numbers of this item annually at a price of Rs. 3000 per piece. The purchase price per piece to the firm is, however, Rs. 2500. The cost of carrying a wardrobe is Rs. 20 per month and the cost of placing an order is Rs. 10.
   (a) What is the total cost associated with placing one, three, six, and twelve orders per year?
   (b) What is the economic order quantity?

8. Friends Electricals require 20,000 units of a certain item per year. The purchase price per unit is Rs. 50; the carrying cost per year is 30 per cent of the inventory value; and the fixed cost per order is Rs. 55.
   (a) Compute the economic order quantity.

(*b*) How many times will the inventory have to be ordered per annum, if the order size is equal to the EOQ?

(*c*) What will be the total ordering and carrying costs of inventories, when 15 orders are placed per annum?

9. Consider the following data for a certain item purchased by Ganesha Stores:

Annual usage	9,000 units
Fixed cost per order	Rs. 50
Purchase price per unit	200
Carrying cost	15% of inventory value

(*a*) What is the economic order quantity?

(*b*) Now, assume that a discount of Rs. 10 per unit is offered, if the order size is 2,000 units. Should the firm avail of the quantity discount? Give reasons for your answer.

10. Park View Stores require 8,000 units of a certain item annually. The cost per unit is Rs. 40, the fixed cost per order is Rs. 40, and the inventory carrying cost is Rs. 8 per unit per year.

The supplier offers quantity discount as per the details given hereunder:

Order Quantity	*Discount Percentage*
2000	6
3000	9

What should the firm do? Give reasons for your answer.

11. The information about annual usage and price for 16 items used by a company is as under:

Item	*Annual Usage (Number of Units)*	*Price per Unit (Rs.)*
1	500	320.00
2	25	250.00
3	7000	52.00
4	950	418.00
5	2200	325.00
6	125	360.00
7	1300	212.00
8	2450	41.00
9	500	54.00
10	300	120.00
11	3900	52.00
12	600	315.00
13	2600	27.00
14	330	140.00
15	545	120.00
16	1000	3570.00

Required

(*a*) Rank the items of inventories on the basis of their annual usage value;

(*b*) Show the percentages of usage of items;

(*c*) Classify the items into three categories: A, B and C; and

(*d*) Justify the basis of such categorisation.

7

FINANCING OF WORKING CAPITAL

A person's treatment of money is the most decisive test of his character, how they make it and how they spend it.

James Moffatt

The Learning Points

The chapter aims at developing the knowledge and facilitating the understanding of:

- Sources: viz.
  - (*i*) Short-term sources of funds, like accruals, trade credits, public deposits, inter-corporate deposits, commercial papers, short-term loans from financial institutions, rights debentures, and factoring; and
  - (*ii*) Long-term sources of funds, like retained earnings, equity share (Ordinary share) capital, preference share capital, debenture capital and term loans.

All the components of working capital, like the raw materials, work-in-process, finished goods and bills receivable, require investment of funds of varying levels from time to time, depending upon the different levels of the individual components. Accordingly, as we have seen in the earlier chapter, the components of working capital should be financed by a suitable and optimal mix of:

(*i*) short-term sources of funds; and

(*ii*) long-term sources of funds.

We shall discuss each of these, one by one, in this chapter.

(A) SHORT-TERM SOURCES OF FUNDS

While the long-term sources of funds are generally raised for financing fixed assets, and for meeting the margin money for working capital loans, as also a portion of the working capital requirements, the short-term sources of funds have to be necessarily and exclusively used for meeting the working capital requirements only, inasmuch as otherwise, as we have already discussed earlier, it may amount to diversion of funds, which is viewed by all the commercial banks with great disfavour. Now, since 1999, the other financial institutions, like IDBI Bank, ICICI Bank, IFCI, have also chosen to finance the working capital requirements, besides granting term loans.

Commercial banks too, in turn, have started granting term loans, along with financing the working capital requirements. The various sources of short-term financing are discussed hereafter.

7.1 ACCRUALS

Accruals are such amounts which the company owes to other persons or organisations, but has not yet paid the amount. For example, wages and taxes. When a labourer works on daily wages basis, and is accordingly paid too, no accrual will take place. But, usually such payments are made weekly, fortnightly or even monthly. In such cases, whatever amounts of expenses have accrued but have not been paid on the date of the balance sheet, would appear therein as accrued wages. Similarly, the income tax is also paid to the government, on quarterly basis, and some other taxes may be payable half-yearly or even annually. Thus, such amounts of taxes, though due, as on the date of the balance sheet, and not paid till then, would be shown in the balance sheet as accrued taxes. All other such items of expenses will also appear in the balance sheet as accrued expenses only.

The quantum of accruals also varies (expands or contracts) in accordance with the rise and fall of the levels of activities of the company. Thus, as these changes take place in direct proportion to the changes (increase or decrease) in the levels of the accruals, these are rightly treated as the automatic and spontaneous sources of finance (for the interim period) between accruals of expenses and their actual payments. Further, as no interest is payable on such accruals, these are accordingly treated as a 'free' source of finance.

But, in actual terms, this may not be the case, because, if the payment is paid to the labourers engaged on daily wages basis, they may be paid daily at a particular rate of daily wages say, Rs. 50 per day. But, if the term of payment be weekly, fortnightly or monthly, it may vary, say from, Rs. 55, Rs. 60 and Rs. 70 respectively per day. Thus, the element of interest for the intervening days does creep in into the labour rate mechanism. So, it may be wrong to treat the accruals as a 'free' source of finance. Similarly, the tax authorities may increase the rate of taxation depending upon whether it falls due for payment, quarterly, half-yearly or yearly. However, one must agree that such element of interest, though real, is only implicit and not explicit. It must also be understood, at the same time, that the accumulation of accrued funds is quite beyond the control of the management, as the period and pattern of payment get fixed by the business practices and the relevant labour laws, etc., and the due date for payment of taxes is established by law, and any defiance or delay may attract fines and penalties.

7.2 TRADE CREDITS

As per the trade practices, all the manufacturers and traders, unless they are in the sellers' market, have to supply a larger portion of their goods on credit basis, whatever the terms may be, depending upon the trend in the specific line of business and/or the market reputation and position of the seller companies. In order to be eligible to avail of the credit facility, the buyers should also have acceptable and dependable credibility and reputation in the market. Here, it may suffice to say that the sellers also assess the credit-worthiness of their prospective buyers as their buyers, in turn, happen to be the sundry debtors to the sellers. Therefore, all the techniques of assessment of credit-worthiness and compilation of an opinion report, as already discussed earlier in the Chapter on Management of Credit, will apply here also. In brief, the various aspects generally examined, analysed and assessed, in this regard, are discussed hereunder:

(*i*) Profitability of the buyers' company is to assess the extent of profitability and prospects of the company. It is also seen with interest as to whether the company has the practice, as on record, to plough back a major portion of the profit in the business, which is viewed with great favour, as it indicates that the company is interested in continuing the business with a long-term perspective.

(*ii*) The liquidity position of the company is also assessed through the ratio analysis, both by way of intra-firm and inter-firm comparisons mainly of current ratio and quick ratio, also referred to as the acid test ratio. These ratios reveal the ability of the company to meet its commitment for payments, as and when these may fall due.

(*iii*) And, most importantly, a prudent and intelligent judgement has to be made in regard to the willingness and honest intentions of the buyers to pay the dues on or around the stipulated date. A perusal of the company's record and personal enquires (in confidence) with the present suppliers may be of great help.

Trade creditors, who are almost an automatic and spontaneous source of finance, which is generally available without much of negotiations (provided the credibility of the buyer is not doubtful), as per the prevalent trade practices. Such trade creditors constitute a very important source of finance, inasmuch as these generally constitute 25% to 50% of the total short-term sources for financing working capital requirements.

Establishing and Sustaining Goods Supplier Relationship

Mostly it takes relatively a much longer time, especially in the business world, to establish one's credibility and reputation in the market. But, it takes just a few moments to destroy and demolish even a long standing reputation. Therefore, all companies, especially the newly established ones, should make it a point to honour the commitments, more importantly, at the initial stages, with a view to stabilising the newly-established relationships with the trade suppliers, so that a strong and long lasting business partnership could be formed on the sound foundation of mutual trust, faith and honesty.

Further, while prompt payments may facilitate further liberalization of the credit terms, unduly delayed payment may adversely affect the quality of supplies and services, as also the competitive pricing thereof. Two diametrically opposite live cases; one of a private sector company in Chennai, and the other of a Public Sector Undertaking (PSU) may bring home these points quite effectively.

Mini Case No.: I

"PRIZE OF PROMPT PAYMENT"

ABC Company (Private) Limited (not the real name) established in Chennai, was procuring one of the main components of its products from only one vendor, PQR Company Limited (again, not the real name). The quality of this item was so vital for the overall quality of the company's products, that it could hardly afford to procure it from any other source, whatsoever. The credit term offered by PQR Company Limited to ABC Company Limited was the same 30 days, as was in the usual cases of other buyers.

The Director (Finance) of ABC Company Limited thought of a very innovative strategy to get the credit term extended from 30 days to 45 days, without any extra cost. By way of a strategic decision, he had issued strict instructions to the officers concerned, both in the finance and purchase departments, to ensure that all the payments due to PQR Company Limited must invariably be made one day prior to the respective due dates, even if it may require borrowing of funds at a very high rate of interest.

This continued for about six months, uninterrupted. In the seventh month, the Director (Finance) instructed the General Manager (Finance) to personally visit the office of the vendor concerned to negotiate with them to grant them the facility of extended credit period (say 45 days, instead of the usual 30 days) as the company had been particularly prompt in the payments for the last six months in a row, and accordingly, it would be ensured that the payments are made all through on the 44th day or latest by the 45th day, and not even on the 46th day ever. And, the deal was struck, to the mutual advantage of both the parties.

By adopting the prudent policy of prompt payment to our sundry creditors, we may also, at the same time, ensure a sure source of finance, in our difficult times. Because, if we were prompt payment party all through, all the sundry creditors would voluntarily supply us the materials for a much longer credit period, at no extra cost, till our financial position improves and comes back to normalcy.

I am saying so because, in my career as a senior Bank Executive with the State Bank of India, I have myself seen happening so in several cases.

As against the Case-I, discussed earlier, the second case, incidentally of a Public Sector Undertaking (PSU) presents a diametrically opposite picture.

Mini Case No.: II

"PRICE PAID FOR PROLONGED PAYMENTS"

A Public Sector Undertaking (PSU) arranged an in-company Management Development Programme (MDP) at its factory premises for its officers. The travel involved a seven hours journey by road. One of the involved faculty members requested the office of the PSU concerned to arrange for a taxi for him on the scheduled date. And, the necessary arrangement was made accordingly. But, the concerned faculty member had a very tough and tiresome journey, as the taxi, arranged by the office of the PSU was one of the condemned ones. And, when the Professor made a complaint to the PSU to this effect, the fact that was revealed to him was really a revealing one. The contractor, who arranged taxis for the PSU confided with the faculty member that as the PSU had not made payments to him for the last over six months, he had decided either not to supply any taxi on the request of the PSU, or else to 'oblige' by providing only one of the condemned vehicles, and that also at a relatively higher price.

Thus, we see that, the practice, of unnecessarily delaying payments for an unreasonably long time, may prove to be a doubly costly and losing proposition in that you may get a sub-standard product or services, and that too at a much higher price.

Cost-Benefit Aspects of Prompt Payments

When goods are supplied on credit, it results in the blockage of funds in the sundry debtors, and the resultant loss of interest and/or opportunity cost, depending upon the period and term of credit. That is why some of the companies quote slightly lower price for cash purchases, inasmuch as, besides the avoidance of the aforesaid costs, the possibility of losses, on account of bad debts, also gets eliminated.

Further, with a view to ensure and encourage prompt payment, earlier than the usual credit period, some companies may prefer to offer cash discount. But then, the prompt payment so received has its price, too, usually a high price. A detailed discussion on cash discount and its financial implications, has already been made earlier, in the Chapter on Management of Credits.

Centralized Payments

As we have observed, it may prove to be highly beneficial if the payments are centralized at the corporate office of the company. The multi-faceted advantages comprise, *inter alia,*

(*a*) Consolidation of funds at one point, at the corporate office;

(*b*) Phasing and scheduling of all payments more effectively and systematically;

(*c*) This may, also, reduce the unproductive blockage of funds spread over several offices/ branches of the company.

(*d*) And, above all, the short-term investment of surplus funds can also be better planned and managed at one central focal point at the Head Office of the company.

It may be all the more beneficial if purchases, or at least their payments, are scheduled, in advance, with the mutual consent in such a way that the due dates of payments almost perfectly match with the position of inflows and outflows of cash, so that most of the payments may fall due for payment when the company's cash position is mostly favourable, and, correspondingly, no payment may fall due when the company is likely to face the phase of some cash crunch.

It may sound difficult but it, any way is possible.

Some other short-term sources of funds have already been discussed, in detail, in the Chapter on Management of Cash. These are:

(*a*) Public Deposits (PDs),
(*b*) Inter-Corporate Deposits (ICDs), and
(*c*) Commercial Papers (CPs).

7.3 SHORT-TERM LOANS FROM FINANCIAL INSTITUTIONS

The financial institutions like those mentioned below:

(*i*) the Life Insurance Corporation of India (LICI);
(*ii*) the General Insurance Corporation of India (GICI); and
(*iii*) the Unit Trust of India (UTI),

also grant short-term finance but only to manufacturing companies, and not to any trading company, and that too to only such manufacturing companies, who have excellent track records.

Eligibility Criteria

The detailed eligibility criteria of having an excellent track record, as stipulated by them, are given hereunder:

(*i*) It must have declared an annual dividend of at least 6% during the last five years. In some special cases, however, companies, who have declared annual dividend of at least 10% but for the last 3 years, may also be considered for short-term financing.

It thus occurs to me that, in any case, the company should have declared an aggregate dividend of minimum 30%, preferably during the last five years, or even during the last three years, but only in special cases.

(*ii*) The debt equity ratio of the company should not be more than 2 : 1.

(*iii*) The current ratio of the company should not be less than 1.33 : 1, as had been the case and was generally being followed by commercial banks in terms of the second method of lending, stipulated in the Tandon Committee Report.*

(*iv*) Further, the interest-coverage ratio for the last three years, on an average, should not be less than 2 : 1.

Special Features of such Loans

The short-term loans, provided by the financial institutions, have certain special features, detailed hereunder:

(*i*) Such loans are invariably in the nature of unsecured loans. Thus, the main loan document is the demand promissory note (DP Note), executed by the borrower company, in favour of the financial institution.

(*ii*) The loan is granted for a period of one year only. It can, however, be renewed but only for two further successive years. Thus, the loans have to be repaid, in full, with interest, within a maximum period of three years, in all. The aforesaid eligibility criteria must be satisfied at the time of renewal of the loan, too, on each such occasion.

---

* It, however, has no longer remained a mandatory stipulation, as the recommendations of the Tandon Committee have now remained just as a guide-line, and thus, no longer need to be strictly adhered to.

(*iii*) Further, after the repayment of the previous loan, the company cannot be granted any fresh and further loan at least for a period of six months.

(*iv*) Interest is charged on the loan at a stipulated rate, with quarterly rests, *i.e.* compounded quarterly. This way, the effective rate of interest proves to be even higher. But, a rebate of one per cent is given for prompt payment, which goes to nullify the compounding factor, to a great extent.

7.4 RIGHTS DEBENTURES

Public limited companies can issue debentures to its shareholders, on rights basis, for financing a part of its working capital requirements, from such long-term sources, too. For issuing such rights debentures the companies must comply with the following main guidelines:

The total amount of such an issue should not exceed;

(*a*) 20% of the gross current assets, loans and advances, less the long-term funds currently available for financing the company's working capital requirements,

OR

20% of the total paid-up share capital, including preference shares and free reserves, whichever is lower.

(*b*) The debt: equity ratio of the company, including the amount of the proposed issue, should not exceed 1 : 1.

(*c*) Such rights debentures will have to be issued first to the Indian resident shareholders of the company, on a pro-rata basis, *i.e.* in proportion to the total number of shares held by them, as on the recorded date.

7.5 FACTORING

A financial institution, rendering services pertaining to the management and financing of sundry debtors is referred to as a factor, and the service rendered in this way is known as factoring. The services of factoring is prevalent in the advanced western countries for long and is, by now, well-established there. In India, however, it is yet at the formative stage. The Reserve Bank of India has authorized only four public sector banks to offer services relating to factoring in the respective regions of the country, viz. State Bank of India (through its subsidiary known as State Bank of India Factoring and Commercial Services Limited), Canara Bank (through its subsidiary company named Canara Bank Factoring Limited), Allahabad Bank and Punjab National Bank to cater to the needs of the western, southern, eastern and northern regions, respectively.

Salient Features of Factoring

Some salient features of the factoring arrangement are given hereunder:

(*i*) The factor does not take the accounts of all the sundry debtors of a company. Instead they, do so on a very selective basis, and also fix up a credit limit in the case of each sundry debtor, depending upon the safety and security, financial stability and credit-worthiness of the respective sundry debtors whose accounts have been selected for factoring.

Thus, it occurs to me that the factor would not like to take up the accounts of such sundry debtors who are not considered to be of sound and stable financial standing. On the other hand, the company, on its part, will not like to part with the accounts of 'A' category sundry debtors to the factors, inasmuch as these may involve no or little risks.

On such an analysis, it may fairly be concluded that both the parties will settle for offering and availing of the factoring facility in respect of sundry debtors, falling under the medium or 'B' category, or at best, the creamy portion of some 'C' categories. Thus, no factor would be ready to accept any of the 'D' category of sundry debtors.

Such selectivity has naturally restricted and limited the number of accounts.

(*ii*) The factoring services pertain to taking up of the responsibility of collecting the amount of bills relating to goods sold on credit to the selected parties. The arrangement usually works like this:

Immediately on taking delivery of the bills from its client company, pertaining to the selected accounts, the factor may give a sum equal to the extent of 70% to 80% of the amount of bills to the company as advance.

This advance is, however, taken as an unsecured loan, as the factor, in the aforesaid circumstances, is only the holder of the relative bills of exchange and not its holder-in-due course. Had the factor paid full amount of the bill in advance (signifying almost the purchase of the bill), it would have become the holder-in-due course. And thus, such an advance would have been treated as a secured loan.

The factor, however, charges interest on such advances, which usually is equal to, or higher than the rate charged by the bank on the Cash Credit Accounts.

Further, immediately on realisation of the bill amount, the factor also pays the balance amount (the remaining 20% to 30%, as the case be) to the client company. In case the realization of the amount gets a little delayed, the factor also undertakes to pay the balance amount of the bill latest by the end of the credit period, stipulated in the bill.

(*iii*) The facility of factoring may be offered to the client company in two ways:

(*a*) with recourse 0to the drawer(s);

OR

(*b*) without recourse to the drawer(s).

In the former case, if the bill amount is not paid by the drawee(s) concerned, the factor has a recourse open to the drawer of the bill, *i.e.* the seller. This means that in the event of the return of the unpaid bill, the factor returns the bill to the drawer and recovers the entire amount, already paid to the sellers, as advance payment. As against this, in the case of 'without recourse to the drawer(s)', no claim could be made on the drawer, once the bill has been taken over by the factor, and in case of non-payment of such bills, the sufferer will be the factor only, as the drawer (seller) concerned is already out of the picture, since the bills have been taken over from him by the factor.

In such a case, the factor runs a much higher risk. And, consequently, more than ordinary care has to be exercised by the factor, and the rate of such service charges will, naturally, be comparatively much higher.

In India, however, as the factoring business is still in its infancy, the facility so far being extended is only on "with recourse to the drawer" basis.

Thus, one may argue and rightly so, that there is hardly any difference between the facility of factoring and the facility of advances against the bills sent for collection (or even purchase or discount of the demand and time bills respectively) extended by Commercial Banks. The only difference, however, lies in the fact that the bank only intimates the drawee of the bill, *i.e.* the buyer, and pays the amount to the seller if the bill is paid, or else returns the bill to the seller, if it remains unpaid. The bank does not make any special effort of follow-up for the realisation of the bill. The factor, however, makes some sincere efforts and attempts for timely payment of the bills.

(*iv*) Further, the factor also charges commission from the client company, which may vary from 1 % to 2% of the face value of the bills factored. This amount of commission is realized over and above the amount of interest received on the amount advanced to the company against the bill factored.

Further, if both the parties (factors and the client company) mutually agree to factor the entire credit bills, the collection department of the company may become quite redundant, resulting in a matching savings for the company, both in terms of its expenses and botheration, as compared to the payment of amount of interest and commission to the factor, even if these may amount to be a little higher than the rate of interest being charged by the banks.

Disadvantages

The disadvantages (or instead let us call these the limitations) of the scheme, too, may be summarized as under:

(*i*) As the factors are very selective in choice of accounts, and the client companies would also prefer to handle the first class accounts themselves, the number and value of the accounts factored may be much lower than the total number and volume of trade bills.

(*ii*) Besides, this would also mean continued maintenance of the credit and collection department of the company, along with the availment of the factoring facilities, resulting in the two-way expenses in respect of the credit collection department of the company, as well as payment of commission and interest to the factors.

Relative Advantages and Disadvantages of Factoring

A. Advantages

The following advantages, pertaining to the facility being offered by the factors, are intended to make the scheme very attractive:

As we have seen earlier, the factor advances a sum of money to the extent of 70% to 80% of the amount of the bill, accepted under the scheme, and the balance amount is also paid on the due date of the credit period or on collection of the amount, whichever is earlier. Thus, the time and volume of cash inflow is known to the company almost in certain terms, whereby it becomes as much easier and accurate for the company to estimate while preparing the cash budget.

B. Disadvantages

But, the very fact that the services of factoring is being offered in India, even as of now, only on "with recourse to the drawer" basis, the risk and botheration of bad debts still remains with the company.

All considered, a modest beginning has been made in India in respect of factoring facilities, and gradually the scheme may pick up the desired pace and become well-established, as is the case in the Western world.

7.5.1 FORFAITING

As we already know, factoring is the facility of collection and/or negotiation (purchase) or discount of demand or time bills of exchange respectively, wherein both the drawers and the drawees are of the same country. But then, if such a facility of collection and/or negotiation or discount, as the case be, is extended in the case of export bills of exchange, this is known as forfaiting. Thus, while factoring pertains to domestic (inland) trade transactions, forfaiting relates to the international trade (export bills). And, the agency extending the facility of forfaiting is known as the forfaiter in the same way as the agency providing the factoring facility is known as the factor.

Further, the services of forfaiting is mostly provided on "without recourse" basis, as against the facility of factoring which is presently being offered in India, and even in most of the other developing countries, on 'with recourse' basis. This way, the exporter is free from both the commercial and political risks, usually inherent in international trade transactions.

In India, the EXIM bank (Export and Import Bank) serves as the nodal agency in respect of the contracts of forfaiting. The forfaiting arrangement usually involves the following main procedures and steps:

1. The contract of sale and purchase is first finalized between the exporter and the importer in regard to the quantity of the order, price, currency of payment, terms of credit, the period of delivery, the nature of documents required, etc.
2. Further, the exporter is required to reveal all the relevant details and information pertaining to the contract, so as to enable the forfaiting agency (the EXIM bank or the Indian agent of the international forfaiter) to reasonably assess and appraise the quantum and extent of the financial (credit) and political risks, and thereby to quote the rate of discount of the export bill.
3. Such quotation of the discount rate requires the approval of the EXIM bank. If, in the considered opinion of the EXIM bank, the quoted discount rate is found to be rather high and not competitive, the exporter has to renegotiate with the same forfaiting agency, or even with some other ones, and an acceptable and reasonably lower discount rate has to be obtained, and, in turn, finally approved by the EXIM bank.

4. It is only then that the exporter is be able to quote the final selling price to the importer, by loading the discount rate to the quotation of the selling price.
5. On finalization of the deal, the following parties, sign the required legal documents:
   (*a*) A commercial contract is signed between the exporter and the importer.
   (*b*) A forfaiting contract is signed between the exporter and the forfaiter, through the EXIM bank.

   Further, the forfaiter issues two certificates pertaining to the
   (*a*) Commitment fees, and
   (*b*) Discount rate.
6. It is only at this stage that the exporter draws the export time (usance) bill and present it to the forfaiter for discount purposes.
7. The forfaiter then presents the bill to the importer on the due date for payment; or may even prefer to sell it in the secondary market.

Advantage of Forfaiting over Export Financing by Banks

(*a*) As we already know, the export finance (post-shipment finance), can be extended by the banks up to 180 days or, in some special case up to the maximum of 270 days, as per the Reserve Bank of India (RBI) guidelines. But then, the contract of forfaiting can be entered into for as long a period as even up to 5 to 7 years.

(*b*) Besides, an Indian exporter can sell the goods to the foreign importers of even such country wherefor export credit guarantee coverage of the ECGC is not available, inasmuch as the forfaiting contract itself covers both the commercial and political risks, as it is entered into on 'Without Recourse' basis).

Cost of Forfaiting

The forfaiting charges comprise:

(*a*) Financing charge, which is computed on the basis of the tenor of the bill, the country risk and the country bank risk. As of now, it usually ranges between 50 to 400 basis points above the LIBOR. Further, it is computed from the date the finance is provided by the forfaiter.

(*b*) The commitment charge, however, depends upon the period of the usance bill and the risk connected with the country of destination.

At present, the commitment charge ranges between 13 to 15 basis points.

It may be pertinent to mention here that, by way of a safeguard and risk management, the forfaiter normally stipulates a ceiling of its exposure for the portfolio of the various countries, separately, commensurate with the extent of the financial and political risks involved.

Working Capital Financing by Banks

As compared to the various aforesaid short-term sources of funds for financing working capital requirements of the companies, the short-term advances by commercial banks is the most popular and prime source of such short-term funds in the business world, even as of now.

We, therefore, propose to discuss separately in detail the various facilities offered by the commercial banks for financing the working capital requirements, in Chapter 8.

(B) LONG-TERM SOURCES OF FUNDS

As we have already seen, in Chapter 2, a prudent business sense calls for financing our working capital requirements from a suitable mix of both short-term and long-term sources of funds.

We would, now discuss, in this section of the Chapter, the following sources of long-term funds:

(*i*) Retained earnings,

(*ii*) Share capital:

(*a*) Equity shares (also referred to as Ordinary Shares),

(*b*) Preference shares,

(*iii*) Debentures, and

(*iv*) Term loans.

7.6 RETAINED EARNINGS

It is again a better business sense to retain a major portion of the net profit, to be ploughed back in the business so as to result in an overall growth of the shareholders' wealth, instead of just the annual income, by way of dividend paid.

By now, it is a well known fact that the Reliance Industries Limited (RIL) had been, by working backwards, investing the required sum of money in expanding and acquiring capital assets so as to avail of the tax concessions, by way of investment allowance, for modernization, etc. Thereby it continues to remain in the zero-tax bracket for several years. Perhaps, it was mainly due to this reason that Section 119J was incorporated in the Income Tax Act, whereby all the companies were, henceforth, necessarily required to pay income tax on their book profit at the specified rate.

All said and done, RIL has, by now, become a great industrial force to reckon with by adopting the policy of ploughing back a major portion of its net profit into the business, to grow into an industrial giant and earn the envious distinction of becoming the *numero uno*, in several areas.

Further, "Berkshire Hathway, the US investment company of Warren Buffett, has its shares quoted at a whopping $ 40,000 per share. It has never given dividend to its shareholders, yet the market price of its share appreciates, as the company's investment portfolio is considered among the most impressive, with the blue chips like Gillette, Coca-Cola, and Washington Post, in its bag", as had once been reported in the *Economic Times*.

But the fact that "the fate of similar investment companies in India, does not inspire much hope" is quite a different matter.

This is so because the shareholders of the aforenamed US Investment Company have full and firm faith that the management of the company can build up much more wealth for them in the company as compared to the income that may accrue to them annually, by way of investment of the amount of dividend, paid to them annually. And, at the end of the day, the shareholders of the company alone are the lone beneficiaries, because the retained earnings (the reserves and surplus of the company) belong to none other than the company's shareholders only and exclusively.

The relative advantages and disadvantages:

(*a*) To the company; and

(*b*) To the shareholders of the company.

A. To Companies

Advantages

(*i*) Retained earnings represent the internal generation of surplus, and to this extent, the company does not have to depend or negotiate with any outsider like the creditors or even the shareholders.

(*ii*) Retained earnings, as aforesaid, represent, in essence, a part of the Owners' Equity (OE) and, in effect, enhance the owners' stake in the business, whereby their capacity to borrow from outside also goes up, as the Debt/Equity Ratio improves. This way, the company's capacity and possibility to expand and modernize goes up along with its prospects.

(*iii*) Retained earnings help the company to avoid issuance of fresh equity shares, which, besides involving the cost related with their issue, eliminates the possibility of downward trend in the price of its shares in the stock market due to the resultant decline in the earning per share (EPS).

(*iv*) This also mitigates, if not fully eliminates, the risks of dilution of the control, resulting from the forced take-over of the company by some other business houses or groups.

Disadvantages

(*i*) The quantum of retained earnings may fluctuate, year after year, if the company prefers to maintain the uniform level of dividends paid, irrespective of the rise and fall in the quantum of net profit or Profit After Tax (PAT).

(*ii*) Besides, the level of profitability of the company, and the quantum of retained earnings is very limited. Therefore the level of retained earnings alone may not be sufficient enough to achieve the expansion and modernization at the optimal level.

(*iii*) As against the external borrowings, the retained earnings are not tax-deductible and, therefore, ultimately, the opportunity cost of retained earnings becomes very high. Besides, the retained earnings, in effect, are the dividends foregone by the equity shareholders and, such a sacrifice, in the present day context, becomes still higher since the financial year 1998-1999, inasmuch as dividends paid are no longer taxable in the hands of the equity shareholders. Instead, the tax on dividends paid, is now payable by the company.

B. To Shareholders of Companies

Advantages

Retained earnings, in effect, reduce the quantum of dividend paid, and thus, the equity shareholders are relieved of the botheration and anxiety of selecting the most advantageous avenues of fresh investments. The case of the US investment company, "Berkshire Hathway of Warren Buffett", which has not paid any dividend so far, right from its inception, as discussed in the foregoing pages, is an apt example to bring home the point amply clear.

Disadvantages

The very fact that the amount of dividend paid is no longer taxable in the hands of the equity shareholders, whereas the capital gains tax is still payable, makes the appreciation of the market value of shares, commensurate with the increase in the level of reserves and surplus and the book value of the shares, less attractive and gainful.

In some cases, the companies have been found to have invested the retained earnings sub-optimally, without fully appreciating and correctly computing the actual opportunity cost of the retained earnings. This, naturally, goes against the financial interest of the shareholders.

7.7 SHARE CAPITAL

There are two types of shares:

(*a*) Equity shares, also known as ordinary shares, and

(*b*) Preference shares.

We shall discuss both these shares separately hereafter.

7.7.1 Equity Share (Ordinary Share) Capital

The equity shareholders of the company are considered to be (though notionally only) the owners of the company, as against the debenture holders, who are, in fact, the creditors to the company. I say 'notionally' inasmuch as, a shareholder, owning just 50 equity shares of say, the State Bank of India, out of its total over 50 crore (around 52.63 crore) issued, subscribed and fully paid up equity shares, of the face value of Rs. 10 each, can hardly exercise any control and have any effective say in the management of the affairs of the company, whatsoever. But then, the shareholder is virtually the owner of the company (though 'collectively'), along with all the other shareholders, collectively owning the entire equity shares of the Bank aggregating 52, 62, 98, 878 shares of Rs. 10 each to be exact, as on March 31, 2000. However, after the issue of the rights equity shares by the SBI recently, the aggregate value of the SBI equity shares has gone up still further.

The fact that the shareholders own the company, they are entitled to all the gains and benefits accruing to the company. But, at the same time, they also share the losses and liabilities of the company in the same way as the proprietor of a proprietary firm or the partners of a partnership firm do. But, of course, with a difference. The liabilities of the shareholders of all the limited liability companies remain confined and restricted only to the extent of their share capital, contributed in such companies.

In the case of unlimited liability company, however, the liabilities of the shareholders remain unlimited. Such companies, however, are extremely rare, almost non-existent, in the real world, for obvious reasons.

That is why, with a view to ensure that all the directors of the company always work with full zeal and enthusiasm, interest and inclination, for the general good and welfare of the company, the banks and financial institutions insist on obtaining a third party guarantee from all the directors in their personal capacity, so as to bind all their personal belongings and assets, too, to recover their dues from the limited liability companies.

Further, before we discuss the special features, connected with the equity shares, it would be better if we discuss some of the terminologies, which are most relevant for any such discussion.

SOME TERMINOLOGIES

(*a*) **Authorised Capital:** Authorised capital, as the name itself suggests, is the maximum amount up to the face value of which the company concerned has been authorised to issue shares including both the equity and preference shares. Here, only the face value of the share is to be taken into account, and not the amount of premium at which the share has been issued.

But, if the bonus shares are issued, by capitalization of the general reserves, such amount (the face value of the bonus shares issued) shall also be taken into account, while computing whether such aggregate amount comes within the ceiling of the authorised capital.

And, if such aggregate amount is to exceed the amount of the authorised capital the letter will have to be suitably augmented and duly authorised by the competent authority.

Take for example, the case of Burroughs Wellcome, who had announced the issue of the bonus shares in the ratio of 1 : 1 *i.e.* one equity share against each equity share held as on the record date in its annual general meeting of the shareholders. But, as the authorised capital of the company, at the material time, was only Rs. 5 crore and the issued, subscribed and paid-up capital was Rs. 3 crore, the issuance of the bonus shares were withheld till the authorised capital of the company was duly raised from Rs. 5 crore to Rs. 10 crore.

This was so because the issuance of the bonus shares would have raised the paid-up share capital of the company to Rs. 6 crore Rs. 3 crore plus Rs. 3 crore (bonus shares)], which would have exceeded the authorised capital (ceiling) of Rs. 5 crore.

Thus, we see that while the declaration of the bonus share is permitted, the actual issuance thereof is not, pending due augmentation of the authorised capital.

(*b*) **Issued Capital:** Issued capital is the amount for the aggregate face value of which the shares have been offered for subscription by the public, or by private placement. This amount (excluding the share premium amount, if any), of course, will have to be well within the amount of the authorised capital.

(*c*) **Subscribed Capital:** Subscribed capital is the amount up to which the shares have been applied for by the investors (in the public issue or by private placement).

(*d*) **Paid-up Capital:** While issuing the shares, the companies, in their prospectus, stipulate as to what percentage of amount of the face value of the shares is to be paid, along with the application (which is known as the application money). It also stipulates as to how much amount (percentage) is payable on allotment, on the first call (say, after six months from the date of allotment) and on the second, third, and the final call (say, after 12 months, etc., from the date of allotment).

Let us now try to understand such provisions with the help of an **illustrative example.**

Example

XYZ Company Limited, having an authorised capital of Rs. 200 million has come out with a public issue on January 1, 2009 to the tune of Rs. 100 million with the undernoted stipulations:

(*i*) 25% of the amount of the face value of the shares is payable with the application;

(*ii*) 25% of the amount on allotment and/or thereafter, by a stipulated date, say, up to February 28, 2009;

(*iii*) 25% of the amount, on the first call, on or before June 30, 2009; and

(*iv*) the balance 25% of the amount is payable on the second and final call, on or before December 31, 2009.

And, supposing if the issue has been fully subscribed, the amount under various heads, discussed earlier, would be as under:

(*a*) Authorised capital: Rs. 200 million

(*b*) Issued capital: Rs. 100 million

(*c*) Subscribed capital: Rs. 100 million

(*d*) Paid-up capital:

- (*i*) Rs. 25 million on application;
- (*ii*) Rs. 50 million (Rs. 25 million + Rs. 25 million) on allotment or by February 28, 2009;
- (*iii*) Rs. 75 million on or before June 30, 2009; and
- (*iv*) Rs. 100 million on or before December 31, 2009.

(Provided, of course, all the investors have paid the required allotment money, and all the call money on time. Otherwise, they may pay it later with penal rate of interest, or else their shares may be forfeited.)

Thus, if some amount of money has not been paid up to February 28, 2009 (allotment money) and/or up to June 30, 2009 (first call money) and/or up to December 31, 2009 (second and final call money), these figures will have to be shown with as much lesser amount (remaining unpaid) on the specific date of the balance sheet, etc.

In the above example, in case only 90% of the issued capital has been subscribed, the position obviously will be as under:

(*i*) Authorised capital: Rs. 200 million (*i.e.* no change)

(*ii*) Issued capital: Rs. 100 million (*i.e.* no change)

(*iii*) Subscribed capital: Rs. 90 million (*i.e.* 90% of Rs. 100 million)

(*iv*) Paid-up capital:

(*a*) Rs. 22.5 million will be adjusted as the application money

(*b*) Rs. 45.0 million on allotment, and/or by February 28, 2009

(*c*) Rs. 67.5 million on or before June 30, 2009

(*d*) Rs. 90.0 million on or before December 31, 2009.

Provided, of course, all the investors make all the payments within the stipulated due dates.

Some of the companies, specially those of good standing and reputation, may stipulate that the full amount is to be payable with the application itself. In such cases, all the aforesaid three categories of capital, viz. issued, subscribed and paid-up capitals, will be the same as the amount of the issued capital, which has necessarily to be well within the authorised capital, provided, of course, the issue gets fully subscribed. For example, the State Bank of India had come out with its first public issue in 1993 at a premium of Rs. 90, *i.e.* Rs. 10 face value share were issued for Rs. 100, *i.e.* Rs. 10 towards share capital and Rs. 90 towards share premium account. And, the full amount was payable along with the application.

As against this, Usha Rectifiers Limited (now changed to Usha India Limited), had come out with a public issue of the equity shares in 1989, at a premium of Rs. 40, *i.e.* Rs. 10 face value share for Rs. 50 each, with the following stipulations in their prospectus:

Only 10% of the amount was payable with the application, and the remaining 90% of the amount was made payable in very easy instalments of convenient percentages of the face value of shares, spread over a longer period. Such a strategy was, perhaps, adopted by the company, as a well thought of market strategy, to make the issue most attractive and easy for the prospective investors. But then, the issue was highly under-subscribed, as most of the enlightened investors had kept their hands off from this issue as, in their considered opinion, the amount of premium was on a very high side. But, the company, on its part, had also proved to be smart enough in that they had, obviously, deliberately, avoided stipulating in their prospectus and the application to the SEBI that, in the event of the issue being undersubscribed, lesser than 90% of the issued capital, the entire application money would be refunded to the applicants. And, on this very plea, the company preferred to retain the entire application money, though the issue was subscribed far under the required minimum 90%.

Whether suitable actions were taken by the SEBI authorities against its erring officials for the aforesaid negligence on their part, however, is not within the purview of the book. But, it was stipulated by SEBI to that in case the subscription to the issue falls short of the 90% of the amount of the issued capital, the entire application money will be refunded to all the investors/applicants.

SOME OTHER TERMS

PAR VALUE (ALSO KNOWN AS FACE VALUE)

Par value is the amount written on the face of the share scrip. That is why, it is also known as the face value. The most popular par values of shares, prevalent in India, as of now, are Rs. 10 followed by Rs. 100. But some of the shares are still having the par value as Re. 1, Rs. 2, Rs. 3,

Rs. 4, Rs. 5, Rs. 20, Rs. 50. Earlier, the shares of ACC had the face value of Rs. 1000, which have since been split into shares of the par value of Rs. 100 and later of Rs. 10 only. Thus, now there is no share left with the face value of Rs. 1000, quoted on the Bombay Stock Exchange (BSE) or the National Stock Exchange (NSE). For details, one may refer to the financial papers like the *Economic Times*, etc., where the companies having the face values of their shares other than Rs. 10 (the most common face value), a specific distinguishing sign is indicated before their names in the daily quotations of the quoted shares published on day-to-day basis.

Recently, the shares of Infosys, of the face value of Rs. 10 have since been split into the shares of the face value of Rs. 5 each.

Some of the companies, whose shares have the face values, other than Rs. 10, are given, by way of illustrative examples, hereunder:

Amount	*Descriptions*
Rs. 100	Madras Cement, Andhra Paper, Bharat Pipe, MICO
Rs. 5	Infosys Technologies, Sterlite Industries
Rs. 4	Mascot Syst
Rs. 2	Cummins India, Wipro
Re. 1	Dabur India, Hindustan Liver Limited, Zee Telefilms,

Book Value

Book value of the shares is the value of each share, inclusive of the aggregate amount of the entire Reserves and Surpluses, as per the books of the company, as all these belong to none other than the equity shareholders alone.

Thus, the book value of each share, in percentage terms, would be equal to

$$= \frac{\text{(Fully Paid-up Equity Share Capital + Reserves + Surpluses)}}{\text{Aggregate face value of such shares}} \times 100$$

Let us elucidate the point with the help of an **illustrative example:**

(*a*) Fully paid-up equity shares of XYZ Company — Rs. 100 million

(*b*) Reserves and surplus — Rs. 400 million

(*c*) Aggregate face value of such shares will be equal to (*a*), *i.e.* — Rs. 100 million

Therefore, the Book Value per Share $= \frac{100 \text{ million} + 400 \text{ million}}{100 \text{ million}} \times 100$

$$= \frac{500 \text{ million}}{100 \text{ million}} \times 100$$

$$= 500\%$$

$$= 5 \text{ times (the face value).}$$

Thus, if the face value of each equity share is Rs. 10, its book value will be Rs. 50, and if it be Rs. 100 or Rs. 5, it would be Rs. 500 or Rs. 25, and so on.

Issue Price

Issue price is the amount at which the shares are offered to the public for subscription. Usually, new companies come out with their first public issue at par value or face value. For example, the first public issue of HDFC Bank in the year 1994 was priced at par value (Rs. 10), though its market price had shot up to Rs. 250.75 and Rs. 251.50, as on Thursday, February 22, 2001, on BSE and NSE respectively, as reported by *The Economic Times* dated February 23, 2001.

Incidentally, the high and low prices of the share of HDFC Bank in the preceding 52 weeks [from 23 February 2001] had, however, been Rs. 296.00 and Rs. 189.00 on Bombay Stock Exchange (BSE) and Rs. 295.00 and Rs. 185.00 on National Stock Exchange (NSE). And again, within less than nine years (*i.e.* as on 18 September, 2009), it had risen to Rs. 1,524.45 on the National Stock Exchange (NSE). [Source: *The Economic Times,* 18 September 2009.]

But, some well established companies, the book value and market price of whose shares are higher than their face value, usually come out with their public issue at a reasonably higher price than the face value of their shares. For example, the State Bank of India had come out with the public issue of its shares of Rs. 10 face value at an offer price (issue price) of Rs. 100, *i.e.* at a premium of Rs. 90. [The amount of the issue price, in excess of the face value of shares is known as the amount of premium. Thus, in the above case of the State Bank of India, the shares of Rs. 10 face value were issued for Rs. 100, *i.e.* at a premium of Rs. 90, *i.e.* Rs. 100 less Rs. 10 equals Rs. 90.

It may, however, be pertinent to mention here that, as per law, the issue price of the share can, under no circumstances, be lower than its par (face) value.

Incidentally, it may also be mentioned here that the first public issue of Garden (manufacturing Garden Brand 'Saris') was issued at Rs. 85, *i.e.* at a premium of Rs. 75, when it was converted from Private Company to Public Company, depending upon its financial stability as also its performance and prospects.

Market Value

Market value of the equity shares, however, is the price at which the shares are being quoted and traded in any stock exchanges (BSE, NSE, etc.). Such prices may be said to be reliable enough, only if the shares are being actually traded daily or at least frequently as also in reasonably large volumes. But, in the case of the shares which are rarely traded and that, too, in a significantly low volume, the price at which these have been traded in the stock exchanges may not be considered to be reliable. One must, however, be cautious enough in this regard, inasmuch as some companies deliberately go on enhancing the price of their shares, gradually, in a calculated manner, if they intend to come out with a public issue of their shares, at a premium of an unreasonably higher level.

The press reports, pertaining to Usha Rectifiers Limited (now Usha India Limited), indicate that it reportedly artificially jacked up the price of its shares in the market from Rs. 20, and Rs. 25 to around Rs. 250, immediately before coming out with its public issue, at a premium of Rs. 40, *i.e.* at a price of Rs. 50.

Soon after its public issue was over, its price came down to its natural level at around Rs. 20 or even lower. It is a separate matter that, due to all these reportedly unfair practices adopted by the company, its shares were highly under-subscribed, which was no where near the stipulated minimum 90% of the total issue amount. And, surprisingly, it did not have to refund the entire application money to the investors, as it had not stipulated in its prospectus, nor in its application to the SEBI anything to that effect.

Thus, the negligence, on the part of the officers of SEBI, proved to be a boon for the company, though a bane for the investors. After seeing through the reported 'game' played by the company, most of the investors preferred not to pay a single amount on any of the further calls and thus, preferred to allow their entire application money to get forfeited by the company.

Public Issue

The issue of shares to the members of the public, through a prospectus, is known as the public issue. This, in fact, is the most popular and important mode of raising funds through issue of share capital.

Private Placement

The sale of shares to one or only a few investors is known as private placement. Such issues do not require the issuance of the formal prospectus nor any underwriting arrangements. Besides, the terms of the issue are also determined through negotiation between the parties, viz. the issuing company and the investing company(ies) or individuals.

Rights Issues

The fresh shares issued only and exclusively to the existing shareholders of the company, as per its register, as on a specified record date, on the rights basis, is known as the rights issue.

The existing shareholders are given the right to apply for a specified number of shares, in proportion to their existing holdings of shares, on pro-rata basis. And, they are assured of allotment of (at least) such number of shares. I say, 'at least', because they also have the option of applying for additional number of shares, over and above the number of shares offered to them on rights basis. And, in the event of some of the existing shareholders opting not to subscribe to the issue or if they fail to apply within the stipulated time period, which is usually 30 days, such un-subscribed portion of the shares may be given to such shareholders who have applieJ for additional shares also, of course, on pro-rata basis, depending upon their current holding of shares.

For example, if the paid-up share capital of a company is Rs. 50 million, and it comes out with a rights issue to the tune of Rs. 25 million, a shareholder owning 100 shares will get the offer to apply for 50 shares on rights basis. And, he may also apply for additional shares, over and above the 50 shares. But then, as only a portion of the additional shares applied for may be allotted to the investor, on pro-rata basis, it may be usually prudent to apply for additional shares only to the extent of around 30%-40% of the total number of shares, offered on the rights basis.

Besides, the rights offers are negotiable, too. That is, a shareholder can sell its rights for some consideration (money), directly to a third person or through a share broker in the secondary market. That is why, when the rights issue opens, the price of such shares are quoted in the secondary market (stock exchanges) as 'cum-rights', that is, the shares purchased by an investor can be got registered with the company and this way, he or she will become entitled to receive the rights offer, too. And, on the expiry of the time period for applying for the shares with the rights entitlement, again the share prices are quoted in the share market (stock exchanges) on 'ex-rights' basis.

Rights issues, as compared to public issues, are more economical and cost-effective, as these do not involve any underwriting, or wide publicity, etc., whereas these are required in the case of public issues.

The company, which has made the rights issue, just sends, invariably by Registered Post, a 'Letter of Offer', along with a composite application form, to all of its existing shareholders only, as on a record date, announced earlier.

The composite application form comprises four pages, divided into four segments, marked Parts A, B, C and D, on one separate page each.

Part A is meant for accepting and applying for the shares offered on rights basis by the existing shareholders only. They may also apply for some additional shares, provided they have applied for the entire number of shares offered to them on the rights basis.

Part B is meant for renouncing the rights by the existing shareholder in favour of some other person. This is duly completed and signed by the existing shareholders and passed on to the other person, when the former wants to sell its rights.

Part C is to be used for application by the renouncee, *i.e.* in whose favour the existing shareholder has renounced his rights, by executing the Part B, as aforesaid.

Part D is in the nature of a split form which is required to be sent to the issuing company within a stipulated time, with a request to send fresh application forms, in the case where the original allotee (existing shareholder) wants to apply for some shares on rights basis as also wants to sell some portion of the rights offer in the secondary market. But, in such cases, as the original allotee is not applying for the full number of the rights shares offered, he is not entitled to apply for any additional shares, whatsoever.

Primary Market and Secondary Market

When shares are issued by way of public issue, rights issue or on private placement basis, and the shares applied for are allotted by the issuing company to the investors, it is know to have been purchased or obtained from the primary market.

And, later, when such original primary investors want to sell their shares to some one else in any stock exchange, through a broker (or even on personal basis to their friends and/or relatives, etc.), such sales and purchases are known to have been transacted in the secondary market.

Advantages and Disadvantages of Equity Share Capital

A. From the Point of View of the Company:

Advantages

(*i*) Equity shares may well be considered as the most significant long-term source of finance, inasmuch as it represents the perpetual and permanent capital of the company and, thus, there is no liability on the part of the company, to repay it at any point in time, during its entire life span.

Earlier, the aforesaid statement could have been absolutely correct inasmuch as till recently, as per the extant laws, no company was allowed, under any circumstances, to dilute the level of its paid-up equity shares, during its continued existence. But, now the companies have since been permitted to buy back their own shares, under certain circumstances, and, of course, at their own option.

(*ii*) Besides, there is no obligation on the part of companies to pay any dividend to the equity shareholders. But, in practice, good companies do not prefer to skip the payment of dividends, unless there are some compelling circumstances to do so. For example, in the year 1994-95, though Kesoram Industries had shown a net loss at the end of the year, it declared a dividend, though at a nominal rate of 10% only, and that, too, out of the dividend equalization reserves.

The companies usually adopt such strategies so as to be able to claim in their prospectus, at the time of their subsequent issues, that the company had consistently been paying dividends for the last so many years. But, even Kesoram Industries could not afford to continue this indefinitely, at all times, and thus, its had to skip the dividend for a year or two.

And, in the most recent and current case of Flex Industries, the company has not been paying any dividend to the equity shareholders for the last around five/six years, though it continues to pay interest on its debentures, every six months, and that, too, by way of Bank Drafts and not by way of the usual interest warrants, on account of the legal obligation to do so, *i.e.* pay periodical interest due on stipulated dates.

However, Burroughs Wellcome, one of the reputed blue chip companies, preferred to skip the payment of dividends to the equity shareholders for a couple of years, as it had sustained very heavy losses on account of its diversification into manufacturing of sports goods. But, later, its financial position improved significantly so much so that not only did it resume the payment of dividends to the equity shareholders, it also declared bonus shares in the ratio of 1 : 1, out of its accumulated free reserves.

(*iii*) Besides, a large equity base goes a long way in enhancing the credit-worthiness of the company, and accordingly, its borrowing powers too. That is why, when the scale of operation of a company goes-up, and its requirements of funds therewith, the banks and term lending institutions insist that the company should enhance its equity base by way of fresh issue of equity shares (or even preference shares, which, too, constitute its net worth), so as to maintain its current ratio and debt/equity ratio, within the permitted parameters.

The equity base is of utmost importance to determine the dependability and bankability of banks too so much so that the Letters of Credit issued, even by the State Bank of India, till late sixties and early seventies, were not being accepted by some of the foreign banks, and they kept on insisting for their confirmation by some known and reputed foreign bank, with sound equity base. This was so, because, at the material time, the equity base (net worth) of State Bank of India was as meagre as under:

Authorised capital: Rs. 200 million (Rs. 20 crore),

Issued, subscribed and paid-up capital: Rs. 56.25 million (Rs. 5.625 crore), and

Reserves and surplus: Rs. 200 million (Rs. 20 crore) approximately.

Thus, the bank's net worth came broadly to around Rs. 250 million (Rs. 25 crore) as against very high levels of its loans and advances.

Therefore, the State Bank of India took a strategic decision to bring back Rs. 200 million (Rs. 20 crore) from its secret reserves each year, for quite sometime. And, with the mega public issue of its equity shares in 1993-94 and the GDR issue, a little later, its paid-up equity share capital now stands at Rs. 5262.989 million (Rs. 526.2989 crore) as on March 31, 2000.

Disadvantages

The cost of equity shares is high, generally the highest, because of the following two main reasons:

(*a*) The dividends payable to the equity (as also preference) shareholders are non-tax-deductible, for the company, and

(*b*) The expectation of the investors in the equity shares are generally high as compared to other categories of investors.

But then, if the company is a reputed one and whose shares are being quoted in the share markets at a much higher price than their face value, it can afford to issue the equity shares with a high premium, whereby these may, in effect, prove to be much cheaper.

For example, the State Bank of India issued its shares of Rs. 10 face value at a price of Rs. 100, *i.e.* at a premium of Rs. 90. Thus, even if the Bank declared a dividend of 50%, it will actually have to pay only Rs. 5 per share to the shareholders, which, in turn, costs to the Bank only 5%, because Rs. 5 have been paid to the shareholders on their investment of Rs. 100 (Rs. 10 + Rs. 90).

Thus, we may qualify the above statement by saying that:

"The equity shares may prove to be the costliest source of funds, if issued at par, unless these are issued at a sufficiently high premium". But, the companies, with a view to maintaining their position and prestige, in the eyes of the public, should not price their shares at an un-reasonably high premium. For example, the IDBI issued its equity shares of the face value of Rs. 10, at a price of Rs. 130, *i.e.* at a premium of Rs. 120. [And, reportedly, it perhaps, forced its borrowers to compulsorily subscribe to its (evidently high priced) shares, well against their free will, failing which its issue would have ended up highly under-subscribed]. It is evident from the fact that the share was initially quoted, on day one, in the Bombay Stock Exchange (BSE) at Rs. 120, *i.e.* well below its issue price. And, as all the investors, mainly perhaps, the IDBI borrowers, started unloading their shares, in the stock market, it closed at Rs. 105 only, on the very first day. And, till February 20, 2001, its shares had hardly crossed the level of Rs. 50 in any of the stock markets. In fact, as on February 20, 2001, it closed at Rs. 31.30 and Rs. 31.10 on BSE and NSE respectively, and its high and low prices, in the preceding 52 weeks, had been Rs. 47.00 and Rs. 18.00 on BSE, and Rs. 49.00 and Rs. 19.00 on NSE. [Source: *The Economic Times,* February 21, 2001]. And, the position had still worsened, if we look at the market price of the IDBI share, both at the BSE and NSE, as at the close of business on October 15, 2001, at as low as Rs. 15.95; while its high and low prices, in the preceding 52 weeks, had fallen far lower at Rs. 35 and Rs. 15 respectively. (Source: *The Economic Times,* October 17, 2001).

This, in my considered opinion, has adversely affected the reputation and prestige of the biggest term leading institution in the country, and, that too, in the public sector.*

(*i*) It would, therefore, augur well if the companies learn the lesson not to repeat the story under any circumstances, whatsoever.

(*ii*) Further, the relatively higher cost of issuing equity shares, as compared to the issue of other securities becomes far too higher, if the cost of commission paid to the underwriters, the brokerage paid to the brokers and the other costs connected therewith are also taken into account.

(*iii*) Moreover, the issue of equity shares to the outsiders also involves the risk of dilution of the control of the existing major shareholders, and forced takeovers.

B. From the Point of View of the Shareholders

Advantages

(*i*) Equity shareholders, by virtue of being the owners of the company (though notionally) enjoy the controlling rights.

(*ii*) Besides, in the limited liability companies, the shareholders' liabilities are limited only to the extent of their shareholdings.

(*iii*) The equity shareholders, being the owners, enjoy the highest reward, though they tend to share the highest risk too.

(*iv*) Further, of late, the dividends, in the hands of the shareholders, are no longer taxable, irrespective of the amount, which is now the added advantage. [But then, in the budget proposals for the financial year 2002-03, the dividends had again been made taxable, in the hands of the shareholders. Now, however, again the dividends in the hands of the equity shareholders are no longer taxable. Further, the dividends in the hands of even the preference shareholders are no longer taxable. But then, now the companies concerned have to pay the tax, on the amount declared as dividends each year.

* The position has, however, since improved inasmuch as the share of Industrial Development Bank of India (IDBI) had closed at Rs. 113.70 on Friday, the 18th September, 2009, on the National Stock Exchange (NSE) [Source: *The Economic Times* dated the 19th September, 2009]. But then, as we may observe, even this price is far below its issue price at Rs. 130 per share.

Disadvantages

(*i*) As the price of the equity shares in the stock market fluctuates widely, this seems to be a rather risky investment.

(*ii*) The common shareholders, holding a very small portion of the total share capital of the company, and being scattered and disorganised, cannot raise any effective voice against the quantum of dividends declared, or even if these are skipped in any of the years, at the sole discretion of the Board of Directors of the Company.

(*iii*) The equity shareholders enjoy the lowest priority over the residual claims on assets, in the event of the liquidation of the company. That is to say that, after all the claims of the central and state governments as also of all the creditors and debenture holders and even the preference shareholders are satisfied, in full (and in that order), then alone comes the turn of the equity shareholders.

But, at the same time, one should not forget that if, at the end, the residual claim and assets are very huge, all these, by and large, belong to the equity shareholders alone, to share all these among themselves, proportionately.

7.7.2 Preference Share Capital

Preference share capital is a queer combination, a synthesis, of the main features of both the equity shares and debentures. This is so because of the following reasons:

(*i*) These are considered as a component of share capital, a portion of the Owners' Equity (OE). That is why, it has been stipulated that the quantum of both the equity shares and the preference shares, taken together, should be within the quantum of the company's authorised capital. Besides, the returns given on the preference shares are treated as dividend (and not interest).

(*ii*) But, while the quantum of dividend payable on equity shares may vary, depending upon the quantum of PAT, year after year, the dividend on preference shares are payable each year at the specific pre-agreed fixed rate, as per the laid down stipulations in the prospectus, published at the time of the issue of such shares.

(*iii*) The dividends on the preference shares are payable prior to the payment of dividends to the equity shareholders. That is, only after the dividends payable to the preference shareholders have been paid, in full, the dividends may become payable to the equity shareholders.

(*iv*) But then, the payment of dividends, payable to the preference shareholders is not compulsory, unlike the payment of interest on debentures, which is obligatory. Instead, it depends very much upon the sole discretion of the Directors of the company.

(*v*) Further, while the amount of interest paid/payable on the debentures are tax-deductible, for the company, the amount of dividend paid on shares (both equity and preference shares) are not tax deductible and have to be paid out of the quantum of 'Profit After Tax' (PAT) only.

(*vi*) Besides, as in the case of the debenture holders, preference shareholders also do not generally enjoy the right to vote.

Types of Preference Shares

There are various types of preference shares, categorised on the basis of their different characteristic features/parameters. They are:

(a) Cumulative and Non-cumulative

In the case of cumulative preference shares, if the amount of dividend payable, remains due, in full or in part, in any of the years, such balance amount gets carried over to the next successive years, till the entire outstandings are cleared.

Let us take an illustrative example. Supposing the "Better than the Best Biscuit Company" has to pay dividends to the preference shareholders @15% per annum. But, if it has been able to pay nil, 5%, 10%, 12% and 14% as dividends during the last five years, the company may have to pay 34% (15 + 10 + 5 + 3 + 1) outstanding dividends, plus 15% for the current year, that is total 49%, during the current (sixth) year.

And, only after the entire amount of dividends, due on preference share, has been paid, up to date, the amount of dividend, if any, may become payable to the equity shareholders. That is, in case, the company does not have sufficient amount of PAT to pay the entire 49% to the preference shareholders, as in the aforesaid example, and has paid say, 45% dividend only, the equity shareholders will not get a 'single paisa' as dividend, even that year, as must have been the case, during all the previous five years, too.

As against this, in the case of non-cumulative preference shares, in case no dividend or some lesser amount (than 15%, as in the previous example) has been paid, the balance amount would not get automatically carried over. This would, instead, lapse during that year.

Thus, in the previous example, the non-cumulative preference shareholders is paid only 15% dividend in the sixth year, and the balance amount pertaining to the last five years is deemed to have lapsed.

In India, however, in most of the cases, the preference shares are in the nature of cumulative preference shares.

(b) Callable and Non-callable

Callable preference shares are such where the amount could be called (*i.e.* paid back) in full or in part, at any time, but at the discretion of the issuing company, of course, at a price, as per such call features stipulated by the company at the time of the offer/issue of such shares. Non-callable preference shares, however, cannot be paid back in full or even in part, before the due dates.

(c) Convertible and Non-convertible

Convertible preference shares are such shares where the holders enjoy the right, of course, at their option, to get their shares converted into equity shares, after the lapse of a certain period (say, after three years) in the pre-settled ratio (say, 1 : 2), but within a specified period thereafter (say, within a period of three months).

As against this, non-convertible preference shares are not to be converted into equity shares at any point of time.

(d) Redeemable and Non-redeemable

Redeemable preference shares are such which are stipulated to be redeemed (repaid or retired) after the lapse of a specified maturity period (say, 10 years, etc.) after the date of allotment, as specified in the issue documents.

In the case of non-redeemable preference shares, however, these are supposed to be perpetual in nature, not to be redeemed (repaid or retired) at any point in time, till the existence of the company. Thus, such shares do not have any maturity period. In India, however, most of the preference shares are redeemable in nature.

(e) Cumulative Convertible Preference (CCP) Shares

This was a unique innovation wherein the features of both the cumulative and convertible preference shares were combined in one instrument. But, unfortunately, it has ultimately proved to be a non-starter so far.

(f) Participating and Non-participating

Participating preference shares entitle the holders thereof to participate in the surplus profit, *i.e.* the balance amount remaining after the dividends, at certain rates, have already been paid each year, on both the equity and preference shares. Similarly, such preference shareholders may also be entitled to the assets that may still be remaining [after meeting all the claims and dues of the governments (both central and state), of all the creditors and the preference shareholders (in that order)], according to some specific formula.

For example, the issue documents may provide that the participating preference shareholders will get a dividend @ 12% per annum and will also be entitled to receive further dividend to the extent of, say, 20% of the dividend paid to the equity shareholders each year.

Similarly, it may be provided that such participating preference shareholders will be entitled to say 10% of the residual assets, left after meeting the claims of the governments and all the creditors, including sundry creditors, banks and debenture holders, etc. but prior to the distribution of the assets among the equity shareholders, who will be entitled to the proportion of their shares, only out of the assets, if at all, still remains.

Shareholders who have been issued non-participating preference shares, however, will, of course, be not entitled to such shares in the surplus profit, nor in the residual assets, at the time of liquidation of the company, as aforesaid.

Rights to Vote

Since the commencement of the Companies Act, 1956 unlike equity shareholders, the preference shareholders no longer enjoy any voting rights. However, they are entitled to vote on every resolution placed before the company under anyone or all of the undernoted circumstances. That is:

(*i*) If the dividend(s) on preference shares is in arrears for the last two years or more, in the case of cumulative preference shares, or

(*ii*) If preference dividends have not been paid for two or more consecutive years in the past, or for an aggregate period of three years or more, in the preceding six years, ending with the expiry of the immediately preceding financial year of the company.

But then, as we all know, the number of preference shareholders is usually too small to let its voice and views be felt, in any way, in any of the meetings of the shareholders of the company.

It will, however, be pertinent to mention here that since the provision had been made in the Union Budget for the financial year 1998-99 to the effect that the dividend payable on shares (both equity and preference shares) will not be taxed in the hands of the shareholders (though the companies were required to pay tax on the amount of dividend paid @ 10% during the year 1998-99, raised to 20% with effect from the year 2000-2001, and again reduced to 10%, the very next financial year) the preference shares have, naturally, gained unprecedented popularity, in absolute preference to debentures and loans, earlier subscribed by the promoters and others.

This is so because, while the income received by way of interest paid on loans and on debentures, payable to the creditors or debenture holders, are taxable, the income by way of dividends are exempt from taxes, to an unlimited extent. It is a different matter that the interest payable on loans and debentures are tax-deductible, for the company, while the dividends paid are not, and, therefore, these have to be paid only after the PAT stage, when even the amount of tax, payable by the company on the amount of dividend declared and payable to the shareholders, has also to be paid by the company, at the prevalent rate. Thus, though the payment of dividend, payable on preference shares, will prove to be costlier to the company, as compared to the loans and advances, it is the other way round from the point of view of the promoters and other investors.

In view of the budget proposals for the financial year 2002-2003, the position was reversed, as has been discussed in the foregoing pages.

Advantages and Disadvantages of Preference Share Capital

(a) From the Point of View of the Company

Advantages

(*i*) The company does not have any legal obligation to pay dividend on preference shares, as against the legal obligation to pay interest on debentures. It can, thus, on its own discretion, skip the payment of dividends to the preference shareholders without running any risk of legal action or facing bankruptcy.

(*ii*) In case of non-redeemable (perpetual) preference shares, the company does not have any responsibility of redeeming the shares, at any stage. Even in the case of redeemable preference shares, its redemption can very well be delayed without incurring any significant penalty.

(*iii*) As the amount of preference shares is also included, while calculating the net worth of a company, it enhances its credit-worthiness too.

(*iv*) As the preference shareholders generally do not enjoy any voting right, there is no risk of dilution of the control involved in the issuance of the preference shares, as against the equity shares.

(*v*) As no security is charged in favour of the preference shareholders, as against the debenture holders, the company's assets remain free to be charged against future loans and advances, and/or debentures and bonds.

Disadvantages

(*i*) As already discussed, the preference shares prove costlier to the company, as compared to loans, advances and debentures, as the amount of interest payable on the latter is tax-deductible.

(*ii*) Though it is within the absolute right of the company to skip the preference dividends, such an action may adversely affect the credit-worthiness and image of the company in the stock market as also in the eyes of the general public and prospective investors.

(b) From the Point of View of the Shareholders

Advantages

(*i*) The preference shareholders (somewhat like the debenture holders) are assured of a fixed amount, by way of dividend.

(*ii*) The income, by way of dividend, even on preference shares, are not taxable in the hands of the shareholders.

Disadvantages

(*i*) Preference shareholders run a very high risk of being deprived of payment of dividend at the sole discretion of the company. And this could be the case even in respect of timely redemption of the redeemable preference shares.

Some empirical studies, like the one conducted by L.C. Gupta, however, have revealed that:

(*a*) Generally speaking, when companies avoid the payment of dividend on equity shares, they usually prefer to skip the dividend in respect of preference shares, too.

(*b*) Further, a substantial amount get accumulated by way of arrears of preference dividend in the case of several companies.

(*c*) Besides, the fluctuation in the price of preference shares is far greater than in that of the debentures.

(*ii*) Till recently, the rate of dividend on preference shares was rather modest. But, now that the dividend paid to the investors on such shares, too, are exempt from income-tax, these are, of late, gaining much popularity and, accordingly, the rate of dividend on preference shares have also been showing some rising trend.

7.8 DEBENTURE CAPITAL

As against the equity shareholders, who are considered to be the owners of the company (though notionally only), the debenture holders are considered to be the company's creditors. That is, while the share capital is the owners' equity, the debenture capital is like the funds lent to the company at an agreed rate of interest, and re-payable after the stated and agreed period, say, after the expiry of the 6th, 7th and 8th year, from the date of allotment, in the ratio of say, 35%, 35% and 30%, respectively. Thus, the debentures are usually issued for raising long-term debts. Besides, the company has the legal obligation to pay the amount of interest at the specified rate and on the specified time, and redeem the debentures on the due date. There is, however, no such legal obligation on the part of the company, in the case of shares, both equity and preference.

However, as in the case of equity and preference shares, debentures can as well be issued by way of:

(*i*) Public issue,

(*ii*) Private placement, and

(*iii*) Rights issue.

Types of Debentures

There are generally, three main types of debentures on the basis of their convertibility (or otherwise) into equity shares. They are:

(*a*) Fully Convertible Debentures (FCDs),

(*b*) Partly Convertible Debentures (PCDs), and

(*c*) Non-Convertible Debentures (NCDs).

(a) Fully Convertible Debentures (FCDs)

As the name itself suggests, the fully convertible debentures, as per the agreement, may be compulsorily and necessarily converted into equity shares at a prestated price, as contained in the issue documents. There may also be cases where the conversion into equity shares may be at the option of the debenture holders, after the expiry of the stated period but, of course, sometime within the stipulated time frame, thereafter, *i.e.* say, any time between three and five years after the date of issue, but within, say three months from the date of such announcement by the company, to be made between three and five years, as aforesaid.

For example, BSES Limited issued fully convertible debentures of the face value of Rs. 140, which were to be compulsorily converted into two equity shares of the face value of Rs. 10, at a premium of Rs. 60 each, *i.e.* at the cost of Rs. 10 + Rs. 60 = Rs. 70, after the expiry of, say two years and three years respectively, from the date of the issue of the debentures. Thus, on the expiry of two years, Rs. 70 (out of Rs. 140), got converted into one equity share of the face value of Rs. 10, and the balance amount of Rs. 60 was credited to the share premium account. Thus, while dividend was, thereafter, payable on the equity share of Rs. 10, interest was payable on the balance amount of Rs. 70 only.

And, on the expiry of the third year, the balance amount of Rs. 70 also got converted into one equity share of the face value of Rs. 10, at a premium of Rs. 60. And, thus, the entire amount of Rs. 140, comprising the fully convertible debentures (FCDs), got repaid and satisfied in full, and all the debenture holders had now become the shareholders of the company.

Some company may prefer to issue FCDs leaving the option of conversion in full, or in part(s), or not at all, on the debenture holder himself. The triple option convertible debentures (TOCDs) issued by the Reliance Petroleum Limited (RPL) is the live example in point. One debenture of total amount of Rs. 60 was issued, out of which two shares were to be issued after expiry of certain period, in two instalments of one share each, of the face value of Rs. 10 each at par. The balance amount of Rs. 40 was stated to be convertible into two shares, at a premium of Rs. 10 each, at the triple options of the debenture holders. That is, the debenture holders had three options:

(*a*) To get the entire Rs. 40 converted into two equity shares, at a premium of Rs. 10 each, or

(*b*) To get one share for Rs. 20 and retain the balance amount of Rs. 20 as the non-convertible portion of the debenture, or even

(*c*) To retain the entire Rs. 40 as a non-convertible portion of the debenture.

Here, as you may recollect, when it was time for the conversion of Rs. 40 into equity shares, the market price, prevailing at the material time, was around Rs. 12-14 only. Under the circumstances, no sane person would have opted for conversion of debentures into equity shares @ Rs. 20 each. The company, therefore, prudently decided, and got it approved in the general meeting of the debenture holders and shareholders that Rs. 40 would now get converted into three equity shares, at an average price of Rs. 13.33 each, instead of only two, as was announced in the issue documents earlier. All the other aforesaid three options and conditions, however, remained unchanged.

(b) Partly Convertible Debentures (PCDs)

Partly Convertible Debentures (PCDs) are usually issued in two parts, viz.,

(*i*) Convertible portion (marked Part-I or Part-A), and

(*ii*) Non-convertible portion (marked Part-II or Part-B).

Further, mostly Part-A, the convertible portion, comprises Debenture-Cum-Share Certificate, wherein it is specifically stated that up to the specified date, the instrument will be deemed as the debenture certificate of the specified number and prime value, *e.g.* 10 PCDs of Rs. 100 each. And, at the lower portion of the document (Debenture-Cum-Share Certificate), it is specifically stated that with effect from the stipulated date, the certificate will be deemed as the share certificate comprising two shares of the face value of Rs. 10, on conversion of Rs. 100 PCDs, at a premium of Rs. 40 each, as had been stipulated in the issue documents.

Further, the non-convertible portion (Part-II or Part-B) throughout remains non-convertible. That is, it is not converted into equity shares at any stage. It is, instead, redeemed after the specified period, say after 6th, 7th and 8th year in the ratio of 35%, 35% and 30% respectively, or @ 1/3rd portion or 33.33% each year, etc.

For example, Ranbaxy Laboratories Limited had issued, in early 1990s, PCDs of the face value, of Rs. 200 each, comprising Part-A and Part-B, *i.e.* convertible and non-convertible portions of Rs. 100 each. And, on the expiry of two years, the convertible portion was to be compulsorily converted into two shares of the face value of Rs. 10 each, at a premium of Rs. 40. The relative portion A of the certificate was issued in the nature of Debenture-Cum-Share Certificate, as discussed in the foregoing pages, and w.e.f. the specified date, the same certificate was to be treated and traded as share certificates of the corresponding number of shares.

The second portion (non-convertible part), however, was redeemed after the expiry of the stipulated period, but at par, as the non-convertible portion had been issued at 'nil' or 'zero' coupon (interest) rate. Even then this rights issue was substantially over-subscribed by the existing shareholders, because they were very well rewarded in the form of equity share itself, at a nominal premium of Rs. 40 only, when the market price of the equity share, in the stock exchanges, was being quoted at a much higher level, at around Rs. 700 each.

(c) Non-Convertible Debentures (NCDs)

The Non-convertible Debentures (NCDs), as the name itself suggests, is not converted into equity shares at any stage.

These are, instead, redeemed after the given period in the given percentage at each stage, as had been stipulated in the issue documents, as has already been discussed earlier, while dealing with the non-convertible portion of PCDs.

It may be pertinent to mention here that the popularity and acceptability of the issues of FCDs, PCDs and NCDs usually prevail in that order, whereby the FCDs are most popular and the NCDs are the least popular. This is so because, while the companies of good standing and repute issue the FCDs and PCDs at very attractive conversion terms, the NCDs do not have any provision for their conversion into equity shares. Therefore, to make the NCDs somewhat attractive, the companies quote somewhat higher rate of coupon (interest rate) for them. The companies, however, prefer to issue NCDs for the undernoted main reasons:

(*i*) The risk of dilution of control of the existing major shareholders is completely avoided; and

(*ii*) The Earning Per Share (EPS) of the company's equity shares do not get adversely affected.

Some Salient Features of Debentures

Security

More often than not, debentures are issued against the security of the charge created by way of an equitable mortgage of the company's immovable properties, both present and future.

Why Equitable Mortgage?

The rationale behind creation of the charge by way of equitable mortgage is the fact that the stamp duty eligible in the case of an equitable mortgage is nominal, *i.e.* the relative documents are required to be stamped as a simple agreement. As against this, the documents pertaining to the registered mortgage have to be stamped *ad valorem, i.e.* as per the value of the document, the debenture deed, which may come to a very huge amount, as the large scale companies usually issue debentures for a substantial amount.

And, if we look at the relative advantage of the registered mortgage, it lies in the fact that such a mortgage has the effect of public notice, and thereby, any subsequent mortgage may not be held valid in the eyes of the law. But then, in the case of limited liability companies, even the charge created by way of an equitable mortgage has to be reported, and registered with, the Registrar of Companies, which, too, has the effect of a public notice. This is so because, all the creditors, before accepting any asset of a company as a security against the advance, are required to make a search in the books of the Registrar of Companies at his Office on payment of a nominal search fee, for this purpose, with a view to ensuring that no prior charge has already been registered in regard to the immovable assets and properties, now being offered by the company as a security against the current advance, now being granted to the company.

How is the Equitable Mortgage Created?

The procedure for creation of the charge by way of an equitable mortgage is simple.

The Director(s) of the Company, duly authorised for this by the company, through a resolution to this effect, passed by the company, approach the Branch Manager of the Bank, at the Branch concerned. He delivers the relative title deed, in original, to the Branch Manager, stating that he/they is/are delivering the relative title deed to the bank on behalf of the company with the intention of creating the equitable mortgage on the same, by depositing the title deed, for the purpose. And the Branch Manager, in turn, accepts the title deed accordingly, and keeps it in his custody on behalf of the Bank.

The aforesaid act takes place in the presence of at least two witnesses, and all of them must be the Bank officials only. Why so? Because, the whole episode is recorded in the Branch Document Register and is duly signed by the Bank Manager as also by the witnesses. And, as all these signatories are signing on behalf of the bank only, no stamp duty is applicable thereon, as it does not amount to an agreement, inasmuch as it has been signed by, and on behalf of, a single party. And, if it were to be signed by the witnesses belonging to both the bank and the borrower, it may have been construed as an agreement, and may have, therefore, to be stamped accordingly.

The borrower company is also required to handover the title deed along with a title deed delivery letter, so as to evidence in writing, that the title deed was actually delivered to the Bank Manager for the aforesaid purpose. Otherwise, the executives of the company may always have the option of taking the plea that the title deed was not actually delivered, but they had, by mistake, left the same at the Bank Manager's office. And, in that event, the equitable mortgage may not be held to be valid, in the eyes of law.

The matter does not end here. The Bank Manager, by way of an abundant precaution, also handsover a printed proforma letter to be duly completed and signed by the Director(s), on behalf of the company, and then to be posted later, per Registered Post, which, too, is recorded at the Branch of the Bank, along with the other relative documents. This, too, is held as an evidence to prove that the equitable mortgage was created with the free will of the Director(s) and that the earlier Title Deed Delivery Letter was not got signed by them under coercion, in which case the contract, as per the Contract Act, may be treated as void, *ab initio*.

And, the relative proforma has also since been printed by way of an Inland Letter, so as to incontrovertibly prove that the same letter had been sent by the company's Director(s), per Registered Post, inasmuch as if sent in an envelope, some unscrupulous companies could as well take the plea that some other letter (and definitely not the Title Deed Delivery Letter) was sent under the cover (envelope) in question, sent per Registered Post.

Trustee

At the time of the issuance of the debentures, a trustee is appointed, by executing a Trust Deed, with a view to safeguard the interests of the debenture holders, that is to ensure that the investors may get the periodical amount of interest regularly and on time, and that the principal amount, too, is duly paid as and when it falls due.

And, generally, the commercial banks, insurance companies or financial institutions are appointed as the trustee and a mention to this effect is also made in the issue documents.

Debenture Redemption Reserve (DRR)

With a view to safeguard the interest of the investing public still further, the companies are required to create a Debenture Redemption Reserve, too, with at least 50% of the amount of the issue, before the process of redemption actually commences. This, however, is required to be done only if the maturity period of the debenture happens to be more than 18 months.

Rate of Interest (or Coupon Rate)

The debentures are issued at a fixed pre-determined rate of interest which is also referred to as the coupon rate. Earlier, a ceiling on the coupon rate used to be stipulated by the Ministry of Finance. But now, no such restrictions exist and the companies are free to stipulate the coupon rate at their own and sole discretion. But then, any prudent company would quote only a reasonable coupon rate, keeping in view the prevailing market conditions and forces, obtaining at the material time.

In some cases, the coupon rate may be 'nil' (zero) too. For example, as has already been discussed earlier, Ranbaxy Laboratories Limited had issued, on rights basis, Partly Convertible Debentures (PCDs) of Rs. 200 face value, wherein the non-convertible portion (Part-B) had a 'zero' coupon rate. And, the PCDs were fully subscribed (in fact, were highly over-subscribed) because the convertible portion of the PCDs had a very attractive term of conversion; that the Rs. 100 was to be converted into two shares at an average price of Rs. 50 only (Rs. 40 being the amount of premium), when the prevailing market price, at the material time, was many folds higher (around Rs. 700). Thus, the investors (existing shareholders) were well rewarded and, therefore, they did not mind the 'nil' coupon rate on the Non-convertible portion of the Debentures (PCDs).

Fixed or Floating Coupon Rate

Generally, the coupon rate is fixed and stipulated in the issue documents. But, in some cases, it may be kept floating, periodically rising and falling with some other benchmark rate, like Bank Rate, State Bank Advance Rate, or a certain percentage higher than the Bank's highest term deposit rate, etc. For example, it was the State Bank of India which had issued unsecured, redeemable floating interest rate bonds, for the first time in the year 1993. Such bonds were in the nature of Promissory Notes and the interest thereon was made payable annually at 3% above the bank's maximum term deposit rate.

Period of Maturity

A company, as of now, is completely free to stipulate any maturity (redemption) period. Earlier, however, the average maturity period for non-convertible debentures could not be more than seven years. For example, it could be made redeemable in the sixth, seventh and eighth years, in the ratio of say. 35%, 35% and 30% respectively. Such restrictions, however, have since been lifted.

Various Variations of Debentures

(i) Deep Discount Bonds

For example, the Small Industries Development Bank of India (SIDBI) had, in the year 1992, issued Deep Discount Bonds with the following features:

Face Value of each Bond	Rs. 1 lakh
Issue Price	Rs. 2,500 only
Maturity Period	25 years
[From the date of allotment (*i.e.* 01.02.1993)]	

Descriptions	*Amount (Rs.)*	*At the End of Years*
Options available to both the investors and the SIDBI to withdrawn or redeem respectively, at the end of the specified period(s) at the specified maturity (redeemed) value(s).	5300 9600 15300 25000 50000	5 9 12 15 20

(ii) Warrant Attached with NCDs

As the Non-Convertible Debentures (NCDs) are generally not considered to be attractive enough, by the prospective investors, with a view to make the offer attractive some companies issue detachable warrant with each NCD or one warrant against every two NCDs. These warrants could be got converted into company's equity shares, at par, after certain specified period, say, after three years but within some specified period of, say three months, from the date of such announcements made by the company.

For example, Flex Industries issued NCDs along with one detachable warrant each (and equity shares with one detachable warrant with every two shares) entitling the investors to apply for one equity share of the company, at par, within a period of, say three months, after the announcement on this behalf was made by the company. And, such an announcement was to be made by the company after, say three years, but well within a period of 5 years, from the date of allotment of such NCDs.

It is quite a different story that, at the material time, the market price of the share of the company had fallen far below par and consequently no prudent debenture holder must have exercised the option.

(iii) Optional Convertibility

Some companies issue debentures with the provision that these would be got converted into shares at the sole option of the debenture holders, after the expiry of a specified period, and in the pre-specified ratio, as stated in the issue documents.

For example, the Straw Products Limited had, in the year 1981, issued 12% secured convertible debentures of Rs. 500 each. Here, the investors were conferred the right to seek conversion of the debentures into a certain number of equity shares of the company, during a specified period, but, at their own sole discretion, to opt therefore or not.

The Triple Option Convertible Debenture (TOCD) issued by Reliance Petroleum Limited (RPL) is one of the recent examples.

(iv) Call and Put Features

Some debentures contain call features or put features:

(a) Call Features

In case the company issues debentures with call features, the issuing company itself enjoys the right of exercising the option to redeem the debentures well before the specified due date of redemption, of course, at a certain price, specified at the time of the issue.

(b) Put Features

As against the call feature, in the case of the debentures issued with 'put' features, the investors, instead, are given the right to exercise their option to ask for the redemption of the amount after the expiry of certain specified period, of course, at the pre-determined prices.

Advantages and Disadvantages

A. From the Point of View of the Company

Advantages

(*i*) As the amount of interest paid on the debentures are tax-deductible, the post-tax cost of debentures is far lower, as compared to the equity and preference shares, inasmuch as the dividends paid thereon were taxable @ 20% (raised from 10%, which was earlier payable in the years 1998 and 1999). The rate of income tax on dividends, payable by the companies, had again been reduced to 10 per cent only, in the Budget for the year 2001-2002. However, as of now (*i.e.* in one financial year 2009-2010), the company has to pay a dividend tax, on the amount it proposes to pay out as dividends to its shareholders, at the rate of 16.995 per cent (*i.e.* 15 per cent + surcharge + cess). Thus, there is an effective indirect tax of 16.995 per cent payable by the compaı.y by way of dividend distribution tax.

(*ii*) Further, and more importantly, the issue of debentures, as against the equity shares even to the general public, does not entail any risk of dilution of control of the current stakeholders, inasmuch as the debenture holders do not enjoy any right to vote in the affairs of the company.

(*iii*) Besides, the pre-determined fixed rate of interest facilitates many companies in the preparation of their cash budget, and future plans of investment and expansion.

Disadvantages

(*i*) As the payment of periodical interest on due time as also that of the amount of the debenture capital on the date of maturity is obligatory on the part of the company, any default in this regard is fraught with grave risk of causing embarrassment and loss of reputation to the company, besides facing legal disputes and actions.

(*ii*) Further, the protective covenants, stipulated at the time of the issue of the debentures, at times, become too restrictive.

B. From the Point of View of the Investors (Debenture Holders)

Advantages

(*i*) As the rate of interest is fixed and the period of payment of the principal amount is pre-determined, the investors can plan their investments or expenses accordingly.

(*ii*) As the company is legally bound to pay the principal and interest, the investment in debentures is a relatively secured channel of investment.

(*iii*) The debenture holders enjoy a very high order of priority, well above the preference and equity shareholders, in the event of liquidation of the company.

(*iv*) The Debenture Trust Deed and the security of equitable mortgage of the immovable assets and properties of the company further secure their interest.

Disadvantages

(*i*) As the element of risk, in the case of debentures, is much lesser, as compared to the equity shares, the gains (returns) thereon are also of the lower level, though at a fixed rate.

(*ii*) Besides, the income by way of interest on debentures is fully taxable in the hands of the debenture holders. The income, by way of dividend on equity and preference shares, however, is not taxable in the hands of the shareholders.

(*iii*) Further, while the equity shares have the prospects of yielding some capital gains, in due course of time, the debentures have to be sold off only at a discount, and the rate of discount may even go up, in line with the trend of rising rate of interest and inflation.

(*iv*) Moreover, the debenture holders do not enjoy any right to vote, except where their own interest is involved, as has been discussed, in detail, in the foregoing pages.

7.9 TERM LOANS

Term loans are generally granted for a period of more than one year but maximum up to ten years, and are made repayable in stipulated instalments, at the stipulated periodical intervals. As these loans are not made repayable on demand, these are not treated as short-term loans (like working capital finance provided by the banks), but as long-term loans, and accordingly, long-term sources of finance.

Purpose

Term loans are granted mainly for the purpose of acquiring fixed assets like plants and machinery, or for the purchase of land and construction of factory buildings/sheds etc. In some deserving cases, the borrowers are also granted term loans for meeting any short-fall in the margin money required for obtaining working capital loans.

Security

Term loans are usually granted by way of secured loans, mainly against the security of the fixed assets that are to be acquired therefrom. Further, while the movable items of machinery are charged by way of pledge or hypothecation, the immovable items of fixed assets like factory land and building, are charged to the bank by way of equitable mortgage.

As we have already seen earlier (in the section on secured debentures), the creation of equitable mortgage is preferred to the registered mortgage because far lesser stamp duty is exigible thereon, as also because such mortgage, in the case of companies, is registered, too, with the Registrar of Companies, which has the effect of public notice. And, for the same two main reasons, the charge by way of hypothecation is preferred to pledge, in the case of movable items of machinery, too, specially in the case of companies.

It will, however, augur well if a rather detailed discussion is undertaken, at this stage itself, to explain the salient features of the different types of securities, obtained by the banks and other creditors, and/or the various types of charges created on the assets of the borrowers, viz. Pledge, Hypothecation and Mortgage, as also some of the related legal ramifications/implications connected therewith.

7.10 PLEDGE, HYPOTHECATION AND MORTGAGE

In all the cases of secured loans and advances, some tangible securities are charged to the bank or to any other secured creditor, for that matter, by way of:

(*a*) (*i*) Pledge, and/or

(*ii*) Hypothecation (of goods, and/or of movable items of machinery, and/or book debts), or

(*b*) Mortgage (invariably of landed properties like land and building, and immovable items of plant and machinery, imbedded to earth).

Let us now discuss, in somewhat greater details, each of these three types of charges.

PLEDGE

What is a Pledge?

Pledge is a bailment of goods, as a security, for payment of a debt, or performance of a promise, against some advances (as per Section 172 of the Indian Contract Act).

This definition leaves us to find out yet another definition, that is, of 'Bailment'.

Bailment

As per Section 148 of the Indian Contract Act, Bailment is the delivery of goods by one person [known as the Bailor or Pledgor, in the case of a pledge] to another person [known as the Bailee or Pledgee, in the case of a pledge], for some purpose, and on the strict understanding that the goods will be returned to the bailor (or otherwise disposed of, as per the direction of the bailor), by the bailee, immediately, when the purpose for which the goods were initially bailed, had been completed.

For example, safe-deposit box, deposited with the bank, for safe custody giving of a watch for repair, lending of book(s) for study and return, etc.

Let us take another example:

If, in a marriage party, some full plates have been hired, this may constitute a bailment, and, accordingly, these plates are required to be returned to the bailor, in good condition, after the occasion, *i.e.* the marriage party, is over.

In the case of such bailment, some charges may, as well, have to be paid. But, if such full plates were borrowed from friends and relatives, free of any charge, such lending may as well constitute a 'bailment', though without charging any fee therefore.

But, then, if one of the porcelain plates gets broken, the cost thereof may have to be compensated to the bailor, in both the cases, *i.e.* whether it is bailed with some fee, or just for free. That is why, the law provides that the bailee must take as much precaution and care of the goods bailed/pledged as a man of ordinary prudence will, under similar circumstances, take in the case of his own goods, of the same bulk, quality and value (Section 151 of the Indian Contract Act).

That is why, when the goods are pledged to the bank, the bank is expected to take as much care as a man of ordinary prudence would take in the case of his own goods of similar nature. For example, if paper has been pledged to the bank, the bank must take care to treat the stocks of paper with termite treatment, and to take care to over-turn the stocks, periodically, to save it from termite attack and/or damage due to dampness, rain, etc.

Let us take yet another example. Supposing a company has pledged the stocks of pig iron and iron ingots. And, as these stocks do not get damaged due to fire, a fire-insurance therefor may not be warranted. But then, if any theft of these goods takes place, and if these were not insured against theft, the bank may be held responsible, and may have to compensate the borrower with the cost of the damages/loss sustained. But again, as we all know, in the event of getting the goods insured against theft, the fire-insurance thereof is a prerequisite, a necessary pre-condition/ requirement. But then, fire-insurance of pig-iron and iron-ingots may be the most unwarranted, and an unwise action. Therefore, the banker, with a view to playing safe, just sends a letter, to the borrower concerned, suggesting therein that, the stocks pledged to the bank may be got insured against theft, if the borrower considered it necessary to do so.

And, the duly acknowledged copy of such letter is kept, along with the other legal documents, so as to prove, in the court of law, at any later date, that the bank had taken due care to forewarn the borrower to get the stocks insured against theft. And, in case the borrower (pledgor) had preferred, not to get the stocks insured against theft, he himself will be held solely and exclusively responsible in this regard, and not the bank (the pledgee).

In Pledge, Delivery of Goods is Essential

In the case of a pledge, the actual delivery, of the goods pledged/to be pledged, is a must. That is why, the bankers prefer to obtain a letter of pledge (usually on a printed proforma), whereby the pledgor (borrower) provides a documentary evidence, in writing, to the effect that the goods, specified, in detail therein, had actually been delivered by the borrower to the creditor bank, with the specific intention of pledging the same with the bank, as a security against the advance. This procedure is meticulously followed by the banks, so that the borrower may not, at a later date, take the plea that the goods, in question, were not willingly delivered but, instead, were forcibly taken possession of by the bank, or by any other creditor.

HYPOTHECATION

As against pledge, in which case, the charge is specific and fixed, *i.e.* it relates only to those specific items of goods actually pledge. The hypothecation is in the nature of a floating charge, in that all the goods that are stored and stocked in the company's godown(s) or factor premises, etc., or even in transit. It automatically gets charged (hypothecated) to the bank, and the moment these stocks are taken out of the company's godowns, factory premises, etc., and/or from the possession of the company, such goods automatically get released, and are, accordingly, deemed to be out of the bank's charge (of hypothecation) too.

Thus, the various items of stocks/goods keep going out and the fresh stocks keep coming in. The moment such goods come in, these get automatically charged, by way of hypothecation, to the bank. And, similarly, the moment these goods are out of the possession of the company, these get out of the hypothecation charge of the bank too. Thus, as the actual (specific) stocks of goods, this way, keep changing and are turnedover, the charge of hypothecation is referred to as the floating charge, an ever-changing charge, over the ever-changing items of goods and stocks.

PLEDGE vs. HYPOTHECATION

(i) Fixed (specific) vs. Floating (fluid, fluctuating, changing) Charge

As we have seen earlier, while the charge, in respect of pledge is fixed and specific, in terms of the specified goods pledged, the charge in respect of hypothecation keeps floating, fluctuating and changing, with each and every 'ins' and 'outs' of the goods. The hypothecation charge, thus, keeps shifting and changing over, with each and every event of the turnover of the goods.

(ii) Sale of Goods Pledged vs. Hypothecated

In case of the goods pledged against advances, the pledgee, in the event of the pledge or failing to pay the debt in time, has the lawful right to sell the goods pledged, without obtaining specific prior permission of the Court. Thus, in the case of pledge, the pledgee can sell the goods pledged, after giving a reasonable notice of such intended sale to the pledgor, as per Section 176 of the Indian Contract Act. The pledgor, however, in turn, has the right to redeem, vide Section 177 of the Indian Contract Act.

But, as against this, in the case of hypothecated goods, these cannot be sold off, to recover the outstandings in the loan account, without prior specific written order of a competent Court, on this behalf. The sale of the hypothecated goods, without the Court permission, may, however, become possible and permissible, provided the charge of hypothecation itself is got converted into a charge of pledge, instead, by the simple act of the delivery of a pledge letter, duly signed by the borrower concerned, to its effect.

But then, a defaulting and recalcitrant borrower may usually be most unwilling to sign such a letter of pledge, so as to convert the charge of hypothecation into that of pledge, inasmuch as this obviously, is going to be well against his own 'interest'.

In such cases, however, some 'prudent and pragmatic' bankers, have acted smartly (or have over-acted, over smartly) by forcing the borrower, under coercion and to perforce sign the letter of pledge, knowing full well that an agreement, signed under pressure, or threat makes such an agreement voidable (not void *ab initio),* at the option of the party whose consent was so caused (vide Section 19 of the Indian Contract Act). But then, such an agreement may turn, and be treated as void, only and only after it is proved to have been obtained under coercion, *i.e.* under threat and/or undue influence.

A live example may illustrate and clarify the point.

SIGN OR DIE

A friend of mine, the Chief Manager of a nationalised bank, once went to the shop a defaulting borrower, and requested him to sign a letter of pledge, converting the charge of hypothecation into pledge. But, the borrower was, naturally, most unwilling and reluctant to do so. When all sorts of appeasements, appeals and pleas failed, my friend lost his temper, and asked his junior officer, accompanying him, to down the shutter of the shop and lock him (the borrower) inside his own shop, and let him die there, for lack of fresh air and oxygen. The junior officer, standing by, got the signal and readily complied with the instructions instantaneously. And, both of them left the place. But then, the prudent and pragmatic officer came back on the advice of the Chief Manager, and started counselling the recalcitrant borrower to come to terms and sign the 'simple' pledge letter, and save his precious life. He shared with him a 'top secret', in a serious and sincere manner, that the bank manager, though apparently a soft spoken and kind hearted person, was, in fact, a very tough and daringly dangerous person, so much so that he had been reported to have been responsible even for three/four murder cases, by now. This, surely and suddenly scared the borrower and he readily agreed to sign the pledge letter, and ultimately did so. And, my friend had all smiles on his face.

One may wonder and start arguing that it was most immoral and illegal on the part of the bank manager of a public sector bank to have acted in such an irresponsible and uncivilised and, above all, in a blatantly illegal and unlawful manner. But then, one must always bear in mind that being in the business or in the bank, one must have some practical and pragmatic business-sense: neither moral nor immoral but, amoral. And, as the adage goes—**"Possession is ninety per cent ownership"**.

Just take a hypothetical case. Supposing a well-built person, lawyer by profession, is walking on the street, and a road-side raffish person pushes him, and slaps him on his face, for no fault of the lawyer, he, too, instantaneously and, by way of a natural reaction and a reflex action, may raise his hand to slap him back. But then, he may stop mid-way, reflecting back, because of his knowledge of law, that slapping him back may tantamount to assault, which is a cognisable and punishable offence under the provision of the Indian Penal Code (IPC), attracting imprisonment or fine, or both.

Such a law-abiding person may be ideal, but, at the same time, too dull and idle, to take prompt and appropriate action, in the right and ripe time, and may be repeatedly slapped for no fault of his own. Because, it may prove to be too difficult, to prove the aforesaid offence in the court of law.

Similarly, if the aforesaid recalcitrant and defaulting borrower may plead in the court of law that he was forced and threatened by the bank manager to sign the letter of pledge, the bank manager may, in turn, plead his case somewhat like:

> My Lord! I am a responsible and law-abiding officer of a public sector bank, and I am not expected to have behaved the way I am being alleged by the defaulting borrower to have done. The allegation is most baseless and fabricated, an after-thought and blatant lie, with a view to avoiding the payment of the loan amount.

And, the honourable judge may, most likely, believe the contention of the bank manager, as against that of the defaulting borrower, the facts of the case being to the contrary notwithstanding.

I am, however, by no stretch of imagination, suggesting that we should always act in the manner my banker fried had done, in the aforesaid case. But then, it is a matter for serious consideration as to how moral and legal is the action and behaviour of the borrower, who is defaulting to repay the loan of a bank, and thereby, defrauding the public money. An 'appropriate' and 'effective' action needs to be taken promptly, with some pragmatic wisdom, depending upon the merit and circumstances of each case.

Suffice it to say that if threat can do the trick, go, do it, or get it done. And, term it as an administrative and business strategy, and mostly a winning strategy at that.

(iii) Priority of Pledge over Hypothecation

As per the legal provisions, the charge of pledge, created even after the creation of the charge of hypothecation, may have the priority and preference thereto (though created afterwards) provided, of course, the pledgee did not have the knowledge and notice of the prior charge of hypothecation.

Registration of the Charge(s) of Hypothecation

Under Section 125 of the Companies Act, 1956, the charges of hypothecation of stocks of inventories and book debts, as also of equitable mortgage, created by the deposit of the title deed, usually original of the immovable property charged must be registered with the Registrar of Companies, within 30 days from the date of the creation of the charge. The application, along with the relative legal agreement document, needs to be filed in the office of the Registrar of Companies concerned. Such an application can, however, be filed either by the borrower or by the creditor (banker) concerned.

Such registered charges may as well be got vacated, but such an application for the vacation of the registered charge can be filed only by the borrowing company, and not by the creditor concerned.

Here, it must be observed and emphasised that, as per the requirement of the law, the application, for the registration of the charge, along with the relevant documents, must be filed with the Registrar of Companies within the stipulated time. It is not necessary that it should be actually recorded and registered by the Registrar of Companies in his books, and/or a certificate of such registration must be issued by the Registrar of Companies, within a stipulated time. Just the act of filing, within the stipulated time of 30 days, is enough.

Such an application, along with the copies of the relative documents (instruments), creating the charge, along with the brief particulars thereof, is to be submitted on Form-8, in triplicate.

[It may, however, be pertinent to mention here that the application for the modification of the charge, or the satisfaction of the charge, is required to be submitted on Form-10 and Form-17, respectively, in triplicate].

Further, the registration of the charge, created by way of pledge of movable items of goods and/or movable items of machinery, etc., is not a statutory requirement, though it is permissible. The words used in the Act are 'not being a pledge', which implied that the intention of the framers of the law was that such a registration should not be necessary, inasmuch as the creditor, in such a case, happens to be in the possession of the goods charged (pledged).

DATE OF NOTICE OF THE CHARGE

Under Section 126 of the Companies Act, 1956, the date of the execution of a charge, *i.e.* the date of the signing of the relative documents, is the date of creation of the charge, for the purpose of computing the time for its registration, prescribed by Section 125.

PRIORITY AMONG CHARGES

A charge executed earlier to another charge, but registered afterwards (of course, within the prescribed time limit of 30 days) will have the priority over the other, it having been registered subsequently, notwithstanding.

For example, the charge executed by ABC Company on 31 October 2008 in favour of one creditor, and again subsequently on 11 November 2008 in favour of yet another creditor, if filed for registration on the 25 and 15 November 2008, respectively, the charge executed on 31 October 2008 will have the priority over the charge executed on 11 November 2008, though it (the charge dated 31 October 2008) was filed for registration, subsequently, *i.e.* on 25 November 2008, of course, within the stipulated time of 30 days.

In view of the aforesaid provisions of law, the banks usually take the following precautions:

Before granting any advance to a company, against the charge of pledge or hypothecation, the banks first undertake a thorough search in the office of the Registrar of Companies, where the company concerned is registered, to ascertain as to what are all the various charges, already created by the company in favour of the other creditors, and whether any of the goods, now being charged to the bank, are already charged to some other creditor(s). And, only if the securities, now being offered are unencumbered, would the bank go ahead with the creation of the charge in its favour, and execute the necessary documents.

The matter does not end here. After the necessary documents are executed by the bank and the borrower, such hypothecation documents are promptly submitted to the office of the Registrar of Companies concerned for the purpose of the registration of the charge in his books.

This is a MUST, inasmuch as such registration is deemed to be a due public notice and, thus, any subsequent charge on the goods concerned will not have any priority, or preference, at all.

Such documents have to be filed in the office of the Registrar of Companies within 30 days raised from 21 days, vide Section 62 and the Schedule to the Companies (Amendment) Act (31 of 1965), w.e.f. 15 October 1965] from the date of its execution (Section 125 of the Companies Act, 1956).

Further, after a month from the date of the execution of the document, yet another search has to be conducted in the office of the Registrar of Companies, this time to ascertain whether any other charge had also been created, a little before the creation of such charge on the goods in favour of the bank, because, in that event, the prior charge of hypothecation will naturally have the priority and, thus, a preferential treatment, *vis-a-vis* the bank's subsequent charge.

This is so, because, the public has been given 30 days time to get the charge registered with the Registrar of Companies. Thus, a charge of hypothecation, created on the 11 November 2008 can well be submitted for the required registration up to 10 December 2008 and, similarly, the hypothecation charge created in favour of the bank on 21 November 2008 can well be filed for registration by 20 December 2008. And, supposing the bank has filed the legal documents for registration of the charge with the Registrar of Companies on the 23 November 2008, and the other (prior) creditor as late as on 10 December 2008, the charge of the other (prior) creditor will have the priority over that of the bank, inasmuch as the priority will be computed from the date of the creation of the charge, and not from the date of the filing of the charge, inasmuch as the filing is valid, in the eye of the law, so long as it is done within the stipulated time, *i.e.* within 30 days from the date of the execution of documents. This is the rationale behind undertaking the second search in the office of the Registrar of Companies, after say, a month or so, of the execution and filing of the hypothecation documents in the office of the Registrar of Companies.

One more word of caution and extra precaution. Usually, the formal recording in the office of the Registrar of Companies may take sometime, may be a couple of months or even more. Therefore, the bank's officer must take care to look into all the other documents filed with the Registrar of Companies for recording in its Register, and are still pending for registration, of course, only such documents which have been filed up to one month after the execution of the documents by the bank. This is so, because of one of the following two reasons:

The two possible conditions are:

(*i*) Either, the documents have been executed well before the bank but the creditor has failed to get them registered with the Registrar of Companies, and the stipulated time of 30 days has lapsed;

(*ii*) Or, the documents have been executed after the date of its execution in favour of the bank.

Thus, in case of (*i*) above, as the stipulated period of 30 days has already elapsed, the same document may not be registered, after the expiry of the stipulated 30 days. Therefore fresh documents will have to be executed, whereby the date of their execution will fall subsequent to the date of the execution of the documents by the bank, and hence the bank's charge will have the priority.

And, in case of (*ii*) above, inasmuch as the documents have themselves been got executed subsequent to the execution of the documents by the bank, these naturally cannot have the priority over those of the bank.

But then, it will augur well if the bank will prefer to have such searches conducted in the office of the Registrar of Companies at regular half-yearly or yearly intervals to ensure that no subsequent charge (even second charge) has been created and registered, or even submitted for registration with the Registrar of Companies. In such cases, the documents pertaining only to the intervening period need to be perused and examined.

POSSESSION AND OWNERSHIP

While in the case of the pledge, the possession of the goods pledged are transferred to the pledgee, in the case of hypothecation, however, possession of goods continues to remain with the borrower (hypothecator); only a floating charge is created thereon in favour of the bank or some other creditor.

And, so far as the ownership of such goods is concerned, it remains with the borrower in both the cases, *i.e.* both in the cases of the pledge and hypothecation.

PLEDGE/HYPOTHECATION vs. MORTGAGE

While the charge by way of pledge and hypothecation is created in respect of movable items only, the charge in regard to immovable property (land and building) or even immovable items of plants and machinery, are required to be created necessarily by way of mortgage only.

Mortgages are broadly of two types:

(*i*) Registered mortgage, and

(*ii*) Equitable mortgage (by deposit of title deeds).

[For a detailed discussion on the topic of mortgage, specially the detailed procedure for the creation of the charge by way of an equitable mortgage, please refer to the earlier pages of this chapter].

Movable Items of Machinery

It may be pertinent to discuss here as to under what circumstances items of machinery may be treated as movable, in the eyes of law, requiring creation of charge by way of hypothecation, not necessitating mortgage.

An asset, embedded to earth, is treated as immovable. But, if say, only the four iron frames/angles are embedded to the earth and the heavy lathe machine's four legs are tightened thereto, with nuts and bolts, so that the lathe machine can easily be removed just by loosening and removing the nuts and bolts, leaving the four iron frames/angles undisturbed, the whole lathe machine is considered to be movable. As against this, if legs of the lathe machine themselves were embedded to the earth, and the machine could not have been removed without digging and disturbing the 'Mother Earth', it would have to be treated as an immovable property in the eyes of law, and, accordingly, necessitate mortgage thereof.

Primary and Collateral (Additional) Securities

A prudent banker always tries to play safe and therefore insists on some collateral (additional) securities, too, in addition to the primary security. To put it differently, a prudent banker wants to tighten his pant, not with belt alone, but with gelles too, so that if one of them incidentally breaks, the other would hold the pant in place. Therefore, the banks usually take additional security by way of:

(*i*) third party guarantee and/or;

(*ii*) equitable mortgage of some fixed assets or immovable properties, in addition to those purchased out of the term loan granted; and/or

(*iii*) by way of pledge/hypothecation of the company's current assets, already charged against working capital loans, by way of the second charge thereon.

Thus, while assets purchased out of the loan amount are considered to be the primary security, any other security, as aforesaid, in addition thereto, is known as the collateral or additional securities.

Similarly, in case of working capital loans, the current assets (like inventories and sundry debtors) may be treated as primary security (inasmuch as on the basis thereof the Drawing Power is determined), and any other security, obtained by way of third party guarantee and/or equitable mortgage of some immovable property would be considered as the collateral or additional security.

Repayment Schedule

Term loans are, generally, made payable in half-yearly instalments, of principal and interest, spread over a period of five to ten years. And, by taking a very pragmatic view, the term lending institutions also provide a moratorium of one to two years to take care of the gestation period.

And thus, the first instalment may fall due for payment after a lapse of one or two years, from the date of the disbursement of the term loan. Further, initially the quantum of instalment may be kept sufficiently lower, in keeping with the cash generation, through the actual production activities.

It has, however, been found that at times some term lending institutions take a very impractical view and fix half-yearly instalments in such a way that the first instalment may fall due exactly after six months from the date of disbursement of the term loan, irrespective of the fact whether the commercial production had actually commenced or not.

> This reminds me of a live case in point. In early 1970s, a young entrepreneur had established a small-scale industrial unit in a rural area. The State Financial Corporation (SFC) granted him a term loan of Rs. 10 lakhs. And, a commercial bank, in the public sector, sanctioned working capital finance to the tune of Rs. 5 lakh.
>
> Further, besides meeting the required margin money on both the aforesaid advances, the entrepreneur invested his own funds for the construction of the factory building, on his own ancestral piece of land.
>
> The term loan was to be paid within five years in half-yearly instalments of Rs. 1 lakh each. The State Financial Corporation, in its own wisdom, stipulated the repayment programme in such a way that the first half-yearly instalment of Rs. 1 lakh, plus interest, was made payable exactly six months after the date of disbursement of the term loan, without caring to see whether the unit will be able to commence its commercial production by then to generate sufficient cash surplus to repay the first instalment of the loan. In fact, the unit could not commence its production, even on trial basis, for two years. But, the State Financial Corporation (SFC) applied its rule, strictly in letter (and not in spirit) and called up the loan, inasmuch as three instalments, in a row, when they became overdue.
>
> Acting swiftly, the SFC locked up the factory too and seized all the items of machinery charged to it against the term loan. The commercial bank too followed suit and called up its working capital loan.
>
> And, all this, without any of the creditors taking care to look into the real cause and genuine difficulties of the borrower. In fact, the borrower had defaulted for no fault of his own, inasmuch as the production could not commence, because the power connection had not been provided to the factory premises till then.

Now, perhaps, the term lending institutions have become far wiser and since then may be scheduling the repayment programme in such a rational way as to match with the level of surplus cash generated in the usual course of business.

Thus, it will augur well if, in the case of a term loan, though made repayable within a period of five years, the instalments are stipulated in a phased manner, both in terms of the period and quantum, so as to synchronise with the expected generation of cash surpluses. Thus, it is quite possible that in some cases, the repayment schedule may be stipulated somewhat as under:

Amount of Term Loan	Rs. 10 Lakh
Term of repayment	5 years
Period of moratorium granted	2 years
Repayment of loan 10% (Plus the amount of interest)	In the 3rd year, in half-yearly instalments,
40% (plus interest)	In the fourth year, and
The balance 50% (plus interest)	In the fifth year.

This arrangement, may make a better sense rather than the repayment schedule that had been stipulated by the SFC in the aforesaid case.

[A detailed discussion on the topic of term loan, like:

(*i*) Project Appraisal, including examination of the technical feasibility and economic viability of the project;

(*ii*) Detailed analysis and interpretation of the projected balance sheets, profit and loss accounts, cash flow and funds flow statements, and such other related financial tools and techniques, etc. have not been discussed here, inasmuch as these are beyond the scope of the book on 'Working Capital Management and Control'].

A SYNOPTIC NOTE (CHAPTER 7 AT A GLANCE)

FINANCING OF WORKING CAPITAL

Working capital requirements of companies are financed by way of two types of sources of funds, viz.,

A. Short-term sources of funds, and

B. Long-term sources of funds.

A. SHORT-TERM SOURCES OF FUNDS

These are the sources of finance, which are required to be paid back within a short period of say, one year, or even on demand.

Long-term sources of funds, however, are made repayable in suitable instalments, spread over a period of three to five years or even more or, may not be during the entire life-time of the company.

VARIOUS SHORT-TERM SOURCES OF FUNDS

(a) Accruals

Accruals constitute the expenses, which have already accrued (for say, services rendered) but the payments are required to be made at a later date. For example, when the labour charges are to be paid weekly or monthly (instead of daily). Similarly, payments of taxes are required to be made quarterly, half-yearly, or even yearly.

And, such accruals are available for use by the company, without payment of any interest or charges thereon. Thus, these constitute the availability of free funds to the company.

But then, in reality, it is not so, inasmuch as, in the cases of payments agreed upon to be made at a later date, *i.e.* not daily but weekly, monthly, quarterly, yearly, etc., the amount of interest so accrued (though notionally) does enter into the rate of wages/taxes, etc.

(b) Trade Credits

All companies, in the buyers' market, are required, as per the market forces, to supply a portion of their sales, on credit basis, of course, on varied terms of payment. The supplies of raw materials, parts, components, etc., on credit, constitute trade credits and the suppliers on credit are referred to as the sundry creditors.

The sundry creditors (sellers) prefer to have some means of assessing the credit-worthiness of the prospective buyers (on credit), known as the sundry debtors. They, therefore, look into the various aspects of the financial stability and strengths of the prospective buyers.

Example

(*i*) Profitability and prospects, and the practice of ploughing back a (substantial) portion of profit into the business;

(*ii*) Liquidity position, e.g., current ratio, quick ratio (intra-firm and inter-firm analyses);

(*iii*) Character and integrity, *i.e.* willingness to pay (besides the capability to pay), through trade enquiries;

(*iv*) Perusal of past records, and their trend of payments to the other existing sundry debtors.

Trade credits are a sure and automatic source of finance, as per the trade practices, and these constitute around 25% to 50% of the total sources for financing the working capital requirements.

The lessons derived out of the two live cases, titled "Prize of Prompt Payments" and "Price of Prolonged (delayed) Payments" must be borne in mind, *i.e.* facilitating the liberalization of the credit terms and ensuring the quality of goods and services, at the same time, or else the other way round.

Thus, the creation and continuation of good suppliers' relationship is a must. Therefore, we should treat them (sundry creditors) as a part of the company and not apart from this.

The relative advantages and disadvantages of centralized vs. decentralized systems of payments (to the sundry creditors) should always be borne in mind. The optimal mix of the two is the most desirable decision.

(c) Short-Term Loans From Financial Institutions Like LIC, GIC and UTI

I. Eligibility Criteria

(*i*) To manufacturing companies only, *i.e.* not to traders;

(*ii*) Must have excellent track records, viz. must have paid dividends for the last six years @ minimum 5% per annum, or for the last three years @ 10% per annum, *i.e.* minimum 30% aggregate dividend must have been paid during the last six years or three years.

(*iii*) Debt: Equity Ratio to be up to 2 : 1.

(*iv*) Current ratio should be minimum 1.33 : 1.

(*v*) Interest coverage ratio on an average should be 2 : 1.

II. Special Features of Such Loans

(*i*) Unsecured loans on execution of demand promissory notes (DP notes).

(*ii*) Loans to be repaid within one year. May be renewed, but for further two successive years only.

(*iii*) After repayment of the loan, there must be a gap of minimum six months.

(*iv*) Interest is charged at quarterly rests, *i.e.* it is compounded quarterly.

(d) Rights Debentures

Rights debentures, *i.e.* the debentures issued to the existing equity share holders on rights basis.

Conditions and Criteria

(*i*) Total issue amount should not exceed 20% of the gross current assets, loans and advances (less) long-term funds available for working capital requirements.

Or

20% of the total paid-up share capital, *i.e.* equity and preference shares, and free reserves.

Whichever is lower.

(*ii*) Debt: Equity ratio, including the proposed issue, should not exceed 1 : 1.

(e) Factoring

Factoring, as of now, is at its formative stage in India.

Reserve Bank of India has authorized four banks in public sector to do factoring business, viz. State Bank of India in the west Allahabad Bank in the east, Punjab National Bank in the north and Canara Bank in the southern regions of the country.

1. Salient Features

(*i*) Factors, *i.e.* the organization undertaking the factoring business, accept the Sundry Debtors' Accounts on selective basis, and that too, within a certain limit, stipulated by them for each account (sundry debtor).

Thus, while the factors do not accept the 'C' category accounts, companies are reluctant enough to give 'A' category accounts to the factors. Thus, only limited accounts under category 'B', or at best, the creamy layers of some of the 'C' category accounts may be got factored.

(*ii*) And, even these are factored on "with recourse to the drawers" basis, and not on "without recourse to the drawers" basis, as is the case in the developed countries like the US, etc. Thus, for the aforesaid two main reasons, the companies will have to still maintain the bills collection department, though on a slightly lower scale.

2. Factoring Arrangements

While accepting the bills for factoring the factors may advance 70% to 80% of the bill amount, and the balance (30% and 20% respectively) is to be paid on realization of the bills or on the due date, whichever is earlier. The rate of interest charged on such advance is equal to or slightly higher than the rate of interest charged on the cash credit account.

3. Factoring vs. Advance Against Bills by the Banks

While banks work only as the collecting agents, they return bills to drawers/parties if some of these remain unpaid without making any effort to get these paid. The factors, however, do make efforts and approaches for getting the bills paid. They, therefore, rightly charge 1% to 2% additional amount as their commission/charges.

And, in all cases where bills are factored on 'without recourse' basis, the rate of commission is naturally higher, as the risk of loss, by way of bad debts due to non-payment of bills, is higher too.

(f) Forfaiting

While factoring pertains to domestic (inland) trade bills, forfaiting relates to the international (export) trade bills. And, the forfaiting agency is known as the "Forfaiter".

It is mostly provided on "without recourse" basis. And, accordingly, the exporter is automatically free from both the commercial and political risks, too.

In India, the EXIM bank serves as the nodal agency, in regard to the contract of forfaiting. And, accordingly, the discount rate requires a prior approval of the EXIM bank.

The contract of forfaiting could be entered into even for as long as five to seven years.

The financing charge is computed on the basis of the tenor of the bill, the country risk, and country bank risk. It usually ranges between 50 to 400 basis points above LIBOR. The commitment charges, however, range between 13 to 15 basis points.

B. LONG-TERM SOURCES OF FUNDS

(a) Retained Earnings

A major portion of net income (PAT), after payment of divided, is retained (ploughed back) in the business, year-after-year, whereby the shareholders' wealth increasingly grows and goes-up.

In this way, the Owners' Equity (OE), or the own fund in the business, goes up gradually, and with it the company's borrowing capacity as the debt: equity ratio improves, too. Besides, this amount does not fall due for payment, at any time, to anyone, and no amount of interest is payable thereon. But, it proves to be a rather costlier source of finance, as it is not tax-deductible. It is all the more disadvantageous in view of the fact that, as of now, the dividends have, of late, become tax-free in the hands of the shareholders. However, the market price of the company's shares does improve and the risk of dilution of control also diminishes.

(b) Share Capital

The two types of share capital are:

(*i*) Equity Shares (or Ordinary Shares), and

(*ii*) Preference Share Capital.

(i) Equity Share (or Ordinary Share) Capital

Equity shareholders are deemed to be the owners of the company (though notionally). Thus, they enjoy the owners' rights and risks, too, in the event of profit or loss.

Some Terminologies

Authorised capital: This is the maximum amount up to the face value of which the company is authorised to issue the share capital. While computing the ceiling, the amount of premium on the shares, if any, is not taken into account. But, the bonus shares issued are taken into account.

Issued Capital: The aggregate face value for which the shares are offered for subscriptions, both by way of the public issue or by private placement.

Subscribed Capital: The amount of aggregate face value of shares accepted and applied (subscribed) for, by the investors.

Paid-up Capital: The amount or percentage of the face value of the shares, which have actually been paid to the company by the investors.

Par Value or Face Value: It is the amount written on the face of the share certificates. The most popular face value is Rs. 10, though some shares do have the face value of Rs. 100, Rs. 50, Rs. 20, Rs. 5, Rs. 4, Rs. 3, Rs. 2, Re 1, etc., too.

Book Value: The paid-up value of shares, and the reserves and surplus, as per the books of the company, [That is (Total Fully Paid-up Equity Share Capital + Reserves + Surplus) × 100] divided by the Total Face Value of such Shares = Book Value (Per Share) in Percentage Terms.

Issue Price: The price (inclusive of premium, if any) at which the share is issued for subscription. It, however, can never be below the face value of the shares, as per law.

Market Value: The price at which the shares of a company are traded (purchased and sold) in the stock market is known as the market price. Usually, the market value of shares of good companies are quoted in the market at above the face value. But, the market price of the shares of some of the companies may be quoted even below par, that is below the face value.

PUBLIC ISSUE

When the shares are issued for subscription by the general public, through the issue of prospectus, etc., it is known as the public issue.

PRIVATE PLACEMENT

However, when the shares are offered to individuals or companies by way of letters addressed by names, it is known as the private placement.

RIGHTS ISSUE

When the shares are issued for subscription by the existing shareholders of the company [as on the announced (record) date] in terms of the percentage/proportion of their share holdings (like 1: 2, 2 : 3, etc.) it is termed as the rights issue.

The shareholders can, however, apply for even lesser or additional shares than offered on the rights basis, and they can sell (renounce) their 'rights', in favour of some one else, even at a price, prevailing in the stock market, at the material time.

PRIMARY MARKET

When at the time of the issue shares are purchased directly from the company, it is known as having been purchased from the primary market.

SECONDARY MARKET

It refers to the stock market, where the shares, after having been issued in the primary market, can be traded in the secondary market, *i.e.* stock market, through brokers, or even on private basis, to the friends and relatives.

(ii) Preference Share Capital

It is a combination of the features of shares and debentures, in the sense that while, like shares, they are treated as a part of the Owners' Equity (OE) and are paid dividend (not interest thereon, like debentures), the dividends (though not interest) are paid at the predetermined fixed rate, and prior to (in preference to) the equity shareholders. Besides, the payment of dividend is not compulsory, as per law, as is the case with the payment of interest on debentures.

But, unlike the amount of interest paid on debentures, the amount of dividend paid on preference shares is not tax-deductible for the company. Income tax @ 10%, however, is payable by the company on the amount of dividend paid on preference shares, too (as in the case of Equity Shares).

TYPES OF PREFERENCE SHARES

(*i*) **Cumulative and Non-Cumulative:** In the former case, the amount of interest not paid in any particular year(s), or if only partly paid, the balance amount gets accumulated and carried over, year after year, for payment of the entire pending dues, in full, before any dividend could become payable to the equity shareholders.

In the latter case, however, the amount of interest not paid in any year, or even if only partly paid, the balance amount lapses during the same year.

(*ii*) **Callable and Non-Callable:** In the former case, the company, at its discretion, can call (*i.e.* pay back) the amount of the preference shares, in full or in part, even prior to the due date, at a price, already stipulated in the issue document.

Non-callable preference shares, however, cannot be called or paid back, prior to the stipulated due date(s).

(*iii*) **Convertible and Non-Convertible:** The former can be converted into equity shares, compulsorily or at the option of the holder, after a certain period, and in the pre-settled ratio.

The latter, however, does not get converted into equity shares.

(*iv*) **Redeemable and Non-Redeemable:** Redeemable preference shares get redeemed, *i.e.* paid back in full, according to the stipulated time, and in the stipulated proportion.

Non-redeemable preference shares, however, are not repaid till the company itself gets liquidated.

(*v*) **Cumulative Convertible Preference Shares:** These shares, combining the features of cumulation and conversion, have been a non-starter in India.

(*vi*) **Participating and Non-Participating:** The shareholders of the former shares are entitled to participate in the surplus profit as also in the residual assets remaining after meeting the dues of all the creditors in full, in the event of the company's winding up or liquidation.

(c) Debenture Capital

The debenture holders are considered as the creditors to the company, as against the shareholders, who are deemed to be the owners of the company, though notionally.

These can also be issued by way of

(*i*) Public issue;

(*ii*) Private placements; and

(*iii*) Rights issue:

TYPES OF DEBENTURES

There are three main types of debentures:

(*a*) Fully Convertible Debentures (FCDs);

(*b*) Partly Convertible Debentures (PCDs); and

(*c*) Non-Convertible Debentures (NCDs).

(a) Fully Convertible Debentures (FCDs)

These debentures are fully and compulsorily converted into equity shares as per the pre-agreed ratios and price.

(b) Partly Convertible Debentures (PCDs)

Only a portion of these debentures are compulsorily converted into equity shares as per the pre-stated ratio and price. Accordingly, these debentures are usually issued in two parts, A and B, being the convertible and non-convertible portions respectively. And, the latter portion is redeemed fully, as per the pre-stated terms and conditions.

(c) Non-Convertible Debentures (NCDs)

These debentures are redeemed fully as per the pre-stated terms and conditions, and no part of such debentures is converted into equity shares at any stage.

SALIENT FEATURES OF DEBENTURES

(*i*) **Securities:** Debentures are usually issued against security, except in the case where the maturity period of debentures is stipulated up to 18 months only, mostly by way of equitable mortgage of immovable properties and other fixed assets embedded to earth, as per the procedure prescribed by law.

Equitable mortgage is preferred to registered one, inasmuch as, in the former case, the documents attract minimal stamp duty, *i.e.* just as an agreement, as against ad valorem (according to value) stamp duty in the latter case. Besides, as the equitable mortgages, created by the companies, are registered in the books of the respective Registrar of Companies, it has the effect of public notice too.

(*ii*) **Trustees:** These securities are charged to, and entrusted with, some trust, usually being banks and/or insurance companies. After creating the equitable mortgage in the office of the banks or the insurance companies, as the case may be, and confirming the same, in writing, the mortgagor companies are required to send yet another proforma confirmation letter, to the bank or the insurance company concerned, on an inland letter form, by registered post, to evidence that the charge was created by the deposit of the title deeds, in original, out of free will and not under coercion.

(*iii*) **Debenture Redemption Reserve (DRR):** DRR is required to be created by companies to the extent of 50% of the issue amount, before the period of redemption the debenture actually commences. This is required to safeguard the interest of investors but only in those cases where the maturity period of debentures is more than 18 months.

(*iv*) (*a*) **Rate of Interest (or Coupon Rate):** It is specifically stated in the issue document itself. It may be, in some cases, 'nil' too. Now, there is no prescribed ceiling on quoting the interest rate, but usually, it is in line with the prevailing trend and interest rates.

(*b*) **Fixed Rate *vs* Floating Rate of Interest:** In most of the cases, the rate of interest is fixed and unchangeable during the whole period. But, in some cases, it may be tied-up with some benchmark, like the highest rate available on the Bank's Term Deposit Receipt (TDR), and it may rise and fall, therewith.

(*v*) **Period of Maturity:** Debentures may be payable after, say, 6, 7 and 8 years @ 35%, 35% and 30%, etc.

DEEP DISCOUNT BONDS

These bonds are issued for a 'deeply' long period of, say, 25 years or so. For example, the one, issued by SIDBI, in 1992, with the face value of Rs. 1 lakh, was issued at a price of Rs. 2500 only, but the same matured after 25 years from the date of allotment. These could, however, be encashed after 5, 9, 12, 15 and 20 years also, at a pre-stated value.

WARRANTS ATTACHED WITH NCDs

To sweeten the NCDs, an innovation of detachable warrants has, of late, been introduced, which entitles the debenture holders to exchange the same with a pre-stated number of equity shares, and at the pre-agreed price.

OPTIONAL CONVERTIBILITY

In some cases, the debentures could be got converted into equity shares, not compulsorily, but only at the option of the holder. There could be cases of multiple options also being made available to the investors, for example, the Triple Option Convertible Debentures (TOCDs) issued by Reliance Petroleum Limited (RPL).

'CALL' AND 'PUT' FEATURES

In 'call' feature, the debentures could be redeemed prior to the due date, but at the sole option of the issuing company.

In the 'put' feature, instead, it could be redeemed prior to the due date, but, at the sole option of the investors.

Such early redemptions are, of course, done at a price, pre-determined, as per the issue documents.

(d) Term Loans

Term loans are granted for a pre-determined term of time (period) ranging from over one year to say, 5 to 7 years, or even more.

Term loans are usually granted for the purpose of capital expenditure, for instance, for the acquiring of fixed assets [*e.g.* land (factory) building, plant and machinery, etc.).

These are made payable, over a period of time, in suitable instalments, which should be fixed reasonably and rationally, keeping in view the productivity and cash inflows, etc.

SECURITY

Term loans are usually granted against the security of equitable mortgage and/or hypothecation of the immovable and movable items of machinery, etc., respectively.

PRIMARY vs. COLLATERAL SECURITIES

Primary securities are those items of assets against which the advance has been granted. And, collateral security (or additional security), in turn, is the charge on some other assets, in addition to the ones advanced against, and/or by way of the third party guarantee.

PLEDGE, HYPOTHECATION AND MORTGAGE

Pledge and Hypothecation

Pledge is the bailment of goods as a security against advances. In the case of pledge, the charge is fixed and the delivery of goods pledged is essential. The pledged goods can be sold out without a specific order from the Court of Law, of course, after serving a reasonable notice of such sale to the pledgor. The pledgor, however, has the right to redeem.

Hypothecation charge, however, happens to be in the nature of a floating charge, whereby all the incoming goods get automatically hypothecated and all the outgoing goods get released from the charge.

Such hypothecated goods cannot be sold out without a specific order from the Court of Law to this effect, unless the charge is converted into pledge, by just getting a letter of pledge, duly signed by the pledgor.

The charge of hypothecation is required to be registered with the Registrar of Companies within 30 days from the date of the execution of the relative legal documents.

This registration has the effect of public notice, whereby any subsequent charge by way of hypothecation, or even by way of pledge, cannot have the priority over the earlier charge of hypothecation.

While the possession of the goods pledged gets transferred to the pledgee, the possession of the hypothecated goods continues to remain with the company. The ownership, however, remains with the company in both the cases.

Mortgage

While the charges, by way of pledge and hypothecation, are created in respect of the movable items of assets, including the movable items of machinery, mortgage has to be created in all the cases of immovable property, like land and building, plant and immovable items of machinery, embedded to earth.

Mortgage is mainly of two types:

(*a*) Registered mortgage, and

(*b*) Equitable mortgage, by deposit of (usually original) title deeds.

The equitable mortgage, however, must be got registered with the Registrar of Companies within 30 days, from the date of creation of such charge, so as to get the effect of public notice.

However, the documents creating the charge of equitable mortgage, is required to be stamped just as a simple agreement and, thus, results in a substantial saving in regard to the stamp duty.

QUESTIONS
(For Self-assessment)

1. Distinguish between
   (*a*) Short-term sources of funds, and
   (*b*) Long-term sources of funds, by giving suitable illustrative examples.
2. Name the various sources of short-term financing.
3. Write short notes on:
   (*a*) Accruals,
   (*b*) Trade credits,
   (*c*) Short-term loans from financial institutions, viz. LIC, GIC and UTI,
   (*d*) Rights debentures, and
   (*e*) Factoring.
4. It is said that the sundry debtors enjoy funds of the sundry creditors, at no cost. Accordingly, it would be a better business sense to delay payments of the sundry creditors, as far as possible, enjoy the related benefits. Do you agree? Give reasons for your answer, with appropriate illustrative examples.
5. (*a*) It is said that the best policy of financial management, specially in the case of cash management, is to have an optimal mix of centralised and decentralised systems of both the receipts and payments. Do you agree? Explain with suitable illustrative examples.
   (*b*) What type of mix of centralised and decentralised systems of receipts and payments would you consider as optimal? Explain, by giving suitable illustrative examples, and also specify the rationale behind your contentions.
6. Discuss briefly the eligibility criteria and special features of short-term loans, provided by the financial institutions, viz. LIC, GIC and UTI.
7. (*a*) Distinguish between:
   Factoring, "with recourse to the drawer", and factoring, "without recourse to the drawer".
   (*b*) Which one of these two forms of factoring are prevalent in India, and in the developed countries.
8. It has been found that, in India, factors usually take bills for factoring, drawn on some selected drawee companies only. And, if such be the case, there is every likelihood that they will accept bills mainly for factoring (or even solely) from the first class ('A' category) companies and from the cream of the 'B' category companies only; and would not accept any bill drawn on 'C' or 'D' category companies or the lower level of even 'B' category companies, where the recovery may be rather doubtful.

   And, on the other hand, companies would not like to give bills of 'A' category drawees, these being 'no risk' or 'low risk' clientele.

   This, in turn, will result in a much lower level of factoring business taking place. This will also mean that companies will have to maintain their credit collection department too, side by side.

These circumstances cannot be conducive for the growth of the factoring business in India.

Under these circumstances, what are your considered opinions and suggestions for making 'factoring' as a gainful alternative arrangement for companies?

9. As of now, the factoring arrangements in India, comprise 'with recourse to drawer(s)' only. Thus, it does not seem to be any different from the credit facilities already being given by the commercial banks, against trade bills. Do you agree? Give reasons for your answer.
10. What are the different sources of long-term financing?
11. 'Retained Earning' is a very valuable source of long-term financing. Discuss.
12. Write short notes on:
    (*a*) Authorized capital,
    (*b*) Issued capital,
    (*c*) Subscribed capital, and
    (*d*) Paid-up capital.
    Elucidate all these, by giving suitable illustrative examples.
13. Distinguish between:
    (*i*) Equity shares and preference shares.
    (*ii*) Par value and market rate.
    (*iii*) Face value and book value.
    (*iv*) Issue price and market price.
    (*v*) 'At par' and 'at premium'.
    (*vi*) Public issue and rights issue.
    (*vii*) Public issue and private placement.
    (*viii*) Primary market and secondary market.
    (*ix*) Below par and above par.
14. (*a*) Distinguish between:
        (*i*) Cumulative and non-cumulative preference shares.
        (*ii*) Callable and non-callable preference shares.
        (*iii*) Convertible and non-convertible preference shares.
        (*iv*) Redeemable and non-redeemable preference shares.
    (*b*) Give suitable illustrative examples to bring home the difference(s).
15. (*a*) Distinguish between:
        Equitable mortgage and registered mortgage.
    (*b*) (*i*) It is a better business sense to create an equitable mortgage by way of deposit of the title deeds, rather than creating a registered mortgage, from the point of view of the borrowal companies as also that of the financing bankers. Do you agree? Give reasons for your answer.
        (*ii*) Would the position be any different in the case of equitable mortgage created by proprietary and partnership firms? Give reasons for your answer, citing suitable provisions of law, prevailing in India.
16. State, in brief, the procedure usually being followed by banks, in regard to the creation of equitable mortgage by way of deposit of title deeds.

17. Give the rationale behind each of the undernoted procedures being followed, and the precautions being taken by banks, in the event of creation of an equitable mortgage:
    (*a*) The banks record (in a Register) the actual happenings of events while the creation of the equitable mortgage, by way of deposit of title deeds, by the borrowal companies take place, recording the full details of the event, in terms of date, time, place as also the persons present, etc. Such details are duly signed by at least two officials of the bank, other than the Chief Manager of the branch, as witnesses.
    (*b*) The bank officers see to it that none of the representatives of the borrowal companies put their signatures in the register.
    (*c*) The bank insists on getting a letter to the effect that the title deed has been duly handed over to the bank for creation of an equitable mortgage by the company.
    (*d*) Further, the bank also gives a proforma letter, to such effect, to be sent by registered post, by the borrowing company (creating the equitable mortgage), at a later date.
    (*e*) Such proforma letter is being printed on the pattern of an Inland Letter, to be duly stamped and posted, instead of on a plain piece of paper, to be posted under a separate cover.
    (*f*) The banks invariably prefer to accept the title deeds, in original, and seldom the duplicate copies thereof, and that, too, as a special case.
18. What is the rationale behind the creation of a 'debenture redemption reserve?
19. Distinguish between 'Fixed' and 'Floating' coupon rates, by giving suitable illustrative examples.
20. What do you mean by the Deep Discount Bonds? Why it has been termed as 'Deep Discount'? Explain, with the help of some suitable illustrative examples.
21. Distinguish between 'Call' features and 'Put' features, in relation to the Debentures/Bonds, by giving suitable illustrative example in each case.
22. The instalments of a term loan, repayable in 5 years, in half-yearly instalments, sanctioned and disbursed on the 1st January, 2009, will automatically fall due for payment on 30th June and 31st December, each year, for 5 years. And, the event of three such instalments falling overdue for payment, will render the account in default, and will be treated as a non-performing asset (NPA). Accordingly, the lending banks and/or financial institutions should, immediately call up the loan. Do you agree? Give reasons by citing some suitable illustrative examples in this regard.
23. (*a*) Distinguish between 'movable' items of machinery and 'non-movable' items of machinery.
    (*b*) While the movable items of machinery may have to be pledged or hypothecated, immovable items of machinery will have to be necessarily mortgaged. Do you agree? Give reasons for your answer.
24. How would you ascertain as to whether the specific item of the machinery is movable or immovable?

PROBLEMS FOR PRACTICE

1. A company has issued Cumulative Preference Shares, on which dividends are payable @15% per annum. The company could not pay any dividend for the first-two years to these shareholders. They were, however, paid dividend @7% for the third year, 10% for the fourth year, and 11% for the fifth year. Luckily for the company, it earned substantial profit in the sixth year, and the equity shareholders were paid the dividend, for the first time, @ 16% that year.

(*i*) How much amount (in Rupees) would Mr Aditya get by way of dividend in the sixth year, if he holds 40,000 cumulative preference shares of the face value of Rs. 10 each?

(*ii*) How much amount (in Rupees) would Mr Rahman get by way of dividend in the sixth year, if he holds 9,000 Non-cumulative Preference Shares of the face value of Rs. 100 each, on which dividend is payable @ 14% per annum, and if he, too, has been paid dividends for the last five years at the same level as Mr Aditya?

2. A company has issued Cumulative Preference Shares on which dividends are payable @ 12% per annum. The company could not pay any dividend for the first year to these shareholders. They were, however, paid dividends @ 6% for the second year, 9% for the third year, and 10% for the fourth year. Luckily, for the company, it earned sufficient profit in the fifth year and the equity shareholders were also paid dividend @ 11% that year.

(*a*) How much amount (in Rupees) would Mr Abhinav get by way of dividend in the fifth year if he holds 3000 cumulative preference shares of the face value of Rs. 100 each?

(*b*) How much amount (in Rupees) would Mr Rohit get by way of dividend in the fifth year, if he holds 7000 Non-cumulative Preference Shares of the face value of Rs. 100 each, on which dividend is payable @ 14% per annum, and if he, too, has been paid dividends in the previous years at the same level as Mr Abhinav?

3. The fully paid-up equity share capital of Arun Software Corporation aggregates Rs. 150 lakh. Its reserves and surplus amount to Rs. 3000 lakh. The face value of each equity share is Rs. 5. Find out the book value of its equity shares, per share:

(*i*) In terms of rupees, and

(*ii*) In terms of percentage value.

4. Arvind Air Coolers (P) Limited has issued Partly Convertible Debentures (PCDs) of Rs. 100 each, to its equity shareholders on rights basis, in the ratio of 1 : 2. Mr Gopal Swarup has 1000 equity shares of the company as on the record date, *i.e.* May 30, 2009. As per the terms of the issue, Rs. 50 had to be compulsorily converted into one equity share of the face value of Rs. 10 each, after the expiry of one year from the date of issue, *i.e.* July 01, 2009. Interest @ 12% per annum is payable on the debentures half-yearly, as on the 30th June and 31st December, each year.

Required

(*a*) Calculate the amount of interest, which will be payable to Mr Gopal Swarup as on December 31, 2009; June 30, 2010 and December 31, 2010.

(*b*) How much dividend will be payable to Mr Gopal Swarup as on December 31, 2009, and December 31, 2010, if the dividends are declared/to be declared by the company @ 20% each year?

8

WORKING CAPITAL ADVANCES BY BANKS

> *Many of the things you can count, don't count. Many of the things you can't count, really count.*
>
> ***Albert Einstein***

The Learning Points

The chapter aims at developing the knowledge and facilitating the understanding of:

- Different Methods for Assessment of Working Capital Requirements by Banks, viz.
  - (a) Projected Balance Sheet (PBS) Method,
  - (b) Cash Budget (CB) Method, and
  - (c) Projected Yearly Turnover (PYT) Method.
- Method of Assessing Working capital Requirements of non-SSI Sectors
- Submission and perusal of Financial Follow-up Reports (FFRs) for Working Capital Finance
- Modifications made in (categorization of) Current Assets and Current Liabilities
- Mode of Computing Commitment Charges
- Methods of Verification of the Levels of Inventories, Receivables and Sundry Creditors
- Bases of bifurcation of Working Capital (WC) limit into Cash Credit Component (CCC) and Working Capital Demand Loan (WCDL) Component
- Rationale behind Bifurcation (of Working Capital Limit) into CCC and WCDL
- Bifurcation of Approved Bank Finance (ABF) of Rs. 2 crore and above, but below Rs.10 crore
- Assessment of Working Capital Requirements of SSI Sector, as per Nayak Committee, w.e.f. June 1993.

In the Monetary and Credit Policy, announced in October, 1997, for the second half of the year 1997-98, the Reserve Bank of India (RBI) withdrew the then prevailing norms for the assessment of the Working Capital Finance, based on the concept of Maximum Permissible Bank Finance (MPBF), mainly based on the Tandon Committee recommendations, regarding 'Inventory Carrying Norms' and the 'Second Method of Lending'. And, at the same time, the RBI had counselled the banks to evolve an appropriate system, for their own objective and rational assessment of the working capital needs of the borrowers.

Accordingly, the banks sincerely endeavoured and finally laid down transparent policy and guidelines for dispensation of credits, pertaining to different categories of economic activities.

It may, however, be pertinent to mention here that the then prevailing policy and guidelines (mainly based on the Tandon Committee Recommendations) were not given a go by. They were, instead, retained intact, in essence and spirit, as these were also based on the sound principles of lending, evolved over a period of time.

The only difference, however, had been (and a significant one at that) that these guidelines were no longer obligatory to be compulsorily followed by the banks. Instead, the banks were now given some freedom and relaxation to evolve their own respective norms:

(*i*) For the assessment of the working capital needs, and

(*ii*) For the post-disbursement supervision and follow-up of advances.

Such modified and flexible norms are discussed hereafter.

8.1 ASSESSMENT OF WORKING CAPITAL REQUIREMENTS BY BANKS

The working capital requirements can be assessed by the banks under three different methods under different circumstances.

They are:

(A) Projected Balance Sheet (PBS) method,

(B) Cash Budget (CB) method, and

(C) Projected Yearly Turnover (PYT) method.

(A) Projected Balance Sheet (PBS) Method

As the name itself suggests, the modified approach of assessment of the credit requirement [in lieu of the Maximum Permissible Bank Finance (MPBF) method], is based on the Projected Balance Sheet of the borrowers, the funds flow planned for the current year and the following years, as also on the examination of the profitability and such other financial parameters. In fact, the PBS method is also based on similar lines, as those of the then prevalent Credit Monitoring Arrangement (CMA) assessment method, of course, with some differences and modifications, with a view to ensuring that all the genuine credit requirements of the borrowers are fully met.

(B) Cash Budget (CB) Method

As against PBS method, in Cash Budget (CB) method, the financial requirements are assessed on the basis of the projected cash flows, and not on that of the projected value of assets and liabilities, as is done under the PBS method. In the case of seasonal industries (like tea, sugar, jute, rubber, etc.), and for construction activities as also in the case of hire-purchase and leasing financing, the CB method continues to be in use. However, in this method of assessment also, besides cash budget, several other relevant financial parameters like the borrower's projected profitability, liquidity, gearing, funds flow, etc. are analysed and evaluated, as is done in the case of the PBS method.

Incidentally, Cash Budget analysis is also used for sanction of ad hoc (*i.e.* temporarily additional) working capital limit, during a year.

(C) Projected Yearly Turnover (PYT) Method

Under the Projected Yearly Turnover (PYT) method, the working capital requirement is assessed on the basis of the value of the Projected Yearly Turnover. Till recently, this method was being used by the banks for assessment of the working capital finance up to a limit of Rs. 1 crore, for both Small Scale and other (non-SSI) borrowers. But now, while the banks have the flexibility to adopt their own criteria for sanction of working capital limit to non-SSI borrowers, the RBI has stipulated that the SSI borrowers will have to be sanctioned the working capital limit up to Rs. 5 crore (raised from Rs. 2 crore earlier), on the basis of minimum 20% of their projected yearly turnover (PYT).

[PYT comprises total annual gross sales, *i.e.* Cash Sales and Credit Sales taken together plus excise duty].

And, the owner's stake (margin) would be 5% of the PYT, and total working capital requirement will be 25% (20% + 5%) of the PYT.

Let us now understand with the help of an illustrative example the procedure of assessing the working capital requirement of SSI units based on PYT method.

Example

Cool Air (Private) Ltd., a small scale industrial (SSI) unit, manufacturing room air-conditioners, has its Projected Yearly Turnover (PYT) [total gross sales, *i.e.* credit sales + cash sales, plus excise duty] of Rs. 20 crore.

Required

(*i*) Compute the quantum of total working capital requirement of the company, the quantum of finance that would be granted to the unit by a bank, as per the current guidelines issued by the RBI for such advances.

(*ii*) Also compute the quantum of owner's stake (margin) in the instant case.

(*iii*) What would be the current ratio in such cases?

Solution

(*a*) Projected Yearly Turnover (PYT)	:	Rs. 20 crore
(*b*) Thus, total working capital requirement would be assessed at	:	Rs. 5 crore
	:	[25% of PYT]
(*c*) Working capital limit to be sanctioned by the bank	:	Rs. 4 crore
	:	[*i.e.* 20% of PYT]
		or
		[80% of Working Capital [requirement]
(*d*) Owner's Equity (Margin) to be brought in by the SSI unit	:	Rs. 1 crore
		[5% of PYT] or
		[20% or working capital requirement]

Thus, we see that, in all such cases, the current ratio (CR) would work out to be invariably 1.25 : 1.00 [*i.e.* CA/CL = 5/4 (*i.e.* b/c, above) = 1.25 : 1.00.

8.2 ASSESSMENT OF WORKING CAPITAL FINANCE TO NON-SSI SECTORS

As regards the assessment of the working capital limit for non-SSI borrowers, most of the banks follow different methods of assessment for the limits of:

(*i*) Below Rs. 25 lakhs, and

(*ii*) Rs. 25 lakhs and over.

Methods of Assessment

(*i*) Limits of Rs. 25 lakhs and above but up to Rs. 4 crores	PBS method
(*ii*) Limits of above Rs. 4 crores	PBS method
(*iii*) Limits of above Rs. 2 lakhs but under Rs. 25 lakhs	Simple assessment

Application Forms

For different categories of borrowers, and for different working capital limit, different application forms [as also different appraisal forms] are generally being used by the banks.

8.3 FINANCIAL FOLLOW-UP REPORTS (FFRs) FOR WORKING CAPITAL FINANCES

The quarterly information system (QIS) pro forma, viz. QIS I, II and III, stipulated by the Tandon Committee, and further streamlined by the Chore Committee, have been dispensed with, since 1st October, 1997. However, some of the commercial banks, in the public sector, have, on their own, designed some follow-up proforma, somewhat on similar lines. Such Financial Follow-up Reports (viz. FFR-I and FFR-II) are required to be submitted in all the cases of working capital limits of Rs. 1 crore and above.

FFR-I: This form is to be submitted by the borrowers on a quarterly basis, within 6 weeks from the close of the quarter.

[This form is a simplified version of the QIS Form II, with certain additional analysis].

FFR-II: This form is required to be submitted by the borrowers, half-yearly, within 8 weeks from the close of the half-year.

[This form is a modified version of QIS Form-III].

Specimen of both the above proforma are placed at Annexures–8.1 and 8.2 (A and B), [and 8.3 (A and B) for Traders and Merchant Exporters], at the end of the Chapter.

8.4 SOME MODIFICATIONS IN CAs AND CLs

Under the PBS method, the criteria for classification of Current Assets (CAs) and Current Liabilities (CLs) have undergone slight modifications.

These are:

C.As

(*i*) Term Deposit Receipts (TDRs) with the banks, Government Securities and other Trust Securities, plus.

(*ii*) All short-term investments made for parking short-term surplus funds, like Money Market Mutual Fund (MMMF), CP, CD, etc., plus.

(*iii*) Margin Money deposited against Letters of Credit (L/Cs) and Bank Guarantees (B/Gs).

NON-CAs

All other investments, like Inter-Corporate Deposits (ICDs), investments in quoted shares and debentures, including investments in subsidiaries and associates.

CLs

Inter-Corporate Deposits (ICDs) accepted by the company.

It may be pertinent to clarify here that, though apparently, there seems to be two contradictory parameters for categorization of similar investments [inasmuch as, while the investments in ICDs by the company in some other companies are taken as non-current asset, ICD's accepted by the company in question are treated as Current Liability], there is a significant and subtle rationale behind such stipulations. This is so because, generally speaking, no company may be sure enough that the investments made by it in the ICDs of other companies would be repaid to it definitely on the due date. In fact, most of the companies are found to have defaulted, though in different degrees. Therefore, it is most rational not to categorize these as Current Assets but only as non-current Assets.

As against this, the ICDs accepted by the companies, as per the usual terms and conditions stipulated, are undertaken to be repaid on the due date, positively. And, such undertakings must be complied with, too. That is why the banks, in their own assessment, take such ICDs, issued by the company under appraisal, as Current Liabilities, and rightly so.

It may further be noted here that the bills drawn under the Letter of Credit (L/C) are computed outside the assessment of the main working capital finance. Therefore, the demand and time bills, drawn under L/C, are not to be included in the Current Assets (CAs). Correspondingly, the drawings made against the limit for negotiation/discount of demand/time bills will not be treated as Current Liabilities (CLs).

8.5 COMMITMENT CHARGES

The commitment charges of 1% p.a., earlier levied on unutilised portion of fund-based working capital limit now stand withdrawn, w.e.f. 1st October, 1997, except in the cases of:

(*i*) Working capital limit of Rs. 20 crore and above, and

(*ii*) Term loan of Rs. 5 crore and above.

Further, the rate of interest charged on additional working capital limit, sanctioned on an ad-hoc basis, will henceforth be the same as was being charged on the usual cash credit account of the company (and not 200 percentage points higher, as was the case earlier).

Rate of Commitment Charge

Utilisation of limit	Rate of commitment charge
A. ***Working Capital***	
(*i*) Above 60%	NIL
(*ii*) 60% and below	0.75% p.a. on the entire portion of the unutilised limit for each half-year ending September and March.
B. ***Term Loan***	
Amount undrawn from the stipulated dates as per the agreed schedule of drawal, which is usually 6 months	1% on the amount undrawn from the stipulated date, with a grace period of one month.

Exemptions

Commitment charges on the Working Capital limits sanctioned for the under-noted purposes are, however, exempt:

(*i*) Working capital limits to SSI,

(*ii*) Export finance,

(*iii*) Limits for the purchase/discount of demand/time bills,

(*iv*) Limit sanctioned against bills sent for collection,

(*v*) Limits sanctioned to commercial banks, financial institutions, cooperative banks and land development banks.

8.6 VERIFICATION OF THE LEVELS OF INVENTORIES/RECEIVABLES AND SUNDRY CREDITORS

Under the PBS method, the levels of projected inventories, receivables and sundry creditors are examined, during the course of the credit assessment exercise, on the basis of the trend of the past levels (historical data or intra-firm data of the past) and the inter-firm comparison of the levels, as was being done earlier, under the MPBF method. But, now the basic and significant difference is that (as against the MPBF method) the inventory norms, laid down on the basis of the Tandon Committee recommendations [vide Annexure: 8.4, at the end of the Chapter] are no longer taken as the maximum (ceiling) level, imposed in strict terms. These are, instead, treated only as a historical reference levels, and the credit needs may now be examined by the banks, independent of the erstwhile laid down inventory norms, which may vary, depending upon the merit of each case. And, in case the projections of Current Assets (CAs) seem to be rather excessive, these may be brought down to realistic levels, in consultation/discussion with the borrowers concerned.

Evaluation of Liquidity

Similarly, the current ratio (CR) of 1.33 and above is now no longer stipulated as the minimum acceptable level. Instead, the CR at 1.33 is now considered only as a bench mark and, therefore, it may be acceptable even at a slightly lower level, depending upon the merit of each case. As we all know, the level of CR may vary, depending upon various factors, like the scale of operation, the nature and duration of the operating cycle, and the overall financial position of the borrowers.

In summary, we may say that, under the PBS method, the level of Working Capital Finance is not determined on the basis of any rigid formula, as was the case earlier, when the CR was required to be not less than 1.33 (as stipulated by the second method of lending). [*All the three methods of lending, however, have been placed at Annexure-8.5, at the end of the Chapter*].

Thus, the 'Assessed Bank Finance' (ABF) [as against MPBF] is now being computed, based on:

(*i*) the duration and nature of the operating cycle,
(*ii*) projected level (scale) of operation,
(*iii*) nature of projected build-up of CAs and CLs,
(*iv*) profitability, and
(*v*) liquidity, etc.

8.7 BIFURCATION OF WORKING CAPITAL (WC) LIMIT

(*i*) CCC [Cash Credit Component], and
(*ii*) WCDL [Working Capital Demand Loan].

It would, however, be quite pertinent, at this very stage, to first understand the salient and distinguishing features of the cash credit, and demand loan, as also overdraft facilities, so as to be well appreciate the rationale behind such bifurcation easily.

CASH CREDIT, OVERDRAFT AND DEMAND LOAN

Cash Credit and Overdraft

Both the cash credit and overdraft accounts are running accounts, in the sense that the amount can be deposited in the account any number of times and the amount can be withdrawn, too, unlimited number of time, of course, within the available drawing power or credit balance.

This much about the similarities between the two accounts. But, the distinguishing features between these two accounts are that while the credit facilities against the security of pledge or hypothecation of inventories and/or book debts are granted by way of cash credit facilities, the advance against the securities, other than the items of inventories and book debts (*e.g.* against the security of Shares and Debentures, Bank's Own Term Deposit Receipts, NSCs, LIC Policies, Units of UTI, etc.), is granted by way of an overdraft.

The difference, thus, is only technical and in terms of terminology and name of the account, to differentiate between the two different purposes, or against two different classes of securities.

SECURED AND CLEAN

Both the cash credit and overdraft may be of two types viz. secured and unsecured or clean, *e.g.*

(*a*) (*i*) Secured Cash Credit or Stock Cash Credit (against the security of stocks of inventories and book debts), and

(*ii*) Clean (or unsecured) Cash Credit against the security of trade bills sent for collection, or just against personal security or the third party guarantee, etc.

(*b*) (*i*) Secured Overdraft, against the security of Bank's Own Term Deposit Receipts, NSCs, etc., and

(*ii*) Clean (or unsecured) Overdraft, against the personal security of the borrower and/or the third party guarantee.

Further, even the overdrafts granted against the security of shares, LIC policies, etc., are treated as clean overdrafts as these have not been classified as authorised securities for the banks.

DEMAND LOAN

The demand loan, on the other hand, is not in the nature of a running account, as against the cash credit and overdraft accounts. This means that while the demand loan may be disbursed in one lump sum or in phases, or in instalments, the amount once deposited in the demand loan account cannot be withdrawn, during the entire currency of the loan. That is, the amount once deposited in the demand loan account is deposited forever, and it goes to liquidate the outstanding on the demand loan account by that much amount.

The concept and position, the system and procedure, can well be appreciated, more clearly, by means of an illustrative example, presented in a tabular form:

Sample of the position/picture of a cash credit or an overdraft account:

Limit : Rs. 10,000

Drawing Power : Rs. 9,000

Date	*Debit*	*Credit*	*Balance (amount in Rs.)*
01.11.2008	8,000		(–) 8,000 (Debit)
12.11.2008		5,000	(–) 3,000 (Debit)
23.11.2008	4,000		(–) 7,000 (Debit)
23.11.2008		9,000	(+) 2,000 (Credit)
27.11.2008	10,000		(–) 8,000 (Debit)
27.11.2008		6,000	(–) 2,000 (Debit)
27.11.2008		7,000	(+) 5,000 (Credit)
30.11.2008	12,000		(–) 7,000 (Debit)
Total	**34,000**	**27,000**	

Sample of the Position/Picture of a Demand Loan Account:

Demand Loan Sanctioned: Rs. 10,000

Date	*Debit*	*Credit*	*Balance (Amount in Rs.)*
01.11.2008	5,000		(–) 5,000 (Debit)
12.11.2008	4,000		(–) 9,000 (Debit)
19.11.2008	1,000		(–) 10,000 (Debit)
27.11.2008		3,000	(–) 7,000 (Debit)

Thus, the amount of Rs. 3,000 deposited on 27.11.2008, goes to reduce the outstanding on the demand loan account permanently, and, thus, it cannot be withdrawn back from the account at any stage, during the entire currency of the demand loan account. In the cases of cash credit and overdraft accounts, however, both the deposits and withdrawals can take place any number of times.

For the first time, in April, 1995, the working capital limit of the borrowers, enjoying WC limit of Rs. 20 crore and above (in aggregate) from the banking system, were bifurcated into:

Cash Credit Component (CCC) and Working Capital Demand Loan (WCDL) in the ratio of 75% and 25% respectively, of the Maximum Permissible Bank Finance (MPBF).

Since then, the WCDL component has been gradually increased (and correspondingly, the CCC has been reduced) over a period of time. A chronological presentation has been placed in **Table 8.1** hereunder:

Table 8.1: Gradual Changes in CCC and WCDL

Period	*Assessed Bank Finance (ABF) (erstwhile MPBF) of Rs. 20 crore and above*		*ABF (erstwhile MPBF) of Rs. 10 crore and above*	
	CCC (Max.)	*WCDL (Min.)*	*CCC (Max.)*	*WCDL (Min.)*
	%	%	%	%
April, 1995	75	25	NA	NA
October, 1995	60	40	NA	NA
April, 1996	40	60	60	40
November, 1996	25	75	40	60
April, 1997	20	80	25	75
October, 1997	20	80	20	80

Thus, the system of bifurcation of WC limit into CCC and WCDL was initially introduced to cover MPBF of between Rs. 10 crore and above but below Rs. 20 crore, too, in April, 1996, in a modest 60:40 ratio, which has been gradually raised to 40 : 60, 25 : 75, and finally at par with the uppermost bracket of Rs. 20 crore and above, at 20 : 80, since October 1997. This was done, simultaneously, with the gradual increase of WCDL component in the case of borrowers with the MPBF of Rs. 20 crore and above, as has been shown in Table 8.1 above.

It may, however, be pertinent to mention here that, at the request of the borrowers, the loan component (WCDL) could be increased with the corresponding decrease in the CCC. The reverse, however, is not permitted.

8.8 RATIONALE BEHIND BIFURCATION INTO CCC AND WCDL

In 1968 the Dehejia Committee, remarked that the bank's cash credit facility, though considered to be in the nature of a short-term loan (as it was specifically stipulated to be "repayable on demand; to be renewed annually, if necessary"), it had virtually become the longest term loan. This was so because, if a company was initially granted a W.C. Cash Credit limit of say, Rs. 1 crore, it was, in actual practice, observed to be gradually raised to Rs. 2 crore, Rs. 3 crore, and so on, of course, subject to the satisfactory conduct of the bank cash credit account as also the gradual increase in the scale of operation of the company. And now, with the introduction of the concept of the WCDL component, a portion of the WC limit has got to be compulsorily repaid, over a period of time, ranging from minimum 15 days to maximum 6 months.

The minimum period, however, has since been reduced even to one single day, by some banks (like SBI), in some cases, at the request of the borrowers, to this effect.

> I, however, do not tend to agree with the comments made by the Dehejia Committee (that the banks's cash credit facility is virtually the longest term loan), in that, with every credit into the borrower's cash credit account, the amount of the loan, withdrawn earlier by the borrower, gets repaid, in full, on the first-come-first-liquidated basis, as per the Clayton's rule. Therefore, provided the credit summations in the respective cash credit accounts are commensurate with the amount of WC limit and the annual sales turnover of the company, the WC advance continues to remain a short-term loan, not only virtually, but actually, too, inasmuch as every withdrawal may constitute, a fresh loan, which gets repaid with every successive deposits in the cash credit account.
>
> But then, in actual practice, most of the borrowers usually do not deposit the entire sale proceeds into their cash credit accounts and, therefore, the contention of the Dehejia Committee may, in a way, be said to be quite correct, in essence and spirit. Therefore, the practice of the bifurcation of the aggregate WC limit into CCC and WCDL is a right step, in the right direction, with a view to enforcing the financial discipline among the borrowers of the banks.

8.9 BIFURCATION OF ABF OF Rs. 2 CRORE AND ABOVE BUT BELOW Rs. 10 CRORE

Since November 1996, the borrowers, availing of the fund-based WC limit of Rs. 2 crore and above, but less than Rs. 10 crore, have also been given the option to avail of WCDL but, at least, in the ratio of 50 : 50, with the option to increase the proportion of WCDL component and with the corresponding decrease in the CCC, but not vice versa.

Exemptions

(a) Export Finance

It may, however, be mentioned here that the entire export finance facilities, both pre-shipment finance (also known as packing credit) and post-shipment finance, *i.e.* purchase/discount of (export) demand and time bills, are exempt from such bifurcation. That is, the entire credit limit of export finance [Export Packing Credit (EPC) and Foreign Bills Discounted (FBD)] could be availed of by the borrowers by way of CCC alone.

Thus, the bifurcation of WC limit into WCDL and CCC, as stated earlier, has to be given effect to, only after excluding export credit limits.

That is why, the interchangeability of the limits of export finance and domestic finance has, ordinarily, been not permitted, except in some deserving cases, depending upon the merit of each case, authorised by a competent controlling authority.

(b) Bills Limit

Further, the Bills Limit for inland sales, including purchase of third party cheques/bank drafts, is allowed to be fully availed of as CCC. But then, the interchangeability between CCC and Bills Limit, is generally not permitted, except in some deserving cases, depending upon the merit of each case, authorised by the competent controlling authority.

The mechanism of computation of CCC and WCDL components, in the case of a borrower, enjoying an Export Credit Limit as also Bills Limit can be well understood with the help of an illustrative example.

Example

Surya Metals Ltd. is enjoying an aggregate WC limit of Rs. 100 crore made up as under:

(*i*) EPC (Export Packing Credit) — Rs. 40 crore

(*ii*) Inland Bills Purchase limit — Rs. 20 crore

(*iii*) Other WC limit — Rs. 40 crore

Required

Please compute the quantum of CCC and WCDL components in this case.

Solution

Export Finance — Rs. 40 crore (A)

Cash Credit — Rs. 12 crore (B)
[20% of (Rs. 100 crore less Rs. 40 crore)
i.e. 20% of Rs. 60 crore]

Bills/Cheques
Purchase Limit — Rs. 20 crore (C)

WCDL — Rs. 28 crore (D)
[(80% of Rs. 60 crore) less Rs. 20 crore
= Rs. 48 crore – Rs. 20 crore)].

Thus, A + B + C + D = 40 + 12 + 20 + 28 = Rs. 100 crore.

Disbursement of WCDL

Since November 1996, the number of WCDL has been restricted to maximum seven accounts. However, under exceptional circumstances, the number could be reasonably increased, in case of large borrowers. Further, in each WCDL account, only one withdrawal is permitted.

Roll-Over

Since November 1996, WCDL has been permitted to be rolled over, at the request of the borrower. The term 'roll-over' means that the due date of repayment of WCDL can be extended by another 45 days/3 months/6 months, provided of course, the conduct of the borrower's cash credit account is regular or is only temporarily irregular (overdrawn). But, in all the cases, where the cash credit account is regularly irregular, *i.e.* where the account continues to be irregular for quite sometime, and the drawings thereon have been restricted, with a view to gradually regularising the position, no fresh WCDL should be created by allowing any further withdrawals, even within the WCDL limit. However, in the case of the current WCDL, part payment and roll over facility may be extended, as usual. The borrower may as well choose to repay the WCDL on due date and draw it again on a later date. Part-payment of WCDL can also be accepted and the balance amount rolled over. But, such roll-over constitutes one account out of the maximum seven accounts permitted in a year.

But, in the case of non-payment and in the event of non-receipt of the request for roll-over of the WCDL from the borrower, on or before the due date, the bank, at its own discretion, rolls over the loan. And, in all such cases, the repayment of the loan has to be made latest by the next due date.

Prepayment

WCDL can as well be repaid well before the due date, but a penalty @ 1.5% p.a. is imposed on the prepaid amount for the entire unexpired period of the WCDL.

Example

Supposing a WCDL for Rs. 100 crore, due for payment on 31.12.2008, is partly paid on the 5th October, 2008, to the extent of Rs. 60 crore. Thus, penal interest @ 1.5% p.a. will be charged on Rs. 60 crore for the unexpired period of WCDL *i.e.* 2 months and 26 days. And, if the entire loan of Rs. 100 crore would have been prepaid on 5.10.2008, the interest @ 1.5% p.a. would have been charged for the period (2 months and 26 days) on the entire amount of Rs. 100 crore.

Ad-hoc Limit

Ad-hoc (additional) Working Capital limit can be granted to the borrowers to meet their temporary financial requirements, but only after both the duly sanctioned CCC and WCDL components of the limit are fully availed of.

Concessional Rate of Interest on WCDL Components

The rate of interest applicable on WCDL components of the working capital finance is quoted at 0.25 percentage points lower than that applicable on the CCC, but only in the cases of the borrowers enjoying aggregate working capital finance of Rs. 2 crore and above but up to Rs. 10 crore only of Assessed Bank Finance (ABF). In all other cases, *i.e.* in the cases, of borrowers enjoying ABF above Rs. 10 crore the same rate of interest is applicable, both on CCC and WCDL components.

Lien for Irregular Portion of the Account

To cover any shortfall in Drawing Power (DP) on the CCC, in relation to the outstandings on the account, a suitable lien should be noted in the borrower's other account(s) maintained at the branch and having some credit balance(s) therein, so as to cover the irregular portion of the account to the maximum possible extent.

Renewal

Working capital finance is a short-term finance, as it is made "repayable on demand, or on the due date in the case of WCDL and to be renewed annually, if necessary". Therefore, the aggregate working capital finance must be reviewed annually, as and when due for renewal, and the reassessed limits should be put in place in time.

8.10 ASSESSMENT OF WORKING CAPITAL REQUIREMENTS OF SSI SECTOR (AS PER NAYAK COMMITTEE), W.E.F. JUNE, 1993

Eligibility

All the units, falling under the SSI Sector (comprising of small scale industries, village and cottage industries, and tiny sector units) — both existing and new having an aggregate **fund-based** working capital limit up to **Rs. 5 crore**, from the banking system, may be provided working capital limits to the extent of **minimum 20% of their Projected Yearly Turnover** [PYT], *i.e.* 'total gross sales', **including Excise Duty.** And, 5% of PYT will be the Owner' Equity margin. Thus, the total working capital requirement of the unit will be 25% (20% + 5%) of the PYT.

Let us now understand the provisions with the help of some illustrative examples.

Example 1

Supposing, Sunrise Industries, a small scale industrial unit, manufacturing nuts and bolts, has a Projected Annual Turnover of Rs. 25 crore. In this case, the minimum fund-based working capital limit would be computed at 20% of Rs. 25 crore, which comes to Rs. 5 crore. Thus, this unit will be eligible to be sanctioned a fund-based working capital limit of Rs. 5 crore, whereas its total working capital requirement would be estimated at Rs. 6.25 crore, *i.e.* 25% of the Projected Annual Turnover estimated at Rs. 25 crore. The proportion of the bank finance and the owners' stake (margin money) would be as under:

(*i*) The SSI unit would be required to bring in 5% of the Projected Annual Turnover (Rs. 25 crore) *i.e.* Rs. 1.25 crore as margin money, and

(*ii*) The bank will sanction a fund-based working capital limit of Rs. 5 crore, *i.e.* 20% of the Projected Annual Turnover.

This means that the margin money and the bank finance will be in the ratio of 1 : 4, *i.e.* the margin stipulated for such an advance would be 25%.

Let us now re-enforce and clarify the aforesaid points with the help of another illustrative example.

Example 2

Stars and Moon (Private) Limited, a small scale industrial (SSI) unit, manufacturing readymade garments for children and ladies, has a Projected Yearly Turnover (PYT) estimated at Rs. 16 crore.

Thus, its total fund-based working capital requirement would be 25% of Rs. 16 crore = Rs. 4 crore. It will be met by way of:

Sl. No.	*Descriptions*	*Amount (Rs.)*
(*i*)	The (fund-based) working capital limit (by bank) to the extent of 80% of Rs. 4 crore , or 20% of Rs. 16 crore , *i.e.*	Rs. 3.2 crore
(*ii*)	Margin money to be brought in by the owner(s) to the extent of 20% of Rs. 4 crore , or 5% of Rs. 16 crore , *i.e.*	Rs. 0.8 crore
	Total	**Rs. 4.0 crore**

The aforesaid relaxation is available only to the units in the SSI sector with the requirement of fund-based working capital limit to the extent of Rs. 5 crore or below. Thus, in the case of even SSI units, having aggregate fund-based working capital limit from the banks in excess of Rs. 5 crore, the working capital requirement would be assessed on the basis of Projected Balance Sheet (PBS) method.

It is, however, very pertinent to mention here that the bank executives should be careful and prudent enough to ensure that the projected annual turnover is reasonable and achievable by the unit, and that even the estimated growth, if any, in the sales turnover [in relation to the previous year(s)] is realistic.

For this purpose, the returns filed by the unit with the sales tax/revenue authorities, may very well serve as useful guiding documents. Besides, the borrowers must be informed that they should deposit the sale proceeds of their entire sales in their account with the bank, which may serve as the documentary evidence of the annual gross sales with the branch of the bank itself. Regular periodical performance monitoring of the units and the scrutiny of the stock statements and the physical verification of the stocks charged to the bank, and the timely realisation of the trade bills, may ensure satisfactory conduct of the units' business and their bank accounts, on a regular and on-going basis.

The other broad parameters of the bank's present appraisal system would remain unchanged. These are:

(*i*) Basic credit decision based on the financial health and prospects of the unit, and

(*ii*) Fixing up the quantum of limit, based on the working capital requirement.

Seasonal Industries

In case of seasonal industries, however, the peak season and off season turnover, instead of the annual turnover may be considered separately for determining the respective 20% levels.

Sundry Creditors and Advance Payments

As these are themselves sources of funds, other than bank finance, these should be substracted from the credit limit to be fixed by the banks, with a view to avoiding double financing.

Borrower's Margin

As we have already seen earlier, the ratio of margin and working capital loan should be 1 : 4. And, the proportion of margin and bank finance may be higher than 1 : 4.

Fixing of Sub-Limits

Banks are free to fix sub-limits for the various components of inventories, viz. raw materials and finished goods, as also for trade/supply bills.

Non-Fund Based Limits (L/Cs and B/Gs)

Non-fund based working capital limits, *i.e.* for letters of credit and bank guarantees, would be assessed separately over and above the fund based working capital limit in the usual manner, as hitherto.

Assessment of Working Capital Limit in SSI Sector

The term 'minimum' working capital limit obviously suggests that there is the possibility of some higher working capital limit being sanctioned to a particular unit, though any lower limit than 20% of the Projected Yearly Turnover is just ruled out.

That is, the assessment of the working capital limit has got to be done both as per the

(*i*) Projected Yearly Turnover Basis, as also the

(*ii*) Traditional/Projected Balance Sheet (PBS) method.

And, if the credit requirements, based on production/processing cycle/projected balance sheet method, happens to be higher than the one assessed on the basis of the Projected Yearly Turnover method, the former quantum of limit would be sanctioned, inasmuch as the 20% of the Projected Yearly Turnover is the minimum (not the maximum) credit requirement.

As against this, if the assessment of credit requirements, based on PBS method, happens to be far short of the one assessed on the basis of the Projected Yearly Turnover, the credit assessment will have to be thoroughly re-examined and properly re-assessed with more than ordinary care, and a realistic working capital limit may be sanctioned. Such a situation may usually arise mostly in the cases of ancillary units, which have the assured supply of raw materials as also the off-take of the finished goods. Similarly, where the working capital operating cycle happens to be shorter than even 3 months, the working capital requirement would, naturally, be less than 25% of the Projected Yearly Turnover, and consequently the limit may be lower than 20% of the Projected Yearly Turnover.

A lower working capital limit can as well be sanctioned if the liquid surplus available with the borrower happens to be more than 5% of the Projected Yearly Turnover, inasmuch as the banks are supposed to meet only the need-based financial requirements of each borrower.

It would, however, be desirable to discuss the matter with each borrower separately and individually, whereby he may be convinced that his actual credit requirement is much lower and, therefore, he should not borrow more funds than required, as in that case he may lose by way of avoidably extra cash outflow in the form of interest payable on the funds borrowed from the bank.

Appendix 8.1

FINANCIAL FOLLOW-UP REPORT (FFR-I)

Report for the quarter ending ______

Period [number of months] ______ ( ) Months

[This report replaces QIS Form-II]

Name of the borrower: ______

A. PERFORMANCE

Activity	*Annual Plan (current year)*	*Actuals (cumulative) up to quarter ending*	*% of achievements*
	1	2	3
(*i*) Production (quantity) (*ii*) Net sales (Rs. in rounded lakh) (*a*) Domestic (*b*) Exports			

B. STATUS OF WORKING CAPITAL FUNDS

(*Rs. in round lakh*)

Particulars	*At the end of the last year (31.3. ___)*	*At the Quarter ending ___/___/___*	*Change during the current year (2 minus 1) (+) or (–)*	*Estimates at the end of current year (31.3. ___)*
	1	2	3	4
Current Assets (CAs) (*a*) Inventories (*b*) Sundry debtors (*c*) Other CAs				
(*d*) Total CAs				
Current Liabilities (CLs) (*e*) Bank borrowings [for working capital] (*f*) Sundry creditors (*g*) Other CLs				
(*h*) Total CLs				
(*i*) NWC ($d - h$) (*j*) Current ratio (d/h)				

C. CURRENT ASSETS—HOW FINANCED?

Particulars	At the end of the last year (31.03.___)	At the quarter ending ___/___/___	Estimates at the end of the current year (31.03. ___)
	1	2	3
(*k*) Bank borrowings (e/d%) (*l*) Sundry creditors (f/d%) (*m*) Other CL's (g/d%) (*n*) NWC (i/d%)			
Total	**100**	**100**	**100**

D. LEVELS OF INVENTORIES/SUNDRY DEBTORS/SUNDRY CREDITORS

Particulars	At the end of the last year (31.03. ___)	At the quarter ending ___/___/___	Estimates at the end of the current year (31.03 ___)
	1	2	3
(*o*) Inventories (*p*) Sundry debtors (*q*) Sundry creditors			
Total			

Notes

1. This report is required to be submitted by the borrowers within six weeks from the close of each quarter.
2. Classification of Current Assets and Current Liabilities should be the same as in the assessment of working capital limits. [Deposits/Instalments of Term Loans (TLs), Deferred Payment Guarantees (DPGs), debentures, etc., due within 12 months from the end of the quarter, should be included in the Other Current Liabilities (OCLs)].
3. The information should be furnished for each line of activity/division/unit separately, as also for the company as a whole.
4. In Section D, the levels in days should be computed for each column as follows:

   For Inventory : (Value × 365) divided by net sales

   For Receivables : (Value × 365) divided by Gross (Credit) Sales

   For Sundry Creditors : (Value × 365) divided by (Credit) Purchases

   (For the above computation, under column 2, sales/purchases for the part of a year is to be analysed).
5. This format is applicable for traders and merchant exporters, too.

Appendix 8.2 (A)

FINANCIAL FOLLOW-UP REPORT (FFR-II)

(THIS REPORT REPLACES QIS FORM-III)
HALF-YEARLY OPERATING STATEMENTS

PART-A

Name of the borrower: ______________________________

A. HALF-YEARLY OPERATING STATEMENT

(Amount Rs. in rounded Lakh)

Activity	*Last Year (actuals)*	*Current Year (estimates)*	*Half-Year Ended ______ (actuals)*
	1	2	3
1. Gross Sales (Net of Returns) (*a*) Domestic (*b*) Exports			
Total			
2. Less: Excise Duty 3. Net Sales (Item-1 – Item-2) 4. **Cost of Goods Sold** (*a*) Raw materials consumption (including consumable stores and spares used in the process of manufacture) (*b*) Other spares (*c*) Power and fuel (*d*) Direct labour (factory wages and salaries) (*e*) Other manufacturing expenses, including depreciation			
Sub-total			
Add: Opening stocks-in-process and finished goods Sub-total *Deduct:* Closing stock-in-process and finished goods 5. Total cost of goods sold 6. Selling, general and administrative expenses 7. Interest 8. Sub-total (5 + 6 + 7) 9. Operating Profit/Loss (3–8) 10. Other non-operating income/expenses – Net (+ / –) 11. Profit Before Tax/Loss (9 + 10)			

Appendix 8.2 (B)

FINANCIAL FOLLOW-UP REPORT (FFR-II)

(THIS REPORT REPLACES QIS FORM-III)

HALF-YEARLY OPERATING STATEMENTS

PART-B

Name of the Borrower: ____________________

A. HALF-YEARLY FUNDS STATEMENTS

(Amount Rs. in rounded Lakh)

Activity	*Last Year (actuals) (audited) Provisions*	*Current Year (estimates)*	*Half-Year Ended ______ (actuals)*
	1	2	3
1. SOURCES			
(*a*) Profit Before Tax			
(*b*) Depreciation			
(*c*) Increase in capital			
(*d*) Increase in term liabilities			
(*e*) Decrease in			
(*i*) Fixed Assets			
(*ii*) Other non-current assets			
(*f*) Others			
(*g*) Total (A)			
2. USES			
(*a*) Net Loss			
(*b*) Dividend payments			
(*c*) Taxes			
(*d*) Decrease in term liabilities (including public deposits)			
(*e*) Increase in			
(*i*) Fixed Assets			
(*ii*) ICDs Placed			
(*iii*) Investments in associates/subsidiaries			
(*iv*) Other non-current assets			
(*f*) Others			
(*g*) Total (B)			

3. Long term surplus (+) / deficit (–) (A – B)
4. Changes in current assets, Increase (+) / Decrease (–)
5. Changes in other current liabilities (other than bank borrowings) Increase (+) / Decrease (–)
6. Changes in WC Gap, Increase (+) / Decrease (–) (4–5)
7. Net surplus, (+) / Deficit (–) (Difference between 3 & 6)
8. Changes in bank borrowings, Increase (+) / Decrease (–)

Notes

(*a*) This report is required to be submitted by the borrower within 8 weeks from the close of each half year.

(*b*) Information should be furnished for each line of activity/unit separately, as also for the company as a whole.

(*c*) Valuation of current assets or current liabilities and recording of income and expenses should be on the same bases as have been adopted for the statutory balance sheets, and as such these should be applied, consistently.

(*d*) Classification of current assets/current liabilities for the purpose of funds flow should be the same as in the case of the assessment of working capital limits and the relevant FFR-I.

(*e*) In respect of traders and merchant exporters, a suitably modified format for Part-A and Part-B should be used, vide Annexures–8.3(A) [TME] and 8.3 (B) [TME] respectively.

Appendix 8.3(A) TME

FINANCIAL FOLLOW-UP REPORT (FFR-II)

HALF-YEARLY OPERATING STATEMENTS

PART-A

This report replaces QIS Form-III for traders and merchant exporters

Name of the borrower: ____________________

A. HALF-YEARLY FUNDS STATEMENTS

(Amount Rs. in rounded Lakh)

Activity	*Last Year (actuals)*	*Current Year (budgeted)*	*Half-Year Ended ______ (actuals)*
	1	2	3
1. (*i*) Gross Income (net of returns)			
(*a*) Domestic Sales			
(*b*) Exports			
(*c*) Sub-Total (*a* + *b*)			
(*ii*) Other Income			
(*a*) Duty Draw Back			
(*b*) Cash Assistance			
(*c*) commission and brokerage received			
(*d*) Sub-Total (*a* + *b* + *c*)			
(*iii*) Total (*i*) + (*ii*)			
2. **Cost of Sales**			
(*a*) Purchases			
(*b*) Other Trading Expenses			
(*c*) Sub-Total (*a* + *b*)			
(*d*) Add: Opening Stock			
(*e*) Sub-Total (*c* + *d*)			
(*f*) Less: Closing Stock			
(*g*) Total Cost of sales (*e* – *f*)			
3. Selling, general and administrative Expenses, including bonus payments			
4. Interest			
5. Depreciation			
6. Operating Profit/Loss (Item 1 minus total of Items 2, 3, 4 and 5)			
7. Other non-operating income/expenses – Net (+/–)			
8. Profit Before Tax/Loss (Item 6 plus 7)			

Appendix 8.3(B) TME

FINANCIAL FOLLOW-UP REPORT (FFR-II)

HALF-YEARLY OPERATING STATEMENTS

PART-B

This report replaces QIS Form-III for traders and merchant exporters

Name of the borrower: ______________________________

A. HALF-YEARLY FUNDS STATEMENTS

(Amount Rs. in round Lakh)

Activity	*Last Year (actuals) (audited)/ (provisions)*	*Current Year (estimates)*	*Half-Year Ended __ 200 __ (actuals)*
	1	2	3
1. SOURCES			
(*a*) Profit Before Tax			
(*b*) Depreciation			
(*c*) Increase in Capital			
(*d*) Increase in Term Liabilities			
(*e*) Decrease in			
(*i*) Fixed Assets			
(*ii*) Other non-current Assets			
(*f*) Others			
(*g*) TOTAL (A)			
2. USES			
(*a*) Net Loss			
(*b*) Dividend Payments			
(*c*) Taxes Paid			
(*d*) Decrease in term liabilities (including public deposits)			
(*e*) Increase in			
(*i*) Fixed Assets			
(*ii*) ICDs			
(*iii*) Investments in Associates/Subsidiaries			
(*f*) Others			
(*g*) TOTAL (B)			

3. Long-term surplus (+)/deficit (–) (A–B)
4. Changes in Current Assets, increase (+)/decrease (–)
5. Changes in other current liabilities (other than bank borrowings) increase (+)/decrease (–)
6. Changes in WC gap increase (+)/decrease (–) (4–5)
7. Net surplus (+)/deficit (–) (difference between 3 and 6)
8. Changes in bank borrowings increase (+)/decrease (–)

Notes

(*a*) This report should be submitted by the borrower within 8 weeks from the close of each half-year.

(*b*) Information should be furnished for each line of activity/unit separately, as also for the company as a whole.

(*c*) The valuation of current assets or current liabilities and recording of income and expenses should be on the same bases as have been adopted for the statutory balance sheets, and these should be applied, as such, consistently.

(*d*) Classification of current assets/current liabilities for the purpose of funds flow should be the same as in the case of the assessment of the working capital limits and the relevant FFR-I.

Appendix 8.4

SUGGESTED NORMS FOR INVENTORIES AND RECEIVABLES AS PER THE TANDON COMMITTEE

Sl. No.	Industry	Raw Materials (including stores and other items used in the process of manufacture)	Stocks-in-process	Finished goods	Bills Receivable, Bills purchased and discounted
	1	2	3	4	5
1.	(a) Cotton and (b) Synthetic Textiles	**(a) Cotton** 2 Bombay and Ahmedabad areas, 3 [Eastern Areas: (Bihar, Orissa, West Bengal and Assam], 2.5, other than the above areas **(b) Other Raw Materials** 2 all over India	0.75, Composite textile mills 0.50, other mills	2.25	2.25
2.	Man-made fibre	1.5	0.5	1.75	1.75
3.	Jute Textiles	2.5	0.25	(a) 1 for domestic sales (b) 1.5 for exports	1.50
4.	Rubber Products	2	0.25	1.75	1.75
5.	Fertilizers	2	0.25		1.75
	(a) for nitrogenous plants	0.75 units near refinery 1.50 units away from refinery	Negligible	1. where stocks are in plant site 1.5 where stocks are also in upcountry centres	1.25
	(b) for phosphatic plants	2 (units in port areas) 3 (units away from port areas)	”	”	1.25
6.	Pharmaceuticals	2.75	0.5	2	1.25
7.	Dyes and Dyestuffs	2.25	1	0.75	2.25
8.	Basic Industrial Chemicals	2.75	0.25	1	1.75

9.	Vegetable and Hydrogenated oils	1	Negligible	0.75	0.75
10.	Paper	2-6, Bamboo and wood (to be built up in stages, from November to May, and thereafter, to be brought down) 2.25, Chemicals	”	1 (for controlled sales and 0.25 for free sales)	0.75
11.	Cement	2.25 Gypsum, 1.25 Limestone 0.75 Coal, 1.5 Packing Materials	0.5	1	1
12.	Engineering (automobiles and ancillaries)	2.25	0.75	2.5	2.5
13.	Engineering (consumer durables)	2	0.75	2.5	2.5
14.	Engineering: ancillaries, other than automobile ancillaries, and component suppliers	2	0.75	2.5	2.5
15.	Engineering: machinery manufacturers and other capital equipment suppliers (other than heavy engineering)**	2.75	1.25	3.5	3.5

16.	Silk and Art Silk Mills (*a*) Weaving mills (*b*) Processing mills (including composite mills and others); (not applicable for job work units)	1. (Synthetic Yarn) 0.5 (Cloth processing mills) 2. (Other raw materials, vide note 1)		(*a*) 0.5 (*b*) 0.75		(*a*) 1.5 (*b*) 2.5	
17.	Woollen Mills	3 (Raw wool, rags and waste) 1 (Synthetic fibre/yam) 2 (Other materials, vide note 1)		1.25 (off season) (busy season)		4 (Apl. to Sept.) (Oct. to Mar.)	
18.	Bulbs, fluorescent tubes and dry cell batteries	4*	2.5**	0.5		3	
19.	Storage Batteries	4*	2.5**		1	3	
20.	Fans	3*	1**		0.5	4@	
21.	Transformers	2*	0.5**	2	1.5	2 @@	
22.	Switchgears	2*	0.5**	0.5	1.5	2 @@	

* Imported ** Indigenous @ in off-seasons @@ during seasons

Notes

(*i*) Raw materials are expressed in terms of "so many months of consumption". These include stores and other items used in the process of manufacture.

(*ii*) (*a*) Stocks-in-process are expressed in terms of "so many months of cost of production".

(*b*) In individual cases, however, the bank may deviate from the norm, for the stocks-in-process, if it is satisfied that the actual process time involved, in any particular unit, say, in view of the nature of production, past experience and technology employed, is more than the norm suggested.

(*iii*) (*a*) Finished goods and receivables are expressed in terms of so many months of 'cost of sales', and 'sales', respectively. These figures represent only the average levels. Individual items of finished goods and receivables, for different periods, could, however, exceed the indicated norms, so long as the overall average level of finished goods and receivables does not exceed the amounts, as determined in terms of the norm.

(*b*)* The norm prescribed for receivables relates only to inland sales, on short-term basis, *i.e.* **excluding** receivables arising out of deferred payment sales and exports.

(*iv*) Stocks of spares are not included for norms, since, in financial terms, they are not significant in many industries. Banks, therefore, ascertain the requirements of spares for individual units. They should, however, keep a watchful eye if the level of spares exceeds 5% of the total inventories.

**(*v*) Heavy engineering include supply of whole or substantial plants, involving long manufacturing period, *i.e.* sugar, cement, steel and textile plants.

Appendix 8.5

TANDON COMMITTEE LENDING NORMS: THREE ALTERNATIVE METHODS

1. FIRST METHOD

Under the first method, the difference between the acceptable level of current assets and the anticipated quantum of other current liabilities, *i.e.* other than bank finance, viz. largely comprising sundry creditors, is calculated, and is termed as the "Working Capital Gap" (WCG). And, the Net Working Capital (NWC) [or the margin, or the Owners' Equity (OE)], should be minimum 25% of the working capital gap. Thus, under the first method, the banker finances maximum up to 75% of the working capital gap.

2. SECOND METHOD

Under the second method, the Net Working Capital (NWC) should be minimum 25% of the total value of the acceptable level of current assets. The remaining 75% is to be financed first by the other current liabilities (mainly Sundry Creditors) and the banker may finance the balance amount of the working capital requirements.

3. THIRD METHOD

The third method is quite similar to the second method, except that the composition of the acceptable current assets is slightly changed. That is, under this method, the acceptable current assets would mean the total current assets (as commonly understood by us) less the value of the Core Assets. And, the Core Assets, according to the Tandon Committee, constitute "the absolute minimum level of the raw materials, goods-in-process, finished goods and stores, which are in the pipe line, so to speak, to ensure a continuity of production". The entire Core Assets, however, are to be financed out of the Owners' Equity (O.E.) only.

These three methods of lending can easily be understood when computed in the following example:

Given

	(Rs. in lakh)
Acceptable Current Assets	160.00
Anticipated Current Liabilities, other than Bank Finance, *i.e.* mainly Sundry Creditors	60.00
Core Assets	20.00
FIRST METHOD	
Current Assets	160.00
(Less) Other Current Liabilities	(–) 60.00
Working Capital Gap	100.00
(Less) Minimum NWC (Margin) @ 25%	(–) 25.00
Maximum Permissible Bank Finance (MPBF)	75.00

SECOND METHOD

Current Assets	160.00
(Less) NWC @ 25% (margin)	(–) 40.00
	120.00
(Less) Other Current Liabilities	(–) 60.00
Maximum Permissible Bank Finance (MPBF)	60.00

THIRD METHOD

Current Assets	160.00
(Less) Core Assets	(–) 20.00
	140.00
(Less) NWC 25% (margin)	(–) 35.00
	105.00
(Less) Other Current Liabilities	(–) 60.00
Maximum Permissible Bank Finance (MPBF)	45.00

The maximum permissible bank finance (MPBF) and the minimum level of net working capital (NWC) under the three methods, in the above example, would, thus, be as follows:

	1st Method	*2nd Method*	*3rd Method*	*[Rs. in lakh]*
MPBF	75.00	60.00	45.00	
NWC	25.00	40.00	55.00	

Thus, the customer gets the largest quantum of bank finance under the first method and the least in the third method.

However, it may be pertinent to mention here that the third method of lending had not been implemented, as it would have resulted in curtailing the bank's finance for working capital, quite considerably. Besides, the determination of the value of core assets would have posed innumerable practical difficulties too.

A SYNOPTIC NOTE
(CHAPTER 8 AT A GLANCE)

WORKING CAPITAL ADVANCES BY BANKS

Since October 1997, the "Suggested Norms for Inventories and Receivables", and the 'Second Method of Lending', based on the Tandon Committee Recommendations, have ceased to be regulatory. These have, instead, since remained just the guiding principles and recommendatory in nature. Reserve Bank of India has, therefore, counselled all the banks to evolve their own norms and methods of assessing the quantum and quality of working capital loans.

1. ASSESSMENT OF WORKING CAPITAL REQUIREMENTS BY BANKS

There are three main methods, viz.,

(*a*) Projected Balance Sheet (PBS) method;

(*b*) Cash Budget (CB) method; and

(*c*) Projected Yearly Turnover (PYT) method.

(a) PROJECTED BALANCE SHEET (PBS) METHOD

In place of Maximum Permissible Bank Finance (MPBF) method, the PBS method is based on:

(*i*) Projected Balance Sheet;

(*ii*) Funds Flow, Planned for the Current Year and the Next Year; and

(*iii*) Profitability and Other Financial Parameters.

(b) CASH BUDGET (CB) METHOD

Under Cash Budget method, however, the financial needs are assessed on the basis of the Projected Cash Flow (as against the value of Assets and Liabilities, as is done under the PBS method). This method continues to be in use mainly for:

(*i*) Seasonal industries; and

(*ii*) Construction work.

Besides Cash Budget (CB), some other financial parameters are also looked into, even under the Cash Budget method viz. Projected Profitability, Liquidity, Gearing, Funds Flow, etc.

(c) PROJECTED YEARLY TURNOVER (PYT) METHOD

This method is adopted for assessing the working capital requirements of small scale industries, up to Rs. 4 crore (raised from Rs. 2 crore, earlier).

Under this method, the total working capital requirement of SSI units is computed at 25% of the PYT. And, out of this

(*a*) 5% of the PYT is the margin or Owners' Equity (OE); and

(*b*) 20% is Bank's Finance.

That is, if PYT is Rs. 100, the working capital requirement is assessed at Rs. 25, out of which the margin is Rs. 5, and the bank finance is Rs. 20. Thus, in such cases, the current ratio is invariably be 25/20 = 1.25 : 1.

ASSESSMENT OF WORKING CAPITAL REQUIREMENTS FOR NON-SSI SECTOR

Usually, most of the banks are following the undernoted norms:

(*i*) Limit of over Rs. 2 lakh but less than Rs. 25 lakh (Simple Assessment)

(*ii*) Limit of Rs. 25 lakh and over, but up to Rs. 4 crore (PBS method)

(*iii*) Limit of over Rs. 4 crore (PBS method)

Different application forms, as also appraisal forms, are generally being used by banks:

(*i*) For different categories of borrowers, and

(*ii*) For different levels of working capital limits.

FINANCIAL FOLLOW-UP REPORTS (FFRs):

FFR-I and FFR-II are now being used by the banks, in replacement of QIS-I QIS-II and QIS-III (which were earlier prevalent as per the Tandon Committee and Chore Committee Recommendations).

The requirements of FFR-I and FRR-II apply to all the working capital advances of Rs. 1 crore and above:

FFR-I: To be submitted by the borrowers quarterly, and within 6 weeks of the close of the quarter.

This form is a simplified version of QIS-II, with some additional information.

FFR-II: To be submitted by the borrowers half-yearly, and within 8 weeks of the close of the half-year. This form is a modified version of QIS-III.

SOME MODIFICATIONS IN CAs AND CLs UNDER PBSS METHOD

CAs INCLUDE

(*i*) Term Deposit Receipts (TDRs) with the banks, government securities and other trust securities;
(*ii*) All short-term investments; like MMMF, CPs, CDs, etc; and
(*iii*) Margin Money, deposited against Letters of Credit and Bank Guarantees.

NON-CAs INCLUDE

Other short-term investments like ICDs, investments in shares and debentures, including Subsidiaries and Associates.

CLs INCLUDE

Inter-Corporate Deposits (ICDs) accepted by the company.

COMMITMENT CHARGE

Commitment charge of 1% is levied on unutilized portion of the fund-based working capital limit, but only in the undernoted cases:

(*i*) Working Capital Limits of Rs. 20 crore and above, and
(*ii*) Term loans of Rs. 5 crore and above.

RATE OF COMMITMENT CHARGES

(*i*) *Working capital limit:* Only if the limit is utilized up to 60% or below, this charge will be @ 0.75% per annum on the entire portion of the unutilized limit, for each half-year ending September and March each year. That is, if the limit is utilized even slightly above 60%, no such charge is levied.
(*ii*) *Term loan:* This charges is levied @ 1% per annum on the amount undrawn from the stated dates of drawal, with a grace period of one month.

Exemption from this charge is available in respect of the working capital loans to;

(*i*) Small Scale Industries (SSIs);
(*ii*) Export Finance;
(*iii*) Bills Purchase/Discount Limit;
(*iv*) Bills sent for Collection Limit; and
(*v*) Advances to commercial banks, financial institutions, cooperative banks, and land development banks.

ASSESSMENT OF WORKING CAPITAL ADVANCES

Under PBS method, the Projected Levels of Inventories, Receivables and Sundry Creditors are examined and verified, with the trend of the past (historical) data, *i.e.* Intra-firm data, as also with the inter-firm data, as was the case under the old MPBF method. But, now the norms of inventories (and Sundry Debtors), laid-down by the Tandon Committee, are no longer obligatory to be followed. But, even till date, the rationale behind the norms hold good as valid guiding principles. Accordingly, the banks no longer insist on current ratio to be minimum 1.33, as per the Second Method of Lending, propounded by the Tandon Committee. Thus, even a lower level of current ratio may be quite acceptable to the banks and the financial institutions.

Now, as against the old MPBF, the Assessed Bank Finance (ABF) is being computed on the basis of:

(*i*) The nature and duration of the operating cycle;

(*ii*) Projected levels of operations;

(*iii*) Nature of build-up of CAs and CLs;

(*iv*) Profitability;

(*v*) Liquidity, etc.

Bifurcation of working capital limit of Rs. 10 crore and above into

(*i*) Cash Credit Components (CCC), and

(*ii*) Working Capital Demand Loans (WCDL),

In the ratio of 20 : 80, since October 1997.

It is definitely quite rational and reasonable, as the WCDL components get compulsorily repaid on a regular and continuous basis.

Exemptions

(*a*) Export Finance: The entire export finance, both pre-shipment as also post-shipment finance, against the purchase/discount of demand/time bills, is exempt from such bifurcation. Thus, the entire export finance can be availed of by way of Cash Credit Components (CCC) only. Accordingly, the 20 : 80 ratio is to be worked out only after excluding the export finance component.

(*b*) Bills Limit: Similarly, the entire inland bills limit can as well be availed of by way of Cash Credit Components (CCC) only.

(*c*) And, in the cases of working capital limits of above Rs. 2 crore but below Rs. 10 crore, the bifurcation could be permitted in the ratio of 50 : 50, or the WCDL component could be even higher than 50%, but not below 50%, in any case.

ROLL OVER OF WCDL

Roll over, however, is permitted in all the cases of WCDL, but with a maximum of seven accounts in a year (one roll over constituting one account).

RENEWAL

Working capital loan is required to be reviewed and renewed annually.

CASH CREDIT, OVERDRAFT AND DEMAND LOAN

Cash Credit and Overdraft

Both these accounts are running accounts in the sense that any number of deposits and withdraws are permitted therein, without any restrictions of withdrawals, of course, within the available drawing power (DP).

Further, while cash credit facility is granted only against the security of inventories and book debts, the overdraft facility is granted against other securities like the bank's own TDRs, shares and securities, units of UTI, NSCs, LIC policies, etc.

Demand Loan

This account, however, is not a running account. That is, the entire sanctioned loan amount has to be withdrawn in one go or, at best, in some reasonable instalments. Further, any amount, once it is deposited in the demand loan account, cannot be withdrawn over again, during the full currency of that very demand loan.

Secured and Unsecured Advances

All the loans and advances, granted against the security of some tangible assets, are known as secured advances. For example:

(*i*) Cash credit facility against the security of inventories and book debts (bills receivables),

(*ii*) Overdraft against the security of the bank's own TDRs, government securities, NSCs, units of UTI, etc., and

(*iii*) Demand loan against any of these securities.

The unsecured (also known as 'clean') cash credit, overdraft and demand loan accounts, however, are such accounts whereon no tangible assets have been provided as a security. And, the only security available in such cases may be by way of (*a*) the third party guarantee or (*b*) the equitable mortgage of some immovable property, as an additional (also known as collateral) security.

ASSESSMENT OF WORKING CAPITAL REQUIREMENTS OF SSI UNITS, AS PER NAYAK COMMITTEE

In the cases of the units under SSI Sector, *i.e.* SSIs, village and cottage industries and tiny sector units, having fund-based working capital need of up to Rs. 5 crore, from the banking sector, their fund-based working capital limit is assessed simply at 20% of the Projected Yearly Turnover (PYT) (Comprising Total Gross Sales, Including Excise Duty). And, the bank finance and OE portion (*i.e.* margin) is in the ratio of 80 : 20.

Thus, if PYT is Rs. 25 crore, working capital limit by bank will be Rs. 5 crore and the OE Component (*i.e.* margin) will be Rs. 1.25 crore. Thus, the level of CA will be (Rs. 5 + Rs. 1.25) Rs. 6.25 crore, CL will be Rs. 5 crore, and CR will be 1.25 : 1.00.

Reserve Bank of India has suggested this level to be the minimum bank finance. Thus, if a higher working capital limit is required by any SSI unit, an assessment will have to be done on the basis of PBS method, and a suitably higher limit will be sanctioned, if so assessed under the PBS method.

But, in all cases, the amount of sundry creditors will have to be substracted from the total working capital requirements, to avoid double financing. And again, if the borrower can bring in more funds as OE, the working capital limit will be reduced accordingly.

QUESTIONS
(For Self-Assessment)

1. Distinguish between:

   (*a*) Projected Balance Sheet (PBS) method and Cash Budget (CB) method;

   (*b*) Projected Balance Sheet (PBS) method and Projected Yearly Turnover (PYT) method.

2. Under the PBS method, the criteria for classification of current assets and current liabilities have undergone slight modifications. What are these modifications?

3. While Inter-Corporate Deposits (ICDs) accepted by own company are treated as Current Liabilities, the investments by the company in other companies are not treated as current assets, but as non-current assets, instead.

What is the rationale behind such discriminatory classification? Do you agree? Give reasons for your answer.

4. (*a*) What is the percentage of bifurcation of Working Capital Component, advanced by banks between Working Capital Demand Loan (WCDL) and Cash Credit Component (CCC) in the following cases?
   (*i*) Working capital advance of Rs. 10 crore and above;
   (*ii*) Working capital advance of Rs. 15 crore and above;
   (*iii*) Working capital advance of Rs. 20 crore and above; and
   (*iv*) Working capital advance of Rs. 2 crore and above.

   (*b*) What is the rationale behind such bifurcation between Rs. 10 crore and above, and below Rs. 10 crore? Do you agree? Give reasons for your answer.

5. (*a*) How many accounts comprising WCDL components can be opened by a company, during the period of one year?

   (*b*) (*i*) What do you mean by the term 'Roll Over' of the WCDL component of an account?
   (*ii*) Is such 'roll over' treated as only one account or more than one account?

PROBLEMS FOR PRACTICE

1. Aditya Chemicals is enjoying an aggregate working capital limit of Rs. 200 crore, made up as under:
   (*i*) Export Packing Credit (EPC) limit: Rs. 75 crore;
   (*ii*) Inland Bills Purchase limit: Rs. 40 crore; and
   (*iii*) Other Working Capital limit: Rs. 85 crore.

Required

Please compute the quantum of Cash Credit Component (CCC) and Working Capital Demand Loan (WCDL) component in the instant case.

2. (*a*) The total Projected Yearly Turnover (PYT) of Friends Fridge and Fans Limited, a small scale industrial unit, is Rs. 24 crore, made up as under:
   (*i*) Cash sales – Rs. 4 crore; and
   (*ii*) Credit sales – Rs. 20 crore.

Compute

   (*i*) The total Working Capital Requirement of the unit [to be assessed by the bank, as prescribed by the Reserve Bank of India (RBI), as per the Nayak Committee recommendations].
   (*ii*) The total fund-based working capital limit to be sanctioned by the bank, and
   (*iii*) The quantum of margin money required to be brought in by the company, from the Owners' Equity (OE).

   (*b*) (*i*) Would the position be any different if the Projected Yearly Turnover (PYT) of the unit would have been Rs. 30 crore, instead of Rs. 24 crore? Give reasons for your answer.
   (*ii*) Compute the following, over again, in the above case:
   (*a*) Total Working Capital Requirement of the company;
   (*b*) Total fund-based Working Capital Limit to be sanctioned by the bank; and
   (*c*) The Quantum of margin to be met by the company, out of the Owner's Equity (OE).

3. (*a*) Tirupati Telecom Limited, a small scale unit, has an annual sales of Rs. 20 crore, excluding Rs. 5 crore excise duty, paid thereon, @ 25%. Compute the following, in the instant case:
   (*i*) Total working capital requirement of the unit,
   (*ii*) Total working capital limit that will be sanctioned by the bank, and
   (*iii*) The quantum of margin money to be brought in by the unit out of the Owner's Equity (OE).

   (*b*) (*i*) Would the position be any different if the annual sales of the unit were Rs. 20 crore, including the excise duty of Rs. 5 crore? Give reasons for your answer.
   (*ii*) Compute all the three, *i.e.* (*a*) (*i*), (*ii*) and (*iii*) above, over again under the changed conditions.

4. Tarun Textiles Limited, manufacturing woollen textiles, have been granted a Working Capital Finance to the tune of Rs. 22 crore by the State Bank of India, Lucknow Main Branch.
   (*a*) What will be the quantum (in Rupees) of the:
   (*i*) Cash Credit Component (CCC); and the
   (*ii*) Working Capital Demand Loan (WCDL) component?
   (*b*) If the bank is charging interest @ 15% per annum on the Working Capital Demand Loan, at what rate will it be charging interest on the Cash Credit Component of the finance?

5. Pushkar Industries (P) Limited, a small scale industrial unit, has an annual sales turnover of Rs. 1000 lakh, out of which Rs. 440 lakh is on cash basis and the balance Rs. 560 lakh is on credit basis, and on these sales the excise duty, too, has been paid aggregating Rs. 600 lakh.
   (*a*) What will be the maximum quantum of Working Capital Requirement (in Rupees) of the company, as assessed by a commercial bank?
   (*b*) What will be the quantum of minimum amount of Working Capital Finance (in Rupees) to be provided by the Bank to the company?
   (*c*) What will be the minimum quantum of margin (borrower's stake) (in Rupees) stipulated in this case?
   (*d*) Calculate the Current Ratio, presuming that there is no Current Liabilities, other than the bank finance, in the present case.

9

MANAGING CREDIT RISKS

Rule No.1: Never lose money. Rule No. 2: Never forget Rule No. 1.	***Arren Buffett***
Loans and debts make worry and frets.	***Saying***

The Learning Points

The chapter aims at developing the knowledge and facilitating the understanding of:

- Historical perspective and concept of Credit Risk Assessment (CRA) system
- Models of Credit Risk Assessment (CRA) pertaining to
  - (*a*) Financial risks: both quantitative and qualitative assessments
  - (*b*) Industrial risks, and
  - (*c*) Managerial risks.
- Overall Financial Risks Assessments
  - (*a*) Quantitative:
    - (*i*) Static–(parameters like, ratio analyses)
    - (*ii*) Dynamic–historical comparison, *i.e.* Intra-firm comparison
    - (*iii*) Dynamic–Industry Comparison, *i.e.* inter-firm comparison
  - (*b*) Qualitatives Financial Factors (negative features only
- Over-all Credit Risks assessment
- Over-all Scoring: A Suggested Pattern

9.1 A NOTE OF CAUTION

Several commercial banks and term lending institutions had been extremely kind and gracious enough to allow me access to their books and records, systems and procedures. They had, however, agreed to do so exclusively on the condition, and commitment on my part, that the actual figures and data will not be made public, under any circumstances, whatsoever. Therefore, in keeping with the trust reposed in me and with a view to ensuring meticulous maintenance of the professional ethics of a professor and academician, I have deliberately modified (or even concealed) some of the facts and figures (as also some details). But, at the same time, ample care has been taken to ensure that the spirit and rationale behind the systems and procedures, in the various areas of credit assessment and management, do not get diluted or distorted, in any manner.

It is, therefore, suggested to the readers (both the practising executives and the promising PGP/MBA students) not to take the data and figures, mentioned herein, for granted, or to necessarily adopt all these exactly in the present form. It will, instead, augur well if the spirit and rationale, lying behind these provisions, are well understood and appreciated and these are adopted only after being suitably ADAPTED and modified, to meet their specific needs, matching with their own specific systems and procedures, organisational culture and convictions.

The reasons adduced by most of the banks and financial institutions are very candid and convincing in that, as the mechanism of assessment of the credit risks, inter alia, includes some judgemental approaches on the quality of management and such other sensitive issues, it would, in their considered opinion, based on their past experience, be prudent enough not to disclose the exact scoring pattern to anyone. The parameters of assessment, however, could broadly be shared (specially with the borrowers) to enable them to improve upon their performance. And, I too, tend to agree with them. Not only that. In my own considered view, based upon my past experience as a professional banker, it is a well-thought-out stand, inasmuch as if all the parameters under consideration, and the bases of the scoring pattern etc., are disclosed, some not-so-honest companies may attempt some intelligent distortions even in their audited balance sheets, to conceal some vital and valued facts and figures, making it even more difficult and well-nigh impossible for the bankers to decipher and detect some negative features connected with the financial position of the company.

And, as is well conceded, some companies do sometimes resort to some sort of window dressing (or creative accounting, as I call it). Therefore, such factors also have to be taken into account, while taking any credit decision.

Introduction

Some scientific and mathematical tools, to measure and assess the credit risks (or credit-worthiness) of the borrowers, both present and prospective, based upon the rich experiences of the past and the excellent expertise of professionals of the present, have, of late, been evolved by some of the premier financial institutions in India, both by some commercial banks and other financial institutions.

9.2 HISTORICAL PERSPECTIVE

Since the year 1992, most of the commercial banks adopted some Credit Rating System (CRS) with a view to assessing the level of credit-worthiness of their borrowers, both present and prospective, based upon certain objective parameters and somewhat scientific scoring pattern, based upon the range of credit-worthiness and financial strength and stability, as revealed by their past performance (of the present borrowers) and the prospects and potentials of the borrowers of the future.

A brief description of the various parameters and the range of the scoring pattern of CRS, as was obtaining in some of the commercial banks, has been given in Annexure 9.1 at the end of the Chapter.

But, during the course of the application of the CRS and the experiences gained therefrom, it was found that the CRS was not serving the full purpose of assessing and managing credit risks on all the related parameters. It (CRS) could, at best, be rated as means and tool just to classify the borrowers under different categories of credit risks (A, B, C, D and E, etc.), and nothing more beyond that. For example, the CRS did not take sufficient care to look into some very relevant and vital aspects for assessment and management of credit risks, like:

(*i*) Profitability,

(*ii*) Repayment capacity,

(*iii*) Effectiveness and efficiency of the management, etc.

Besides, the CRS did not take into account a comparative study of the historical data of the unit and/or the industry, *i.e.* the intra-firm and inter-firm comparisons, qualitative aspects of the management and the specific characteristics and benchmark of a particular industry. With a view to revamping the credit risk assessment and management process, some of the commercial banks and financial institutions have evolved and introduced a more comprehensive and scientific system of Credit Risk Assessment (hereafter referred to as CRA), since the year 1996.

9.3 CREDIT RISK ASSESSMENT (CRA) SYSTEM

With a view to taking all the relevant factors and parameters into account, to arrive at a comprehensive opinion about a borrowal unit, the CRA system enlists the following:

(*a*) The rationale,

(*b*) The various parameters to be considered, and

(*c*) The scoring methodology, etc.

Broadly speaking, the CRA is applicable to all the segments of advances, viz. Large Scale Industrial (LSI) segment, Small Scale Industrial (SSI) segment, Agricultural (Agrl.) segment, as also the trade advances. The only difference, however, lies in fixing the minimum and the extent of rigour of Credit Risk Assessment (CRA) parameters and scoring patterns.

9.4 CONCEPT OF CRA

As per the CRA system, while, at the first stage, the risk rating has to be compiled, at the second stage of the credit process, an assessment has to be made on the industry and management factors, and a judgemental scoring has to be given. Both these scorings must conform with each other.

Extra care, however, has to be taken to ensure that each borrower scores at least the minimum permissible score, under both the Industry and Management factors, to be eligible to be granted new advance or even to continue the current credit facilities. Thus, a proposal for fresh credit facilities, which does not score even the minimum permissible grades, viz. Working Capital 6, and Term Loan 6, will not be entertained. But then, if an existing borrowal unit, already on the bank's books, happens to score such a low grade, as aforesaid, any proposal for enhancement of the working capital limit will not be entertained. The management of the unit should, however, be counselled to improve upon certain parameters and that, too, within a stipulated time schedule. Care should, at the same time, be taken that the methodology of rating and the weightage allotted on different ranges of score, etc. are not disclosed to the units.

Besides fixing the minimum eligibility rating of WC6 and TL6, other minimal eligibility ratings and standards pertaining to:

(*i*) Financial,

(*ii*) Industrial, and

(*iii*) Managerial risk parameters are also built in, in the CRA system.

9.5 CREDIT RISKS ASSESSMENT (CRA) MODEL

The various factors which go into appraising the credit risks, associated with any loan, have broadly been classified under three main heads, viz.,

A. Financial risks,

B. Industrial risks, and

C. Managerial risks.

And, all these have to be first rated separately, and thereafter, each of these must be duly weighted and then aggregated to arrive at a single point indicator of the risks, associated with a particular credit decision.

We therefore, discuss the risk dimensions pertaining to all these three categories as under:

9.6 FINANCIAL RISKS ASSESSMENT

The assessment of financial risks involves:

A. Quantitative assessments, and

B. Qualitative assessments.

A. Quantitative Assessment

The quantitative assessments comprise the appraisal of the financial strengths of the company, based upon its past performance and various other financial indicators. The standard measures of financial strength mainly are:

(*i*) liquidity ratios,

(*ii*) profitability ratios,

(*iii*) gearing ratios, and

(*iv*) turnover ratios.

Further, while analysing the ratios, both

(*a*) Intra-firm comparisons of the same company, *i.e.* the performance of the unit this year as compared to the previous years, and

(*b*) Inter-firm comparisons, *i.e.* to appraise as to how this company, under appraisal, is performing in comparison to some other companies in the same or similar lines of business and the similar scale of operation, etc.

Here, both the positive and negative factors are taken into account in the appraisal exercise.

B. Qualitative Assessment

Besides such quantitative appraisal and assessment, certain qualitative factors are also assessed and analysed to form a comprehensive opinion about the company. These factors are:

(*i*) Accounting policies,
(*ii*) Policy and provision of bad debts,
(*iii*) Arrears of depreciation,
(*iv*) Contingent liabilities and claims, and
(*v*) Auditor's remarks, as contained in the annual report of the company.

9.7 OVERALL FINANCIAL RISKS ASSESSMENT

The overall financial risk assessment comprises four parts, viz.

A. (*i*) Quantitative (static) – Parameters like ratio analysis,
(*ii*) Quantitative (dynamic) – Historical comparison, *i.e.* intra-firm comparison,
(*iii*) Quantitative (dynamic) – Industry comparison, *i.e.* Inter-firm comparison.

B. Qualitative Financial Factors (negative only).

Let us now discuss all these four parameters, in greater detail.

A. (i) Quantitative (Static) Parameters: Ratio Analysis (Out of Aggregate Score of 50)

Under this head, six financial ratios may be analysed, on the basis of the latest audited financial statements of the borrowers. And, on the basis of the figures of the various ratios arrived at, specific scores are assigned to each of the ratios, depending upon the specific scoring rate, fixed on the pre-determined range of the ratios, which may generally range on a five point scale, *i.e.* minimum zero and maximum 4. But, we should not stop here. Instead, we should also allot specific weightage to each of these six ratios, depending upon the degree of the importance and ramifications of each ratio.

Now, let us identify all the six ratios and then decide about the weightage to be assigned to each of them.

The six ratios are:

(*a*) Current Ratio,
(*b*) TOL/TNW (Total Outside Liabilities to Tangible Net Worth),
(*c*) (Inv. + BR)(365)/Sales (days) [(Inventory + Bills Receivable)(365) to sales],
(*d*) PBITD/interest (times)
[Profit Before Interest, Tax and depreciation to interest],
(*e*) PAT/Net Sales (%), and
(*f*) ROCE [Return on Capital Employed] (%).

When we look at these six ratios, we observe from our experience that the first two ratios (*a* and *b*) are of the highest importance, deserving the highest weightage, followed by the third one (*c*). And, out of all these, the last three, (*d*, *e* and *f*) deserve the lowest weightage. We may, therefore, summarise the scores and weightage, based upon our personal experience, as under:

Table 9.1

Sl. No.	*Ratios*	*Score*			*Maximum Score (Aggregate)*
		Minimum	*Maximum*	*Weightage*	
(*a*)	Current Ratio	0	5	5	25
(*b*)	TOL/TNW	0	5	5	25
(*c*)	(Inv.+BR)(365)/Sales [days]	0	5	4	20
(*d*)	PBITD/Interest [Times]	0	5	2	10
(*e*)	PAT/NET SALES (%)	0	5	2	10
(*f*)	ROCE (%)	0	5	2	10
	TOTAL				100

Thus, we see that, while the liquidity ratio and debt:equity ratio should attract the highest weightage, immediately and closely followed by the extent of blockage of funds in inventory and sundry debtors, the profitability ratios need to be given the lowest weightage.

Further, the parameter of ratios being of great ramifications, these may be given the 50% of the aggregate overall scores. Thus, the total scores arrived at, as above, should be divided by two.

(ii) Quantitative (Dynamic)

Historical Comparison (Intra-firm comparison) [Max. aggregate score-8]

Under this head, the undernoted four of the aforesaid ratios may be compared for the last 3 to 5 years, based upon the figures of the latest available audited financial statements of the company.

Table 9.2

Sl. No.	*Ratios to be compared*	*Basis of Comparison*	*Scores Awarded*	
			Minimum	*Maximum*
(*a*)	Current Ratio	[Latest ratios compared with those for the last 3 to 5 years (average)]	0	2
(*b*)	TOL/TNW	”	0	2
(*c*)	PAT/Net Sales	”	0	2
(*d*)	(Inv.+BR)/Sales	”	0	2
	TOTAL		0	8

(iii) Quantitative (Dynamic)

Industry Comparison (Inter-firm comparison)

Under this head also the same four ratios are considered and compared, taking into account the latest available audited financial statements of the borrower, vis-à-vis such ratios of similar industries.

To put these in a tabular form, the position will look as under:

Table 9.3

Sl. No.	*Ratios to be compared*	*Basis of Comparison*	*Scores Awarded*	
			Minimum	*Maximum*
(*a*)	Current Ratio	[Latest ratios `compared to the Industry Ratios]	0	2
(*b*)	TOL/TNW	"	0	2
(*c*)	PAT/Net Sales	"	0	2
(*d*)	(Inv.+BR)/Sales	"	0	2
	TOTAL		0	8

B. Qualitative Financial Factors (Negative only)

Under this category, only negative scores are awarded, depending upon the extent of the various unfavourable factors and the negative impacts and ramifications expected to be felt by the company in the near future. Thus, depending upon the quantum of adverse impact expected, a company may be accorded a negative score, ranging from 1 to 10, denoting little (or almost nil) risk to very high risk and the extent of its adverse impact on the company's performance and prospects.

Take, for instance, the adverse factors like extent of losses suffered, year after year, having an adverse impact on Tangible Net Worth (TNW). And, depending upon the extent and quantum of the damage, the scores may be awarded, which may range from 1 to 10, as aforesaid. Then, if the score awarded is 1, no negative marks would be awarded, whereas if the score is as high as 10, the highest possible negative marks (*i.e.* 10) would be accorded. That is to say that, if the adverse impact on TNW is to the extent of 10% this year, and if there is about 50% possibility of its recurrence, the highest negative marks of 10 may be given. But, as against this, if only 10% adverse impact is expected on the company's TNW, no negative marks need be allotted. But, it must be well understood here that all these assessments and quantifications (in terms of scores) are only judgemental, depending upon the prudence and expertise of the decision making authority concerned.

Parameters

The various parameters on the basis of which such judgemental decisions may be taken are:

(*a*) Contingent liabilities under excise duty/tax disputes, bank guarantees being given by the company, etc.

(*b*) Auditor's qualifying remarks.

(*c*) Accounting policies, *e.g.* in regard to the valuation of inventories (like FIFO, LIFO or Weighted Average), capitalisation, depreciation, revaluation of fixed assets, etc.).

Such qualitative risks have two distinct factors, viz. industrial risks and management risks.

9.8 INDUSTRIAL RISKS

Different industries have different factors of risks and in varying degrees. These parameters must also be taken into account in our Credit Risk Assessment (CRA) exercise.

Industry risks may broadly be classified as under:

(*a*) Market competition.

(*b*) Cyclicality of industry.

(*c*) Regulatory risks.

(*d*) Technology and obsolescence risks.

(*e*) Availability of raw materials and other inputs and their pricing.

(*f*) Substitute risks of finished goods, etc.

Under each of the above parameters, the risks may be assessed on a five point scale, ranging from 0 to 4, and the scores may be given accordingly. In case of a multi-product companies, like Reliance Industries Ltd., L & T, Kesoram Industries, etc., the various industry risks could be separately analysed and the figures could be suggested in the end, with due weightage, depending upon:

(*a*) The turnover, or

(*b*) Funds employed, in each industry.

Some illustrative value statements (though not exhaustive) pertaining to industrial risks, are placed at annexure 9.2 at the end of the chapter.

9.9 MANAGEMENT RISKS

One may also argue that the management risk need not be assessed separately, inasmuch as the level of financial efficiency, stability and profitability themselves may be good indicators of managerial efficiency or otherwise. But then, they may not be quite right in taking such a stand. As we all know, with the news of the withdrawal of Choksys from Asian Paints, the profitability and prospects of the company had been assessed to be on the downward trend, which had resulted in the marked slide in the company's share price in the stock exchanges. Similarly, even a rumour of Dhirubhai Ambani's failing health, immediately affected the share price of the company, the Reliance Industries Ltd., and even of other companies of the group. Though I admit that these are the extreme examples, these, at least, serve the purpose of bringing home the points of imperative need of assessing management risks separately.

Let us first clarify as to what do we mean by the term 'management'. Management is said to comprise promoters, directors, partners and the key functionaries of the unit. The traits and characteristics of one set of management can be different from the other, and it is on these factors that the profitability and prospects of a company largely depend.

The various sets of parameters that can be gainfully used to assess the management risks have been listed hereafter.

Here again the risk could be computed on a five point scale, ranging from zero to 4, as in the case of assessing industry risks. The various parameters are:

(*a*) Integrity and honesty,

(*b*) Track record,

(*c*) Organisational structure and system,

(*d*) Expertise, competence and level of commitment, and

(*e*) Perception in the capital market.

Some illustrative value statements (though not exhaustive) to assess the management risks have been given at Annexure 9.3, at the end of the Chapter.

It would augur well for the credit granting institutions (commercial banks and other financial institutions) to formulate and compute their own list of such value statements, based upon their own specific experience and organisational culture, as also the risk-taking pattern and capacity.

9.10 OVERALL CREDIT RISKS ASSESSMENT (CRA)

As we may observe, the old Credit Rating System (CRS), adopted by most of the commercial banks, had been based mainly on a quantitative and mathematical (and, therefore, somewhat objective) model. But, the current shift to the present Credit Risk Assessment (CRA) system is a combination of both quantitative and qualitative, an objective and subjective (or judgemental or value based) system. We must, however, take care that the element of objectivity in the credit appraisal system should not disappear or even get indirectly diluted. To this end in view, it will augur well if the factors/parameters of objective and subjective evaluations are combined in the ratio of 2 : 1. That is, out of the total score of 100, while the quantitative (objective) dimension should be allotted 2/3rd or 66.6 per cent or say, 66 or 67 marks, the judgemental (qualitative and subjective) factors must be allotted only 1/3rd or 33.33% or say, 34 or 33 marks only.

This is so because, in the case of the existing companies, several historical data are available to form opinion on objective basis.

But, in the case of new companies (that is, the newly established companies) approaching any bank for credit, there is no background or historical data available to go back to. Thus, the whole judgemental process depends upon estimates of projected production, sales and profitability, making the subjectivity and intuition the primary base of all evaluations and assessments.

Similar is the position in the case of term loans, granted for procurement of fixed assets, like capital goods, etc. Therefore, here also the elements of subjectivity will be more pronounced.

Therefore, in case of CRA, pertaining to Working Capital advance, the financial risks w ould contain 2/3rd portion of the full marks 100; *i.e.* say, 66 (min. 25). These full marks (66) may be further bifurcated as under:

1. Static ratios will be allotted one half portion of the full marks 100, *i.e.* 50, and
2. Historical (intra-firm) trends and industry (inter-firm) trends, will share the balance 16 marks equally, *i.e.* 8 marks each, which comes to 16.

And, the balance marks 34 (100-66) may further be bifurcated as under:

(*i*) Industry risk — 24 (min 10)

(*ii*) Management risk — 10 (min 5)

Minimum scores in parentheses indicate minimum acceptable hurdle rate, below which a proposal may usually be rejected.

As against such allotments, in the case of working capital advances to new companies, as also in the case of term loans to all companies, in the absence of any available historical data, the financial risk factors should be allotted only 1/4th or 25% of the full marks. And, the balance 3/4th portion, or 75% marks, may be further bifurcated into industry risk and management risks, roughly in the ratio of 2 : 1 or say 50 and 25, or some slight variations thereof, like 48 and 27 or 46 and 29 or 45 and 30, depending upon the administrative decision of the banks concerned.

The aforesaid allotments of marks may be summarised in a tabular form as under:

Table 9.4: Working Capital Advances to Existing Units

(A)	*Financial Risks*	*66 (min. 25)*
	(*a*) Static Ratios —	50
	(*b*) (*i*) Historical Trends	8
	(*ii*) Industry Trends	8
	$(a + b)$	66
(B)	Industry Risk	24 (min. 10)
(C)	Management Risk	10 (min. 5)
	Total (A + B + C)	= 100
(D)	Qualitative (negative only)	(–10)

Table 9.5: In Cases of Granting Working Capital Advances to New Companies, and Term Loans to all Units (i.e. both existing and new)

Financial Risk	— 25 (min. 10)
Industry Risk	— 50* (min. 20)
Management Risk	— 25* (min. 12.5)

(* or any variations thereof, as aforesaid, like 49/26, 48/27, 47/28, 46/29, 45/30, etc.). However, the minimum scores may be left undisturbed so as to avoid confusions and complicated calculations).

9.11 OVERALL SCORE

The overall aggregate score of all risks may be further rated on a 9 or 10 point scale. And, such ratings say, on 9 point scale, may be categorised as per Table 9.6.

9.12 PRICING MECHANISM OF ADVANCES

The CRA ratings, besides assessing the credit risks, also serves as a reasonable basis for pricing each category of advances. And, all such pricing policies are determined on the basic principle of 'higher risk, higher price'. Thus, if the prime lending rate of a commercial bank happens to be say 15% p.a., and the aggregate spread is restricted to say 3.5 percentage points, the rate of interest, to be made applicable on various grades (categories) of advances, may be presented (only illustratively, and not necessarily specifically) as in the undernoted Table 9.7, just for the purpose of understanding the mechanism a little better.

Table 9.6

Score Range	*Working Capital Loans*	*Term Loans*
90 and above	WC1	TL1
80–89	WC2	TL2
70–79	WC3	TL3
60–69	WC4	TL4
50–59	WC5	TL5
40–49	WC6	TL6
30–39	WC7	TL7
20–29	WC8	TL8
10–19	WC9	TL9

Table 9.7: Pricing Mechanism of Advances

WC1 & TL1	PLR (presumed to be say, 15%)	
WC2 & TL2	PLR + 0.50 (percentage point)	(=15.5%)
WC3 & TL3	PLR + 1.00	(=16%)
WC4 & TL4	PLR + 1.50	(=16.5%)
WC5 & TL5	PLR + 2.00	(=17.0%)
WC6 & TL6	PLR + 2.50	(=17.5%)
WC7 & TL7 and below	PLR + 3.50	(=18.5%)

As the provision of interest tax (*i.e.* income tax surcharge @ 2% on the income of the bank, earned by way of interest charged (on loans and advances, etc.) has since been removed, with effect from the financial year 2000-2001, such factor has not been taken into account.

Minimum Cut-Off Point

It may be further decided by the banks, administratively, as to what should be the minimum range of eligible score (minimum pass marks, so to say) below which no advance proposal should be entertained, as it may be said to be falling 'below the medium risk range,' and bordering on the high risk category. And, this is a very vital decision to be made by the CEO, of course, in consultation with the other TOP executives.

In my own considered personal view, minimum 40 marks may be said to be a reasonable cut-off point, the minimum hurdle rate. And thus, the units scoring an overall rating of minimum WC6 and/or TL6 should only be entertained, below which the proposal must be tactfully declined, unless some extra financial and strategically compelling circumstances exist, but only at the sole discretion of the CEO or, at least, one of the top executives of the bank. However, in the case of existing borrowal units, scoring an overall rating of below WC6 and/or TL6, we cannot do anything about it, except exercising more than ordinary care and closer supervision and follow-up in the case of such advances, on an ever alert basis. But, in such cases, the working capital limit should not be enhanced, nor any proposal of fresh term loans should be entertained, unless as already mentioned earlier some other compelling and convincing reasons exist.

Appendix 9.1

BANK'S CREDIT RATING SYSTEM (CRS): PARAMETERS AND [RANGE OF SCORING PATTERN OF CRS]

RATES OF INTEREST

Rate of interest goes up usually @ 0.50 percentage points each, as the credit rating goes down.

*Rating**	*Score (Total)*	*Rate of Interest (only illustrative)*
I		X% (Prime Lending Rate) [PLR]
II		X + 0.50%
III		X + 1.00%
IV		X + 1.50%
V		X + 2.00%
VI		X + 2.50%
VII		X + 3.00%
VIII		X + 3.50%

*[For the purpose of ratings, various banks have, of course, used different terminologies to describe different categories].

Scoring pattern for credit rating has been used by the banks, w.e.f. 1.1.1992. But, this has been done by the various banks on their own choice, and not under any RBI directive, whatsoever. The CRS has, in fact, been evolved by banks, based upon their own long and varied experiences.

Parameters	*Range*	*Score*
	[Only min./max. ranges and scores have been indicated here]	
1. Current Ratio [Actual/not Projected Fig.]	1.34 and above	15
	below 1.00	0
2. Debt (Total Outside Liability): Equity Ratio (Actual)	2.5 and below	15
	5.01 and above	0
3. QIS and Renewal Data	Timely submission	5
	Non-submission [for over 1 month for QIS and Over 3 months for renewal data]	0

4.	Negative (–ve) variance in net sales (Higher of the Two): [Quarterly information systems and credit monitoring arrangement]	Up to 10% Over 25% (*i.e.* QIS and CMA)	5 0
5.	Non-compliance of inventory norms [Including 20% deviation allowed by RBI]	Generally complied with [*i.e* up to 20%] Over 50%	5 0
6.	Instalment on [deferred payment Guaranteed/term loan]	Timely repaid 3 or more instalments overdue	5 0
7.	Compliance with covenants and other terms and conditions	Promptly Non-responsive (Regarding dividend, etc.)	5 0
8.	Irregularity, including not meeting Letters of Credit (L/C) commitments	Regular for 1 year or irregular up to 2 occasions, not over 15 days on each occasion [occasion here means month] Irregular on more than 4 occasions or over 60 days	5 0
9.	Average utilisation of limit, based on weekly outstandings	Above 85% Less than 70%	5 1

Parameters for Negative Scores

	Parameters	*Range*	*Score*
1.	Fall in Current Ratio due to diversion of funds	[Only max. and min. have been given here] [(*i*) From above 1.33 to below 1.33 (*ii*) From below 1.33 to up to 1.30]	–1
		1.15 and below	–5

2.	Non-fund/ancillary business transacted through non-consortium banks		–5
3.	Delayed submission of stock statements (by more than 15 days)	Up to 2 occasions more than 4 occasions	–1 –5
4.	If credit facility released and documentation pending for over 30 days		–5
5.	Merchant banking business going past the bank (or consortium banks, if consortium advance is involved).		–5

Penal Rate of Interest

1.	Delayed submission of QIS forms I, II and III even by one day	1.25%
2.	Delayed submission of stock statements (say, by 15 days)	1.25%
3.	Delayed submission of renewal data (say, by I month)	1.25%

Maximum penal rate of interest, to be charged on the account would, however, not exceed 2.25% (even if all the 3 defaults are involved).

But, if the account is irregular on more than two occasions in the last 12 months (one occasion means during 1 month, even for 1 day or for all the days in the month) an additional penal rate of interest @ 1.25% would be charged, over and above the ceiling rate of 2.25% [*i.e.* 2.25% + 1.25% = 3.50% maximum).

APPENDIX 9.2
VALUE STATEMENTS OF INDUSTRY RISKS
AN ILLUSTRATIVE (NOT EXHAUSTIVE) LIST

VALUE STATEMENTS

Sl. No.		*Descriptions*
1.	**Competition and Market Risk**	
	A.	– Monopoly or Oligopoly situation.
		– High entry barriers into the industry.
		– Company is one of the lead players or has an exclusive niche market or brand equity.
		– Has a market share, which is growing faster than the industry.
		– Does not depend on one or few buyers.
		– Has a range of products.
	B.	– Few large players in the market.
		– There are some barriers to entry.
		– Company is one of the top three players.
		– Has an established brand which is well received in the market.
		– Has a share which is steadily growing, apace with the industry growth rate.
		– Has a large area of operation.
		– Has adequate orders on hand.
	C.	– Competition heating up but, by and large, the demand still exceeds supply.
		– Virtually no entry barriers.
		– Company is one of the average players.
		– Its products are reasonably well received and have some image.
		– Company's market share is steady though there is recession in the market.
		– Depends on one or few buyers.
	D.	– Supply exceeds demand but regional/product niches still exist for exploitation.
		– Specialised niche oriented firms making an entry.
		– Company is a minor player but has some regional brand equity/the market share is declining.
		– Insufficient orders in hand.
		– Recession in the market.
	E.	– The industry has a problem of oversupply and/or low capacity utilisation.
		– The company is an insignificant player with no distinguished product.
		– Market share is insignificant.
2.	**Industry Cyclicality**	
	A.	– Long-term prospects of the industry are excellent.
		– Fairly stable industry cycles.

(Contd...)

Sl. No.		Descriptions
B.	–	Long-term industry.
	–	Outlook stable.
	–	Modest industry cyclicality.
C.	–	Long-term outlook stable, but for some critical factors.
	–	Industry cycle on the upswing.
D.	–	Susceptible to unfavourable changes in the economy; high degree of cyclicality.
	–	Cycle on the downswing.
E.	–	Industry in the startup or declining phase.
	–	Long-term outlook uncertain.
3.		**Regulatory Risk (Incorporating Aspects of Labour and Environment)**
A.	–	Business not affected by the regulatory framework.
	–	Operations are not hampered by lack of skilled labour.
	–	Harmonious labour relations and no stoppages due to labour unrest.
	–	All environment/pollution related clearances have been obtained.
B.	–	Regulatory and legislative issues create some vulnerability but potential impact on the company not significant.
	–	The issues can be tackled appropriately.
	–	There have been no stoppages on account of labour unrest.
C.	–	Demanding environment, labour and regulatory scenario.
	–	Can be problematic, if the company does not take care.
	–	Profitability has not been affected so far.
D.	–	Legal, labour or regulatory environment may create a difficult and problematic situation.
	–	Frequent stoppages on account of labour unrest.
	–	Can deliver shocks, affecting the viability of the company.
E.	–	The company/firm/unit is unable to cope with the Labour/Regulatory/Legal scenario.
4.		**Technology and Quality Control**
A.	–	World-class technology or tie-up with a World-Class Major; there is no problem relating to transfer of technology.
	–	Adequate measures for quality control are in place.
	–	Maintenance of Plant and Machinery is in good condition.
	–	Premises are suitable for current production and immediate expansion plans.
	–	Capacity utilisation is high.
B.	–	Technology proven. Not subject to any vast changes in the medium term.
	–	No change in the product line is expected in the medium term.
	–	Maintenance of Plant and Machinery is satisfactory; breakdowns have not affected production schedules.

(Contd...)

Sl. No.	*Descriptions*
C.	– Technology is likely to undergo changes which could affect the company/firm.
	– Product has substitutes and the unit is finding it difficult to manage in the face of competition.
	– Quality control measures require to be tightened.
	– Capacity utilisation is satisfactory.
D.	– Technology could face severe competition from the improved versions of global players.
	– Tie-up is essential.
	– Product innovations are changing the face of the industry.
	– Substitutes emerging.
	– Plant and Machinery require frequent repairs.
E.	– Outdated technology or technology subject to very fast obsolescence or, technology as yet untried and untested.
	– Severe threat of substitute products.
	– Frequent breakdowns in Plant and Machinery leading to stoppages over long periods.
5. User Profile	
A.	– Engineering/industrial product of wide acceptance/usage.
	– The product is distinctive.
	– There are no complaints about rejection of the company's products.
	– The company's products are protected by patents.
	– There is a wide area of operation.
B.	– There is a large number of buyers for whom the input is critical.
	– The users of the product have no substitutes.
	– The company is able to adhere to the delivery schedules.
C.	– The user industry is increasingly going in for backward integration in order to maintain their spreads; therefore, the demand for the unit's products is falling.
	– The user industry is employing alternate inputs to be able to compete.
	– The company is struggling to meet the delivery schedules.
	– Off-lake dependent on government spending.
D.	– Packaging, after sales service, etc., are material to the sale of the product and the company is unable to meet customers' requirements regarding the quality of packaging.
	– Company is falling behind in meeting delivery schedules.
	– Frequent rejections of the company's products.
E.	– Sale is seasonal.
	– Consumer product heavily dependent on promotion, back-up, image, tastes, styles and perceptions of the buyers.
	– Product is custom made to specifications and has no alternate use.
	– Company is unable to meet the delivery schedules.

(Contd...)

Sl. No.		Descriptions
6.	**Inputs Profile**	
	A.	– Raw materials – easily available.
		– Steady price.
		– No risk of sourcing by alternate users or more profitable usages elsewhere.
		– Substitutes of inputs available.
		– There is no risk in sourcing the imported raw materials.
		– Appropriate price escalation clauses have been provided.
	B.	– Raw material – generally available.
		– Price more or less steady.
		– Has few other usages but supply is adequate.
	C.	– Raw material availability ensured by tie-ups with suppliers.
		– There are no substitute inputs.
		– There is difficulty in ensuring that customers agree to price escalations.
	D.	– Timely availability is critical and there have been slippages on account of inadequate supplies.
		– Needs large stocking levels, and planning needed to prevent stock-outs.
		– Industry highly dependent on critical raw materials.
		– Price variations are not fully passed on to the consumers (Price escalation clause is inadequate).
	E.	– Availability extremely seasonal.
		– There are extreme price fluctuations.
		– Production loss has occurred on account of scarcity of raw materials.
		– Input prices controlled.
		– Alternate uses for the raw materials exist.

APPENDIX 9.3

VALUE STATEMENTS OF MANAGEMENT RISKS [AN ILLUSTRATIVE (NOT EXHAUSTIVE) LIST]

VALUE STATEMENTS

Sl. No.		*Descriptions*
1.	**Integrity**	
	A.	– No fraudulent deals/connections.
		– On no occasion has any unsatisfactory feature of the management come to light.
		– Integrity and character of the management is beyond reproach.
	B.	– Full history of the management not available but the management is reportedly reliable and is of good integrity.
		– Features revealed by reports on conduct of accounts/stock audit/inspector's remarks, etc., do not indicate doubtful integrity.
	C.	– There are apparently no adverse reports about the integrity of the management/ promoters.
	D.	– Features revealed by reports on conduct of accounts/stock audit/inspector's remarks, etc., could be pointers to doubtful integrity.
		– There are reasons to doubt the integrity of the promoters/management.
	E.	– Could be dubious.
		– History indicates antecedents of being involved in civil/criminal suits and questionable deals.
2.	**Expertise, Competence/Commitment**	
	A.	– Highly qualified professionals working as a team.
		– Record of timely execution of projects.
		– The management has well defined strategy for the future.
		– The line of succession is well established.
	B.	– The company has professionals in the key areas under the overall control of owners who function independently.
		– The projects undertaken are executed in time and well.
		– Promoters/management have the relevant experience.
	C.	– The company has very few professionals (less than 25% of the top management) owners; however, the management is satisfactory.
		– The line of succession is unclear for the present but there are appropriate plans on the anvil.
	D.	– Projects are delayed for various factors, which reveal inadequate planning process.
		– Diversification based on ad-hoc decisions revealing no clear game plan or strategy.
	E.	– The management centres around one or two people only. Projects are inordinately delayed.
		– There is an unrelated diversification planned by the management at an extremely fast pace.

(Contd...)

Sl. No.		Descriptions
3.	**Track Record**	
	A.	– Achieves sales projections, maintains financial discipline.
		– No irregularities/developments of Letter of Credit (L/C) in the account.
		– Record of meeting commitments to lenders and creditors is excellent.
		– No defaults in group companies.
		– Credit summations are adequate.
		– Management have adequate measures for warding off takeover threats.
	B.	– Achieves sales projections except for unexpected external factors.
		– Accounts are regular.
		– Repayment of loans sometimes delayed.
		– Some group companies are not doing well but the management is cooperating with them in reviving/settling them.
	C.	– Sales projections have fallen short but this is a short-term phenomenon.
		– The accounts are satisfactory.
		– Repayments delayed but account continues to be a standard asset.
		– Overall group/associate company record is average.
	D.	– Accounts maintained mostly irregular but remain standard. Loans rescheduled and are running regular.
		– Instances of returned bills constitute more than 25% of the total bills.
		– Delayed submission of reports/statements.
		– Sales projections are not achieved.
	E.	– Not amenable to financial discipline, like submission of statements, adherence to covenants, etc.
		– Diversion of sale proceeds through other banks on record. Cash, liquidity management problems.
		– Accounts are frequently irregular aggregating more than four months in a year.
		– A few group companies have been/are in default; their loans are doubtful.
4.	**Structure and Systems**	
	A.	– Adequate delegation has taken place, sound budgeting/MIS/reporting/costing systems are in place.
		– Statutory requirements are met.
	B.	– Key positions are owner driven but, by and large, the top and senior management take independent decisions.
		– Well laid down systems of reporting, etc.
	C.	– Systems relating to budgeting, costing are in place but usually, are not strictly adhered to.
	D.	– Management has a lot of other interests and bestows only limited control/interests in the unit.
		– No adequate second line of command.
		– Some system areas are inadequate, *e.g.* costing, receivables/invoice follow-up, etc.
	E.	– All decisions are dependent on one person. Reporting system non-existent.

(Contd...)

Sl. No.		Descriptions
5.		**Capital Market Perception**
A.	–	The company/management/group has successfully tapped the capital market in the past three years and the subsequent performance shows achievement of the plans given to the market.
	–	The company is improving its Earning per Share (EPS); has a good record of dividend payments and is not in default with FIs/Banks/Stock Exchanges.
B.	–	The company/management/group has successfully tapped the capital market in the past.
	–	The track record vis-à-vis plans is not yet known. However, the project is on schedule and there are no adverse features.
C.	–	The company/management/group has been able to tap the market in the past.
	–	Their recent performance sales/profits/EPS, etc., have not been entirely as per the projections, but the outlook still remains positive.
D.	–	The company/management/group are approaching the capital market for the first time.
	–	Their track record and other features carry indications of some adverse features, which could affect the market perception.
E	–	The company/management/group have not been able to adhere to their plans in the past.
	–	Their accounts have run into default and their ability to reach the market is in doubt.

A SYNOPTIC NOTE
(CHAPTER 9 AT A GLANCE)

MANAGING CREDIT RISKS

Historical Perspective

Since 1992, most of the banks had adopted some Credit Rating System (CRS) for assessing the extent of credit-worthiness and financial strength of the borrowers, on some 5 to 0 points scale, as also for stipulating the rate of interest, *i.e.* so much basis percentage points higher than the Prime Lending Rate (PLR), accordingly. This exercise had some objective parameters for giving the positive and negative scores, and taking a decision, based on the net score (points).

But, it was later realised that the CRS was, at best, just enough to assess and classify the borrowers under different categories of credit risks, but was not good enough to facilitate the overall management of credit risks.

This was so considered, and rightly so, inasmuch as the following vital parameters were not taken into account, viz.,

(*i*) Profitability;

(*ii*) Repaying capacity;

(*iii*) Effectiveness and efficiency of management of the borrowal companies; and

(*iv*) The inter-firm and intra-firm comparisons and analysis, based on the historical data, specially pertaining to the qualitative aspects of management and prospects based upon some acceptable and reasonable benchmarks.

This, naturally, gave rise to a better and comprehensive system of analytical assessments (both quantitatively and qualitatively) of the borrowers, both present and prospective. This system is commonly known as **Credit Risk Assessment (CRA)** System, supplementing and not replacing, the earlier parameters, pertaining to the Credit Rating System (CRS).

What is the Credit Risk Assessment (CRA) System?

It has two steps:

Step I

Risk rating is computed.

Step II

(*i*) Assessment is made, based on the (*a*) industry; and (*b*) management factors; and

(*ii*) Judgemental (not mechanical) scorings have to be given to both these aspects, separately.

And, the two must also match.

Besides, minimum permissible score has also been laid down for both the parameters, viz. (*a*) and (*b*) above, for any company to be eligible for consideration for granting fresh advances (to the prospective companies) and even for the renewal and continuation of the existing advances by the bank, or at least, for any enhancement of the credit limits, in regard to both the working capital and term loan facilities.

Different parameters and their different ranges of scores have also been given different weightage. The methodology adopted is not shared with the borrowers, though the various parameters of assessment, as such, are made known to them. They are counselled, from time to time, to improve upon certain parameters, on which they may be lacking, and that, too, within a stipulated time-frame.

Besides fixing the minimum overall eligibility ratings, the banks have also allotted some minimum eligibility ratings and standards, to the undernoted three main heads, both individually and collectively:

(*i*) Financial risks pertaining to the company;

(*ii*) Industrial risks pertaining to the industry; and

(*iii*) Managerial risks relating to the effectiveness of the company's management.

All these three are first:

(*i*) Rated separately on a credit risk dimensions, and then

(*ii*) Duly weighted, and thereafter

(*iii*) All the weighted scores are totalled and then the

(*iv*) Single point risk indicator is arrived at, and lastly, the

(*v*) Final credit decision, is taken.

The methodologies and parameters, as also the rating patterns, of course, vary from bank to bank, but the underlying principles behind all these are almost the same.

Financial Risks Assessment

It involves:

(*a*) Quantitative aspects parameters; and

(*b*) Qualitative aspects (parameters).

(a) QUANTITATIVE ASPECTS (PARAMETERS)

These are based on the analysis and interpretation, mainly of the following ratios:

(*i*) Liquidity ratios;

(*ii*) Profitability ratios;

(*iii*) Gearing ratios; and

(*iv*) Turnover ratios.

Both

(*a*) Intra-firm, and

(*b*) Inter-firm comparisons are done taking into account both the positive (+ve) and negative (–ve) aspects thereof:

(b) QUALITATIVE ASSESSMENTS

These comprise an analytical study of:

(*i*) Accounting Policies;

(*ii*) Bad Debts (Policy and Provisions);

(*iii*) Arrears of Depreciation;

(*iv*) Contingent Liabilities and Claims; and

(*v*) Auditor's (Adverse) Remarks, if any, in the Annual Report.

(c) OVERALL FINANCIAL RISK MANAGEMENT

This comprises three parts:

(*i*) Quantitative (Static) aspects, *i.e.* ratio analysis;

(*ii*) Quantitative (Dynamic) aspects, *i.e.*

- (*a*) Historical (or Intra-Firm) comparison; and
- (*b*) Industry (or Inter-Firm) comparison.

(*iii*) The third part is qualitative area comprising qualitative financial parameters, viz.

- (*a*) Contingent Liabilities under excise duty/tax disputes, guarantees given by the company, etc., and the
- (*b*) Accounting Policies, regarding:
  - (*i*) Valuation of inventories (*e.g.* LIFO, FIFO, weighted average, etc.);
  - (*ii*) Capitalization;
  - (*iii*) Depreciation;
  - (*iv*) Revaluation of fixed assets, etc.

Such qualitative risks, however, are assessed only on negative parameters, and are allotted negative scores, ranging from zero to ten (0–10) only.

Under the quantitative aspects, the following six ratios are studied (comprising both intra-firm and inter-firm comparisons).

And, these are given different weightages (in percentage terms), as per the suggested norms.

The maximum marks allotted to these aspects (being most vital and of utmost ramifications) are given 50% marks, out of the overall total of 100%.

The six ratios are:

(*i*) Current Ratio;

(*ii*) TOL/TNW;

(*iii*) [(Inventory + BR) × 365] / Sales (No. of Days);

(*iv*) PBITD/Interest (times);

(*v*) PAT/net sales (%);

(*vi*) ROCE (%)

While all the 6 ratios are assessed in the range of minimum zero (0) and maximum five (5), the weightages given to them vary, depending upon their respective impact and influence on the overall financial strength of the company.

That is, while the first two, *i.e.* (*i*) and (*ii*) above, are given the weightage of 5 each, the last three, *i.e.* (*iv*) to (*vi*) are given the weightage of only 2 each.

The third one, however, is given the weightage of 4.

Thus, in the aggregate, these comprise (Though suggestively only):

(5 × 5) × 2	= 50
(5 × 2) × 3	= 30
(5 × 4) × 1	= 20
TOTAL	= **100**

And, the overall proportion, allotted to these ratios, is 50%. Thus, total score, in absolute term, here will be 50 only.

The two Dynamic Aspects in the Quantitative Area (*i.e.* Intra-firm and Inter-firm comparisons) are given, say, the total score of 8 each, aggregating 16.

Here, however, only 4, out of the 6 ratios, noted above, are taken into account (*i.e.* PBITD/Interest and ROCE are excluded). All these four ratios may be given the score of 2 each, which means (2 × 4) × 2 = 16.

The qualitative risks comprise two distinct features, viz.,

(i) Industrial Risks

(*a*) Market Competition;

(*b*) Regulatory Risks;

(*c*) Technological Obsolescence Risks;

(*d*) Scarcity of Raw Materials; and

(*e*) Substitute Risks of Finished Goods.

(ii) Managerial Risks

(*a*) Integrity and Honesty;

(*b*) Track Record;

(*c*) Organizational Structure and System;

(*d*) Competence and Commitments of the Personnel (of the company); and

(*e*) Perception (of the company) in the Capital Market, etc.

Overall credit risks assessment:

These comprise:

(*a*) Quantitative (or objective) aspects; and

(*b*) Qualitative (or subjective) aspects.

These may, therefore, better be given a weightage in the ratio of 2 : 1 (or 2/3 and 1/3), *i.e.* 66 and 34, 65 and 35, 67 and 33, and so on. These could be divided into (50 + 8 + 8) + (10 + 24), and so on, *i.e.* the division could be like: pertaining to the Ratio Analysis (50), Intra-Firm and Inter-Firm Comparisons (8 each), and Industry Risks (24), and Management Risks (10), negative only.

QUESTIONS

(For Self-assessment)

1. In what ways is the Credit Risks Assessment (CRA) system a marked improvement over the earlier Credit Ratings System (CRS)?
2. Under the Credit Risks Assessment (CRA) model, the appraisal of Credit Risks, associated with any loan, has been classified into the undernoted three main heads:

   (*a*) Financial risks;

   (*b*) Industrial risks; and

   (*c*) Managerial risks.

   Which one of the following pattern of percentage distribution should generally be adopted among these three?

   (*i*) 50 : 25 : 25 (*ii*) 33.3 : 33.3 : 33.3

   (*iii*) 66 : 24 : 10 (*iv*) 65 : 25 : 10

   (*v*) 60 : 30 : 10

   Give reasons for your answer.
3. Financial Risks Assessment must be divided under two broad heads, viz.

   (*i*) Quantitative assessment, and (*ii*) Qualitative assessment.

   What overall weightage should be given to each of these parameters?
4. What are the main six ratios considered under the quantitative (static) parameters?
5. What weightage should be allotted to the undernoted three dimensions of the overall Financial Risks Assessment (out of the total 100 points)?

   (*a*) Quantitative (Static) parameters like ratio analysis;

   (*b*) (*i*) Quantitative (dynamic) [intra-firm comparison]; and

   (*ii*) Quantitative (dynamic) [inter-firm comparison].
6. What are the main parameters/factors, on the basis of which the qualitative (judgemental) decisions must be taken, for assessing and awarding (negative) scores?
7. What are the main factors/parameters to be considered under the following heads?

   (*i*) Industrial risks; and

   (*ii*) Managerial risks.

10

DISBURSEMENT AND FOLLOW-UP OF WORKING CAPITAL FINANCE BY BANKS

> *The use of money is all the advantage there is in having money.* — ***Benjamin Franklin***

The Learning Points

The chapter aims at developing the knowledge and facilitating the understanding of:

- System of Objective Appraisal of Projects by Banks
- Methodology Adopted by Banks for Assessing Working Capital Requirements of the Prospective Borrowers
- Rationale behind Phased Disbursement of Loans
- System of Supervision and Follow-up of Advances, and Performance Monitoring of Units, usually adopted by Banks
- Desirability of Timely Detection of early Symptoms of Sickness
- Supervision and Control of Irregularities in the Advances (at the banks' branches) at the Controlling Office
- Early Rehabilitation of Viable Sick Units by Banks

INTRODUCTION

Realistic assessment and sanction of credit needs, phased disbursement of loans, and post-sanction supervision and follow-up of advances are the main facets of credit risk management by commercial banks (as also by the other financial institutions). And, the efficiency and effectiveness of the credit risk management largely depends on the following seven factors:

1. Prompt and realistic appraisal of projects, on receipt of the loan applications along with the project reports.
2. Prompt and realistic assessment of the credit requirements, both short-term (working capital) and long-term (term loan).
3. Phased disbursement of loans to ensure proper end-use of funds.
4. Effective supervision and follow-up of advances, and periodical performance monitoring of the companies through intelligent scrutiny of their books of accounts, stock statements, financial statements, etc., coupled with personal dialogues with the owners and/or managers of the companies.
5. Timely detection of early symptoms of sickness at the incipient early stage itself, and prompt and effective implementation of suitable remedial measures to put the companies back to its financial health.

6. Effective supervision and control of irregularities in the advances at the branches by the controlling authority.
7. Prompt decision and action in regard to the rehabilitation of viable sick units or calling up of the advances of non-viable sick units.

These seven factors have been discussed seriatim in the following pages:

And, such discussions have broadly been classified under the following four segments:

(*i*) What are the objectives (rationale) behind each of the instructions/systems and procedures, laid down by the banks?

(*ii*) What are the actual practices obtaining at most of the branches of banks?

(*iii*) What are the main reasons for the flaws/gaps between the banks' instructions/laid down systems and procedures, and the actual practices being followed at most of the branches of the banks?

(*iv*) Some pragmatic suggestions for bridging such gaps, if any, effectively and fruitfully.

10.1 PROJECT APPRAISAL

Objectives

Project appraisal is the process of critical examination and analytical evaluation of a loan proposal for a project to see whether funds, if lent, can be repaid out of the profit generated within a reasonable time. It provides an analytical base for the decision making process.

The main objectives of project appraisal are:

(*a*) To assess whether the entrepreneurs are technically and managerially equipped to execute the project, and whether their antecedents like character, credit-worthiness, integrity, etc., are satisfactory.

(*b*) To examine the technical feasibility of the process of manufacturing the product and the availability of the infrastructural facilities, raw materials, etc.

(*c*) To realistically determine the market demand for the proposed product and the achievability of the projected sales.

(*d*) To estimate the quantum of bank finance required.

(*e*) To assess the profitability of the project on a realistic basis and the adequacy of the cash surplus for repayment of the loan within a reasonable time.

Flaws Observed in the Banks' Project Appraisal

Instead of making independent and realistic estimates of the projected sales and profitability, keeping in view the technical competence of the entrepreneurs and the quantum of demand for the products, extent of competition, etc., the operating staff at the banks are largely guided by the estimates of entrepreneurs, as incorporated in the project reports. These initial lapses, at the project appraisal stage itself, naturally led to the steady deterioration of the financial health in most of the units, as has been revealed in several empirical studies on the subject. Such units had ultimately fallen sick, beyond rehabilitation, as these were facing serious marketing problems and could not overcome such problems even at any later stage.

Flaws generally observed in the Project Appraisal by the Bank Officers

The sales of some of the units had fallen short of the projected levels, estimated in the project reports, due to stiff competition in the market. The extent of competition and the level of achievable sales were not thoroughly examined by the bank officers independently, on a realistic basis, at the project appraisal stage. Some other units also initially faced some competition in the market but the entrepreneurs concerned strived hard and ultimately succeeded in establishing themselves in the market, by adopting suitable marketing strategies and/or by improving the quality of their products.

The products of some units could not pick-up in the market due to their poor quality, ultimately resulting in the sickness of these units. As the entrepreneurs concerned could not improve upon the quality of their products, even at a later stage, their units became non-viable and the loans were called up by the bank. The bank officers had thus failed to properly assess the technical competence of the entrepreneurs at the project appraisal stage.

The bank officers did not forewarn the entrepreneurs at the project appraisal stage, regarding the pitfalls of over-dependence on one or a few bulk buyers, viz. government departments or large scale industries. They too could have counselled the entrepreneurs to explore an alternative broad-based clientele in the open market.

Some units, which initially depended on government departments or a large scale industry and had fallen sick due to change in the government policy or the failure of the parent unit, could be rehabilitated by the bank as the entrepreneurs could subsequently find some alternative buyers to establish themselves in the open market. Some units, however, steadily grew and prospered, as they were selling their products right from the beginning to the government departments as also in the open market.

Bank's Systems and Procedures for Project Appraisal

All the relevant factors required to be considered by the entrepreneurs while preparing the project report, and to be examined by the bank officers, while appraising the project reports, are contained in various loan application forms prescribed by the banks for different quantum of advances. For example, say,

(*i*) over Rs. 2 lakh and up to Rs. 5 lakh;
(*ii*) over Rs. 5 lakh and up to Rs. 10 lakh; and
(*iii*) over Rs. 10 lakh, where Tandon Committee norms earlier applied.

These application forms well serve the purpose of check lists to verify whether all the relevant factors have been duly considered.

Example:

This reminds me of a manufacturing company, which had, in the year 1972, constructed the factory building from its own resources, with an investment of Rs. 5 lakh. The commercial bank had also disbursed a working capital loan of Rs. 10 lakh and the State Financial Corporation had disbursed a term loan of Rs. 15 lakh. But, as the company had defaulted in the payment of the half-yearly instalments for three consecutive half-years, the State Financial Corporation had called up the loan and had locked up the factory premises. The commercial bank also, in turn, had called up the loan. And, the company had to suffer, for no fault of its own, inasmuch as the reason for the default was that the machines had not become operative till then for want of power connection. Thus, the commercial banks, having learnt the good lesson the hard way, have, in their loan application form itself, stipulated, inter alia, as under:

(*a*) Is power connection required to run the machines?

(*b*) If so, whether the power connection has already been given?

(*c*) If not, by when is the power connection expected? (Also state the basis on which the expected date is given. Please enclose copies of the letter/document in support of your contention).

Thus, the application form itself served as a check list. Had such comprehensive application forms been there in place even earlier, the aforesaid unit might not have suffered so hard, and for no fault of its own.

It also serves as a lesson for the financial institutions and commercial banks that, though they might have sanctioned loans (as they had rightly done), they should not have disbursed loans, in full, unless the basic pre-conditions, like, say, installation of power connection for the commissioning of the plant and machinery, would have been fulfilled. Besides, the quantum and period for the payment of half-yearly instalments of the term-loan also seems to have been fixed arbitrarily, just by counting exactly six months from the date of the disbursement of the loan. Further, while the term loan should have been disbursed in a phased manner, with a view to ensuring the right end-use of funds, the working capital loan, too, should have been released in phases, and the borrowers should have been counselled to withdraw the loan amount not in one go, but only in stages, depending upon the requirements, specially during the initial period of commencement of its production, so as to avoid payment of huge amount, by way of interest, unnecessarily.

But, unfortunately, even now, in many cases, due attention is not being paid to these crucial factors by some bank officers.

Suggestions

(*a*) It is, therefore, suggested that the bank officers should pay due attention and importance to the project appraisal, so crucial and critical for the success of an enterprise. They must meticulously appraise the technical feasibility and economic viability of the projects and objectively assess the entrepreneurs' managerial competence. The bank managers should seek help and guidance from the specialists in the bank's consultancy services cell for conducting the detailed techno-economic viability study of new units, involving highly technical and complex manufacturing process, where the experience of the branch staff may be considered inadequate.

(*b*) It is a well-known fact that no industrial unit can work on sound and profitable lines unless it is able to market its products in sufficient quantity and at a price higher than its cost of production. The bank officers should, therefore, assess the cost of production and marketability of the products of units on a realistic basis.

(*c*) They must do the break-even analysis on the basis of actual (not conservative) costs and reasonable (not over-ambitious) estimates of sales, with a view to ensuring that the unit was breaking-even at a reasonably lower level so as to be able to withstand the initial shocks of lower sales and profitability.

(*d*) They would do well to ensure that the entrepreneurs undertake a market survey, or a quick market census/scanning, to ascertain the actual demand of their products and the extent of competition from the multinationals and the large, medium and small scale sectors.

Example:

In 1974, a young entrepreneur had been sanctioned a working capital limit of Rs. 5 lakh by a commercial bank, for establishing a unit near Lucknow (U.P.) to manufacture collapsible tubes. The unit had projected its sales based merely upon the number of units located in and around Lucknow, manufacturing pharmaceutical products, without verifying and realising as to how many of them were manufacturing ointments, to be packed in collapsible tubes. At a later stage, however, the entrepreneur was advised by the bank to undertake a market scanning (not a detailed market survey) and to endeavour to obtain some firm orders. He was naturally very much annoyed with the bank officer for his so-called 'delaying tactics' to disburse the loan. But, soon he had realised that his sales projections were not based on sound facts and ground realities, inasmuch as even a handful of units in U.P., which were manufacturing ointments, did not require the collapsible tubes as the packing material. Because, even such units were manufacturing ointments for ringworm and they had found the tiny tin containers much cheaper and far more popular, as these could well be used later by farmers, who mostly suffered from such disease, as a handy container to keep some lime for mixing with their chewing tobacco.

(*e*) Banks should suggest to the prospective entrepreneurs to explore and tap some alternative broad-based customers also, to the extent of say, 50% of their production, so as to guard against the imminent risk of over-dependence on one or a few bulk buyers, like the government or some large industries.

Example:

The ancillary units of Scooters (India) Limited, Lucknow, and those of AP Scooters Limited, Hyderabad, as also those of the Indian Telephone Industries (ITI), Raebareli, etc., had, in turn, suffered severe financial losses, and most of them had to face even closure of their units, as and when their parent companies had failed to do well in the market. But, one of the ancillary units of AP Scooters, Hyderabad, manufacturing clutch assembly for two wheelers, could survive the shock as it had already been selling its products to some other companies, too, in the private sector.

I also know of a company, manufacturing agricultural implements and steel storage bins, etc., who could sell its products well, inasmuch as the State Government of Uttar Pradesh had been giving a subsidy to the extent of 50% of the cost of these products, by way of incentives. But, suddenly the government had decided to withdraw the subsidy scheme and the unit, naturally, suffered a great loss, as it had to perforce sell most of its finished goods at a huge discount. The unit, however, with the unstinted support of the commercial bank, could survive the shock and avoid its imminent closure.

(*f*) Further, they (bank officers) should impress upon the entrepreneurs the desirability of maintaining the quality of their products up to an acceptable standard so as to pick up in the market, even in the face of competition. They must make the entrepreneurs realise that a substandard product may fail in the market, and that even the supply of such products on credit terms may give rise to disputed bills and accumulating sundry debtors, resulting in liquidity problems, with other ramifications, ultimately leading to the steady deterioration in the financial health of the unit.

(*g*) They must also advise the entrepreneurs to first get the samples approved by the parent units or the bulk purchasers, before going in for mass production, so as to guard against mass rejection and the adverse ramifications connected therewith.

Examples:

A small scale unit in Hyderabad, manufacturing plastic components for a large scale company, manufacturing refrigerators, suffered a great financial loss, as its very first consignment worth over Rs. 5 lakh was rejected due to sub-standard quality of the products, not conforming to the required specifications.

As against this, the Assistant General Manager (AGM) of a commercial bank invested some of his valuable time, while sanctioning loans to four young entrepreneurs, owning ancillary units of ITI, Raebareli, to get the samples of their products tested by the parent unit well before going in for mass production. That is why, I have deliberately used the term 'invested' (and not spent) his valuable time, because, this way, a lot of the precious moments of the AGM were saved from being unproductively wasted in the recovery proceedings of the loan amount, as had already happened in the aforesaid case of the unit manufacturing plastic components for the refrigerators.

(*h*) Bank officers should also guide entrepreneurs in identifying viable projects and assist them in preparing the project reports on a realistic basis. Banks should develop their own data banks on some selected industries, on an on-going basis, and have a list of other banks and institutions maintaining the data banks on some other industries. This may help the bank officers in guiding entrepreneurs in the preparation of the project reports, as also while appraising the projects. Bank's consultancy services cell could render the necessary help and guidance, wherever required. Besides, the bank may have a panel of some reputed management consultants to refer to the prospective borrowers, or even to consult them on some highly technical projects.

(*i*) Many senior retired officers of banks and term lending institutions, with sufficient financial and technical background, were found to be keen on establishing their private consultancy services. Banks may help them in doing so by rendering them the necessary guidance and even some financial assistance, if necessary. They may, as well, design and conduct a short-duration course for them for this purpose.

(*j*) The bank officers should apprise entrepreneurs of the imminent risks, if any, in the project, which may ultimately result in the sickness of the unit. They should also counsel entrepreneurs, wherever necessary, to start the project on a scale that they may manage effectively, and to go in for expansion and diversification only after acquiring some insight and experience in the line of the business.

Example:

A team of five young engineers had established a small scale unit under the Entrepreneurship Scheme, as banks and term lending institutions were granting loans on very liberal and concessional terms, under the scheme. This unit had already been sanctioned a term loan of Rs. 25 lakh and a working capital limit of Rs. 20 lakh. The unit had, however, (mis) utilised the working capital loan for the purpose of payment of the three half-yearly instalments of its term loan so as to impress the financial institution, though the unit had not even commenced its production till then. They were, however, disbursed yet another term loan by the financial institution to establish yet another unit, and this unit had already purchased some land therefrom for the purpose. Both the units, however, had soon fallen sick and were ultimately closed down.

(*k*) Personal interviews with the prospective entrepreneurs would provide bank officers with some valuable information regarding the competence and commitment of entrepreneurs to run their units on sound lines. A visit to a factory site by the branch operating staff and an informal dialogue with the managers/workers of the unit, at the project appraisal stage, would also reveal some valuable and vital facts and facets, which usually may not be available in the project report or other statements.

Examples:

A company had stated in the loan application that they were already manufacturing and making bulk supplies to government departments. But, the bank officer, on his visit to the unit, found that a thick layer of dust had gathered on all the machines, signifying that none of these had been operated for quite sometime. The bank officer rightly declined the loan proposal.

As against this, in another case, a working capital loan was sanctioned by the same bank officer, on the spot, during his visit to the unit's factory, as the young proprietor of the firm, though quite new to the line of the business, had been found to be very pragmatic, cautious and careful, to start his business on a much smaller scale, to begin with, and had some realistic expansion plans, too, to be undertaken later, after gaining some useful experience and expertise in the line of his business.

10.2 ASSESSMENT OF WORKING CAPITAL REQUIREMENTS

Objectives

Prompt and realistic assessment of working capital requirements by banks is crucial for the success of a unit, inasmuch as while over-financing may lead to diversion of funds and avoidable interest burden, under-financing may cause financial constraints and avoidable hardship to the unit.

It has been usually observed that whenever a borrowal unit is granted a higher amount of loan than actually required, most of the borrowers tend to avail of the entire loan amount and divert surplus funds for renovation/repair of their residential buildings or for purchase of car or such other consumer durables, making the conduct of the account irregular *ab initio*.

And, I personally feel that the act of under-financing (though not desirable) is, after all, a much lesser evil, as the borrower soon start feeling the brunt of shortage of funds, and, therefore, may have to come back to the bank for some more financial help. In such a case, the bank officer would do well to reassess the credit needs, based upon the actual performance and the actual level of activities of the unit, based on its past experience, though short, but significant.

Components of Working Capital

As we all know, the working capital finance is required to meet the cost of production and sales so as to keep the production cycle moving on an on-going basis. It is, therefore, intended to finance the five components of the production cycle, viz.

1. Raw Materials as also consumable stores and spares.

2. Stocks-in-process
3. Finished goods.
4. Bills receivable.
5. Cash (and near cash).

Factors Determining the Quantum of Working Capital

The quantum of funds required to finance the aforesaid components of working capital depends on the nature and level of the activity of the unit and the prevailing market conditions, which are discussed hereunder:

1. Raw Materials (and Consumable Stores and Spares)

The amount of funds required for holding stocks of raw materials and consumable stores and spares depends mainly on the undernoted factors:

(*a*) Availability of raw materials in the market and proximity to their sources.

(*b*) Seasonal availability of raw materials.

(*c*) The normal lead time of delivery, *i.e.* average time taken for raw materials to reach the factory after an order is placed.

(*d*) The maximum lead time of delivery.

(*e*) Minimum order quantity stipulated by the suppliers.

Example:

A Public Sector Undertaking (PSU), manufacturing warships had to purchase some high value items of raw materials from Steel Authority of India Limited (SAIL) in much larger quantity than actually required, because it was not found economical for the SAIL to produce any quantity lesser than the lot size. And, as these items were not available elsewhere, the ship manufacturing company had no alternative but to order for the purchase of the full lot size, and thereby had to incur unnecessarily very high inventory carrying cost.

It, however, occurs to me that both the PSUs could have mutually agreed to produce and purchase only the required quantity (much lower than the minimum economic lot size). The SAIL could have, however, charged a proportionately higher price, so as to yield the same percentage of profits. This would have suited the ship manufacturing company, too, as the proportionately higher price paid would have ultimately proved to be much lower than the avoidable and disproportionately higher inventory carrying costs.

(*f*) The quantity that can be transported economically, and the discount available on bulk orders could be valid reasons for making some bulk purchases, provided the amount saved by way of such bulk purchase is sufficient to cover the interest on the funds blocked, as also the other items of inventory carrying costs.

A mutually advantageous deal could be to make a bulk order for the total annual requirement (say, worth Rs. 12 lakh) but with the condition that the goods worth Rs. 1 lakh only should be supplied each month. This will entitle the buyer company to avail of the bulk discount, and, that too, without incurring any extra inventory carrying cost. And, this may suit the seller company, too, as they will not have to produce and store the goods till the full bulk quantity is produced, and kept ready for dispatch. The policy of bulk order with phased delivery could, thus, be a win-win situation for both the buyer and the seller companies.

(*g*) Government quotas and controls.

The sale and supply of certain items of raw materials, being in short supply, may be brought by the government within the purview of control and quota system. Thus, depending upon the installed capacity and the annual consumption of such items of raw materials by the respective units, a quota may be fixed for the manufacturers to meet their quarterly requirements. They may further be required to lift the quota only once per quarter, either in full or only a part thereof, whereby the balance quantity of the quota for the quarter may lapse. Under such circumstances, the company may have to, per force, keep the quarterly requirements of raw materials, though just one month's stock would have usually been sufficient.

Further, with a view to holding the price line of some essential commodities in an inflationary situation, the Reserve Bank of India (RBI) may resort to the policy of selective credit control in respect of such commodities. In such cases, the company may not hold more than the maximum permissible quantity, though a much larger quantity of the commodity would have been more economical for the company.

(*h*) In the case of imported raw materials, the time taken for the issuance of import licence, lead time and such other relevant factors.

(*i*) The normal rate of consumption of raw materials, depending upon the level of activity.

(*j*) Fluctuations in the requirements of raw materials.

(*k*) Seasonal peak requirements, if any.

(*l*) Safety level of stocks to take care of delay in supply or high consumption of raw materials to meet an urgent order.

(*m*) Storage facility available.

(*n*) Economic order quantity, based on cost considerations, *i.e.*, cost of holding and carrying the inventory versus cost of frequent ordering.

2. Stocks-in-process

The level of stock-in-process depends on the following main factors:

(*a*) Manufacturing process.

(*b*) Manufacturing time.

For example, the manufacturing time (and consequently the operating cycle) of units producing bread may be very small (say, 2 days), while it may be much longer (say, 8 to 12 months) in the case of a company manufacturing heavy electrical or heavy engineering items or even plants and pipes for sugar industries, made to order and special specifications. The manufacturing time for units manufacturing textiles or plastic goods, however, may vary say, from one month to three months. Therefore, the quantum of working capital requirements may vary with the varying period of operating cycle or manufacturing time.

(*c*) Batch quantity, *i.e.* number of units manufactured in a batch.

3. Finished Goods

The stocking period of finished goods usually depends on the factors given hereunder:

(*a*) Delayed inspection by the government officials/customers.

Example:

A unit manufacturing wheels for goods trains was required to submit the bills to the railway authorities, invariably accompanied by the inspection note, duly signed by a Railway Officer, authorised on this behalf. However, on some occasions, for some unavoidable (or even avoidable) reasons, the transportation of the manufactured goods were unduly delayed due to the delay in their prior inspection and thereby the delay in the issuance of the required inspection note.

The enlightened banker, however, understood the genuine difficulties of the borrowers and accordingly cooperated with them by allowing retention of the finished goods inventories even beyond the maximum permissible limit, as a special case.

Incidentally, even while the norms of the Tandon Committee were in full force, deviations from the laid down inventory norms were made permissible, under such special circumstances, too.

(*b*) Time involved in the preparation of documents.

(*c*) Average minimum quantity of despatch.

(*d*) Transportation facilities.

(*e*) Market demand (only in the case of goods manufactured against anticipated orders).

(*f*) Purchasing pattern of buyers.

(*g*) Storage space/facility available.

(*h*) Seasonal demand, like for firecrackers, calendars, room-heaters, woollens, etc.

(*i*) Maximum shelf life of the product, if perishable, *e.g.* fruits or even papers, cement, medicines, food-stuff, etc.

(*j*) Seasonal availability of raw materials.

(*k*) Extent of competition, forcing stocking of higher level of stocks of finished goods to ensure prompt supply to the buyers.

Example:

I know of a company who had manufactured and stored a large number of a particular model of machinery so as to supply these instantaneously from the ready stock, and thereby to have an edge over its competitors. But, unfortunately, with the change in the technology, this particular model had become obsolete, resulting in a heavy loss to the company on this single count. It would, therefore, augur well if, under such circumstances, only a small quantity of products are kept in ready stock, so as to meet the immediate demand and thereafter the balance quantity could be supplied by manufacturing these on a priority basis. This way, both the risks, *i.e.* (*a*) of losing the prospective buyers; and (*b*) of losing on account of obsolescence of the stock, could well be avoided.

4. Bills Receivable

The amount of advance required against bills receivable largely depends on the undernoted factors:

(*a*) Percentage of credit sales to total sales.

(*b*) Period of credit allowed as per the existing business practices.

(*c*) Normal realisation time as determined by the existing business practices.

Bank's Systems and Procedures for Assessment of Working Capital Requirement

In most of the banks, the instructions are clear and detailed, covering all the foregoing points, for consideration by the operating staff, while assessing the total working capital requirements. The banks also prescribe separate detailed loan application forms for the purpose, for different levels of such financial requirements, as discussed earlier.

Further, bank officers are required to consider the various factors for the assessment of the total working capital requirements, as per the proforma given in Table 10.1.

Table 10.1: Factors to be Considered by Bank Officers for the Assessment of the Total Working Capital Requirements

A Anticipated monthly sales Rs. ________

B. Cost of raw materials per month Rs. ________

C. Total expenses per month Rs. ________

D. Cost of production per month Rs. ________

No.	*Item*	*Period of Stocking/ Realisation of payment*	*Working Capital Requirement*	*Margin %*	*Value*	*Permissible Limit*
			–	%	–	–
	1	2	3 Rs.	4	5 Rs.	6 = (3 – 5) Rs.
(*a*)	Imported raw materials	month(s)	–	%	–	–
(*b*)	Indigenous raw materials	month(s)	–	%	–	–
(*c*)	Stock-in-process	week(s)	–	%	–	–
(*d*)	Finished goods	month(s)	–	%	–	–
(*e*)	Bills receivable	month(s)	–	%	–	–
(*f*)	Expenses	month(s)	–	100%	–	NIL
	Total		–		–	–

Flaws generally observed in the assessment of working capital requirements by the officers of the banks

A proper assessment of the working capital requirements by the banks depends on the realistic assessment of two main factors, viz.,

(*i*) Anticipated monthly sales; and

(*ii*) Period of stocking of the various components of inventories and the terms of credit sales.

On perusal of records of some of the banks, it has been observed that in most of the cases the level of estimated sales was taken on an over-ambitious basis, as projected in the relative project reports, resulting in over-financing and extra interest burden and even diversion of funds, ultimately resulting in the deterioration of financial health of the units. Bank officers did not make their own independent estimates of sales on a realistic basis at the project appraisal stage itself, keeping in view the installed capacity, the demand for the product, the extent of competition in the market, etc.

It was further observed that bank officers usually arrive at the total working capital requirements on an ad-hoc basis, and thereafter compute the period of stocking/payments and/or realisation of sundry debtors, so as to conform to such figures. In some cases even this exercise is not done and only the total working capital requirement is put in the assessment form.

Main reasons for such flaws in the assessment of working capital requirements by the bank officers

Personal interviews with the bank officers have revealed that the system of realistic assessment of working capital requirements, though meticulously laid down by banks, was not being followed at the branch level, mainly due to:

(*i*) lack of job knowledge and skills in these areas on the part of the operating staff at the branches; and

(*ii*) ever-increasing work-load in branches, which is not commensurate with the staff strength. The problem is further accentuated with the implementation of the Voluntary Retirement Schemes (VRSs) by various banks in the public sector.

Suggestions

(*a*) It is, therefore, suggested that the operating staff, lacking in such job knowledge and skills, should be imparted the required institutional training in these areas in the Bank's Staff Colleges and Staff Training Centres.

(*b*) On perusal of the existing curricula and programme designs of such in-house training programmes, it has been observed that these were more theory based and academic in character. These should, therefore, be suitably modified so as to provide the required pragmatic orientation to the operating staff by including more inputs by way of practical exercises, live case studies, group discussions, etc., instead of only the lecture method. The involved members of the faculty who would do well to prepare some relevant exercises, live case studies, and a list of common discrepancies, usually found in the working capital assessment, by visiting some intensive centre branches and controlling offices.

(*c*) It has also been observed that some of the officers, who had attended special programmes on industrial financing, were subsequently transferred to agricultural branches or were posted in some such other assignments, where the training could not be put to much practical use. It is, therefore, suggested that, barring some exigencies of circumstances, the post-training assignments should be so planned as to enable the trained officers to make full use of the training in their respective areas of specialisation.

(*d*) It is further suggested that banks should come out with some sort of Handbook by updating and consolidating instructions, wherever necessary. They should print sufficient number of copies thereof, so that each and every officer of the bank who deals with industrial advances, may have a personal copy for his/her guidance and reference purposes. A sufficient number of extra copies should also be kept in stock to be promptly supplied to the other officers as and when they get inducted into the work connected with industrial financing. Such measures will provide a good back-up system to the institutional training, imparted to the bank officers, and the incidence of industrial sickness, caused by lack of experience and expertise on their part, would be curbed to a large extent.

It has been observed that some commercial banks have prepared a very short and crisp, systematically compiled and lucidly written Handbook in the area of industrial finance, which has been found to be of great help and guidance to the operating staff. But, unfortunately, a very small number of copies of the Handbook had been got printed which fell far short of the demand.

It is, therefore, suggested that a much larger number of copies of such Handbooks may be got printed so as to be freely distributed among the officers and employees, of course, for internal circulation only. We should appreciate that if banks have preferred to spend a substantial amount of money on the institutional training of members of their staff, Handbooks, though not a substitute for the institutional training, would prove to be a good post-training back-up, or even of some guidance, prior to the institutional training, to the operating staff, and that, too, at a much lower cost of say, hardly Rs. 50 or even Rs. 100 per copy of the Handbook.

(*e*) It is further suggested that, based on relevant factors, the banks should build up a data bank on some selected industry groups, on an on-going basis, wherein the inventory norms, the position of demand for the product in the market, the extent of competition and such other relevant information and data could be available, for use by the operating staff.

Some banks have built up such data bank in respect of a few industry groups and the work in respect of some other industry groups is in progress.

The concept of data bank has proved to be of practical utility to the operating staff. It is, therefore, suggested that other banks should also initiate such good work, if not already done. It would also be a good idea for all banks, specially in the public sector, to coordinate amongst themselves so that each bank may undertake the task of building up data banks in respect of different selected industry groups, most relevant for the particular region, and this information/data should be freely shared and exchanged amongst themselves. The Reserve Bank of India or the Indian Banks' Association (IBA) could undertake the responsibility of coordinating such activity.

(*f*) As regards the problem of paucity of staff, banks may consider the desirability of suitably augmenting the staff strength, particularly of the field staff, at the branch level, specially at the intensive centre branches, based on the merit of each case.

(*g*) Another strategy could be to reduce the work-load at the branches, wherever possible, specially at the intensive centre branches. One such strategy could be to take a policy decision not to entertain any small loan under the government sponsored schemes, like Self-Employment Scheme for Educated Unemployed Youth (SESEUY), Self-Employment Programme for Urban Poor (SEPUP), etc., at intensive centre branches, already burdened with high-value advances. Such schemes could, however, be financed by other neighbouring branches of banks. This would be on the similar principle on which some banks have set up industrial finance branches in large cities (Lucknow, Hyderabad, Mumbai, Chennai, Delhi, Kolkata, etc.), exclusively for the borrowers enjoying credit facilities with any bank to the tune of Rs. 1 crore and above.

Example:

While I was posted as the Chief Manager at one of the intensive industrial finance branches in Kanpur (U.P.), my Assistant General Manager (AGM) sent me a letter exhorting me, too, to finance some rickshaw pullers in the locality or vicinity of the branch under the Differential Interest Rate (DIR) Scheme, by citing some commendable work done by some of the local branches, operating in the residential areas. And, I distinctly remember to have convinced my AGM that such DIR advances would, unnecessarily and avoidably be an uneconomical and imprudent extra burden on the branch, which had already been quite short of the sanctioned staff strength. And, it was really great of the AGM to have seen through the reasoning and rationale behind such arguments, way back in the year 1972.

10.3 PHASED DISBURSEMENT OF LOANS

Objective

The objective of phased disbursement of loans is to ensure the proper end-use of funds. The bank officers are, therefore, required to disburse the working capital loans in a phased manner, in accordance with the gradual increase in the scale of operations of units and the levels of their stocks of inventory and book debts. Due care is to be taken to avoid double financing of goods supplied on credit. Further, term loans are required to be disbursed in instalments, commensurate with the progress made in the implementation of the project.

Flaws observed in the disbursement of loans by bank officers

On perusal of books and records of some banks, it has been observed that in most cases, bank officers had allowed the entrepreneurs to withdraw the entire amount of the working capital loans soon after these were sanctioned to them, resulting in avoidable extra interest burden on them. Further, most of them had resorted to diversion of funds, *i.e.* short-term sources of funds (working capital loan) for long-term uses, *e.g.* for acquiring fixed assets or for unplanned expansion/ diversification. This led to the problem of paucity of working fund, adversely affecting the operating cycle with other ramifications, ultimately resulting in the steady deterioration in their financial health, beyond rehabilitation. In some cases, it was observed that though the entrepreneurs had stated, in the application form, that the required quantum of own fund (equity) would be invested by them in the venture, they actually did not do so in full measure, or else they later gradually withdrew their own fund from the business. In some cases, bank officers even end up advancing against goods supplied on credit, amounting to double financing.

Suggestions

(*a*) It is, therefore, suggested that bank officers should allow drawings in the working capital loan accounts in a phased manner, commensurate with the gradual increase in the scale of operations of the new units and the levels of their stocks of inventory and book debts. This way, they would be able to ensure the end-use of funds and guard against the risk of diversion of funds by the entrepreneurs.

(*b*) Further, bank officers should get the required margin money for working capital loans deposited in cash with the bank in the accounts of the units, before releasing the loan amount to them. The margin money so deposited by the entrepreneurs should also be reflected in their books of accounts.

(*c*) Besides, while encashing cheques, specially those drawn in favour of the entrepreneur and/or in round thousands, bank officers would do well to satisfy themselves, beyond doubt, that the amount was being withdrawn for genuine business transactions and not for the purpose of siphoning off of the entrepreneur's own fund from the business.

(*d*) Due care must be taken by bank officers to avoid double financing against the goods supplied to the units on credit. This can very well be done by perusing the relative in, voices for goods purchased on cash payment basis, or already paid for, when due. Better if such bills are routed through the bank. The perusal of books of accounts of the company may as well clarify the position.

(*e*) Term loans, of course, should be disbursed in instalments, commensurate with the stages of progress in the implementation of the project. Payments should preferably be made direct to suppliers of the machinery, etc. Proportionate amount of margin for term loans should be got deposited with the bank before disbursement of each instalment of the loan amount.

10.4 SUPERVISION AND FOLLOW-UP OF ADVANCES AND PERFORMANCE MONITORING OF UNITS

Objectives

The objectives of post-sanction supervision and follow-up of advances are:

(*a*) To check the end-use of funds.

(*b*) To verify the quantity and quality of assets charged to the bank and to ensure that the outstandings in the accounts are fully covered by the securities of adequate value.

(*c*) To regularly monitor and assess the financial health of the unit and to take timely preventive or corrective measures, wherever called for.

Types of Supervision and Follow-up

Post-sanction supervision and follow-up could broadly be classified under two categories, viz.

1. Quantitative or security oriented, and
2. Qualitative or activity oriented.

1. Quantitative or Security-oriented supervision and follow-up

This helps the bank officers to ensure that

(*a*) the condition of the factory premises, machinery and equipment, financed by the bank, is in order, (*b*) the machinery is intact and in good working condition,

(*c*) stocks of inventory charged to the bank are adequate to cover the outstandings in the account, and

(*d*) the insurance cover is adequate.

Stocks of inventory charged to the bank are to be verified with the latest stock statements, which should, in turn, be reconciled with figures in the company's books and records, as on the date of the inspection.

2. Qualitative or activity oriented supervision and follow-up

It is heartening to note that the emphasis on the bank's supervision and follow-up of advances has undergone a healthy change, from security-based inspection to activity-based supervision, from mere physical verification of assets to the monitoring of the performance and prospects of companies.

The key indicators of performance are the levels of activity (production and sales) and profitability of units. Some banks have, therefore, laid down the following guidelines for the inspecting officers:

(*a*) The books of accounts, like cash book, sales, purchase and stock registers, should be maintained by companies/firms properly and kept up-to-date. Invoices may be checked by the inspecting officers at random to know the mode of purchase (on credit or cash basis), and the terms of purchase and payment.

(*b*) Stocks should be regularly turned over. If there is any accumulation of slow-moving/non-moving items of finished goods, semi-finished goods and raw materials, reasons therefore should be enquired into, and remedial measures suggested.

Examples:

A company, manufacturing aluminum fittings, for supply to the State Electricity Board, had a number of items, which had not been taken delivery of, since long. It later transpired that these were the items rejected by the State Electricity Board, as they were not up to the desired specifications. The company, however, continued to avail of the Drawing Power (DP) against such rejected stocks also, at their full value, though these were now left worth scraps only. Fortunately, a branch of another bank was later opened in the vicinity of the unit's factory, and the former bank, most willingly and readily, transferred the account of the company to the other bank, the day such a request was made by the company.

This example is cited only to highlight and stress the point that if some stocks are not moving at all for long, or has slow moving items, there must, undoubtedly, be something wrong somewhere, worth enquiring into.

It reminds me of yet another case. A cycle manufacturing unit had huge stocks of some non-moving items of bicycle parts, like hubs, chain, wheels, spokes, etc. On enquiry, however, the Managing Director of the company confided with me that these were the high value and scarcely imported items and so these were being used very sparingly. But, when I asked him to show me an 'imported' bicycle assembled with these non-moving items, he had to confess that these constituted only the few odd parts of the erstwhile imported bicycle, and, as, such, these were of no value, whatsoever. Thus, sometimes it pays if pleas advanced by the borrowers are not taken at their face value. Instead, a cross-examination may help us to get some hidden facts and facets revealed, to the advantage of the bankers and other creditors.

(*c*) Where the number of items charged to the bank is large, the inspecting officers may check such items on the principle of 'ABC Analysis', whereby all 'A' class (high value) items may be checked thoroughly during each visit. Only a certain percentage of 'B' and 'C' class items, however, may be checked during each visit so that all such items may be covered within, say six months. Goods should be stocked according to volume or size, weight, lots, groups, etc., to facilitate the inspection.

Example:

While verifying the stocks, at one of the godowns, a bank officer got more than 10 lakh pieces of pocket combs physically counted and detected a shortage of some 4000 pieces. He pointed this shortage to the borrower with a 'victorious' smile on his face, despite the fact that the entire shortage accounted for hardly Rs. 400, @ Rs. 100 per thousand pieces. The borrower naturally felt sorry and belittled, but instantaneously brought back a big box full of such pocket combs containing roughly more than a lakh pieces.

Such low value 'C' category items should have better been verified with eye estimates, rather than wasting the valuable time on counting of such lowest of the low value items, piece by piece.

Similarly, it will augur well if bank officers could acquire the skill and expertise to find out an approximate weight, in case of very heavy-weight items (like iron ores and ingots, stocked in heaps of say, 5 tonnes each, or steel strips of varied thickness and width stocked in coils, etc.), just through an eye-estimate. Adopting a very time consuming and expensive process of getting the entire stocks physically weighed each time, may prove to be very impractical and even imprudent. But, such an expertise may be acquired by bank officers through constant practice and experience. The inspecting officers of companies, too, may adopt such techniques while verifying the company's stocks of inventories and stores periodically.

(*d*) Stocks-in-process should be in proportion to the time required for conversion of raw materials into finished goods.

(*e*) Activity level may be assessed from the order book, daily production register, general tempo of the activity in the unit, number of shifts, etc.

(*f*) Outstandings in loan accounts should be related to the activity level, and actual activity levels should be compared with the projected levels. Reasons for major adverse variance, if any, should be enquired into. Debit and credit summations on the accounts are also good indicators of the level of production and sales of units.

(*g*) When there is a decline in sales, production and/or profitability, the reasons therefore should be ascertained, and remedial measures should be taken promptly.

(*h*) Idle machinery, rejected items, and additions or disposal of fixed assets, should also be checked.

(*i*) Unit's accounts should be scrutinised periodically and where the accounts are irregular due to non-payment of instalments or excess drawings, the entrepreneurs should be promptly advised to regularise the position urgently.

(*j*) Bills outstanding in Cash Credit (Bills) account beyond a reasonable period (depending upon the lead time and transit time) need enquiry.

(*k*) Sales through associate or sister concerns, and the bills drawn on them for the purpose, should be monitored with extra care.

(*l*) The reasons for the return of bills or undue delay in their payments should be enquired into.

(*m*) Bills outstanding in the bank's books should be compared and cross checked with the unit's bills receivable registers.

(*n*) The position of orders pending, being executed and anticipated, should be enquired into and matched with the production and sales. This should be followed up in subsequent inspections.

(*o*) The inspecting officers should discuss with the company's management the general trend in the market, the unit's problems regarding supply of raw materials, labour and infrastructural facilities, performance of the unit's competitors, future plans, etc., and share their own experiences of other similar units. This would give them a clue to the imminent problems of the unit, if any.

(*p*) Surplus cash generated, its utilisation, the management of cash and working capital should be monitored.

(*q*) Where goods are stored in different places, inspection of all the godowns should be conducted simultaneously on the same day.

While taking over the charge of an industrial finance branch of the State Bank of India in Kanpur, I inspected one of the godowns of a borrowal unit and wanted to verify the stocks stored in the other godown too the same evening. The Managing Director of the company, however, suggested to me to defer the inspection to the next morning, as it had already been quite late in the evening.

I agreed, though reluctantly. The very next morning, I inspected stocks stored in other godown of the same borrower and immediately thereafter proceeded to inspect the first godown, too, though I had already verified the stocks stored therein only last evening. And, my suspicion came true; the entire stock of the first godown had been shifted to the second one overnight.

(*r*) Market enquiries may also be made about the unit.

(*s*) Inspection card/register should be filled in after each inspection.

(*t*) Godown cards should also be properly placed in godowns, duly tied or pressed, to avoid their loss or destruction.

Example:

One of the borrowers of the State Bank of India (SBI) had fraudulently taken concurrent borrowings from another bank also, on the security of pledge of the same stocks stored in the same godown, having two entry doors on the opposite sides of the godown. One day, when the godown-keeper of State Bank of India (SBI) had gone to effect the delivery of some stocks from the godown, he, to his utter surprise, happened to see that the godown-keeper of the other bank had also come to the godown premises. And, on enquiry he found that the same stocks were pledged to the other bank, too. Being a smart and intelligent person, he immediately rushed to his branch office, took the required number of locks, engraved with the name of the bank thereon, and locked all the entrances to the godown from outside, even over and above the locks of the other bank, wherever these were found. Besides, all the doors were locked from inside, too, which could be used as an incontrovertible evidence as to which of the two banks actually had the entry into the godown. Further, as per the practice of State Bank of India (SBI), the godown card was also kept inside the godown, wherein the entries, matching with the entries in the godown register, appeared on a day-to-day basis.

Thus, in the court of law, the State Bank of India (SBI) could prove, beyond doubt, that the officials of State Bank of India (SBI) alone had the entry inside the godown, and that the other bank apparently and obviously had put on its lock later, and that, too, only from outside, as there was no documentary (or even circumstantial) evidence to prove that its officials had ever gone inside the godown.

It is, therefore, suggested that bank officers must invariably make a thorough inspection of godowns (in a completely empty state) wherein goods are proposed to be stocked and stored, and ultimately pledged to the Bank, so that all the entries into the godown, from outside, could be thoroughly checked. Further, all doors and locking arrangements should be verified to be strong enough to prevent any easy unauthorised entry into the godown. As a matter of abundant precaution, all the entry doors and windows of the godown should be locked from inside, too, to prevent any unauthorised entry from outside. And, all the locks affixed therein must bear the bank's name prominently engraved thereon, so as to constitute as a public notice that stocks stored therein are already pledged to the bank. A prominently painted sign board should also be distinctly displayed at the main entrance to the godown, as also on the other side walls, etc.

(*u*) All units should be advised to maintain visitors' books at the place of business and the inspecting officers should note down irregularities observed during the inspection. On return to the bank, the entrepreneurs should be advised, in writing, about the irregularities observed, with a request to set right the position immediately. During their next visit, attention should be paid to check the progress made in regard to the rectification of irregularities observed, during the previous visits.

The above instructions of the bank, regarding periodical supervision and follow-up of advances, are considered sufficiently detailed, clear and effective, with a view to ensuring the safety of the bank's advances, and the health of the units, on an on-going basis. The banks have also been reasonable in stipulating that such detailed supervision and follow-up were required to be done by the inspecting officers in case of advances of higher value like over Rs. 2 lakh or so.

Frequency of Inspection

The frequency of inspections, for different quantum of advances, may be fixed by banks somewhat on the following lines:

Sl.No.	*Quantum of Advances*	*Frequency of Inspection*
1.	Loans, say up to Rs. 2 lakh	Once in 3 months by the field officers
2.	Loans, say above Rs. 2 lakh and up to Rs. 5 lakh	Once in 2 months by the field officers
3.	Loans, say above Rs. 5 lakh	Monthly by the field officers

Chief managers of branches with SBI Division, SBI branches and special branches, and managers/deputy managers of SBI Division may, however, be required to inspect units with loans above Rs. 5 lakh, once in 9 months and 6 months respectively.

For the first-four months of disbursement of the loan, however, inspection should be done by the field officers on a monthly basis in all cases, inasmuch as more than ordinary care needs to be exercised to monitor activities of new units and to rectify initial difficulties, if any.

In case of unsatisfactory accounts, the inspection is required to be carried out at shorter intervals, irrespective of the loan amount, till the units are nursed back to health or the loans are called up and recovered.

The Branch Manager is required to verify the Inspection Register each month to find out the units not inspected during the previous month, and to ensure that such units are inspected during the current month.

Flaws Observed in the Supervision and Follow-up of Advances by the Bank Officers

Systems and procedures laid down by banks for supervision and follow-up of advances, as discussed in the foregoing pages, are found to be sufficiently exhaustive and clear, with a view to detecting early signals of sickness, and arresting and rectifying the malady in time, at the incipient stage itself, so that all units, financed by banks, could perform on healthy lines, on an on-going basis. But, there seems to be something significantly wanting in the implementation of these systems and procedures by the bank officers. For example:

(*a*) In some cases, stocks of inventory, charged to the bank, get depleted, completely or substantially, over a period of time.

(*b*) In some other cases, the bank officers allow frequent overdrawings on the accounts, well above the drawing powers, and even, sometimes, above the sanctioned limits.

Reasons for Lack of Effective Supervision and Follow-up of Advances by Bank Officers

Personal interviews with bank officers, both at the branch level and by controlling offices, have revealed that the extant instructions regarding the supervision and follow-up of advances were not being meticulously and effectively followed by bank officers at the branches for several reasons, viz.

1. Lack of job knowledge and skills on the part of the field officers.
2. Paucity of field officers to cope with the ever increasing work-load at the branches.
3. Lack of willingness on the part of the field officers to inspect units periodically, as stipulated by the bank.
4. Lack of efforts on the part of the bank officers to apprise the entrepreneurs of adverse effects and ramifications of non-adherence to the bank's financial discipline.

Suggestions

1. Suggestions for Improving the Job Knowledge and Skills of the Field Officers

(*a*) It is suggested that banks should impart institutional training to field officers who are lacking in the job knowledge and skills, in the areas of supervision and follow-up of advances. These areas may be covered in the special courses for industrial finance, but, with a shift in the emphasis from imparting conceptual knowledge through theoretical lectures, as at present, to developing the required skills and pragmatic approach through practical exercises, live cases, and visits to the units.

(*b*) Besides the institutional training, branch managers and managers (SBI Division) should invest some of their valuable time in imparting practical training to the field officers. They should, for the first few months, take field officers along, while going for inspection of some units, for imparting on-the-job training to them. This way, the managers would become 'gurus' (teachers) to the members of the staff, and would enjoy 'personal power', in addition to their 'position power', making them more effective in the discharge of their managerial role and responsibility.

2. Suggestions for Solving Problems of Paucity of Field Officers at Branch Level

Problems of paucity of field officers at the branch level may better be tackled by the bank from two directions simultaneously:

(*i*) By suitably augmenting the strength of the field officers at the branches, and

(*ii*) By rationally reducing the work-load of field officers.

(i) Augmenting the Staff Strength at Branch Level

(*a*) It is suggested that the required number of additional field officers should be posted at the branches, specially at the intensive centre branches, having sufficiently large number of units enjoying credit limits, say of over Rs. 2 lakh, so that each field officer may be required to effectively supervise only a limited number of units, as stipulated by banks.

(*b*) Personal interviews with bank officers have revealed that at some branches, specially at the urban and metropolitan centres, the staff position was rather comfortable, as compared to most of the branches in the semi-urban and rural areas. It is, therefore, suggested that the bank should rationally deploy the staff amongst its branches.

(ii) With a view to rationally reducing the work-load of Field Officers, the banks may consider the following suggestions

(*a*) Small loans under the government sponsored schemes like SEEUY, SEPUP, etc., may not be encouraged at the intensive centre branches, already burdened with high-value advances. Such advances may, instead, be diverted to other neighbouring branches. Siphoning off of such existing small loans, from the intensive centre branches to some neighbouring branches, may as well be considered. This would save sufficient time of the field officers at the intensive centre branches to effectively supervise the advances of higher value.

(*b*) Further, while the field officers may be required to supervise advances of, say, Rs. 1 lakh and over, the supervision and follow-up of the other smaller advances, say, below Rs. 1 lakh, may be delegated to other junior officers.

(*c*) Moreover, the frequency of inspection of units by the field officers may be modified somewhat on the lines, as suggested in Table 10.2.

Table 10.2: Present and Proposed Frequencies of Inspection of Units by the Field Officers

Sl. No.	*Quantum of Loans*	*Present Frequency of Inspection (Presumed)*	*Proposed Frequency of Inspection*
(*i*)	Loans up to Rs. 1 lakh	Once in 3 months	Once in, say, 6 months
(*ii*)	Loans above Rs. 1 lakh and up to Rs. 5 lakh	Once in 2 months	Once in, say, 4 months
(*iii*)	Loans above Rs. 5 lakh and up to Rs. 10 lakh	Once in 2 months	Once in, say, 3 months
(*iv*)	Loans above Rs. 10 lakh and up to Rs. 20 lakh	Once in 1 month	Once in, say, 2 months
(*v*)	Loans above Rs. 20 lakh	Once in 1 month	No change suggested

(*d*) In addition, branches may categorise their advances into:

(*i*) satisfactory,

(*ii*) temporarily irregular, and

(*iii*) unsatisfactory, and gradually increase the rigour of their supervision and follow-up, accordingly.

3. Suggestions for Enforcing Discipline Among Field Officers

(*a*) Insincere and recalcitrant field officers deserve to be dealt with firmly. **Where persuasion fails, punitive measures must prevail.** Any dereliction of duty must be dealt with severely.

(*b*) Branch managers should not pass the TA bills of field officers without perusing their Inspection Diary and satisfying themselves that the necessary corrective steps have been initiated by the field officers, wherever necessary.

4. Suggestions for Enforcing the Bank's Financial Discipline on the Entrepreneurs

(*a*) It is suggested that bank officers should apprise the prospective entrepreneurs of the dangers and adverse ramifications of diversion of funds, frequent and excess over-drawings on the account, and such other violations of the bank's financial discipline, and counsel them to guard against them.

(*b*) It would also be a good idea to arrange a one-day seminar (a banker-borrower meet), branch-wise, in the branch premises or in some hotel. It would serve as a good forum for an interface between the branch staff and the borrowers enabling them to appreciate the problems of, and expectations from, each other. The presence of the Regional Manager or the Assistant General Manager, in such meets, would give even the controlling office a first-hand feedback regarding the position of advances at the branches and the practical difficulties being experienced by the borrowers.

(*c*) Regional managers and assistant general managers, during the course of their periodical visits to the branches, would do well to visit some high value units and discuss the problems and prospects with the borrowers. This way, the borrowers will feel that they are being cared for by the bank, and the regional managers and the assistant general managers would get to know of the unsatisfactory features, if any, attached with such advances.

5. Suggestions for Streamlining the Bank's Performance Monitoring of Units and Management Information System (MIS)

With a view to streamlining the bank's system of performance monitoring, a follow-up form may be introduced by the bank on the lines of the suggested proforma placed at Annexure-10.1 at the end of the chapter.

The proforma contains three parts:

Part-I: Control Card (The Unit at a Glance)

It contains particulars about the unit, relevant for the effective control and security of the advance. It may be got printed on a hard paper and placed in the relative files of the unit concerned, for perusal and review of the position of these accounts by the bank's inspecting officers at regular quarterly intervals.

Part-II: Performance Monitoring of the Unit

This part includes main indicators of the unit's performance, viz. levels of activity (production, sales, etc.), profitability, cash management, liquidity position, etc. This part is required to be compiled by the bank's inspecting officers.

Part-III: Quarterly Information System (QIS Form)

This part also contains all the particulars provided in Part-II, except Item No. 5, and is required to be submitted by the borrowers to the Branch Manager at regular quarterly intervals. This would give a meaningful feedback to the entrepreneurs also, as to in which area(s) they were faltering.

Further, keeping in view the quantum of work at the branches, it is suggested that such statements may be submitted only by the units enjoying aggregate credit limits of over Rs. 2 lakh or even over Rs. 5 lakh, and that too, at regular quarterly intervals. These statements should be thoroughly and meaningfully examined at the branch level and need not be sent to the controlling office. Any adverse features observed therein should be looked into and necessary remedial measures initiated, in consultation with the borrowers concerned. Such regular performance monitoring undertaken, both by the bank and the borrower, and timely corrective actions taken, in mutual cooperation of each other, may go a long way in ensuring the financial health of the companies, on an on-going basis.

10.5 TIMELY DETECTION OF EARLY SYMPTOMS OF SICKNESS

Objective

The objective of timely detection of early symptoms of sickness by bank officers, as also by industries, should enable them to take timely corrective actions, in close coordination with each other, so as to remedy the malady at the incipient stage itself.

Reserve Bank of India, in their circular letter dated January 03, 1987, had rightly advised all the banks that "a culture of identifying the sickness symptoms of assisted units and rendering possible assistance with speed has to be enforced to prevent increasing sickness due to delays and consequent burden to the borrowers and losses to the bank."

Symptoms of Sickness

Symptoms of sickness can be detected in the following areas:

1. Conduct of Bank Accounts by Unit

(*i*) Non-routing of sale proceeds through the account, *i.e.* credit summations in the account, are not commensurate with the total sales.

(*ii*) Frequent requests for excess drawings.

(*iii*) Non-payment of term loan instalments.

(*iv*) Non-payment of interest applied periodically.

(*v*) Irregular or non-submission or delayed submission of stock statements and/or financial statements.

(*vi*) Frequent removal of bills from the cover.

(*vii*) Frequent dishonour of bills or cheques.

(*viii*) Raising of accommodation bills or cheques.

(*ix*) Progressive reduction in the number and amount of bills lodged with the bank.

(*x*) Repetition of the same item in the stock statements or in the list of sundry debtors, indicating non-movement of stocks and poor recovery of sundry debtors.

2. Levels of Unit Activities

A. Production

(*i*) Low capacity utilisation (of both men and machines).

(*ii*) Frequent closure of units.

(*iii*) Fluctuations in the capacity utilisation in non-seasonal activities.

(*iv*) High internal rate of rejection of products.

(*v*) Inadequate maintenance of machinery, resulting in frequent breakdowns.

B. Sales

(*i*) Decrease in sales turnover.

(*ii*) Inability to meet delivery schedule.

(*iii*) Frequent customer complaints.

(*iv*) High external rate of rejection of products.

(*v*) Non-moving/non-usable stocks.

3. **Financial Indicators**

(*i*) Negative liquid surplus, *i.e.* current ratio less than one.

(*ii*) Increase in sundry creditors and sundry debtors.

(*iii*) Increase in debt/equity ratio.

(*iv*) Decrease in net profit to sales ratio.

(*v*) External borrowings at exorbitant rates of interest.

(*vi*) Excessive drawings by promoters or directors.

(*vii*) Changing pattern of cash to credit sales.

(*viii*) Non-payment of statutory dues.

(*ix*) Sale of fixed assets.

Reasons for Non-detection of Early Symptoms of Sickness by the Bank Officers

Personal interviews with bank officers have revealed that the branch field staff avoided to record and refer such unsatisfactory features to the higher authorities as it involved more work for them by way of closer performance monitoring of such units, failing which they could be held personally responsible by the bank.

Personal interviews with entrepreneurs, however, have revealed that instead of discussing their genuine problems and financial difficulties with bank officers, freely and frankly, they preferred to conceal them, at the initial stages, apprehending that the bank may adopt a strict and unhelpful attitude towards them.

In the process, the small maladies, not tackled and remedied at the incipient stage, keep on accumulating and ultimately the units become non-viable, beyond rehabilitation, to the mutual detriment of both the banks and the borrowers.

Suggestions

(*a*) It is, therefore, suggested that the bank officers should work in close coordination with entrepreneurs, in an atmosphere of mutual trust and confidence, and with the positive attitude of timely and sustained help and cooperation towards each other, based on the genuineness of the problem and sincerity of purpose. Bank officers may, however, bear in mind that the symptoms of sickness, discussed earlier, are sometimes found even in healthy units. They may, therefore, take suitable action, based on the merit of each case.

(*b*) Further, the cases of dereliction of duty on the part of the operating staff, in regard to detection of early symptoms of sickness and initiation of suitable remedial measures in time should be severely dealt with by the banks.

10.6 SUPERVISION AND CONTROL OF IRREGULARITIES IN ADVANCES (OBTAINING AT THE BANK'S BRANCHES) BY THE CONTROLLING AUTHORITY

Objectives

Objectives of the system of reporting irregularities in advances by branches to the controlling authority, at periodical intervals are:

(*a*) To provide the controlling authority with the total picture of the position regarding the irregular accounts at branches for control and monitoring purposes.

(*b*) To enable the controlling authority to help and guide branches in taking some further suitable corrective measures, in addition to the those already initiated by the branch staff, to regularise the position of the accounts, and to keep the interest of the bank, as also that of the borrowers, safeguarded at all times.

Suggestions

During the course of discussions with the bank officers, it has been gathered that the controlling office, in its over-anxiety to exercise rather absolute control over the advances at the branches, was gradually loosening its grip thereon. It was generally felt that the system of control, prevalent in the sixties and seventies, may not necessarily prove effective in the new millennium too. The circumstances have changed. The delegation of power of the bank officers has recently been suitably revised upward to cope with the ever increasing quantum of advances. The level of trust reposed in bank officers also needs to go up accordingly. Consequently, the extent of control over the branches by the controlling office may be reduced suitably, somewhat on the lines suggested hereunder:

(*a*) Only the undernoted category of irregular accounts may be reported in detail by the branches to the controlling office as on the last Friday of each quarter:

All accounts with credit limits of over Rs. 2 lakh standing irregular, as on the date of the statement, by more than 10% of the amount of the sanctioned limit, or in excess of some specified amount, in case of each branch, whichever is lower.

(*b*) Irregularities due to application of interest for the quarter in question may not be reported.

(*c*) Irregularities allowed during the quarter, within the discretionary powers of the Branch Manager, and subsequently rectified as on the date of the statement, may not be reported.

(*d*) Irregularities allowed on the accounts beyond the discretionary powers of the Branch Manager, however, may continue to be reported separately in each case, for reporting and ratification purposes.

(*e*) In the case of loans up to Rs. 2 lakh, a summary of accounts irregular by more than 10% of the sanctioned limit, may be enclosed to the main statement.

(*f*) All irregular accounts not reported in the statements must be got rectified at the branch level within a reasonable period, under the direct supervision of the Branch Manager.

(*g*) A separate summary of loans up to Rs. 2 lakh, which are persistently irregular for more than three quarters, inclusive of accounts, which are irregular for more than three quarters due to application of interest, should be enclosed to the quarterly statement of, say June, every year.

(*h*) In the case of such persistently irregular accounts of over Rs. 2 lakh, each case must be reported to the controlling office separately, with reasoned recommendations whether to treat the unit as sick or otherwise, and if declared sick, whether considered viable for rehabilitation or rated as non-viable, justifying calling up of the loan. The required action must also be initiated promptly.

The suggested changes in the quarterly statements of irregular accounts, excluding smaller accounts and smaller irregularities in other accounts, would considerably reduce the quantum of work involved, facilitating its submission by branches regularly thereby ensuring effective control of the advances by the controlling office. Further, the non-submission or inordinately delayed submission of these statements must be taken up with the defaulting branches strongly and dealt with severely.

10.7 REHABILITATION OF VIABLE SICK UNITS BY BANKS

Objectives

The objective of bank's rehabilitation programme is to bring the viable sick units back to health by restoring their capacity to generate internal cash surplus. It has been mostly observed and widely accepted that in most of the cases, the commercial banks take unduly long time in identifying and declaring a borrowal unit as sick, to the mutual disadvantage of the bank and borrowers. And, by the time any unit is declared sick, its ailments turn into terminal cancer, and that too, mostly of the last stage.

The effective measures for, and the management of, a comprehensive package and programme for the rehabilitation of sick units, however, is not the scope of the book. The readers interested in some detailed discussion on this topic may look to the other book by the author, '*Sickness in Small Scale Sector: Causes and Cures*' (with special reference to the role of commercial banks), published by Concept Publishing Company, New Delhi (1999).

However, as rigorous and regular monthly monitoring and review of the performance and progress of sick industrial units, under the bank's rehabilitation programme, are of great significance and value for the success of the revival of the unit, a suggested proforma for 'Monthly Performance Report', to be submitted by;

(*i*) the unit to the bank (Part-I) and;

(*ii*) by the branch to the controlling authorities (Part-II), is placed at Annexure 10.2, at the end of the chapter.

Appendix 10.1

FOLLOW-UP FORM FOR USE BY THE BANK'S INSPECTING OFFICERS

PART-I: Control Card

(The Unit at a Glance)

1. Name of the unit
2. Constitution
3. Address
   (*i*) Office
   (*ii*) Factory
4. Telephone Number [Fax Number] E-mail
   (*i*) Office
   (*ii*) Factory
5. (*i*) Name(s) of the Proprietor/Partners/Directors
   (*ii*) Name(s) of key person(s)
6. Products manufactured
7. Installed capacity
   (*i*) Quantity per annum
   (*ii*) Value per annum (Rs.)
8. Credit facilities

Facility	Limit
(*a*)	
(*b*)	
(*c*)	
(*d*)	

9. Date of sanction/last renewal
10. Collateral security
11. Due dates
    (*a*) For renewal of documents
    (*b*) For renewal of insurance policies
    (*c*) For renewal of working capital limits
    (*d*) Of medium term loan instalments

Amount (Rs.)	Due Date

12. Inspection due in the month of	Inspection conducted on (date)
______________________	______________________
______________________	______________________
______________________	______________________
______________________	______________________

PART-II: Performance Monitoring of the Unit

(For use by the Bank's Inspecting Officers for units enjoying working capital limits of over Rs. 2 lakh)

Name of the Unit: Messrs ____________________

Report for the quarter ended ____________________

1. Production

Budgeted	Actual	Variance	Reasons for variance
Quantity/	Quantity/	Quantity/	
(Value Rs.)	(Value Rs.)	(Value Rs.)	

2. Sales

Budgeted	Actual	Variance	Reasons for variance
Quantity/	Quantity/	Quantity/	
(Value Rs.)	(Value Rs.)	(Value Rs.)	

3. Purchases

Budgeted	Actual	Variance	Reasons for variance
Quantity/	Quantity/	Quantity/	
(Value Rs.)	(Value Rs.)	(Value Rs.)	

4. Performance of Working Capital Loan Account

(*a*) (*i*) Drawing power Rs.

(*ii*) Debit balance Rs.

(*iii*) Amount of irregularity, if any, Rs.

(*iv*) Reasons for the irregularity

(*v*) Remedial measures taken for regularising the position

(*b*) (*i*) Debit summations for the period under review Rs.

(*ii*) Credit summations for the period under review Rs.

(*iii*) If credit summations are not commensurate with the actual sales for the period, the reasons therefore

5. Review of Bills Receivable

	No.	Value (Rs.)
(*i*) Bills withdrawn from the cover during the period under review		
(*ii*) Reasons for delay in payment		
(*iii*) Bills returned unpaid during the period under review		
(*iv*) Reasons for such return		

(*v*) Does the frequency of withdrawals/return of bills [specially those drawn on one or a few drawee(s)], reveal any unsatisfactory features? If so, what corrective steps have been taken?

6. Performance of Term Loan Account

(*i*) Are the Instalments (with interest) paid up-to-date? YES/NO

(*ii*) If reply to 6(*i*) is 'NO', the position of overdue instalments No. of instalments....... Amount of Principal (Rs.).......
Amount of Interest (Rs.) ....

(*iii*) Reasons for non-payment of instalments

(*iv*) Steps taken to regularise the position

7. General Remarks

PART-III: Quarterly Information System (QIS Form)

(To be submitted to the Bank Manager by Units enjoying Working Capital limits of over Rs. 2 lakh)

Name of the Unit: Messrs ______________________________

For the quarter ended ______________________________

1. Production

Budgeted	Actual	Variance	Reasons for variance
Quantity/ (Value Rs.)	Quantity/ (Value Rs.)	Quantity/ (Value Rs.)	

2. Sales

Budgeted	Actual	Variance	Reasons for variance
Quantity/ (Value Rs.)	Quantity/ (Value Rs.)	Quantity/ (Value Rs.)	

3. Purchases

Budgeted	Actual	Variance	Reasons for variance
Quantity/ (Value Rs.)	Quantity/ (Value Rs.)	Quantity/ (Value Rs.)	

4. Performance of Working Capital Loan Account

(*a*) (*i*) Drawing power Rs.

(*ii*) Debit balance Rs.

(*iii*) Amount of irregularity, if any, Rs.

(*iv*) Reasons for the irregularity

(*v*) Remedial measures taken for regularising the position

(*b*) (*i*) Debit summations for the period under review Rs.

(*ii*) Credit summations for the period under review Rs.

(*iii*) If credit summations are not commensurate with the actual sales for the period, the reasons therefore

5. Review of Bills Receivable

	No.	Value (Rs.)
(*i*) Bills withdrawn from the cover during the period under review		
(*ii*) Reasons for the delay in payment		
(*iii*) Bills returned unpaid during the period under review		
(*iv*) Reasons for such return		

6. Performance of Term Loan Account

(*i*) Are the instalments, (with interest) paid up-to-date? YES/NO

(*ii*) If reply to 6(*i*) is "NO", the position of overdue instalments No. of instalments....... Amount of principal (Rs.)....... Amount of interest (Rs.) ....

(*iii*) Reasons for non-payment of instalments

(*iv*) Steps taken to regularise the position

7. General Remarks

Note: Simpler forms, on the suggested lines, may be designed and used by the bank concerned, for small advances say, up to Rs. 2 lakh.

Appendix 10.2

MONTHLY PERFORMANCE REPORT

For the month of ____________________ 20__

PART-I: INFORMATION FROM THE UNIT

(To be submitted to the Bank Manager by the Unit under the Bank's Rehabilitation Programme)

Name of the Unit: Messrs ____________________

Name of the Branch (of the Bank) ____________________

Date of Implementation of the Rehabilitation Programme ____________________

1. Production and Sales

(Rs. in lakh)

Item	*Actuals from the month of April (progressive figures)*	*Performance during the month under review*			*Budgeted level for the next month*
		B*	A*	V*	
1	2	3	4	5	6
1. Production					
(*a*) Quantity					
(*b*) Value (Rs.)					
2. Sales					
3. Receipts/Realisation					
4. Payments					
5. Sundry debtors					
6. Sundry creditors					

* B* Budgeted; A* = Actual; V* = Variance

Comments on adverse variances, if any:

2. Cumulative Position

(*i*) Projected Annual Sales – Rs.

(*ii*) Sales up to the last month – Rs.

(*iii*) Sales in the current month – Rs.

3. Break-even Level

(*i*) Projected

(*a*) per annum

(*b*) per month

(*ii*) Actual (average) per month

4. Break-up of the Outstanding Accounts Receivable (Sundry Debtors or Bills Receivable)

Age	*No.of Bills*	*Amount (Rs.)*	*Expected Date of Realisation*
(*i*) Over 1 year (*ii*) 181 days to 1 year (*iii*) 91 days to 180 days (*iv*) 61 to 90 days (*v*) 31 to 60 days (*vi*) up to 30 days			

4.1 Position of bills returned unpaid

	No. of Bills	*Amount*
(*i*) Total bills submitted from April 1 to the current month		Rs.
(*ii*) Total bills returned unpaid		Rs.
(*iii*) Percentage		
(*iv*) Reasons for return of such bills		
(*a*)		
(*b*)		
(*c*)		

5. Break-up of Stocks

(*i*) Total value of stocks Rs.

(*ii*) High-value stocks Rs.

(*iii*) Slow-moving/Non-moving stocks (*i.e.* value of stocks stored for more than 3 months)

(*a*) Raw Materials Rs.

(*b*) Finished Goods Rs.

6. Current Financial Position of the Unit

Current Liabilities (C.L.)			*Current Assets (C.A.)*		
Previous month	*Items*	*Current month*	*Previous month*	*Items*	*Current month*
	• Bank Borrowings • Sundry Creditors • Statutory Dues • Others			• Stocks of Inventory • Sundry Debtors • Cash and near cash • Advances • Others	
	TOTAL			**TOTAL**	

6.1 ***(i)*** **Liquid Surplus (CA-CL)** (*a*) Estimated; and (*b*) Actual

(ii) **Current Ratio (CA-CL)** (*a*) Estimated; and (*b*) Actual

7. Order Book Position

7.1 Pending Orders

Name of buyers Amount (Rs.) Expected date of completion of orders

7.2 Expected Orders

Name of prospective buyers Amount (Rs.) Date by when expected

8. Performance Statement for the Month of ________________, with Projections for the Next Month

	Current Month		*Next Month*
	Projections 1	*Actuals* 2	*Projections* 3
(*i*) **Raw Materials**			
Opening Stocks			
Purchases			
Consumption			
Closing Stock			
(*ii*) **Stocks-in-Process**			
Opening Stock			
Additions			
Conversions			
Closing Stock			
(*iii*) **Finished Goods**			
Opening Stock			
Production			
Sales			
Closing Stock			
(*iv*) **Sundry Creditors**			
Opening Balance			
Purchases (Credit)			
Payments			
Closing Balance			
(*v*) **Sundry Debtors**			
Opening Balance			
Sales (Credit)			
Receipts			
Closing Balance			

9. Cash Flow Statement for the Month of ____________________, with Projections for the Next Month

	Current Month		Next Month
	Projections 1	*Actuals* 2	*Projections* 3
(*i*) **Cash Inflow**			
Cash Receipts			
Bill Realisations			
Miscellaneous			
Others, *e.g.* fresh capital			
TOTAL (A)			
(*ii*) **Cash Outflow**			
Cash Purchases			
Creditors			
Consumable Stores			
Fuel			
Wages and Salary			
Administrative Expenses			
Power			
Maintenance, etc.			
Miscellaneous			
Bank Interest			
TOTAL (B)			
Surplus/Deficit (A–B)			
Outstandings in the Bank account at the end of the month			

(Signature of the Unit's Representative)

Date: ____________

PART-II: INFORMATION FROM BRANCHES OF THE BANK

(To be submitted to the Controlling Office by the Branch Manager along with PART-I)

10. Position of Accounts as on ________________ 20_

Facility and Limit	*Market Value of Stocks*	*Advance Value of Stocks*	*Drawing Power*	*Outstandings*	*Irregularity*	*Clean*
TOTAL						

11. Date of Stock Statements: ____________________________

12. Summations

Sl. No.	*Period*	*Debit Summations*	*Credit Summations*
(*i*)	From April up to the last month		
(*ii*)	During the current month		
	TOTAL		

13. Date of the Last Inspection of the Unit

(*i*) By the Field Officer

(*ii*) By the Manager (SIB)

(*iii*) By the Branch Manager

14. Comments/Reasons for Irregularities, if any, under each facility.

15. General comments on the 'conduct of the account' and the 'implementation of the rehabilitation programme.'

(Signature of the Branch Manager)

Date: ____________

Note: Simpler forms, on the suggested lines, may be designed and used by the banks for small advances up to Rs. 2 lakh.

A SYNOPTIC NOTE
(CHAPTER 10 AT A GLANCE)

Disbursement and Follow-up of Working Capital Finance by Banks

Main Features of Credit Risk Management

They are:

(*a*) Realistic assessment and speedy sanction of credit needs;

(*b*) Phased disbursement of loans; and

(*c*) Post-disbursement supervision and follow-up of advances, *i.e.* periodical monitoring of the financial health of the units.

These are the three main features of effective credit risk management, both by the banks and industries.

The success depends on the following series of seven steps, viz.

(*i*) Prompt and realistic project appraisal, including, inter-alia, the economic viability and technical feasibility;

(*ii*) Prompt and realistic appraisal of credit needs;

(*iii*) Phased disbursement of loans, ensuring proper end-use of funds;

(*iv*) Effective supervision and follow-up of advances, *i.e.* periodical performance monitoring of units, both (*a*) security based, and (*b*) activity based, *i.e.* in quantitative and qualitative terms respectively;

(*v*) Timely detection of early symptoms of sickness, at the incipient stage itself, and prompt remedial measures for rehabilitation;

(*vi*) Effective supervision of irregularities in advance at the branches by the controlling authorities; and

(*vii*) Prompt decision regarding viability or otherwise of the sick units, and speedy initiation of rehabilitation measures or recovery proceedings accordingly.

For effective implementation of all these seven steps in the right earnest, the banks, as also the industrial units, must properly understand and appreciate the following factors connected therewith:

(*a*) Objectives;

(*b*) Rationale behind such laid down systems and procedures by the banks;

(*c*) Presently prevailing positions in branches of banks;

(*d*) Flaws observed in (*c*) above;

(*e*) Reasons for such flaws; and

(*f*) Pragmatic remedial measures in realistic terms.

Both the banks and industries must be well aware of the various early signals and symptoms of sickness of units, and they must take early and effective steps, in full cooperation and coordination with each other, to remedy the situation at the earliest, to save the unit from falling seriously, chronically and terminally sick, beyond rehabilitation and recovery.

And, the term lending institutions should also realise that unless the working capital is well managed by units, they cannot earn sufficient profit to repay the periodical instalments on their term loans.

Thus, if a full and continued coordination and cooperation, with mutual trust and interdependence, are taken by banks (*i.e.* B), entrepreneurs (*i.e.* E) and term lending institutions (*i.e.* T), I 'BET' the incidence of industrial sickness can well be mitigated, and controlled, if not eliminated, altogether. Amen!

QUESTIONS
(For Self-assessment)

1. On what seven significant parameters/factors does the effective 'Credit Risks Management' largely depend?
2. (*a*) Discuss the rationale behind each of the undernoted seven factors for ensuring an effective Credit Risks Management (CRM) by the banks:
   (*i*) Prompt and realistic appraisal of projects, on receipt of the loan applications, along with the project reports.
   (*ii*) Prompt and realistic assessment of the credit requirements, both short-term (working capital) and long-term (term loan).
   (*iii*) Phased disbursement of loans to ensure the proper end-use of funds.
   (*iv*) Effective supervision and follow-up of advances and periodical performance monitoring of companies through intelligent scrutiny of their books of accounts, stock statements, financial statements, etc., coupled with personal dialogues with the owners and/or managers of companies.
   (*v*) Timely detection of early symptoms of sickness at the incipient stage itself, and prompt and effective implementation of suitable remedial measures to put companies back to health.
   (*vi*) Effective supervision and control of irregularities in advances by branches as also by the controlling authority.
   (*vii*) Prompt decision and action in regard to the rehabilitation of viable sick units, or calling up of advances of non-viable sick units.

   (*b*) What are the flaws generally observed in the actual implementation/execution of each of them in the present practices, prevailing at most of the branches of banks, specially in the public sector banks; and.

   (*c*) Your own pragmatic suggestions for mitigation (if not complete elimination) of flaws, pertaining to each of the aforesaid seven areas.
3. (*a*) Bring out the salient features connected with the following:
   (*i*) Quantitative (or security oriented) supervision and follow-up; and
   (*ii*) Qualitative (or activity oriented) supervision and follow-up of advances.

   (*b*) Which one of these two, in your own considered view, is more important and valuable? Give reasons for your answer.
4. What is the rationale behind the phased disbursement of working capital loans? Elucidate by citing suitable illustrative examples.

PART TWO

NON-FUND BASED WORKING CAPITAL FINANCING

11

LETTERS OF CREDIT

> *The best way to save money is not to lose it.* — ***Les Williams***

The Learning Points

The chapter aims at developing the knowledge and facilitating the understanding of:

- Rationale behind treating letters of Credit and Bank Guarantees as Non-fund based Financing of Working Capital
- Purpose of Issuing a Letter of Credit and its Contents
- Procedure for Issuing Letters of Credit
- Deposit of Margin Money against Letter of Credit
- Management of Credit Risks by banks while issuing Letters of Credit
- Different types of Bills of Exchange, like Demand and Time Bills of Exchange
- Definitions of Bill of Exchange, as per the Negotiable Instruments Act
- Different slabs of Stamp Duty Exigible on time (Usance) Bills of Exchange
- Detailed procedure for Calculation of Due Date of a Bill of Exchange made payable after a Specified Number of Days or Months
- Mode of presentation of Time Bills of Exchange for Acceptance and Payment
- Desirable mode of Acceptance of (Time) Bills
- Different Types of Letters of Credit, including Revolving Letters of Credit

Non-fund based working capital financing comprises:

(*i*) Letters of Credit (L/Cs), and

(*ii*) Bank Guarantees (B/Gs).

11.1 WHY CALLED NON-FUND BASED?

These are called non-fund based financing (or quasi-credit facilities) because, at the time of opening of the L/C or B/G, no amount, as such, becomes immediately payable. But, these facilities do involve some financial commitment on the part of the bank inasmuch as the bank is required to pay the amount of the bill (drawn under the L/C, and in meticulous compliance of all the terms and conditions stipulated therein), in the event of the applicant (borrower) refusing or being unable to honour the bill on presentation, at the material time.

The bank, however, is within its rights to proceed legally against the applicant (borrower) on the basis of the Letter of Request (counter guarantee and indemnity) executed by the applicant, at the time of the issuance of the Letter of Credit, on a duly stamped paper.

Similarly, no amount becomes payable by the bank at the time of execution of the B/G, but as per the undertaking (commitment) given by the bank, under the B/G issued, the bank will have to make payment of the amount, covered under the B/G, in the event of the invocation of the B/G by the beneficiary concerned. The bank may make the required payment by debit to the applicant's account, even if sufficient balance may not be available therein. The amount so overdrawn may have to be deposited by the applicant, in due course, failing which the bank may prefer to file a civil suit against the applicant to recover the amount, on the basis of the counter-guarantee executed by the applicant on the stamped paper, at the time of the issuance of the Bank Guarantee.

Thus, it is for the aforesaid reasons that the L/C and B/G are referred to as non-fund based working capital financing. And, accordingly, one should not harbour any misconception that L/Cs and B/Gs do not involve any financial commitments and risks. These facilities (L/C and B/G) are also referred to as Quasi-(or Semi) Credit Facilities for the same reasons.

And, as these facilities also involve financial risks, the amount, and the terms and conditions of the L/C and B/G, are also determined by the bank concerned, on the basis of all precautions taken, as is done at the time of granting fund based credit facilities (like stock cash credit), whereby the borrower gets the right to withdraw the amount immediately after sanction of the limit, of course, within the overall credit limit sanctioned and the Drawing Power (DP) available at the material time. Accordingly, the limits for L/C and B/G were also being stipulated well within the Maximum Permissible Bank Finance (MPBF). But now, the limits of L/C and B/G are sanctioned separately and are independent of the Assessed Bank Finance (ABF).

11.2 WHY LETTERS OF CREDIT (L/Cs)?

The buyer usually prefers to first receive goods to be bought and only after satisfying himself of the quality and quantity of goods supplied, he would like to make the payment. As against this, the seller usually prefers to first receive the full payment for goods to be supplied, and only then he would like to deliver the goods. And, if such a mutual distrust continues, the business transaction can hardly take place.

Here comes the facilitating role of the banking system which serves as a bridge (a common link) between the buyer and the seller, as both of them should be having their full faith in the banking system and the bank concerned.

The mechanism, used by the banker in this regard, is the Letter of Credit.

11.3 WHAT IS LETTER OF CREDIT (L/C)?

A Letter of Credit (L/C) is a written document issued by the Buyers' Banker (BBk), at the request of the buyer (B), in favour of the seller (S), whereby the buyer's banker (BBk) gives an undertaking to the seller (S) that, in the event of the seller tendering the Bill of Exchange to the seller's banker (SBk), along with all the required documents, in strict compliance of all the terms and conditions stipulated in the L/C , the entire amount of the bill is paid to the seller by the seller's banker (SBk), on behalf of the buyer's banker (BBk) immediately, as has been, in turn, undertaken by the buyer to his own banker (BBk).

The L/C is usually issued by the buyer's banker in quadruplicate. The buyer's banker sends the original and three copies to the respective parties involved, as under:

(*i*) The original L/C is sent to the paying (seller's) banker;

(*ii*) One copy is sent to the seller through his (seller's) banker, for his information and further necessary action;

(*iii*) One copy is sent to the buyer (B) for his information; and

(*iv*) One copy is retained by the issuing banker (BBk) for his office records and reference, whenever the documents, drawn under the L/C, are received for payment, or for issuance of amendments thereto, etc.

While the original L/C is duly stamped, as per the Indian Stamp Act, the other copies are unstamped; they are just marked as Not Negotiable copies, meant for the buyer, seller, and office copy.

The original L/C is sent by the buyer's banker, to the seller's banker, authorising him to make the full payment of the Bill of Exchange to the seller, provided all the documents, tendered by the seller, are in strict conformity with the terms and conditions stipulated therein (L/C). And, in the event of any of the terms and conditions, howsoever minor or apparently insignificant, being at variance with those stipulated in the L/C, the seller's banker should decline to make any payment to the seller against the documents tendered under the L/C in question.

The paying banker (seller's banker) should, instead, point out the deficiency/deficiencies found in the documents to the seller, suggesting to him either:

(*a*) to rectify the irregularities observed, or

(*b*) to contact the buyer, to approach his (buyer's) banker and arrange for the required amendments to the L/C, so that the paying (seller's) banker could honour and make payment against the bills drawn under the L/C. And, if so requested by the buyer, the buyer's banker may issue the required amendment, which can well be done by means of a simple letter on the letterhead of the bank (unstamped). Such an amendment letter is also sent by the buyer's banker to all the involved parties, as is usually done in the case of the issuance of the L/C, *i.e.*:

   (*i*) Original letter is sent to the seller's banker;

   (*ii*) One copy is sent to the seller's banker for onward transmission to the seller for his information and necessary action;

   (*iii*) One copy is sent to the buyer; and

   (*iv*) One copy is retained by the issuing (buyer's) banker for office records.

Under certain special circumstances, if so requested by the seller (preferably in writing, and that too, supported by the execution of a duly stamped indemnity bond), the paying (seller's) banker may make the payment to the seller in full, but 'under reserve'; that is, in case the payment is refused by the buyer, on the plea that some specific terms and conditions, stipulated in the L/C, were not fulfilled, the seller's banker will have the right to recover the amount (paid earlier 'under reserve'), immediately after coming to know of such refusal of the payment by the buyer.

The point may well be understood, with certainty, by citing a live case law in this regard.

11.4 CASE LAW

TO RETURN OR TO PAY

[*Source:* State Bank of India Monthly Review, Vol. 31 No. 5, May, 1992]

Riyadh House Establishment, Riyadh, Saudi Arabia (buyers),

Japson International, Ambala, India (seller),

National Commercial Bank, Riyadh (issuing banker, who had issued the L/C at the request of the buyer).

State Bank of India (the Paying Banker or Seller's Banker)

The Buyer's Banker had sent the L/C to The State Bank of India, Overseas Branch, Mumbai, who, in turn, had sent the L/C to The State Bank of India, Ambala Cantt. for onward transmission to the seller (the beneficiary of the L/C).

The seller opened a current account with State Bank of India, Ambala Cantt. branch and sent his first consignment of goods to the buyer at Riyadh.

But, when he handed over the documents, drawn under the L/C, the Chief Manager, State Bank of India, Ambala Cantt., pointed out the various discrepancies therein, which were not in strict conformity with the terms and conditions, laid down in the L/C. The Chief Manager, therefore, rightfully, declined to negotiate the bills and documents under the L/C.

Thereupon, the seller submitted a letter of request to the bank to the effect that the bank may negotiate the documents at his (seller's) risk and responsibility, despite the discrepancies.

Besides the letter of request, the seller executed an indemnity bond, too. And thus, the bank negotiated the documents 'under reserve' and credited the seller's account. The seller later sent the second, third and fourth consignments also, and in each case the banker pointed out the discrepancies and each time he had negotiated the documents 'under reserve', on the basis of the letter of request and the indemnity bond executed by the seller, in each case.

But, when the consignments reached Riyadh, the buyer refused to take delivery of the goods and honour the documents. The Chief Manager, State Bank of India, Ambala Cantt., in turn, informed the seller of dishonour of documents and requested him to pay back the entire amount paid 'under reserve' as aforesaid, along with the incidental changes. But, the seller failed to do so.

Therefore, the bank, after notice, filed a civil suit for recovery of the amount with interest. The bank also filed an application to the court, praying for an injunction restraining the partners of the seller-firm from withdrawing the amount lying to their credit with the bank, in the form of term deposits and current accounts in their personal names. The trial court, finding the balance of convenience in favour of the bank, granted the ad interim injunction.

The seller-firm, in turn, filed a revision petition against the grant of injunction and contended that the letter of credit was confirmed and irrevocable and imposed upon the banker an absolute obligation to pay. The bank disputed the fact that the letter of credit was properly confirmed.

Judgement of High Court

The Court held that it is evident from the fact that, as and when each of the four invoices and the bills of lading were sought to be negotiated by the seller through State Bank of India, it pointed out the discrepancies which existed in the description of goods as mentioned in the documents, in comparison to those given in the letter of credit. It was on realisation of this position that the seller made an endorsement every time to the effect that the documents should be negotiated at his risk and responsibility in view of the discrepancy therein and further supported the same by an indemnity bond. Yet again, the payment was made or the amount was credited to the current account of the seller by the State Bank of India 'Under Reserve', and at the cost and risk of the seller. The Court did not consider it either expedient or advisable to return a definite finding on the question as to whether or not the letter of credit was a confirmed letter of credit.

Prima facie, in such a situation, when the bank was not in a position to realise the proceeds of the documents negotiated, from the Riyadh Bank, it could fall back upon the above undertaking and indemnity of the seller and recall the payment made by it 'Under Reserve'. The balance of convenience clearly lay in allowing the normal banking transaction to go on, and upheld the lower Court's order of injunction restraining the seller from alienating fixed deposits and other amounts to the credit of the seller with the bank.

In this case, the Court had relied on the Supreme Court ruling in United Commercial Bank vs. Bank of India [(1982) 52 Company Case 186], wherein the Supreme Court had held that a payment 'Under Reserve' is understood in banking transactions to mean that the recipient of the money may not deem it as his own but must be prepared to return it on demand.

The above cited case also strikes a point of caution for the paying banker to release the payment, even 'Under Reserve':

(*i*) as a very special case, and

(*ii*) invariably after getting a duly stamped indemnity bond, executed each time afresh, and

(*iii*) as a matter of abundant precaution, after crediting the amount so paid 'Under Reserve', a suitable lien, for such amount, should be noted in the account of the seller, whereby the amount so paid, through credit to the account, may not be released, unless a confirmation has been received by the paying (seller's) banker, through the issuing (buyer's) banker, to the effect that the bill has been duly honoured (paid) by the buyer concerned, despite the involved discrepancy(ies). No relaxation should be permitted in such cases, under any circumstances, unless the seller concerned is a very valuable and highly credit-worthy and trust-worthy client of the bank.

11.5 HOW LETTERS OF CREDIT ARE ISSUED?

We may well understand and appreciate the system and procedure, involved in the issuance of an L/C (step by step), with the help of a schematic representation, as given hereunder:

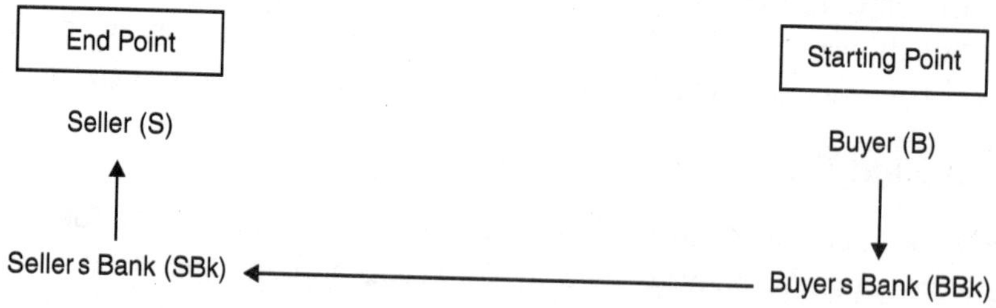

Fig. 11.1: Issuance of the L/C

As has been indicated in Figure 11.1 above, at the request of B, the BBk issues the L/C favouring S and sends the original L/C to SBk and (through SBk) a copy is sent to S, for his information and further necessary action.

The letter of request, to be submitted by B to BBk, is written on a prescribed printed application form, duly stamped, which reads somewhat as under:

"In consideration of your having agreed to issue the L/C in favour of (the name and address of the seller) as per the text given hereunder:

> [And, the full text of the required L/C is already printed in the proforma; only the terms and conditions, and such other specific details are to be incorporated therein, at the appropriate space, meant for the purpose].

And, on the basis of such a request, the BBk issues the L/C in the required form which, too, is on a pre-printed proforma. The original L/C is also required to be stamped.

It may be mentioned here that the Letter of Request, executed by the buyer, on a duly stamped paper, in effect, constitutes a 'Counter Guarantee cum indemnity', an undertaking by the buyer, to indemnify the bank of any loss or losses, suffered or to be suffered by it (the bank) in this regard.

Now, let us understand, with the help of yet another schematic representation, the entire procedure (step by step) involved at the time of the payment of the amount of the Bills of Exchange, drawn under the L/C, immediately on presentation, along with other relative required documents, in strict compliance of all the terms and conditions stipulated in the L/C.

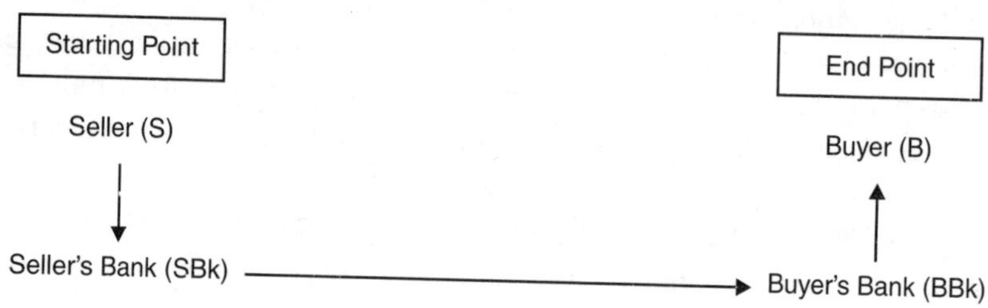

Fig. 11.2: Payment made under the L/C

Step 1

S draws the Bill of Exchange (superscribed as "drawn under L/C No. _______ dated _____") and submits the same, along with all the required documents/papers to the SBk.

Step 2

SBk, thereupon, scrutinizes all the documents, carefully and meticulously, so as to satisfy that all the terms and conditions, stipulated in the L/C, have been fully and perfectly complied with.

On being fully satisfied to this effect, SBk releases the full payment of the bill to S by crediting the amount to the account of S, maintained with SBk. And, immediately thereafter, SBk sends all the documents/papers to BBk for reimbursement of the entire amount to SBk (including all the charges of SBk). Thus, on receipt of the full payment, S is out of the picture.

Step 3

BBk, on its turn, again meticulously scrutinizes all the documents/papers and on being fully satisfied to the effect that all the terms and conditions, stipulated in the L/C, have been strictly complied with, debits the account of B, and remits the amount to SBk. Thus, SBk, and BBk, too, come out of the picture.

Step 4

The relative documents are then sent by BBk to B, along with the advice that the account of B has been debited with the relative amount.

Thus, BBk has also been able to realize the full payment from B, and ultimately, B has made the payment for goods purchased and all the relative documents received.

However, if BBk detects some discrepancy in documents/papers (howsoever small or minor) it first brings it to the notice of B, and if B agrees to honour (*i.e.* pay the amount of) the bill in question, the payment is effected, as aforesaid.

> [Here, it must be clarified that a reference may have to be made to B, only if some discrepancy is observed. That is, if everything is found to be in perfect order, the account of B is debited with the amount of the bill, without any prior reference made to B. And, even if sufficient amount is not available in B's account, at the material time, the account is even then be debited with the full amount, all the same. However, the irregularity (of over-drawings) so caused in the account, will have to be adjusted and the position regularized by B in due course of time, failing which the BBk may prefer to file a civil suit against B, for the recovery of the (balance) amount (with interest) on the basis of the stamped letter of request submitted by B at the time of the opening of the L/C].

11.6 MARGIN MONEY AGAINST LETTER OF CREDIT

That is why, BBk insists on retention of some margin money to the extent of a certain percentage of the amount of L/C (*i.e.* 100%, 50%, 25%, 10% or even zero), depending upon the level of the credit-worthiness of the specific buyer (borrower), B.

Example

If, for example, an L/C is to be issued on behalf of some very valued constituents like ONGC, FCI, IOC, TISCO, L&T, RIL, etc., the banks may decide to retain 'nil' margin, as all the aforenamed companies enjoy very high ratings in the eyes of the bankers, in terms of their credit-worthiness and trust-worthiness.

As against this, the bank may prefer to retain 100% margin for issuance of an L/C, if the applicant is not considered to be sufficiently credit-worthy (and trust-worthy). But, usually the bank may decide not at all to entertain such request from such parties.

Usually, an L/C is opened only at the request of the parties who are already enjoying some credit facilities with the bank. And, no bank grants any credit facility to a person or company, if the credit-worthiness, and, above all, the honesty and integrity of the party, are even somewhat doubtful.

And usually the banks do not retain margin money more than the percentage of margin retained on the stock cash credit account, *i.e.* the advance granted against pledge or hypothecation of stocks of inventory, etc., which, again, does not, generally speaking, exceed 25%. As a general practice, however, the percentage of margin money varies from 10% to 20% and maximum 25%. Further, in case of import L/C (under which some scarce goods are being imported), a lower margin of, say only 10%, may be retained, as the possibility of the buyer not retiring and honouring the relative bill (under the L/C) is rather remote, inasmuch as some premium goods are involved.

And, for that matter, a seller can afford to demand issuance of an L/C only if such party is operating in the sellers' market and, therefore, the possibility of honouring and retirement of such bill by the buyer is very high. But, a word of caution here may be very pertinent.

Example:

I know of a party, who got an L/C issued by a bank, in favour of one of its own associate firms, and thereby had defrauded the bank with a handsome amount.

The fraud connected with the L/C issued by State Bank of India in favour of a company of the Middle East, for the supply of urea, is also a case in point.

Where to Deposit the Margin Money?

Margin money is usually deposited by the buyer with the bank in the form of a term deposit (and not in the current account, as it does not earn any interest). Better still, if the margin money is deposited in the cash credit account of the company, allowing a lien to be noted thereon, for the full amount of the margin money, so as to save the maximum possible amount by way of interest on the amount of the margin money.

[For a detailed discussion on the mechanism and procedure, pertaining to the noting of the lien on the cash credit account, please refer to the Chapter 4 dealing with the Management of Cash as also the Case Study titled 'Margin Money Makes Money' and a suggested solution thereto, in the same Chapter].

Thus, though the issuance of the L/C is a very lucrative and profitable activity, with a very small degree of risks, this business also involves some risks, requiring the bank to be always alert and watchful, while issuing the L/C.

Further, though the opening of L/C is considered to be a non-fund based working capital credit facility (or quasi-credit facility), it should not be misunderstood as not involving any fund or money, whatsoever. It is known as non-fund based credit facility only because the funds are not to be released immediately (as is done in the case of working capital demand loan and working capital cash credit), but only at a much later date, when the bills and documents, drawn under the L/C are received, for payment. And, if all the documents/papers received under the L/C are in perfect order, the bank has no option but to pay the amount to the seller through seller's banker, as aforesaid. And, if the bank fails to realise/recover the amount from the buyer, it will have to sustain the losses, in full or in part, as the case be.

The bank may, however, file a civil suit against the buyer on the basis of the stamped application form, executed by the buyer, at the time of the issuance of the L/C, whereby the buyer had undertaken to indemnify the bank of any loss that may be incurred by the bank. But, if the buyer can successfully prove that there had been some discrepancy in the relative documents/papers, and if the issuing (buyer's) banker had already paid the amount to the seller, through seller's bank, the issuing bank will have no recourse to law left and will have to sustain the entire loss all alone. The amount so debited (wrongfully) to the buyer's account, in that event, will have to be credited back to the account of the buyer.

11.7 MANAGEMENT OF CREDIT RISKS PERTAINING TO LETTER OF CREDIT

As the issuance of L/C involves some credit risks, the banks take following precautions while issuing an L/C:

(*i*) L/C is generally issued at the request of only genuine borrowers of the bank, who are, by and large, found to be conforming to the bank's laid down financial discipline, and who conduct their WCDL and cash credit accounts in a satisfactory manner.

(*ii*) A suitable L/C limit is also sanctioned in favour of the borrower, along with sanctioning the over-all working capital finance, taking into consideration, the genuine requirements of the party concerned, based upon its scale of operation, and the level of its credit-worthiness.

(*iii*) Further, with a view to assessing and estimating the possibility that the party (buyer) will be able to generate sufficient cash so as to have sufficient funds at the time the documents, drawn under the L/C, are received at the branch for payment, the banks undertake the following studies/exercises:

(*a*) Preparation of cash budget, and

(*b*) Preparation and study of cash/funds flow statements of the company.

(*iv*) A suitable amount of margin is also insisted upon by banks to be deposited usually by way of TDR (or even by way of noting a lien in the cash credit account, but, of course, in the case of very valued parties only).

In fact, when documents negotiated under the L/C are received at the branch, the relative goods, covered thereunder, will ultimately be charged to the bank, as a security against the loan, and a suitable Drawing Power (DP) will be allocated in the account. Thus, the borrower may be required to deposit only that much of amount in the account which constitutes the stipulated percentage of margin on the cash credit account, because, in the event of pledge or hypothecation of goods received under the L/C arrangement, this would ultimately go to suitably enhance the DP, and thereby the position of the account would automatically get regularized.

(*v*) That is why, while ascertaining the quantum of L/C limit as also the amount of each L/C, the bankers take into consideration the genuine requirements of goods involved (commensurate with the scale of operation) and the expected cash position of the company at the material time, by means of cash budget exercise.

(*vi*) Collateral (Additional) Security: By way of an abundant precaution, the bankers usually insist for some collateral (additional) security too. The primary security comprise:

(*a*) the pledge/hypothecation of goods covered under the L/C, and

(*b*) the execution of the duly stamped counter guarantee agreement by the applicant (buyer) at the time of issuing the L/C.

The collateral (additional) security is obtained by way of:

(*a*) Equitable mortgage of some landed property (like land and building, plant and machinery embedded to earth, etc.) and/or

(*b*) Third party guarantee of the partners/directors of the firm/company in their personal capacity, or even from their friends and relatives.

[Equitable mortgage is preferred by banks as an additional security (as against the registered mortgage) inasmuch as the stamp duty exigible on such document is only as much as is exigible on a simple agreement, prevalent in the respective states. Besides, the equitable mortgage created by a company gets registered with the Registrar of Companies concerned, whereby a public notice is deemed to have been served about the charge of mortgage created on the specific property. In case of firms (proprietary firm or partnership firm), however, such facility of public notice by way of registration is not available].

However, the bankers insist on equitable mortgage of immovable properties, by way of deposit of title deeds, even in the case of firms, because:

(*a*) It is just a collateral security, in addition to the primary security, and

(*b*) The fact of creation of an equitable mortgage may have some psychological pressure on the applicant (buyer), whatever be the legal position and validity of the equitable mortgage.

[Here, it may be pertinent to mention that, while in USA the term 'collateral' stands for both primary and additional security, in the Indian context, it signifies only the additional security taken, over and above the primary security. These two are, thus, different in the Indian context].

(*vii*) Above all, the bankers invariably ensure that the applicant of L/C is not only capable of honouring the documents drawn under the L/C, but is also willing to pay, and always has good intentions to honour the documents. That is why, the bank does not open L/C (or even entertain request for granting any credit facilities) in the case of parties who are habitual litigants or are of even slightly doubtful integrity.

11.8 TYPES OF BILLS OF EXCHANGE

On the basis of different parameters, letters of credit may be divided into various categories, as detailed under Section 11.14. But, before doing that, let us first understand the distinguishing features of Demand Bills of Exchange and Time Bills of Exchange.

Demand and Time Bills of Exchange

The Bills of Exchange (B of E), broadly speaking, are of two types.

(*i*) Demand Bills of Exchange; and

(*ii*) Time (usance) Bills of Exchange.

The demand bills of exchange are such bills which are made payable on demand. These are also known as sight bills. The time bills of exchange (also known as usance bills) are, instead, drawn payable after some specified days or month(s) from the date of the bill, or from the date of acceptance of the bill.

A **specimen** of each of the Demand Bill and Time Bill is given hereunder:

On Demand* Pay to *State Bank of India* or Bearer/Order a sum of Rupees *One lakh* only for value received.

Rs. 1,00,000

To,
M/S XYZ Company Limited,
5/55, Hazratganj,
Lucknow-226001

For ABC Company Limited
Signature
DIRECTOR

* In some of the Demand Bills, the term 'At Sight' is used instead.

Fig. 11.3: Specimen of Demand Bill of Exchange

60 Days	after	*Date*
2 months	after	*Sight/Acceptance*

Pay to State Bank of India or Bearer/Order a sum of *Rupees One lakh* only for value received.

Rs. 1,00,000

To,
M/S XYZ Company Limited
5/55, Hazratganj,
Lucknow-226001

For ABC Company Limited
Signature
DIRECTOR

Fig. 11.4: Specimen of Time (Usance) Bill of Exchange

In the case of 'after date', the due date will be counted from the date of the bill of exchange, while in the case of 'after acceptance' (or 'after sight'), it will be calculated from the date of acceptance of the bill of exchange.

11.9 DEFINITIONS OF BILL OF EXCHANGE, CHEQUE, BANK DEMAND DRAFT (AS ALSO PROMISSORY NOTE) AS PER THE NEGOTIABLE INSTRUMENTS ACT, 1881 (NI ACT, FOR SHORT)

Section 5: *Bill of Exchange*

"A 'Bill of Exchange' is an instrument in writing containing an unconditional order, signed by the maker, directing a certain person to pay a certain sum of money only to, or to the order of, a certain person or to the bearer of the instrument."

Section 6: *Cheque*

"A 'Cheque' is a bill of exchange drawn on a specified banker and not expressed to be payable otherwise than on demand."

Section 4: *Promissory Note*

"A 'Promissory Note' is an instrument in writing (not being a bank-note or a currency-note) containing an unconditional undertaking, signed by the maker to pay a certain sum of money only to, or to the order of, a certain person, or to the bearer of the instrument."

Section 85 A: *Draft drawn on one branch of a bank on another payable to Order*

"Where any draft, that is an order to pay money, drawn on one office of a bank upon another office of the same bank, for a sum of money payable to order on demand, purports to be endorsed by or on behalf of the payee, the bank is discharged by payment in due course."

Thus, we see that a bill of exchange has three parties:

(*i*) The drawer, usually the seller (in the specimen stated as ABC Company Limited), who draws the bill on, or orders, the drawee, to pay the amount to the payee mentioned therein.

(*ii*) The payee (*i.e.* State Bank of India in the specimen), whose name appears in the Bill of Exchange and to whom the amount specified in the bill of exchange is required to be paid.

(*iii*) The drawee (usually the buyer, *i.e.* XYZ Company Limited in the specimen) to whom the drawer of the bill of exchange (usually seller) has ordered to pay the specified amount to the payee.

The bill of exchange could be drawn either as an order or bearer instrument.

Incidentally, it may be mentioned here that cheque is also a bill of exchange but it is invariably a demand bill of exchange only, wherein the drawee is always a bank and the drawer is the account holder of the same branch of the bank.

And, a bank draft is also a bill of exchange, invariably a demand bill of exchange, wherein both the drawer and the drawee are the two branches of the same bank or of two different banks, *e.g.*,

(*i*) a bank draft issued by The State Bank of India, Lucknow, on The State Bank of India, Bangalore, or else;

(*ii*) by The State Bank of Hyderabad, Lucknow, on The State Bank of India, Bhopal; or by Grindlays Bank, New Delhi, on The State Bank of India, Sitapur (by a special arrangement between the two banks).

It must also be borne in mind that while cheques may be drawn as either order or bearer, the Bank Draft, as per law, has necessarily to be drawn payable on order only (and never in the form of a bearer draft). Why?

Because, in that event, the Bank Draft could as well be used as a currency note, as the title to a '(bearer) bill of exchange' gets transferred merely by delivery, and no endorsement, whatsoever, is required. Thus, in the case of Bank Draft (an order), the title cannot get transferred merely by delivery (as is done in the case of the currency notes issued by the Reserve Bank of India, *i.e.* currency notes of Rs. 2 and above [and not Re. 1 note, which are issued under the signature of the Finance Secretary, instead]. The currency notes are issued in the form of a Promissory Note, under the signature of the Governor, Reserve Bank of India (RBI). Incidentally, it may be mentioned here that, in the case of Promissory Notes (both Demand and Time) there are only two parties (instead of three, as in the case of Bills of Exchange). They are drawer and payee only (no drawee being there). And, in the case of Reserve Bank of India currency notes, the drawer of note is the Reserve Bank of India and the payee is the bearer of the currency note. That is why, a currency note is invariably drawn in the form of a Demand Promissory Note (DP Note) payable to the bearer, wherein it reads as under:

"I promise to pay the bearer the sum of ____ Rupees". ['*Here the amount of the respective denomination of the currency note is specified*'].

(*Signature*)
Governor

11.10 STAMP DUTY EXIGIBLE ON USANCE BILLS

Further, the Demand Bills are expected to be paid immediately on demand. But usually, some specified period, say of 30 days or 45 days, etc., are granted by the drawer to the drawee to make the payment by that time, whereafter some overdue interest may become chargeable at the specified rate.

Further, the Demand Bills of Exchange do not attract any stamp duty. As against this, stamp duty is invariably exigible on all the Time Bills of Exchange, which varies in terms of the amount and the period after which the amount is made payable, as per the Indian Stamp Act, *i.e.* the stamp duty is exigible at the same rate all over India. (The rate of stamp duty payable under State Stamp Acts, however, vary from State to State, *e.g.* stamp duties payable on Agreements, Pledge documents, etc.).

The **Table of Stamp Duty**, exigible on Time (Usance) Bills of Exchange, as per the Indian Stamp Act, is given hereunder:

Table 11.1: Stamp Duty Exigible on Time (Usance) Bills of Exchange [Vide Section 13 of Indian Stamp Act]

Sl. No.	*Descriptions*	*Rupees*
6(*b*)	Where payable otherwise than on demand:	
(*i*)	Where payable not more than three months after date or sight:	
	if the amount of the bill or note does not exceed Rs. 500;	One Rupee
	if it exceeds Rs. 500 but does not exceed Rs. 1,000;	Two Rupees
	and for every additional Rs. 1,000 or part thereof in excess of Rs. 1,000.	Two Rupees
(*ii*)	Where payable more than three months but not more than six months after date or sight:	
	if the amount of the bill or note does not exceed Rs. 500;	Two Rupees
	if it exceeds Rs. 500 but does not exceed Rs. 1,000;	Five Rupees
	and for every additional Rs. 1,000 or part thereof in excess of Rs. 1,000.	Five Rupees
(*iii*)	Where payable more than six months but not more than nine months after date or sight:	
	if the amount of the bill or note does not exceed Rs. 500;	Three Rupees
	if it exceeds Rs. 500 but does not exceed Rs. 1,000;	Seven Rupees
	and for every additional Rs. 1,000 or part thereof in excess of Rs. 1,000.	Seven Rupees
(*iv*)	Where payable more than nine months but not more than one year after date or sight:	
	if the amount of the bill or note does not exceed Rs. 500;	Five Rupees
	if it exceeds Rs. 500 but does not exceed Rs. 1,000;	Ten Rupees
	and for every additional Rs. 1,000 or part thereof in excess of Rs. 1,000.	Ten Rupees
(*v*)	Where payable at more than one year after date or sight:	
	if the amount of the bill or note does not exceed Rs. 500;	Ten Rupees
	if it exceeds Rs. 500 but does not exceed Rs. 1,000;	Twenty Rupees
	and for every additional Rs. 1,000 or part thereof in excess of Rs. 1,000.	Twenty Rupees

A discussion regarding the mode of calculation of the due dates of time bills of exchange, as laid down in the Negotiable Instruments Act, may also be quite appropriate here.

11.11 CALCULATION OF DUE DATE OF A BILL OF EXCHANGE MADE PAYABLE AFTER THE SPECIFIED NUMBER OF DAYS OR MONTHS

Example 1

A Time Bill of Exchange is dated February 1, 2008, and is made payable 60 days after date and has been accepted on February 05, 2008.

Calculation of Due Date

Now, in the instant case, let us calculate, step by step, the due date of the bill.

Step 1

Find out the starting point. In the instant case, it is given as 01.02.2008.

Step 2

Exclude the starting point, *i.e.* 1st February, and count the days now remaining in the month of February, *i.e.* 29 days less one day = 28 days. As the year 2008 is a leap year, because it is divisible by 4, the month of February 2008 will have 29 day. (But the full century, like 2400, should be divisible by 400, and not just 4. Thus, the month of February 2400 will also have 29 days, because it is a full century and is also divisible by 400, and not only 4. But the month of February 2100 and 2200 will not have 29 days, but only 28 days, because 2100 and 2200 are full centuries, and these are not divisible by 400.

Step 3

Now, add 31 days of March to the balance 28 days of February, *i.e.* 28 + 31 = 59 days.

Step 4

Now, how many more days need to be added from the next month, *i.e.* April, to make it a complete 60 days' period.

That is 60 – 59 = 1 day.

Step 5

Finally, the due date comes to 59 + 1 = 60 days, *i.e.* on 1st April, 2008.

Days of Grace

But, the matter does not end here. One more step remains to be computed, that is, granting of three days of grace. As per the NI Act, 3 days of grace has invariably to be granted, while calculating the due date of a Time Bill of Exchange.

Step 6

Thus, finally, the 3 days of grace has to be granted, and accordingly, added to the due date calculated earlier, *i.e.* 1st April, 2008 + 3 days = 4th April, 2008.

Thus, finally the due date comes to be 4th April, 2008 in the instant case.

But, the exercise has not ended up even here; because one more step still remains.

Step 7

If the due date, finally calculated, including the three days of grace, happens to be a public holiday, what shall be the due date, under such circumstances?

The NI Act provides that the Bill of Exchange, in such a case, will fall due on "the next **preceding** business day."

Here, the terms 'next' and 'preceding' are of great significance. That is, if the 4th April, 2008 happens to be a public holiday, the due date will be the next (*i.e.* immediately) preceding (and not succeeding) business day, *i.e.* the 3rd April, 2008. The term, 'next preceding' days should not be confused with the term 'next' day which means the next 'succeeding' day. And, the term used in the NI Act is 'the next preceding business day' which means that if the 3rd April, 2008 also happens to be a public holiday, the due date will be the 2nd April, 2008 instead. And, if the 2nd April 2008 also happens to be a public holiday, the due date will be deemed to have fallen on the 1st April, 2008, and so on.

[In the case of the Bank's Term Deposit Receipts (TDRs), however, if the due date falls on, say, the 4th April, 2008, and if 4th April, 2008 happens to be a bank holiday, it will be deemed to have matured for payment on the next succeeding business day, instead, *i.e.* on the 5th April, 2008, and so on].

Example 2

Now, let us take another example, where the bill is made payable so many months after date or sight (acceptance).

Supposing the bill is drawn payable 2 months after date and is dated 01.02.2010 and has been accepted for payment on 05.02.2010.

Calculation of due date:

Step 1

The starting point will be, in this case, the date of the bill, *i.e.* 01.02.2010. [If the bill was drawn two months after sight (or acceptance), the starting point would have been 05.02.2010 instead.

Step 2

Add 2 months to the starting point, *i.e.* 01.02.2010 + 2 months = 01.04.2010.

Step 3

Add 3 days of grace, *i.e.* 01.04.2010 + 3 days = 04.04.2010.

Step 4

And, if 04.04.2010 happens to be a public holiday, then 03.04.2010, and so on, as has been shown earlier, in the case of Example-1.

Extracts from the Negotiable Instruments Act, 1881

Section 22: Days of Grace

"Every promissory note or bill of exchange which is not expressed to be payable on demand, at sight or on presentment, is, at maturity, is due on the third day after the day on which it is expressed to be payable."

Calculating Maturity of Bill or Note Payable so many months after date or sight

Section 23

In calculating the date at which a promissory note or bill of exchange is made payable, a stated number of months after date or after sight, or after a certain event, is, at maturity, the period stated shall be held to terminate on the day of the month which corresponds with the day on which the instrument is dated, or presented for acceptance or sight, or noted for non-acceptance, or protested for non-acceptance, or the event happens, or, where the instrument is a bill of exchange made payable a stated number of months after sight and has been accepted for honour, with the day on which it was so accepted. If the month in which the period would terminate has no corresponding day, the period shall be held to terminate on the last day of such month.

Illustrations

(*a*) A negotiable instrument dated 29th January 1878 is made payable at one month after date. The instrument is at maturity on the third day after the 28th February 1878.

(*b*) A negotiable instrument dated 30th August 1878, is made payable three months after date. The instrument matures on 3rd December 1878.

(*c*) A promissory note or bill of exchange, dated 3rd August 1878 is made payable three months after date. The instrument is at maturity on 3rd December 1878.

Calculating Maturity of Bill or Note payable so many days after date or sight

Section 24

In calculating the date at which a promissory note or bill of exchange is made payable a certain number of days after date or after sight or after a certain event is at maturity, the day of the date, or of presentment for acceptance or sight, or of protest for non-acceptance, or on which the event happens, shall be excluded.

When Day of Maturity is a Holiday

Section 25

If the day on which a promissory note or bill of exchange is to mature is a public holiday, the instrument shall be deemed to be due on the next preceding business day.

Explanation

The expression 'public holiday' includes Sundays and any other day declared by the Central Government, by notification in the Official Gazette, to be a public holiday.

It may be pertinent to mention here that Time Bills of Exchange have invariably to be presented to the drawee for acceptance purposes, to hold the drawee liable for dishonour of the bill of exchange for non-acceptance and/or for non-payment. And, if the bill is refused to be accepted by the drawee, it would be deemed to have been 'dishonoured for non-acceptance' instead. In such cases, the bill may have to be noted (or protested, if no notary public is available in the area of the drawee's place of business), to proceed further against the drawee in the Court of law.

11.12 PRESENTATION OF TIME BILLS FOR ACCEPTANCE AND PAYMENT

The time bill should be presented for acceptance (and payment) at the usual place of business of the drawee during the usual business hours, or else, at a mutually agreed reasonable place and at a reasonable time (*i.e.* not at the burning ground or grave yard at 12 O' clock at night, and the like).

11.13 MODE OF ACCEPTANCE OF TIME BILLS

Supposing the bill is accepted for payment in the following manner:

Accepted
For XYZ Company Limited

Signature

DIRECTOR
05.02.2010

In such a case, the bill will have to be presented again on the due date for payment at the usual place of business, of the drawee, and the payment collected there itself, which may have to be brought back to the branch of the bank, at the risk of the bank, for deposit at the branch.

With a view to avoiding such a situation, it would be preferable to get the time bill accepted and made payable at the specific branch of the bank concerned. For example:

Accepted for payment at State Bank of India, Hazratganj, Lucknow.
For XYZ Company Limited

Signature

DIRECTOR
05.02.2010

In such a case, the drawee will have to come to the branch of the bank on the due date and make the payment of the bill, in full.

In must also be ensured that the time bill, while being accepted, also clearly bears the date of its acceptance, whether the bill is made payable so many days or months after date or after acceptance of the bill. This is a legal requirement, perhaps to stand as an evidence that the bill was accepted for payment on the specific date.

Where should the acceptance of the bill be written on the bill?

The acceptance of the time bill must be stated on the face of the bill and not on the reverse of the bill.

[I do not intend to go any further to discuss various other legal provisions in this regard, and the legal implications and ramifications thereof, as, I think, our purpose is well served by the detailed discussions made on the topic so far].

11.14 TYPES OF LETTERS OF CREDIT

(A) *Demand L/C and Time L/C*

We have already discussed the distinguishing features of 'Demand' and 'Time' (usance) Bills of Exchange, in Section 11.8 earlier.

The Letters of Credit, accompanied by Demand Bills of Exchange are known as Demand L/Cs, while those accompanied by Time (Usance) Bills of Exchange are called Time (usance) L/Cs.

(B) *A 'DA' Bill L/C and 'DP' Bill L/C*

As per the instructions of the drawer, the documents, pertaining to the time bill, *i.e.* the documents to the title to the goods (like Railway Receipt, Lorry Receipt, Bill of Lading, Air-way Bill, etc.) may be required to be delivered against acceptance of the Bill of Exchange [*i.e.* Delivery against Acceptance (DA for short)]. As against this, in some cases, the documents, pertaining to the time bill, *i.e.* the documents to the title to the goods, may be required to be delivered against full payment of the amount of the Bill of Exchange (DP for short), *i.e.* Delivery against payment. These are, thus, known as DA Bills or DP Bills respectively, and the relative L/C is also termed accordingly.

(C) *Documentary L/C and Clean L/C*

A documentary L/C is one which is **accompanied** by the relative title to goods (as aforesaid), which may have to be delivered against acceptance or payment of the bill, as required by the drawer. But usually, time bills are made DA, *i.e.* Delivery against Acceptance, so that, on acceptance of the bill, the relative documents to the title to the goods could be delivered to the drawees, duly endorsed in their favour. This way, the drawees will be able to get delivery of goods, well before making payment of the amount of the bill, either all before selling them entirely or its large quantity, well before the due date for payment. Such sale proceeds, thus, could well be used by the drawees for making the payment of the bill on the due date.

Banks not responsible for Quality of Goods

Here, it must be clarified that the bank's responsibility is only to the extent of ensuring that the documents to the title to goods are genuine, *i.e.* that the goods have actually been transported/ shipped/or air-lifted. But, the bank cannot be held responsible for the quality (or even quantity) of the goods so dispatched. Accordingly, if the buyers prefer to get the quality and quantity of the goods inspected and verified before dispatch, he should make his own arrangements to have his own representative to do the prior inspection of goods, or he may have some arrangement made with some agencies, undertaking such jobs, on agency basis, to save on the travel expenses, specially in the case of Import L/C.

In such cases, however, one of the terms and conditions, stipulated in the relative L/C, is that the documents should also accompany an inspection note, certifying the quantity and quality of goods dispatched, duly signed by the officer/agent authorized by the applicant (buyer) on this behalf.

As against this, the Clean L/C is the one which is not accompanied by any document to the title to the goods, like Railway Receipt (RR), Lorry Receipt (LR), Air-way Bill, Bill of Lading, etc. That means that such documents have already been sent to the drawee concerned direct by the drawer of the bill. It may, however, so happen only in such cases where the drawee is considered to be highly credit-worthy by the drawer, who also has full faith in the integrity and honesty of the drawee.

Further, it may as well be possible under such cases where the product of the drawer concerned enjoys a very high demand in the market, and no drawee will ever like to dishonour the bill, lest he may be blacklisted by the drawer, and his agency/dealership arrangement may get cancelled for ever. Nirma Industries (manufacturing detergent powders and soaps) may be one of the several such examples. Similar may be the case when DA (Documents against Acceptance) term is stipulated in the Letter of Credit.

(D) *Inland (Domestic) L/C and Foreign L/C*

Inland (also known as domestic) L/C is one wherein both the drawers (sellers) and the drawees (buyers) are of the one and the same country, say India. For example, an L/C opened on behalf of XYZ Company Limited, Lucknow, in favour of TISCO, Jamshedpur, both the parties being Indians and located in India.

As against this, in the case of a foreign L/C, the drawers and the drawees belong to two different countries.

For Example

(*i*) The L/C, issued on behalf of XYZ Company Limited, Lucknow (India) in favour of Suzuki Motors, Japan, or else,

(*ii*) The L/C issued at the request of a German Company, located in Berlin (Germany), in favour of an Indian Company located in Mirzapur (India), for supply of woollen carpets.

Both these cases are the examples of foreign L/Cs.

Thus, there may be two types of foreign L/C.

(*i*) Import L/C, and

(*ii*) Export L/C.

When Indian party is the buyer (applicant for the L/C) and foreign party is the seller (beneficiary of the L/C), it is known as the Import L/C, as an import of certain goods to India are involved. As against this, in the example number (*ii*) above, the applicant (buyer) is a German Company and the beneficiary (seller) is an Indian Company, whereby export of carpet (from India to Germany) is involved. It is, thus, known as the Export L/C.

(E) *Revocable L/C and Irrevocable L/C*

A revocable L/C, as the name itself suggests, is one which can be revoked (cancelled) by the issuing banker, any time after it is issued. In such a case, the L/C may not serve much of a useful purpose. As against this, an irrevocable L/C cannot be revoked by the issuing banker, once it has been issued and delivered/communicated to the beneficiary concerned. Such L/C stands as an irrevocable undertaking by the issuing banker to make the full payment to the beneficiary of the L/C (the seller), of course, provided all the terms and conditions, stipulated in the relative L/C, have been fully complied with.

Thus, it will always be beneficial for the beneficiary of the Letter of Credit to ensure that the L/C is irrevocable and not revocable.

(F) *With Recourse to Drawer L/C, and Without Recourse to Drawer L/C*

In case of 'With Recourse to Drawer' L/C, after the payment of the bill, drawn under the L/C, has been made to the drawer of the bill (seller), he or she is still under the liability to refund the payment so made earlier, if the drawee (buyer) [for some valid reason(s) or even otherwise] refuses to honour (pay the amount of) the bill. Such an L/C, thus, does not serve much useful purpose to ensure a guaranteed payment to the seller.

But, in the case of an L/C 'Without Recourse to the Drawer', once the payment has been made to the beneficiary (seller), he is finally out of the picture and can, under no circumstances, be made to refund the amount so paid earlier, even for some valid reasons or otherwise.

[Of course, the position will certainly be different, if the payment has been released 'under reserve', as has already been discussed, in detail, in the foregoing pages].

Thus, the beneficiary will do well to invariably ensure that the L/C issued in his favour is specifically mentioned to be 'Irrevocable, Without Recourse to the Drawer' (and NOT Revocable, with Recourse to the Drawer).

Let us bring home the point, a little further, with the help of a case study, given hereunder:

11.15 MINI CASE STUDY

"AKANKSHA ADVISES AKASH"

(A CASE STUDY ON LETTER OF CREDIT)

Mr. Akash came home from office a little early. He was very happy. He had a big export order, backed by a foreign Letter of Credit (L/C). His wife, Ms. Akanksha was obviously happy.

After rejoicing and relaxing for sometime, Akanksha wanted to peruse the contents of the Letter of Credit, a prudent and experienced banker as she was. But, Akash convinced her that there was nothing unusual in the L/C; the terms and conditions stipulated in the L/C were the usual ones as are commonly found in most of the export L/Cs.

For Example

A. The documents, negotiated under the L/C must include:

(*i*) Demand Bill of Exchange.

(*ii*) Bill of Lading.

(*iii*) Certificate of Origin.

(*iv*) Insurance Policy covering fire and pilferage risks for full value of goods shipped.

(*v*) Inspection Note, duly signed by an authorised officer, on behalf of the importer company.

B. Some other conditions stipulated in the L/C included

(*i*) Transshipment not permitted.

(*ii*) Partshipment permitted.

C. Further, the heading of the L/C, too, was the usual one, as it read 'Revocable Letter of Credit with recourse to drawer(s)' – Akash stated emphatically.

D. And, with a glee on his face, Akash reiterated that, as the issuing bank of the importer's country was not of a great financial strength and standing, the L/C was duly confirmed by the State Bank of India, Lucknow.

Ms. Akanksha patiently and attentively heard Akash. At the end, however, she counselled Mr. Akash very convincingly to immediately send an e-mail to the importer concerned requesting him to send some material amendments to the L/C in question.

Mr. Akash got the point crystal clear, and he immediately sent an e-mail to the foreign importer, as suggested.

Issues to be discussed

What all Ms. Akanksha would have explained to Mr. Akash so convincingly? Could you guess? Please do, and explain the same, in detail, clearly bringing out the distinctive features and the ramifications of the suggested amendments to the Letter of Credit (L/C).

Suggested Solution*

Thus, we see that everything is in order in the relative L/C, issued in favour of Akash except that it is 'Revocable and With Recourse to Drawer', which does not serve any useful purpose of guaranteed payment of the bill drawn under the relative L/C. Thus, Akanksha must have advised Akash to get the L/C amended to read as 'Irrevocable, Without Recourse to Drawer'.

(G) *Confirmed L/C and Unconfirmed L/C*

A confirmed L/C is one, which has been confirmed by yet another banker, in addition to the issuing banker of the buyer. This may become necessary if the seller may not be having much faith in the financial standing and stability of the issuing banker of another country. So, he may insist that some banker, preferably of his own country, confirms the L/C, undertaking thereby that the issuing banker is financially sound and in the event of the issuing banker somehow failing to honour the commitment to honour the bill, the confirming banker [of his own country, in whom the seller (beneficiary of the letter of credit) must be having full faith] will make good the payment. In such cases, the buyer will have to bear the cost of commissions and bank charges of both the issuing banker and the confirming banker.

* One of the approaches to the Case Study, as suggested by the author.

* Please note that there is no single approach/solution to a case study.

It may be recalled that in 1970s, in some cases, though rare, the L/C issued even by the State Bank of India was required to be confirmed by a local banker of repute of the exporter (seller) country, inasmuch as its Authorized Capital, at the material time, was only Rs. 200 million and the issued, subscribed and paid-up capital was just Rs. 56.25 million, and the Reserves and Surplus aggregated around Rs. 200 million [not-so-strong a financial position, by any standard]. Therefore, the State Bank of India started bringing in some substantial amount from its Secret Reserves, to the General Reserves, at an average rate of, say Rs. 200 million per year, by way of a well thought of strategy, so as to strengthen its financial position, as revealed in its Balance Sheet. And later, in the year 1993, it came out with a mega (huge) public issue of Rs. 10,000 million (Rs. 1,000 crore) at a premium of Rs. 90, *i.e.* Rs. 10 (face value) shares were issued at a price of Rs. 100, when its Rs. 100 (face value) shares were being quoted in the stock market at around Rs. 2,500, *i.e.* much above the average issue price. The mega issue was, accordingly, highly over-subscribed (two times) and the bank's equity base went further up. And, with the issue of ADR/GDR, its equity capital has, by now, gone up dramatically.

The share capital of State Bank of India, as on the 31st March 2000, was substantial and respectful: Rs. 5263 million (Rs. 526.30 crore). [A quantum jump from Rs. 56.25 million (Rs. 5.625 crore) in 1970s.] And, with the recent rights issue, it has gone up even further.

Reserves and Surplus

Besides, its reserves and surplus have also gradually gone up very high at Rs. 116,210 million (Rs. 11,621 crore), as on 31.03.2000, raised from Rs. 74,509 million (Rs. 7,450.90 crore) as on 31.03.1997, Rs. 90,819 million (Rs. 9,081.90 crore) as on 31.03.1998, and Rs. 98,760 million (Rs. 9,876 crore) as on 31.03.1999.

Thus, when the share capital of The State Bank of India has further gone up, from its previous level of Rs. 5263 million, with the recent rights issue at a premium, its Reserves and Surplus are going up and up every year, which is a very healthy sign indeed.

It is, therefore, natural that in the case of The State Bank of India, the L/Cs are no longer required to be confirmed by any other foreign bank of a higher financial standing. Thus, the L/Cs, which are not confirmed (or let us say, which are not necessarily required to be confirmed) is known as an unconfirmed L/C. The seller must, therefore, ensure that the unconfirmed L/C should be accepted only if it is issued by a bank of an undisputedly sound and stable financial standing, like The State Bank of India. But, in case the financial standing of some other bank, say in India, are considered somewhat weak and unstable, the seller must insist that it should be confirmed by The State Bank of India or any other bank in the country of the seller (exporter).

11.16 REVOLVING LETTER OF CREDIT: SALIENT FEATURES

A revolving L/C is one which rolls over; that is, under which any number of bills could be negotiated a number of times, within a specified period, but only up to a specified aggregate amount, and with the further condition that the aggregate amount of bills, outstanding at anyone time, should not exceed the stipulated amount.

Example

A revolving L/C has been issued on the 1st January, 2009, for a period of one year, for an aggregate amount of Rs. 10 lakh, with the condition that the aggregate amount of the outstanding bills, negotiated under the L/C, does not exceed Rs. 1 lakh at any one time.

Let us restate the example in a simpler (tabular) form, when we get the undernoted conditions, stipulated (and implied) in the revolving L/C:

Table 11.2

Sl. No.	*Descriptions*	*Valid for (Period/Amount)*
1.	Validity of the period of the L/C	Up to 31.12.2009 (*i.e.* one year from 01.01.2009; it being the date of issue of L/C)
2.	Aggregate amount of bills that could be negotiated under the L/C	Rs. 10.00 lakh
3.	Total amount of bills, negotiated under the L/C, outstanding at anyone time	Rs. 1.00 lakh
4.	Total number of bills that could be negotiated under the L/C	Unlimited
5.	Total occasions on which such bills could be negotiated under the L/C	Unlimited

Let us now attempt to solve a practical problem to understand the mechanism of the systems and procedures, adopted by the banks in this regard.

Problem

Lucknow Iron Works (Private) Limited (LIW) wants to procure raw materials from TISCO, Jamshedpur, to the tune of Rs. 10 lakh, to meet its annual requirements. TISCO, in turn, asks LIW to open an L/C for Rs. 10 lakh in its favour, valid for a period of one year, to enable it to dispatch the goods to LIW in the required quantity, from time to time, within the overall limit of Rs. 10 lakh. LIW, accordingly, approaches the bank, say State Bank of India (SBI), Lucknow, with a request to open an L/C for an amount of Rs. 10 lakh for a period of one year in favour of TISCO, Jamshedpur.

The State Bank of India, on its own objective estimation and appraisal, does not find LIW credit-worthy enough for a big sum of Rs. 10 lakh. So, the Chief Manager, State Bank of India, Lucknow, suggests to LIW to get a Revolving L/C opened, instead, for Rs. 10 lakh for a period of one year, only with an added stipulation that the total value of outstanding bills, negotiated under the L/C, should not exceed Rs. 1 lakh at anyone time. And, LIW readily agreed, as it did not ever require to get supplies for more than Rs. 1 lakh, at anyone time, as the stocks of one month consumption of raw materials was considered to be good enough. Moreover, the amount of commission payable on the revolving L/C and the usual L/C also remains the same.

Thus, we see that, it is under such circumstances that the Revolving L/C proves to be handy.

Soon after the opening of the Revolving L/C, the following transactions have taken place between LIW and TISCO, during the period 01.01.2009 to 30.04.2009.

Table 11.3: Negotiation of Bills Under the Revolving L/C

Sl. No.	*Date*	*Amount (Rs. in Thousands)*
1.	10.01.2009	50
2.	15.01.2009	40
3.	20.01.2009	30
4.	05.02.2009	50
5.	25.02.2009	35
6.	06.03.2009	70
7.	29.03.2009	55
8.	30.03.2009	60
9.	15.04.2009	55
10.	30.04.2009	70

Table 11.4: Receipt of Payment Advices at State Bank of India, Jamshedpur, from State Bank of India, Lucknow

Sl. No.	*Date*	*Amount (Rs. in Thousands)*
1.	18.01.2009	50
2.	25.01.2009	40
3.	07.02.2009	30
4.	19.02.2009	50
5.	16.03.2009	35
6.	27.03.2009	70
7.	15.04.2009	55
8.	20.04.2009	60
9.	30.04.2009	55

Required

How would these transactions relating to negotiation of bills under the Revolving L/Cs, on different dates by the State Bank of India, Jamshedpur, and the respective payment advices, received (from the State Bank of India, Lucknow, at State Bank of India, Jamshedpur, would appear in the books of the bank at its Jamshedpur branch.

Solution

A solution has been attempted in Table 11.5.

Table 11.5: Negotiation of Bills under L/C and Receipt of Payment Advices, as Recorded In the Books of the Bank

Revolving L/C - Limit: Rs. 1.00 lakh at any Time; Over-all Limit: Rs. 10.00 lakh

(Rs. in thousands)

Sl. No.	*Date*	*Debit*	*Credit*	*Balance and Remarks, if any (Rs. in Thousands)*
	Balance		100	(+) 100
1.	10.01.2009	50		50
2.	15.01.2009	40		10
3.	18.01.2009		50	60
4.	20.01.2009	30		30
5.	25.01.2009		40	70
6.	05.02.2009	50		20
7.	07.02.2009		30	50
8.	19.02.2009		50	100
9.	25.02.2009	35		65
10.	06.03.2009	70		(Lien 5) (–) 5
11.	16.03.2009		35	(Lien Lifted) 30
12.	27.03.2009		70	100
13.	29.03.2009	55		45
14.	30.03.2009	60		(Lien 15) (–) 15
15.	15.04.2009		55	(Lien Lifted) 40
16.	15.04.2009	55		(Lien 15) (–) 15
17.	20.04.2009		60	(Lien Lifted) 45
18.	30.04.2009	70		(Lien 25) (–) 25
19.	30.04.2009		55	(Lien Lifted) 30
	TOTAL	**515**	**545**	

A SYNOPTIC NOTE
(CHAPTER 11 AT A GLANCE)

LETTERS OF CREDIT

Why are the letters of credit and bank guarantees called non-fund based CREDIT:

Because, though these also involve financial commitments, the funds are actually required to be paid not immediately, on the opening or issuance of the letters of credit and bank guarantees, but only at a later date, *i.e.*

(*i*) When the bills, drawn under the letters of credit, are received at the issuing bank, and

(*ii*) When the bank guarantees are invoked, if at all.

WHY LETTERS OF CREDIT?

Buyers usually prefer to receive the goods in good order, first, before making any payment therefor. Sellers, however, insist on getting an advance payment, to avoid any risk of non-payment and bad debts.

Thus, the bank comes as an intermediary and issues letters of credit at the request of the buyer, in favour of the seller, through the seller's bank. That is the rationale behind the need for issuance of the letters of credit.

WHAT IS A LETTER OF CREDIT?

Letter of Credit is a letter of undertaking issued by the bank, undertaking to make payment of bills, drawn under the Letter of Credit, on first demand, provided all the terms and conditions, as stipulated in the relative Letter of Credit documents, are complied with, completely and in toto, inasmuch as even any small and minor deviation therefrom may render the bills liable to be dishonoured by the buyers and, in turn, by the buyers' banker.

AMENDMENTS TO LETTERS OF CREDIT

However, the necessary amendments to the terms and conditions of the letters of credit can be made by the issuing banker, but at the instance (request) of the buyers. Therefore, the seller has to approach the buyer concerned, to get the needful done, before the bills could be presented to the sellers' banker for payment. Such amendments could be done just by exchange of letters on a plane letterhead (unstamped) of the issuing banker concerned.

LETTERS OF CREDIT ARE USUALLY ISSUED IN QUADRUPLICATE

(*i*) The original letter of credit, along with its one copy, is sent to the sellers' banker for retention of the original with them, and passing on the copy to the seller (the beneficiary) for information and record.

(*ii*) One copy is given to the buyer (the applicant).

(*iii*) One copy is retained by the issuing banker for its record.

PAYMENT UNDER RESERVE

Under special circumstances, at the request of the sellers, and on their specific undertaking (preferably on stamped paper), to the effect that the bills drawn under the letter of credit may be negotiated (paid) under the Letter of Credit, though some minor points are at variance with the terms and conditions of the Letter of Credit, on their (sellers') specific undertaking that such payment be made only with the specific provision of 'under reserve'. That is, if the buyer refuses to pay the amount of the bill, due to such deviation from the terms and conditions of the Letter of Credit, the seller will refund the amount, paid to him under reserve, immediately, on demand made by the bank.

MARGIN MONEY

Banks insist on some margin money to be deposited by the buyer, which may range from nil to cent per cent. However, usually the margin stipulated on the working capital loan is stipulated in the case of issuance of letters of credit.

LIEN ON CASH CREDIT ACCOUNT FOR MARGIN MONEY

The margin money deposited by way of the lien, noted on the cash credit account, has proved to be more economical and gainful for buyers, in comparison to getting the amount of margin money deposited by way of the Bank's Term Deposit Receipts.

MANAGING CREDIT RISKS OF BANKS

Besides insisting on obtaining some margin money, the bank also takes the following precautions to safeguard its interest, viz.,

(*i*) The party should be enjoying the working capital loan facility from the bank, and must be conducting its account, maintained with the bank, in a satisfactory manner, and following the financial discipline stipulated by the bank.

(*ii*) A suitable limit for letters of credit is allocated, along with the requirement of the fund-based working capital limit, based on its scale of operation and credit-worthiness.

(*iii*) (*a*) Preparation of cash budget, and

(*b*) Study of the cash flow position to ensure that the buyer will have sufficient funds to honour the bill, negotiated under the Letter of Credit, when it is expected to arrive at the branch.

(*iv*) Obtaining some collateral (additional) security by way of

(*a*) Third party guarantee; and/or

(*b*) Equitable mortgage of immovable properties.

TYPES OF LETTERS OF CREDIT

1. **Demand and Time.** It depends on whether the accompanying Bill of Exchange drawn is payable on demand or after the stipulated period, *i.e.* days or months.

   Time bills, however, attract some stamp duty, as per the Indian Stamp Act and also involve calculation of due date, as per the Negotiable Instruments Act. Time bills are also required to be accepted by the drawees on the face of the bill, preferably stating "accepted payable at ABC Branch of XYZ Bank," so that the payment is to be made by the drawee at the bank's branch only.

2. **Documentary and Clean:** Whether the documents pertaining to the letters of credit include some documents to title to goods, viz. Railway Receipt, Truck Receipt, Bill of Lading or Airway Bill or not. Banks, however, do not take any responsibility about the quality, or even quantity, of goods. For this, the buyers have to make their own arrangements and insist on 'Inspection Notes' as one of the documents required to accompany the bill drawn under the letter of credit.

3. **Delivery Against Acceptance (DA) and Delivery Against Payment (DP):** This means whether the documents are to be delivered just after acceptance of the time bill or against its full payment on or before the due date.
4. **Inland (Domestic) and Foreign:** If both the sellers and the buyers are of the same country, it would be the case of an inland or a domestic letter of credit. But, if one of them is of some other country, it would be the case of a foreign letter of credit.

   Further, foreign letter of credit may be import Letter of Credit, if the buyer is an Indian and the seller is of some other country. And, it would be export letter of credit if the seller is an Indian and the buyer is of some other country.
5. **Revocable and Irrevocable:** It implies whether the Letter of Credit can be revoked (cancelled) at any time, at the discretion of the issuing banker, or it cannot be revoked (cancelled), at any later date, once it has been issued by the bank.
6. **With Recourse and Without Recourse to the Drawer:** It means whether the amount of the bill negotiated under the Letter of Credit and paid to the seller can be recovered from the drawer of the bill, *i.e.* the seller, at a later date or not. That is, whether the bank still has the recourse and remedy open to the drawer of the bill seller. Thus, for obvious reasons, the seller, to be on the safe side all through, invariably insists on the issuance of an "Irrevocable Letter of Credit, without Recourse to the Drawer".
7. **Confirmed and Unconfirmed:** It shows whether the Letter of Credit has been confirmed by a well known bank, too, in addition to the issuing banker or not. Confirmation by another banker is insisted upon, and that, too, in the case of a foreign letter of credit, when the issuing banker is not a well-known and stable banker, in the specific foreign country, and the seller, thus, insists for the confirmation of the Letter of Credit by another banker, preferably of his (seller's) choice. Such other bank, of course, charges some commission for the service, in addition to the commission recovered by the issuing banker.

REVOLVING LETTERS OF CREDIT

Supposing an industry in Lucknow wants to get supplies of raw materials from a company, which insists on opening of a Letter of Credit by the buyer in its favour and the annual requirement of the material of the buyer company is, say Rs. 10 lakh, but, the bank does not consider the buyer to be worth the amount. Thus, as the average monthly requirement of the buyer, in the instant case, may be one lakh, the bank, instead of issuing one Letter of Credit for Rs. 10 lakh, may prefer to issue a revolving Letter of Credit with the following terms and conditions:

Date of Issue	– Say 01.07.2009
Validity Period	– One year, up to 30.06.2010
Negotiation of bills outstanding at anyone time	– Maximum Rs. 1 lakh
The aggregate amount to be negotiated under the Letter of Credit	– Maximum Rs. 10 lakh

Thus,

(*i*) The next bill will be usually negotiated only when the earlier bill has been paid and the outstanding, as on date, is well within Rs. 1 lakh.

(*ii*) The letter of credit will lapse:

(*a*) As at the close of business on 30.06.2010 (the date of issue being 01.07.2009); or

(*b*) When the bills aggregating Rs. 10 lakh have been negotiated under the letter of credit, whichever of the two [*i.e.* (*a*) and (*b*) above] is earlier.

QUESTIONS
(For Self-assessment)

1. (*a*) Why is the Letters of Credit (L/C) known as non-fund based working capital finance?

   (*b*) Will it be right to suggest that the L/C does not involve any financial obligation or risk on the part of the issuing banker?
2. What is the main idea/purpose behind the evolution of the instrument like the Letter of Credit (L/C)?
3. What are the main undertakings of the issuing banker in the case of a Letter of Credit (L/C)?
4. Distinguish between the following types of Letters of Credit (L/C):

   (*i*) Demand and Time,

   (*ii*) Documentary and Clean,

   (*iii*) Delivery Against Acceptance (DA) and Delivery Against Payment (DP),

   (*iv*) Inland and Foreign,

   (*v*) Revocable and Irrevocable,

   (*vi*) 'With Recourse to the Drawers' and 'Without Recourse to the Drawers', and

   (*vii*) Confirmed and Unconfirmed.
5. (*a*) It is said that the margin money against the Letters of Credit (L/C) must be deposited with the issuing banker by way of the bank's Term Deposit Receipt (TDR) instead of in the current account. Do you agree? Give reasons for your answer.

   (*b*) Can you think of even a better and more gainful way, than the bank's TDR, for the deposit of the required margin money? Explain, in detail, as to how and why, do you consider your suggestion to be a better business sense?
6. What special precautions should the bank take to manage the financial risks connected with the issuance of the Letters of Credit (L/C)? Give reasons for your answer, citing suitable examples to illustrate the points.
7. Banks usually insist that the drawee(s) of the bill must accept the time (usance) bills of exchange preferably in the following form:

   "Accepted payable at ____________________ at its ____________________ branch"

   (*name of the bank*) (*name of the branch*)

   Is it a reasonable and rational stand on the part of the bank? Give reasons for your answer.
8. What are the salient features/provisions/procedures pertaining to the Revolving Letter of Credit? Explain by citing suitable illustrative examples, wherever possible.
9. The Letter of Credit (L/C) can be amended only at the request of the buyer and not the seller. Do you agree? Give reasons for your answer.
10. What do you understand by the term payment made 'Under Reserve'? Explain, by giving suitable illustrative example.
11. (*a*) The banks invariably take the stand that they would not be responsible for the quality and quantity of goods, covered under the Letter of Credit (L/C), opened by them.

    Do you think that the such a stand of the bank is reasonable enough? Give reasons for your answer.

    (*b*) Keeping in view the aforesaid stand of the bank, what precautionary measures would you suggest to the buyer company, so as to ensure the quality and quantity of goods dispatched under the Letter of Credit (L/C)? Give reasons for your answer.

PROBLEMS
(TO PRACTISE FOR PERFECTION)

1. Terms and conditions of a Letter of Credit (L/C) required that the relative documents should comprise, inter alia, a clean bill of lading. But, accidentally, one of the drums got damaged, whereby the liquid material, contained in the drum, started leaking, though very mildly. And, thus, the Bill of Lading had made a special mention in the document, to this effect.

   On this very trifle little ground, the seller's banker refused to negotiate the bill under the L/C, unless a proper amendment to the L/C, to this effect, was duly received by him, from the issuing banker, inasmuch as the L/C had specified a Clean Bill of Lading, as one of the accompanying documents.

   The CMD of the exporting company, however, personally met the Chief Manager of the seller's bank, and assured him that he had a telephonic conversation with the buyer, and he had agreed to honour the bill, despite the Bill of Lading being conditional and qualified, as aforesaid. At this, the banker, in good faith, negotiated the bill drawn under the L/C, and duly paid the amount, of course, by credit to the exporter's current account.

   But, ultimately, the export bill, negotiated under the L/C, came back unpaid, as the importer refused to honour the bill, inasmuch as the Bill of Lading was not clean, as required under one of the specific laid down conditions.

   (*a*) What, in your considered opinion, will be the liabilities of the various parties involved in the present case?

   (*i*) Buyer (Importer),

   (*ii*) Buyers' banker,

   (*iii*) Seller's banker, and

   (*iv*) Seller (Exporter).

   (*b*) What specific precautions, if at all, the seller's banker should have taken, in the instant case, to safeguard its interest? Give specific reasons for your answer.

2. A Bill of Exchange for Rs. 43,946 has been drawn payable after seven months from the date of its acceptance and is, therefore, required to be duly stamped, as per the Indian Stamp Act? How much stamp duty will be exigible in the instant case and why?

3. A Bill of Exchange for Rs. 5,33,349.50 has been drawn and made payable at sight.

   (*i*) What shall be the stamp duty exigible on such instrument?

   (*ii*) Whether the provisions of the Indian Stamp Act or State Stamp Act will be applicable in the instant case?

4. A Bill of Exchange for Rs. 5,555 dated 04.05.2009 has been made payable 90 days after acceptance and it has been duly accepted (for payment) on May 14, 2009.

   (*i*) When will the bill actually fall due for payment? Give reasons for your answer.

   (*ii*) When will the bill fall due for payment if it is made payable 100 days after date if other particulars remain the same? Give reasons for your answer.

   (*iii*) What amount of stamp duty will be exigible on the Bills of Exchange mentioned at 4 (*i*) and 4 (*ii*) above, if the

   (*a*) Bill is drawn in Mumbai and is payable in Lucknow, and (*b*) Vice Versa?

5. A Bill of Exchange dated 23.7.2009, made payable four months after date, has been duly accepted for payment on 30.07.2009. What will be its actual due date of payment? Give reasons for your answer.

6. A Bill of Exchange dated 15.08.2009 and accepted on 23.8.2009 has been made payable 120 days after date. When will this bill fall due for payment? Give reasons for your answer.

12

BANK GUARANTEES

> *A person who can't pay gets another person who can't pay to guarantee that he can pay.*
>
> ***Charles Dickens***

The Learning Points

The chapter aims at developing the knowledge and facilitating the understanding of:

- Different types of bank guarantees: financial and performance
- Different types and purposes of issuing financial bank guarantees
- Special characteristics and greater financial risks inherent in performance bank guarantees
- Restrictions imposed by the Reserve Bank of India (RBI) on banks for Issuing Performance Bank Guarantees
- Calculation of the Validity Period of the Bank Guarantees, Legal Implications inherent in Bank Guarantees, particularly pertaining to Performance Bank Guarantees

12.1 TYPES OF BANK GUARANTEES

There are two types of bank guarantees (B/Gs):

(*a*) Short-term Bank Guarantee, which is usually issued for a period ranging to 3 years; and

(*b*) Long-term Bank Guarantee. It is also known as Deferred Payment Guarantee (DPG)]. It contains an undertaking given by the bank that the amount of instalments, stipulated by the Term Lending Institutions, for repayment of the term loans, sanctioned to the applicant borrower, would be paid by the borrower concerned on the due dates, on time, failing which the bank itself will make payment of the instalment on the due date.

Thus, the long-term Bank Guarantee (being in the nature of a term loan) does not come within the purview of working capital financing. We will, therefore, confine ourselves to the discussion on short-term bank guarantee only.

Short-Term Bank Guarantee (B/G)

Short-term Bank Guarantee usually is of two types:

(*i*) Financial bank guarantee; and

(*ii*) Performance bank guarantee.

As the name itself suggests, the Financial Bank Guarantee is issued in lieu of the deposit of required amount in cash, or for facilitating the release of some withheld payment.

As against this, the Performance Bank Guarantee is issued, guaranteeing the timely performance of a job/task, as also of the required standard and quality, to the entire satisfaction of the beneficiary of such bank guarantee, as is mutually agreed upon.

Thus, the Performance Bank Guarantee involves much higher risks and commitment on the part of the banks. That is why, under instructions from the Reserve Bank of India (RBI), such a guarantee is required to be issued usually on the prescribed proforma (specially designed for the purpose) and against much stricter conditions, and retention of a much higher percentage of the amount of the guarantee (even cent per cent, in some cases) by way of margin money, and that, too, on behalf of very valued constituents of high integrity and financial stability and standing.

12.2 TYPES (AND PURPOSES) OF FINANCIAL BANK GUARANTEES

1. In Lieu of Earnest Money

While submitting a tender, say, for supplying some items, like furniture, electric fittings, or for undertaking some job, like construction of a building, installation of a sprinkler system for lawns, etc., the applicants are invariably required to deposit some amount in cash or by way of Bank Term Deposit Receipts (TDRs), on the condition that if the tender of a particular person/company is accepted and the person/company eventually backs out, the amount so deposited, would be forfeited. This is so, with a view to ensuring that only such parties, who are serious and sincere enough, about rendering the required supply and/or services, must file the relative tenders, quoting some reasonable terms and conditions.

In such cases, some persons/companies may prefer to offer a bank guarantee, instead, stipulating the undertaking, given by the bank, on behalf of the person/company, that in the event of their tender being passed and accepted, and they, in turn, preferring to back out from the compliance of the terms and conditions of the tender, the bank would pay the amount of the required earnest money, as stated in the bank guarantee. Such bank guarantees can, however, be invoked by the beneficiaries, only if it is established that

(*i*) the tender concerned was accepted, and

(*ii*) the relative party had since backed out.

2. In Lieu of Security Deposit

Food Corporation of India (FCI), for example, usually issues stocks of paddy to the rice mills, registered with them, so that they may process the paddy and return the rice to FCI. But, as the stocks of paddy of high value, are generally issued, FCI may insist that some security money (to the extent of say, 10% or 20% of the value of the paddy, to be supplied at anyone time, from time to time), could be deposited with the FCI, so that the party may give back the rice of the required value, and any shortage could be recovered from such security deposits. But, making such a huge deposit even by way of Bank's Term Deposit Receipts (TDRs) may not be as easy or gainful for companies. They may, therefore, approach their bankers and apply for the issuance of a Bank Guarantee for the amount, instead of depositing the cash or the TDR, as the security deposit.

3. Advance for Supply of Raw Materials

Some companies insist on advance payment in cash or by way of a bank draft towards the cost of goods to be supplied. For example, in early 1970s, TISCO did insist on advance payment of the full amount involved, in cash or by way of a bank draft. This naturally means loss of interest on the amount so paid in advance and/or would involve the opportunity cost, besides blockage of funds. In such cases, the buyers prudently prefer to give the bank guarantees, instead, which is issued by the bank on retention of only a percentage of the cost of goods to be supplied, as the margin money, rather than the full cost thereof. In terms of such bank guarantees, the banks undertake to make the required payment to the supplier company in case the buyer company fails to honour the bill. Thus, the financial implications do come in the case of financial bank guarantees, but only in the event of the default, if any, on the part of the buyer company.

4. Part-payment for the Incomplete Job

Bank guarantees may as well be issued to enable organizations to make part-payment against some jobs only half-done. Most of the organizations would be cautious enough, not to release any part-payment, if the job is only half-done. For example, if some of the items of furniture, being manufactured by a contractor, be in the work-in-process stage, and if the contractor, in the mean time, gets some more lucrative job, he may leave the job in hand half-way through, making it all the more difficult for the organization to get the job (somehow) completed by some other contractor, which may, possibly, prove to be even more expensive, besides being bothersome. Thus, in such an unhappy eventuality, the interest of the beneficiary of the bank guarantee would be fully protected as he can invoke the bank guarantee and get the amount, stipulated therein, by way of compensation for the resultant extra cost and botheration.

5. Release of 10% Withheld Payment, Pending Testing of the Performance/ Quality of Items of Machinery/Goods Supplied

As per the usual practice, when some items of machinery are supplied, the buyer companies release only 90% of the amount of the cost of the relative goods supplied. The retained 10% amount is usually released after, say six months, only after the relative machines have been commissioned and found to be running satisfactorily. But, in the case of high value supplies, running into crores of rupees, even 10% thereof may mean quite a substantial amount, involving heavy losses by way of interest or opportunity cost. (For example, BHEL, supplying huge turbines to the State Electricity Boards). The supplier company may, therefore, request its banker to issue a bank guarantee for the required amount. And, the buyer company may not hesitate to release the amount, withheld earlier, as its interests are fully protected by the relative bank guarantee.

6. Bank Guarantee in Lieu of Deposit of Cash with the Court

In early 1970s, there was a legal dispute pending with the Court of Law between the Excise Department and the Sugar Industries regarding some amount of excise duty payable by the sugar industries. The Court, however, ordered that, pending disposal of the case, the sugar industries must deposit the amount in question with the court in cash or by way of Bank Term Deposits, so that the amount could be paid to the excise department or refunded to the sugar industries, depending upon as to which one of the two parties ultimately wins the case. But, in that event, the sugar industries would have lost a handsome amount by way of interest, etc.

Therefore, the sugar industries instead offered to deposit bank guarantees of the like amount. And, the Court agreed to the proposal, and accepted the bank guarantees issued in its favour, to the effect that in the event of the sugar industries losing the case, the amount specified in the bank guarantee, would be immediately paid to the court by the bank on first demand, on invocation of the bank guarantee by the Court. And, as there were 50-50 chances of the sugar industries winning the case, banks had noted lien on the cash credit accounts of the sugar industries to the extent of the full amount, for which the bank guarantees had been issued. This way the company could save a lot of amount by way of interest and the court also got the surety that, in the event of the sugar industries losing the case, the full amount would be paid by the bank, for onward payment to the excise department.

7. Bank Guarantee to Honour Credit Notes of a Particular Party

The Food Corporation of India (FCI) usually has to transport huge stocks of foodgrains (mostly full goods-train load of stocks) from one place to another, which, of course, involves a huge sum of money by way of freight charges, payable to the railway authorities.

The railway authorities, however, seemed reluctant to accept cheques from the FCI for such a heavy amount, so frequently, almost all the year round. Therefore, FCI requested its bankers to issue a bank guarantee to the effect that on presentation of the credit notes, issued by the officer of the FCI, authorized on this behalf, the bank would make payment of the amount specifically mentioned in the credit note, within a maximum period of, say 15 days from the date of the presentation of the credit notes, of course, up to a maximum aggregate amount, as stipulated in the bank guarantee, issued to this effect.

Such bank guarantees may be issued by one of the branches of a bank for an aggregate amount of, say Rs. 5,000 million, by the State Bank of India, New Delhi Main Branch. This may, however, be fragmented into a number of bank guarantees for specific amounts, of course, within an overall limit of Rs. 5,000 million, made to be valid for payment of the credit notes at various important stations like Hyderabad, Chennai, Mumbai, Bangalore, Kolkata, Guwahati, Bhubaneshwar, for Rs. 400 million each, aggregating (Rs. 400 million × 7) Rs. 2,800 million, and the balance amount of Rs. 2,200 million being available for payment of the credit notes at New Delhi Main Branch.

12.3 PERFORMANCE BANK GUARANTEES

Let us first try to understand the main distinguishing features of financial bank guarantee and performance bank guarantee.

It is now clear that in all the different cases of financial bank guarantees, the bank undertakes to immediately make payment of the specified amount to the beneficiary of the bank guarantee, in the event of some failure or lapse on the part of the applicant. For example; the applicant submits the tender and in case his tender has been accepted but he himself backs out from taking up the job, the earnest money, if deposited in cash, would have been forfeited. Now that a financial bank guarantee has been issued, instead of deposit of earnest money in cash, the bank guarantee would be invoked on the default of the applicant, and the bank will have to make payment of the entire specified amount to the beneficiary.

But, in all such cases, some lapse or fault must take place on the part of the applicant or in the quality and performance of goods and machines supplied. Thus, in the case of financial bank guarantee, the alleged lapse or failure, on the part of the applicant, must take place, and that it must be established, too, that it has actually taken place.

As against this, in the case of the Performance Bank Guarantee, the payment has got to be made and that too on the first demand and without any demur (that is, no questions to be asked or any plea advanced), and that, too, at the sole discretion and judgement of the beneficiary, that the performance has fallen short of the stipulated and agreed terms and conditions, about the quantity, quality and timely supply of goods, at the specified place, etc. In such cases, the beneficiary does not have to necessarily establish, beyond doubt, that some breach of some terms and conditions have actually taken place. Because, as per the wording of the performance bank guarantee, in the event of invocation of the bank guarantee, the contention and stand taken by the beneficiary that the applicant had failed to fulfill one or more of the conditions stipulated for performance of the job or for the supply of goods of the required quality, quantity, etc. on time, is considered good enough, and no further probing and proving of the lapse is called for at all. Only in some rare cases, if, in the sole assessment of the judge, there seemed to be a prima fact case of some fraud, corruption and/or vigilance angle involved in a particular case, he may prefer to pass an injunction order, as a special case. Otherwise, no such injunction order would, any longer, be passed by any Court of Law. Some live case laws on the subject can very well be quoted in this regard.

Thus, we see that the risk factors involved in the case of Performance Bank Guarantee (as against the Financial Bank Guarantee), are various and varied, and, above all, of a much higher degree.

Examples

(*i*) In the case of the Financial Bank Guarantee, a stipulated sum of money is payable by the bank, and that too, in the event of some failure, on the part of the applicant, to comply with a condition like honouring an accepted tender, completing unfinished work, rectifying defects in (or replacing) the items of machinery, etc.

As against this, in performance bank guarantee, it is not only a financial undertaking but also a sort of certification, on behalf of the applicant, that the entrusted job is done professionally, with due skill and dexterity, as per the given specifications, regarding quantity, quality and within the given time frame.

(*ii*) In the case of financial guarantee, the bank's liability to pay the specified amount does come but only after some defaults/failings on the part of the applicant are duly established.

But, in the case of a performance bank guarantee, the beneficiary's dissatisfaction and the contention that the job has not been done satisfactorily [in terms of the specifications, quality, quantity, and within the given time frame—anyone or more of such violations], the bank (as per the undertaking given in the bank guarantee) has to pay the amount, in the case of invocation of the bank guarantee, on the very **first demand,** *i.e.* immediately on receipt of the invocation letter, without demur (*i.e.* without asking any questions or pleading verification of the beneficiary's contention), and even without reference to the applicant.

Thus, we clearly observe that the bank's responsibilities and liabilities in the case of performance bank guarantee are far greater in comparison to those in the case of financial bank guarantee.

That is why, it has been so very pertinent and pragmatic, on the part of the Reserve Bank of India (RBI) to have stipulated the undernoted strict and stringent conditions on banks, in respect of issuance of performance bank guarantee right from 1960s.

12.4 RESTRICTIONS IMPOSED BY THE RESERVE BANK OF INDIA (RBI) ON THE ISSUANCE OF PERFORMANCE BANK GUARANTEES

1. Banks are to avoid issuance of Performance Bank Guarantees.
2. Further, such bank guarantees, if at all, should be issued on behalf of very valuable constituents only, whose credit-worthiness, honesty and integrity are of very high order.
3. Such bank guarantees must be issued only as per the proforma bank guarantee circulated by the Reserve Bank of India (RBI) to all the banks. However, some minor variations/ amendments may be allowed, but only in some special cases (usually in the case of PSUs) but, only after fully ensuring that the proposed changes do not adversely affect any of the interests of the bank, in any way, whatsoever. It should further be ensured that the spirit, contained in the text of such amended bank guarantees remained unchanged.
4. Moreover, such amendments must be duly approved by the bank's controlling authorities concerned, as the branches have not been entrusted with any discretionary powers to allow such changes in the bank guarantee proforma.
5. Performance bank guarantee, being pregnant with high risk factors, must usually be issued in the case of valued constituents only, and that too, mostly on retention of the full amount of the bank guarantee as the margin money.

12.5 VALIDITY PERIOD OF THE BANK GUARANTEES

Bank guarantees (both financial and performance bank guarantees) are usually issued for a period of one year. Thus, bank guarantee issued on 01.01.2009 for 12 months would be held valid till the close of the bank's business hours on 31.12.2009. Therefore, any cause of complaint, arising during the aforesaid period only, will be covered under the respective bank guarantees. That is, if the cause for complaint arises on 01.01.2010, such complaint will not be deemed to be covered under the bank guarantee.

But, as per the Indian Limitation Act, the bank guarantee can be invoked (of course, for the complaints arising within the validity period of the bank guarantee) up to a period of 3 years from the date of expiry of the bank guarantee, *i.e.* up to 31.12.2012. And, in the case of government departments (of both the Central and the State Governments) the limitation period, as provided by law, is 30 years. The law, however, provides that the usual stipulated limitation period of 3 years (or 30 years) can be reduced up to a much shorter period, mutually agreed upon, between the parties concerned. And, taking advantage of such legal provisions, the banks invariably stipulate, in all the bank guarantees, that the claim, if any, arising out of the bank guarantee, during its validity period, can be made to the bank within a period of say, 3 or 6 months, from the date of the expiry of the bank guarantee, *i.e.* up to 31.03.2010 or 30.06.2010, respectively. Such provisions, like the period (3 months/6 months) and the specific date (31.03.2010/30.06.2010) are specifically and clearly stipulated invariably in all the bank guarantees. And, the Supreme Court of India, in '*State of Maharashtra vs. Dr. M.N. Kaul*' (AIR, 1967; S.C., 1634), held that it was impossible to ignore the time limit which was the integral part of the guarantee, and upheld the bank's contention that the guarantee was no longer enforceable after the expiry of the time period, as was specifically stipulated in the bank guarantee concerned. These views have again been subsequently endorsed in '*Kerala Electric and Allied Engineering Company Limited vs. Canara Bank*' (AIR, 1980; Kerala, 151).

The bank guarantees can, however, be renewed, usually for a further period of one year, at a time, on payment of the usual bank charges, provided the financial position and standing of the applicant have not deteriorated in the mean time.

Amount: The amount guaranteed under each bank guarantee is specifically and clearly mentioned therein, in each case.

Return of Cancelled Bank Guarantee

The banks also insist that the bank guarantee, after the expiry of its validity period, must be returned to the bank by the beneficiary, duly cancelled, for record at the branch. This is so because, in that event the bank will be fully satisfied to the effect that no claim would be filed with the bank by way of invocation of the respective bank guarantee. The procedure, however, does not seem to be of much significance for the bank, except by way of an abundant precaution.

Many beneficiary companies, however, prefer to retain the bank guarantee with them even after the expiry of its validity period, on the plea that just in case it may, somehow, prove to be of some use, though such a likelihood is negligible. I, on my part, do not want to interfere with the aforesaid prevalent (unnecessarily, notwithstanding) practice on the part of the beneficiary companies (as also the banks). But, I would definitely like to counsel them (beneficiary companies) to keep such expired (and so, worthless) bank guarantees under separate files or in a separate cupboard, so that the valid and current bank guarantees may not get mixed up with them.

"I am Authorized to Sign the Bank Guarantee"

Some of the beneficiary companies insist that in the bank guarantee the bank officer, signing the bank guarantee, should specifically state and certify to the effect that "I/we am/are authorized to sign the bank guarantee on behalf of the bank", under the full signature.

But, it does not seem to make much of a sense except that, in most of the organizations, the officers/employees are required to declare, at the end of their TA Bills, that all the expenses claimed in the TA Bill have actually been incurred. The only idea behind such declaration seems to be that, at the time of signing such a declaration, the person will think twice whether it would be proper and correct for him to do so, whereby his or her honesty and integrity could be doubly checked and ensured.

12.6 LEGAL IMPLICATIONS/RAMIFICATIONS OF BANK GUARANTEE

As we have already observed, the prime purpose of a bank guarantee is that the bank hereby undertakes to pay, on demand, a certain sum of money, specified therein, to the beneficiary concerned, immediately, on the very 'first demand' of the beneficiary, 'without any protest or demur', and even without any reference to the applicant, on whose behalf the bank guarantee has been issued. Most of the bank guarantees include a clause to the effect that the demand notice of the beneficiary, specifying that a default (by way of non-performance or unsatisfactory performance of a contract, etc.), has occurred, would itself be considered as a 'conclusive evidence' that a default has occurred, justify the invocation of the bank guarantee. And, such a clause has been upheld by courts, too, as valid.

Here, I will like to share a practical experience of mine, while I was posted as the Chief Manager at one of the branches in Kanpur (U.P.)

Example:

One fine morning, I received a registered letter from a government undertaking, invoking a bank guarantee, which was issued by me only a couple of months back. I naturally got too worried. So, I immediately sent for the applicant concerned. He, however, counselled me not to take the matter so seriously and, at the same time, he assured me that, latest by 4:00 p.m., he would come back with an injunction order, issued by a competent court. And, to my most pleasant surprise, he was back in my office, by around 3:00 p.m., with a valid injunction order. But, I just could not believe this. I, in fact, wanted to get the signature of the judge verified by a local branch of the State Bank of India so that I could be fully satisfied about the veracity of the injunction order. Therefore, I got the judge's signature duly verified by the Branch Manager of a local branch of the State Bank of India, dealing with the government business, and, thus, paying the salary bills of all the judges, too, every month.

But, the verification was done only in pencil, which could be easily erased, if required to be submitted in the Court. Because, otherwise, the verification of the signature of the judge and the seal of the Court may amount to Contempt of Court.

I, therefore, immediately sent a copy of the injunction order to the beneficiary concerned. And, the matter ended there.

But then, it was in the year 1972, and I was a little fortunate, too. Because, nowadays, the courts, in their judgements, have clearly indicated that the banks are obliged to make the payment of the guaranteed amount to the beneficiary when he prefers to invoke the bank guarantee, unless the bank has a notice of a clear fraud.

The extracts of a portion of the court judgement in the case *HOWE Richardson Scale Company Limited vs. Plimex-Cekop and National Westminister Bank*, reported in 1978, I Lloyd's Law Reports 161, clarifies the points beyond any possible doubt and dispute:

> The bank, in principle, is in a position, not identical with but very similar to the position, of a bank which has opened a confirmed irrevocable letter of credit. Whether the obligation arises under a letter of credit or under a guarantee, the obligation of the bank is to perform that which it is required to perform by that particular contract, and that obligation does not, in the ordinary way, depend on the correct resolution of a dispute as to the sufficiency of performance, by the seller to the buyer or by the buyer to the seller, as the case may be, under the sale and purchase contract.

Further, the bank guarantee is independent of the primary contract of sale between the buyer and the seller. As was decided by the Calcutta High Court, in the case, *Texmaco Limited vs. State Bank of India* (AIR, 1979, Calcutta-44) that, as the obligation was undertaken by the Bank to repay the amount on 'First Demand, and "Without protest, demur and without questioning the legal relationship subsisting between the STC and Texmaco", the bank was liable to make the payment to the beneficiary, irrespective of any disputes between the parties. And, therefore, the Court did not issue injunction in this case.

Further, in *Centex India Limited vs. Vinmar Impex Inc. and Others* (1987, 61, CC697) the Supreme Court of India laid down that the Guarantee must be allowed to be honoured free from interference by the courts and the Bank is liable to honour it, regardless of the controversy between the buyer and the seller.

It would, therefore, augur well for banks to insist to get a clause incorporated in the counter-guarantee and indemnity, executed by the applicant (on the basis of which the bank guarantee is issued) to the effect that notwithstanding any dispute between the applicant (customer of the bank) and the beneficiary of the bank guarantee, the reasonableness, propriety or validity of any payment, made by the bank to the beneficiary, in terms of the bank guarantee, shall not be questioned by the applicant (bank's customer).

But, if the bank guarantee specifically stipulates that it is enforceable on proof of the breach of the primary contract between the applicant and the beneficiary, the beneficiary will have to prove the actual damage or loss, suffered by him and the onus (burden) of proof will also lie with the beneficiary. We have observed that the courts have always decided the cases keeping in view the words used and the terms stipulated in the impugned bank guarantee.

Thus, generally speaking, there are two types of bank guarantees:

Type 1: The bank guarantee, which is **'absolute'** and, thus, is encashable on the very first demand made by the beneficiary, which itself is conclusive in terms of the bank guarantee, whereby the beneficiary himself is the sole judge as to whether there has been any breach of the primary contract on the part of the other parties, as also as to how much amount falls due for payment to him.

Type 2: The other type of bank guarantee is **'conditional'**, that is, the one whereby it is not encashable without proof of breach of the primary contract between the two parties (the applicant and the beneficiary to the bank guarantee).

It may, however, be pertinent to mention here that there is only one exception to the absolute right of the beneficiary in the first type of bank guarantee, stated earlier, enunciated by the Supreme Court of India in the case *United Commercial Bank vs. Bank of Baroda* as has been quoted hereunder: "Except possibly in clear cases of fraud, of which the banks have notice, the courts will leave the merchants to settle their disputes under the contract by litigation or arbitration, as available to them, or as stipulated in the contracts." Such fraud must, however, have direct connection with the contracts of guarantee and not the primary contract. Because, in that case, even the absolute bank guarantee (Type-I) will get reduced to the status of conditional bank guarantee (Type-2).

A Word of Caution

It will augur well for all the beneficiaries of the bank guarantees never to part with the original bank guarantee to the bank, lest the bank officers, in order to save their skin, may destroy the bank guarantee and ask for the original bank guarantee to enable them to honour the commitment, if any. It would, however, be out of place to argue that banks are not supposed to act so irresponsibly and dishonestly, because, there are some live cases where bank officers (and not the banks, as such) had destroyed the original bank guarantee, whereby a lot of valuable time (and the amount of interest, etc., therewith) was avoidably lost in forcing the bank to honour the bank guarantee, as per the office copy thereof, which, as a regular practice, must be on record at the branch.

12.7 MINI CASE STUDIES

Let us now endeavour to understand and appreciate some legal aspects and ramifications, pertaining to bank guarantees through some live case studies.

Mini Case Study No. 1

"PILLARS AND POLES PROTEST"
(A CASE STUDY ON INVOCATION OF A BANK GUARANTEE)

Aloke Electricals Limited (AEL), a Public Sector Undertaking (PSU) was executing a Government contract for electrification in some rural areas of Himachal Pradesh. Pillars and Poles (Private) Limited (PPL), the manufacturers of tubular poles, received a large order from AEL, for the supply of tubular poles of different sizes and thickness. In this connection, PPL furnished a Performance Guarantee for Rs. 5 lakh, issued by a scheduled bank to the effect that "the applicant (PPL) will deliver the specified numbers of different sizes of poles, as per the required specifications, at the site of work, failing which the beneficiary (AEL) had the absolute right, in its sole discretion, to invoke the bank guarantee, and the bank would make the payment of the full guaranteed amount to AEL immediately on first demand, without any demur or protest, and without any prior reference to the applicant."

However, after sometime, within the validity period of the bank guarantee, the bank received a Registered Letter from AEL, invoking the bank guarantee (which, too, was enclosed, in original) stating that PPL had failed to supply the goods as per the terms of the order and contract.

The Bank Manager was surprised to receive the letter of invocation. However, as PPL was a valued customer of the bank, the Branch Manager informed them about the invocation of the bank guarantee, and further stated therein that in case the bank did not hear from them anything in this regard, within a week, the payment would be made to the beneficiaries (AEL). And, accordingly, the bank made the payment to AEL, by debit to the cash credit account of PPL immediately after a week.

Thereafter, PPL filed a civil suit in the court of law challenging the payment made by the bank, terming it as wrongful, illegal and arbitrary, and prayed that the bank should be instructed to credit the amount back into their account.

Issues to be Discussed and Decided Upon

(*i*) What, in your considered opinion, are the chances of PPL winning the court case? Give sound reasons in support of your answers.

(*ii*) One may argue that, after having written a letter to PPL, the bank should have waited for the confirmation from PPL, before making the payment under the bank guarantee.

Do you agree? Give reasons in support of your arguments.

(*iii*) Some may suggest that on receipt of the letter from the bank, PPL should have immediately approached the court and got an injunction order issued, on the plea that there was no breach of contract and the goods were supplied at the site, strictly as per the order and the contract.

Do you subscribe to the suggestions? Give reasons in support of your stand.

(*iv*) AEL were very happy on receipt of the amount from the bank against the bank guarantee. But, they had very well realized that there had been some small but significant 'imprudent act' on their part, too, which could have jeopardised their interest and claim against the Bank Guarantee itself. They were just fortunate that nothing untoward happened.

Identify the small but significant 'Imprudent Act', and justify as to why do you consider it as such?

Mini Case Study No. 1

"PILLARS AND POLES PROTEST"

A SUGGESTED APPROACH*

(*i*) There is no chance of PPL winning the case, inasmuch as it has been specifically mentioned in the guarantee document as under:

"......failing which, the beneficiary (AEL) had the absolute right, in its sole discretion, to invoke the bank guarantee, and the bank would make the payment of the full guaranteed amount to AEL immediately, on first demand, without any demur or protest."

There are several case laws, where the learned judges have held that the bank guarantee is, though not the same, but quite similar to the irrevocable letter of credit, and therefore, it should comply with its undertakings, as stipulated in the bank guarantee document, *i.e.* to pay the full amount to the beneficiary on first demand, without any demur or protest, as specifically stated, in very clear terms, in the guarantee document.

(*ii*) I do not agree at all inasmuch as it was, in fact, not necessary for the bank to have even referred the matter to the applicant (its customer). And, as the learned judge in a legal case, *Alliance Mills (Lessees) Private Limited vs. Union of India and others* [(1986) 59, Comp Cas 194 (Cal)] says:

> It is surprising that although it was specifically mentioned in the bank guarantee that before making the payment, no reference would be made to the petitioner company (PPL in the instant case), even then the Allahabad Bank, for reasons best known to them, without encashing the bank guarantee, intimated the petitioner company (PPL in the instant case) about the demand made by the Government Company", the beneficiary (*i.e.* AEL in the instant case).

It has, however, been found that usually banks issue bank guarantees on behalf of their customers (borrowers). Therefore, with a view to maintain good relations with them, bank managers usually inform the applicant in this regard, so that if they were to prefer any legal action, they could proceed accordingly. But, in fact, it is not proper to do so in such cases of absolute bank guarantees. Sometimes, the bank managers seek instructions from the controlling office before making the payment, which, too, results in some avoidable loss of time, which is not proper, either, in the eye of the law. Therefore, as a prudent act, the bank manager may contact the applicants (bank's customers) but not in writing, but only over telephone, with a view to alerting them in this regard, and thereby maintaining good relations with them, and, at the same time, without inviting any adverse remarks from the learned judges in the court cases.

(*iii*) It may not be considered as a prudent act to file a suit in the Court of law for seeking an injunction order, because there are several case laws to support the view that Courts should not issue injunction order in such cases of 'absolute' bank guarantee, which means that such bank guarantees stand on their own, independent of whatever may be the terms and conditions in the primary contract, entered into between the applicant and the beneficiary of the bank guarantee. The Court decides only on the basis of the terms and conditions of the bank guarantee in question, which clearly states, in unequivocal terms,

* One of the approaches to the case study, as suggested by the author.

* Please note that there is no single approach/solution to a case study.

that "the beneficiary has the absolute right, in its own discretion, to invoke the bank guarantee" and ask the bank to pay the full amount without any protest or demur. And, rightly so, because, if Courts issue injunction order in such cases of absolute bank guarantee (which is held by the Courts, in several cases, being similar, if not identical with irrevocable L/C), the bank guarantee will cease to be even worth its name, and may have to be referred to, by the aggrieved parties, at least, as a non-bank guarantee, instead.

It may, however, be mentioned here that banks are within their rights, in refraining from making the payment to the beneficiary, "possibly in clear cases of fraud, of which the banks have notice." In such, Courts leave the merchants to settle their disputes under the contract by litigation or arbitration, as available to them, or as stipulated in the contracts", as has been held by the Supreme Court of India in *United Commercial Bank vs. Bank of Baroda*, as has already been mentioned earlier.

Further, banks need not go into the question whether there had been some breach of conditions, contained in the primary contract between the applicant and the beneficiary of the bank guarantee, in such cases of absolute bank guarantees.

The bank is, thus, required to look into such disputes only in the case where terms and conditions of the bank guarantee specifically mention that "its encashment is subject to proof of performance of the underlying contract", *i.e.* the primary contract, which has given rise to the issuance of the bank guarantee. [*Banwari Lal Radhey Mohan vs. Punjab State Cooperative Supply and Marketing Federation Limited* (1955) 58, Comp Cas 210 (Delhi)].

(*iv*) The blunder committed by officers of the beneficiary company was that they had sent the original bank guarantee to the bank, at the time of its invocation, as it was fraught with grave risk of its being destroyed by the bank officers, thereby causing a lot of avoidable delay (and the consequent loss of interest), and long drawn correspondence and dispute.

Mini Case Study No. 2

"TO PAY OR NOT TO PAY"

(A Case Study on Bank Guarantees)

Ram Gopal, Chief Manager, Azadnagar Branch, Bank of Hindustan (a nationalised bank) issued 10 bank guarantees aggregating Rs. 91.50 lakh during the period March 2008 to March 2009, in favour of Diamond Development Commission (a public sector undertaking), on behalf of three parties, viz. M/s Anand Ahuja and Company and M/s Alpana Ahuja and Company and M/s Adarsh Ahuja and Company (all sister concerns), as per details given in Annexure 12.1.

With a view to exercising more than ordinary care, the Regional Manager, Diamond Development Commission, sent a letter dated 23 October 2008 to Ram Gopal, requesting him to confirm that the seven bank guarantees, aggregating Rs. 54 lakh (enclosed in original) were bonafide and were duly signed by him at the branch. On 24 October 2008, the Regional Manager received a letter duly signed by Ram Gopal to that effect. Again, by way of an abundant precaution, the Regional Manager sent a letter dated 11 March 2009, addressed to the aforesaid branch, with a request to confirm that all the 10 bank guarantees aggregating Rs. 91.50 lakh (enclosed in original) were bonafide and duly issued at the branch. The letter, however, was signed by the Regional Manager on 12 March 2009. The letter, in original, as also the enclosures, were returned by the aforenamed branch duly confirmed by Ram Gopal, the Chief Manager, the same day, under his full signature, by affixing the branch rubber stamp.

On 11 April 2009, two senior officers from the Head Office of the Bank of Hindustan, called on the Regional Manager, Diamond Development Commission, to enquire about the bank guarantees issued in their favour by the local branch of the bank. Further, on 14 April 2009, when a senior officer from the Regional Manager's office contacted the bank for extension of the validity period of bank guarantees, expiring shortly, it transpired that the office copies of all these guarantees were not available on record at the branch. The bank, therefore, declined to extend the validity period of bank guarantees in question.

Further, the bank, vide their letter dated the 17 April 2009, refused to honour guarantees for the following reasons:

(*i*) Ram Gopal, Chief Manager, was not authorized to issue bank guarantees for such large amounts. He had acted beyond his discretionary power, delegated to him and, therefore, the bank could not be held responsible.

(*ii*) As per the practice of the bank, all guarantees are required to be signed jointly by the Chief Manager and the Accountant, whereas all these were signed by the Chief Manager alone. This should have given rise to the doubt in the minds of beneficiaries of guarantees.

(*iii*) The beneficiaries of guarantees should have assessed the credit-worthiness of the respective three associate firms, before accepting and acting upon the bank guarantees of such large amounts.

As the bank had disowned its obligation to honour all the 10 bank guarantees in question, the officials at the Regional Manager's office initiated prompt action, immediately on receipt of the letter from the bank to this effect on 17 April 2009. They had sent a telegram to their Head Office on 19 April 2009, advising them the facts contained in the bank's letter dated the 17 April 2009. They had also intimated all the Depots in the Region on 22 April 2009, about the incident, instructing them to exercise more than ordinary care, while dealing with the three parties in question. And, all transactions, viz. issuance of stocks, were discontinued promptly thereafter. Further, all payments to these three parties were also impounded at the various depots, with immediate effect, thereafter.

Please Examine

The accountability and responsibility of various parties concerned, viz.

(*a*) Of the bank officers; *i.e.*

(*i*) The Chief Manager at the bank's branch;

(*ii*) The officers at the bank's Head Office;

(*b*) Of the officers of the Diamond Development Commission; *i.e.*

(*i*) The officers at the Regional Manager's office;

(*ii*) The officers at the various Depots;

(*c*) The stands taken by the Bank; and

(*d*) The actions initiated by the officers of the Commission.

Appendix 12.1

Anand Ahuja and Company

Sl. No.	Date of Issue	Value of Guarantee (Rs. in lakh)	Validity Period	Extended Date
1.	11.03.2008	30.00	10.03.2009	09.09.2009
2.	11.03.2008	0.50	10.03.2009	09.09.2009
3.	09.03.2009	22.50	08.09.2009	—
		Total: 53.00 lakh		

Alpana Ahuja and Company

Sl.No.	Date of Issue	Value of Guarantee (Rs. in lakh)	Validity Period	Extended Date
I.	16.10.2008	15.00	15.04.2009	—
2.	16.10.2008	0.50	15.04.2009	—
3.	09.03.2009	7.50	08.09.2009	—
		Total: 23.00 lakh		

Adarsh Ahuja and Company

Sl. No.	Date of Issue	Value of Guarantee (Rs. in lakh)	Validity Period	Extended Date
1.	16.10.2008	4.50	15.04.2009	14.10.2009
2.	11.09.2008	3.00	10.03.2009	09.09.2009
3.	11.09.2008	0.50	10.03.2009	—
4.	09.03.2009	7.50	08.09.2009	—
		Total: 15.50 lakh **Grand total: 91.50 lakh**		

Mini Case Study No. 3

"TO PAY OR NOT TO PAY"

(A SUGGESTED APPROACH)*

Lapses of the Chief Manager of the Bank

(*i*) The Chief Manager of the Bank has unauthorisedly exceeded his discretionary power while issuing bank guarantees in question.

* One of the approaches to the case study, as suggested by the author.

* Please note that there is no single approach/solution to a case study.

(*ii*) He has not taken due care to properly appraise the financial position and stability of all the sister concerns, at the request of whom bank guarantees for the amount in question, were issued which later transpired to be well above their estimated financial standing and credibility.

(*iii*) The very fact that the office copy of bank guarantees, in question, were not available in records at the branch of the Bank, goes to suggest some wilful and deliberate foul play on the part of the Chief Manager, perhaps, in connivance with the three sister concerns.

All the aforesaid lapses, on the part of the Chief Manager, provide sufficient and valid grounds to initiate departmental proceedings against him, and to take suitable disciplinary action against him, so that even other officers of the Bank may refrain themselves from indulging in such acts of gross indiscipline and misconduct.

It, however, has not been understood as to how did the Chief Manager return all the seven and ten bank guarantees, when these were sent to him on two different occasions, all in original, on both the occasions, for some confirmation.

Lapses of the Officers of the Commission at the Regional Manager's Office

(*i*) One fails to understand as to what purpose would have been served by obtaining the required confirmation about the validly and genuineness or otherwise of bank guarantees from the same person, who had issued all these bank guarantees. Efforts, instead, should have been made to obtain such confirmation from some independent authorities, other than the Chief Manager himself, preferably from his controlling office.

(*ii*) And, at the same time, due care should have invariably been taken by officers of the Diamond Development Commission to send only xerox copies of bank guarantees, and not the original ones, on any occasion, under any circumstances. Because, if the Chief Manager would have destroyed all bank guarantees and would have feigned non-receipt of documents, the Commission would have got involved in some avoidable trouble and complications.

(*iii*) The letter dated 11 March 2009, requiring reconfirmations of the validity of Bank Guarantees, instead of having been signed and sent the same day, was signed a day later, as if it was also one of the usual routine letters. The officer concerned should have personally taken the letter to the Regional Manager and got it signed by him on an urgent basis, and must have initiated further necessary action on top priority basis.

(*iv*) When bank authorities had declined to renew bank guarantees, the Commission should have invoked all the ten bank guarantees, thereby making the renewal of bank guarantees unnecessary. And, all bank guarantees would have remained in full force, as all these had already been invoked well within their validity period.

Under such special circumstances, it would not be prudent enough to waste some valuable time in ascertaining whether there had actually been some lapse on the part of all the three Ahuja firms, justifying the invocation. Here, the invocation has, instead, been forced on the Commission by the Bank itself, by declining to renew bank guarantees. And, whether the beneficiaries have resorted to such invocation justifiably or otherwise, is not relevant here. Besides, bank guarantees can be renewed by the Bank at its sole discretion, and that too, only at the request of the applicants (Ahujas), and not the Commission. And, thus, with a view to keeping the interest of the Commission safeguarded at all times, in respect of bank guarantees, the Commission was left with no alternative but to invoke all the bank guarantees, well before the expiry of the dates, within which bank guarantees could be invoked and claims filed.

And, when we look at Annexure-12.1, we find that as on 14 April, 2009, when the Commission had requested the bank to extend the validity period of the ten bank guarantees, one bank guarantee dated 11.09.2008 for Rs. 50,000 had already expired on March 10, 2009, and the other two bank guarantees, both dated 16.10.2008 for Rs. 15 lakh and Rs. 50,000, respectively, were about to expire on 15 April 2009.

But then, as we already know, usually a period of three months or six months are specifically mentioned in bank guarantees within which (even after the expiry of the validity period of bank guarantees), the claim can be filed, by invoking the bank guarantees.

[Incidentally, it may be recalled that by mutual agreement between the two parties, the limitation period can well stand reduced to a specified period of time, well below the usual three years, in the case of the general public, and 30 years in the case of the Central and State governments, as stipulated in the Indian Limitation Act].

Here, it may be reiterated that the cause for default must, of course, take place within the validity period of bank guarantees. And, therefore, the Commission should have taken the stand that the cause for default, warranting the invocation of bank guarantees, had taken place well within the validity period of bank guarantees, *i.e.* on or before 10 March 2009. Now, whether the claim is tenable or not, is decided in the Court of Law. But, at the same time, the problem of non-renewal of bank guarantees would have very well been taken care of, by invoking bank guarantees.

Lapses of Bank's Officers at the Head Office

All the three contentions of the Bank for refusing to honour bank guarantees are unreasonable and untenable for various reasons as discussed hereunder:

(*i*) The contention that Ram Gopal was not authorised to issue bank guarantees for such large amount will not be tenable on the principle of **'indoor management,'** inasmuch as, the general public is not supposed to know the internal administrative arrangements, like the discretionary and/or financial powers of the various officers of any organization. In fact, it is for the officers of the organisation to know their specific discretionary powers, and they must themselves guard against exceeding these. And, in the case of any default on the part of the officer, suitable disciplinary action should be taken against such an erring officer. But, so far as members of the general public are concerned, the authorities of the organization (the bank in the instant case) are bound to honour all action and decisions taken by its officers, as per the Law of Agency, contained in the Indian Contract Act, whereby the Agent's actions bind the Principal, unless due public notice is given regarding the withdrawal of the Agency right from such an officer. Thus, the Bank is bound to honour bank guarantees issued by Ram Gopal, when he enjoyed full agency rights on behalf the Bank, in the eyes of the general public.

(*ii*) Likewise, the second stand taken by the Bank that Bank Guarantees were required to be signed by both the Chief Manager and the Accountant jointly is also untenable, in the eye of the law on the principle of ***'caveat emptor'***, which means ***'buyer be ware'***. That is, unless, in the printed proforma of bank guarantees, some specific spaces were provided, meant for two signatures, *i.e.* of the Chief Manager and the Accountant, the members of the general public may not be expected to know that the documents needed two signatures. And, obviously in bank guarantees in question, no such specific spaces were provided, otherwise the space meant for the signature of the Accountant would have remained blank and unsigned. Because, if such would have been the case, the Bank would have taken such specific plea, instead of the general plea, in vague terms, as indicated in its letter dated 17 April, 2009.

As we must have observed, bank drafts, issued by Tellers, specifically state as under: "The Draft will not be valid unless signed by the Teller."

This is so because, with a view to facilitate and hasten the process of the issuance of the Bank Draft, a bunch of blank security forms (Bank Draft proforma) is given to the Teller, duly signed by the authorised officer, well in advance.

Similarly, in some dividend warrants or interest warrants, it is stated that "two signatures are required if the amount exceeds, say Rs. 5,000" or "a manual signature is also required, if the amount exceeds Rs. 50,000", and so on.

Some companies, like Lakme, issue and dispatch Dividend Warrants well in advance bearing earlier dates, but it is specifically stated thereon reading such as "Not payable before, December 01, 2009", etc. Such is the case in regard to the salary cheques issued by the Defence Departments, etc.

(*iii*) The third contention of the Bank, that the Commission should have independently assessed and ascertained the credit-worthiness and financial position of all the three Ahuja firms, does not seem to be plausible at all, inasmuch as, if the beneficiary itself would be certain and assured of the financial standing and stability of firms, there may hardly be any need for the issuance of bank guarantees. And, the very fact that the Commission insisted on the issuance of bank guarantee, and their renewals, goes to indicate that the Commission wanted the guarantee from the side of a reliable party like the nationalized bank, as all the three Ahuja firms were not considered to be financially extra sound, beyond doubt. Because, if such would have been the case, bank guarantees would have been unnecessary.

In fact, it is the sole duty and responsibility of bank officers to assess and ascertain the financial strength and stability and the standard of credit-worthiness of parties on whose behalf bank guarantees are required to be issued. The Bank's act of shirking its sole responsibility and contending that the Commission should have ascertained the credit-worthiness of the firms, before acting upon bank guarantees, amounts to nullifying the value and credibility of bank guarantees issued by responsible officers of the issuing Bank itself. Does it not sound ridiculous; to put it mildly?

'Prompt' action on the part of officers at the Regional Manager's office

The action taken by any officer of the Regional Manager's office were far from 'prompt', by any standard, keeping in view the urgency and seriousness of the matter. As the interest of the Commission was in great jeopardy, a swift action was warranted.

It is surprising to find that though the Bank's letter dated 17 April was received on the same day, the Head Office was informed after a lapse of full two days, and that too just by telegram, not even by fax or phone, leave alone e-mail. In my considered view, a Senior Officer from the Regional Office must have been deputed by the Regional Manager himself to go to Head Office by taxi and discuss the matter in greater detail with officers and legal experts at the Head Office. And, he must have come back the same day with full brief and sound strategies chalked out at the Head Office. I presume that the Commission's Head Office was situated around 200/300 kms. away from the Regional Office.

Furthermore, all depots in the region were advised after full five days to exercise more than ordinary care while dealing with all the three Ahuja firms in question. And, the practice of issuance of stocks of rough diamond was discontinued even thereafter. All payments (cheques) of these parties were impounded, but, after some undue delay. Besides, no effort seems to have been made to instruct the branch of the bank concerned to urgently stop payment of all the cheques already issued in favour of all the three Ahuja firms.

All the aforesaid delays seem to be deliberate and intentional, with some ignoble and fraudulent intentions, and these also smack of some illegal connivance with the three Ahuja firms. It may very well occur to us that more than sufficient time had wilfully been allowed to the various Depots so that all the pending stocks of rough diamond could have been issued to the Ahuja firms and all the pending cheques, too, meant for them, were issued and encashed, well before the official instructions and directions for initiating the aforesaid preventive measures, could be communicated to them, in writing, to be placed on record. Thus, the case also leaves much scope for initiating vigilance enquiry along with the usual departmental enquiries against all the delinquent employees and officers of the Commission.

A SYNOPTIC NOTE

(CHAPTER 12 AT A GLANCE)

BANK GUARANTEES

Types of bank guarantees:

(*i*) Short-term Bank Guarantee; and

(*ii*) Long-term Bank Guarantee;
(or Deferred Payment Guarantee).

Short-term Bank Guarantee is again of two types:

(*i*) Financial Bank Guarantee; and

(*ii*) Performance Bank Guarantee.

(i) Financial Bank Guarantee

It is issued for the following purposes:

(*a*) In lieu of the earnest money, while submitting tenders for undertaking some job/work.

(*b*) In lieu of security deposits, say, with the Food Corporation of India, for obtaining stocks of paddy (by rice mills) for milling and return.

(*c*) In lieu of advance payment for supply of raw materials, *e.g.*, when bank guarantee was insisted upon by TISCO for supplying materials in early 1970s, at a time when iron and steel products of TISCO were in short supply and in high demand.

(*d*) To release part-payment for the job only half-completed, *e.g.*, by the contractor for construction of the factory premises, half done, or some items of furniture only partly completed, and still in the process of production.

(*e*) For releasing 10% payment withheld, pending satisfactory commissioning and performance of the items of machinery supplied.

(*f*) In lieu of deposit of the amount in cash. For example, in early 1970s, bank guarantees were given to the court by the Sugar Mills, in the court case, on the dispute of the levy of Excise Duty by the Excise Department.

(*g*) To assure the payment of 'credit notes' of a particular party, *e.g.*, bank guarantee issued on behalf of the Food Corporation of India by the State Bank of India, in favour of Indian Railways for payment of freight charges for the transportation of food grains, etc.

(ii) Performance Bank Guarantees

These bank guarantees are still more tricky and, therefore, more risky, inasmuch as in such bank guarantees the timely performance [of the specific task/supply by the suppliers (bank's party)], on due time, as per specifications, in regard to the quality and quantity, at the specified place, and, above all, to the entire satisfaction of the beneficiary, and at his/her sole discretion and judgment. And, the bank further usually undertakes that it will make the payment, on the very first demand, by the beneficiary, without any demur (or asking any questions) and without any reference being made to the applicant concerned. Accordingly, such a bank guarantee is known as 'Absolute' Bank Guarantee, and the primary contract (between the buyer and the seller) does not form part thereto.

And, as such, bank guarantees involve high risk factor. The Reserve Bank of India has stipulated certain safety conditions/measures in this regard; viz.

Such Bank Guarantee must be issued by the bank in the case of only first class borrowers, preferably on deposit of cent per cent or very high margin money, and on the lines of the proforma prescribed by the Reserve Bank of India, in this regard, to keep the interest of the Bank fully safeguarded at all times.

And, if some valued parties insist on some different bank guarantees as per proforma specially designed by them, it must be got approved by the bank's controlling office, who should, in turn, take special care to see that no provision exists in the proposed proforma, which may go against the interest of the bank.

Here it must be borne in mind that there are two types of performance bank guarantees. They are:

(*i*) Absolute Bank Guarantee; and

(*ii*) Conditional Bank Guarantee.

In Case (*i*), the primary contract between the buyer and the seller is not to be taken into account.

In Case (*ii*), it has to be taken into account too.

GENERAL

Validity Period

Bank guarantees are usually issued for a period of one year and the expiry date so arrived at is also specifically mentioned in them.

At the same time, the time frame (like three months/six months) is also stated in the bank guarantee, within which period, the claim, if any, must be filed by the beneficiary with the bank, whereafter it may get time barred, under the provisions of Limitation Act.

This way, the provision of the Limitation Act, of the validity period of 3 years in general and 30 years in the case of government, is reduced, as per the mutual agreement, as per the Contract Act. However, please note that a cause for complaint, for invocation of the Bank Guarantee must occur within the currency (validity period) of the bank guarantee, as specified in the bank guarantee, though the claim may be filed by the beneficiary within the stipulated time period, *i.e.* the reduced limitation period of 3 or 6 months, from the date of the expiry of the Bank Guarantee.

The banks also insist that bank guarantees, if not invoked, should be returned to the bank, duly cancelled by the beneficiary. Some beneficiaries, however, prefer to keep it with them, though it is to them of no value. Accordingly, if at all, it has to be retained, it should be kept away from the valuable documents like the valid bank guarantees, to avoid any mix-up.

As a matter of precaution, the beneficiaries of bank guarantees should not send the Bank Guarantee, in original (but only Xerox copy thereof). I say so, because some bank officials have feigned as if the original bank guarantee, said to have been sent by the beneficiary, had not been received by them, causing avoidable delay and correspondence.

QUESTIONS

(For Self-assessment)

1. Distinguish between

Financial Bank Guarantee and Performance Bank Guarantee.

2. (*a*) For what specific purpose is the following types of Financial Bank Guarantee issued?

(*i*) In lieu of earnest money,

(*ii*) In lieu of security deposit,

(*iii*) In lieu of advance payment for supply of goods,

(*iv*) To release the part payment towards jobs, only half done,

(*v*) To release the 10% of the full payment withheld, pending satisfactory commissioning and performance of certain items of machinery,

(*vi*) In lieu of the deposit of the required amount in cash, in a court of law, and

(*vii*) To honour credit notes issued by a certain company in favour of another.

(*b*) Explain each of the aforesaid types of bank guarantees by giving suitable illustrative examples in each case.

3. Why are bank guarantees known as one of the non-fund based working capital financing?

4. (*i*) What are the special salient features of Performance Bank Guarantee, as against the Financial Bank Guarantee?

(*ii*) In what ways are the performance bank guarantees considered to be a far greater financial risk for the issuing bankers?

(*iii*) What are the special safety measures/safeguards prescribed by the Reserve Bank of India (RBI) to keep the interest of banks issuing the performance bank guarantees, for safeguard at all times?

5. (*a*) Why is it that banks invariably insist on recording, on the body of bank guarantees, the specific time frame (beyond the specified validity period), within which a Bank Guarantee must be invoked and claims filed, if at all, with the issuing banker?

(*b*) Are they justified in doing so, in the eye of the law? Give reasons for your answer.

6. The issuing banks insist that the Bank Guarantee, after the expiry date, must be returned to the bank, by the beneficiaries, duly cancelled. But, most of the beneficiaries, prefer to retain them, just in case .... (it may prove to be of some use, at some later date).

(*i*) What is the possible rationale behind the aforesaid stance taken,

(*a*) By the bank, and the

(*b*) Usual response/reaction of beneficiaries, as aforesaid?

(*ii*) What sincere advice will you like to give to beneficiaries of bank guarantees, who invariably prefer to retain all expired bank guarantees, over a period of time, which keep getting piled up?

7. It is generally suggested that while invoking bank guarantees, beneficiaries should take care not to send the Bank Guarantee, in original, to the issuing banker, for the purpose.

Do you agree with such a contention? Give reasons for your answer.

PROBLEMS

(TO PRACTISE FOR PERFECTION)

1. A Performance Bank Guarantee for Rs. 3 lakh had been issued by the National Bank of India on behalf of Arjuna Opticals, Lucknow, in favour of Arun Jaipuria and Company, Delhi, on July 1, 2009, for a period of one year, and the documents had specified, in clear terms, that the claim, if any, pertaining to the Bank Guarantee should be filed within 6 months from the date of the expiry of the Bank Guarantee. Accordingly, the beneficiary preferred to invoke the Bank Guarantee saying that the goods supplied by the applicant, as on 11 July 2009, did not conform to the specifications agreed upon. The Bank Guarantee was in the nature of an absolute Bank Guarantee and the bank had undertaken, inter alia, to make the payment, immediately on invocation of the Bank Guarantee, on first demand, without demur and without making any reference to the applicant company to this effect. But, the Bank Manager made a reference to the applicant, who, in turn, asked the Bank not to make any payment against the Bank Guarantee, inasmuch as speedy arrangements were urgently being made to obtain an injunction order, in this regard, from a competent court of law. And, accordingly, the bank refused to make the required payment to the beneficiary of the Bank Guarantee, on receipt of the injunction order, and that too, after getting the signature of the Judge, duly verified by a competent officer of the local branch of the Bank, transacting the government business.

Thereupon, the beneficiary of the Bank Guarantee preferred to file a civil suit in the competent court of law, (*a*) for the vacation of the injunction order, as also

(*b*) for the recovery of the amount of the Bank Guarantee from the Bank.

What are the chances of the beneficiary's winning the case?

Give reasons for your answer.

2. The National Bank of Hindustan had refused to renew the Bank Guarantee, issued by it earlier, in favour of Zenith and Company, on behalf of Horizon and Brothers, despite repeated requests from Zenith and Company, in this connection.

   (*i*) Is the bank justified in such acts? Give reasons for your answer.

   (*ii*) Would the position be any different, if Horizon and Brothers would have made such a request, instead?

   (*iii*) Is the Bank under obligation to necessarily renew the Bank Guarantee, if so required by the applicant concerned? Give reasons for your answer.

PART THREE

CASE STUDIES ON WORKING CAPITAL MANAGEMENT AND CONTROL WITH SUGGESTED APPROACHES

13

CASE STUDIES

Error is discipline through which we advance.	***William Ellery Channing***
Money without brains is always dangerous.	***Napoleon Hill***
Money will come to you when you are doing the right thing.	***Michael Phillips***

The Learning Points

Chapters 13 (A), 13 (B) and 13 (C), aim at developing knowledge, art and skill of decision-making, by applying the various relevant managerial principles, tools and techniques, in the given business situations and circumstances, by way of live case studies. Further, the cases are written not to reflect either the apt or inapt handling of administrative situations, but only to serve as the training material, purely for educational purposes.

It would augur well if readers can first study cases and formulate their own strategies/ approaches in each case independently. Only thereafter, they may prefer to go to next chapter 14, and compare their own approach with that of the author, in each case, given at chapters 14 (A), 14 (B) and 14 (C), respectively. This is being suggested so that they may derive maximum learning from each case.

Incidentally, please note that names of companies, and those of their executives, used in all the three case studies are pseudonyms. Even the stand taken and the lines of action initiated by the company executives are fictitious and, any resemblance thereto, is just coincidental. Further, no part of case studies should be reproduced in any form, or even quoted, without the specific and express permission of the author in writing.

13(A). INDIAN AUTOMOBILE INDUSTRY LIMITED*

The undernoted documents/papers of the Indian Automobile Industry Limited are placed below:

(*i*) Abridged Balance Sheets of the Company for the last two consecutive years. [Appendix 13 (A).I].

---

* One of the approaches to the case study, as suggested by the author, appears at Chapter 14 (A).

* Please note that there is no single approach/solution to a case study.

(*ii*) Profit and Loss Accounts of the company for the last two consecutive years. [Appendix 13 (A). 2].

(*iii*) An extract from the Directors' Report pertaining to the current year [Appendix 13 (A).3].

Required

1. Based on the given balance sheets of the company, reclassify items under the various categories of Liabilities [viz. Current, Deferred and Owners' Equity (OE)], and Assets (*i.e.* Current, Fixed, Miscellaneous and Intangible Assets).
2. Calculate the various relevant ratios pertaining to the following areas/parameters.
   (*i*) Liquidity ratios,
   (*ii*) Turnover/productivity ratios,
   (*iii*) Leverage/financial structure ratios,
   (*iv*) Profitability ratios,
   (*v*) Valuation ratios, and
   (*vi*) Coverage ratios.
3. Based on the above data/dimensions, critically evaluate the financial performance of the company with special reference to the management and control of its working capital.
4. What are your comments/observations on the claims/remarks made in the extracts of the Directors' Report?
5. What specific recommendations would you like to make with a view to streamlining the Working Capital management and control of the company?

Appendix 13(A).1

INDIAN AUTOMOBILE INDUSTRY LIMITED

BALANCE SHEET AS AT 31ST MARCH

(A) SOURCES OF FUNDS

(Rupees in crores)

	Current Year	*Previous Year*
1. Shareholders' Funds		
(*a*) Capital		
(*i*) Equity	103.67	62.97
(*ii*) Preference	1.34	1.34
(*b*) Reserves and Surplus		
(*i*) Share Premium Reserve	100.54	12.54
(*ii*) Capital Redemption Reserve	0.99	0.99
(*iii*) Revenue Reserve	172.22	147.93
(*iv*) Revaluation Reserve	—	—
(*v*) Surplus in Profit and Loss Account	33.65	13.45
	412.41	239.22
2. Loan Funds		
(*a*) Debentures (FCD) due after 12 months	155.05	283.75
(*b*) Public Deposits due after 12 months	63.93	53.54
(*c*) Secured Loans (other than Debentures) due after 12 months	71.04	64.07
(*d*) Unsecured Loans, due after 12 months	33.94	42.70
	323.96	444.06
Total of (1) and (2)	**736.37**	**683.28**

Appendix 13(A).1

INDIAN AUTOMOBILE INDUSTRY LIMITED

(B) APPLICATION OF FUNDS

(Rupees in crores)

	Current Year	Previous Year
1. Fixed Assets		
(a) Net block (original cost less depreciation)	403.69	351.44
(b) Capital Work-in-Progress	46.26	59.48
	449.95	410.92
2. Investments		
(a) Government Securities	—	—
(b) Investments in Subsidiary Companies	—	—
(i) Quoted	22.88	—
(ii) Unquoted	1.41	—
(c) Investments in other companies	—	—
(i) Quoted	—	1.02
(ii) Unquoted	115.75	48.53
	140.04	49.55
3. (I) Current Assets, Loans and Advances		
(a) Inventories	304.72	255.15
(b) Sundry Debtors*	207.44	206.67
(c) Cash and Bank Balances	21.26	25.75
(d) Other Current Assets	—	—
(e) Loans and Advances		
(i) To Subsidiary companies	—	—
(ii) To others	67.71	57.32
	601.13	544.89
Less		
(II) Current Liabilities and Provisions		
(a) Liabilities	399.21	298.51
(b) Provisions	55.54	23.57
	454.75	322.08
Net Current Assets (I – II)	**146.38**	**222.81**
4. Miscellaneous Expenditure to the extent not written off or adjusted	—	—
5. Profit and Loss Account	—	—
Total of 1 to 5	**736.37**	**683.28**

*Includes Sundry Debtors outstanding for over 180 days.	1.49	2.37

Appendix 13(A).2

INDIAN AUTOMOBILE INDUSTRY LIMITED

PROFIT and LOSS ACCOUNT FOR THE YEARS ENDED 31ST MARCH

(Rs. in crores)

	Current Year	Previous Year
I. Income		
Sales/Services rendered	1638.51	1375.46
Dividend	0.52	0.43
Interest	5.26	2.18
Other Income	32.13	24.48
Total Income	**1676.42**	**1402.55**
II. Expenditure		
Cost of goods consumed/sold		
(*i*) Opening stocks of Work-in-Progress and Stock-in-Trade	142.15	142.68
(*ii*) Purchase/consumption of Raw Materials and Components	842.48	710.43
Total (*i*) + (*ii*)	984.63	853.11
Less: Closing Stocks of Work-in-Progress and Stock-in-Trade	(147.74)	(142.15)
(Net Result)	836.89	710.96
Manufacturing, administration and selling expenses	496.35	420.82
Salaries, wages and other employee Benefits	199.43	160.46
Managerial Remuneration	0.34	0.13
Interest	59.07	77.58
Depreciation	43.15	38.22
Auditor's Remuneration	0.14	0.11
Provisions for:		
(*i*) Doubtful Debts	0.50	3.78
(*ii*) Other Contingencies	—	—
Any other expenses	—	—
Less: Expenditure transferred to		
Capital Account	(44.58)	(41.56)
Total	**1591.29**	**1370.50**

(*Contd...*)

PROFIT AND LOSS ACCOUNT FOR THE YEARS ENDED 31ST MARCH *(continued)*

(Rs. in crores)

	Current Year	*Previous Year*
III. Profit/Loss before tax (PBT) (I – II)	85.13	32.05
IV. Provisions for taxation	15.10	5.10
V. Profit/Loss after tax (PAT)	70.03	26.95
VI. Adjustment of depreciation relating to previous years	—	(0.05)
VII. Investment allowance reserve account	(21.55)	—
VIII. Investment allowance reserve account written back	2.51	5.38
VIX. Tax for previous years	(1.10)	(3.23)
X. Balance brought forward from previous years	13.45	3.91
XI. Debenture redemption reserve	—	(1.95)
XII. Proposed dividend:		
— Preference shares	(0.20)	(0.20)
— Equity shares	(24.24)	(13.36)
	(24.44)	(13.56)
XIII. Transfer to reserves	(5.25)	(4.00)
XIV. Balance carried to the balance sheet	**33.65**	**13.45**

Appendix 13(A).3

NATIONAL AUTOMOBILE INDUSTRY LIMITED

EXTRACTS FROM THE DIRECTORS' REPORT

1. Once again, there was substantial improvement in the company's turnover and profits. Sales turnover increased by 19.5% to Rs. 1676.42 crore. The profit after tax improved by 160% from Rs. 26.95 crore last year to Rs. 70.03 crore. Increased sales, better margins and stringent cost reduction contributed to this achievement.
2. A good monsoon and an overall upturn in the economy resulted in a sharp surge in the demand for freight movement. Consequently, this year, the company achieved an all-time record sale of 61,691 vehicles (including 10,943 LCVs) as compared to 56,168 (including 8,808 LCVs) in the previous year. For the first time in the last five years, the growth in the Medium and Heavy Commercial Vehicle segment exceeded that in the LCV segment of the domestic market. Exports rose by 63% to Rs. 81.40 crore, and spare part sales reached a peak of Rs. 68.20 crore. A resurgence in excavator sales brought the number of machines sold to 176 as against 168 in the previous year.
3. Steep increases in levies and materials costs, particularly steel and non-ferrous metals, more than neutralised savings arising from the cost reductions achieved during the year. The company was, therefore, obliged to revise the selling price of its LCVs and medium and heavy commercial vehicles.
4. The improved profitability during the year, the availability of funds for capital expenditure programmes from the Debenture Issue two years back, and the strict control over working capital requirements, resulted in a comfortable funds-flow situation. The interest cost, therefore, came down from Rs. 77.58 crore last year to Rs. 59.07 crore this year.
5. Conversion of Part "B" of the company's 12.5 % Convertible Debentures into shares was effected on 1st October, last year. After the allotment of these shares, the ordinary share capital of the company stands at Rs. 103.67 crore. Funds raised through these debentures are being used for the company's capital expenditure requirements and for working capital.

Appendix 13(B). NATIONAL IMPEX COMPANY*

Mr. Rakesh Dayal had recently taken over as Director (Finance) in the National Impex Company. As he had grown with the organisation, he had come to realise that the Company had a proactive style of management, in that it was more a 'performance oriented' company, rather than a 'procedure oriented' one. He was fully aware of the fact that the company had been steadily making profits and had been marching ahead, from strength to strength, over the years. He also had in mind some of the highlights of the achievements of the Company given hereunder:

(*a*) The Company's Profit After Tax (PAT) had registered a significant increase of 84.3% from Rs. 4,194 lakh in 1990 to Rs. 7,728 lakh in 1991.

(*b*) The Company had declared a divided of Rs. 1,000 lakh in 1991, as compared to Rs. 700 lakh for the past 9 years in a row, since 1982.

(*c*) With the declaration of the bonus for the 7th time, the initial paid-up capital of Rs. 300 lakh had gone up further to Rs. 3,500 lakh up to 1990, and to Rs. 5,000 lakh in 1991, and had, thus, touched its authorised capital level.

(*d*) The net worth (Capital + Reserves + Surplus) of the Company had also gone up from Rs. 28,279 lakh in 1990 to Rs. 35,007 lakh in 1991, registering an increase of 23.79 per cent.

(*e*) Exports at Rs. 1,32,490 lakh represented a growth of 15.4 per cent in 1990-91, which was higher than the growth of 10.3 per cent in the total turnover at Rs. 5,62,300 lakh the same year.

(*f*) The Company had received the Prime Minister's Award for MoU for 1989-90.

While Mr Dayal naturally felt proud of these achievements, he did not like his people to feel complacent about it. He, therefore, first wanted to acquaint himself with the state of affairs pertaining to the financial management in the Company. With this end in view, he asked Mr. Vikas Mehrotra, General Manager (Finance), to furnish him with certain information.

Mr. Mehrotra, accordingly compiled the undernoted papers for submission to the Director (Finance):

(*a*) Abridged Balance Sheets of the Company as at the 31st March, 1988, 1989 and 1990 [Annexure-13(B). 1]

(*b*) Some schedules pertaining to Balance Sheets of the Company for the years 1989 and 1990 [Annexure-13(B). 2].

(*c*) The analysis of Balance Sheets of the Company for the years 1989 and 1990, as also the relevant ratios for these years pertaining to the financial management of the Company. [Annexure-13(B). 3 and Annexure-13(B). 4, respectively].

(*d*) Abridged Balance Sheets of the Company as at the 3st March, 1990 and 1991, as also the increases/decreases over the last year pertaining to certain items [Annexure-13(B). 5], and

(*e*) Miscellaneous information [Annexure-13(B). 6].

On perusal of these papers, Mr. Dayal felt that there was sufficient scope for further streamlining the working capital management and control of the Company.

He had, therefore, advised Mr. Mehrotra accordingly and had also asked for some further information/break-ups from him. He also requested Mr. Mehrotra to develop his own ideas in the matter and to come for a detailed discussion with him, on the subject, after two days.

---

* One of the approaches to the case study, as suggested by the author, appears at Chapter 14 (B).

* Please note that there is no single approach/solution to a case study.

Required

If you were the Director (Finance) of the Company:

[A] What steps would you have initiated with a view to further streamline the Working Capital management in the Company in the areas of:

(*a*) Cash Management

(*b*) Investment Management

(*c*) Inventories Management, and

(*d*) Sundry Debtors management?

[B] What further information/break-ups would you have called for from the General Manager (Finance)?

Appendix 13(B).1

BALANCE SHEET OF NATIONAL IMPEX COMPANY

As on 31st March

(Rs. in lakh)

Liabilities	*1988*	*1989*	*1990*
(*a*) Paid-up Capital	3,500	3,500	3,500
(*b*) Reserves and Surplus	18,780	21,285	24,779
$(a + b)$ = (Net Worth) (A)	22,280	24,785	28,279
(*c*) Secured loans (Cash Credit)	1,355	1,769	1,044
(*d*) Unsecured loans (from Banks)			
(*i*) Over-draft	350	—	39
(*ii*) Short-term Loan (Under Banker's Acceptance Schème)	6,803	32,386	100,931
(*iii*) Deferred Payment Liability (including payable within one year, shown in parenthesis)	565 (271)	666 (271)	489 (271)
(*e*) Other Current Liabilities [Sundry Creditors, Advances from customers, etc.]	31,806	35,527	43,486
(*f*) Provisions for Taxation, Bonus, Proposed Dividend, etc.	—	1,227	1,049
$[c+d+e+f]$ (B)	40,879	71,575	147,038
Total Liabilities (A + B)	63,159	96,360	175,317
Assets	*1988*	*1989*	*1990*
(A) Fixed Assets			
Gross Block	974	1,703	2,364
Less: Depreciation (–)	272	359	959
Net Block	702	1,344	1,405
Capital Work-in-Proggress (+)	165	138	126
(A)	867	1,482	1,531
(B) Investments (B)	5,606	11,079	16,606
(C) Current Assets, Loans and Advances			
Interest Accrued on Investments		274	442
Inventories		27,879	41,547
Sundry Debtors		18,245	31,255
Cash and Bank Balances		21,646	59,375
Loans and Advances		15,755	24,561
(C)	56,686	83,799	157,180
Total Assets (A + B + C)	63,159	96,360	175,317

Some selected figures from the Company's Profit and Loss Accounts for the years ended 31st March, 1989 and 1990

		1989	*1990*
Sales	—	3,87,997	5,09,725
PBIT	—	9,371	15,677
Interest Paid	—	2,464	7,164
PAT	—	3,205	4,194
Dividend	—	700	700

Appendix 13(B).2

BALANCE SHEET OF NATIONAL IMPEX COMPANY AS AT THE 31ST MARCH

(Rs. in lakh)

Schedules		*1989*	*1990*
Share Capital			
Authorised Capital		5,000	5,000
Issued, Subscribed and Paid-up Capital (including Bonus Shares, Rs. 3,200)		3,500	3,500
Investments			
Shares in the Subsidiary Company (unquoted)		808	808
Bonds of Public Secter Undertakings @ 9%-10% (Tax-Free)		10,271	13,743
Units of UTI		—	2,055
		11,079	16,606
Inventories			
Stocks-in-trade and Goods-in-Transit		27,879	41,547
Sundry Debtors			
Outstanding for over 6 months		6,123	9,490
Less: Considered Doubtful Provided for	(–)	689	792
		5,434	8,698
Other debts (up to 6 months)	(+)	12,811	22,557
		18,245	31,255
Further break-ups of Sundry Debtors as on 31.3.1990			
Period		Govt. Dept.	Pvt. Parties
6 Months – 1 year		NA@	NA@
1 Years – 2 years		3,182	373
2 Years – 3 years		265	205
3 Years and above		706	428
		4,153	1,006

@ Total 6 m — 1 year – (8,698) – (4,153 + 1,006) = 3,539.

Cash and Bank Balances

	1989	*1990*
Cash, Stamps and Cheques-in-hand	201	81
In Current Account	160	4,287
In Cash Credit Account and Telegraphic Transfers (T.Ts.) in Transit	—	1,289
Short-term Deposit with Banks	20,975	53,450
(A)	**21,336**	**59,107**
Term Deposit Receipts as Security Deposit with the Municipal Corporation, Delhi	3	3
With S.B.I. as per Court Order	7	7
Deposit with IDBI for	243	195
Surcharge on Income Tax in foreign countries	57	63
(B)	310	268
Total (A) + (B)	**21,646**	**59,375**

Appendix 13(B).3

ANALYSIS OF BALANCE SHEET OF NATIONAL IMPEX COMPANY AS ON 31ST MARCH

(Rs. in lakh)

Liabilities		*1989*	*1990*
(A) Current Liabilities (including Deferred Liabilities due within one year, *i.e.* Rs. 271)	71,180	146,820	
(B) Deferred Liabilities (excluding D/L due within one year, *i.e.* Rs. 271)		395	218
(C) Owner's Equity (Capital, Reserves and Surplus)		24,785	28,279
Total Liabilities (A + B + C)		**96,360**	**175,317**
Assest	*1989*	*1990*	
(A) Current Assets		83,799	157,180
Add: Investment in UTI Units	(+)	—	2,055
		83,799	159,235
Less: Sundry Debtors of over 6 months	(–)	5,434	8,698
Total Current Assets **(A)**		78.365	150,537
(B) Fixed Assets **(B)**		1,482	1,531
(C) Miscellaneous Assets			
Investments		11,079	16,606
Less: Investment in UTI	(–)	—	2,055
		11,079	14,551
Add: Sundry Debtors of over 6 months	(+)	5,434	8,698
(C)		16,513	23,249
(D) Intangible Assets **(D)**		—	—
Total Assets (A + B + C + D)			**96,360 175,317**

Appendix 13(B).4

RATIO ANALYSIS OF NATIONAL IMPEX COMPANY AS ON 31ST MARCH

	1989		1990	
1. Liquidity Ratios				
1.1. Current Ratio:				
$\frac{CA}{CL}$	$\frac{78365}{71180}$	(1.10)	$\frac{150537}{146820}$	(1.03)
1.2 Quick Ratio:				
$\frac{QA\ (i.e.\ CA - INV)}{CL}$	$\frac{50,486}{71,180}$	(0.71)	$\frac{108990}{146820}$	(0.74)
2. Turnover/Productivity Ratios [Times]				
2.1 $\frac{\text{Sales}}{\text{Capital Employed}}$	$\frac{387997}{25180}$	(15.41)	$\frac{509725}{28497}$	(17.89)
2.2 $\frac{\text{Sales}}{\text{Net Fixed Assets}}$	$\frac{387997}{1482}$	(261.80)	$\frac{509725}{1531}$	(332.94)
2.3 $\frac{\text{Sales}}{\text{Inventory}}$	$\frac{387997}{27879}$	(13.91)	$\frac{509725}{41547}$	(12.27)
*2.3 (a) $\frac{\text{Inventory} \times 365}{\text{Sales}}$	$\frac{27879 \times 365}{387997}$	26.22 (days)	$\frac{41547 \times 365}{509725}$	29.75 (days)

*[In my considered opinion, the **Inventory Turnover Ratio**, in terms of **No. of Days** may give a more comprehending and clear position, for quick decision-making, as compared to **No. of Times.**]

	1989		1990	
2.4 $\frac{\text{Sundry Debtor} \times 365}{\text{Sales}}$	$\frac{18245 \times 365}{387997}$	17.16 (days)	$\frac{31255 \times 365}{509725}$	22.38 (days)
3. Leverage or Financial Structure Ratios				
3.1 $\frac{\text{(Long-term) Debt}}{\text{Equity}}$	$\frac{395}{24785}$	(0.02)	$\frac{218}{28279}$	(0.01)
$\frac{\text{Total Liabilities}}{\text{Equity}}$	$\frac{96360}{24785}$	(3.89)	$\frac{175317}{28279}$	(6.20)
$\frac{\text{Net Fixed Assets}}{\text{Long-term Debt}}$	$\frac{1482}{395}$	(3.75)	$\frac{1531}{218}$	(7.02)
4. Profitability Ratios				
4.1 $\frac{\text{PBIT} \times 100}{\text{Sales}}$	$\frac{9371 \times 100}{387997}$	(2.42%)	$\frac{15677 \times 100}{509725}$	(3.08%)
4.2 $\frac{\text{PBIT} \times 100}{\text{Total Assets}}$	$\frac{9371 \times 100}{96360}$	(9.72%)	$\frac{15677 \times 100}{175317}$	(8.94%)
4.3. $\frac{\text{PBIT} \times 100}{\text{Capital Employed}}$	$\frac{9371 \times 100}{25180}$	(37.22%)	$\frac{15677 \times 100}{28497}$	(55.01%)
4.4 $\frac{\text{PAT} \times 100}{\text{Net Worth}}$	$\frac{3205 \times 100}{24785}$	(12.93%)	$\frac{4194 \times 100}{28279}$	(14.83%)

(Contd...)

	1989	1990
5. Valuation Ratios		
5.1 $\frac{\text{PAT} \times 100}{\text{Equity Share (Total Face Value)}}$	$\frac{3205 \times 100}{3500}$	$\frac{4194 \times 100}{3500}$
i.e. Earning per Share (%)	(91.57%)	(119.83%)
5.2 $\frac{\text{Net Worth} \times 100}{\text{Equity Share}}$	$\frac{24785 \times 100}{3500}$	$\frac{28279 \times 100}{3500}$
i.e. Book Value (%)	(708.14%)	(807.97%)
6. Coverage Ratios		
6.1 $\frac{\text{PBIT}}{\text{Interest Paid}}$ (Times)	$\frac{9371}{2464}$	$\frac{15677}{7164}$
(*i.e.* interest cover)	(3.80 times)	(2.19 times)
6.2 $\frac{\text{PAT}}{\text{Dividend}}$ (Times)	$\frac{3205}{700}$	$\frac{4194}{700}$
(*i.e.* dividend cover)	(4.58 times)	(5.99 times)
HUMAN ASPECTS OF BALANCE SHEET (Rs. in lakh)		
Number of Employees	3827	3825
Sales per employee	Rs. 100.30	Rs. 133.00
Expenses per employee	1.20	1.30

Appendix 13(B).5

BALANCE SHEET OF NATIONAL IMPEX COMPANY

AS ON 31ST MARCH

(Rs. in lakh)

Liabilities	*1990*	*1991*
(A) Own Funds		
Paid-up Capital	3,500	5,000
Reserves and Surplus	24,779	30,007
(A)	28,279	35,007
Book Value of Share	(8 times)	(7 times)
[Initial Equity Rs. 3 crore + Rs. 47 crore (bonus)] Rs. 50 crore		
(B) Loan Funds [mostly Current Liabilities, except say, 271 (Deferred Liabilities)]		
Secured Loans	1,044	2,006
Unsecured Loans	101,459	98,010
Other Current Liabilities		
(Sundry Creditors, etc.)	43,486	83,532
Provisions	1,049	1,451
(B)	147,038	184,999
Total Liabilities (A + B)	**175,317**	**220,006**
Assets		
Fixed Assets (Net)	1,531	1,646
Investments	16,606	22,458
Current Assets, Loans and Advances	157,180	195,902
Total Assets	**175,317**	**220,006**

Appendix 13(B).5 (Contd.)

BREAK-UP OF CURRENT ASSETS OF NATIONAL IMPEX COMPANY

(Rs. in lakh)

	1990	1991	(+)/(–)
Interest Accrued on Investments	442	667	(+51%)
Inventories	41,547	53,123	(+28%)
Sundry Debtors	31,255	69,858	(124%)
Cash and Bank Balances	59,375*	22,251	
Loans and Advances	24,561*	50,003	
	157,180	195,902	
* These two figures differ in the Balance Sheet of the year 1991, due to some adjustments.			
Trading and Profit and Loss Account of National Impex Company			
Net Sales	509,725	562,298	(+10.3%)
Cost of Sales	497,550	542,994	(+9.1%)
PBIT	15,677	28,781	(+83.6%)
PAT	4,194	7,728	(+84.3%)
Interest Paid	7,164	14,442	(+101.6%)
Appropriations of PAT			
Proposed Dividend	700	1,000	
Transfer to Reserves	3,494	6,728	
Transfer to Reserves (÷) PAT	(83.3%)	(87.1%)	

Appendix 13(B).6

MISCELLANEOUS INFORMATION

(*i*) Under the Banker's Acceptance Scheme, payments for the imported commodities are made by bankers of the Company on presentation of documents but the Company's Cash Credit Account is debted after 180 days. This resulted in substantial cash surplus with the Company, which is being invested mainly in term deposits for 46 days with the bank at say, 12.0 per cent per annum.

(*ii*) As revealed in Balance Sheets of the Company since 1985, the inventory level had been reduced from 22 days sales in 1985 to 21 days sales in 1986. In the year 1987, however, though inventories had come down in terms of value, compared to 1986, these had gone up marginally as a percentage of sales from 5.8 per cent to 5.9 per cent.

(*iii*) The increase in the level of inventory for the year 1990 had mainly been due to higher stocks of Zinc and Nickle. In the year 1991, the higher level of inventory mainly comprised Copper, Zinc, Lead, Iron Ore, as also goods-in-transit, viz. Sulphur, Phosphoric Acid, Ammonia, etc.

(*iv*) The increase in the Sundry Debtors had mainly been due to outstanding bills with the Ministry of Agriculture, so much so that as on 31 March 1991, bills aggregating Rs. 36,470 lakh were outstanding with them alone.

(*v*) A large portion of the Company's sales to the private parties (non-governmental agencies) is mostly on cash payment basis or even against advance payment, in some cases.

(*vi*) Further, with the concerted efforts made by the Company, to realise its long outstanding bills, the level of Sundry Debtors had got reduced from Rs. 12,773 lakh in 1986 to Rs. 10,219 lakh in 1987 which, in terms of percentage of sales, came down from 4.2 per cent to 3.7 per cent. The achievement seems to be far more impressive when we compare the level of Sundry Debtors in 1986 and 1987 with the Sundry Debtors at Rs. 25,920 lakh in 1985.

Appendix 13(C). POPULAR PUMPS AND PARTS LIMITED*

Popular Pumps and Parts Limited (PPP for short), manufacturing water lifting pumps of different specifications and strengths, and the respective spare parts, was established in March 1994. By virtue of the high quality of its products, the timely delivery, and prompt and efficient after—sales service, coupled with the price structure, suiting different classes of the society, it had been able to capture a major portion of the market share, within a short span of time. And, as a result, its financial strength and stability had always been maintained on sound and healthy lines.

But, of late, for the last three years to be exact, it had started facing some financial difficulties, specially in the area of working capital financing. Some of the relevant data of the company, given hereunder, amply establish the point:

The Company was experiencing shortage of funds to meet its Working Capital requirements on a continuous and progressive basis for the last three years. Earlier, the financial position of the Company was quite smooth and strong, in that it was generating sufficient cash surplus from its internal sources, by ploughing back a substantial portion of its net profit in the business, year after year.

Trade credits constituted the other major source of financing its Working Capital requirements, but, of late, it had also started dwindling down. The Company was, therefore, naturally very much concerned about such state of affairs, and was trying its best to reach the root cause(s) of the present malady as also to evolve and implement some effective remedial measures so as to overcome the present financial difficulties.

Accordingly, Mr. Manmohan Dalmia, Managing Director of the Company, had asked Mr. Gautam Mishra, General Manager (Finance), to conduct a thorough and intense study of the working of the Company, for the last five years, with a view to establishing the specific cause(s) of such pitiable state of affairs so as to take urgent and immediate corrective steps.

The various financial facts and figures of the Company, on various financial parameters are given at Annexures-13(C). 1 and 13(C).2, at the end of the Chapter.

As if this much of the financial hardship of the Company was not enough, the bank had also been pressing hard for the repayment of the bridging loan, disbursed to the Company some three years back. But, the Company, in fact, had hardly any face, to face the authorities of the bank, inasmuch as the Company had been postponing the repayment of the bridging loan, which it had initially taken, only for a short period of just six months. The Company, instead, had been approaching the bank quite frequently for extending the repayment period of the bridging loan. Besides, it had been requesting the bank, on a continuous basis, to enhance its Working Capital Limit, granted

---

* Based on the presentation of the Case in the 'Case Colloquium' of the Fifth Convention and National Seminar on "Competitiveness 2010: Prospects, Tasks and Challenges", organised by the Strategic Management Forum, at the Management Development Institute (MDI), Gurgaon, during April 25 to 27, 2002.

* One of the approaches to the case study, as suggested by the author, appears at Chapter 14 [C].

* Please Note that there is no single approach/solution to a case study.

against the security of hypothecation of its stocks of inventories (that is, of the raw materials, work-in-process and finished goods) and the trade bills.

Such frequent requests for enhancement of the Working Capital limit, or for granting of some over-drawings on the account, and/or extension of the repayment schedule of the bridging loan had, naturally, alerted the bank and, therefore, the bank had, of late, started taking a very stiff and tough stand for regularisation of the position of the various accounts of the Company, and had even threatened not to extend any further credit facilities to the Company, whatsoever.

Mr. Manmohan Dalmia had, by now, fully realised the meaning and essence of the oft-repeated adage. **"The bank lends the umbrella while it is a bright sunshine, but takes it back immediately when it starts raining."**

One day, in September, 2000, while dictating a strongly worded letter to the company (on the dicta phone) to regularise its various accounts with the bank, Mr. Chandra Prakash Malviya, the Chief Manager of the Bank, on perusal of the latest Annual Report of the Company, for the year ended 31st March, 2000, was rather surprised to find that, all said and done, the Company was still earning sufficient and progressively increasing profit, year after year, though its various accounts with the bank were running irregular for quite sometime now.

He, therefore, gave up dictating the letter and, instead, called Mr. Dalmia, the M.D. of the Company, to come to the bank for a detailed discussion with him, after three days, in view of the aforesaid apparently incompatible situations, viz. paucity of funds and profitability of the company.

Mr. Dalmia, being a professional, did a lot of home work during the three days, allowed by the Chief Manager, Mr. Malviya, and came to the bank, well prepared with the relevant facts and figures of the Company, for the last five years, for a very significant and detailed discussion with Mr. Malviya on the appointed date and time.

During the course of the discussion between the two, some significant and revealing information and dimensions came to light.

Mr. Dalmia assured Mr. Malviya that his Company had adopted several innovative and effective strategies which may go a long way in bringing about the turn-around of the company, in the near future.

When Mr. Malviya wanted Mr. Dalmia to be rather specific about the strategies, adopted and executed by the Company, Mr. Dalmia started emphasising his vast and varied experience as a Director (Finance) in some other multinational company of repute, prior to joining this company, by virtue of which he was fully aware of the importance and imperative need of evolving a sound and appropriate working capital policy, specially in a rapidly growing business like that of the Popular Pumps and Parts Ltd. Further, he went on to emphasise that the working capital policy, under such circumstances should, invariably be flexible enough so as to easily and swiftly adapt to the fast changing circumstances and business conditions. Such Working Capital Policy should also take into account the strategies to be adopted by the Company, so as to adjust itself to the fluctuating demands and requirements of the working capital finance. And, he was very assertive in stating that he was very well aware of the fact that several business houses had become sick, and finally got wounded up, just because they had not understood and realised the importance of skilfully handling the situations pertaining to the rapidly growing nature of business, and the fast changing business scenario.

He further went on to point out that, besides well considered working capital policy, the formulation and following of a long-term financial strategy, too, was of essence and importance, inasmuch as, procuring and financing several items of fixed assets, from time to time, on an ad-hoc basis, may give rise to all sorts of financial problems and bottlenecks for the company.

But, by this time, Mr. Malvia was hardly left with any patience to bear the monotony of the long winding monologues of Mr. Dalmia. He was, thus, left with no alternative but to intervene and firmly ask Mr. Dalmia to be specific and precise in stating the various strategies adopted by the Company.

Mr. Dalmia, intelligent and sharp as he was, immediately realised his folly and instantaneously started specifying the various strategies adopted by the Company in the area of marketing, so as to boost up its sales, and profitability therewith.

Formulation and Implementation of Strategies

"At the very outset I would like to share with you, Sir, the salient features of some of the steps and strategies that our company has adopted, for formulation and implementation, pertaining to different departments and areas, for an all round progress and prosperity of the company" said Mr. Dalmia, with a sense of great pride. And, he went on and on, explaining the various steps and strategies adopted by the Company, department-wise and area-wise, in a sequential order, as follows:

Marketing

The General Manager (Marketing) had been experiencing the ever increasing pressure of competition in the market for the last three/four years. He had also observed that some of the competitors had been able to supply the goods to their customers off the shelf, instantaneously, and, therefore, they were having an edge over other companies including PPP. In the foregoing circumstances the General Manager (Marketing) wrote to the General Manager (Production) to produce a large quantity of 1 H.P. water lifting pumps, so as to enable the Marketing Division to supply them to the customers immediately, on demand, and, thereby, arrest the dwindling trend of our own market share.

And, the General Manager (Production) was left with no alternative but to comply, inasmuch as the organisational culture of the company had been the 'principle of non-interference' in the respective area/department, and, accordingly, all the departmental heads had absolute power and authority for taking the decisions pertaining to their own area of operation, quite independently, and with absolute and full discretionary powers.

It, however, is a different matter that some technological changes came in, fast enough, and a very large portion of such bulk production had become obsolete soon enough, and caused some good losses to the company.

A detailed statement pertaining to the levels of production and sales of 1 H.P. Water Lifting Pumps appear at Annexure-13(C).3 at the end of the Chapter.

And, as such study had, incidentally, shown some revealing facts and position, I had called for such detailed and in depth study of the volume of production and sales in respect of other items, too, produced by our Company, as also to study the systems and procedures being followed in respect of formulating and executing such policy decisions.

Further, cash and credit sales of the Company were in the ratio of 30 : 70; which can well be considered to be satisfactory, and commensurate with the scale of operations and sales of the Company. But, the level of collection of credit sales had, of late, been showing some declining trends, mainly for the following reasons:

(*a*) The cash discount had been reduced from '3/10 net 30' to '2/10 net 30';

(*b*) The rebate of 0.5% allowed on payment on or before the due date, however, had, of late, been discontinued.

These twin decisions were taken by the General Manager (Marketing) in his sole discretion and good business sense, as this task, too, pertained to his exclusive area of operation.

Besides, the credit period for a large number of customers was enhanced from 30 days to 60 days, and this single strategy had resulted in the increase in the volume and value of the sales by as much as 10%. But then, the level of collection of sundry debtors had gone down proportionately. Further, the Company had been resorting to cash purchases in excess of its own cash sales. Thus, these two factors had created fresh financial pressure on the company, which was already facing the cash crunch.

But then, as these decisions were taken by the General Manager (Marketing) in his own exclusive powers (as all these pertained to his area of operation, viz. Marketing) the General Manager (Finance), could hardly do anything about it, except to recast his cash budget and arrange for fresh bank finance; the bank pressurising for an early payment of the bridging loan and other over-dues, notwithstanding.

Purchases

Some imported parts of pumps and fans worth Rs. 160 lakh and Rs. 100 lakh respectively, were purchased by the General Manager (Purchases) from the open market, inasmuch as these were available at the material time, at a reasonable price, as compared to the market price. Besides, these scarce imported items were luckily available readily with one of the parties locally. And, as is well-known, the lead-time, involved in directly importing these items is far too long. Besides, such a decision on the part of the General Manager (Purchases) had saved the company of all the big botheration connected with the issuance of the import licenses, and arranging for the required foreign exchange.

Incidentally, it may be mentioned that the actual consumption of these items in the years 1994 and 1995 had been to the tune of Rs. 35 lakh and Rs. 40 lakh for the spare parts of the pumps, and Rs. 15 lakh and Rs. 25 lakh for the spare parts of the fans. But, the outflow of cash of such a large amount, during the current year was most unexpected and, accordingly, it was not budgeted for. And, this single decision, though pertaining to the area of purchases, had disturbed and dislocated the entire exercise of cash budgeting, at least for the current year.

The General Manager (Finance), had, consequently, been having a really very tough time to manage the financial requirements of the company, in its full measure, and well in time.

After having apprised Mr. Malviya of the prevailing financial position and the problems of paucity of funds, being faced by the Company, Mr. Dalmia, in all his earnestness and sincerity, requested Mr. Malviya to consider the Company's case sympathetically and favourably, and grant the required financial help and concessions, so that the Company could come out of its current financial difficulties, and may start having a smooth functioning, without any further financial constraints.

Mr. Malviya had been listening to Mr. Dalmia all through, with all sincerity, and with full and concentrated attention, and had even been making some personal notes for his own use. And, at the end, he made some valuable suggestions to Mr. Dalmia, to evolve some other strategies pertaining not only to the area of finance, but also in regard to all the other pertinent areas like production and purchases, materials and marketing, etc., and again come back to him, after a week, along with all the General Managers in the Company, when the matter could be discussed over again, at length, and a final financial and the related strategies could be formulated, and the quantum of the bank's fresh loans, and the repayment programmes, could be decided, too.

At the end, Mr. Malviya had made it amply clear to Mr. Dalmia that the bank will extend its full cooperation to the company, provided the company, too, in turn, cooperated with the bank, in formulating and implementing a fresh and appropriate working capital policy, and streamlining its system of working capital management and control, in the right earnest.

Issues for Discussion

1. Critically examine the extant:
   (*i*) Working capital policy, and
   (*ii*) Working capital management and control by the Company.
   Your analysis should cover:
   (*a*) Problems,
   (*b*) The factors that may have caused them, and
   (*c*) Whether they relate to the policy deficiencies or operational snags, or both?
2. Examine and comment on some of the important operational decisions taken in the Company and analyse their impact on its working capital requirements.
3. How will you rate the financial policies and various other strategies of the Company?
4. Also suggest all possible suitable changes which Mr. Dalmia may consider and put forward to Mr. Malviya for finalisation and implementation.
   Support your recommendations with sound reasonings, in each case.

Appendix 13(C).1

POPULAR PUMPS AND PARTS LIMITED

BALANCE SHEETS AS AT 31ST MARCH, 1996-2000

(Rupees in million)

	2000	*1999*	*1998*	*1997*	*1996*
LIABILITIES					
Share Capital	100	100	100	100	80
Reserves and Surplus	278	202	148	108	82
Public Deposits	8	6	4	4	0
Secured Loan from ICICI @ 14 % p.a.	160	168	176	184	192
Total Non-Current Liabilities [A]	**546**	**476**	**428**	**396**	**354**
CURRENT LIABILITIES					
Sundry Creditors	20	24	22	18	10
Acceptances	22	6	14	8	6
Creditors for Expenses	20	14	14	18	12
Short-term loans from Bank	110	34	0	0	0
Bridging loan from Bank	80	50	0	0	0
Interest payable	12	12	14	14	8
Dividend payable	12	12	20	16	12
Tax payable	34	42	50	54	48
Total Current Liabilities [B]	**310**	**194**	**134**	**128**	**96**
Total Liabilities [A + B]	**856**	**670**	**562**	**524**	**450**

(Rupees in million)

	2000	*1999*	*1998*	*1997*	*1996*
ASSETS					
Net Fixed Assets (Gross Fixed Assets, Less Depreciation) **[C]**	176	170	160	180	168
Investments [D]	0	4	16	14	10
CURRENT ASSETS					
Raw Materials	206	142	106	78	50
Consumable Stores and Spares	26	14	10	8	6
Work-in-Process	110	86	70	54	54
Finished Goods	102	76	66	56	44
Sundry Debtors	168	120	78	72	54
Prepaid Expenses	60	48	46	32	30
Marketable Securities	0	0	2	24	28
Cash and Bank Balances	8	10	8	6	6
Total Current Assets [E]	**680**	**496**	**386**	**330**	**272**
Total Assets [C + D + E]	**856**	**670**	**562**	**524**	**450**

(Rupees in million)

	2000	*1999*	*1998*	*1997*	*1996*
Details Regarding Equity Shares					
No. of shares outstanding (in 000)	10,000	10,000	10,000	10,000	8,000*
Dividend per share (Rs.)	2.4	2.4	2	1.6	2
Earnings per share (Rs.)	10	7.8	6.2	6.2	5
Market Price (in Rs.)					
High	138	122	148	116	64
Low	94	74	84	96	42
Average	116	98	116	106	53

* The Company had issued Bonus Shares in the ratio of 1 : 4 in 1997. Face Value per Share — Rs. 10.

Appendix 13(C).2

POPULAR PUMPS AND PARTS LIMITED

PROFIT AND LOSS ACCOUNTS FOR THE YEARS ENDED 1996–1999

(Rs. in million)

	1999	*1998*	*1997*	*1996*
Sales*	1060	840	700	600
Other Income	18	16	18	22
TOTAL	1078	856	718	622
Less: Cost of Goods Sold:				
Raw Materials	422	314	262	218
Excise Duty	58	34	28	22
Salaries, Wages and Bonus	210	188	164	142
Consumable Stores and Spares	44	24	18	18
Power and Fuel	4	4	4	2
Repairs and Maintenance	4	2	4	2
Insurance	4	4	2	2
Rent, Rates and Taxes	6	6	4	4
Other Works Expenses	36	32	24	18
General Adm. Expenses	44	44	42	34
Interest	60	44	28	32
Depreciation	72	62	50	32
TOTAL	964	758	630	526
Less:				
Increase in work-in-process	–24	–16	–16	0
Increase in Finished Goods	–26	–10	–10	–12
Total Cost of Goods Sold	914	732	604	514
Operating Profit	164	124	114	108
Misc. Operating Exp.	4	4	4	4
Profit Before Tax (PBT)	160	120	110	104
Tax	60	42	50	42
Profit After Tax (PAT)	100	78	60	62
Dividend	24	24	20	16
Transfer to:				
General Reserve	76	54	40	46
	674	534	412	354

* Including Credit Sales.

Appendix 13(C).3

Detailed Statement Pertaining to the Levels of Production and Sales of 1 H.P. Water Lifting Pumps

(Rs. in lakh)

1996	*Value of Production*	*Cost of Sales*	*Closing Stocks*
April	24.00	24.00	—
May	26.40	20.40	6.00
June	38.40	33.60	10.80
July	42.00	26.40	26.40
August	44.40	60.00	10.80
September	80.40	26.40	64.80
October to December	76.40	49.40	91.80

Appendix 13(C). 4

Summary of the various credit facilities obtained from the Bank by the Company, from time to time, and the present position of such bank accounts:

(*a*) In April 1995, a bridging loan was granted by a bank to the company for Rs. 500 lakh with interest @ 18% per annum, with quarterly rests, to be repaid by the end of July 1995.

Note: The Company had agreed to such a repayment programme, inasmuch as it had expected to generate sufficient internal cash surplus by that time, coupled with a planned reduction of a portion of its inventories.

(*b*) In mid-July 1995, however, the Company found that it would not be able to repay the Bridging Loan by 31 July 1995, in any case. Accordingly, it preferred to request the bank, well in advance, to extend the repayment of the Bridging Loan up to March 1996, *i.e.* by another eight months.

The bank, however, was left with no alternative but to accede to the request, because, as we all know, if any bank lends, say Rs. 1 lakh, it controls the borrower, but when the bank lends, say in crores of rupees, the borrower controls the bank.

Not only that. Yet, another fresh overdraft to the tune of Rs. 200 lakh was also disbursed to the company, against the security of hypothecation of stocks of inventories, which, by the end of November 1995, got further enhanced to Rs. 400 lakh, to meet its ever increasing working capital requirements.

Besides, as the company continuously faced financial difficulties, the payment of the bridging loan had to be further extended by the bank, by another one full year, though reluctantly.

Thus, by June 1996, the total outstandings on the bank's various accounts stood at Rs. 900 lakh. And, based upon the latest cash flow position of the company, the bank had to agree to grant a further bill discounting facility to the company to the tune of Rs. 240 lakh.

By August 1996, the quantum of the bridging loan went up to Rs. 800 lakh, inasmuch as the capital expenditure was found to have been rather under-estimated earlier, and there had been some cost over-runs, too.

Based on all the anticipated expenditures and financial requirements of the company, the total amount of bank credit aggregated Rs. 1500 lakh, made up as under:

Particulars of Loan Account	*Amount*
Bridging Loan	Rs. 800 lakh
Loan against Hypothecation of Stocks of Inventories	Rs. 400 lakh
Bill Discounting Facility	Rs. 300 lakh
Total	**Rs. 1500 lakh**

And, by now, the rate of interest, chargeable on all the loan accounts, had been revised upward by the bank to 16% per annum, raised from 15% per annum earlier.

14

SUGGESTED APPROACH TO THE CASE STUDIES

Let our advance worrying become advance thinking and planning. ***Winston Churchill***

Capital can do nothing without brains to direct it. ***J. Ogden Armour***

The Learning Points

- Chapters 14 (A), 14 (B) and 14 (C), aim at enabling the readers to compare their own approaches in the case studies, given at Chapters 13 (A), 13 (B) and 13 (C), respectively, with that of the author, in each case.
- However, while doing so, they must bear in mind that the approach suggested by the author is just one of the possible approaches to the respective case study, inasmuch as, there cannot be a single approach/solution thereto. This small but significant point has, therefore, been reiterated, even for the sake of repetition, at the beginning of each case study.

14(A). INDIAN AUTOMOBILE INDUSTRY LIMITED*

Before attempting an evaluation of the financial performance of the company, we must reclassify its various assets and liabilities under the

1. three different categories of liabilities; and
2. four different categories of assets, viz.,

(*a*) (*i*) Current Liabilities,
(*ii*) Deferred Liabilities, and
(*iii*) Capital, Reserves and Surplus,

and (*b*) (*i*) Current Assets,
(*ii*) Fixed Assets,
(*iii*) Miscellaneous Assets, and
(*iv*) Intangible Assets.

---

* One of the approaches to the case study, as suggested by the author.
* Please note that there is no single approach/solution to a case study.

Rationale Behind Such Reclassifications

As we all known, companies are required to present their Balance Sheets as per the proforma prescribed in the Companies Act, 1956. But then, the proforma requires the companies to present their total loan amount under two categories only; viz.

(*i*) Secured Loans, and (*ii*) Unsecured Loans.

But then, this does not give an idea just at a glance to the general public, as to what extent are these payable within 12 months, from the date of the Balance Sheet and beyond, whereby these could be classified as current or deferred liabilities. Such a categorization is a must, inasmuch as by taking the current liabilities, as these are presented in the Balance Sheet (without adding thereto the short-term loan components of both the secured and unsecured loans), the liquidity ratios, viz. current ratio and quick ratio. And, so will be the interpretation and conclusion about the financial position of the company.

Similar is the case in respect of investments, which, too, have to be bifurcated into short-term and long-term investments, so as to be classified under the categories of current assets and miscellaneous assets.

Similarly, the aggregate sundry debtors may also have to be bifurcated into two groups, based on these being outstanding for (*i*) up to 180 days and (*ii*) beyond 180 days, and classified as current assets and miscellaneous assets.

For a detailed, but crisp, discussion on the conditions and criteria of classifications of different categories of assets and liabilities, illustrative examples are placed at Annexure-14(A).1.

And, the actual recasting and corresponding categorization of assets and liabilities of the Indian Automobile Industry Limited (IAIL) is placed at Annexure-14(A).2.

Similarly, the criteria (formula) of computation of various types of the ratios, under six different categories (like, liquidity ratios, profitability ratios, etc.), as also the various ratios of the IAIL, calculated on such bases, have been placed at Annexure-14(A).3.

We would now proceed to do the critical examination, analysis and interpretation of the various ratios, and thereby shall endeavour to assess and ascertain the financial position and prospects of the company on different dimensions.

Further, we would also attempt to give some useful suggestions for adoption and implementations by the Company, with a view to consolidate, and improve upon, its financial health, wherever considered necessary.

RATIO ANALYSIS

14.1. LIQUIDITY RATIOS

14.1.1 Current Ratio

Let us first attempt to comment upon the current ratio of the company, which goes to indicate its liquidity position. That is to say, as to how (financially) liquid the company is, *i.e.* how promptly and with ease would the company be able to meet its liabilities, specially, short-term liabilities, on due date.

We see that the Current Ratio (CR) of the company (as presented in Annexure 14(A).3) during the two consecutive years (*i.e.* the present and the past, or say, the current and the previous years) are 1.32 : 1 and 1.69 : 1 respectively. That is, the Current Ratio (CR) has come down from 1.69 to 1.32, which may not seem to be a satisfactory position. But then, if we re-examine the matter, we find that the Current Ratio (CR) has come down, of course, but not to an alarming degree. Because, as we have seen in earlier chapters, the Current Ratio (CR), as per the second method of the (erstwhile) Tandon Committee Report, should be 1.33, and this is the benchmark, which all the banks, financing Working Capital requirements of companies, had been insisting upon, under the (erstwhile) guidance of the Reserve Bank of India (RBI). Thus, any Current Ratio (CR) far beyond 1.33 level may not be said to be a prudent business sense, because higher the Current Ratio (CR), higher will be the level, mainly of Inventories and Sundry Debtors, which, in turn, involves the loss by way of inventory carrying cost and opportunity cost (or loss of interest) respectively.

Thus, the very fact that the Current Ratio (CR) has come down from the very high level of 1.69 to a reasonably lower level of 1.32, which is very close to the benchmark of 1.33, may well be said to be a better feature.

The Directors' Report, as per the extract given in the Case, also claims that the interest outgo has been much less in the current year (down from Rs. 77.58 crore in the previous year to Rs. 59.07 crore in the current year), mainly because of the fact that the company had been able to manage and control its Working Capital more effectively and efficiently. And, such a claim of Directors, read with the facts and figures, quoting the quantum of interest outgo, seems to be quite convincing.

But, if we endeavour to probe the matter a little more closely and critically, we will find that all is not right with the company, so far as the management and control of the Working Capital of the company is concerned.

Now, let us see, how do we make such a contrary claim, to refute the claim of Directors. First of all, we should always bear in mind that we should not come to a hasty conclusion, based on the Current Ratio (CR) in isolation. We should, instead, try to see how is the Current Ratio (CR) composed of. That is, we should also try to examine the quantum of increase and decrease in the levels of the Current Assets (CAs) and the Current Liabilities (CLs) in the two years, in question.

And, we see that the Current Ratio (CR) has come down this year, mainly because the Current Liabilities (CLs) have gone up substantially, as compared to the last year (by around Rs. 100 lakh), which would mean an outgo of a larger fund, by way of interest on short-term borrowings.

And, this is further substantiated by the fact that the current liabilities (mostly comprising the short-term bank borrowings), increased from Rs. 298.51 crore to Rs. 399.21 crore in a span of two years in succession, and accordingly, the amount of interest paid (to the bank) on such loans must also had gone up.

But then, when we look at the figures of interest paid by the company at Rs. 59.07 crore only (reduced from Rs. 77.58 crore in the past year) we start wondering how and why such a situation existed.

But, the real reason is not too far to seek. This is so mainly because of the conversion into equity shares of the first portion of the Fully Convertible Debentures (FCDs) of the company amounting to Rs. 128.70 crore (Rs. 283.75 crore was outstanding in the previous year, which was reduced to Rs. 155.05 crore only after year). And, as no interest was payable on such converted portion of the FCDs [since converted into equity shares, increased from Rs. 62.97 crore to Rs. 103.67 crore in one year, plus share premium reserve Rs. 88 crore (Rs. 100.54 crore – Rs. 12.54 crore)], [that is, (Rs. 103.67 crore – Rs. 62.97 crore + Rs. 88.00 crore = Rs. 128.70 crore)], the quantum of total outgo, by way of interest, has actually gone down.

So, we can undoubtedly and incontrovertibly prove that the amount of interest outgo has gone down, not because of better and effective Working Capital Management and Control (as 'falsely' claimed by the Directors), but, mainly because of the conversion of a major portion of the FCDs, into equity shares.

[Such deliberate attempt on the part of the Directors to give some wrongful information by twisting and misrepresenting and/or misinterpreting certain pieces of information, given in the Balance Sheet, may safely be termed as an apt example of 'window dressing', which I prefer to refer to as the 'Creative Accounting', instead].

14.1.2 Quick Ratio (or Acid-test Ratio)

It is indicative of the ability of the company to meet its urgent and emergent financial obligations, in a much shorter span of time than the other current assets (mainly inventories) can do, in the usual course of business, during the operating cycle.

That is why, by way of a thumb rule, the Quick Assets are taken to comprise all the current assets less (mainly) the inventories, as these alone contribute a major portion of the current assets, other than the quick assets (viz. cash, near cash and sundry debtors.

The Quick Ratio (QR) of the company has come down from 0.90 : 1 to 0.65 : 1, which may apparently seem to have deteriorated. This may be perceived as such if one may take 1 : 1 to be the benchmark for the Quick Ratio. But, this is so in the U.S. and not in India. Similarly, the US banks insist on the Current Ratio (CR) being at least 2 : 1, whereas in India, it has been 1.33 : 1, as per the second method of lending, stipulated by Tandon Committee Report. Now that the provisions of the Tandon Committee Report have remained more as advisory guidelines, rather than mandatory measures, most of the banks may no longer insist on a CR of 1.33 : 1, but may even accept 1.25 : 1 or so, to be good enough.

And, in the same spirit, in my own considered opinion, a Quick Ratio (QR) of 0.3 to 0.5 may be considered to be good enough. Why do I hold such a view, you may very well ask? This is so because, the components of the Quick Assets (QA) comprise mainly cash, which does not give any yield by way of interest, or near cash, like government securities, etc., which give comparatively lower yield, and the outstanding sundry debtors, which mean blockage of funds and loss of opportunity cost, connected therewith.

In the foregoing circumstances, one may be inclined to believe that lower the Quick Assets (QA) the better. But then, the companies do have to keep some cash (in hand and/or in banks) to meet the day-to-day requirements of cash. Similarly, companies will have to sell a portion of their goods on credit basis, and thereby, they will always be having a certain level of sundry debtors too, so long as they are in the buyer's (and not in the seller's) market. Therefore, it should better be kept at the minimal possible level. Thus, the coming down of the Quick Ratio to 0.69 (from 0.90) may be said to be a better sign for the company, except for the fact that this has been so mainly because of the increased level of current liabilities (in the denominator) and the higher level of inventories reduced from the total current assets in the numerator.

14.2. TURNOVER RATIOS (OR PRODUCTIVITY RATIOS)

These ratios are indicative of the turnover or productivity of the various liabilities (sources of funds) and assets (uses of funds), in relation to the single measuring scale, *i.e.* the annual sales. Thus, the higher ratios represent the coverage of more mileage, *i.e.* being so many times, during the year, in relation to the annual sales.

14.2.1 Capital Employed Turnover Ratio

This has gone up from 2.01 times to 2.23 times. The annual sales of the company have been 2.23 times the quantum of capital (or long-term sources) employed, as compared to only 2.01 times the sales, during the previous year. This means that the capital (*i.e.* long-term sources) have been put to use, more effectively and profitably this year, as compared to the last year.

The same way we can find out the turnover ratio in terms of the effective use of:

(*a*) Short-term sources of funds, as also of the,

(*b*) Total funds (or total liabilities) being employed and invested in the business.

The formula in these cases will be:

(*a*) Sales ÷ short-term sources of funds; and

(*b*) Sales ÷ total sources of funds (or total liabilities).

And, this way, we may compute numerous ratios. But then, as prudent financial analysts, we should endeavour to avoid unnecessary duplications, as far as possible.

14.2.2 Block Capital Turnover Ratio

This has also shown an improvement at 3.64 times, as compared to 3.35 times last year. That is, the fixed assets have also been put to more effective use.

It will, however, be pertinent to discuss here about the differences of opinion as to whether in the denominator we should take;

(*i*) The net fixed assets as also the capital work-in-progress; or

(*ii*) The net fixed assets only, already put to productive use, *i.e.* exclusive of the capital work-in-progress, inasmuch as these are yet to be commissioned and become operative and productive.

And, in my considered opinion, there is sufficient weight in both these points of view.

For example, in support of the first contention, one may argue as well that if we do not take the capital work-in-process into consideration, the turnover ratio that may result may be quite comfortable, whereby one may (sometimes), tend to lose sight of the fact that a substantial sum of money is already invested in the capital Work-in-Progress. And, taking this, too, in the denominator, it will result in a much lower turnover ratio which will keep us ever alive to the fact that we should endeavour hard to complete the project and make it fully operative and commercially productive, sooner the better.

For example, supposing you have already invested a sum of Rs. 10 lakh for the construction of the house, which is lying incomplete, say for the last five years. Thus, you are not getting any return on your existing investment of Rs. 10 lakh. And, if you invest, say another Rs. 5 lakh towards completion of the wood work and other finishing touches required for the completion of the house for living purposes, you may rent it out on completion, and thereafter, may start getting some reasonable return on your total investment of Rs. 15 lakh, instead of getting 'nil' return on your substantial investment of Rs. 10 lakh, as aforesaid.

But then, the second argument of excluding the capital Work-in-Progress cannot be brushed aside, either, for the simple reasons, as aforesaid, that is, that these have yet to be put to any productive use.

All considered, I am of the firm opinion that we may calculate the block capital turnover ratio in both the ways, so that we may not lose sight of the urgency of completion of the project in time, and, at the same time, we may get a realistic picture of the productivity of the net fixed assets already in the productive use.

14.2.3 Inventory Turnover Ratio

The inventory turnover, however, has marginally gone down from 5.39 times to 5.38 times. But then, a prudent Financial Manager should not just brush it aside as being just marginal, because, every company must endeavour to improve upon the turnover of inventories, year after year, and even any stagnation (leave alone the marginal decline) should be enquired into, in depth, and suitable corrective steps should be taken in this regard.

And, as we have already seen, during our detailed discussion on the current ratio, an unreasonably higher blockage of funds in inventories must be endeavoured to be put under strict control. And, if this is done, the inventory turnover will definitely improve substantially.

The inventory turnover can, as well, be calculated in terms of number of days, which also will reveal the identical position, *i.e.* marginal deterioration from 67.71 days to (a slightly higher) 67.88 days.

But, in my considered opinion, the inventory turnover ratio, calculated in terms of number of days, may give a more comprehensive and clear position. And, the same may, as well, be said to be true for calculating the Average Collection Period or turnover. However, I leave it on to the mature and seasoned readers to form their own opinion in this regard.

14.2.4 Average Collection Period

This has, of course, come down from 54.84 days to a substantially lower level at 46.21 days. And, I say, 'substantial', keeping in view the fact that this is so despite the fact that the sales turnover has gone up by around 20% (19.5% to be exact as per paragraph number one of the Directors' Report).

Further, the provision for doubtful debts has also substantially, gone down from Rs. 3.78 crore to just Rs. 0.50 crore, which comes to around 13% of the level of the previous year. And, as one does not have any doubt, about its being realistic and reasonable, in the absence of any adverse or qualifying remarks in the Auditors' Report, whatsoever, the Auditors' Report being clean and unqualified, the company does deserve a pat on the back, so far as its collection efforts, in particular, and the credit policy, management and control, in general, are concerned.

14.3. LEVERAGE RATIOS (I.R)

Leverage ratios or the financial structure ratios are indicative of the fact as to the mix of own fund of the company, and the loan funds, invested in the business.

14.3.1 (a) Debt/Equity ratio

This ratio has come down from 1.86 last year to 0.79, *i.e.* less than half, during the current year, which is a very positive sign and is also indicative of the fact that the company may now be able to procure even further term loan, with great ease, for its capital expenses, as and when the need may arise. True. But, here, one must not lose sight of the fact that this position has emerged not because of the repayment of any long-term loan, out of the internal cash generation. This has, instead, resulted from the fact of conversion of the major portion of the Fully Convertible Debentures (FCDs) into equity shares (with premium), this year.

But then, there is no denying the fact that the company's capacity to borrow long-term funds has substantially improved, now, for whatever reason it may be.

(b) Total Liabilities/Equity

This ratio is indicative of the proportion of the Owners' Equity (OE) (*i.e.* the owners' stake in the business) to the total liability.

Hence, we may come to a quick conclusion that higher the OE portion, the better it is. But then, it may not be so, inasmuch as the OE is non-tax-deductible and, therefore, may not be a prudent business sense to invest funds in the business by way of OE, beyond an optimal level. It may be true in the case of the issue of the equity shares even at a reasonably high premium, because, even in this case, the risk of forced takeover may become imminent.

In the instant case, we find that the proportion of OE has improved from 4.20 : 1 to 2.89 : 1. or, to put it differently, it has gone up from around 24% (23.8% to be exact, viz. 23922/100536), to around 35% (34.62% to be exact, viz. 41241/119112).

But then, on further examination and scrutiny, we find that this has resulted mainly due to the conversion of FCDs (borrowed funds) into equity shares (owners' funds) whereby, while the nominator (total liabilities) has almost remained at the same level, the denominator has substantially increased, by the amount of fresh shares issued (at premium) on conversion of a major portion of FCDs.

And, this way, the risk of forcible takeover has also been kept under check, to some extent, and more so, if the FCDs were issued on rights basis.

(c) Net fixed assets/(Secured)/Long-term debt

We find that in the given formula, the denominator comprises only the secured long-term debt, and not any unsecured one.

Why? This is so because, this ratio gives an indication to the creditors, who have given secured term loans to the company, whether the outstanding balance on the term loan account is fully covered by the depreciated (net) value of the fixed assets financed by way of the term loan. This also indicates whether all the instalments on the relative term loan have been duly paid inasmuch as if there will be some overdue instalments, the ratio will be less than one, as the outstandings on the term loan account (inclusive of the instalments overdue) will be higher than the net (depreciated) value of the fixed assets, charged to the bank, as the primary security against the term loan. This ratio has gone up from 1.18 to 1.99, which is quite satisfactory, inasmuch as the fixed assets financed, fully cover the present outstandings on the term loan, to a still greater extent this year.

14.4. PROFITABILITY RATIOS

We observe that while in the first three profitability ratios, PBIT has been taken in the nominator, in the fourth one, PAT has been taken into account. Why?

The reason, of course, is obvious. Profitability ratios, in essence, are indicative of the managerial efficiency, too. And, therefore, to have an objective and realistic comparison of the managerial efficiency during the successive years, we should take only such parameters into consideration, which are well within the control of the management. Thus, we see that the rate of interest and the rate of income tax are well beyond the control of the management, inasmuch as while the rates of interest are determined by the Reserve Bank of India (RBI), the commercial banks and other financial institutions, the rate of income tax is determined by the Government of India.

For example, in the budget presented in the Parliament by the Union Minister of Finance, on February 28, 2001, for the financial year 2001-2002, the surcharge on income tax had been proposed to be reduced to 2% only, instead of 17% [15% + 2% (to finance the earthquake rehabilitation measures in Gujarat)] levied during the previous financial year. Thus, during the year the Profitability After Tax (PAT) was much higher for all the companies, but for no act on the part of the management of companies. And, therefore, to have given any credit therefor to the management of the company could be inappropriate and misplaced.

Similarly, with the rate of interest reduced by all banks, the quantum of interest was expected to come down, thereby resulting in a corresponding increase in the net profitability of the company. And, yet again, for no act on the part of the management.

Thus, it is more appropriate to compare the profitability of the company at the pre-interest and pre-tax stage, so as to compare the effectiveness of the successive managements in the successive years, on 'even comparing field', *i.e.* at the PBIT stage itself.

As against this, we take the PAT stage, while working out the return on the Net Worth, because it is the net profit that, in fact, is the net income or net return on the net worth or on the Owner's Equity (DE), to be distributed to shareholders, by way of dividend, or retained in the business by way of reserves and surplus, which, too, belong to the shareholders (mainly to the equity shareholders) only.

Now, we shall evaluate the financial performance of the company by interpreting the various profitability ratios hereafter.

14.4.1 PBIT/Sales

We observe that the profitability as a percentage of sales has gone up by around one per cent (from 7.97% to 8.80%) or by around 12%, as compared to the previous year. And, it is still more creditable, inasmuch as there has been a substantial increase, despite the fact that the value of sales has also gone up substantially by around 19.5%.

14.4.2 (a) PBIT/Total Investment, and (b) PBIT/Capital Employed

We further observe that the returns on (*a*) total funds employed, and on; (*b*) long-term sources employed, have also gone up correspondingly, which, too, is a satisfactory feature. This is so mainly because while there has been only marginal increase in the total funds employed, as also in the long-term funds employed, the PBIT of the company has registered a significant growth of 19.5%.

14.4.3 PAT/NW

This ratio has gone up substantially by 5.71 per cent (from 11.27% to 16.98%) or by around 50%, as compared to the previous year. This achievement becomes even more significant when we see that the substantial 50% increase has been registered, despite the fact that the Net Worth (NW) itself (in the denominator) has gone up by around 75%, mainly due to the conversion of a major portion of FCDs into equity shares.

This is so, mainly because there has been a substantial increase of around 160% in the level of PAT itself this year, as compared to the previous year.

14.5. VALUATION RATIOS

Valuation of the equity share or its market value or its price in the stock market is determined mainly on the basis of:

(*a*) its earning per share, commonly known as EPS Ratio; and

(*b*) on the book value per share.

And, we see that both these have registered a satisfactory increase. The EPS has gone up from 42.48% to 67.36%, that is, by 24.88 per cent (or around 60%) as compared to the last year.

And, as regards the book value of shares, this has, however, gone up from 379.90% to 397.81 %, that is, by 17.91 per cent, or only marginally by around less than 5%, as compared to the earlier year.

Here, it may be observed that the EPS and the book value per share have been computed not in terms of rupees but in percentage terms instead. This measure has been adopted, a little away from the conventional method of computing these in rupee terms, mainly to simplify the process of arriving at the increase/decrease in these valuation ratios in just one stroke, as against first finding the value in terms of rupees and then converting the same in terms of the face value of the shares. But, by way of the slightly modified method adopted by us, we get the percentage change in the value, whatever be the face value of shares, this being virtually immaterial for the instant purpose. However, for the sake of convenience of some of our readers, the calculation has been done by the conventional method, *i.e.* in terms of rupees, vide Appendix-14(A).3, item 5.2(*a*).

The present face value of the shares of the company has been taken at Rs. 100 per share.

14.6. COVERAGE RATIOS

Coverage ratios signify as to how many times the payments of (*i*) Interest; and (*ii*) Dividends, are covered by the respective measuring parameters viz. (*a*) PBIT and (*b*) PAT.

To put it differently, it indicates that if the PBIT and PAT, decline the company would be able to meet its obligation of payment of (*i*) Interest and (*ii*) Dividend, at the extant levels.

Thus, higher the coverage ratios, the better it is.

14.6.1 Interest Cover

In the present case, we find that the interest cover ratio has gone up from 1.41 times last year to 2.44 times during the current year, which is a very positive sign. But, here one must not lose sight of the fact that it is so, mainly because a major portion of FCDs has been converted into equity shares during the current year, whereby the interest outgo (on FCDs) has gone down correspondingly.

14.6.2 Dividend Cover

But, again when we see the dividend cover ratio we find that this too has gone up from 2.00 times in the previous year to 2.88 times next year, which was quite satisfactory. It is still more significant keeping in view the fact that this was so despite the fact that a major portion of the FCDs had been converted into equity shares in the year, whereby the quantum of equity shares had gone up correspondingly. Thus, though the denominator (level of equity shares) had gone up, the nominator (PAT), too, had gone up to a far greater extent and hence the end result too, showed a significant improvement, as compared to the earlier.

Here, it may be quite pertinent to examine that though the differences in the end-results in all the three cases 6.2 (*i*), (*ii*) and (*iii*) are quite insignificant, mainly because the quantum of Preference Shares in comparison to that of the equity shares, which one of these three should actually be considered to be representing the most realistic picture.

To this end, we may argue that as the rate of dividend payable on preference shares is already pre-fixed and this has got to be paid to the preference shareholders on priority basis (prior to the payment of the dividends to the equity shareholders), we should take into consideration the "PAT less the amount of the dividend payable on preference shares", in the nominator. And, correspondingly, in the denominator we should take the quantum of payment of dividends on the equity shares only, *i.e.* exclusive of the preference dividends. Thus, the formula 6.2 (*i*) seems to be the most realistic, reaionable and rational one, in comparison to the other two, viz. 6.2 (*ii*), and 6.2 (*iii*).

Appendix 14(A).1

ANALYSIS OF BALANCE SHEET—A BRIEF OUTLINE

Liabilities (or Sources of Funds)	
1. Current Liabilities	i.e. *Loans and Advances, repayable within a period of one year, from the date of the Balance Sheet, e.g.* (*i*) Short-term bank borrowings for working capital requirements. (*ii*) Sundry Creditors. (*iii*) Instalments of Term Loans (with interest) due, within a period of one year, from the date of the Balance Sheet. (*iv*) Loans and Advances from friends and relatives, repayable within one year. (*v*) Public Deposits, maturing within one year. (*vi*) Provisions for taxes, dividends, gratuity, pension, etc.
2. Term Liabilities or Deferred Liabilities	i.e. *Loans and Advances, falling due for payment* after a period of one year from the date of the Balance Sheet, *e.g.* (*i*) Instalments of Term Loans (and interest) falling due for payment, after one year, from the date of the Balance Sheet. (*ii*) Debentures not due within one year. (*iii*) Other Loans and Advances (from friends and relatives) not payable within one year, specifically undertaken by them in writing.
3. Capital, Reserves and Surplus or Owner's Equity (O.E.)	i.e. *Own funds, invested in the business, and the surpluses generated and retained in the business (also known as Owner's Equity (OE), or Shareholders' Funds, or Net Worth, or Own Fund, or Capital Base or Equity, etc.), e.g.* (*i*) Paid-up Capital (Equity Shares and Preference Shares). (*ii*) Capital Reserves. (*iii*) Revenue Reserves or General Reserves. (*iv*) Profit and Loss A/c Surplus (+).

ANALYSIS OF BALANCE SHEET—A BRIEF OUTLINE (Continued)

Assets (or Uses of Funds)	
1. Current Assets	i.e. *Cash and other assets, which are converted into cash, in the normal course of business, during the operating cycle, e.g.*
(*a*)	Cash in Hand, Cash in Bank, Marketable Securities (*e.g.* Government Securities, Other Trust Securities, Quoted Shares, excluding those of the company's subsidiaries), Bills Receivable, outstanding for not more than 180 days.
(*b*)	(*i*) Stocks of Raw Materials and Consumable Stores and Spares, Work-in-Process, and Finished Goods [*i.e.* Inventories]. (*ii*) Loans and Advances given to the suppliers, etc. (*iii*) Pre-paid Expenses, etc.
	Quick Assets These constitute that part of the Current Assets which are convertible into cash rather more quickly than the other items thereof And, the items shown in (*a*) above, are Quick Assets.
Note: Quick Assets are usually computed to comprise Total Current Assets *(less) Inventories,* inasmuch as the remaining items of Other Current Assets [viz. (*b*) (*ii*) and (*b*) (*iii*) above] constitute a relatively much lesser percentage therefore.	
2. Fixed Assets	i.e. *Tools of Business, not intended for resale.* *e.g.* Land and Building, Plant and Machinery, Tools and Transport, Furniture and Fixtures, etc.
3. Miscellaneous Assets	i.e. *Assets which are neither Current, nor Fixed, nor Intangible, e.g.*
(*i*)	Investments in and/or Advances to Subsidiaries and/or Affiliates, including even quoted shares of its subsidiary companies).
(*ii*)	Investments in non-marketable securities unquoted shares), Advances to Directors or employees, Non-Consumable Stores and Spares, Bills Receivable outstanding for more than 180 days, etc.
4. Intangible Assets	i.e. Expenditure incurred for acquiring invisible assets, *e.g.*
(*i*)	Goodwill, Patent, Copyright, Trade Mark.
(*ii*)	Preliminary Expenses, Losses incurred by the Company, etc.

Appendix 14(A).2

INDIAN AUTOMOBILE INDUSTRY LIMITED

ANALYSIS OF THE BALANCE SHEETS

Sl.No.	Descriptions		Current Year	Previous Year
LIABILITIES				
A.	Current Liabilities **(A)**		45475	32208
B.	Deferred Liabilities **(B)**		32396	44406
C.	Capital, Reserves and Surplus (OE) **(C)**		41241	23922
	TOTAL LIABILITIES (A + B + C)		**119112**	**100536**
ASSETS				
D.	Current Assets		60113	54489
	Add: Quoted Shares (Others)	(+)	—	102
	Sub-Total		60113	54591
	Less: Outstanding Sundry Debtors for over 180 days	(–)	149	237
	TOTAL	**(D)**	**59964**	**54354**
E.	Net Fixed Assets	**(E)**	**44995**	**41092**
F.	Miscellaneous Assets			
	Total Investments		14004	4955
	Less: Quoted Shares (Others)	(–)		102
	Total		14004	4853
	Add: Outstanding Sundry Debtors for over 180 days	(+)	149	237
	TOTAL	**(F)**	**14153**	**5090**
G.	Intangible Assets	**(G)**	—	—
	TOTAL ASSETS (D + E + F + G)		**119112**	**100536**

Appendix 14(A).3

INDIAN AUTOMOBILE COMPANY LIMITED

FINANCIAL ANALYSIS USING RATIOS AS ON 31ST MARCH

Sl.No.	Descriptions	Current Year	Previous Year
1.	**Liquidity Ratios**		
	1.1 Current Ratio Current Assets ÷ Current Liabilities	59964 ÷ 45475 (1.32)	54354 ÷ 32208 (1.69)
	1.2 Quick Ratio (or Acid-test Ratio) Current Assets (less) Inventories ÷ Current Liabilities	29492 ÷ 45475 (0.65)	28839 ÷ 32208 (0.90)
2.	**Turnover/Productivity Ratios**		
	2.1 Capital Employed Turnover (Times) Sales ÷ Capital employed (Long-term sources)	163851 ÷ 73637 (2.23)	137546 ÷ 68328 (2.01)
	2.2 Fixed Assets Turnover (times) Sales ÷ Net Fixed Assets	163851 ÷ 44995 (3.64)	137546 ÷ 41092 (3.35)
	2.3 Inventory Turnover (times) Sales ÷ Inventory	163851 ÷ 30472 (5.38)	137546 ÷ 25515 (5.39)
	2.3 (a)* Inventory Turnover period (No. of days) (Inventory × 365) ÷ Sales	(30472 × 365) ÷ 163851 (67.88)	(25515 × 365) ÷ 137546 (67.71)
	2.4 Average Collection Period (No. of days) (Accounts Receivable × 365) ÷ Sales	(20744 × 365) ÷ 163851 (46.21)	(20667 × 365) ÷ 137546 (54.84)

(Contd)...

* In my considered opinion, the inventory turnover ratio, in terms of number of days, as against number of times, may be more easily and clearly understood, facilitating quick and considered decision-making process.

Sl.No.	Descriptions	Current Year	Previous Year
3.	**Liverage/Financial Structure Ratios**		
	3.1 Debt: Equity Ratio Debt = (Long-term Debt) Equity = [Share Capital, Reserves and Surplus (less) Intangible Assets]		
	(*a*) Debt ÷ Equity	32396 ÷ 41241 (0.79)	44406 ÷ 23922 (1.86)
	(*b*) Total Liabilities ÷ Equity	119112 ÷ 41241 (2.89)	100536 ÷ 23922 (4.20)
	(*c*) Net Fixed Assets ÷ Secured Long-term Debts (Secured Term Loans)	44995 ÷ 22609 (1.99)	41092 ÷ 34782 (1.18)
	3.2 Net Working Capital [CA (less) CL] to Current Assets (%) (Net Working Capital × 100) ÷ Current Assets	14489 ÷ 59964 (24.16)	22146 ÷ 54354 (40.74)
4.	**Profitability Ratios**		
	4.1 Profit Margin (%) [Profit Before Interest and Tax (PBIT) × 100] ÷ Sales	14420 ÷ 163851 (8.80)	10963 ÷ 137546 (7.97)
	4.2 Return on (Total) Investment (%) [Profit Before Interest and Tax (PBIT) × 100] ÷ Total Assets	14420 ÷ 119112 (12.11)	10963 ÷ 100536 (10.90)
	4.3 Return on (Long-term) Investment (%) [Profit Before Interest and Tax (PBIT) × 100] ÷ Capital Employed (Long-term Sources)	14420 ÷ 73637 (19.58)	10963 ÷ 68328 (16.04)
	4.4 Return on Net Worth (%) [Profit After Tax (PAT) × 100] ÷ Net Worth (Capital ÷ Reserves ÷ Surplus)	7003 + 41241 (16.98)	2695 ÷ 23922 (11.27)

(Contd)...

Sl.No.	Descriptions	Current Year	Previous Year
5.	**Valuation Ratios**		
	5.1 Earning Per Share (%) [PAT (Less) Preference Dividends] × 100 ÷ Equity Shares (Total Face Value)	6983 ÷ 10367 (67.36)	2675 ÷ 6297 (42.48)
	5.1*a* Earning Per Share (in Rs.) [PAT (Less) Preference Dividend] (÷) No. of Equity Shares	6983 ÷ 10367 (67.36)	2675 ÷ 6297 (42.48)
	5.2 Book Value Per Share (%) (Net Worth × 100) ÷ Equity Shares (Total Face Value)	41241 ÷ 10367 (397.81)	23922 ÷ 6297 (379.90)
	5.2*a* Book Value Per Share (In Rs.) Net Worth ÷ No. of Equity Shares	41241 ÷ 10367 (397.81)	23922 ÷ 6297 (379.90)
6.	**Coverage Ratios**		
	6.1 Interest Cover Profit Before Interest and Tax ÷ Interest	14420 ÷ 5907 (2.44)	10963 ÷ 7758 (1.41)
	6.2 Dividend Cover		
	(*i*) @ (Profit After Tax – Preference Dividend) ÷ Dividend on Equity Shares	6983 ÷ 2424 (2.88)	2675 ÷ 1336 (2.00)
	(*ii*) Profit After Tax ÷ Dividend on Equity Shares	7003 ÷ 2424 (2.89)	2695 ÷ 1336 (2.02)
	(*iii*) Profit After Tax ÷ Dividend on Equity and Preference Shares	7003 ÷ 2444 (2.87)	2695 ÷ 1356 (1.99)

@ In my considered opinion the formula appearing at 6.2 (*i*) seems to be most appropriate and reasonable, as has already been explained, in detail, in the foregoing page, immediately preceding the Annexure 14 (A).1.

Appendix 14(A).4

Some Searching Questions that can very well be Raised by Shareholders of the Company in the Annual General Meeting

1. As has been claimed in the Directors' Report, the increase in the sales by 19.5% was due to higher demand, caused by good monsoon, leading to an overall upturn in the economy and the increased demand for freight movements. True.

   But, is it mainly (if not solely) due to the increase in the selling price of vehicles?

   That is, is the overall quantity (number) of the various models of vehicles, produced and sold during the current year, are the same or higher, as compared to the previous year? And, if not higher, even in the case of a few items only, why so, despite such favourable economic conditions?
2. Interest burden is less. True. But is it due to better working capital management or due to the conversion of FCDs into shares?
3. P.A.T. has increased by 160%. But, is it due to
   (*a*) Increased sales;
   (*b*) Better margin due to the price revision; or
   (*c*) Cost reduction, by virtue of better management of inventories and sundry debtors, *i.e.* better working capital management, as claimed by the Board of Directors? Perhaps not, as has already been discussed in the previous pages.
4. Analysis of Expenses Items
   (*a*) The consumption of raw materials, as a percentage of sales, is 51 % and 52%, *i.e.* almost the same as it had been in the previous year. But, the price revision has been effective in the current year. Thus, the number of vehicles produced this year might have been lesser. And, if such be the case, obviously the quantum of raw materials consumed per unit seems to be relatively on the higher side, which, in turn, speaks of the lack of exercising cost effectiveness measures, though it has been claimed as such by the Board Directors.
   (*b*) Managerial remuneration to Directors has gone up from Rs. 13 lakh to Rs. 34 lakh (*i.e.* by around three times). Why?
   (*c*) Likewise, the substantial rise in manufacturing, administrative and selling expenses also needs to be probed into, as has been suggested in the case of item 4 (*a*) above.
   (*d*) Provision for doubtful debts, this year, as compared to the last year, is less by a substantive 7.56 times. That is, it is only 13.22%, in comparison to the last year. Good. But, one must take care to verify whether the figure is genuine or is again an attempt of window dressing?

Appendix 14 (B). NATIONAL IMPEX COMPANY*

A. Cash Management

(*i*) Under the "Bankers' Acceptance Scheme", the payment for imported commodities are made by bankers of the company on presentation of documents, and the company's cash credit account is debited after 180 days. This has resulted, in substantial cash surplus with the company, which they have invested mainly in term deposits for 46 days with the bank, attracting interest @ 12% p.a. It is for consideration whether such an arrangement is beneficial to the company inasmuch as the bank must be charging a higher exchange rate, which may not compare favourably with the rate of interest on the term deposits. Further, why not take TDRs for 180 days, attracting higher rate of interest, instead of 46 days TDRs, renewed 4 times.

(*ii*) The credit balances on the company's current account and cash credit account, which together aggregated Rs. 5576 lakh as on 31.03.1990, could have been gainfully invested in the bank term deposits, as far as possible, in a phased manner, keeping in view the expected requirement of funds in the near future. In case of emergency, a loan could as well be raised against the term deposits to the extent of even up to 100%, or else, payment of full amount of some term deposits could be obtained with some forfeiture of interest, depending upon the quantum of funds required, and the amount of interest lost in each case.

(*iii*) The company may as well consider giving bank guarantees to the Municipal Corporation, as also to the High Court, in lieu of the Term Deposit Receipts (TDRs) lodged with them. The amount, thus released, may be more gainfully employed by the company elsewhere.

B. Investments

(*i*) The company may consider the desirability of disinvesting units of the UTI amounting to Rs. 2,055 lakh as on 31.03.1990 and use the funds, so released, for reducing the quantum of short-term loans, thereby reducing the quantum of the interest outgo thereon. It may further be observed that the amount of interest paid in the year ended 31.03.1991 at Rs. 14,442 lakh has registered an increase of over 100%, as compared to the previous year which was Rs. 7,164 lakh.

(*ii*) The company has invested in Indian Railways Finance Corporation, Railway Bonds (unquoted) at 10% (tax free) and some other Bonds (tax-free) at 9% p.a. viz. Railway Bonds, NHPC Bonds, HUDCO Bonds, MTNL Bonds, NTPC Bonds, etc. These investments, as it occurs to us, might have been made more under some pressure from government authorities, rather than by way of a deliberate investment decision by the company. The company may, therefore, endeavour (if such be the case) to disinvest such ungainful investments also at the earliest possible opportunity, and use the funds, so

* One of the approaches to the case study, as suggested by the author.
* Please note that there is no single approach/solution to a case study.

released, to reduce its loan liabilities and thereby save on the amount of interest paid, as aforesaid.

C. Inventories

Inventories have steadily increased from Rs. 27,879 lakh in 1989 to Rs. 41,547 lakh in 1990 and Rs. 53,123 lakh in 1991, which represent sales of 26 days, 30 days and 35 days respectively. The increase in the level of inventory for the year 1990 has been mainly due to higher stocks of Zinc and Nickle. In the year 1991, the higher level of inventory comprised mainly of copper, zinc, lead, iron ore, as also goods-in-transit, viz. sulphur, phosphoric acid, ammonia, etc. Further, when we look at the Balance Sheets of the company since 1985, we find that the inventory level was reduced from 22 days of sales in 1985 to 21 days of sales in 1986. In the year 1987, however, though inventories had come down in terms of value, as compared to 1986, these had gone up marginally as a percentage of sales from 5.6% to 5.9%. Sincere efforts, therefore, needs to be made by the company to maintain the level of inventories at the lowest possible level so as to reduce the inventory carrying costs, including the interest burden on current liabilities, and thereby increase the profitability of the company still further.

D. Sundry Debtors

(*i*) The level of Sundry Debtors has also steadily increased from Rs. 18,245 lakh in 1989 to Rs. 31,255 lakh in 1990 and Rs. 69,858 lakh in 1991, which represents an increase from 17 days sales in 1989 to 22 days sales in 1990 and 45 days sales in 1991. The increase in the Sundry Debtors has mainly been due to outstanding bills with the Ministry of Agriculture, so much so that as on 31 March 1991, the bills aggregating Rs. 36,470 lakh were outstanding with them alone. It would, therefore, augur well for the company to vigorously pursue the matter of early payment of bills, particularly with the Ministry of Agriculture, so as to save the interest loss caused due to long outstanding bills. Rigorous follow-up of Sundry Debtors is also expected to reduce the quantum of bills outstanding for more than 180 days (for more than one year to over 3 years in some cases) to minimise the risk of bad debts, and making provisions therefore, year after year.

(*ii*) It may be pertinent to mention here that, with the concerted efforts made by the company to realise the long outstanding bills, the level of Sundry Debtors was reduced from Rs. 12,773 lakh in 1986 to Rs. 10,219 lakh in 1987 which, in terms of percentage of sales, came down from 4.2% to 3.7%. The achievement seems to be far more impressive when we compare the level of Sundry Debtors in 1986 and 1987 with the Sundry Debtors at Rs. 25,920 lakh in 1985. It, thus, goes to indicate that with the much-needed concerted efforts, the level of Sundry Debtors of the company can well be reduced substantially. This may go a long way in increasing the liquidity as also the overall profitability of the company, at a still higher level.

(*iii*) It further occurs to us that a large portion of the company's sales to the private parties (non-governmental agencies) are on cash payment basis or even against advance payments. Therefore, with a view to arrive at a more realistic picture, the company would do well to compare the level of Sundry Debtors with the level of Credit Sales only, that is, Total Sales less Cash Sales, instead of Total Sales.

(*iv*) The bifurcation of the Sundry Debtors (party-wise) into (*i*) dues from the Ministry of Agriculture, and (*ii*) dues from others, as also the age-wise analysis of the outstanding bills are the steps in the right direction. These may continue with still further age-wise break-ups, so as to give the right focus for vigorous follow-up for the realisation of the long outstanding bills, period-wise and party-wise, as also percentage-wise.

E. Concluding Remarks

All considered, achievements of the company are substantial and significant by any standard, for which its people have every reason to feel proud of. But one should always bear in mind that

"There is no room on earth, bigger than the room for improvement."

(*i*) And, therefore, if the company earnestly endeavours to manage its working capital more effectively, by implementing the aforesaid suggestions, the performance and profitability of the company would definitely scale new heights in the years to come. And, as I have always been telling:

"It is good to be excellent, but too bad to be complacent."

(*ii*) **Further information/break-ups:** The Director (Finance) may like to call for from the General Manager (Accounts):

1. (*a*) Cost/Benefit analysis of the 'Bankers' Acceptance Scheme.'
   (*b*) Reasons for its manifold increase, since 1988.
2. Why avail of cash credit limit at a higher rate of interest and invest surplus funds in term deposits at a lower rate?
3. Reasons for the steep rise of Sundry Debtors in 1991.
4. Break-ups of Inventories: Commodity-wise and age-wise.
5. (*a*) Further break-ups of Sundry Debtors:
   (*i*) Party-wise, viz. government, public sector, private sector and others;
   (*ii*) Age-wise; and
   (*iii*) Percentage-wise.
   (*b*) Percentage of Sundry Debtors to **credit** sales (and not total sales)
   (*c*) (*i*) Party-wise break-up of bad debts provided for;
   (*ii*) Specific reasons for bad debts. Is it due to poor follow-up also, in some cases?
   (*iii*) Suggestions for containing the level of bad debts.
6. (*a*) Why a major portion of cash and bank balances (these being substantial) are not deposited with the bank in term deposits to earn some interest?
   (*b*) Why not explore the possibility of giving bank guarantees, instead of term deposits, to the Municipal Corporation as also to the Court?
7. (*a*) Break-up of Public Bonds;

(*b*) Cost-Benefit Analysis thereof vis-à-vis other avenues of investment yielding a better return;

(*c*) Possibility of disinvestments of public bonds and units of UTI to reduce the quantum of short-term loans and thereby the interest outgo thereon, and, above all, to enhance the liquidity and financial stability of the company.

8. The levels of Inventories and Sundry Debtors have gone up substantially in 1991. What are the reasons therefore, and what remedial measures could be initiated in the interest of the company?
9. Interest coverage ratio has deteriorated due to more interest outgo. What measures could be taken to keep the interest outgo at the minimal level by better management of cash, bank balances and investments, as also of loans and advances?

Note: The aforesaid information/break-ups would provide further facts, and reveal a fuller picture of affairs of the company. The management may, therefore, initiate further corrective steps, based thereon, with a view to manage its working capital more effectively, increase the productivity, and financial gains that go therewith.

Appendix 14 (C)

POPULAR PUMPS AND PARTS LIMITED*

Background

Popular Pumps and Parts Limited (PPP), had been facing Working Capital problems only for the last two years. Earlier, the company was able to meet its Working Capital requirements out of:

(*i*) Internal sources like sufficient retained earnings, etc.,

(*ii*) Sundry creditors, and

(*iii*) Marketable securities.

Negative Features

But, for the last two/three years, the company started experiencing some cash crunch and lack of Working Capital Funds, so much so that it had to approach their bank for enhancement of the Working Capital Limit. Besides, it had been approaching the bank for four to five times a year, with some request or the other, like:

(*a*) Grant of some more loan to meet the working capital gap;

(*b*) For further extension of time for the repayment of loans, which had already become overdue;

(*c*) It had taken abridging loan, too, in the third year, with the undertaking to repay it within four months, but had not been able to pay it back till then;

(*d*) Instead, it requested the bank to grant some more loans with a view to tide over its financial difficulties.

But, the Bank was, naturally, reluctant to accede to such requests, keeping in view the company's past performance, and frequent violation of its undertakings, from time to time. Instead the bank, pressed hard for realisation of its dues (say over-dues) at the earliest.

Positive Features

But, at the same time, the company enjoyed several positive features, too. For example:

(*i*) The level of its Profit After Tax (PAT) steadily grew, so much so that it registered an increase of around 150% in its PAT level.

(*ii*) Besides, some of its products had been very well received in the market and enjoyed a popular brand equity, by virtue of their:

(*a*) Good quality,

(*b*) Timely delivery, and

(*c*) High customer satisfaction due to their efficient (after-sales service).

(*iii*) Further, they ploughed back a substantial percentage of the profit in the business every year.

---

* One of the approaches to the case study, as suggested by the author.

* Please note that there is no single approach/solution to a case study.

But, perhaps, they lost sight of one of the most important principles of working capital management that the working capital policy should be flexible enough so as to swiftly respond to the changing economic and marketing conditions like:

(*a*) The ever-increasing competition, and

(*b*) The rapid growth in terms of:

I. The quantum of working capital requirements, which, in turn, depends on the levels of;

(*a*) Raw materials;

(b) Finished goods;

(*c*) Sundry debtors; and

(*d*) Sundry creditors,

II. An optimal mix of various sources of finance (both short-term and long-term), and

III. The cardinal principle of not indulging in the malpractice of diversion of funds, at any time, inasmuch as it is viewed with great disfavour by any short-term lender, be it commercial bank or even other financial institutions. The case of J.K. Synthetics, discussed earlier in the book, is the live example, to bring home the point amply.

IV. And, most importantly, ensuring repayment of bank loans on time, as per promise, failing which the company may lose its face and its credibility, too, in the eyes of the bank, and the other creditors.

Now, let us examine the operational aspects and the prevalent practices of the company in regard to its working capital policy.

As we all know (and must realise too) the management of Working Capital is not the sole role and responsibility of the Finance Manager alone. The realistic implementation of any working capital policy, and the effective working capital management, instead, requires a team effort, a synergy among the personnel of the purchase, materials, production and marketing departments, who must always work in perfect coordination and full cooperation among themselves.

For example, the purchase decision must be taken jointly by the purchase and production departments, in consultation with the materials department. Similarly, production decision must be taken jointly by the production and marketing departments, in consultation with purchase and materials departments. And, the marketing decisions, in turn, must be taken jointly by the marketing and production managers in consultation with materials and purchase managers.

[For a detailed discussion on building an effective team and sustaining the team spirit (emanating synergy) in a high-performing organisation, the readers may refer to the Chapter titled, "Three Plus Three Makes Nine", in an other book of the author, *Mentoring Mantras for Indian Managers*, Matrix Publishers, New Delhi, 2010.

But, when we look at the affairs of the PPP, we are dismayed to observe that the purchase decision has been taken unilaterally by the purchase department alone. In fact, there does not seem to be even a pretence of any tentative system of decision-making, and/or even a consultation mechanism, leave alone their effective implementation.

Let us now substantiate the aforesaid statements by citing the relevant facts and figures, as has been given in the Case Study.

It is amply anguishing and astonishing to observe that the company has taken a decision to purchase huge stocks of certain items of imported goods locally, in a most uneconomic and unprofessional manner, mainly for the following reasons:

1. It is anybody's guess that items must have been imported earlier by some local businessmen or industrial house, which they would prefer to sell at some higher price to earn some profit. And thus, it would have definitely been far more cost-effective and therefore, sane and sensible, if the company would have imported these materials direct.
2. Further, it would have made a much better business sense, if a small quantity of such imported materials had been purchased locally to meet the urgent and emergent requirement thereof. And, simultaneously, the necessary steps should have been initiated for the direct import of materials in the required quantity.
3. It is further disquietening to note that the local purchases of the two imported materials, appearing at items marked (*a*) and (*b*) below, have been made in the successive two years, when the purchases made during the previous year itself were considered sufficient enough to meet its requirements for around five and eight years respectively. And, even if the rate of consumption had substantially gone up the very next year, the purchases still represented around four years of consumption.

A. Pockets of Problems of Purchases

Imported Items	*Amount*	*Annual Consumption in the year*		*Remarks*
Purchased locally	*(Rs.)*	*1994 (Rs)*	*1995 (Rs)*	
(*a*) Parts of pumps	160 lakh	35 lakh	40 lakh	(Representing 4 year's consumption)
(*b*) Parts of fans	100 lakh	15 lakh	25 lakh	(Representing 4 year's consumption)

And, it is just not surprising inasmuch as the decision to purchase the imported items (*a*) and (*b*) in such a huge quantity has been taken by the Production Manager alone, obviously, not in consultation with the Finance Manager.

The arguments put forth by the Production Manager in favour of the local purchase that such stocks were readily available, and that, too, at a reasonably fair price, are most unconvincing. His further plea that the import of these goods would have involved a very long lead time is also far from truth when the procedures and provisions of imports have, of late, been substantially streamlined and simplified.

An Objective Evaluation of Decisions

When we look at such decisions in an objective and professional manner, we find that the purchase of such a huge stock of raw materials will avoidably increase the inventory carrying cost, resulting in unnecessary drop in profit, in addition to the imprudent blockage of funds, resulting in the overall working capital problems in various directions and dimensions. And, the fact that the import will be cheaper enough is just a common sense.

B. Problems Pertaining to Production

Earlier, the company had been producing heavy-duty diesel-driven water-lifting pumps on receipt of firm orders. But, of late, it had started production of such pumps in large quantity and had been keeping them in huge ready stock with a view to effect a prompt delivery thereof, thereby to have an edge over its ever-growing competitors.

This decision was also taken by the Marketing Manager, all by himself, and was forced on the Production Manager without taking into consideration the involved inventory carrying cost and even the risk of obsolescence. He could not appreciate that this may result in the avoidable blockage of funds, which, in turn, could as well lead to some serious working capital shortage. Had the marketing people cared to consult the Production Manager, and, above all, the financial experts, they would have naturally given the sound professional advice, and the company would have been saved of a lot of its financial difficulties.

C. Pockets of Problem Pertaining to Sundry Debtors (S/Ds)

The collection of bills had fallen far short of the budgeted level, mainly because of one or more of the following reasons:

(*i*) The cash discount, allowed to ensure prompt payments of bills, had been reduced from 3% to 2%, if paid within 10 days;

(*ii*) Besides, the cash discount of 0.5% allowed earlier, if the bills could be paid on due dates, had also been withdrawn; and

(*iii*) The credit period had been increased from 30 days to 60 days, which had resulted in the increase of sales, but by 10% only.

And, all these decisions were taken by the Marketing Manager in isolation, which were apparently wrong specially when the company faced cash crunch and severe paucity of Working Capital funds. These steps led to further blocking of funds in sundry debtors to the extent of Rs. 18 lakh.

From the point of view of high cost of cash discount, its reduction from '3/10 net 30' to '2/10 net 30' proved to be sub-optimal, if not absolutely wrong for the following reasons:

The cost of the discount term '(3/10 net 30)', comes to 54% per annum, while that of '(2/10 net 30)', comes to 36% per annum (taking 360 days in a year), whereby both these prove to be unreasonably high, in view of the prevalent advance rates. The cash discount should, therefore, have been completely withdrawn or, at least, could have been reduced to '1/10 net 30', instead, whereby the effective cost by way of interest would have come down to 18%, which seems to be along the line of the prevalent level of cost of capital, provided, of course, such strategy would have produced the desired result, *i.e.* the increase in sales to the expected levels. The company, therefore, should have carefully monitored the developments and should have withdrawn the cash discount, if such a decision would have proved to be more beneficial.

Operating Cycle [vide detailed calculations in Annexure-14 (C).1]

	2000	*1997*
Raw Materials	152	113
Work-in-Process	49	48
Finished Goods	48	46
Sundry Debtors	50	39
Total	**299 days**	**246 days**

Thus, we see that the duration of the operating cycle has worsened by (299−246) 53 days or, say, by around 2 months, mainly due to an increase in stocks of raw materials and sundry debtors. The position revealed may, perhaps, be still worse, if the monthly and/or the weekly averages are taken instead.

The aforesaid position, thus, calls for an effective working capital management and control, with a view to ensuring possible reduction in the duration of the operating cycle, whereby a substantial quantum of blocked funds could be got released for better and optimal use elsewhere. The aforesaid strategies may go a long way in tiding over most of the problems of working capital funds.

Besides, the payments to the creditors may also be restricted and phased out, so as generally to coincide with the level of the cash position, as per the cash budget.

It may further be observed that by taking suitable steps for bringing down the stocks of raw materials and the outstandings in the sundry debtors at the minimal possible level (say, which actually obtained in the year 1997), as has been revealed by the relevant figures given below, we find that the quantum of funds so released (*i.e.* Rs. 40.91 lakh) happens to be a little higher than the total amount of bridging loan (Rs. 40 lakh) granted by the bank, and which the company has not so far been able to repay, despite 'false' promises, several times, resulting in loss of its credibility and credit-worthiness, in the eyes of the bank. The position of the company may, thus, improve significantly, if it tightens its control just on the two fronts, viz. the stocks of inventories of raw materials and the outstandings in the sundry debtors.

Raw Materials

(1.28 ÷ 2) or 0.64 × (152 – 113 days) = 0.64 × 39 = 24.96

Sundry Debtors

(2.90 ÷ 2) or 1.45 × (50 – 39 days) = 1.45 × 11 = 15.95

total = 40.91

Some Other Sources of Raising Additional Funds, *from Long-Term Sources*

(a) By Raising Term Loans

We find that the Debt: Equity Ratio (*i.e.* 84:189 = 0.44) is considered quite favourable, so that any financial institution like ICICI, IDBI, IFCI, would be willing enough to grant suitable term loans to finance its proposed capital expenditure.

(b) By Issuing Fresh Share Capital

To our pleasant surprise, we observe that despite the aforesaid unsatisfactory financial features of the company, its financial standing, in reality, is still sound enough, whereby it may very well be able to raise sufficient long-term funds by way of raising equity capital, and that too, even on rights basis.

With this end in view, we may suggest to the company to adopt the following financial strategies:

Step 1

First of all, the company should issue bonus shares in the ratio of 1 : 2, so as to please the existing shareholders so that they may repose further faith in the company and may be willing to subscribe to the further share capital, whenever issued, by way of rights, or even public issue.

Step 2

The company should, thereafter, issue Fully Convertible Debentures (FCDs) of the face value of Rs. 100 each, for Rs. 100 million, at a coupon (interest) rate of, say 12% per annum, to be compulsorily converted into two equity shares of the face value of Rs. 10 each, at a premium of Rs. 40 (*i.e.* at the price of Rs. 50 per share), after two years.

Step 3

On conversion of the FCDs into equity shares, after two years, the position would emerge as under:

Sl.No.	*Position*	*Share Capital*	*Reserves*	*Total (Rs.)*		*Book Value per Share of Rs. 10 face value*
I.	Before Bonus	50	139	189	189/50	37.80
II.	After Bonus	+25	–25	0		
		75	114	189	189/75	25.20
III.	After Conversion	+20	+80*	100		
	TOTAL	95	194	289	289/95	30.42

* Share Premium Reserves.

A suggestion has deliberately been made to issue FCDs (instead of equity shares) as an intermediate step (before its conversion into equity shares), so that

(*i*) The existing shareholders will continue to get the dividend at the current rate together with interest on the FCDs at periodical (half-yearly) intervals for two years. And, after these two years, when the expansion programme of the company becomes operative, and the commercial production commences, the company's production, sales and the resultant profit will go up along with the PAT and the dividend paying capacity.

Thus, the company may be able to maintain payment of the dividend on conversion at the same level, even on the enhanced equity shares.

Thus, we observe that after the issue of the bonus shares in the ratio of 1 : 2, the book value of shares comes down proportionately, *i.e.* from Rs. 37.80 per share to Rs. 25.20 per share. But then, on conversion of FCDs into equity shares, at a premium of Rs. 40 per share, it again goes up to Rs. 30.42 per share, which is well above the post-bonus level (Rs. 25.20), though below the pre-bonus level (Rs. 37.80).

But then, we have seen that after the declaration of bonus shares, the market price of shares comes down (mostly proportionately) in the immediate post-bonus stage, but gradually its price starts picking-up over again. The bonus shares issued by Reliance Industry Limited (RIL) in the ratio of 1 : 1 in the year 1997 is one of the cases in point.

On the news of the company's proposal to declare a bonus in the ratio of 1 : 1, the price of its shares started rising steadily and, at one point, it touched a peak price of around Rs. 440. And, on declaration of the bonus, the ex-bonus price gradually came down to Rs. 225, Rs. 200, and Rs. 180, in stages. The price of these shares, too, remained at a much lower level during the bearish period at the stock exchanges for a couple of years. But, later its share price went up to around **Rs. 430** as on Friday, 16 February 2001, in Bombay Stock Exchange (BSE), as also in National Stock Exchange (NSE). This, in terms of pre-bonus level, may be notionally computed at double the price at around **Rs. 860,** as this is the price after the issuance of the bonus shares in the ratio of 1 : 1.

It is, therefore, expected that after the issue of the bonus shares of PPP also, its share price may come down initially, but then, may go up again, as has been seen in the aforesaid case of Reliance Industries Limited (RIL), and several other companies too.

That is why, the pricing of shares, on rights basis, at Rs. 50, as against the book value of around Rs. 25, is well justified, inasmuch as it has been observed that, in most of the cases, the issue price is usually kept at almost double the book value of shares.

Based on the general trend, it has further been presumed, that the prevailing price of the company's shares in the market would be well above Rs. 50 (the proposed issue price), which is quite a reasonable expectation, keeping in view the reputation and prospects of the company and the market price of its shares in the recent past, *i.e.* at Rs. 138 (maximum), Rs. 94 (minimum), and Rs. 116 (average), during the year 2000, as has been cited in the case study, itself.

By way of yet another well considered financial strategy, we have not proposed the issue of Partly Convertible Debentures (PCDs), mainly for the following reasons:

(*i*) The issue of PCDs may not prove to be as attractive to the existing shareholders, which may adversely affect the success of the issue.

(*ii*) Moreover, the payment of dividend on the shares, on full conversion of FCDs into equity shares, issued at a substantial premium of 400%, may prove to the company to be much cheaper than the amount of interest payable on the non-convertible portion of the PCDs @12% per annum, for a much longer period.

We are saying so, because even if the company announces a dividend @ 30% per share of Rs. 10, it would be paying Rs. 3.00 only per share, which, in effect, will mean an outgo of Rs. 3.00 per Rs. 50 (*i.e.* the price at which the shares have been issued), which comes to 6% only.

And, as against this, the amount of interest payable on the non-convertible portion (though tax deductible) on the PCDs will be 12% per annum, which is double the actual amount payable on shares, as these have been issued at a substantially high premium of 400%.

The undernoted calculations will justify the stand beyond doubt:

Situaton (A)

(*a*)	Interest Payable on PCDs @ 12% per annum	Rs. 12
(*b*)	(Less) Savings effected by way of Income Tax @ 33.3% (it being tax deductible).	(–) Rs. 4
	Effective Net Cost	Rs. 8

Situation (B)

(*a*)	Dividend payable on Equity Shares @ 30%, *i.e.* Rs. 3.00 per share (sold @ Rs. 50/-) means an effective cost to the company	Rs. 6.00
(*b*)	(Add) Tax payable on the dividend payable by the company @ 10%	(+) Rs. 0.60
		Rs. 6.60

And, this is well below Rs. 8.00.

Appendix 14(C).1

POPULAR PUMPS AND PARTS LIMITED

OPERATING CYCLES FROM 1997 TO 2000

(Rupees in million)

Sl.No.	*Descriptions*	*2000*	*1999*	*1998*	*1997*	*1996*
1.	**Raw materials, Consumable Stores and Spares**					
	(*a*) Closing Inventory	232	156	116	86	56
	(*b*) Average	194	136	101	71	
	(*c*) Consumption	466	338	280	236	
	(*d*) Consumption Per Day	1.28	0.92	0.76	0.64	
	(*e*) Days	(152)	(148)	(133)	(113)	
2.	**Work-in-Process**					
	(*a*) Closing Balance	110	86	70	54	54
	(*b*) Average	98	78	62	54	
	(*c*) Cost of Goods Produced	730	574	482	406	
	(*d*) Cost of Goods Produced Per Day	2.0	1.58	1.32	1.12	
	(*e*) Days	(49)	(49)	(47)	(48)	
3.	**Finished Goods**					
	(*a*) Closing Balance	102	76	66	56	44
	(*b*) Average	90	72	62	50	
	(*c*) Cost of Goods Sold	680	548	456	394	
	(*d*) Cost of Goods Sold Per Day	1.86	1.50	1.24	1.08	
	(*e*) Days	(48)	(48)	(50)	(46)	
4.	**Sundry Debtors**					
	(*a*) Closing Balance	168	120	78	72	54
	(*b*) Average	144	100	76	64	
	(*c*) Total Sales	1060	840	700	600	
	(*d*) Total Sales Per Day	2.90	2.30	1.92	1.64	
	(*e*) Days	(50)	(43)	(40)	(39)	
5.	**Sundry Creditors and Acceptances**					
	(*a*) Closing Balance	42	30	36	26	16
	(*b*) Average	36	34	30	21	
	(*c*) Purchases	542	378	310	266	
	(*d*) Purchases Per Day	1.48	1.04	0.84	0.72	
	(*e*) Days	(24)	(33)	(36)	(30)	
Ratios						
	1. Current Ratio	2.19	2.55	2.88	2.58	2.83
	2. Quick Ratio	0.76	0.92	1.00	1.05	1.23

PART FOUR

SOME OTHER SHORT-TERM FINANCING

15

EXPORT FINANCING

> *One can pay back the loan of gold, but one lies forever in debt to those who are kind.*
> **Malayan Proverb**
>
> *Money speaks sense in a language all nations understand.* **Aphra Behn**
>
> *He who gathers money little by little makes it grow.* **The Bible**

The Learning Points

The chapter aims at developing the knowledge and facilitating the understanding of:

- Main characteristics of Export Financing
- Assessment of Export Financing Requirements:
  - (*a*) Basis of assessment
  - (*b*) Mechanism of assessment
  - (*c*) Post-disbursement Supervision and Follow-up of advances.
- Pre-shipment Finance (or Packing Credit, *i.e.* for the purpose of Production, Processing and Packing of the goods for export)
  - (*i*) Main characteristics of a bill of lading
  - (*ii*) Distinction between clean and qualified bill of lading
- Post-shipment Finance
- Mechanism of Payment of Pre-shipment Finance
- Procedure of Granting Advances against Export Bills sent for Collection
- Procedure of Granting Export Finance in foreign currency
- Procedure of Granting Advance against Duty Drawback, Cash Subsidy, etc.
- Procedure and Purpose of Policies issued by the Export Credit Guarantee Corporation (ECGC), covering:
  - (*i*) Commercial risks, and
  - (*ii*) Political risks

15.1 WHAT IS EXPORT FINANCING?

It is financing for export purpose. Everything is the same, as it is, in the case of the usual working capital financing, except that the goods, so produced, are not meant for domestic sales, but only and exclusively for export purposes.

But then, a question may arise, as to why at all do the Indian banks have to segregate the two; why don't they combine these both as one single credit facility? This is so, because, some financial concessions are allowed in India only on the entire export financing, which are:

(*a*) A concessional rate of interest is charged on the entire export finance, *i.e.* @ 100 basis percentage points below even the Prime Lending Rate (PLR). Thus, if the PLR, stipulated by a bank, is 13.5% p.a., the rate of interest applicable on the export finance to the company will be 12.5%, even if the usual rate of interest, applicable on the cash credit account of the company be 15% p.a., or even more.

(*b*) A lower percentage of margin, too, is required to be retained in such a case.

(*c*) Some other financial facilities and incentives are also available, in such cases, so as to encourage export activities, *e.g.*

(*i*) Duty drawback,

(*ii*) Cash subsidy,

(*iii*) Issue of import license,

(*iv*) Facility of repo, etc.

Such financial concessions have been allowed because, due to highly competitive global economy and market, the exporters may, usually, have to sell their products in the international markets at a much lower rate, as compared to the price they could easily charge in their home land. But then, with a view to maintaining a favourable balance of payment position, our exports have got to be more than the imports.

That is why the banks insist that the stocks of raw materials, goods-in-process, and even the lots of finished goods, must be kept separately, well segregated from the other such stocks of inventories, charged to the bank, against the domestic working capital finance.

15.2 ASSESSMENT OF EXPORT FINANCING REQUIREMENTS

A. Basis of Assessment

The assessment of the quantum of finance, in the case of export financing, is simple enough, inasmuch as the very starting point for the purpose, that is, the quantum of sales, both in terms of volume (quantity) and value, is well known, well in advance, in definite and sure monetary terms (*i.e.* in terms of Indian Rupees, or some foreign currency, whose rupee equivalent can easily be ascertained).

And, the documentary evidences of such sales value is:

(*a*) Letter of Credit, which is the most popular basis for export financing, and

(*b*) Firm Export Order, which is that is, a firm supply order, on the company's letterhead, from some well known foreign company of repute, like Glaxo (UK), Unilever (UK), General Motors (USA), Sony (Japan), LG (Korea), etc. This is so, because a reputed company, with a view to maintaining its reputation, is not expected to go back, on its supply order, though it may be on its letterhead only, and not on a duly stamped legal document (like the Letter of Credit), having recourse to the court of law. But then, it naturally does have some elements of risk. Therefore, the bankers would do well to ascertain the antecedents and background, financial position and reputation of the company, and must safeguard against all possible risks, even if there is some doubt.

B. Mechanism of Assessment

Now, suppose the Letter of Credit (L/C) has been issued for Rs. 1,00,000, for the supply of woolen carpets from Mirzapur, Varanasi or Bhadohi. That is, the sale to the extent of Rs. 1 lakh is assured. Then, the very first step is to ascertain the quantum of the required raw materials, and other consumable items like colours, chemicals, etc., and, above all, the labour charges. And, suppose, the cost of goods to be sold is expected to be to the tune of, say Rs. 80,000. Thus, after retaining a margin, say, 20%, an export finance limit of Rs. 64,000 (Rs. 80,000 less Rs. 16,000), or, say, in round figure of Rs. 65,000, it may be sanctioned by the bank.

But then, the bank may not disburse the entire amount in one go. It has to be, instead, disbursed in phases, and gradually, commensurate with the stages and progress of production, so as to ensure the proper end-use of funds.

C. Post-disbursement Supervision and Follow-up of Advances

As the eternal vigilance is the price of safety and· security of bank advance, the importance of post-sanction and post-disbursement supervision and follow-up thereof, can hardly be over-emphasised, both in (*a*) quantitative, and (*b*) qualitative terms. However, detailed discussion on this aspect of financing appears in Chapter 10 of the book.

15.3 PRE-SHIPMENT FINANCE (ALSO KNOWN AS PACKING CREDIT, i.e. FOR THE PURPOSE OF PRODUCTION, PROCESSING AND PACKING OF THE GOODS FOR EXPORT)

On disbursement of the loan, the exporting unit starts the manufacturing process, after the purchase of stocks of raw materials and consumable stores, like colours, chemicals, etc. The goods-in-process, as also the stocks of finished goods, as and when these keep getting ready, are stored and stacked separately, segregated from the stocks of such inventories meant for domestic sales.

After the stocks of finished goods get finally ready for the purpose of export, these are first securely packed so that the packing may withstand the stress and strain of the long journey abroad, by ship or by air or, maybe, even by road, depending upon the destination country and the approach and the route.

If stocks are to be exported by ship (which mostly is the case), goods have first to be transported by truck and/or train, up to the port-town, whereafter these are put on board the ship. On receipt of such goods, the exporter is first issued a 'Mate's Receipt', which is a 'Kachcha' acknowledgement of goods on board, pending issuance of a proper Bill of Lading, duly signed by the Captain of the ship.

And, after the consignment is thoroughly inspected and checked by officials of the ship, and are found to be in proper order, free of any apparent packing defects, etc., a document, known as the Bill of Lading, is issued under the signature of Captain of the ship.

What is a Bill of Lading?

A Bill of Lading (B/L) is a document to the title to goods, as is the Railway Receipt and the Truck/Lorry Receipt. The Bill of Lading is a legal document which is a written undertaking, given on behalf of the shipping company, to the following effects:

(*i*) It is a written acknowledgement of goods, duly packed, etc., in the specified quantity, volume, value, packets, drums, etc., as specifically mentioned in the document.

(*ii*) It is an undertaking to ship the entire consignment to the desired destination, as mentioned therein.

(*iii*) It is also an undertaking to the effect that goods so carried will be delivered only to the consignee, as specifically mentioned in the document (B/L) or to his/their order, on production of the Original Bill of Lading, marked 'Original Negotiable' copy.

Clean vs. Qualified Bill of Lading

A Bill of Lading, containing some qualifying/adverse remarks (like, received ten drums, one drum leaking; or received five bales duly packed and tightened with steel strips, except one loosely packed; or received fifteen wooden boxes out of which one is damaged on two sides, etc.) is known as a qualified (not clean) Bill of Lading. Accordingly, the Bill of Lading, free of any of such qualifying remarks, incorporated on the body of the document, is known as a 'Clean Bill of Lading.'

Thus, if one of the conditions, contained in the Letter of Credit, stipulates that a clean Bill of Lading should be one of the documents mentioned therein, the Bill of Exchange may not be accepted by the bank for negotiation under the Letter of Credit, if a qualified Bill of Lading instead is submitted therewith.

15.4 SHIPMENT STAGE

When raw materials are processed and finally produced in the form of finished goods, ready for export, and these are duly packed, transported to the port-town and put on board the ship, and the Bill of Lading is issued, the pre-shipment finance stage, *i.e.* the first stage of the export finance, is completed and comes to an end. And, accordingly, from now on, begins the post-shipment stage.

15.5 POST-SHIPMENT FINANCE

The post-shipment finance, as the name itself suggests, starts after the stage of shipment and the issuance of the Bill of Lading.

At this stage, the Bill of Exchange is drawn by the exporter (seller/drawer) on the importer (buyer/drawee), and the same is submitted to the bank for payment. Such payment, to be effected by the bank, may be classified under two types, viz.

(*a*) Negotiation of the bill, and

(*b*) Collection of the bill.

(*a*) Under the negotiation of the Bill of Exchange, *i.e.* purchase or discount of the demand and time (usance), Bill of Exchange respectively, the payment of the bill is immediately and instantaneously made by the bank, on submission of such bill, by credit to the account of the exporter, maintained with it. The amount of bank charges as also the amount of discount, in the case of discounting of the time bills, however, is usually recovered from the exporter. In some cases, these charges may have to be recovered from the importer, in which case such bank charges are added to the net amount of the Bill of Exchange, and the aggregate amount is to be recovered from the drawee of the bill.

The bills, however, are usually negotiated by banks, as aforesaid, in the cases where such bills are drawn under some Letter of Credit (L/C). In such cases, the Bill of Exchange is superscribed. "Drawn under Letter of Credit No .... Dated ....; issued by .... Bank."

But then, as we have seen earlier, the export finance can be granted against a Letter of Credit or even against a firm export order, of course, of a company of an undisputed reputation and of a sound financial standing.

In such cases, normally, banks may prefer to send the bill on collection basis, and it is only after the bill has actually been paid by the drawee thereof, the bank may release the relative payment to the drawer (exporter) on receipt of an authenticated payment advice from the paying banker concerned. This may, of course, take 10 to 15 days, or even more.

But, if the drawer of the bill (the exporter) is also a very renowned party, of high creditworthiness and financial standing and stability (like, Reliance Industries Ltd., Bombay Dying, L&T, Infosys, Wipro, ONGC, IOC, GAIL, etc.), the bank may prefer to negotiate even such bills (though not drawn under any Letter of Credit), inasmuch as the bank is doubly sure that the amount so paid to the drawer (exporter) may well be recovered from him in case the drawee (importer), somehow, fails to honour the bill, *i.e.* to make the payment of the bill, when required to do so.

15.6 HOW IS THE PRE-SHIPMENT FINANCE REPAID?

On presentation of the Bill of Exchange, pertaining to the goods exported, the bank may purchase or discount the demand or time bill, as the case be, and make immediate payment of the bill, or else may prefer to make the payment of the bill only on receipt of the payment advice, as aforesaid.

Whatever be the case, such payment is not released by the banker straight and direct to the exporter, but, instead, it is routed through the pre-shipment or packing credit account. This way, the entire outstanding amount on the account, up to date, comprising the principal amount, advanced by way of the export finance earlier, plus the amount of interest accrued thereon, as also the banker's charges like, commission, discount, etc., get paid and wiped of, and the net balance, so remaining, only becomes available now for the exporter to draw from the account.

This may well be explained and understood by way of an illustrative example.

Example

An exporter company, Portex India Limited, Moradabad, received a Letter of Credit for Rs. 1,00,000, for export of brass wares to Germany. The bank granted it an export finance, by way of the packing credit, or pre-shipment finance of Rs. 80,000. The company, in due course of time, manufactures the required good, and ships these to Germany, and thereafter, comes back to the bank with a demand Bill of Exchange, drawn on the German Importer for Rs. 1,00,000, and submits it along with the relative Bill of Lading and all the other required documents to the bank, for negotiation. The bank, scrutinises the documents, and finding these to be in strict conformity with the terms and conditions, stipulated in the Letter of Credit (L/C), negotiates the demand bill and credits the entire proceeds of the Bill of Exchange, so drawn, to the 'company's Pre-shipment Account." And, as on that day, the current outstandings [including the amount of interest for the period (say, Rs. 4,000), and all other bank charges, up to date (say, aggregating Rs. 1,000], standing at Rs. 85,000, on the account, now gets converted into a net credit balance of Rs. 15,000 (Rs. 1,00,000 less Rs. 85,000). Thus, the exporter company can now withdraw the net credit balance of Rs. 15,000 only, any time, as this entire balance amount belongs to it and, at its exclusive disposal. And, the bank's entire amount of the advance (principal, plus interest and all other bank charges also), get paid back to the bank in full.

It is said that the pre-shipment finance automatically gets repaid out of the post-shipment finance. This is the reason why banks insist that both the pre-shipment finance and the post-shipment finance must be obtained by the exporter from the same bank and, preferably, at the same branch.

The transactions/entries that take place in the books of the bank, in the above example, may well be explained and demonstrated clearly with the help of the following table:

Table 15.1

Portex India Limited: A/C Export Finance, Pre-shipment Finance (Packing Credit)

Limit : Rs. 80,0000

Drawing Power : Rs. 80,000.

(Amount in Rs.)

Particulars	*Debit*	*Credit*	*Balance*
B/F	80,000		(80,000) (Debit)
To amount of interest	4,000		(84,000) (Debit)
By proceeds of export Bill of exchange		1,00,000	(16,000) (Credit)
Bank charges (exchange and commission, postage, etc.)	1,000		(15,000) (Credit)
Total	**85,000**	**1,00,000**	

15.7 ADVANCE AGAINST EXPORT BILLS SENT FOR COLLECTION

Banks may even decide to advance a certain percentage (say 75%) of the amount of the export bills, sent for collection. But then, this amount of advance will be credited to the packing credit account of the borrower, and would be utilised for the liquidation or reduction of the outstandings, already existing on the account. And, if some credit balance may happen to be still available on the account, such amount can very well be withdrawn and utilised by the borrower. But then, when the entire sale proceeds of the bill is credited to the account, on receipt of the relative payment advice, the entire credit balance is placed at the disposal of the borrower, and the drawing power (to the extent of a certain percentage, say 75%, as aforesaid), allotted on the account earlier, will be consequently cancelled. But if such an export bill happens to be returned unpaid, the amount (say 75% of the export bill) advanced to the exporter borrower earlier, will be recovered from him. And, by way of exercising an extra precaution, the banker may prefer to exercise more than ordinary care at the time of deciding whether to advance any amount against the export bill(s) of such party, being sent for collection.

15.8 EXPORT FINANCE IN FOREIGN CURRENCY

Since 1993, banks have been permitted by the Reserve Bank of India to grant the pre-shipment (export) finance even in the foreign currency, if so desired by the exporter. In such cases, the banker may have to borrow the relative foreign currency in the euro-market, and may, in turn, lend it to the exporter, but with a spread (profit margin) not exceeding 2% of its own borrowing cost.

The exporter may, sometimes, prefer to go in for foreign currency export finance, provided it may prove to be cheaper, taking into account the rate of interest prevailing in the euro-market as also the amount of premia on the foreign currency, ruling at the material time. This loan, however, has got to be repaid and liquidated out of the sale proceeds, as is done in all the cases of the pre-shipment export finance, and that, too, in the Indian currency.

Further, of late, even the post-shipment finance can be granted in any foreign currency of the choice of the exporter, which need not necessarily be the same currency in which the invoice/bill has been drawn.

This way, the exporter has been given an opportunity to make use of his experience and expertise, and make some speculative profit, by virtue of taking some intelligent foreign exchange risks. But the borrowers will do well if they resist from the temptation of becoming greedy and taking more than the fair business risks.

15.9 ADVANCE AGAINST DUTY DRAW-BACK, CASH SUBSIDY, ETC.

With a view to giving a boost to the level of our exports, the Government of India gives some cash incentives to the exporters by way of:

(*i*) **Cash subsidy,** to compensate for selling goods in the foreign market at a lower rate than the rate prevailing in the domestic market, due to global competition, and (*ii*) **Duty draw-back** (that is, giving some concessions/discounts in the amount of import duty, payable by the exporter concerned), and such other facilities/concessions.

But then, some valuable time may be involved in the issuance of the relative cheque for the amount by the government departments concerned. Thus, with a view to tiding over the financial difficulties of the exporter, the bank may even pay him such amount (of cash subsidy, duty draw-back, etc.) by way of an advance, pending receipt of the relative cheque for the amount.

But, in such cases, the banks prefer to play safe and, accordingly, insist that:

(*i*) Such eligible export bills should be routed through the bank concerned. This way, the bank may know, for sure, as to the amount of the cash subsidy, duty-draw-back, etc. that would become payable to the exporter in due course.

(*ii*) Besides, an undertaking is executed by the exporter/borrower in favour of the bank to the effect that the amount of cheque/payment so received by him from the government department concerned will immediately be deposited in his account, towards repayment of the advance. Such advance is granted by the bank for a very short period, for say, 180 days, when the relative cheque/payment is expected to be received.

The pre-shipment finance, granted for the purpose of production and export of goods, is usually advanced for a period of 180 days, though in some cases it may be allowed to be repaid even in 270 days, depending upon the time usually taken in production and in receiving the payment.

15.10 EXPORT CREDIT GUARANTEE CORPORATION (ECGC)

The Export Credit Guarantee Corporation (ECGC) is a Government of India Undertaking. It has been set up under the Ministry of Commerce, with a view to providing insurance cover to the Indian exporters of goods and services, against the risks of non-payment of bills.

The ECGC usually covers two types of risks:

(*i*) Commercial risks insurance, and

(*ii*) Political risks insurance.

(I) Commercial Risks Insurance

When an exporter procures a commercial risk insurance policy from the ECGC, he is assured that the corporation will make the payment of the bill to the extent of 90% of the amount of the bill, in case the foreign importer fails to honour and pay the amount of the export bill.

(II) Political Risks Insurance

The Commercial Risks policy, however, does not cover the political risks, for which a separate (political risks) policy has got to be obtained. Such a policy, as the name itself suggests, covers the risk emanating from, or caused by, some political upheaval, changes and turmoil. For example, some payments of huge amount, pertaining to the U.P. Bridge Corporation was impounded by Iraq, during the Iraq-Kuwait War. And, as the U.P. Bridge Corporation had obtained both the commercial and political risk policies from the ECGC, it got a major portion of losses, so sustained, well compensated by the ECGC, of course, after making great efforts and sustained pursuance and persuasions.

A SYNOPTIC NOTE
(CHAPTER 15 AT A GLANCE)

EXPORT FINANCING

What is Export Financing?

1. It is the usual working capital financing, but with a difference. That is, it is granted only and exclusively for the export purposes, and not for production and sale in the domestic market.
2. But then, why at all it is treated and transacted as an exclusive and separate account by the banks? Because, some special financial concessions/facilities are granted in the case of the export finance, so as to give some incentives for export promotion.

   They are:

   (*a*) A concessional rate of interest, *i.e.* 100 basis percentage points (one per cent) below even the Prime Lending Rate (PLR).

   (*b*) A lower percentage of margin,

   (*c*) Some other financing incentives, such as

   (*i*) Duty draw-back

   (*ii*) Cash subsidy

   (*iii*) Issue of import licence, and

   (*iv*) Facility of Repo, etc.

   to compensate the Indian exporter for the loss suffered due to the sale at below domestic price, due to the global competition.
3. Assessment of export financing requirements:

   (*a*) Basis of assessment

   (*i*) Letter of Credit;

   (*ii*) Firm Export order.

   (*b*) Mechanism of assessment:

   Cost of sales (less) margin

   (*c*) Post-disbursement supervision and follow-up
4. Pre-shipment finance (packing credit):

   (*i*) For purchase of raw materials and consumable stores and manufacturing of the goods for exports;

   (*ii*) For transportation and other charges up to the boarding of goods on ship, etc., and the issue of the Bill of Lading (B/L).
5. What is a Bill of Lading (B/L)?

   It is a document for title to the goods comprising

   (*i*) Acknowledgement of goods, duly packed, etc.;

   (*ii*) Undertaking to take it to the desired destination; and

   (*iii*) To deliver these to the consignee, or according to his/her specific written order, on production of the original negotiable copy of the B/L.

Types of B/L:

(*i*) Clean or unqualified B/L wherein no defect whatsoever has been mentioned in the B/L.

(*ii*) Qualified B/L wherein some defects in goods/packing, etc., received for shipment, have been mentioned in the B/L.

6. Shipment Stage:

This stage is the stage after the pre-shipment stage is over, and the post-shipment stage begins.

7. Post-shipment finance:

(*i*) Negotiation or discount of demand or time bill of exchange respectively, or

(*ii*) Advance to the extent of certain percentage of the amount of the Bill of Exchange, sent for collection, instead of being negotiated/purchased/discounted.

8. Repayment of pre-shipment finance:

It is repaid out of the sale proceeds of the Bill of Exchange pertaining to the actual export of goods: These proceeds are credited to the pre-shipment finance account of the exporter, and thereby the entire outstanding amount in the account, comprising the principal loan amount plus interest and all the other bank charges, up-to-date, get automatically liquidated, that is, the pre-shipment finance gets fully repaid.

9. Export finance in foreign currency:

Since 1993, the export finance (pre-shipment finance) can be granted in a foreign currency as well, of the choice of the exporters. In such cases, the bank is allowed to charge a spread of just 2% only, over its actual cost of borrowing the foreign currency.

The repayment of the finance, however, has to be made in the Indian currency only. Further, the post-shipment finance can, as well, be given in any foreign currency, other than the one in which the Bill of Exchange has been drawn, at the sole option of the exporter borrower.

10. Advance against:

(*i*) Duty draw-back;

(*ii*) Cash subsidy, etc.;

are granted on the condition that

(*a*) The eligible export bills must be routed through the bank.

(*b*) An undertaking is given by the exporter borrower that cheques, when received from the government department, will be immediately deposited on the respective loan account with the bank. Such advance is usually granted for a period of 180 days; in some special cases, up to 270 days.

11. Export Credit Guarantee Corporation (ECGC):

The ECGC policies generally cover two types of risks, viz.,

(*i*) Commercial risks, and

(*ii*) Political risks.

(*a*) Under the commercial risks policy, in case the foreign importer fails to make the required payment, the ECGC undertakes to make the payment up to 90% of the amount of the bill.

(*b*) Under the political risks policy the ECGC undertakes to make good the losses incurred due to non-payment of the amount of the bill due to some political upheaval/turmoil/disturbances, etc.

QUESTIONS
(For Self-assessment)

1. What do you mean by export (pre-shipment) finance? How does it differ from the usual short-terms (working capital) finance by banks?
2. What are the various concessions available to the exporter in the case of export finance, viz., in terms of the rate of interest, and the percentage of margin?
3. What special safeguards/precautions does the bank take, while financing against:
   (*i*) Duty draw-back, and
   (*ii*) Cash subsidy?
4. All banks insist that stocks of inventory (raw materials, work-in-process and finished goods) pertaining to the export finance, must be stored and stacked separately, well away from those pertaining to the usual working capital finance. What in your opinion could be the rationale behind such a stipulation?
5. On what basis is the quantum of export (pre-shipment) finance assessed by the banker?
6. What is a bill of lading? What are the various stipulations/undertakings contained therein?
7. Distinguish between qualified bill of lading and unqualified (clean) bill of lading. Elucidate your point by citing some illustrative examples.
8. It is said that the pre-shipment finance automatically gets repaid by the post-shipment finance. Discuss by citing some illustrative examples, wherever applicable.
9. Distinguish between
   (*i*) Negotiation and discount of bill of exchange.
   (*ii*) Negotiation and collection of bill of exchange.
10. (*i*) "Export (pre-shipment) finance cannot be granted in foreign currency." Do you agree? Give reasons for your answer.
    (*ii*) "Post-shipment finance cannot be granted in any foreign currency." Do you agree? Give reasons for your answer.
11. Export Credit Guarantee Corporation (ECGC) mainly covers two types of risks:
    (*i*) What are these?
    (*ii*) What types of risks do each of them cover?

16

FINANCING OF INFORMATION TECHNOLOGY (IT) AND SOFTWARE INDUSTRIES

Thought, not money, is the real business capital. **Harvey S. Firestone**

Money never starts an idea; it is the idea that starts the money. **W. J. Cameron**

Money is like a sixth sense without which you cannot make a complete use of the other five.
W. Somerset Maugham

The Learning Points

The chapter aims at developing the knowledge and facilitating the understanding of

- Salient Features of Software Industries
- Indian Advantages and Disadvantages
- Critical Success Factors and Key Risk Factors in the Software Industry
- Facilitating Factors for Fresh Exposures
- Working Capital Financing of IT and Software Industries (RBI Guidelines)

16.1 INTRODUCTION

The Software Industry, the driving force in the Information Technology (IT) industry, has rightly been called the 'growth sector of the millennium.' This sector requires highly skilled manpower, and it is heartening to note that in India, in the initial period itself, the sector had grown almost 50%, and that too, during the short span of just five years, *i.e.* from the year 1992 to 1997.

Accordingly, the Government and the Reserve Bank of India are earnestly seeking to improve and facilitate the easy and adequate financing of the software activities, inasmuch as, this sector, *inter-alia*, is expected to make a major contribution in the export earnings of the country, both in the short and medium terms.

16.2 SALIENT FEATURES OF SOFTWARE INDUSTRY

(a) Manpower Intensive

The key feature of the industry is that it is highly manpower intensive, and that too requiring proficient and skilled professionals. Thus, the availability and cost of such manpower, and the productivity and turnover of the unit, are most critical to the success of a software venture.

The most sought after personnel for the sector are:

(*a*) Programmers (65%–70%);
(*b*) Data-based analysts (25%–30%);
(*c*) MIS professionals (15%–20%); and
(*d*) Coders (around 15%).

The productivity and performance of these professionals require high intensity, and immense concentration, coupled with continued long-hours of work, with flexible work-schedule.

And, the scarcity of competent and skilled professionals is the main impediment to the growth and success of the software units. Thus, as the supply is far lesser than the demand, it is no wonder that the price (market value) of software engineers and experts has, of late, rocketed to new heights.

(b) High Capital Output Ratio

As it is a highly skilled manpower intensive sector, its critical inputs and assets are more in the nature of intangibles and, consequently, their assessment becomes more subjective and judgemental, than objective and analytical, as has been the case in respect of the conventional industries. The units engaged in the business of assembly of hardware or consultancy assignments or rendering programming services, in fact, require a relatively small quantum of capital investment and outlay. Consequently, the mushroom growth of such units could hardly be arrested. But, as is well known, it is only the innovative and dynamic units, like, Infosys, Wipro, TCS, HCL-HP, etc., that could flourish and generate high cash inflows and cash surpluses, in a relatively much lesser span of time. But, such cases are more rare than rule. And, thus, it is, in fact, in these special areas that the real skill and acumen, experience and expertise, of financial risk assessment and management, on the part of the bankers and other financial institutions lie.

(c) Fast Changing Technology and Shorter Life-Span of Products

In the modem age and era of rapidly changing technology, like DOS, windows, etc., most of the software products often become obsolete and outdated. Thus, the market share of a product may be gained and lost overnight. This sector can, therefore, rightly be marked as the 'high-risk-high-reward' sector.

(d) Project Appraisal

The assessment and appraisal of the technical feasibility and economic viability of a software project is very tough and tricky, inasmuch as it involves more intuitional and judgemental skills (the sixth sense, rather than the usual business sense), on the part of the traditional and conventional bankers and other creditors.

16.2.1 Advantages In India

1. It is very heartening to note that a World Bank Study of the US companies, pertaining to country preferences for outsourcing softwares, has ranked India as the first choice.
2. In the year 1997 alone, 131 of the Fortune 500 companies outsourced their software requirements from India, and the credibility of the Indian Software capability is, by now, well established, the world over. Besides, as many as 25 of the Fortune 500 companies comprise the regular client list of Infosys alone.
3. These are rather natural, inasmuch as, on a cost-quality coordinates grid, India occupies a unique position in the High Quality, Low Cost quadrant (as against Ireland, Singapore, and Israel in the High Quality, High Cost Quadrant, and countries like China, Philippines, and Hungary in the low quality, low cost quadrant.
4. The major Indian companies have started successfully executing large projects, involving more than 200–300 man years.
5. Over 60 Indian companies have ISO 9000 series certification, out of which as many as 41 companies export to the tune of US $ 3 million annually.
6. India can rightly boast of the availability of large manpower resources of English-speaking, technically proficient personnel, recognised globally as being endowed with high mathematical and logical expertise and, above all, at rather competitive salaries.
7. The 12-hour time zone difference between India and the US (US is the largest software market in the world today and is a net importer to the tune of over US $ 40 billion annually) has been successfully leveraged by the bigger Indian companies into offshore software project work. The work is carried out from India through high speed data communication satellite links on US client mainframes on US downtime (night time), thereby creating extended 'virtual' software arms for the client companies, equipped to even troubleshoot overnight and deliver solutions without loss of daytime working hours for the US company.

16.2.2 The Indian Disadvantages

1. The rising manpower costs/wage structure, coupled with stiff competition from other countries like Ireland and Israel, Singapore and China, Taiwan and Philippines, have, of late, been creating some problems for the sector.
2. Besides, the low market shares, at the higher ends of the value addition chain, have given rise to a greater vulnerability and lower level of consolidation in the industry.
3. Lower rate of technology/enterprise return to home country by the expatriate entrepreneurs, as compared to Taiwan, Korea, Singapore, etc. (*i.e.* lower 're-export' of talent and capital) is yet another disadvantage, India is confronted with.

   These aspects have been cited by some foreign journals as also by Prof. C.K. Prahalad, the renowned 'Strategy Guru'.

16.3 CRITICAL SUCCESS FACTORS IN THE SOFTWARE INDUSTRY

(a) The CEO and the Team of Professionals

The team of software engineers and professionals, in general, and the Chief Executive Officer (CEO) in particular, constitute a very critical and crucial factor for the success, progress and prosperity of the rapidly changing, highly competitive, and manpower intensive software industry.

Most of the Chief Executive Officers (CEOs) of the software companies have generally been found to be technopreneurs and/or highly empowered persons, inspiring team leaders, and persons with vision and mission, drive and urge to prove, progress and prosper. And, above all, all professionals in the organisation keep working as a well-knit-team, complementing and supplementing the efforts and achievements of each other, inasmuch as they fully realise that in the software industry, in particular, they all are destined to sail or sink together; sell or fail enblock. The organisational structure of the units in this sector is relatively flat, and is conspicuously characterised by a youthful workforce of around 30s and 40s, with an egalitarian approach and attitude, and work-culture.

(b) Recruitment and Retention of Human Resources

The success, especially of a software company, to a large extent, depends on its ability to recruit, enable, empower and, above all, retain its employees. Work demands in the industry are uniquely creative and stressful, too, requiring round-the-clock work schedules, to meet the deadlines and time-bound programmes. Successful companies, therefore, have always to resort to some innovative retention strategies.

Of late, the Employee Stock Option Plans (ESOPs) initially introduced by Microsoft, *et al.*, have become popular enough, and have given rise to several variations like stock option build-up over-time, with additional options extended after additional years of service, etc. And, as we all know, many of the Infosys employees have, by now, become millionaires, mainly through their ESOP.

16.4 KEY RISK FACTORS

The software industry is characterised by higher-than-average financial risks. The key components of financial risks are given hereunder:

(a) Intangible Current Assets

The tangible current assets, like inventories (raw materials, work-in-process, and finished goods) are conspicuous by their absence. The current assets of software companies, instead, comprise mostly intangibles, the intellectual capital or property. And, the other current assets (OCAs) are also those that are not generally considered as very significant components of the operating cycle, viz. prepaid expenses, rent advances, employee related advances, etc.

(b) Obsolescence

The most important fixed assets of software companies, viz. the computer hardware, depreciate fast enough. This fact tends to make financial institutions both wary and worried. The other fixed assets, other than land and buildings, comprise the auxiliary equipments like the generators, UPS, furniture and fixtures, etc.

Further, as the risk of obsolescence of software techniques is rather too high, it calls for the scarce virtue of very quick adaptability as also the zeal and preparedness to learn and remain most up-to-date all the time.

(c) Low Initial Capital Investment

Low initial capital requirements of the software sector is more a vice than virtue, inasmuch as it gives rise to a low entry barrier, leading to a mushroom growth of small and medium units, which, in turn, makes it difficult to assess the risks, and predict the success. This accounts for uncomfortably high rate of mortality of the software firms.

(d) Long Gestation Period

Besides, the jobs at the higher end of the value chain, *i.e.* software products have rather long gestation period, carrying very high developmental costs, and that too mostly intangible in nature. And, the risk and threat, that the end-product, being developed, may itself become a non-marketable product, at the end of the long gestation period, is very real and repetitive. The stiff and cut-throat competition in this sector is an added disadvantage, pregnant with high financial risks.

(e) Marketing

It has been observed, over a period of time, that though some companies had developed high quality products, its marketing called for a higher degree of dexterity of product commercialization, in of fierce competition specially in the overseas markets. Lack of a well-developed domestic market is yet another constraint for the industry to attain the required depth, even on the home front.

(f) Some Other Risk/Threat Factors

(*i*) Fierce competition, resulting in erosion of margins, may, in turn, inhibit the ability of the Indian Software companies to invest for growth and upgradation.

(*ii*) Ever-rising cost of manpower, which comprises highly qualified skilled professionals.

(*iii*) Ever-increasing preference of users, in the western markets, for packaged, standard software products, rather than for the customised softwares development. The Indian software companies are best in this.

16.5 FACILITATING FACTORS FOR FRESH EXPOSURES

Some facilitating factors, which have encouraged banks and the other financial institutions to go in for fresh financing and exposure to the software sector may be summarized as under:

(*i*) Software industry in India has since stabilised and strengthened.

(*ii*) Threats of failure of software industries in India have shown marked decline, since early 1990s.

(*iii*) The skill and expertise of the Indian software engineers and professionals have gained high recognition in the overseas markets, as being of high quality and cost competitive, too.

(*iv*) The STPs have dramatically facilitated and improved satellite-based telecommunication facilities in India, enabling on-line work-access to the clients, etc. thereby expanding business opportunities.

(*v*) Besides, the rapid growth and development of foreign markets have given rise to outsourcing, wherein India has emerged as the country of the very first choice. It is evident from the fact that 131 Fortune 500 companies had outsourced softwares from India, way back in 1997, as already explained.

(*vi*) Moreover, with the improvement in the client profiles, the financial risks, like delayed, or even non-payment of bills, have substantially reduced.

(*vii*) Indian software industry has attained perfection and quality, whereby the risk of rejection is rather remote.

(*viii*) Further, the continued exposure to the world markets has given several Indian software units a rigorous commercial education and expertise, relevant for the global marketplace. Accordingly, their business perspective has broadened and their goals and strategies have stabilised, too.

(*ix*) Distinct hierarchies have since emerged among the Indian software units, which have facilitated the benchmarking as also a much better credit risk appraisal and assessment.

(*x*) Besides, the margin of profit of the Indian software industry, too, has increased, which has given added financial strength to the unit concerned, and has brightened its prospects and profitability.

16.6 WORKING CAPITAL FINANCE FOR INFORMATION TECHNOLOGY AND SOFTWARE INDUSTRIES

Reserve Bank of India (RBI) Guidelines

Financing of the four Segments of the Information Technology (IT) and Software Industries

The various segments of the information technology and software industries could broadly be classified under the following four categories:

(a) Software Services

This means staffing services and programming services

These services, also known as the manpower exports, involve deputation of professionals for delivering programming services at the customers' locations, within and outside the country under different types of contracts.

The working capital requirements for these services would, therefore, be in the form of initial travel costs and living expenses of the personnel, deputed for executing the orders. The party may, in some cases, receive some amount by way of advance payment from the clients, which would be specifically mentioned in the contract. The contract would also indicate the mode of payment, *i.e.* whether by way of monthly/periodical payments or payment in lump-sum, after the execution of the contract.

Thus, the working capital requirements of the company would, *inter-alia*, depend upon the gap in the inflows of cash.

(b) Project Services

These may usually have three categories:

(i) Customized Software Development

These services provide solutions to the specific problems of the customer concerned, which would be utilised by the corporate main frame and the mini-computer users. These services could be rendered either at the customer's location or may be delivered on physical magnetic media (like floppies and diskettes) or even through satellite communication networks. This service is normally offered under special contracts, which provide for 'mile-stone' payments.

In these cases, too, the working capital requirements would be for meeting gaps, as is apparent by the company's cash flow statements.

(ii) Systems Solution and Integration

This involves providing a complete business solution, using information technology. Here, the integrator addresses a business problem of the client and offers an IT-based business solution. The work involves programming, testing, documenting customized software solution for clients, and integration of this programme with the client's existing IT system, as also with the systems of the client's parties and associates.

Working capital requirements in such cases, however, would arise mainly on account of expenditure on professionals, and purchases of software packages and tools.

(iii) Maintenance of Software

In this category, the party takes up an assignment for maintenance of the client's software. Typically, it takes on the complete responsibility for maintaining a suit of software of the client. These contracts cover trouble-shooting operations and, at times, even updation of the software.

Working capital for this activity is needed mainly for meeting the expenditure on the professionals.

(c) Software Products and Packages

These comprise:

(*i*) **Systems Software**, viz. Operating System Software, conversion of programmes and utilities, which enhance the computer's capabilities, and (*ii*) **Application Software**, which lets the computer perform specific functions. The packages like the word processing, graphic design, financial analysis, etc., come under this category.

These products are prepared to meet the standard requirements of end-users, and are sold as packaged units, comprising software manual and other user aids (tutorials). The development of these products involve fairly large scale investment, the return on which can be realised only after the product is fully developed and sufficient demand is generated therefore. By and large, no payment by the buyers is involved at any stage of the development, and the developer receives payments only when the interested buyers purchase products.

In such cases, working capital requirements is mainly for meeting the expenditure like salaries and expenses of professionals associated with the development of products. The period required for the development of course, vary and, in some cases, may extend up to 24 months or even more.

As regards the financing of the working capital requirements of this category, it would have to be funded as a venture financing, which naturally involves considerable financial risks.

(d) Information Technology Related Services (IT Services)

IT services, such as call centres, monitoring, teleconferencing, tele-medicine, etc., result from the use of any IT software, over a system of IT products, for realising the value additions.

Working capital requirements, under this segment, may arise for meeting the expenditure, incurred in respect of providing these services. However, these may not be of any significant scale.

16.7 OPERATIONAL GUIDELINES FOR EXTENDING WORKING CAPITAL FINANCE TO INFORMATION TECHNOLOGY (IT) AND SOFTWARE INDUSTRIES

(a) Eligibility

Banks may consider the sanction of the working capital finance, irrespective of the business age of the borrower unit, and/or the quantum of turnover achieved by it, in the previous year(s), in respect of its business activities.

While considering applications for credit facilities, they may be guided by the track record of the promoters, their group affiliations, the management team, academic/professional qualifications and work experience, particularly in the software writing/development/marketing, besides the infrastructure available with the unit.

(b) Methodology for Assessment of Working Capital

The monthly cash budget system has been considered by banks to be ideal for arriving at the permissible bank finance. A specimen of the proforma statement has been circulated by the Reserve Bank of India (RBI) to banks for obtaining the cash budget from the borrowing units. The financing banks may, however, adopt the proforma, with suitable changes, to suit their specific requirements.

The working capital needs of borrowers may be assessed on the basis of 20% of the projected turnover for those units, which may be having working capital limits of up to Rs. 2 crore. And, the assessment of Permissible Bank Finance (PBF) on cash budget basis may be confined to the borrowers having working capital limits of over Rs. 2 crore. Further, while the peak deficit in the cash budget would determine the PBF, credit is made available on the basis of deficits shown at the relevant points in time. Cash budgets may, however, be reviewed, if the underlying presumptions have undergone some significant change, and the credit limits may have to be modified/revised accordingly.

Working capital credit needs of borrowers, with credit limits up to Rs. 2 crore may as well be assessed even on cash budget system, if they would so desire. Further, software products and packages, which are normally financed out of equity, seed money, venture capital, etc., may be considered for finance, on a case to case basis.

(c) Documents to be Submitted for Credit Appraisal Purposes

To enable banks to appraise the credit requirements of any unit, the following documents are obtained by them from the borrowers:

(*i*) (*a*) Operating statement; and

(*b*) Note on assumptions, underlying the operating statement.

(*ii*) Balance sheet.

(*iii*) Cash budget;

[This form, however, is required only in such cases where the working capital gap is to be financed on the basis of the cash budget].

(*iv*) Statement of economics.

Every proposal for the financial assistance must be accompanied by a detailed project report and a business plan. Besides, the documents must, clearly and specifically, describe the short-term, and long-term goals of the unit, the strategies proposed to develop and market the softwares, the stage-wise financial outlays and the revenue/cost projections. The basis for seeking the proposed limits from the bank needs to be clearly spelt out.

As the activity involved in such cases is different from the conventional activities (with which a banker is quite familiar), a detailed plan needs to be drawn up for evaluation of the progress made by the unit. The plan may provide for milestones to be delineated, which could then be appraised.

(d) Nature of Credit Facilities

In respect of credit facilities below Rs. 10 crore, banks have the freedom to sanction the credit facility by way of cash credit facility or overdraft. However, in respect of credit facility of Rs. 10 crore and above, banks are required to restrict the Cash Credit component (CCC) to 20% of the aggregate credit limit, after, of course, excluding the export credit component. The balance 80%, however, has to be disbursed by way of a Working Capital Demand Loan (WCDL) component. The borrower could, as well, be sanctioned appropriate credit facility by way of bills purchased/discounted and invoices drawn.

In the case of specific orders received from abroad, the credit provided would amount to export finance; pre-shipment or post-shipment finance, as the case may be.

(e) Margin

It is open to banks to stipulate a reasonable promoter's contribution, which would serve as the margin.

(f) Security

The process of development of software does not generate tangible goods, as is the case, in the case of the other manufacturing activity, and the value of the end-product depends upon its acceptability to the client users. Further, as the success of the activity depends largely upon the skills of professionals/promoters, banks have to carefully evaluate the promoter's track record, their competence, their stake in the business, marketing strategies, etc. It is also open to banks to obtain some collateral (additional) security, wherever available. The first or second charge, on the current assets, if available, may also be obtained.

(g) Rate of Interest

(*i*) In respect of pre-shipment and post-shipment credits, extended for financing of the exports, the concessional rate, as applicable for such credits, could be charged, provided all the conditions stipulated for the concessional credit are complied with.

(*ii*) For all other types of advance, the rate will be as prescribed by the Reserve Bank of India (RBI), for the general category of borrowers, and, accordingly, no concession would be available.

(h) Periodical Reporting System

In order to verify whether the actual cash flows are in conformity with the projected ones, banks may periodically, say once in a quarter, obtain from the borrower, the statement of actual cash flows, so that the mid-course corrections can be made in respect of further cash budgets, if necessary. However, in respect of borrowers, where cash budget is not the basis for the sanction of the limit, banks may devise a suitable reporting system, as they may deem fit.

(i) Follow-up

Considering the risk associated with this activity, and the fact, that banks naturally take sometime to gain the necessary insights into the intricacies in financing the same, additional attention has to be paid to these advances, and tailor-made follow-up systems may have to be evolved for this purpose by banks themselves.

(j) Administrative Arrangements

As banks are already aware, the Indian software industry is essentially export oriented, and, accordingly, these contribute substantially to the country's FOREX earnings. It is, therefore, necessary that efforts of the industry are supplemented by providing timely and adequate quantum of credit. Banks, therefore, have to streamline their administrative arrangements. They may, therefore, identify centres, where the IT software and service units are sufficiently large in number, and create IT financing cells in the identified branches, at such centres. Banks may also consider constituting appropriate screening committees for appraisal of credit proposals and monitoring the progress/performance of the units.

As regards the training of the bank executives, as an input, banks may arrange for a requisite in-house training programmes on the IT and software industries. It may, as well, augur well to depute the bank staff and officers to the seminars/workshops, conducted by the industry associations, and such other agencies, from time-to-time.

INDEX

A

B

C

D

P

Q

R

S

T

U

V

W

Z